D1324447

The Chinese City in Space and Time

YINONG XU

The Chinese City

University of Hawai'i Press / Honolulu

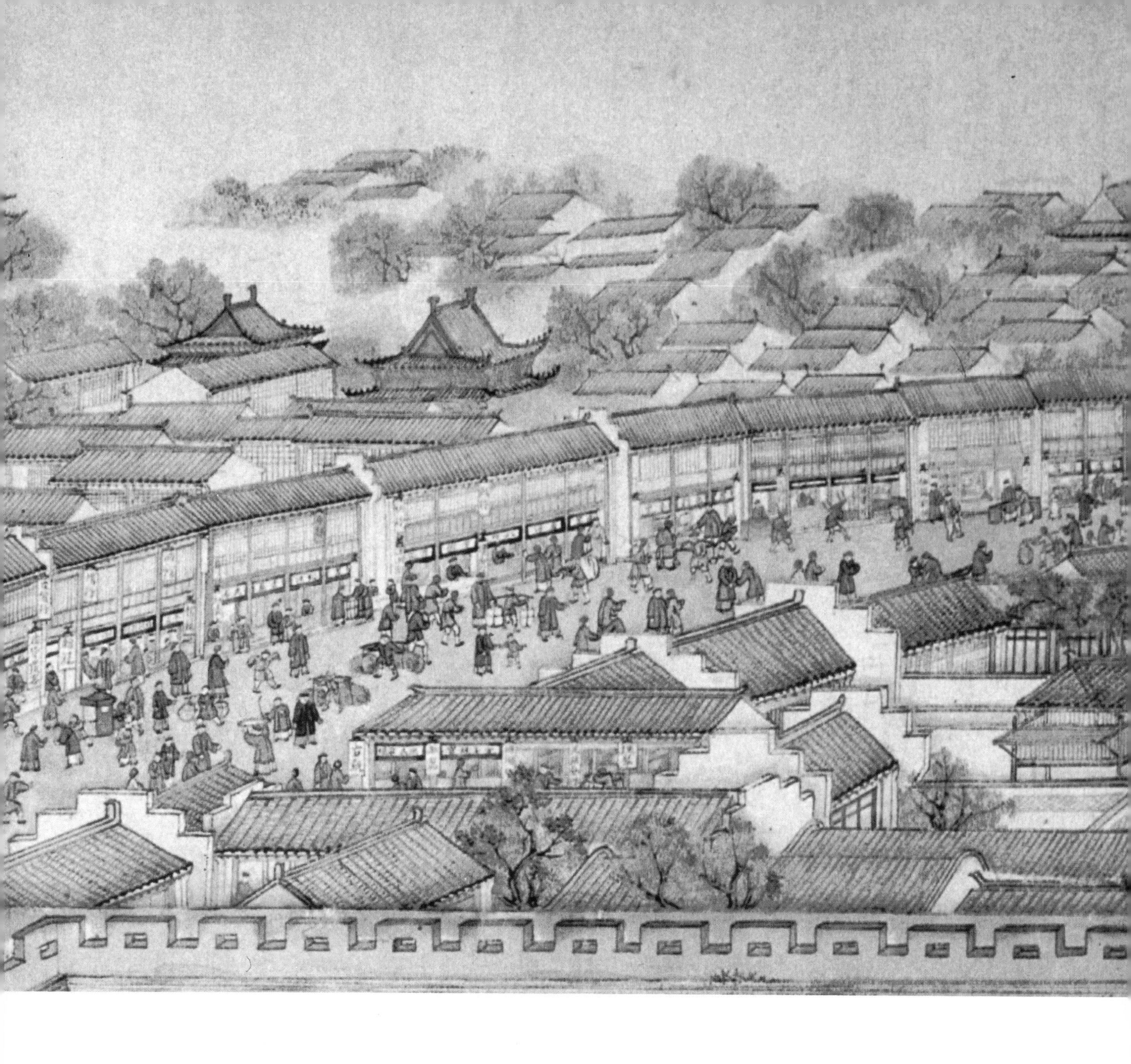

in Space and Time

The Development of Urban Form in Suzhou

Printed in the United States of America

05 04 03 02 01 00 5 4 3 2 1

Library of Congress Cataloging-in-Publication Data
Xu, Yinong, 1961–
The Chinese city in space and time : the development of urban form in Suzhou / Yinong Xu.
p. cm.
Includes bibliographical references and index.
ISBN 0-8248-2076-2 (alk. paper)
1. City planning—China—Suzhou (Jiangsu Sheng)—History. 2. Urbanization—China—Suzhou (Jiangsu Sheng)—History. 3. Suzhou (Jiangsu Sheng, China)—History. I. Title. II. Title: Development of urban form in Suzhou.

HT169.C62S999 2000
307.1'216'0951136—dc21 99-37240
CIP

Publication of this book has been assisted by grants from
The Chiang Ching-kuo Foundation for International Scholarly Exchange and
Furthermore, the publication program of The J. M. Kaplan Fund

University of Hawai'i Press books are printed on acid-free paper and meet the guidelines for permanence and durability of the Council on Library Resources.

Designed by Diane Gleba Hall
Printed by The Maple-Vail Book Manufacturing Group

Contents

Illustrations

Figures *(North is to the top of the page for all plans and maps unless otherwise specified.)*

Tables

Acknowledgments

RESEARCH FOR THE DISSERTATION ON WHICH THIS BOOK IS BASED was conducted first under the direction of the now late Professor Christopher Barrie Wilson and then of Dr. Angus J. MacDonald. I express my deep gratitude to Dr. A. W. E. Dolby and David Ellis for proofreading. Dr. Nicholas Tapp, Professor Iain Boyd Whyte, and Dr. Frances Wood kindly offered constructive suggestions on revisions. I was helped at various points with the collection of materials by Qiu Xiaoxiang, Xu Minsu, Liu Guchuan, Professor Ho Puei-peng, John P. C. Moffett, Zhu Ruiping, Professor Zhu Xiaojian, Kim Migyung, and Liu Li.

Research at the University of Edinburgh from 1990 to 1993 was made financially possible by the Edinburgh University Postgraduate Studentship, ORS Award Scheme, and Edward Boyle Scholarship. During the academic year 1993–1994, I was aided by an award from the Henry Lester Memorial Trust; and in 1995 I was supported by the Michael Ventris Memorial Trust at the Architectural Association for the completion of a self-contained piece of work that is closely related to a particular chapter of this book.

My special debt is to Professor Ronald G. Knapp, who not only commented on my dissertation but also thoughtfully recommended it to the University of Hawai'i Press for publication. I am also very grateful for the helpful comments and criticisms from the two manuscript reviewers, Professors Frederick W. Mote and Nancy Shatzman Steinhardt, who kindly revealed their identities to me. I was able to incorporate most of their suggestions into the amended and corrected version. During the revision of the work, I continued to profit from their expertise. Nor would my acknowledgments ever be complete without mention of my gratitude to my editor at the press, Patricia Crosby, for her suggestions, support, and patience, and to my copyeditor Robyn Sweesy, for her commitment to the improvement in the style and presentation of the manuscript. All the comments I received have carefully been considered; what errors remain are mine.

Finally, I thank my wife, Jing; my parents, and my sister for their love, goodwill, and confidence in my academic endeavor. Jing has shown extraordinary fortitude and stamina in supporting our life in Edinburgh.

Introduction

THIS BOOK EXAMINES THE FORMATION AND TRANSformation of the urban form and space of the city of Suzhou up to the early twentieth century.[1] The purpose of the study is not to produce a comprehensive historiography of the city, but rather, by taking Suzhou as a specific case, to address a number of important characteristics of city building and development in premodern China. Because the research has been shaped by my training in the fields of architecture and city planning, all but the most general remarks on the social and economic history of Suzhou, important as these topics are, have had to be passed over. It is hoped that this work will serve as a starting point from which a sound historical approach to studies of traditional Chinese cities may emerge.

Two major considerations determine the choice of this particular city. The first is a historical one. The city claims a past going back to the late sixth century B.C., and its later development has been regarded as a physical continuation of this earliest construction. The point is not just that the city had a very early beginning but that it is a physical entity that by the early twentieth century had existed continuously for nearly two and a half millennia. This long history was characterized by, among many other events, the sociopolitical transition from the multitude of states contending against each other for survival to the unified imperial structure in the Qin (221–206 B.C.) and Han (206 B.C.–A.D. 220), by the medieval urban revolution from the second half of the eighth century to the Southern Song (1127–1279), and by the development of the market economy and of a matured hierarchical system of cities and market towns in the Ming (1368–1644) and Qing (1644–1911). In this sense, this city itself, in the course of its rise and decline, can be treated as an object of as well as a witness to this important period of China's complex urban history.

The second consideration is associated with the place of the city of Suzhou in pre-modern China. In theoretical terms, the largely fictional accounts by the Eastern Han (A.D. 25–220) scholars of its earliest construction were so important to the tradition of Chinese city building that, as an example of a distinctive experience, the city figures in all the encyclopedic works of the imperial era. In practical terms, although the city was not an imperial capital of China, it was the hub of a large region on which the economic and cultural flourishing of the whole Chinese empire had increasingly depended to a phenomenal extent from as early as the ninth century. Thus, the transformation of the city of Suzhou in history was not an isolated case that happened to be in the Chinese urban context but often represented a leading force in the development of an urban China. Also because of the prominence of the city and the region in which it is situated, sources for the study of its urban development are abundant, as a remarkably large collection of records of its history, customs, and, of course, urban construction has been produced and kept.

At the inception of a study, a basic question usually has first to be answered: Is its topic worth the effort? In our case, this question may have had to be answered in length had it been mooted thirty years ago. Yet the necessity for studies of China's urban past has been averred by many distinguished sinologists, so there seems no need now to spend more space on it.[2] Instead, I should only emphasize that the importance of studies of Chinese urban history lies not only in its distinctiveness from that of the West but in the fact that the range and variety of Chinese experience in building, adjusting, governing, and inhabiting cities, as well as in relating cities to the rest of society, is by far the largest block of such human urban experience. It therefore constitutes an indispensable parameter of comparison for urbanism in other cultural spheres and is a rich source of suggestion and of inspiration.

To illustrate this, an obvious and revealing example can briefly be cited here. One standard view of preindustrial European cities is that they usually possessed separate legal and political status as organized entities, which set them apart from the countryside. In the introduction to his masterly survey of a thousand years of urban architecture in western Europe, Wolfgang Braunfels has gone so far as to argue that the reasons for the urban failure and disorder in the modern era, for which architects and urban designers have partly been responsible, must be sought in changes in the general political function of cities:

> Cities no longer form unities but serve both the interests of the individual and those of the state with its manifold business, the new "one world." They represent only to the most limited extent an independent body corporate, for their areas of existence are interwoven in different ways, with the states to which they are subordinated and with the rural areas that surround them.[3]

Interestingly, no Chinese city in the imperial era was ever a corporate entity of its own; nor did any of them have the organizational features that set European cities apart in legal and political ways. The Chinese city was an instrument of the imperial government and thus an integral part of the "one world"; its area of existence was more than interwoven with the state to which it was subordinated and with the rural areas that surrounded it. Yet one can hardly deny that such a city captured "the imagination with its order" as much as any preindustrial European city is believed by Braunfels[4] to have done. Paradoxically, it is the cities of modern China that have evinced a kind of urban-rural dichotomy and at the same time show marked disorder in urban architecture. Whether the reasons for the modern failure on both sides of the world lie more in the process of rapid change itself than in the direction of change falls beyond the scope of the present study. Suffice it to say that Chinese urban history deserves much more attention than it is presently given in the academic field of architecture.[5]

As I have already stated, my treatment of Suzhou as a particular case is an attempt to sketch a few important features of an approach to urban history appropriate to traditional Chinese cities. I make no claim to provide an ideal construct to explain the varied and complex history of urban China. Most sinologists, in fact, realize that simple, undifferentiated models of "the Chinese city" are untenable.[6] An epistemological question then arises: how can we draw from the study of this single city general conclusions about the history of Chinese urban construction and development as a whole? For all the various historical reasons, Chinese culture has been characterized for the last two millennia by both its extreme diversity and its high integration. Its cities were products of this complex culture. Thus, two important and interrelated ideas come to inform this methodological issue. First, although the histories of these cities were profoundly differentiated from each other in space and time, common features must have existed to make them recognizable as culturally Chinese. It should be valid, then, to treat the city of Suzhou axiomatically as *a* Chinese city in the sense that, even with all the unique factors of its own history, it was firmly embedded in the urban context of pre-modern China.

The second idea is that the city of Suzhou, like any other Chinese city, was given form not only by the practices and ideas that derived from its particular social, economic, and political circumstances but also by a set of changing values and beliefs that were an integral part of a widely shared worldview of the traditional Chinese as a whole, a characteristic way of both looking at and shaping the world. It is for the purpose of this study that the pragmatic examination of the city in its various historic contexts is frequently accompanied by an inquiry into the conceptual realms of the Chinese. Consequently, how the city in all its varied, specific aspects was perceived by the Chinese in history is taken as no less important than what the city really looked like. The common features in China's urban history are therefore found mainly in the areas of attitudes, principles, and symbolic functions, whereas this particular city was surely differentiated to various degrees from other Chinese cities in such aspects as form, spatial disposition of urban components, specific historic events, and its political and economic significance.

Although works of Western scholarship on urban development in traditional China have markedly increased in the past few decades, there seem to exist at least two biases apparent in them. One appears to be either that sociological interests override careful examinations of the formation and transformation of the spatial and physical features of the cities or that an overemphasis of the cities' formal and technological aspects detaches them from social contexts. Can urban phenomena be sufficiently explained solely in either social or formal terms? On this issue, Bill Hillier and Julienne Hanson's work throws important light. Any architectural structure, they argue, "is an object whose spatial form is a form of social ordering."[7] The social and the spatial cannot be treated as distinct, separate entities, because human societies are spatial phenomena. Thus not only does society have a certain spatial logic, but space has a certain social logic to it.[8] If this line of argument is valid, a sensible understanding and discussion about cities should therefore employ a two-way approach: to study the social contexts that create and order the spatial and formal elements into patterns as a part of society *and* to study the spatial and formal features that not only reflect the social phenomena but are themselves characters of social ordering. The other bias is that attention is more often paid to the imperial capitals than to local cities. A noticeable deficiency in this scholastic imbalance is that the imperial capitals, important as they are to our understanding of the history of Chinese city planning, do not constitute the whole picture of China's urban experience. There are two basic reasons for this understanding. The first is the plain fact that the vast majority of urban centers in the premodern era were not imperial capitals. The second reason lies in the realization that, as I will develop in Chapter 3, the idea of building the imperial capitals, especially in its cosmological aspects, is profoundly different from that of building, maintaining, and governing local cities. This book responds to these concerns as well.

Chapter 1 is an introduction to the historic background against which the city of Suzhou rose and declined. In the first section of this chapter, I introduce the general geographic, cultural, and socio-political conditions under which the city was believed to have been built for the first time in 514 B.C. as the capital of the state of Wu situated on the fringe of by then the nominal Zhou (ca. 1040-256 B.C.) hegemony, and eventually to have fallen in 473 B.C. when Wu was destroyed by its chief enemy, the neighboring state of Yue. In the second section, I present an overview of the development of the city and the prefecture of which it was an administrative center in the imperial era. Since important growth of the city did not start until the mid-Tang, and since sources are very few prior to that period, the cursory description of its economic growth, population, cultural transformation, and urban features observed by Chinese and foreign visitors focuses on the second half of the imperial era, from the eighth century.

The main body of the book is composed of three parts. The first part, Chapter 2, focuses on the earliest construction of the city of Suzhou in the late sixth century B.C. and on the perceived cosmological symbolism of its form. This chapter does not present a historical study but formulates the conception of this city and its symbolism, which had accumulated and was fairly systematized by the Eastern Han period. This methodological orientation is the result of extremely scarce archaeological discoveries, to date, pertaining to the building of the Wu capital and the fact that the main texts from which the information about this early city is extracted are from the Eastern Han dynasty, more than half a millennium after the event of its building. A historical approach would create serious latent problems such as how later accounts can be used to reconstruct the form of the city and how the particular way in which the city form was symbolically perceived at the time of its building can be identified. Because of these two problems in our sources of study, the subject of this chapter is what was perceived in a systematized written version of the building of the city by the authors of the Eastern Han documents and not what it was in physical reality.

Consequently, the conceptions and ideas revealed in the accounts of the initial building of the city should not be severed from the traditions of city planning and construction, which, by the Eastern Han, had evolved for two thousand years. They almost certainly reflected, consciously or unconsciously, not only the value system and moral judgment of the Han but the syncretized cosmology of city building of the Han. Thus, examination of the form and symbolism of the Wu capital is preceded by a discussion of the prescriptive components of city planning characteristic of the Han synthesis, into which a considerable body of lore, practices, and ideas connected with city building had accumulated by the end of the Warring States (481–221 B.C.). This synthesis is epitomized in the classical source of city theory, the *Zhou li,* and its last section in particular, the "Kaogong Ji."

The chapter then focuses on its major concern, the construction of the Wu capital and its cosmological symbolism as elaborated in Eastern Han texts. This "history" may be seen as a construct devised by the authors of these later documents to express the historical struggle for survival between the states of Wu and Yue. Whatever the authenticity of this "history" may prove to be, it later came to be viewed as an authoritative historical source and continued to inform the city's further development in subsequent dynastic periods. Since the main purpose of this study is to identify a number of important features of urban transformation in premodern China, Chapter 2 focuses on investigating *what* the significant aspects of this "history" are rather than *how* it was devised, although a few suggestions are made on the possible origins of some of its elements. This investigation is supplemented by a brief discussion of other fictional accounts of the capital city of Yue.

Chapter 3 functions as a theoretical link between the discussion of the city in connection with the fictional accounts of its earliest construction and its development in the imperial era. The Qin unification in 221 B.C. is often taken as a turning point in Chinese history, as it was in this year that the first strongly centralized Chinese empire was brought into being. Along with the far-reaching social and political transformation of that time, there occurred a profound change in the nature of China's city system. China's urban history throughout the subsequent two-thousand-year imperial era was characterized by both its remarkable continuity and its great complexity. The development of the city of Suzhou is to be regarded not only as an integral part but as a particular instance, of that history. Since there are fundamental differences in how sinologists interpret the cities of imperial China and their development, it is necessary to delineate these differences and to clarify my views on them before proceeding to examine the city of Suzhou more closely.

To pursue this task, I first consider some general attributes of the regional and local cities as centers of imperial administration, emphasizing the variability of their form in space, and arguing that a fundamental distinction should be drawn between these cities and the imperial capital, particularly in their symbolic roles. Second, I deal with the overall evolution of urban planning and governing principles during the period of the medieval urban revolution and urban development in the midst of the socioeconomic change in the Ming and Qing periods. Third, I discuss some aspects of the distinctive urban-rural relationship in imperial China and suggest that the role of the city walls in society was more of a symbolic than pragmatic one. Fourth, I attempt a preliminary explanation of the coexistence of the stability of form of the walled city in time and the urban expansion in space.

Chapters 4, 5, 6, and 7 comprise the third and final part of the book, concentrating on the major aspects of urban transformation of the city of Suzhou in the imperial era. Examination of the development of the walls and gates of the city in Chapter 4 is given pride of place because of their physical and symbolic significance as much in Suzhou's history as in the whole urban history of traditional China. In this chapter, I first describe the temporary transference of the city to a new site in A.D. 591 and its return to the old site within a period of about thirty years. After analyzing the major pragmatic reason for the resumption of the old site, (that is, the imbeddedness of the city in its natural surroundings where history had been deposited), I suggest a deeper implication of this event: the conceptual and possibly institutional inseparability of the walled city from its status as the regional or local administrative center of the imperial government. Second, I review the history of the reconstruction of the city walls and note a peculiar fact that, unlike previous ones, major reconstruction works during the Ming and Qing occurred in the early years of the dynasty. Third, I examine the length of the walls in each dynastic period and argue that the overall position of the city walls and thus the general form of the city have remained basically unchanged from 1229, or probably even a few centuries earlier, throughout subsequent history. Fourth, I briefly sketch the physical structure and configuration of the walls on the basis of both written records and pictorial evidence from the 1229 picture map and the scroll paintings of the Qing. Finally, I discuss the transformation of the city gates. Emphasis is laid on their symbolic meanings, and, in particular, on how their cosmological aspect is profoundly different from that in the accounts of the earliest construction of the city.

Chapter 5 focuses on the transformation of the overall urban structure of the city of Suzhou. Three prominent features are examined. The first is the development of the network of city canals. After a brief review of the possible process of its formation by the year 1229, I demonstrate that this canal system functioned as a framework for the spatial organization of city structures from the pre-Tang era to the end of the Southern Song. I also argue that the partial decay of the canal network and the unusually frequent efforts to maintain it by the local government in the first half of the Qing reflect the enormous economic and demographic pressure on the existing water system. The second feature is the fate of the geometrical center of the city. By showing how it was demoted from being the location of the prefectural offices to a state of dereliction, and describing the tragedies that ensued upon an attempt at rebuilding the offices on this particular site in the early years of the Ming, I propose that this apparently unique event in Suzhou's history might have carried with it some significant implications that fell within the general sociopolitical context of urban experience in imperial China. The third feature is the partitioning of urban space into three main districts from the mid-Ming onward. Special attention is then directed to the development of the city's west suburbs as a major outcome of the urban expansion in the late imperial period, which, in a modern sense, may be regarded as more "urban" than most areas enclosed by the city walls. Here I venture to explain why such an evident contradiction could have existed between the remarkable stability of the city form defined by the largely unaltered position of the city walls, and a process of steady urban growth in space in the last centuries of the imperial era.

In Chapter 6, I seek to resolve two apparently simple, but actually complicated, issues. One concerns architectural forms and styles of buildings in the city in relation to those in rural areas. This issue is approached by unraveling the relationship between form and function and by analyzing the compositional traits of building complexes in the tradition of Chinese architecture. On the one hand, it is then suggested that the lack of discernible difference between the forms and styles of Chinese urban and rural buildings was fundamentally determined by a characteristic absence of formal bond between building types and social institutions, and, on the other hand, that the distinctiveness of a few types of urban structures was brought about by the formal attributes of the city walls or wall-like structures but not by the buildings incorporated in these urban structures. The other issue discussed in this chapter is the use of public urban space. It is shown how the courtyard of Xuanmiao Guan, a renowned Daoist temple located in the city of Suzhou, was used for public purposes in the late imperial period. Two possible explanations are presented: first, the traditional Chinese concept of socialized space determined that any space of a considerable size facilitating social interactions in a man-made environment had to be defined both nominally and physically, the courtyard being the most appropriate space of this kind, and second, the public nature of the temple, the spaciousness of its courtyard, and the psychologically and practically maintained accessibility of all sections of both urban and rural societies to it, made this particular use a convenient option.

Finally, in Chapter 7, I discuss the position of *fengshui* (Chinese geomantic) ideas in the history of the city of Suzhou. I consider this issue as important not only because *fengshui*, as a system of adapting the residences of the living and the dead to the natural environment, was supposed to be extensively applied to site selection, site adjustment, and the construction of tombs, houses, gardens, villages, and many other kinds of structures in traditional China, but also because of an implicit (in some cases, even explicit) assumption currently held by many students of Chinese urban history and sociology that the building of traditional cities in China was often, if not always, influenced by *fengshui* ideas. This assumption may have derived from reading expositions in *fengshui* manuals that its principles should ideally operate in man-made construction of all kinds and right down the scale, from cities to individual buildings and tombs. In practice, however, evidence indicates that the assumption is very questionable as far as regional and local cities are concerned. By analyzing the relevant materials contained in a number of local documents on the history of the city of Suzhou and the development of its urban elements, this chapter aims at tentatively answering the following questions: to what extent and in what way were *fengshui* ideas applied to its urban construction and transformation? What physical and psychological effects could they have had on the city? How significant may this aspect prove to be in studies of traditional urban China?

Chapter 7 begins with a cursory examination of the problems concerning the origins of *fengshui* as a set of newly elaborated cosmological ideas and the principles of its two major schools from the Tang period onward. Then I consider the one and only extant documented instance of active *fengshui* advice on the urban construction of the city of Suzhou and discuss the social and historical implications of its eventual failure. In the third section of this chapter, I deal with three cases of *fengshui* interpretations of the natural setting, form, and urban spatial pattern of the city. The question concerning the applicability of *fengshui* ideas to the physical construction of regional and local cities at an urban level is mooted in the fourth section. A tentative answer to this question is made on the basis of an analysis both of the collective ambiguous attitudes of the imperial scholar-officials toward *fengshui* and the particular social and ideological context of regional and local governments that were staffed by these scholar-officials and housed in these cities. In the fifth and final section, I extensively analyze *fengshui* involvement in the construction of a major bridge across the city moat and suggest that the exertion of the influence of *fengshui* ideas on building activities in the city probably varied in intensity at different levels of the interests of sociopolitical groups.

CHAPTER 1 Historical and Cultural Background

BOASTING A HISTORY OF OVER TWO AND A HALF millennia, Suzhou is situated at the center of the Yangzi delta, in the southeast of present-day Jiangsu province. As Figure 1.1 shows, the River Yangzi flows eastward over sixty kilometers to the north. About twenty kilometers to the southwest lies Lake Tai, the great drainage basin of the Southeast region, out of which flow innumerable streams north to the Yangzi or east to the sea. The region around Lake Tai has been the richest rice-growing bottom land in all of China; it is also a region of great scenic beauty, with mountains and hills and thousands of islands. It provided water routes connecting to all the important cities of the Southeast as well as to the Grand Canal and Yangzi arteries. As background information for our discussion of the construction and transformation of the city, the first part of this chapter introduces the general geographic, cultural, and political conditions under which the city was believed to have been built for the first time in 514 B.C. This is followed by a brief description of the development of Suzhou in the imperial era, primarily from the ninth century to the turn of the twentieth century.

Background of the Beginning of the City

Tradition holds that the city of Suzhou was originally built in 514 B.C. as the capital of the state of Wu.[1] It was then called Helü Dacheng (the Great City of Helü). In the first half of the Eastern Zhou (770–256 B.C.), known as the Spring and Autumn period (770–476 B.C.), Wu occupied a territory spreading out from the Yangzi delta and gradually extended in almost all directions except for the eastern seaward one (see Figure 1.2). From a strategic point of view, this central area in which the city was built had the

Figure 1.1 Present topographical features around the city of Suzhou. Redrawn from Jiangsu sheng ditu ce *1990, pp. 5–6, 48–49.*

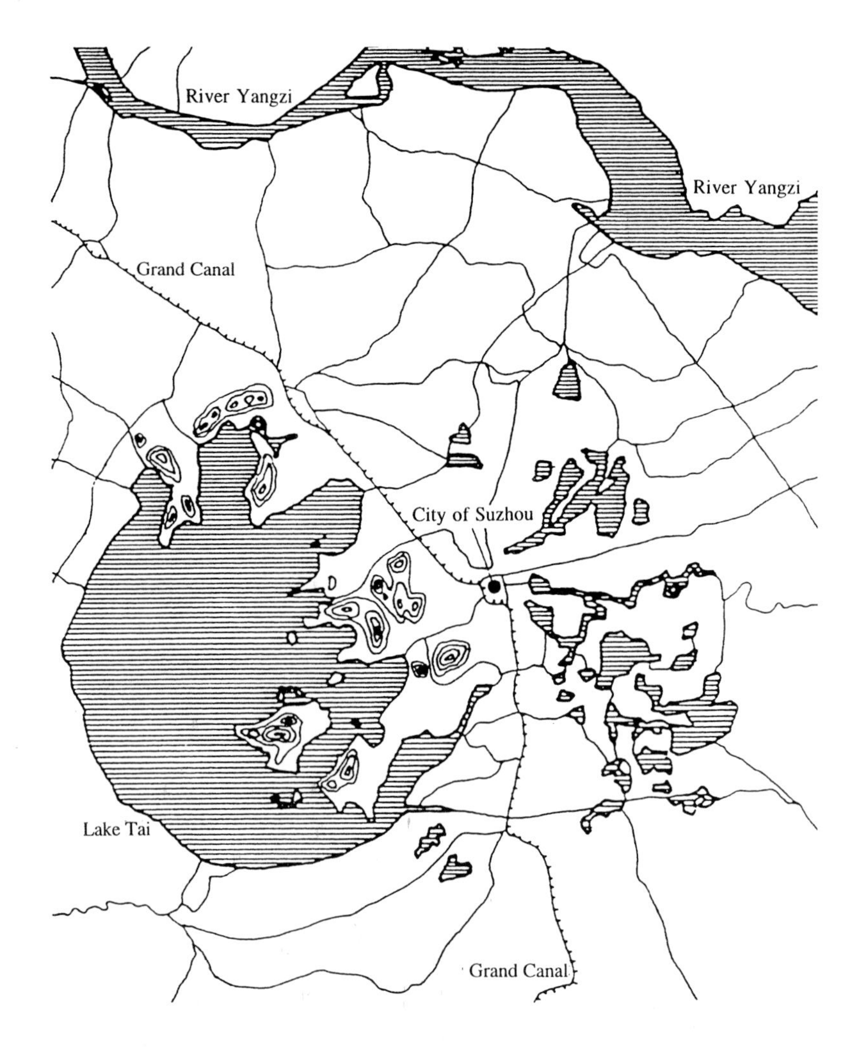

advantage of being protected by the River Yangzi at its back to the north, extending southwest to the shore of Lake Tai, and controlling the sea to the east by reaching across the mouth of the Yangzi. This advantage was summarized by an early Qing geographer, Gu Zuyu (1624–1680):

> From Wu [i.e., Suzhou] prefecture northward across the River [Yangzi], Huainan [present-day Yangzhou] could be annexed; southward by sea, Ming [Ningbo] and Yue [Shaoxing] could be taken over; upstream along the River Yangzi, Sheng [Changzhou] and Run [Zhenjiang] could be possessed; further across Lake [Tai], Tiao [Wuxing] and Zhe [Hangzhou] could be reached. Zhexi[2] is a wealth-concentrated, heavily taxed region, whereas the Wu prefectural city is the metropolis of the Zhexi region. In the matter of all-under-Heaven, how can Wu prefecture not be considered as a place of priority![3]

The vast delta plain, with the hilly land to its west periphery and the coastal islands to its east end, is, in contrast to Central China, characterized by myriad waters and lakes, fertile soils, rich natural resources, and a genial climate. From the evidence revealed by archaeological excavations and in literary records, it is certain that the main contemporary agrarian produce of this region included rice and flax, kudzu vine, and mulberry leaves, providing raw materials for textile manufacture. Fishing and stock raising were also prominent activities for providing daily necessities. Rich bronze and tin resources yielded abundant supplies for tools and to arms foundries.[4]

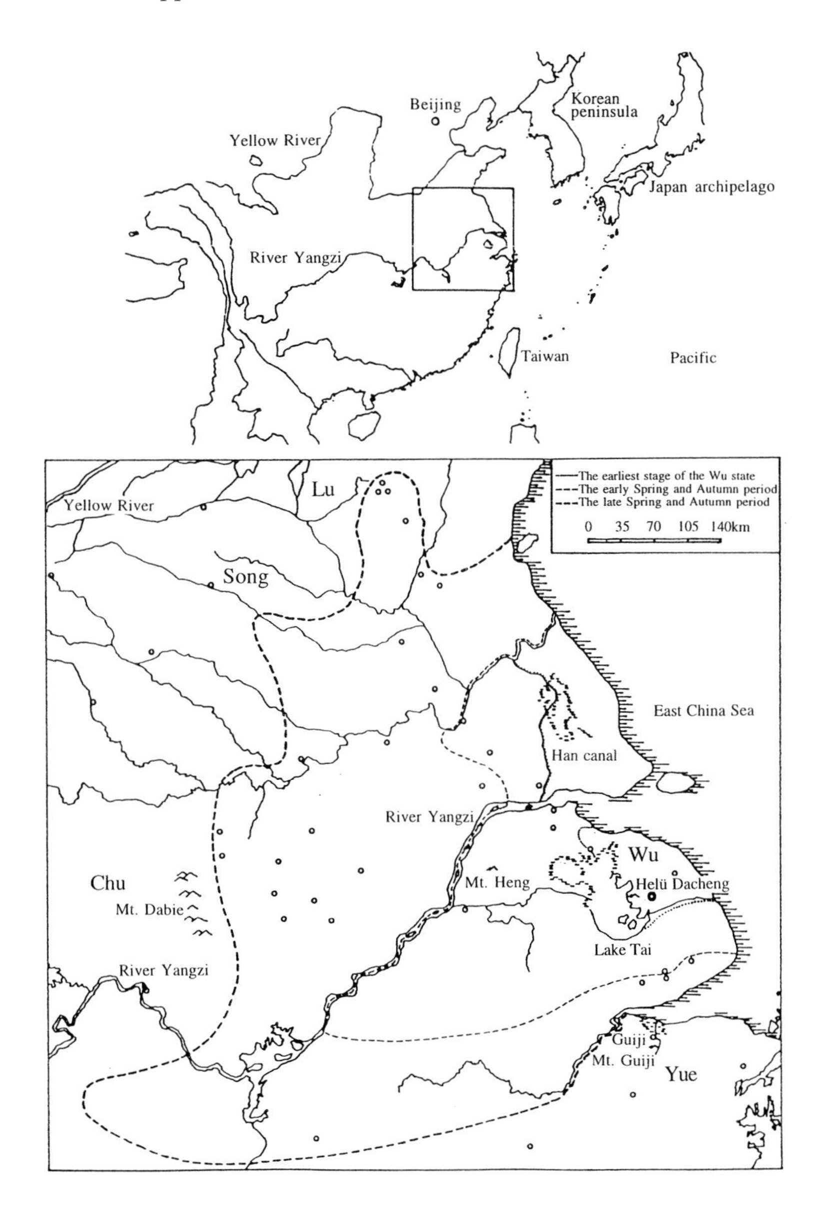

Figure 1.2 *Geographical locations of the state of Wu at three historical stages in relation to its neighboring states. Helü Dacheng was the capital city of Wu from 514 to 473 B.C. Redrawn from Wei 1988, p. 122, by reference to Cao and Wu 1986, p. 27; Guo 1979, pp. 15–16; and Tan 1982, vol. 1, pp. 20–21, 29–30.*

The origin of the Wu tribe is not very clear, but we may surmise that, as Granet has suggested, it was formed by tattooed people with short hair.[5] Wu culture may have originated in the Ning-Zhen area (around present-day Nanjing and Zhenjiang), where the Neolithic period seems to be represented by a phase of development known as the Beiyinyangying and characteristic of patriarchal tribe society, when the practice of bronze metallurgy may have begun.[6] Large amounts of archaeological evidence, including the remains of relatively permanent settlements and cemeteries, tools, ornaments, spindle whorls, and pottery, have been found to support such a hypothesis.[7] A successor to the Beiyinyangying phase, the Hushu culture, shared the source of Wu culture with the Maqiao phase in the area around Lake Tai, which developed directly from the Liangzhu phase. The early period of the Hushu stage was approximately at the time of transition from the Shang (*c.* sixteenth to the eleventh centuries B.C.) to the Zhou, while its later period was at the time of the Spring and Autumn period when the Wu culture had become fairly developed.[8]

Although some mutual influence between these semibarbarian chiefdoms and Central China from as early as the Shang period on is suggested by both ancient literature and archaeological discoveries,[9] and although the House of Wu is supposed to have issued from the same ancestors as the royal House of the Zhou, Wu culture did retain its separate identity and developed in its own way. When Taibo, the eldest son of Danfu,[10] came with his brother Zhongyong to the Wu area in the late Shang, they had to adapt themselves to aboriginal customs.[11] Therefore, it seems possible that, as suggested by Wheatley when he refers to all the territories directly or indirectly controlled by the Zhou, neither was the aboriginal culture replaced by the Zhou nor can the basic establishments of its settlements be regarded as having been created *de novo* by the Zhou aristocrats.[12] It is only possible that at the time when King Wu of Zhou posthumously enfeoffed Taibo in Wu, Taibo had already long been supported and chosen by the aborigines as head of the tribe.[13] The enfeoffment was actually a part of the Zhou's policy of placing most settlements of any size under a Zhou chieftain or a Zhou adherent so that the Zhou themselves could concentrate on maintaining direct control of their homeland in the Wei valley.[14]

The Wu culture had its closest affinity rather with that of Yue in the south, which shares a border with Wu, and to a degree with that of Chu in the west. All three were parts of the Bai-Yue[15] (Hundred Yue peoples), who were spread over a vast area of southern China. Apart from the same geographical and climatic conditions, they shared direct communications, similar customs, and possibly a common language.[16] It would be impossible to deal with all aspects of Wu's distinctive cultural development not only because of the paucity of evidence, which impedes detailed speculation, but also because of the great extent of the area, which would inevitably take us well beyond the scope of the current topic. However, a short discussion on the characteristic use of animal themes by the people of Wu in their social activities would be helpful, as it directly concerns the topic of discussion in the following chapter.

The peoples of Wu and Yue, and those further south, whom the Chinese of the Central Plain pejoratively called "southern barbarians" (*nanman*) in contrast to themselves, the "civilized men" (*ren*), were regarded by the latter as progenies of the snake.[17] This designation may have derived from the extensive application of the snake to supramundane accounts, architectural decorative themes, and the general tattoo pattern in these areas, as recorded in many writings. The most prominent and interesting records concerning the snake are those that give an interpretation of the snake pattern tattoo: since people in the South frequently conducted their livelihood activities in the water, either to grow rice or to go fishing, they were commonly tattooed with such patterns as small dragons (*longzi*) or snakelike creatures with scales so as to avoid harm from aquatic beings including water snakes or sea snakes.[18] As discussed in the section on symbolism in the recorded building of the Wu capital city, these snakelike themes were depicted as being employed in the construction and decoration of significant city gates and thus were characteristically integrated in the application of cosmological motifs.

The first known written record of direct influence from Central China on Wu's social development is one that describes the immigration of Taibo and Zhongyong to this peripheral area. One may be inclined to speculate that Taibo and Zhongyong passed on their experience of advanced cultivation, irrigation, poultry and livestock raising, and of bronze foundry, to the aborigines, since at the end of the Shang, Central China was possibly more developed in most material ways than its peripheral areas.[19] It also seems likely that the tribe led by Taibo became the most advanced in the Lower Yangzi area and laid a foundation for its further development.

In 770 B.C., barbarian invasion drove the royal court of Zhou eastward and its hegemony was crumbling. The fiefs emerged as *de facto* independent states, and the historical stage known as the Spring and Autumn period started. From that time, the Wu and Yue tribes were probably in some degree of subjection to Chu in the west,[20] until 585 B.C. when Shoumeng (?–561 B.C.), the nineteenth successor of the chiefdom, took the title of *wang* (king) formerly reserved for the Zhou ruler who was regarded as the Son of Heaven, or the overall ruler of China. It is also from then on that the chronicle years are precisely recorded for Wu. Wu established a close relationship with the state of Jin in Central China, which intended to unite with Wu so as to neutralize Chu's threat to the north. With the help of Jin from around the 580s B.C., especially in the matter of imported advanced techniques of archery, charioteering, and battle formation, the rapidly developing state of Wu started to attack Chu and dispossessed Chu of all its vassals in the Southeast. Consequently, Wu became more powerful and made frequent contact with other states in Central China. It thus took an active role in the struggle for the hegemony.[21]

Whereas wars between the states of Wu and Chu were frequent, culminating in the former's great victory over the latter in 506 B.C. when Chu's capital city, Ying, was temporarily captured,[22] the history of Wu from the late sixth century B.C. was in a sense a history of its struggling for supremacy against its chief enemy, the state of Yue in the south. According to the *Zuo zhuan* and *Shi ji*,[23] after decades of skirmishes on the borders between the two states, King Helü (?–496 B.C.) of Wu initiated a full-scale offensive against Yue for the first time in 510 B.C. In 505 B.C., when Wu's main force remained in Chu, Yue seized the opportunity to make a major incursion into Wu.[24] In retaliation for this action, Helü led Wu's forces once again in an attack on Yue in 496 B.C., and they battled at Zuili (to the southwest of present-day Jiaxing in Zhejiang). But this time Helü was defeated and died of a severe wound in the same year.[25]

To avenge his father's death, Fuchai (?–473 B.C.), who succeeded to the throne in 495 B.C., waged a bitter war against Yue in the following year and won a decisive victory at Fujiao (a mountain island in present-day Lake Tai), which he followed by a hot pursuit of Yue's forces to Guiji, at present-day Shaoxing. King Goujian (?–465 B.C.) of Yue was forced to surrender and subsequently came to the Wu palace, serving there as a hostage.[26] Although, after his three-year period as a hostage in Wu, Goujian was allowed to return home once again as the king of Yue, it became at this point a *de facto* vassal state of Wu. A hidden peril then remained for Wu. It was acknowledged by Wu Zixu (?–484 B.C.), a prominent minister of Wu, that in this narrow southeast corner, the two states could never co-exist forever; eventually, either Wu annexed Yue, or Yue subjugated Wu.[27] In 473 B.C., Wu was at last destroyed by Yue.[28]

Suzhou Prefecture in the Imperial Era

After the subjugation of Wu by Yue in 473 B.C., the city of Suzhou was left as a remote local town of little importance, in the successive possession of Yue and Chu, until the prime minister of Chu, Lord Chunshen (?–238 B.C.), was enfeoffed in the Wu area in 248 B.C., and took the city as his capital.[29] After the Qin unification in 221 B.C. and the abolition of the fief system, the city constantly housed the seat of a prefecture,[30] or even of a higher administrative unit, notably during the Ming and Qing periods. However, the Suzhou region did not markedly develop in the early imperial period. According to Sima Qian (ca. 145–ca. 85 B.C.), the Jiangnan region in which Suzhou is situated remained sparsely populated in the second half of the Western Han period (206 B.C.–A.D. 9), and the primitive method of cultivation, known as *huogeng shuinou* (plowing after burning [the field] and weeding with water) was still widely in practice; people were living at such a moderate standard that "no one froze or starved, but no family had great wealth either."[31] It was only from the early fourth century when the royal court of Jin fled to the Yangzi valley, accompanied by the exodus of the population of northerly China to the south because of the famine and the political, economic, and administrative chaos that prevailed in North China, and of the occurrence of the tribal rebellions there, that agriculture of this region, especially the area known as San Wu (the Three Wu), started to boom.[32] Yet significant growth of the city in both economic and cultural terms did not occur until the demographic center of the whole of China began to shift to the Yangzi provinces in the ninth and tenth centuries.

Economic Growth

Suzhou's substantial economic growth started during the Tang period (A.D. 618–907). In the second half of the eighth century, the development of the rice-growing areas of the Yangzi basin and South China had begun to gather impetus with the adoption of the technique of planting out seedlings and the appearance of new tools for tilling and irrigating the soil.[33] The superiority of this region in agriculture to any other areas in China became obvious as rice, the yield of which is in fact the highest of all the major cereals (roughly twice that of the millet usually grown in the north) began to dominate the nation's food crop production.[34] The region south of the Yangzi thus became the richest area, one on which the empire economically relied; Suzhou prefecture was at the heart of it and regarded as the most prominent part of the region.[35] After the mid-eighth century, for example, the total amount of tax annually paid by the Liang-Zhe region,[36] consisting only of thirteen prefectures but heavily levied, was 6,650,000 strings of cash (*guan*), while 1,050,000 *guan* were collected from Suzhou—the amount was twice the average from each prefecture in the Liang-Zhe region, and made up 3.5 per cent of the contemporary annual Inland Revenue.[37]

During the course of the following centuries, this upsurge of rice growing continued and expanded.[38] As extensive water conservation projects were carried out during the Song period (960–1279)[39] and progress in methods of rice cultivation continued, the economic strength of Suzhou prefecture further increased to such an extent that the following two proverbs came into circulation:

> Above in Heaven there is the celestial palace, below on Earth there are Suzhou and Hangzhou. [*Tianshang tiantang, dixia Su-Hang.*]
>
> When the harvest of Suzhou and Huzhou is ripe, the whole realm has enough. [*Su-Hu shu, tianxia zu.*][40]

Rice growing made it possible to release a large number of people from working the soil, and the surplus production of the plains to the south of the Lower Yangzi favored the development of interregional trade, the commercialization of agricultural produce, an upsurge in the number of craftsmen, and the growth of big urban centers, such as Suzhou. For Suzhou, however, the currency of the proverbs marked the beginning of a new stage in the city's development, not its culmination. In both economic and demographic terms, it could not match Kaifeng during the Northern Song period (960–1126), nor could it rival the Southern Song capital at Hangzhou.[41]

During the Yuan period (1279–1368), the Hangzhou region stagnated as a result of the center of political power being located by the Mongol rulers on the North China Plain. By contrast, Suzhou prefecture experienced dramatic growth,[42] probably brought about by the government's decision to send southern grain north by sea.[43] A temporary setback for Suzhou occurred in the second half of the fourteenth century when repeated wars broke out in the region, followed by the exile or execution of its social, economic, and cultural elites and by the higher taxes imposed on it by Zhu Yuanzhang (1328–1398), the founder of the Ming (1368–1644), who tried to punish the big landowners of Suzhou for supporting his chief rival, Zhang Shicheng (1321–1367).[44] Yet, as Marmé emphasizes, late fourteenth-century Suzhou was no longer the half-submerged, underpopulated and semideveloped area that it had been at the beginning of the Southern Song in the early twelfth century. When the imperial capital was formally transferred from Nanjing to Beijing in 1421, the rise of Suzhou became clearly visible in its key role in the integration of China's now separate economic and political centers, which was ensured by the extensive use of the Grand Canal.[45]

I have noted that beginning as early as the Northern Song, the increased productivity of agriculture freed the rice-producing farmers from the necessity to retain the main portion of that basic crop for their own subsistence. During the Ming, ever larger numbers of persons in the growing population could engage in secondary production and in distribution. The production of luxury goods and the rapid growth of textile industries were typical of the Suzhou area.[46] Thanks to the convenience and economy of water transport that characterized this region, the city of Suzhou played an organizing role in the aggregation of raw materials and the distribution of finished products around an ever larger hinterland. By the sixteenth century, Suzhou had emerged as the economic and cultural center of China's richest, most urbanized and most advanced region. Continuously developed during the Qing period (1644–1911), it remained the central metropolis integrating and dominating that region well into the 1860s when the Taiping Rebellion brought its prominence to a disastrous end and its leading role was overtaken by Shanghai.[47]

Suzhou's economic domination was indeed partly reflected in its annual land tax payment to the state, unquestionably the highest among all prefectures. Accounting for around 1.16 percent of the registered cultivated land in the whole empire, in 1393, Suzhou prefecture was taxed 9.55 percent of the state's total land tax; in 1491, 7.81 percent; in 1578, 7.86 percent; in the early seventeenth century, 12.39 percent; and in 1820, 9.85 percent.[48] Thus, the following metaphorical assessment of the prefecture by Gu Zuyu can hardly be seen as exaggerating:

> The prefecture takes the River [Yangzi] as its pillow [at its back] and lies adjacent to Lake [Tai]. It enjoys the plenitude of [resources provided by] the sea and mountains, and embraces the benefits from the fertility of the soil. People are wealthy and numerous, and produce is abundant. The amount of tax [collected] from it is constantly above the highest [amongst all prefectures]. Some commentators have remarked that Wu [i.e., Suzhou] prefecture's [relationship] to the world is like the storehouse of a ménage, and the chest and stomach of a man.[49]

Although Suzhou remained the great city of the region, urban growth from the Tang onward occurred in Jiangsu province south of the Yangzi as a whole and was not isolated to a single city. For centuries, the Lower Yangzi had been settled gradually by migrants from North China, but it was above all during the Tang that its city system was fleshed out and showed rapid growth. Skinner has addressed some of the characteristics of the general process of the city system development in the economically advanced regions of imperial China from the mid-Tang onward. Although a fundamental component of the urban revolution in the medieval era was the development of a more fully differentiated hierarchy of economic central places articulating the various regional economies, this city system was immature and uneven: capitals and market towns were only very imperfectly meshed into an integrated system, and the urban population as a whole was concentrated in the largest cities. By contrast, the city systems of the late imperial era were better integrated into a single hierarchical system, and the total urban population was more evenly distributed throughout the hierarchy, but the levels of urbanization were lower than in the medieval era.[50]

The urbanization of the area around the city of Suzhou, which had long functioned as an economic apex, was typical of this process of city system development.[51] Three features of this process can be identified. First, a cluster of secondary cities around Suzhou grew from the mid-Tang onward into the ten thousand class in and after, if not before, the sixteenth century. They included not only county cities of Suzhou prefecture in the Ming period, such as Kunshan, Changshu, Taicang, Jiading, and Wujiang, but also those of adjacent prefectures, notably Wuxi and Jiangyin. The second feature was the burgeoning of market towns in the hinterland of Suzhou after the mid-Tang. The number of these market towns, as was the case in the other more economically advanced parts of China, began to multiply extensively some time in the course of the seventeenth century, many of such towns being reputed in their specialized, notably cotton and silk, industries and trade.[52] All of these market towns helped the flow of persons, goods, money, and ideas locally, regionally, and nationally. Third, the spillover of the city from within its walls may have occurred as early as the mid-Tang period. The most remarkable commercial suburbs developed first outside Chang Gate in the west by north of the city walls and later in Ming times outside Xu Gate in the west by south, both providing access to the Grand Canal, which functioned as the major trade route. And these spawned suburbs, which were connected with the market towns such as Fengqiao, Hengtang, and Mudu in the further west, seem to have formed a larger area of conurbation. The geographical conditions of the hinterland and accessibility to the major trade route conversely had a great impact on the general pattern of the partitioning of urban space based on occupations. Thus, by the nineteenth century, the area of Suzhou, like other more advanced parts of the country, witnessed what Elvin calls "the perfection of a network of local and regional markets, efficiently connected and functionally differentiated."[53] It was on this market network that subsidiary peasant handicrafts relied, providing the main portion of the industrial output.[54]

Population

The first marked demographic growth in the Suzhou area occurred in the early fourth century A.D. when the flow of Chinese population from the north to the south started.

From then on, it continued to grow, though fluctuating as famines, epidemics, and wars periodically took a catastrophic toll of human lives. By the late imperial period, the population density of the prefecture became the highest among all prefectures in the empire. Take the figure for 1820, for instance: the population of Suzhou prefecture stands in fourth place behind Wuchang, Guangzhou, and Chengdu, but its population density was the highest, at 1,073 persons per square kilometer, followed by that of nearby Jiaxing prefecture at 719 persons per square kilometer.[55] This figure is in sharp contrast to the ones for Han times, estimated by Liang Fangzhong, namely 12.3 persons per square kilometer in A.D. 2 and 18.1 persons per square kilometer in A.D. 140.[56]

Of course, the size of the prefectural territory varied immensely. In fact, in the development of field administration of Suzhou prefecture there was a process of the "shrinking" of its territory as a result of the continuous division of counties under the jurisdiction of the prefecture and of the reduction of the area of the prefectural territory. All the local documents inform us that, once the population and economic condition of one of Suzhou's counties reached a certain point, its territory was divided and a new county was subsequently established. In a similar way, the prefectural territory was deducted from some of its old counties being reorganized to form a new prefecture. To illustrate this process visually, Figure 1.3 juxtaposes diagrammatic maps of the area under the jurisdiction of Suzhou prefecture during the Eastern Han, Tang, Song, and Qing periods. In fact, as Naquin and Rawski also have noted, Suzhou from 1724 onward was the only city in the empire to be the seat of three counties, and Jiangsu after 1760 was the only province with two financial commissioners.[57] This pattern of change may have been exceptional in the history of Chinese field administration, if Skinner's argument proves the case that the number of county-level units in the whole of China throughout imperial history was remarkably stable; consequently, since new counties were continually being founded as the boundaries expanded, the number of counties in the already settled areas was being regularly reduced rather than increased, and the average area of counties over the dynasties gradually increased rather than decreased.[58] If we assume that under premodern conditions, population was a reasonable mirror of the size of an economy, these aspects tell us how advanced Suzhou's economy was during the late imperial period as compared to other regions in China.

As for the population of the city itself, because Chinese cities were not corporate entities, Chinese statistics usually do not preserve separate figures for the population of what we would call the cities but include the strictly urban population figures within the statistics for the administrative units to which they belonged, that is, the counties or prefectures. Therefore, it is not surprising that, among all the statistic records available to us, the only figure that appears close to representing the urban population of Suzhou is the one obtained in 1906, when the police examined the house numbers within the city and its near suburbs, which stood at 32,994 households.[59] Even this figure can hardly be seen as accurate, for many shabby dwellings simply did not have number plates on their doors. Nevertheless, Mote estimates that the population of the city of Suzhou in 1229 was about three hundred thousand, and it had probably already reached this size

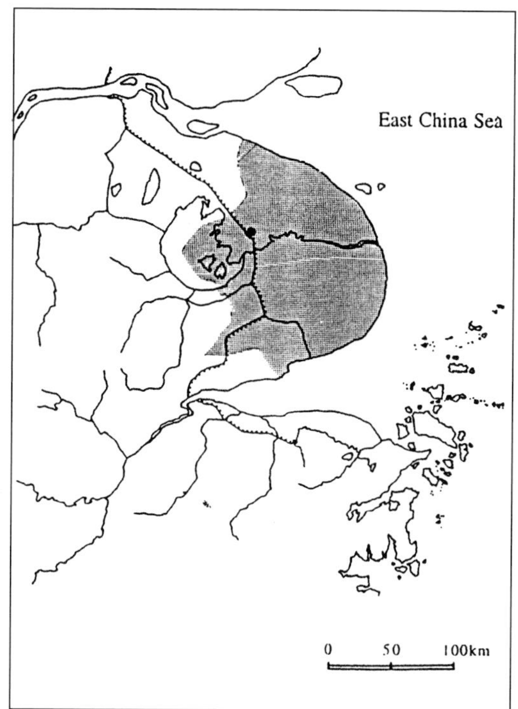

Figure 1.3 *Territories of Suzhou prefecture during the Eastern Han (top left), Tang (top right), Song (bottom left), and Qing (after 1724, bottom right) periods. Adapted from Tan 1982, vol. 2, pp. 24–25; vol. 5, pp. 21–22; vol. 6, pp. 24–25; and vol. 8, pp. 58–59.*

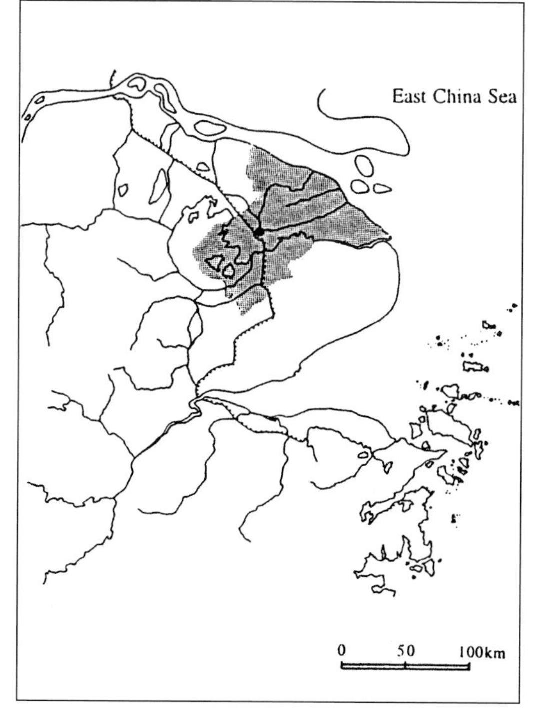

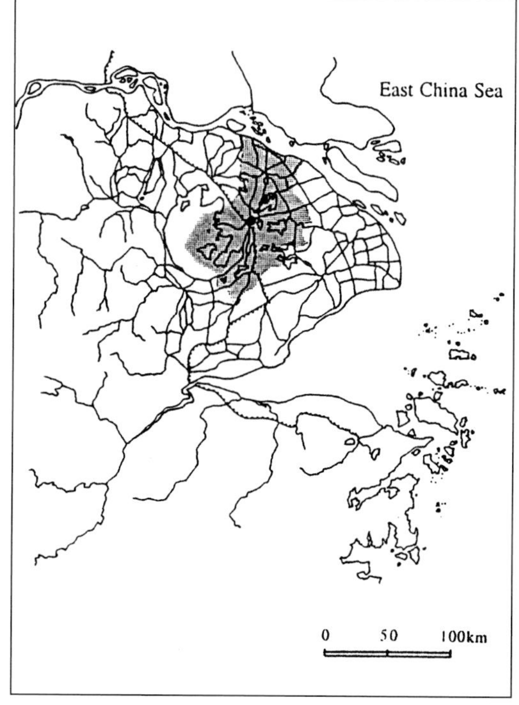

several hundred years before that year. He also suggests that it probably reached the half-million mark in the sixteenth century and may have been close to one million just before the Taiping Rebellion.[60] The city population in 1911, including the suburbs, was estimated at seven hundred thousand by an American Presbyterian missionary named Hampden C. du Bose who lived in Suzhou at that time, while it remained between a half-million and six hundred thousand in the Republican era.[61] Whether these figures are accurate is less important than the fact that Suzhou, starting at the size it had reached by the twelfth or thirteenth century, has continued in stable, if slow, growth, remaining always one of the major cities of its region, throughout the last seven or eight centuries.[62]

Cultural Transformation

Accompanying the economic growth was the gradual change in the social values and conduct of this region. Information about local customs in the Qin and Han periods is summarized in the *Han shu*:

> Gentlemen in [ancient] Wu and Yue were all fond of gallantry. Thus the people there nowadays still relish the practice of swordplay; take death lightly and get agitated easily.[63]

This statement seems to indicate, although apparently without any deprecation, that it was fighting rather than intellectual pursuits that was notable there, and thus this area remained in the eyes of the "civilized men" of Central China as much culturally semi-barbarian as economically underdeveloped.

As more people from North China migrated southward and the economy, especially that of agriculture, boomed in the South, the insemination of Confucian values was accelerated in this area. Therefore, although in the Sui period (581–618), it is still recorded that "the people of this region all practiced the arts of war, and were reputed to constitute the crack troops of the world," a new assessment is also documented:

> [Amongst] the people there, nobles uphold *li* [proper ritual], and commoners are innocent and honest. Thus the customs are those of the unblemished and unsophisticated, whilst the intensity and appropriateness of the teaching of the principles of life are what its general mood esteems.[64]

The rooting of the Confucian ideology in the social life of this area is further stressed by Zhu Changwen (1041–1098), a prominent local scholar of his time. After mentioning a saying said to have been current in the Eastern Han about contemporary commendable customs, he writes in his *Wujun Tujing xuji*:

> Thus that the people of Wu are more taken up with Confucian doctrines and fond of believing [in Buddhism] and giving alms, probably has its evolved reasons. Yet [their present inclination to] boasting wealth and indulging in luxury

> and extravagance already had its precedents in the past. . . . As this dynasty has enjoyed lasting stability and peace, people are courteous and moral; every child has a knowledge of diction, calligraphy and painting, and the old cannot distinguish a dagger-axe from a lance. . . . Within the territory there is no serious banditry, and around the neighborhoods there is no rape or killing; it can be said that [here] is a land of happiness under Heaven.[65]

This passage reveals two related, but in a sense contradictory, aspects of change in social customs, namely achievements in culture on the one hand and extravagance in life on the other.

Confucian values were gradually implanted in every corner of the social life of the locals; literature and arts as the very epitome of Chinese High Culture prevailed, and using swords and spears for fighting as a distinctive character of the ancient local customs became faint memories. The acquisition of wealth by trade and from the textile industry and the production of other luxury goods generally did not lead to systematic capital formation and to the deployment of resources to economic activities of the greatest return. Before the late imperial period, Suzhou was typical in its use of capital in that it poured the excess of its great wealth mostly into land and cultural attainments. Both, in the long term, were secure and reliable investments in status and in assisting access to moderate wealth; both reinforced the normative component of Chinese civilization and its predilection for cultural conservation.

Learning was continuously encouraged in Suzhou as one of the Confucian principles; and it was arduously pursued by many as a theoretical and very practical path to higher social status and official careers as well as a prestige affectation of all who could afford it. This was especially true after Emperor Wen (541–604) of the Sui in 587 introduced the imperial examination institution for the recruitment and promotion of civil servants (*keju*) to replace the old system of official recommendation and selection (*xuanshi*).[66] It was in the Song age, as noted by Gernet, that the system of recruitment competitions actually reached its greatest perfection.[67] Education in the Suzhou area was further promoted when Fan Zhongyan (989–1052) established for the first time the prefectural school in the southern part of the city. This establishment was even seen as setting a model that was about to be followed by all other prefectures, according to the memoir written by Zhu Changwen.[68] Accordingly, academic success became highly significant. Figures for the distribution of *jinshi* (presented scholars, or highest examination graduates) degree-holders during the Qing period, for example, reveal that Jiangsu and Zhejiang ranked first and second for all of China.[69] Suzhou was undoubtedly one of the leading prefectures of Jiangsu in this respect. Elman indicates that Han Learning (*Hanxue*), a school of scholarship that was prominent in the Qing, came into fashion in Suzhou in the eighteenth century and soon swept through the academics there, often replacing Song Learning (*Songxue*) as the vogue of instruction in many other Southeast schools.[70]

Elman also points out that a close overlap existed between the book trade in China and the high level of cultural achievement in the Southeast and that Suzhou was one of the book-collecting and printing centers in the Lower Yangzi for centuries. Hu Yinglin (1551–1602), one of the most famous scholars-book collectors during the Ming, regarded Suzhou as the center for quality printing during the late Ming period, it being a place where printing shops were staffed by outstanding xylographers. Lu Wenchao (1717–1796) noted the centrality of Suzhou scholar-bibliophiles since the Ming dynasty and held that the Suzhou book collections added immeasurably to the stature of the prefecture as a cultural center.[71] Other cultural activities were also outstanding. Painting, for example, flourished in Suzhou from the Yuan onward, as did the related handicraft industries. The Wu School (*Wupai*) of painting started by Shen Zhou (1427–1509), Wen Zhengming (1470–1559), and Tang Yin (1470–1523) became so celebrated during the period between 1567 and 1644 that it was followed by hundreds of well-known scholar-painters. These three artists, together with their contemporary in Suzhou, Qiu Ying (?–ca. 1552), were later called in praise "the Four Painters of the Ming" (*Ming sijia*).[72] Thus, by the late imperial period, Suzhou was not only fostering the arts of China—literary arts, music, painting, calligraphy, craft arts, decorative arts, and minor arts contributing to elegant life—but was also lavishing wealth on gardens, art collections, and religious institutions. Its residents' dress, their mansions, their delicate foods, their pleasure boats and pleasure houses, and their theatricals and festivals were reputed to be the finest in China.

On the other hand, however, long periods of relative peace and social stability and great wealth engendered arrogant and extravagant habits that were at odds with the ideal morality advocated by the Confucians. This trend seems to have been aggravated in the Ming and Qing dynasties when the prefecture reached the peak of its economic and cultural development. Not only did Suzhou have the lasting reputation from the Song to the Ming that people there conducted their lives "commonly more in prodigality than in frugality, competed in festivities and possessions, and indulged in strolls and sightseeing,"[73] but great wealth came to be lavished, in the eyes of many scholars of the Ming and Qing, solely for pleasure. Many of the activities that resulted were nonproductive, resulting only in dissipation or exhaustion of resources and energies. This customary feature of Suzhou was implicitly condemned in the mid-Ming in 1475 by Lu Rong (1436–1494) in his *Shuyuan zaji*:

> Suzhou and Hangzhou are equally renowned as the famous prefectures of Jiangnan. However, the wealthy of the city of Suzhou and its county cities generally enjoy the splendors of pavilions, lodgings, flowers and trees. Nowadays there are none of these in the city of Hangzhou. This indicates that in the frugality of customs, Hangzhou surpasses Suzhou.[74]

This is certainly not a lone voice of discontent with the prodigal way of life in Ming Suzhou. The criticism in 1641 from Gui Zhuan (1613–1673), a scholar of Kunshan county, sounds much more severe:

> Nowadays the arrogance and self-indulgence of customs of Suzhou are well over the limit. Within the city of several *li* across, gardens are facing one another; fertile land is turned to hills and gullies. [Everywhere are] exquisite and ornate buildings, and luxuriant flowers and trees. [The people] indulge themselves intemperately with ephemeral pleasures of strolls and sight-seeing, worrying about nothing else. Alas! Vitiating the useful into the useless, and pursuing the nonbeneficial to damage the beneficial, how can they be imprudent to such an extreme extent![75]

The custom of Suzhou in the Qing period was judged in 1765 by Gong Wei (1704–?) as "being second to none in profligacy under Heaven; and it worsens day by day, but [the people] are unaware that it should turn back."[76] Ironically, the extravagant life drew even larger amounts of labor into the production and distribution of luxury goods. Gu Gongxie witnessed this state of affairs in the second half of the eighteenth century and pointed out its paradoxical social implication in his *Xiaoxia xianji zhaichao*:

> [If] there is a life of luxury and extravagance for thousands, then there is means of livelihood of [other] thousands. Should [we] intend to convert the luxury and extravagance of thousands back to purity and honesty, the means of livelihood for the survival of [other] thousands would certainly be almost cut off. This is [part of] the unchangeable structure [of nature] in which reduction and production revolve and exchange in the world.[77]

We may conclude with Mote that Suzhou "was infamous in the seventeenth and eighteenth centuries as a dissolute city."[78] It is the other side of the coin.

The City Observed

In the fifth month of the year 825, Bai Juyi (772–846), one of the great poets of the Tang, was appointed as the prefect of Suzhou. On the ninth day of the ninth month that year, he held a banquet in a grand multistory hall known as Qiyun Lou on the north wall of the inner enclosure in the city and wrote a poem capturing moments of this experience and reflecting on his career. What he perceived there of the city is depicted in the following stanzas:

> Half inebriated, I lean on the railing and look around:
> Seven weirs, eight [city] gates and sixty residential wards.
> Far and near, high and low, emerge scattered [Buddhist] temples,
> From east to west, from north to south, gazing upon each other are bridges.
> On the arteries and veins of waters the boats are lined up like fish scales,
> Within the oblong city walls residential wards are arranged like a chess-board.
> Filled with houses and trees leaving no gaps,

> The expanse of ten *li* looks all bluish green.
> I ask myself, "What talent and deeds do I have [to deserve to participate in administration],
> And dwell in these grand halls at the center [of the city]?"[79]

In the first half of the ninth century, Suzhou had already emerged as one of the biggest cities in the South east. "Densely populated," as observed again by Bai Juyi, "it surpasses Yangzhou; bustling with noise and excitement in its residential quarters, it matches half of Chang'an."[80] Apart from the increased population and busy urban life, Bai draws—certainly not without hyperbole—a vivid picture of the city in his time: within the city walls that were laid out regularly in rectangular shape and in which there were eight gates, residential wards were orderly and tightly distributed with abundant vegetation; rivers and canals crisscrossed the whole city, and across them numerous bridges were built; temples dotted this vast urban area, with the official prefectural residence situated at the center of the city.

Of all these features, the bridges across myriad rivers and canals probably were most fascinating. In 1072, on his way northward along the canal to the famous Buddhist center on the Wutai Mountains in Shanxi, the Japanese Buddhist monk Seijin passed through the city. As he traveled from Hangzhou toward Suzhou, he wrote in his diary: "There are wooden bridges and there are stone bridges; there are bridges of such number that I would not be able to know how many." He then spent two days there and recorded what he saw in the city:

> All the government palaces and residences are similar in grandness and extent to those in Hangchow [i.e., Hangzhou]. The commerce in the markets is beyond imagining. There are 360 large stone bridges, for on [*sic*] east and west, on [*sic*] south and north, there are canals all about.[81]

Twelve years later, Zhu Changwen eulogistically depicts the city in his *Wujun Tujing xuji*:

> Throughout this period of a century,[82] the wealth of all settlements [of this area] has surpassed that in the Tang period. The city [of Suzhou] not only is fully filled within its walls but spills out beyond them. Multi story halls are facing one another; flying bridges are like rainbows. [Houses are densely aligned together and widely spread out like] the teeth of a comb and a chessboard. Even the narrow alleys in the near suburbs are all paved with bricks. For great number of high officials and prominent figures, [Suzhou] ranks first in the Southeast. This is really a time of peace and prosperity.[83]

In the twelfth month of 1275, Suzhou surrendered to the Mongols without a fight. A few years later, a Venetian merchant, Marco Polo (1254–1324), allegedly visited the city.[84] In his travel book, he writes:

> Suju [i.e., Suzhou] is a large and very noble city. They are idolaters, are subject to the Great Kaan, and have paper currency. They have immense quantities of silk. They live by trade and handicrafts. They make a great deal of silk cloth for clothes. There are great and wealthy merchants. It is so large a city that it has a circuit of sixty miles. The population is so immense that it is beyond all counting. I assure you that, if they were soldiers, the men of Manji[85] would conquer all the rest of the world. But they are no soldiers; instead they are wise merchants, and clever in all handicrafts; and among them there are great natural philosophers, and great leeches who are learned in the secrets of nature. There are many magicians and diviners.
>
> You must know moreover that in this city there are quite 6000 stone bridges,[86] under which, one, and even two, galleys abreast might pass. . . .
>
> . . . Know, too, that this city has sixteen other cities dependent upon it, all large and thriving with trade and handicrafts.[87]

In spite of his exaggerations,[88] Marco Polo's descriptions indicate how large and how thoroughly urban in character the city of Suzhou, together with many other contemporary Chinese cities, was in the Yuan period. Two new, important aspects of Suzhou in this period are revealed here: the first is the apparent multitude of wealthy merchants in and around the city; the second is the continued expansion of urban settlements well beyond the area previously enclosed by the city walls.[89]

The city's recovery after the harsh years of the early Ming became substantiated in the second half of the fifteenth century. Wang Qi (1433–1499), a native scholar of Changzhou county, noted the fact that Suzhou "was always reputed as prosperous and flourishing" and that it remained desolate for over half a century after the Ming conquest. He witnessed the partial resurgence of its economy and urban life during the reign-periods Zhengtong (1436–1449) and Tianshun (1457–1464) but emphasized that substantial rejuvenation came only during the Chenghua reign-period (1465–1487). By the late fifteenth century, Suzhou was in his eyes once again a thriving city. He writes:

> The eaves of houses converge like the spokes of a wheel at the hub, and tens of thousands of tiled roofs are as densely packed as fish scales. From the corners of the city wall to the tributaries of the city moat, pavilions and multi-storey buildings spread out so densely that there is no unoccupied place left. Horse-drawn carriages, mixing with those carrying various food or gift containers, speed up and down the streets and alleys that extend in all directions; all are lustrous and dazzling. Ships gliding around hills and pleasure-boats blossoming with singing girls are flowing one after another through the green waves and the vermilion multi-storey buildings. The melody of musical instruments, of songs and of dances mingle with the noises of the market.[90]

Suzhou by this time had, as recognized by Ch'oe Pu (1454–1504), a Korean official who praised Suzhou's splendor and renown in 1488, truly become the cultural center of the empire, home to a large number of scholars. It was a place where every kind of manufactured article, cheap or expensive, could be found and the destination of all the most skillful craftsmen and wealthiest merchants. The city was noted for the widespread, densely packed houses and shops, "like the stars"; for the numerousness of water courses running through it; and for the extravagance of its residents and the splendor of their mansions. Most important, he mentions the development in the area outside Chang Gate in the west city wall: "At the port of Chang Gate, merchant ships hailing from Hubei and Fujian gather thickly like clouds."[91]

The city throughout the second half of the Qing undoubtedly made deep impressions on British, French, and American visitors. William Alexander, an artist who accompanied the British ambassador Lord Macartney, recorded that he traveled there on November 7, 1793, and "at 2 P.M. arrived at the famous and flourishing city of Soutcheou [i.e., Suzhou], passing through but a portion of it where the canal is close under the walls of the city . . . many houses project over the canal reminding me of Canaletto's views of Venice . . . ."[92] This is not the lone voicing of comparison between Suzhou and Venice. Laurence Oliphant's record made in the mid-nineteenth century, for instance, contains the following lines:

> It has been compared by the French missionaries to Venice,[93] with this difference, that Súchau [i.e., Suzhou] is two days distant from the sea, being accessible only by small inland water, [*sic*] communications. . . . Its situation in the midst of large channels of water is beautiful; the country all around is very pleasant; its climate is delightful, and it is said by many to be the most populous city of the empire . . . .[94]

He continues to remark on other features of the city:

> Súchau is like Hángchau [i.e. Hangzhou] not only a town of large commerce and great silk manufactures, but a place of diversion and pleasure. "Above," say the Chinese, "is paradise, below are Sú and Háng." . . . In fact, Súchau has a high reputation throughout China, for the magnificence of its ancient and new marble buildings, the elegance of its tombs, the multitude of its granite bridges and artificial canals, the picturesque scenery of its waters, streets, gardens and quays, the politeness of its inhabitants, and especially for the beauty of the female sex.
>
> It is said that the city contains a "million of inhabitants," and that there are other millions in its vicinity. Indeed there are several towns included in one, comprising what is called Súchau. First the city proper, inclosed with high walls which are about ten miles in circumference. Second, the suburbs, which are four distinct towns, especially one in the west part,[95] which is about ten miles in length and nearly the same in breadth, and is separated from the city proper by the great imperial canal. Third, the population residing on the water which is very numerous.

> . . . Having entered by the eastern gate, he [i.e., Isidore Hedde, a French commercial delegate] passed out through the famous western gate,[96] and visited there the most interesting part of Súchau, the focus of Chinese industry.[97]

Even at the end of the Qing period when Shanghai by many measures had quickly surpassed Suzhou, the latter's business or wealth was not sucked away. Hampden C. du Bose, who lived in Suzhou through the last of the nineteenth century and into the first decade of this century, describes in a small guidebook to the city[98] the elegant mansions of the rich and tells about the cultivation of the Suzhou people, their refined tastes in rich dress and delicate foods. By noting the great accumulations of capital in the local silver shops and native banks, he sees clearly that the basis of this wealth was the amazingly productive rice culture of the Lower Yangzi delta, coupled with the skills of weavers and artisans, and the entrepreneurial acumen of the businessmen. The opening lines of du Bose's book, written in 1911, run:

> On the banks of the Grand Canal eighty miles west of Shanghai, twelve miles east of the Great Lake [Tai], and forty miles south of the Yangtze, stands a far-famed city, the silk metropolis of the Orient. Even in this hurried twentieth century a crowd of admirers stands with reverent awe around the statue of antiquity, and gazes upon its towering heights, which seem to pierce the clouds.[99]

It is very likely that, as Mote suggests,[100] by "the statue of antiquity," the author refers to the seventy-six-meter tall pagoda, located within the precincts of the large Buddhist temple compound called Baoen Si, popularly known as North Temple (Bei Si), in the north part of the city. Again, canals and bridges cannot but be emphasized:

> Our city stands upon the great artificial highway of the Empire, the Grand Canal, which is from fifty to one hundred yards wide and is spanned by magnificent stone arches—one of these bridges, near Soochow [i.e., Suzhou], has fifty-three arches[101]—and when on this great stream the white sails of the junks and small craft are spread to the winds, and the trackers along the path are towing in the opposite direction, it is a beautiful sight. In regard to inland navigation, Soochow is at the hub, and from it great and wide canals diverge as spokes in every direction, each of these being, as the Chinese boatmen say, "a centipede," from the innumerable streams diverging to the right and left, so there is not a city or town or village or hamlet which cannot be reached by boat in this well-watered plain, so inviting to the itinerant.[102]

Yet du Bose is so amazed by the pagoda that he regards it as "the glory of the capital [of Jiangsu]." "Stand near it," he exclaims, "and behold one of the great wonders of the world! Count the stories, note the verandahs, see the doors, as so many pigeon-holes, and men as pigmies on those giddy heights!"[103] Then he does not hesitate to spend a long passage describing the architectural and decorative details of this huge structure. Mote is right in noting that this American was indeed a perceptive observer, because from the top of the pagoda, one could have a perfect overview of the entire city and what lay beyond:

> Walk around these porches; see the city lying at your feet; the Dragon Street running south to the Confucian Temple; the busy north-west gate; the pile of buildings constituting the City Temple; the Great Lake to the west; the range of hills and the picturesque pagodas that crown the jutting eminences; the plain dotted every fourth mile with hamlets. See the pagoda to the south,—it marks the city of Wukiang [i.e., Wujiang]. Follow the Shanghai canal glistening in the sunlight to the east till your eye rests on a hill,—that is Quensan [i.e., Kunshan]. At the foot of that mountain, thirty miles to the north-east, is Changsoh [i.e., Changshu], a city of 10,000 inhabitants. Look north-west up the Grand Canal, thirty miles,—that is Mount Wei 'tsien. There is Wusih [i.e., Wuxi], with a population of 150,000, and within this radius of thirty miles are one hundred market towns of from one thousand to fifty-thousand inhabitants and probably 100,000 villages and hamlets—five millions within the range of vision![104]

Du Bose does not mention the west suburb outside Chang Gate, because this once prosperous area had not recovered from the devastation brought about fifty years previously by the wars of the Taiping Rebellion.

CHAPTER 2

The City in Its Beginning

TRADITION HOLDS THAT THE WU CAPITAL, Helü Dacheng, at the site of present-day Suzhou was founded in 514 B.C. and that, twenty-four years later, the Yue capital was constructed at the site of present-day Shaoxing. Both events occurred at the time of Confucius when philosophical expositions and disputes amongst various schools of thinking were about to begin. Pervasive ancestor worship appears to have long been the main religious orientation, though this worship existed in constant interplay with concerns about spirits of rivers, mountains, earth, wind, rain, and heavenly bodies, and about Heaven (Tian), which was supremely powerful over both the divine realm and the human world.[1] The cosmological symbolism in the foundation of the Wu capital, and, to a lesser degree, the capital of Yue as Wu's rival state, was seen as expressive of the ambitions of the king of Wu in the struggle for hegemonic power during the Spring and Autumn period. This chapter focuses on the construction of the state capital of Wu, a "history" that was devised by the authors of the Eastern Han documents. However, the problems concerning the sources for the examination of this earliest city and a proper methodology should be discussed first.

Sources of Information and Methodological Approach

This chapter, unlike following chapters, does not present a historical study of the city at its earliest construction. Instead, it aims at formulating the *conception* of its urban form and symbolism, which, by the Eastern Han period, had accumulated and was fairly systematized. This methodological orientation is determined, first, by the lack of archaeological evidence. As Wheatley states when discussing the cities of the Zhou period, the only material that can be regarded as primarily relevant for the study of urbanism in ancient times is properly attested archaeological evidence, while the transmitted texts must be considered as only of secondary importance. In these circumstances, it is very unfortunate that archaeological discoveries pertaining to the Zhou era are extremely scarce.[2] The study of the Wu capital is similarly difficult. One of the reasons for this turns out to be that the site of the capital has most probably been occupied successively by the dynastic and present-day city and has thus been reconstructed again and again. Another related reason may lie in the ephemeral building materials applied in almost all Chinese city construction, which could easily be destroyed by wars and fires. Thus, archaeological investigation is often limited to chance exposures revealed during construction work, and some remaining pieces of past dynasties have been excavated from several layers of a rubble seam of three to four meters in thickness beneath the present ground surface of the city.[3] Consequently, an examination of this early city has to rely only on the traditional written information.

The methodological orientation for this chapter is further determined by the fact that, to my knowledge, the earliest documents providing relatively extensive and systematic information are the *Yue jue shu* and the *Wu Yue chunqiu,* both written in the Eastern Han period,[4] more than half a millennium after the founding of the city. Therefore, it is difficult to distinguish authentic accounts of the city's construction as historical fact from amendments or even concoctions. Changes to these texts may have taken place partly through unconscious processes natural to the passage of time and partly through historiographical editing and exegesis not only designed to afford support for later value systems and moral judgments but also reflecting the cosmological synthesis of the particular time. Serious problems would then ensue in a historiographical approach to the building of this city. For example, how can later accounts be used to reconstruct the form of the city, and how can the particular way in which the city form was symbolically perceived at the time of the building be identified?

It is because of these limitations that this chapter does not aim at examining what the Wu capital was in physical reality or how and to what extent the history of its earliest building was devised by the authors of the Eastern Han documents to express Wu's historical struggle for survival against other states, most notably against the state of Yue. Instead, this chapter describes what was perceived of the city as revealed in this earliest, systematized version of its beginning. A few suggestions only are randomly made on the possible origins of some of its elements. This orientation of the study is justified by the context of the present study, its main purpose being to sketch a number of important features of urban transformation in premodern China. It is evidenced by all the local gazetteers and many other documents produced in subsequent history that this earliest version was traditionally accepted through the ages. It constitutes an archetypal construct that has been transmitted from the remote past and can therefore be regarded as a conceptual beginning of the city. The authority of the past has been a more cumulative phenomenon for the Chinese, who have possessed a particularly strong sense of continuing tradition. Whatever the authenticity of this version may prove to be, it later came to be viewed as a source of historical authority and continued to inform the city's further development. After all, "history," as Sivin indicates, "unlike science, is not the study of physical things, but of how human beings conceive them."[5]

Nevertheless, the earliest accounts in the Eastern Han documents of the event of the building of the Wu capital in the late sixth century must have been produced in the social and theoretical context of the time of the writing. Thus, the following section examines the canonical principles of city planning recorded in the *Zhou li* and, in particular, its last section, "Kaogong ji." They not only reveal a considerable body of lore, practices, and ideas connected with city building accumulated by the end of the Warring States but are strongly characteristic of the Han synthesis. In discussing these principles, I rely not only on my reading of the Han texts but also on the pioneering efforts mainly of Arthur F. Wright and Paul Wheatley.[6]

The Locus Classicus

Whereas some passages, or their underlying ideas, may be of early date, the basic structure of the *Zhou li*, and the numerical-symbolic references in particular, date from about the time of Han Wudi (156–87 B.C.). There is little doubt at present that the *Zhou li* was not known before the Western Han. It gives an elaborately laid out and detailed description of what purports to be the governmental and administrative structure and organization of the royal Zhou. Yet it is of utmost importance to note that, since the text as it now stands was arranged, interpolated, and partly invented by the architects of the Han syncretic ideology and cosmology, it is normative and prescriptive, not historical. The *locus classicus*[7] for the ideal layout of the Zhou capital city is the "Kaogong ji" section. This section was thought by Jiang Yong (1681–1762) to be a work of the late Warring States period, compiled by a person from the state of Qi. It was substituted for the original sixth, and last, section on "Dongguan" (Winter offices), which had already been lost at the time when the *Zhou li* first became known in the Western Han.[8] For convenience, I have grouped the characteristic features of the principles of city building prescribed in the "Kaogong ji" into four categories: choice and preparation of the site, cardinal orientation, city layout, and disposition of principal structures.

Choice and Preparation of the Site

Ideally, the city has to be at the center of the land. The precise position of this cosmic pivot should be calculated, as explained in the *Zhou li*, by the official known as the Da Situ, with the gnomon shadow template (*tugui*), the length of the gnomon being one *chi* five *cun:*

> [The Da Situ], with the *tugui* method, measures the length of the sun's shadow on the earth [*tushen*]. [He] seeks [the place where] the sun's shadow [*riying*] stretches in the true north and equals the gnomon in length, so as to find the center of the earth. . . . The center of the earth is [that place where] the sun's shadow at the summer solstice is one *chi* five *cun*. [This is the place] where earth and sky

> meet, where the four seasons merge, where wind and rain are gathered in, and where *yin* and *yang* are in harmony. Therefore the myriad things are at peace. Thus [it is here that] the royal capital is to be built.[9]

Wright suggests that the second half of this passage is an expression of the systematized organicism characteristic of Han Confucian ideology. It makes the capital city a cosmic focal point, a center from which the forces of nature may be adapted to or controlled in the interests of the whole realm. Here, the siting of a capital was seen, in Wright's words, "in relation to the forces of nature and to the hypostasized powers that govern all phenomena."[10] It was at this quintessentially cosmic pivot that the royal palace was raised. Here resided the king, the Son of Heaven, who upheld and represented the harmony of macrocosm and microcosm. Such a proper siting was regarded as responsible for aligning the human realm with the moral patterns of the cosmos. Such emphasis was placed on this idea that each of the six sections of the *Zhou li*—corresponding to Heaven, Earth, and the four seasons—opens with the same following statements:

> It is the king alone who establishes the [capital of his] state, discerns the directions of the four quarters, and puts right the proper positions [of the Royal Palace and Ancestral Hall]; he gives to the city its principle layout and to the fields their proper divisions; he devises the offices and apportions their positions; so that the center is established to which the people turns.[11]

The centralism is clearly characteristic of Han ideology. It makes the capital the epicenter of an orderly spatial grid extending to the boundaries of civilization.[12] From this carefully determined site, the powers of cosmic order should spread outward to the four quarters of the world, and the outward degressive potentialities will be formed into a harmonious system and thus brought into full play.

Before any social activity is conducted, certainly including construction of a new city, or a transference of the capital, or even an alteration at the site of the capital, auguries should be taken by milfoil and then by tortoise shell. Once the site has been decided, the first step of the construction work is to survey the contours of the site by the use of plumb lines and water levels at its four corners and then to grade the site to a level piece of ground, as recorded in the "Kaogong ji."[13] This record is regarded by Wright as "a straightforward description of procedures for preparing a building site that were no doubt of great antiquity."[14]

Cardinal Orientation

The orientation of the city to the four cardinal points is omnipresent in the construction of almost all the Chinese capitals. An ode entitled "Ding zhi fangzhong" evokes the scene of the building of a new capital by the people of the state of Wei in 660 B.C. at the site called Chu:

When [the constellation] Ding[15] had attained the zenith,
They began to build the Ancestral Hall at Chu.
When they had calculated [the cardinal orientations] by the sun,
They began to build the palaces and houses at Chu.[16]

Wheatley observes that prominent among the morphological features that the ideal-type Chinese city shared with a majority of the great capitals of Asia were cardinal orientation, cardinal axiality, and a more or less square perimeter delimited by a massive wall. There was, however, a difference of emphasis in one important feature of their plans: much greater significance was given to the main processional axis running from south to north, "the celestial meridian writ small," as Wheatley calls it, than to any avenue running from east to west."[17] The preference of the south-north axiality may, on the one hand, come from the basic pragmatic requirement of buildings' southern exposure for biological reasons, which later gave rise to the general conceptual partiality of the Chinese for facing the south. On the other hand, this preference may come from the equatorial character of Chinese astronomy, which concentrates attention on the Pole and circumpolar stars, as opposed to the ecliptic-emphasizing nature of Greek and medieval European astronomy and to astronomy based on azimuth and altitude as practiced by the Arabs.[18] The concept is fairly clear, as recommended in the "Kaogong ji":

> They [the artificers] erect a post [at the center of the leveled ground], taking the plumb lines to ensure its verticality, and with it observe the sun's shadow [*riying*]. They take it as the determinator of the shadows of the sun at its rising and setting and discern their midpoint [indicating the true north]. In the daytime, they consult the sun's shadows at noon; in the nighttime, they study the pole star, so that [the orientation of] true east and west, [and south and north] is precisely fixed.[19]

The pole was connected therein with a background of microcosmic-macrocosmic thought and thus corresponded to the position of the emperor on earth, around whom the vast system of the bureaucratic agrarian state naturally and spontaneously revolved.[20] This was metaphorically stressed in a passage in the *Lun yu*:

> He who exercises government by means of his virtue may be compared to the north polar star, which keeps its place while all the stars turn round it.[21]

Since this earthly center reproduces the order of the wider cosmos, the city draws forth the power of that order into the city and the kingdom of the earth.[22] In this sense, the Son of Heaven throned facing southward, corresponding to the pole star that at the axis of the universe watched over the southerly world of men, ruled all the people on earth who "face the north to acknowledge their allegiance as his subjects" (*beimian chengchen*).

City Layout

The ideal layout of the city is summarized in the following passage of the "Kaogong ji":

> The artificers, as they built the capital, demarcated it as a square with sides of nine *li*, each side having three gateways. Within the capital there were nine meridional and nine latitudinal avenues, each of the former being nine chariot tracks wide.[23]

Figures 2.1, 2.2, and 2.3 show three drawings of the ideal royal Zhou city, produced in the mid-tenth century, in 1408, and in the second half of the eighteenth century, respectively. Whereas the problem of layout concerning the proportion of subdivision has evoked controversial speculations,[24] there is no question that this idealized urban plan relied on the same principle of subdivision as the old well-field (*jingtian*) system of land settlement and cultivation, as Granet has noted.[25] In cosmological terms, this aspect might turn out to have been more significant in the city as a microcosm and the very center of the earth than in the methodological application of the well-field system in city layout, in that the ruler of all-under-Heaven was expected to reside in a structure that was a symbol of the earth. First, since the ancient Chinese perceived the earth as a square checkerboard, the form of a square was obviously taken to be a prerequisite for the general morphology of an ideal capital that would be a replica of the earth.[26] Second, and perhaps more profoundly, the layout of the city was analogous to the administrative subdivision of the royal territory and further to the conceptual subdivision of the whole world. According to the "Yu gong" section of the *Shang shu*, Yu, a legendary hero-emperor, divided the land of China into nine regions, or nine provinces (*jiuzhou*), after having mastered the waters.[27] Furthermore, the Middle Kingdom (Zhongguo, also denoting present-day China) was thought to hold a central place among the nine greater regions of the whole world.[28] It is therefore reasonable to think of the city that

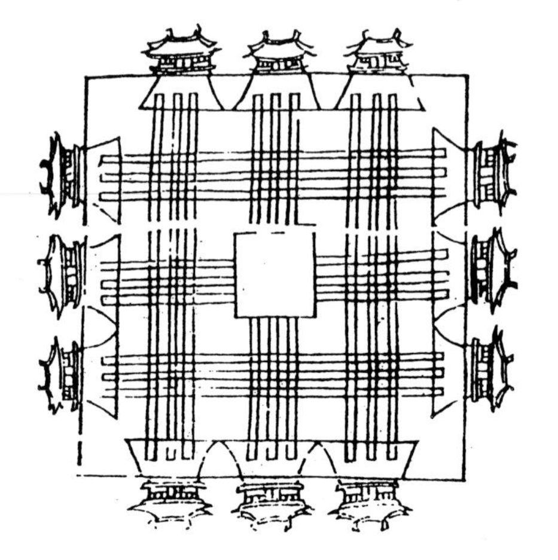

Figure 2.1 Canonical plan of the royal Zhou capital (Wangcheng) in the Sanli tu jizhu *(juan 4.3b), produced in the mid-tenth century.*

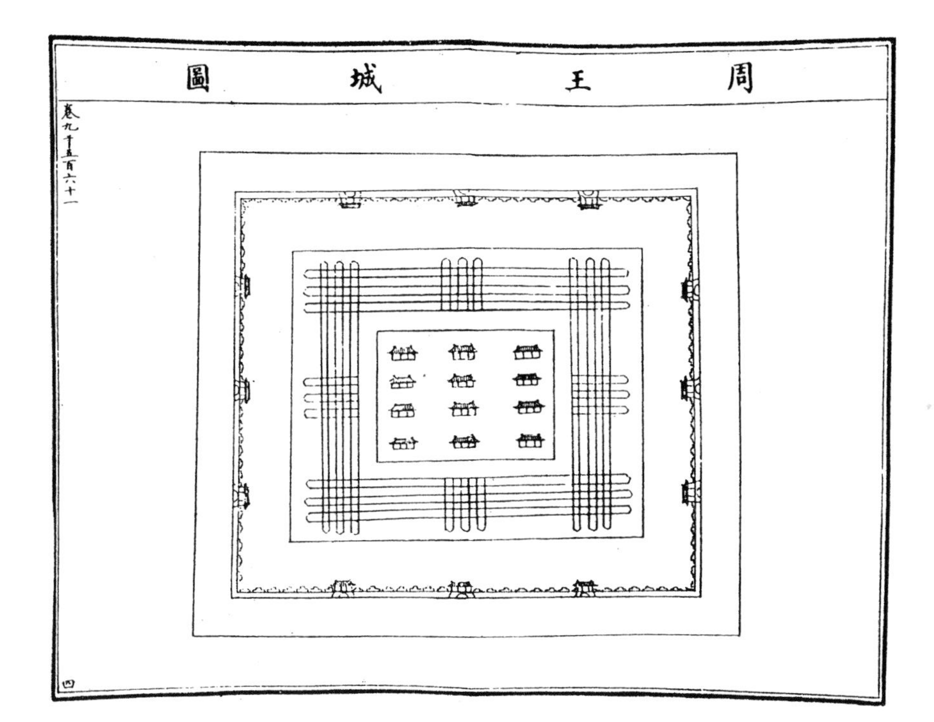

Figure 2.2 Canonical plan of the royal Zhou capital in the Yongle dadian *(*juan *9561.4a–b), produced in 1408.*

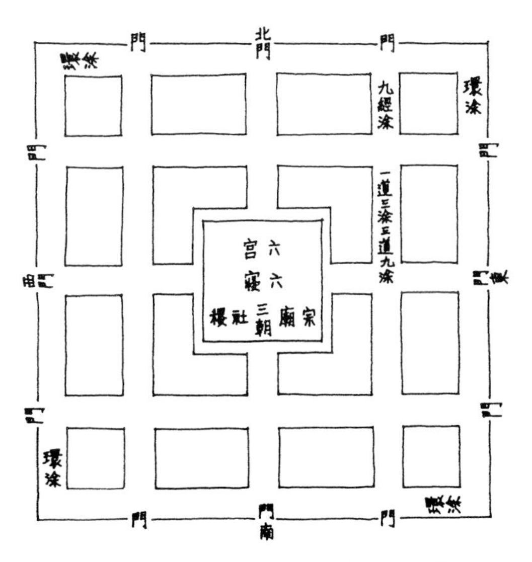

Figure 2.3 Canonical plan of the royal Zhou capital in the Kaogong ji tu *(B, p. 110), produced in the second half of the eighteenth century.*

was subdivided into nine units, with the royal palace in the center, as a microcosm embedded in a concentric system, from the Chinese empire up to the scale of the whole world, on the pivot of which resided the Son of Heaven. The third significance lies in the network of the well-field system into which the capital city is embedded. The capital (*guo*) was constructed in such a symbolic way that the grid scheme of its subdivision and the units of its measurement were identical with those of the country field (*ye*),[29] and the perspective of this checkerboard pattern radiated from the capital outward, ideally in all directions to the frontiers of the world.

Wright, after citing a passage from Granet's "Les Nombres" on the emblematic numbers, argues that the systematic application of numbers to the city layout is a product of the second half of the Western Han. Among them three, nine, and twelve are particularly significant: *three* represents the three sectors of the intelligible universe (heaven, earth, and man); *nine* symbolizes the ancient Chinese world (the nine provinces as established by the Emperor Yu); and *twelve* is the number of months in a year. "Thus it follows that the ruler, who is seen by the Han theorizers as uniting in his person the three sectors of the universe and presiding over the nine provinces, during the sequence of twelve months in each year, should have the numbers three, nine, and twelve in the symbolism of his capital."[30]

Here it seems worth emphasizing the exclusive application of the number *nine* for the capital and the decreasing arithmetical progression for other cities in the hierarchical range. Odd numbers were regarded as of *yang*, and nine, the largest of odd numbers, was the supreme *yang* number denoting Heaven and was thus associated with the Son of Heaven. As in other civilizations, the larger and higher the construction is, the higher the number employed in it and the more noble and majestic it is considered to be rendered. In China, this hierarchy was constitutionalized in detail as formal rituals (*li*) as early as the late Zhou.[31] In the case of city construction, for instance, a passage in the *Zuo zhuan* explains:

> The walls of any state capital which exceed a hundred *zhi*[32] [in circumference] constitute a danger to the state. According to the institutions of the former kings, the walls of a city of the first order must not exceed one-third the length of that of the capital, that of a second-order city one-fifth, and that of third-order city one-ninth.[33]

By the Han period, the basic formula of this matter became fairly standardized, and, as recorded in the *Han shu*, "it is a matter of the *li* that from the higher to the lower [the number employed in any event] descends with a difference of two."[34] This ritually classified order was also expressed in many other aspects of city construction, with the city where the Son of Heaven resided on the top of the hierarchy.

Disposition of Principal Structures

The "Kaogong ji" states that the Ancestral Hall (*Zu*) shall be on the left, that is, the east, and the Altar to the God of the Earth (*She*) on the right, or the west. This prescription, of course, places the south-facing royal palace at the center and the point of reference. Thus, the passage continues, "In the front [i.e., the south] is the Imperial Court [*Chao*], while at the back [i.e., the north] lies the market [*shi*]."[35]

As mentioned earlier, ancestor worship dominated since the earliest known times of Chinese civilization, and it is extremely possible, as Wright assumes, that the cult of ancestors is as old as Chinese culture itself.[36] Thus for the Zhou, the ancestral temple of the princely line (*zongmiao*), wherein the commemorative tablets of the royal lineage were enshrined, with the high ancestor of the lineage as the focus of the cult, was a building of the highest importance in religious, political, diplomatic, and military terms and became a crucial criterion for a city or settlement to be regarded as a proper capital. A passage in the *Zuo zhuan* explicitly states that

> All *yi* [settlements] having an ancestral temple, with the Spirit-tablets of former rulers, were called *du* [state capital]; those without such a temple were called *yi*. Walling a *yi* is called *zhu*; walling a capital is called *cheng*.[37]

The Han documents therefore prescribe that some significant events should be reported at the *zongmiao* in appropriate formulas, and an elaborate annual calendar of sacrifices was also formulated. This was regarded as necessary ceremony and etiquette in accordance with the *li*.[38]

For the Han synthesizers, another ubiquitous cult in the early Zhou, the Altar to the God of the Earth, laid with the soils of five colors symbolizing the territories in the five directions (four quarters and center),[39] should always be kept open

> To receive the hoar frost, dew, wind and rain, and to allow free access to the *qi* [cosmic breath] of Heaven and Earth. Hence the extinguished state's *she* shall be roofed over so as for it not to receive the *yang* influence from Heaven. . . . Offering sacrifice to the God of the Earth is thus to praise the *Dao* [Way] of the sacred Earth. The Earth carries the myriad things, and the signs descended from Heaven. It is from the Earth that the myriad things are obtained [by men], and it is from Heaven that the order comes that is followed [by men]. Therefore [to offer sacrifice to the God of the Earth] is to show reverence for Heaven and to be on intimate terms with the Earth, and is to teach the people to remain in gratitude.[40]

Again, the symbolic importance of the altar was not new to the Han. During the Zhou period, enfeoffment had to be carried out with a symbolical handful of earth taken from the part of the king's great altar with the relevant direction.[41] Since the earth was of utmost importance to the state in every sense, the Altar to the God of the Earth, like the Ancestral Temple, functioned as one of the loci of the state's affairs. An annual calendar of sacrifices was elaborated, and it was at the Altar of the Earth that various important events started or ended. There, for example, the armies of a state sacrificed before the start of a campaign; there they presented captives and offered sacrifices after a victory; and there the ruler beat the drum or offered sacrifice when abnormal natural phenomena occurred.[42]

It seems possible, however, that the specific positions assigned to both the Ancestral Hall and the Altar to the God of the Earth, were outcomes of the Han synthesis, even though they may have reflected a concept of the Zhou people. The *Yi Zhou shu* states:

> The *Dao* of Heaven esteems the left [position], [hence] the sun and moon move westward. The *Dao* of Earth esteems the right [position], [hence] the waters flow eastward. The *Dao* of Man esteems the central [position], [hence] the ears and eyes serve the heart.[43]

The ancestors, on the one hand, like the father to his son, the husband to his wife, and the king to his subjects, are of *yang* character, and therefore analogous to Heaven.[44] On the other hand, with their previous meritorious and glorious deeds, they obtained the Mandate of Heaven as the source of legitimate authority to rule the world and thus were seen by their descendants as closely associated with Heaven.[45]

Both the Ancestral Temple and the Altar of the Earth and Grain were jointly regarded as the loci of the symbol of the continuing power of the state.[46] When the king of Yue recalled the total defeat that he suffered in the war in 493 B.C. against Wu and the devastation that his state had undergone, he said, "What the state of Wu did was immoral and evil. [They] sought to maim my Ancestral Temple and my Altar of the Earth and Grain and to raze them to the ground, not letting [my ancestors and the gods] enjoy blood sacrifices."[47] The symbolic significance of these two cults for the city and state is more convincingly illustrated by an incident of 548 B.C. recorded in the *Zuo zhuan*, which has come to epitomize the idealized proprieties of military conflict in those times and has been quoted by both Wheatley and Wright. It tells how the conqueror of Chen was met at the royal court in the capital by the defeated ruler, wearing mourning, and his chief staff, who bore in their arms the image of the God of the Earth and the ritual vessels used in the Ancestral Temple.[48] When the conqueror received these two objects—the respective supreme symbols of sustenance and government—it signified that the entire state had passed into his hands.[49]

The market was given the place of least honor and minimum *yang* influence by being located in the northern extremity of the city, in contrast with the southern location of the royal hall of audience. The prescription of the layout of an ideal city reflects to a degree the value system of the pre-Han period, which was later fully elaborated by the Han Confucians.[50] The market was highly supervised and controlled, according to the *Zhou li*, by the "market supervisor" (*sishi*),[51] the principle of this system lasting until the mid-Tang. Even though commerce was granted a rather low status in social life in contrast with other matters in the city, the running of the market may still have reflected a typical Chinese attitude toward social life and the natural world, that is, to paraphrase Graham, to treat opposites as complementary rather than conflicting.[52] This attitude has been described very persuasively by Wright:

> In another passage,[53] under the duties of the *nei-tsai* [*neizai*], the *Chou li* [*Zhou li*] tells us that this official is to assist the empress in establishing a market, to attend to its layout and regulations, and then to dedicate it by the *yin-li* or female ritual. The commentary of Cheng Hsüan [Zheng Xuan] (2nd century A.D.) explains that in establishing the capital of a state the emperor builds the palaces whereas the

> empress establishes the market, and that this is to represent the harmonious complementarity of the male and female principles (*yang* and *yin*). That this ever happened is doubtful, to say the least, but the additional theorizing tends to underscore the *yin* character of the market location in the classical plan.[54]

One of the most notable and important features in the mode of the canonical disposition of these principal urban structures, and, indeed, in the whole set of city planning principles prescribed in the *Zhou li*, ideal as they were,[55] is the proper, symbolic positioning of every physical element of the city by reference to cardinal orientation, with an emphasis on the south. It formed an order that was seen as durable because it was not arbitrary but based on an understanding of Nature, the eternal standard. As the *Zhou Yi qianzaodu*, possibly written in the first century B.C., expounds,

> What does not change [in the universe] is the proper position [of each of the myriad things]. Heaven is above; Earth is below. The monarch faces south; the subjects face north. The father sits and the son prostrates himself. These are what do not change.[56]

The canonized principles of city planning, as many other institutions of the state, were defined by defining the order of Heaven and Earth, to paraphrase Sivin, who concisely interprets one of the passages on this point by Dong Zhongshu (179–104 B.C.).[57]

The Wu Capital

Although from the early sixth century B.C. on, intensified contact between Wu and Central China introduced much Zhou high culture to these southern peripheral regions, Wu may still have preserved some aspects of local customs. One of these customs was using the theme of the snake, which pervaded myths and the general tattoo pattern. This custom is consciously incorporated by later scholars into the reconstructed history of the building of this earliest city. At the same time, the rulers of Wu, no longer seeing themselves as enfeoffed tribal groups with allegiance to the Zhou, took the title of king, and like other states and tribes, joined in the struggle for power that was taking place everywhere across the area of present-day northern and central China.[58] Their endeavor is made symbolically manifest again by the authors of the *Yue jue shu* and *Wu Yue chunqiu* in the construction of their capital city.

Choice of Site

In the early summer of 515 B.C., during the reign of King Liao, a long premeditated palace coup brought to power a new, ambitious king, Helü.[59] At this time, the Wu capital was probably no more than a fortified center for agricultural, military, and perhaps ceremonial purposes, and its site had by now been changed several times. Although the exact locations of the capital are a matter of academic dispute, it has been suggested by a number of scholars, on the basis of early documents and the results of archaeological work, that the trend of the movement of the capital was southeastward.[60] Xiao Menglong suggests that there may have been two pragmatic reasons for the transference of the capital in this direction.[61] One was considerations of military strategy. During the Spring and Autumn period, military conflicts were extremely frequent.[62] If the assumption that the city and state were practically and symbolically one can only be applied to some of the smaller Chinese states, the idea of the city being regarded as stronghold for the state's defense may largely have reflected the reality at that time, as a line in the *Zuo zhuan* runs, "I am charged with the capital to defend the state."[63] The strategic position of the capital, then, became a crucial criterion for the survival of the state.

In the area of the middle and lower reaches of the River Yangzi at that time stood the states of Chu, Wu, and Yue, with Chu being the strongest and Yue the weakest. It is possible that, in order for Wu to fulfill its ambition of seeking hegemony over China, strategic measures had to be taken in dealing with these two enemy states. Although serious threats posed by Yue during the early reign-period of Helü may not have appeared as imminent as those by powerful Chu, the former was regarded by Wu as "a serious disease in its vital organs." The author of the *Yue jue shu* later embroidered this documented concern of Wu by putting the following words in the mouth of Fan Li:

> The *qi* [cosmic breath] of kingly hegemony is visible at [the area of] the Gate of Earth [*Dihu*]. . . . [T]he occupant of [the area of] the Gate of Earth must be either Wu or Yue.[64]

Consequently, the Wu capital may have moved southeastward, further from Chu in the west but closer to Yue in the south. This move geographically retained for Wu the option of either continuing to challenge and exhaust powerful Chu in the west whenever conditions were suitable, while avoiding a direct attack on it, or watching and menacing the weak but potentially dangerous Yue in the South in a most convenient way (see Figure 1.2).

The other pragmatic reason was the need for the development of the economy of the state of Wu. It seems to have been taken as a logical principle for the capital of an agrarian state to have been built in an area of fertile soil and rich resources, as is advocated in the *Guanzi*, "so that the natural conditions can be relied on, and the productive advantage of the land can be beneficial, which will support the people's life there and provide for raising livestock."[65] A similar proposition can be found in the *Wei Liaozi* written in the Warring States period:

> The fecundity of the soil is examined so as to establish a settlement and build a city, and therefore to protect the land by virtue of the city, to support the people by virtue of the land, and to produce crops by virtue of the people.[66]

The transference of the Wu capital from the hilly area in the northwest toward the Taihu (i.e., Lake Tai) plain in the southeast, with its fertile land, rich natural resources, and geographically convenient transport systems, may have been one of the important factors that finally boosted Wu's agricultural production and foundry industry, which in turn supported its bid for hegemony.[67] Since the state of Wu was regarded by the authors of the Eastern Han documents to be on the southeast fringes of ancient China, in territories that were essentially barbarian in character, and as a newcomer to Chinese diplomacy, it is not surprising that in the *Wu Yue chunqiu* and *Yue jue shu* there is no account of the pursuit of the centrality of the city prescribed in the *Zhou li*. Locally, however, the site was regarded by scholars of later periods as endowed with considerable potentialities for the city's later development. Zhu Zichang of the Yuan dynasty, for example, summarized the idea about this locational quality:

> Wu has the superior terrain conditions [*xingsheng*][68] of the Three Rivers and the Five Lakes.[69] Hence its land has been powerful and prosperous from the past to the present.[70]

No process of divination for the choice of the site of the Wu capital is recorded. The only implicit reference relevant to this issue is that when Wu Zixu (?–484 B.C.) was authorized to plan the new capital, he asked the experts "to survey the terrain of the land and taste the waters [*xiangtu changshui*]."[71] The character *xiang* here implies a twofold meaning, namely, to survey *and* to divine, and there is no doubt that such an implication is of great antiquity.[72] Yet the phrase *xiangtu changshui* as a whole was probably of Han origin. In fact, from the *Han shu* a similar account is found in Chao Cuo's (200–154 B.C.) enunciation of the procedure of building a new city on a new site:

> [One should first] survey [*xiang*] the harmonious aspects of its [site's] *yin* and *yang*, taste [*chang*] its waters, examine [*shen*] the suitability of the soil, and observe [*guan*] the exuberance of its vegetation. After this, [one may] build the city and erect its walls.[73]

City Layout

The authors of the *Yue jue shu* depict Helü Dacheng as a city with three layers of walls. The middle city wall (*dacheng*) enclosing the city proper measured 47 *li* 210 *bu* 2 *chi* (approximately 20.18 kilometers by the Eastern Han standard) in perimeter.[74] Ji Yuyi, who, to my knowledge, is the first scholar to treat this matter of the recorded measurements of the city critically, suggests that the record of "47 *li*" might be a faulty transcription of "37 *li*," and that thus the perimeter of the wall would have been less than 16 kilometers.[75] If this were true, the measurement of the *dacheng* would have been roughly in accordance with what was stated in the *Zhou li*, that is, 36 *li* in perimeter ("a square with sides of 9 *li*"). According to the *Yue jue shu*, the outer city wall *(guo)* measured 68 *li* 60 *bu* (approximately 28.85 kilometers) in perimeter, its proportion to the wall of the city proper (*dacheng*) being approximately consistent with that of its contemporary cities in Central China.[76] The same text also states that the wall of the inner enclosure (*xiaocheng*), actually the king's palace (*gong*), was 12 *li* (approximately 5.08 kilometers) in perimeter,[77] which again is in line with that of the canonical Zhou royal capital idealized by the Han synthesizers.

Little is known about the sectional dimensions of the walls of the *dacheng* and *guo*. The *Yue jue shu* claims that the walls of the *xiaocheng* measured 2 *zhang* 7 *chi* (approximately 6.3 meters by the Eastern Han standard) thick at the base, and 4 *zhang* 7 *chi* (approximately 11 meters) high.[78] Yet since the canonical planning principles of the royal Zhou capital recorded in the "Kaogong ji" prescribe that the walls of the city proper should be two *zhi*[79] higher than the walls of the palace enclosure, the sectional dimensions of the walls of the city proper may have been larger than those of the inner enclosure.

The positions of these enclosures relative to each other and the exact form of the city are uncertain due to the paucity of information concerning them. The early documents do not give any explicit account of the position of the wall of the inner enclosure in relation to that of the wall of the city proper and of the city proper to that of the outer city wall, but it is very possible, as has been traditionally accepted, that they formed a three-layer concentric enceinte, which was a fairly common feature of city planning in the pre-Qin era.[80] The accounts of the lengths of the four sides of the wall of the city proper in the *Yue jue shu,* however, seem to imply that the form of the city was a four-sided, if deformed, square. I assume that these aspects of the city may have been regarded by the authors of the Eastern Han documents as *sine qua non* for anything that could properly be termed a city, and ink would therefore not necessarily have been wasted on them.

Because of the lack of archaeological evidence, it is impossible to tell from these accounts of the physical form of Helü Dacheng which part of them reflects the actual city in the late sixth century B.C. and was transmitted through time to the authors of the *Yue jue shu* and *Wu Yue chunqiu*, and which part was based on their own perceptions of it in their time. Figure 2.4 presents a conjectural diagrammatic plan of this recorded city, which is based on literary information and the city maps of later dynastic periods. The lengths of the three walls retain the proportions accorded them by the descriptions in the *Yue jue shu.* However, only the form of the city proper can be regarded with some certainty to be close to that perceived by the author of the Han document, and that only so as long as the speculated position of the city gates is considered to be acceptable[81] and the *Yue jue shu*'s record of the measurements of its four sides and its main streets is reliable.

Except for the walled inner enclosure (*xiaocheng*), which was without exception the king's main palace complex, and a couple of small building compounds serving as the temporary royal abodes, other essential features of Helü Dacheng and Yue's capital, such as the Ancestral Temple, the Altar to the God of Earth and Grain, and the market have not directly been described in any early document. However, their existence is concomitantly implied in the narration of certain historical events. Although the Ancestral

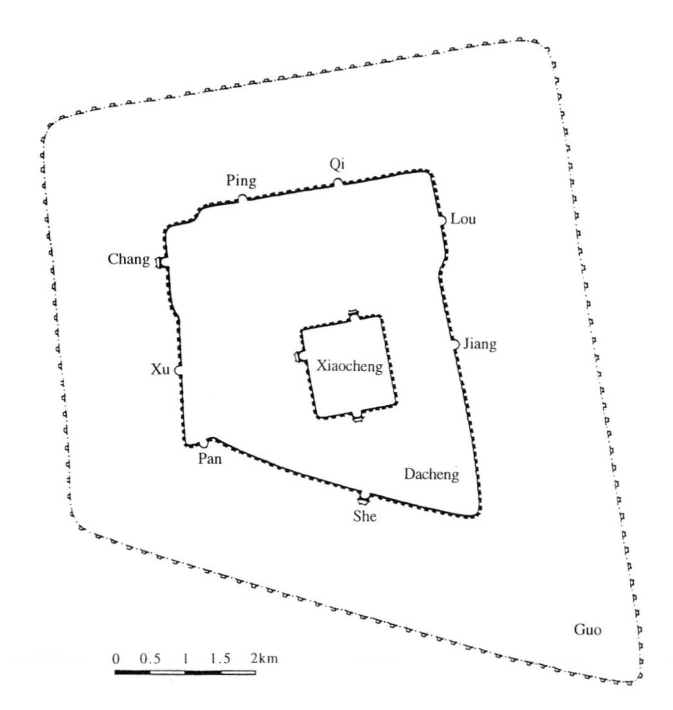

Figure 2.4 Conjectural diagrammatic plan of Helü Dacheng. Based on literary descriptions, mainly in the Yue jue shu *and* Wu Yue chunqiu, *and on the city maps of later dynastic periods. I have also consulted the diagrammatic plan of the city as speculated by Cao and Wu 1986, p. 30, which may contain some serious errors in the scale and proportion of the length of the walls due to the adoption of faulty literary records and the incorrect conversion of ancient length units.*

Temple and the Altar of Earth and Grain are mentioned many times in the *Yue jue shu* and the *Wu Yue chunqiu*, especially when the survival or destruction of cities are concerned,[82] little information about their formation and positions can be extracted. It is quite possible that they may have been seen to conform to the canonical principles advocated in the *Zhou li*, a conformity that was regarded as common sense in city construction. Thus, as in the case of the morphology of the city, there would have been no need to describe them in the documents.

In speculations on the location and formation of the market in Helü Dacheng, we face a similar situation. A market is mentioned several times in both the *Yue jue shu* and *Wu Yue chunqiu* without detailed information. Nevertheless, one can at least infer that an appointed official, known as the *shizheng* or *shili*, supervised the activities in the market, which would be quite crowded in the daytime and where public gatherings would be held and criminals punished or executed in front of crowds. One can also speculate, though with less certainty, that the market was probably established, approximately as in the ideal city according to the *Zhou li*, in the north of the city.[83]

The City as a Cosmic Center

Heaven and Earth

According to the *Wu Yue chunqiu*, Wu Zixu was commissioned by the king of Wu to rebuild the capital: "[He] followed the forms manifested in Heaven and the processes taking place on Earth [*xiang-Tian fa-Di*], and then constructed the great city wall [*dacheng*]."[84] This passage reminds us of a passage in one of the appendices of the *Zhou Yi*, concerning the mythical emperor Fu Xi devising the eight trigrams:

> In antiquity, when Pao Xi [i.e., Fu Xi] had come to rule all under Heaven, he looked up and contemplated the forms exhibited in Heaven, and he looked down and contemplated the processes repeated on Earth. He contemplated the patterns of birds and beasts, and the properties of the various habitats and places. Near at hand, in his own body, he found things for consideration, and the same at a distance, in events in general. Thus he devised the eight trigrams, in order to enter into relations with the virtues of the numinous and the bright, and to classify the relations of the ten thousand things.[85]

Thus the construction of the capital was seen as having been pursued, like other human activities, in accordance with the cosmic order revealed in the recurring rotational processes of Nature. Consequently, the city became not only a replica but also an integral, harmonious part of the cosmos, drawing forth the power of that order into the city and the state in the same way that Wu Zixu is said to have convinced the king that Wu possessed "the ordained fate from Heaven [*Tianqi zhi shu*] of threatening its neighboring states."[86]

Again, from the *Wu Yue chunqiu*, we understand that one of the ways in which the city was believed to have been constructed following the cosmic order was that "eight land gates [were built] to symbolize the eight winds from Heaven [*Tian zhi bafeng*], and eight water gates [were built] to imitate the eight intelligent attributes of Earth [*Di zhi bacong*]."[87] Similar measures are described to have been applied in the construction of the Yue capital as the first step toward the rejuvenation of that state after a total defeat by Wu.[88] The concept of the eight winds from Heaven must have been formed well before the Han period,[89] and the lone appearance of the description in all early texts of the correlation of the eight heavenly winds with the gates of both the Wu and Yue cities seems to suggest the possibility of a local tradition, although it is yet not clear whether or how much, if any, this depicted scheme was influenced by the syncretic cosmology of the Han. Nevertheless, with this cosmological symbolism, the city is perceived as having condensed and represented the world in order to establish a link between the world of man and the world beyond.[90]

Still another mode of symbolism is described in the *Wu Yue chunqiu*. Fan Li, the chief minister of the king of Yue, being ordered to take charge of building the capital, "observed the forms manifested in Heaven, and constructed the inner city wall [*xiaocheng*] by imitating the Purple Palace [Zigong] [of Heaven]."[91] The Purple Palace is also known as the Purple Forbidden Palace (Ziweigong) or the Purple Forbidden Enclosure (Ziweiyuan), which designates the central celestial area around the polar star, and was believed to be where the celestial High God resided.[92] By being a replica of the God's palace, the king's earthly palace and city were imbued with the sacred celestial order and thus instilled with vitality and cosmic power.[93]

City Walls

Despite Wu's progress over the preceding decades, it still lagged behind the larger states in Central China in such aspects as its politics, the economy, and military. In this circumstance, Helü consulted Wu Zixu, as the *Wu Yue chunqiu* claims:

> "I intend to strengthen the state and seek hegemony. . . . But my state stands in the out-of-the-way southeast where the terrain is complicated and cut off, and where the air is humid and the land is constantly devastated by flood from the rivers and the sea. There are neither adequate fortified defense works for the king, nor enough measures for the guarantee of security for the people's life. The granaries are short of grain, while the soil is largely left uncultivated. How can our ambition be realized?" Wu Zixu replied, "I have learned that putting the ruler in a secured, supreme place and the people in reasonable order, is the priority in the *dao* of ruling a state. . . . The way to attain this *dao*, to seek hegemony, and to extend your dominion from those near to those afar, must be firstly to erect city walls [*chengguo*], set up a system of defense, replenish the stocks, and manage the arsenals."[94]

The same document also states that once the king of Yue was released from Wu after his three-year hostageship, he consulted Fan Li:

> "Now [I] intend to stabilize the state and erect city walls [*dingguo licheng*];[95] yet the people are not enriched, their achievements are unable to be enhanced; how can we accomplish our tasks?" Fan Li replied, "Yao and Shun surveyed and divined the land; the Xia and Yin demarcated territories; Gugong[96] constructed his city; and the sacred power of the Zhou capital at Luo prevailed over ten thousand *li*, and its moral influence reached the eight farthest ends [*baji*]. Were [these activities] meant to defeat powerful enemies and to annex neighboring territories?"[97]

It is clear then that constructing city walls was interpreted as equivalent to establishing the state, and founding the capital was thus regarded as the very first step toward an idealized order. This order may be interpreted not only in social but also in cosmic terms.

I have noted repeatedly that the symbolism of the center at which the king resided was in correspondence with his moral and social position at the pinnacle of the social hierarchy. The form of concentric city walls ideally embodied such a conception and was symbolized in the pictograph *guo* in its archaic form.[98] Of course, the concentricity of the city walls derives from considerations of security, as the *Wu Yue chunqiu* states explicitly:

> Gun[99] constructed the *cheng* so as to defend the ruler, built the *guo* so as to guard [*shou*] the people, and these are the origin of the city walls [*chengguo*].[100]

Yet this sense of security must not be interpreted only in practical terms. Arguing that since the city is an orderly cosmos, Eliade writes that any attack from without threatens to turn it into chaos:

> It is highly probable that the fortifications of inhabited places and cities began by being magical defenses; for fortifications—trenches, labyrinths, ramparts, etc.—were designed rather to repel invasion by demons and the souls of the dead than attacks by human beings. . . . [T]he result of attacks, whether demonic or military, is always the same—ruin, disintegration, death.[101]

This is not to say that the purpose of defending against *either* demonic *or* human attacks is the first consideration for fortifications. It seems reasonable to assume that the ancients conceived of the natural world as an extension of their own personalities and consequently apprehended it in terms of human experience. Thus, in the mind of the ancients, the "real" world transcended the material realm of textures and geometrical space and was perceived schematically in terms of a cosmic experience.[102]

The sacred and the profane are not to be seen as a dichotomy; in fact, in human thinking there is no difficulty in associating the human enemy with the devil and death. For the ancient Chinese in a ritualized society, the line between the divine (or demonic) and the human indeed was not sharply drawn. As the *Zuo zhuan* records, when two snakes were found fighting each other at the south gate of the Zheng capital, and the one inside the gate was killed, the Duke of Lu asked Shen Xu whether it meant there were monsters and monstrous events (*yao*) present. Shen Xu replied,

> Monsters and monstrous events take their rise from men. When men did not have blemishes, they do not arise of themselves. When men forsake the constant course [*chang*], then monstrosities appear. Therefore it is that there are monsters and monstrous events.[103]

Therefore, what is divine (or monstrous) would fully converge with what is human into the proper rituals and moral righteousness, and the bright gods (*mingshen*) would descend from Heaven either to examine the morality of a flourishing city or state, or to inspect the viciousness of a perishing city or state.[104] In this sense, the city walls appear to some extent to have been constructed as much for symbolic meaning in the affirmation of the power of the state and of the centrality of the king as for practical military defense, since what really mattered was social order and morality within the state and within the city, which had to be in accordance with the cosmic order and potency, an order that could not be defended with material fortifications alone.

The association of social order and cosmic order is reflected in the Chinese preoccupation with city walls.[105] The character for *cheng* came to denote both "city" and "city wall."[106] It can even be detected from the definitions of the terms *cheng* and *guo* by Xu

Shen (ca. A.D. 58–147), the great philologist of the Eastern Han. "*Cheng*," he explained, "is [applied to mean] to hold [*cheng*] people. [It] contains [the radicals of] 'earth' [*tu*] and 'to achieve' [*cheng*]." Duan Yucai (1735–1815) commented on this association by quoting a passage from the *Zuo zhuan*, "The sage king first helped the people to make achievements [*chengmin*], then put forth their strength in [serving] the spirits."[107] This passage does not indicate a sequential order in which the sage king accomplished his tasks, but, since the essentials and situations (*qing*) of the demons and gods would vary in correspondence with the conditions of the people, to promote people's achievements meant simultaneously to be reverent to the demons and gods.[108] As for the term *guo*, Xu Shen defined it as "to rule by institutionalized order [*du*], [and thus it is] where the people live in institutionalized order."[109] The city, the orderly cosmos, had to be protected against any threat from without, whether natural calamity or military attack, and this threat always carried a demonic implication to the people within, since any destruction of the city, in a sense, was equivalent to a retrogression to chaos. The city must also be guarded against any danger of either degradation or dysfunction from within that would mark the beginning of the deterioration or the waning of the existing order and eventually lead to death and decay. The city walls, together with the city moats, which will be discussed in the next section, symbolize such protection from the perils both without and within.

Since the construction of the Yue capital was preceded by a total defeat by Fuchai, and since at that time Yue became a *de facto* vassal state of Wu, the form and scale of the city walls are said to have been fairly modest compared with Helü Dacheng's.[110] Probably Yue could have been forced to make no more humiliating a gesture, signifying Yue's subjection to Wu in the very construction of its capital, than the recorded reversing of the city's orientation. The *Shui jing zhu* states:

> Therefore [the king of Yue] set its [main city] gate in the north, taking the east as [his] right side, the west as [his] left side. Thus the pair of *que* was [erected] outside the North Gate.[111]

A capital was supposed to be aligned in accordance with the position of the king, that is, facing the south at the center of the city, with the east on his left side and the west on his right side, as indicated by the description of the layout of an ideal Zhou royal city recorded in the "Kaogong ji." The reason why Li Daoyuan (A.D.?–527), the author of the *Shui jing zhu*, mentions the reversal and the right/left sides is simply to stress how grave a humiliation it was for Yue to face the north in acknowledgment of its allegiance to Wu.

City Moats

Whereas in the *Yue jue shu* and *Wu Yue chunqiu* there is no particular description of the city moats of Helü Dacheng, the multiplicity of water gates suggests that the walls of both the city proper and the inner enclosure may have been surrounded by moats. Indeed, the *Shi ji* records: "Wu has city walls [*cheng*] that are thick and lofty, and city moats [*chi*] that are wide and deep." This statement was made by Zigong (520–? B.C.), one of Confucius' disciples, who in around 484 B.C. shuttled between the states of Qi and Wu trying to persuade Wu to attack Qi so as to save Lu from the latter's threat.[112] In fact, city moats have been so important that the characters *cheng* and *chi* for "city wall" and "moat"[113] also jointly connote "city" (*chengchi*). It seems logical that the city walls would have been accompanied by moats: in terms of building technique, much of the earth applied to the construction of the wall conveniently came from the moat that was dug out beside it;[114] and in terms of defense, the addition of a moat simply doubled the fortifications. Yet what seems more significant is that symbolically the moats were no less important than the walls in defending the established cosmic order within the city. In one of the Appendices of the *Zhou Yi*, the "Xiang zhuan," which may be dated within the few decades on either side of 200 B.C.,[115] we read, "The [earth of the] wall [collapses and] returns into the moat, [this indicates that] the mandate has been in disorder." Also in the *Zhou Yi,* Kong Yingda commented in the seventh century,

> If the mandate is to be kept from being in disorder, the subjects should assist the ruler [in governing the state] as the earth supports the wall. If the mandate is left deranged and in disorder, the lower will not respect the higher as the earth will not support the wall, leading to its [the wall's] [collapsing and] returning into the moat. This is why it is termed "the mandate being in disorder."[116]

Therefore, if the wall collapses and its earth refills the moat from which it came, the eclipse of the orderly is seen as a deterioration and eventually a retrogression to chaos, and the existence of the city or state will be brought to an end. In this sense, the wall and moat both symbolically represent and protect the existing order ordained from Heaven.

Cosmological Symbolism and the Chinese Cosmogony

I have demonstrated that Helü Dacheng was depicted by the authors of the Eastern Han documents as having been built as both a replica of the universe and a cosmic center. I will show that this scheme is further enhanced by the symbolism of the city gates.

At this point, however, it is necessary to emphasize the importance of not confusing the modes of cosmological thinking revealed in the records of the building of Helü Dacheng with the cosmological attitudes of many other cultures. To illustrate this crucial point, I refer to assumptions made by Eliade, who seeks to determine the general pattern of specific characteristics of the religious experience. "The discovery or projection of a fixed point—the center—is," he declares, "equivalent to the creation of the world."[117] For Eliade, an unknown and unoccupied territory must be consecrated so as to become an inhabited one, a cosmos:

> By occupying it and, above all, by settling in it, man symbolically transforms it into a cosmos through a ritual repetition of the cosmogony. What is to become "our world" must first be "created," and every creation has a paradigmatic model—the creation of the universe by the gods.[118]

For many other cultures, these statements appear to have some validity; but they are utterly inapplicable to Chinese experience simply because, for the Chinese, man and the universe are uncreated. This phenomenon in Chinese cosmological thought is stressed by Mote, who has presented himself as one of the few forerunning scholars advocating conscious awareness of a "cosmological gulf" between China and the West. Indeed, the High Culture of China is probably unique in having no creation myth. For the Chinese, the world and humans were uncreated but constituted a cosmos having no creator, god, ultimate cause, or will external to itself. "The genuine Chinese cosmogony," Mote continues, "is that of organismic process, meaning that all of the parts of the entire cosmos belong to one organic whole and that they all interact as participants in one spontaneously self-generating life process."[119]

Thus, for the Chinese (at least for the classically educated), the discovery or projection of a fixed point was equivalent not to the creation of the world but to the *finding* of the world order. A settlement—a house or a city—was not "the universe that man constructs for himself by imitating the paradigmatic creation of the gods, the cosmogony,"[120] for nothing is really created in the world, and the world was not created either.[121] Rather, the universal organism—uncreated but generated from Nature itself, whose every part, by a compulsion internal to itself and arising out of its own nature, spontaneously performed its functions in the cyclical recurrence of the whole—was mirrored in human society by a universal ideal of mutual good understanding.[122] It was only by imitating this universal organism that the cities were constructed in the cosmic order. As we read in the *Zhou Yi:*

> Therefore as nature produced the divinational things [tortoise shells and milfoils], the sages formulated them; as Heaven and Earth produced changing processes, the sages imitated them; as the auspicious and ominous signs descended from Heaven, the sages made symbols of them. . . . In great antiquity [people] lived in caves in the wild countryside. Later the sages converted the caves into buildings, with beams at the higher [position] and eaves at the lower [position], to withstand the wind and rain.[123]

In Chinese experience, therefore, the religious moment (in the broadest sense of the word)—in this case, the founding and consecration of a city—did not imply the cosmogonic moment at which the God creates the world, as Eliade advocates, but rather the typical moment in the natural rotational process and the moment of the early sage kings' work following the order of Heaven.

Symbolism of the City Gates

Great attention was paid to the symbolism associated with the erection of the city gates of Helü Dacheng, and long explanations of the gates are contained in almost every imperial or local document about this city. The construction of the gates, as vehicles of passage from the one space to the other, was a most serious business indeed, as Granet has recognized.[124] Therefore, a heightened symbolic significance was inevitably embodied in city gates, not only in their usual massive construction, which far exceeded that necessary for the performance of their mundane function of granting access and affording defense,[125] but also in the names they were bestowed and, to a lesser degree, in their decorative elements, which corresponded with their positions and directions. The city gates, by virtue of their symbolic meaning, not only distinguished but also linked the inside with the outside of the city and the state, this world with the world beyond—the cosmos.

In the mind of the ancient Chinese, the naming of an artifact had to have an acceptable reason behind it, so that it could be justified logically and historically. In other words, the proper link between the name and what is named was held crucial in the matter of putting the world in order. This predilection seems to have been very much associated with one of the Confucian intellectual preoccupations in governing society, that is, the correspondence of name and reality. Language was viewed as embodying its own reflection of the true order, and if language were not used in ways that conformed to its correct implicit meanings, the entire human order would become disjointed. Consequently, a discrepancy between name and reality was seen as one of the sources of conceptual disturbance, for it was evidence of a breakdown at the top, and "a world without order" was seen as its result.[126] This may have been part of the reason for the fact that it was the names of the city gates of Suzhou, rather than their form and style, that were one of the major topics of description and argument in local gazetteers of all periods of history. Thus, the significance of these artifacts to the Chinese always lay more in their supposed origin, in the various transcendental or spiritual meanings they transmitted and in the historical or legendary events associated with them, than in their physical traits. In this section, I discuss only those gates whose symbolism had direct cosmological bearings.[127]

Cosmic Schemes

We have already discussed the general cosmic symbolism embodied in the establishment of the city gates in both Helü Dacheng and the Yue capital, as systematized by the authors of the Eastern Han documents. Now it is time to investigate the specific implications incorporated by these authors in some of the city gates. One of the outstanding gates of Helü Dacheng was Chang Gate, said to have been built in the north section of the west wall, which, as the character of the gate's name itself denotes, symbolizes the Gate of Heaven (*Tianmen*). It was constructed in order to open up and let in the wind of the Changhe, which is one of the eight winds from Heaven, and thus to let in the heavenly *qi* (cosmic breath).[128] Similar symbolic representation is claimed to have been applied in the Yue capital, where Fan Li "constructed in the west by north [of the inner city wall] a tower with dragons with spreading wings on it so as to symbolize the Gate of Heaven."[129]

Changhe is the name of the first gate leading to Heaven and also the name of the gate of the celestial Ziweigong, which, as has been discussed earlier, is at the center of the universe and is where the High God resides. The notion of the Changhe as the Gate of Heaven seems more prominent in earlier times in the southern Chu, as revealed by a stanza in the poem "Li sao" by Qu Yuan (ca. 340–278 B.C.) in the anthology *Chu ci*:

> I asked the gatekeeper of the High God to open the Gate [of Heaven],
> [But he] leant against the *Changhe* and eyed me churlishly.[130]

Xu Shen holds that the term *changhe* was used in Chu to denote any gate or door in general.[131] It is very probable that notions similar to those present in Chu were to a degree also embodied in the life of the people of Wu and Yue, which as neighboring states of and through frequent interaction with Chu shared most of its customs and religious activities. I would therefore suggest that the application of the idea of the Changhe to Wu and Yue's city gates may have been a valid use of cosmological symbolism at the time of the building.[132]

The subject of cosmic schemes becomes even more interesting as we read further in the *Wu Yue chunqiu*, "The reason for establishing [in the south by east of Helü Dacheng] the Snake [*she*] Gate is to symbolize the Gate of Earth [*Dihu*]."[133] A similar symbolic gesture is described for the Yue capital: "In the southeast a stone funnel was set up to symbolize the Gate of Earth."[134] The notion of the Gate of Heaven in the northwest and the Gate of Earth in the southeast may closely relate with the mythical account of the cosmological idea, which certainly derived from the natural phenomena observed from the geographical position in China. That is, on the one hand, the sun and the moon were certainly seen as moving from east to west, and the inclination of the polar axis and the celestial bodies were seen as rotating around the Pole Star in the north; on the other hand, the altitude of the terrains in the southeast is generally lower than of those in the northwest. Therefore the *Huainanzi* explains:

> In ancient times Gonggong, striving with Zhuanxu to be world-ruler, with anger smote Mt. Buzhou. The pillars of Heaven were broken, and the guy ropes of Earth ruptured. Heaven leaned over to the northwest, hence the sun, moon, stars and planets shift [in that direction]; and Earth became empty in the southeast, and hence the waters and dust flow in [this direction].[135]

Commenting in the *Zhou li* on a passage describing how to determine the center of the earth, Jia Gongyan declared that "Heaven in circular form covers and Earth in square form carries." He quoted this from the *Hetu kuodi xiang*, a document that has long been lost:

> Heaven is not fully filled in the northwest, Earth is not fully filled in the southeast. The northwest is the Gate of Heaven, the southeast is the Gate of Earth. The Gate of Heaven does not have limit upward, the Gate of Earth does not have limit downward.[136]

By symbolizing the city gate in the northwest as the Gate of Heaven and the gate in the southeast as the Gate of Earth, the city could be interpreted as a replica of the cosmos at the very axis of the universe. In this sense, the city gates seem to have been viewed as equivalent to the cosmic openings through which communication passed between this world, which was seen as existing in a cosmic order, and the numinous world above and below. The city itself therefore functioned as a link between the three cosmic planes.

Cosmology and Politics

Politics was, and still is, expressed through symbolism.[137] Since the survival of the state was closely related to its success in the earthly world of contests between rival states, the state's intention of gaining an upper hand over its foes was unsurprisingly manifested in the cosmic symbolism elaborated on its city gates. The most salient enemies of Wu were Chu and Yue. Thus the *Wu Yue chunqiu* embroiders the symbolic meanings of three particular gates of the Wu capital:

> Helü intended to expand westward and defeat Chu. Chu was in the northwest, therefore [he] established Chang Gate in order to open up the *qi* from Heaven, and gave it another name—the Gate of Defeating Chu [*po-Chu*].[138] [He] intended to expand eastward and annex Yue. Yue was in the southeast, and therefore [he] established She [snake] Gate in order to subdue that enemy state. Wu was in the *chen* position, which corresponds to that of dragon, hence on the south gate of the inner enclosure wall [*xiaocheng*] the roof corners [of the tower] were bent upward in the form of a stickleback, so as to symbolize dragon horns. Yue was in the *si* area, which corresponds to the position of snake, hence on the south gate [i.e., She Gate] of the wall of the city proper [*dacheng*] was placed a wooden snake facing north, so as to signify the affiliation of Yue to Wu.[139]

The implication in the symbolic construction of She Gate of Helü Dacheng was said to have been countered by Yue by means of a Gate of Thunder (*lei*), which was erected in its capital and wherein a huge drum was set.[140] The elaborated symbolic implications carried by the city gates must not be interpreted as primarily concerned with practical matters with some cosmic significance added, nor should they be seen as superstitious expressions of the king's political ambitions, for kings' ambitions or actions were *them-*

selves expected to follow the pattern of the universe and thus to be in harmonious correspondence with the cosmic order.

Cosmological and political symbolism of the city gates was not new to the authors of the Eastern Han documents. The gates were the thresholds that evinced the solution of continuity in space immediately and concretely. Hence their symbolic prominence. Therefore, it is not surprising to discover that ceremonies could be performed at the city gates, such as in the autumn of 669 B.C., when the state of Lu suffered severe flooding and sacrifices were offered at both the Altar of Earth and the city gate.[141] It is also understandable that when Song, leading the forces of other princes and dukes, conquered Zheng in the winter of 698 B.C., they burned down Qu Gate of the Zheng capital and carried with them the rafters dismantled from Zheng's Ancestral Temple to rebuild Lu Gate of its own capital.[142] The account of this act certainly emphasizes the symbolic significance of the Ancestral Temple and city gate to these two states in both defeat and victory rather than the timber quality of the rafters or the shortage of building materials in Song territory.

Conclusion

In this chapter, I have examined a number of salient features of the Wu capital, Helü Dacheng, believed to have been constructed in 514 B.C. on the site where the city of Suzhou has stood throughout subsequent history. The prominent aspects of the notional reconstruction of Helü Dacheng are both physical and conceptual. The accounts of the physical features—in particular, the site and form of the city and the measurements of its walls—by the authors of Eastern Han and even later documents may have constituted a combination of what had been transmitted, either textually or orally or both, to these authors with what they themselves perceived of the city in their time. The conceptual aspect hinges on the idea that the city was built as a cosmic center, a symbolism of city building that most probably came from diverse sources. It might have drawn elements from the local traditions; it could have been influenced by the culture of Central China as it had developed from as early as the Shang period; and, more importantly, it must have involved the cosmological synthesis of the Han.

Because the main purpose of this book is to present a study of the development of the urban form and space of the city of Suzhou, from which a number of important characteristics of urban transformation in premodern China can be sketched, this chapter has not aimed at investigating *how* this construct was devised by the Han scholars but at *what* was exhibited in it. The main reason for this choice of methodological orientation is that, no matter how reliable the various elements of this construct may eventually prove to be, it was later constantly being viewed as a source of historical authority and continued to inform the city's further development. In other words, for the rise and decline of this city in later historical periods, what the physical city really looked like in the late sixth century from an archaeological point of view, what kind of symbolism was actually applied to its construction, and to what extent the Eastern Han construct of the beginning of the city truly reflects the reality of half a millennium earlier are less important than the content of this construct itself, which was later *believed* to have been true.

The emphasis in this chapter has been the cosmological symbolism of this city. The construction of the city walls was regarded as the first step toward the establishment of not only the state but also an idealized order, an order of both social and cosmic significance that would hopefully lead the king of Wu to hegemony. The walls were depicted as having been built in a symbolic manner, following celestial and terrestrial formations. The eight land gates of the city were said to have been arranged in such a way as to symbolize the eight winds from Heaven, and the eight water gates to imitate the eight "intelligent attributes" of Earth. Thus the city may be interpreted as a replica of the universe, and the parallelism between the macrocosms and the microcosms may be seen as thus having been established. This cosmic scheme was further enhanced by the symbolic correspondence between two particularly important gates, namely Chang Gate, symbolizing the Gate of Heaven in the northwest, and She Gate, symbolizing the Gate of Earth in the southeast. The application of this symbolism, closely associated with an ancient cosmological conception, was largely brought about by their nomenclature correlating with their positions. The city in this way appeared to be a cosmic center. It was supposed to be at this center that the king of Wu was striving for power in the historical context of the conflict between rival states.[143]

The reconstructed "history" of Helü Dacheng and the Yue capital during the late Spring and Autumn period was characterized indeed by an intense struggle between the states of Wu and Yue, which ended when Wu was finally conquered and annexed in 473 B.C. I have argued that any struggle against human enemies was viewed as isomorphic with that against demonic forces, and any attack from without was seen as threatening to uproot the city and thus the state from the cosmic center and turn it back into chaos. Hence the struggle against the enemy was in a sense regarded as an endeavor to protect the established center of the cosmos. Goujian was determined to rejuvenate his state and wipe out the humiliation of a total military defeat by Wu and his three-year hostageship in Helü Dacheng. For this matter, he consulted his ministers, and, as the *Guo yu* records, declared:

> What Wu did in the past was immoral and evil. [They] sought to maim my Ancestral Temple and my Altar to the Gods of Earth and Grain, and to raze them to the ground, not letting [my ancestors and the gods] enjoy blood sacrifices. [Therefore] I am determined to vie [with Wu] for the cosmic center. . . .[144]

The existence of the city, the orderly cosmos, was symbolized by the ritual maintenance of the Ancestral Temple and the Altar to the Gods of Earth and Grain, and the real victory over enemies could only be gained when the cosmic center was taken over, whereupon the ruler's purpose in life could be realized. The human and supernatural matters were virtually part of each other.

Due to the purposefully thematic nature of the *Wu Yue chunqiu*, this received "history" of the construction of Helü Dacheng can only be regarded as "semilegendary." Nevertheless, it is these accounts of a legendary nature that, as a sort of authority from the past, conceptually formed the bases for the city's later transformation. In the opening passage of the "Chengchi" section in the *Wuxian zhi*, this aspect has been explicitly stated:

> As a famous capital and prestigious city, [it] assembles the cultural relics. At its beginning, [Wu] Zixu, following the forms manifested in Heaven and the processes taking place on Earth, constructed the city walls and dug the city moats for [the capital of] Wu. [Whereas it] was meant to strengthen [the state] at that time, [the form of the city] then became the *fixed institution* [in its urban transformation] from antiquity to the present time.[145]

The glories of the city in later periods have always been seen as having derived their impetus from the past, especially from the legends of its foundation, as Zhu Changwen sums it up: "Had not the wise created it at the very beginning, and the able followed on [with it], how would [the city] have been able to reach such [perfect] status?"[146]

CHAPTER 3 Cities in the Imperial Era

HELÜ DACHENG'S EXISTENCE WAS SHORT-LIVED. From its earliest recorded construction by Wu Zixu in 514 B.C. to the conquest of the state by Yue in 473 B.C., the city as the capital of Wu probably existed for only forty-one years. The site of Helü Dacheng since then has been seen to be occupied successively by the dynastic and present-day urban settlement that we call the city of Suzhou, and the largely fictional history of this early city provided a conceptual and possibly physical basis for its later development in the imperial era. Along with the social and political innovation at the time of the Qin unification in the third century B.C., there occurred a profound change in the nature of China's city system. Urban history in the imperial era was characterized by remarkable continuity and great complexity. In this book, the city of Suzhou is treated not only as an integral part but as a particular instance of that history. This chapter discusses a number of important aspects of the general development of cities in imperial China, which will form a larger historic context in which to place the transformation of the city of Suzhou. How some of these aspects should be interpreted remains disputable among students of China's urban history; thus in order to examine the city of Suzhou more closely, I will introduce these problems and clarify precisely my position.

Regional and Local Governmental Centers

There seem to be two tendencies observable in studies of city form and space in imperial China: making sweeping generalizations about *the* Chinese city as if there were few changes or variations in time and space; and concentrating on *only* imperial capitals as the focus of the study and regarding other cities—notably regional and local administrative centers—merely as miniatures of imperial capitals. Such approaches overlook the fact that cities in imperial China were significantly differentiated in time and space and ignore that fundamental distinctions, as far as cosmological conceptions in imperial China are concerned, existed between imperial capitals and other cities.

Imperial Administrative Hierarchy

Apart from imperial capitals, whose location and design through history were characterized by the persistence of a long tradition of city cosmology,[1] there existed hundreds of cities spread across the country that housed regional or local governmental seats. In the history of Chinese field administration, the constant and basic administrative unit of the empire was represented by the institution of the *xian* (usually translated as "county"), the capital of which constituted the lowest level of the urban hierarchy through which the central government directly exercised its authority. This governmental instrument, along with that of the *jun* (or *fu* in later times, usually translated as "prefecture"), a higher administrative unit than the *xian* since the Qin unification, can be regarded as a legacy of the late Zhou. Localizing and dating the origin of the *xian* have been problematic issues,[2] but it seems certain that an embryonic form of the so-called Prefecture-County System appeared during the Warring States period. Subsequently, a system of local administration was formalized by the Qin unifiers, the principal pattern of which was to last for the entire imperial era.[3]

Although the structure of those administrative units above the *xian* was often highly complex, and their names varied over time, the standard hierarchy of province-prefecture-county was constructed, as Skinner observes, in a manner familiar to us in most modern administrative arrangements. Skinner has also summarized the pattern of governmental organization in this system: the territory of a province was entirely made up of prefectural-level units, and the capital of one of these also simultaneously served as the provincial capital. Similarly, the territory of a prefecture was entirely made up of county-level units, and the capital of one of these also simultaneously served as the prefectural capital. Thus, every provincial capital had a minimum of three administrative seats known as *yamen*, one each for the provincial governor, the prefect, and the county magistrate; and every prefectural capital had minimally two *yamen*, one each for the prefect and the county magistrate.[4] Moreover, the capital of a prefecture that was economically and culturally advanced and densely populated often served as the capital of more than one county. In the case of Suzhou prefecture, there were three county *yamen* in the city from 1724,[5] and the county boundaries ran through the city, and the *yamen* of each county was located in the appropriate sector. Thus during the second half of the Qing period, for example, when the provincial government of Jiangsu resided in Suzhou, the city housed five *yamen* (one provincial, one prefectural, and three county) plus, one imperial examination office of the province, two *yamen* of the textile industry of the Southeast, and some other offices in charge of specialized regional business regulated by the state. This situation not only shows the city's political importance but also corresponds with the economic strength of the prefecture.

Nature and Form of Regional and Local Cities

To introduce some of the problems that exist in interpreting the general traits of these regional and local cities, I will begin by quoting two passages from an article entitled "City as a Mirror of Society: China, Tradition and Transformation," written in 1984 by Rhoads Murphey. As a distinguished urban historian of China, Murphey ardently advocates impartial studies and open-minded understandings of Chinese culture.[6] The reason for selecting these two particular passages lies not only in the fact that the points presented in them are crucial for the present discussion—some being valid with more clarification and some representing certain dubious conceptions—but also as an acknowledgment that this work of Murphey's is beyond doubt a great achievement. With regard to cities in general in the imperial era, Murphey writes:

> The traditional-imperial Chinese city . . . lasted in fact, essentially unchanged, well into the present century in many parts of the country; many of its outlines are thus still observable, . . . These traditional cities were primarily centers of imperial authority imposed in a uniform plan to a varied landscape, symbolic monuments of the power and majesty of the Chinese state and of Chinese culture over which it presided.[7]

He then describes the county capitals:

> While the *hsien* [i.e., *xian*] city was, of course, the commonest, it reflected, on a smaller scale, the superior hierarchical models of the provincial and national capitals, whose managerial and cosmic rôles were exercised over progressively larger spheres, until, in the case of the imperial capital, it encompassed "all under heaven," the name by which the Chinese called their empire and its surrounding, but far lesser, tributary states.[8]

Three important questions arise out of Murphey's statements. Were cities in imperial China uniform in plan? Should regional and local cities be perceived as imperial capitals in miniature in cosmological terms? And how should urban development be interpreted, or more specifically, should changes in the nature and general arrangement of urban space of these cities be regarded as essential? I shall try to answer the first two questions in this section; the third question will be dealt with in the two following sections.

To address the first question, I would take a more cautious approach than the one reflected in Murphey's statement that the cities in imperial China were "imposed in a uniform plan to a varied landscape."[9] It seems possible that, in order to illustrate effectively his central point that these cities, having continuously functioned as administrative centers, bore the strong "imperial imprint," Murphey makes this statement in an overemphatic manner. In another work that he produced exactly thirty years ago, he declared, "local defensive terrain, such as at Chungking [i.e., Chongqing], occasionally made this common plan unsuitable, but the stamp of governmental uniformity is nonetheless apparent."[10] I would say that variations of the cities in their actual form and plan should be viewed as having existed more than "occasionally" if we talk about Chinese urban phenomena as a whole. Such variations were largely brought about by local topographical conditions, economic situations, and the specific process of city construction. This idea has succinctly been dealt with by Mote, who, in terms of the basic trends of urban form and space transformation, sees that cities in imperial China appear to be of three types: the planned, regular city; the unplanned, sprawling large town; and the hybrid created when some degree of planning was superimposed on the natural city but too late to be thoroughgoing.[11] Mote then points out a general schematic differentiation between the form of cities in the South and the North: the degree of irregularity in form was greater in the South, where topographical conditions were complex, than in the North, where the cities were older and therefore further from their presumed origins as natural cities.[12]

Uniformity in plan and layout was indeed one of the characteristics of many cities on North China Plain, where variations must have occasionally occurred. The plans of two exemplary cities in the late imperial period, Pingyao and Taigu, situated in present-day Shanxi province, are presented in Figures 3.1 and 3.2. The plan of a typical city of the North, however, was common only in certain regions, and should therefore not be extended to account for all cities in China. Cities in the South, as Liu Zhiping has noted, markedly varied in form, and geometrical regularity was never a common urban feature.[13] The comparatively geometrically regular form of the city of Suzhou appears to have been one of a few notable exceptions among the cities south of the River Yangzi. This is abundantly evidenced both by the city maps contained in numerous local gazetteers and by their present configurations, which most directly bear the marks of their past.

Ideally, of course, any Chinese city would have been built on a plan of square or rectangular form. Such a preference is reflected in the way in which some of the irregularly formed cities were presented by the authors of local gazetteers. The city of Shaoxing in the late imperial period, for instance, was often mapped in oblong plans (see Figures 3.3 and 3.4), although its shape was highly irregular in reality (see Figure 3.5). Another example is illustrated by the two contrasting maps of Hangzhou shown in Figures 3.6 and 3.7.[14] Yet informative of the Chinese mentality toward city building as it is, an ideal pattern does not explain the cities in their complexity. A simple, undifferentiated model of "the Chinese city" would not help us understand China's urban experience any better.

A few more words are needed for answering the second question, whether regional and local cities should be viewed as imperial capitals on smaller scales. The hierarchy of the imperial administration in China was developed into a well structured system, and the imperial cosmological symbolism was, to various extents, applied to the imperial capitals. These two facts tend to lead to an easy and seemingly plausible conclusion that the cosmic role of local and regional capitals was the same as that of the imperial capitals but merely conducted on smaller scales; in other words, local and regional cap-

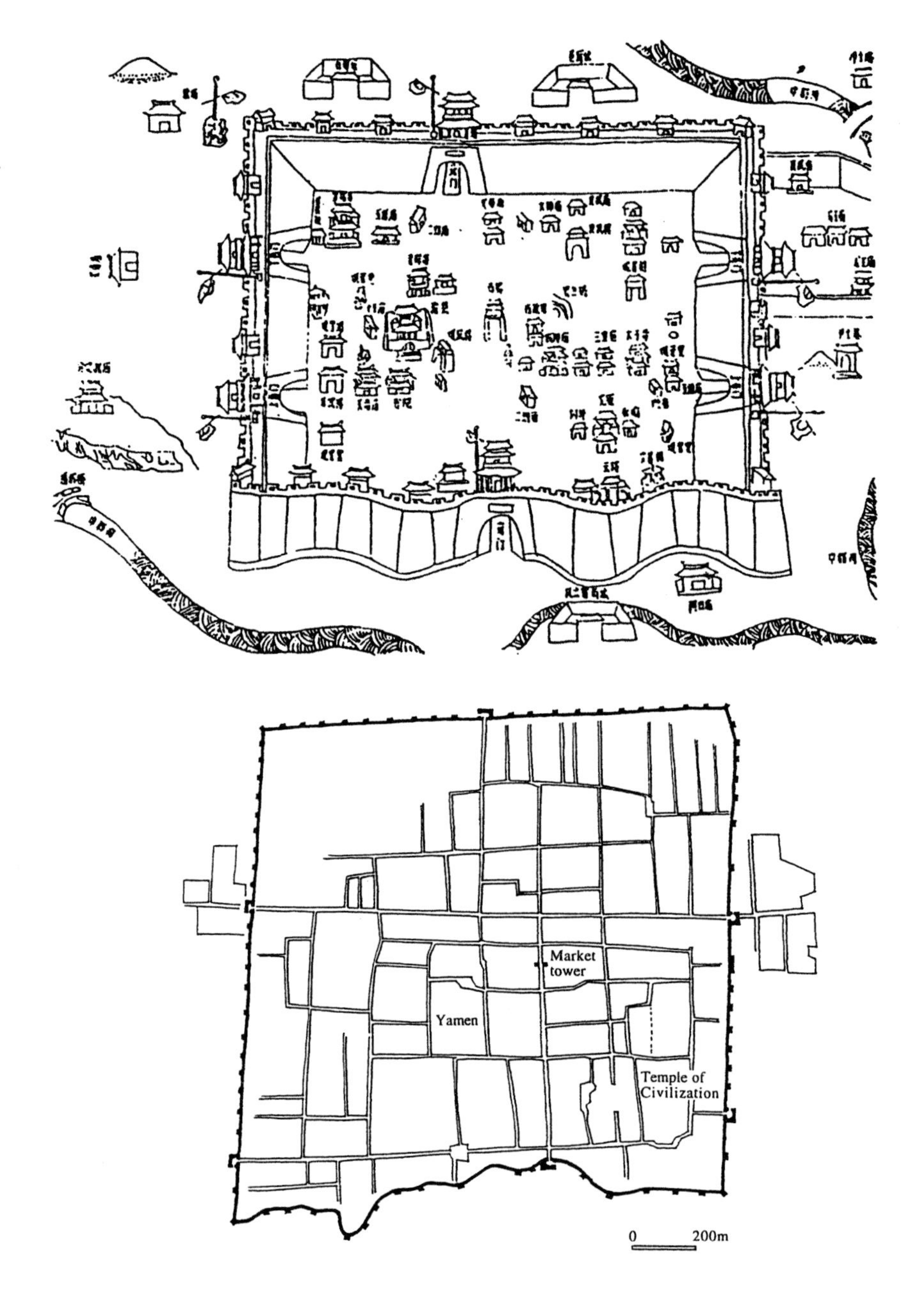

Figure 3.1 *The city of Pingyao in present-day Shanxi province. Top: picture map of the city contained in a local gazetteer of 1707. Adapted from Dong and Ruan 1981, p. 25. Bottom: the city at the end of the Qing. Redrawn from Dong and Ruan 1981, p. 25.*

itals were endowed with the sacred power emanating progressively to larger spheres in accordance with their administrative jurisdictions, until, in the case of the imperial capitals, "all under Heaven" was encompassed.

However, the validity of drawing a parallel between the hierarchy of the imperial administration system and the hierarchy of cosmological symbolism of cities—if there was one—is very much in doubt. It should be noted, first, that the fundamental role of

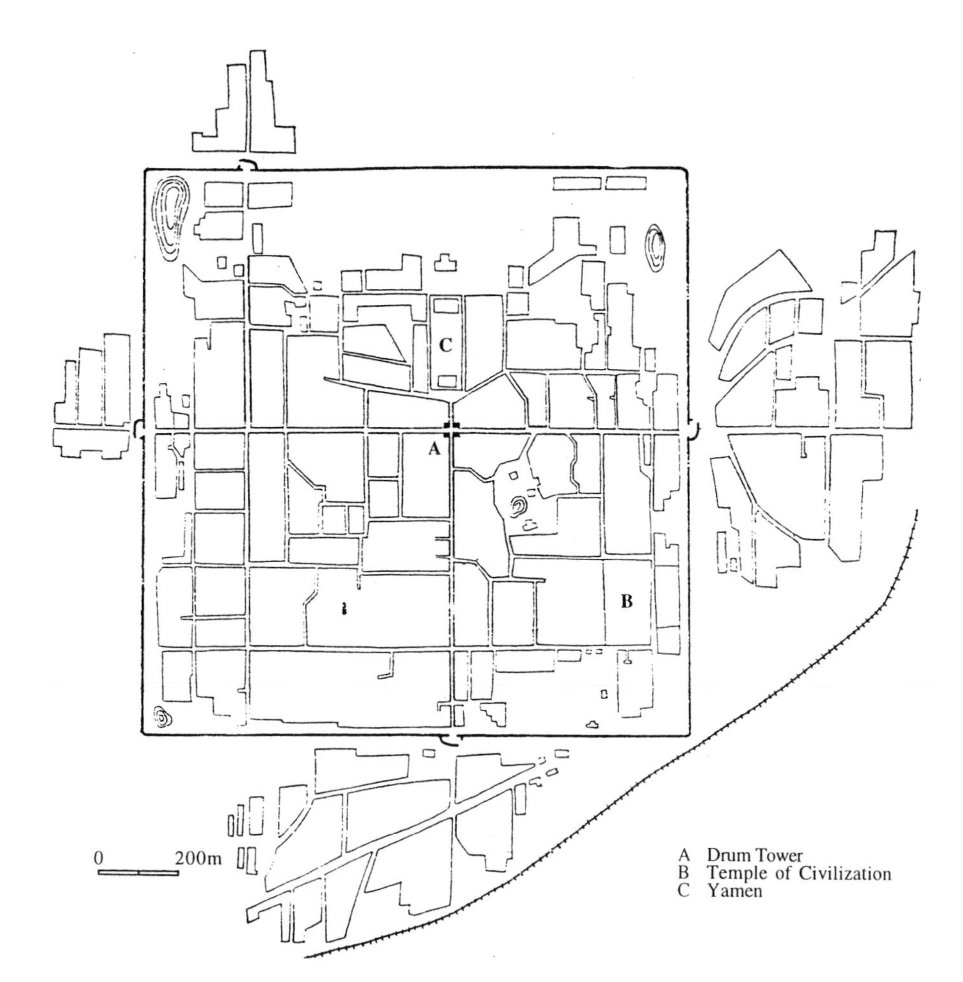

Figure 3.2 The city of Taigu in present-day Shanxi province in 1964. Adapted from Dong 1982, p. 109, fig. 1-7-33.

the post of regional and local governmental seat is entirely different from that of the imperial throne. The ruler ensconced on the throne was perceived as the Son of Heaven at the pivot of the four quarters, who, in Meyer's words, "was commissioned by Heaven to rule China, pacify the outlying territories, and ultimately to set such a shining example of perfect government that the whole world would come to the foot of his throne and offer submission."[15] By contrast, provincial governors, prefects, and county magistrates were merely agents of the imperial authority empowered with the duty to govern the country. If the emperor was ordained on the imperial throne by the Cosmic Order, by Heaven, imperial officials were appointed to their posts by the central authority on earth. The fundamental distinction between the imperial throne and the posts of regional and local government thus lies not in the size of their ruled area but in the symbolic nature of the two categories.

This distinction is most clearly marked by the *de jure* absence in regional and local cities of the unique type of urban structure in Chinese history that was built exclusively in the southern suburb of the imperial capital, namely the Altar of Heaven.[16] This struc-

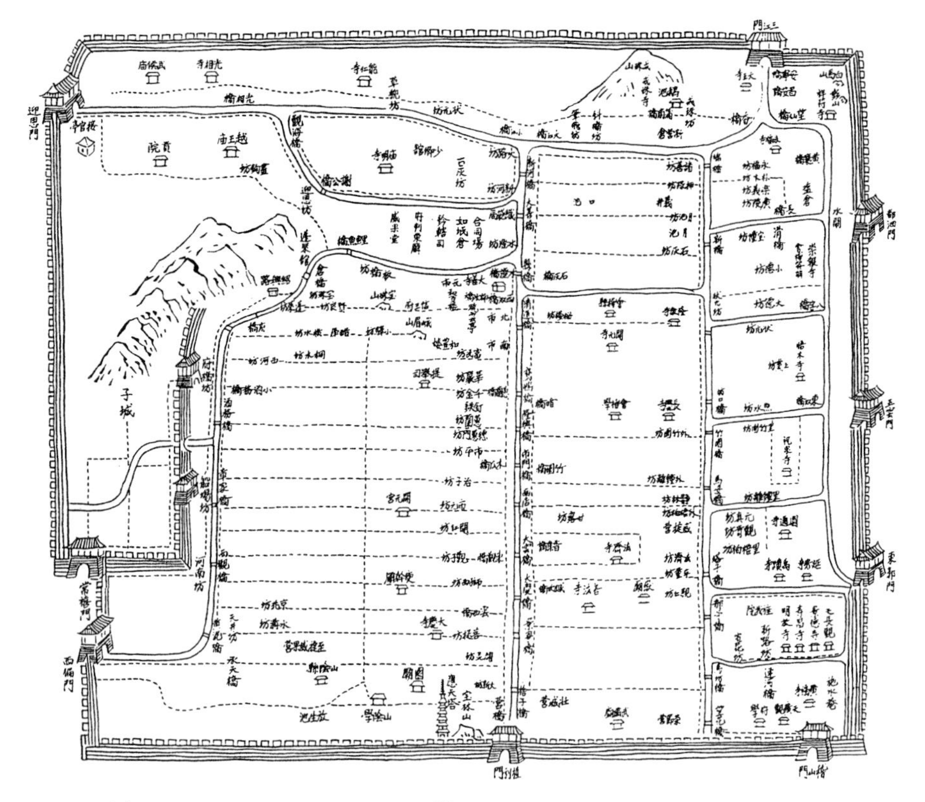

Figure 3.3 Map of the city of Shaoxing during the Yuan period, presented in Shaoxingfu zhi, juan *1. Adapted from Wei and Xu 1986, p. 22.*

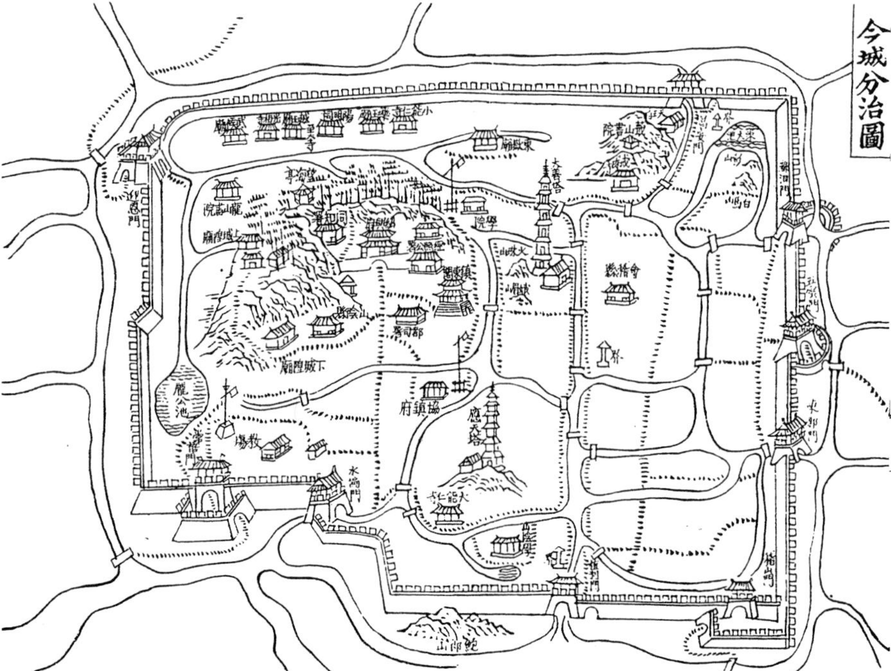

Figure 3.4 Map of the city of Shaoxing in the mid-Qing, presented in Shanyinxian zhi, juan *5. Adapted from Wei and Xu 1986, p. 23.*

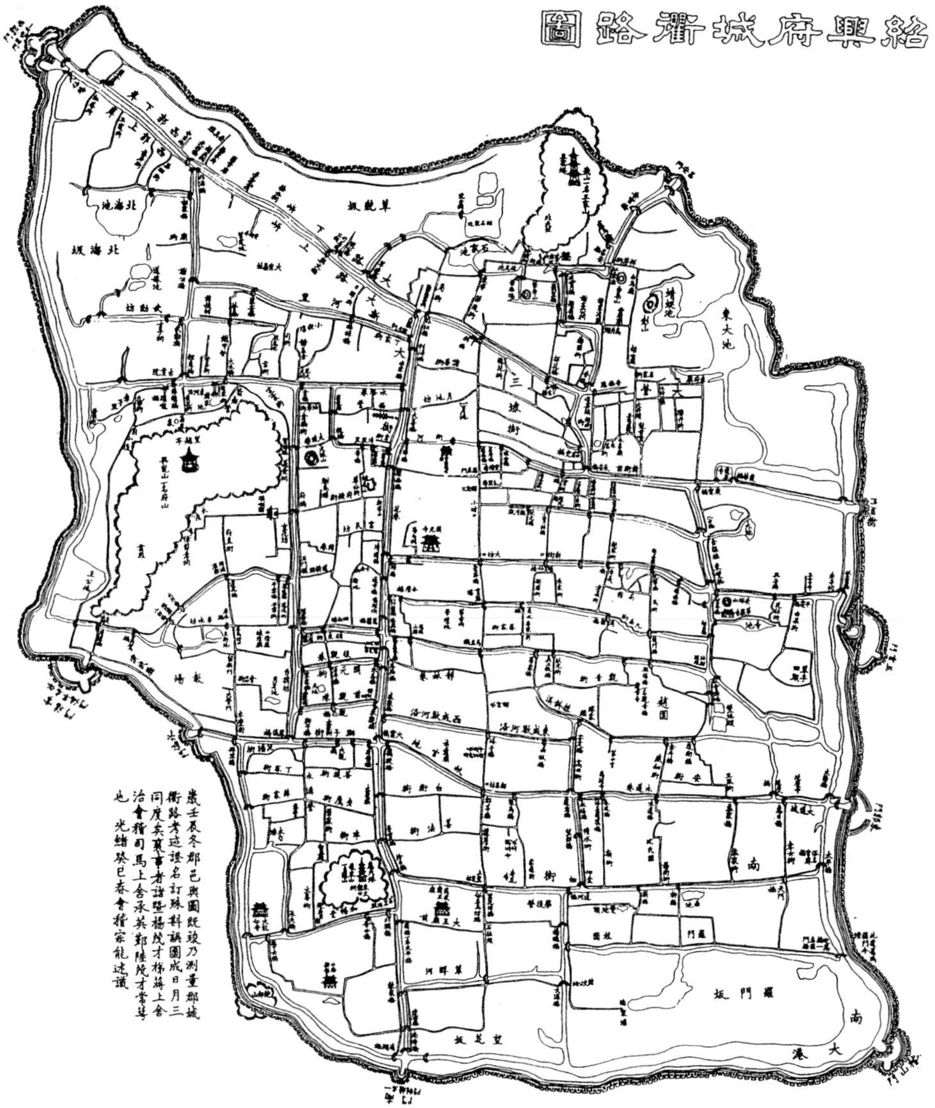

Figure 3.5 *Map of the city of Shaoxing produced in 1893. Adapted from Wei and Xu 1986, p. 24.*

ture epitomized, by name and by rituals conducted on it, the Emperor's revered, unique position on earth as the "cosmic pivot" and his intermediary role between Heaven and the world at large. Therefore, one may proclaim that it is the attribute of the imperial capital as a sacred city to be at the center of the world, just as it is the endowed right of the Emperor, holder of the Mandate of Heaven, to claim that "all [lands] under Heaven are the soil of the King; [all people] within the boundary of that soil are the subjects of the King."[17] Similarly, to regard other cities wherein regional and local governmental seats resided as cosmic centers on smaller scales would appear to be misleading, just as claims of a similar kind by imperial officials on the Emperor's soil, even though on

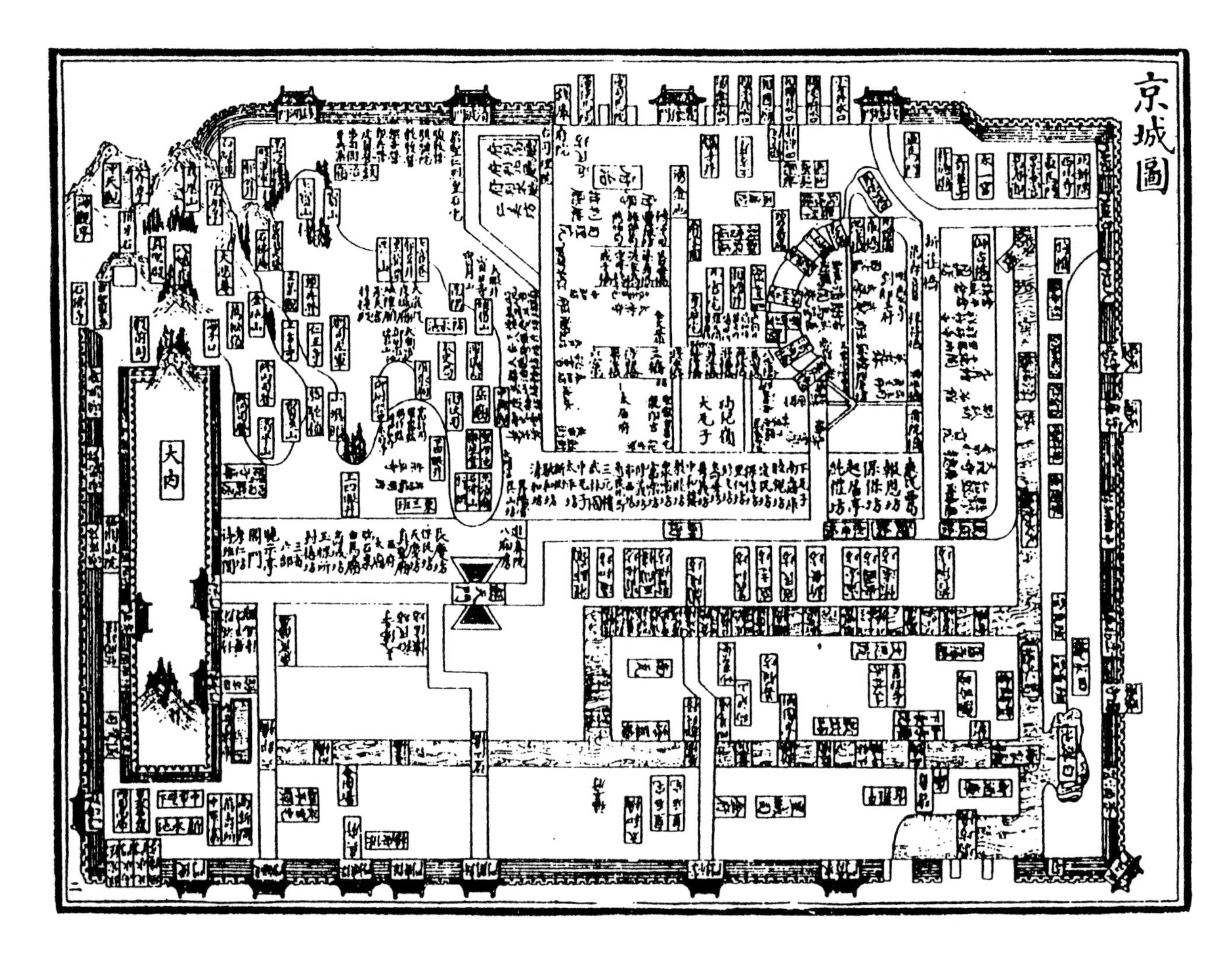

Figure 3.6 Map of the city of Hangzhou (known as Lin'an in the Southern Song), presented in Xianchun Lin'an zhi, juan *1.3. North is to the right of the page.*

smaller scales, would be totally contradictory to the conception and nature of the imperial system.[18]

Furthermore, it is our understanding that the religious orientation to ancestor worship is omnipresent and central to the development of Chinese civilization. Ancestral temples were ubiquitous in settlements at all levels, from imperial capitals down to regional and local cities, market towns, villages, and large houses. They were certainly family-based religious establishments. In the transient world of man, the relatively fixed point on earth, from which one could depart to all directions and to which one could return, would, from the traditional Chinese point of view, be where one's ancestral temple stood, wherein families could properly worship. This was the place at which one's roots would surely be found. Therefore, the centrality of a settlement was to a large extent occasioned by the presence of the ancestral temple as a symbolically dominant structure of the settlement, one which stood for the good of all members of the community, and by the regular worship performed in it. In relation to the rise of the city, Schwartz has emphasized that if the city in Mesopotamia was centered on the city god or goddess who was a nature-related deity, then in China, cities would seem to have been centered on the ancestral cults of the royal lineage and the lineages of the associated nobility.[19]

This religious nature of Chinese cities persisted after the Qin unification but was only present in imperial capitals, where the royal ancestral temple was always one of the principal urban structures; that is, the royal ancestral temple was constructed as an important part of the overall scheme of capital city planning. Although the imperial ancestral temple was established exclusively to house the shrine of the predecessors of the royal family, in which usually only the Emperor was entitled to lead worship, the symbolic significance of the temple reached out to the destiny of the whole world and thus to the welfare of all people "within the four seas." No regional or local administrative center, to my knowledge, possessed an ancestral temple as one of its principal urban structures with such an overwhelming social and religious influence over the city as a whole, except for ancestral temples built and attended by discrete social groups and families in the city.

The lack of such an urban element in regional or local centers seems attributable to the fact that, unlike a village or a house wherein all members were identified as having common ancestors, a Chinese city was merely an administrative center of an area that was largely rural and not an entity of its own;[20] also, its residents were hereditarily heterogeneous and socially discrete. One may also try to seek a similar symbolic significance in the ancestral temples of regional or local officials to that of the Emperor's by drawing a parallel between the ruling role of the Emperor and the governing duty of the imperial officials. Yet since by the rule of "avoidance," these officials were in most cases not assigned to their home areas, and since their positions and posts constantly changed,

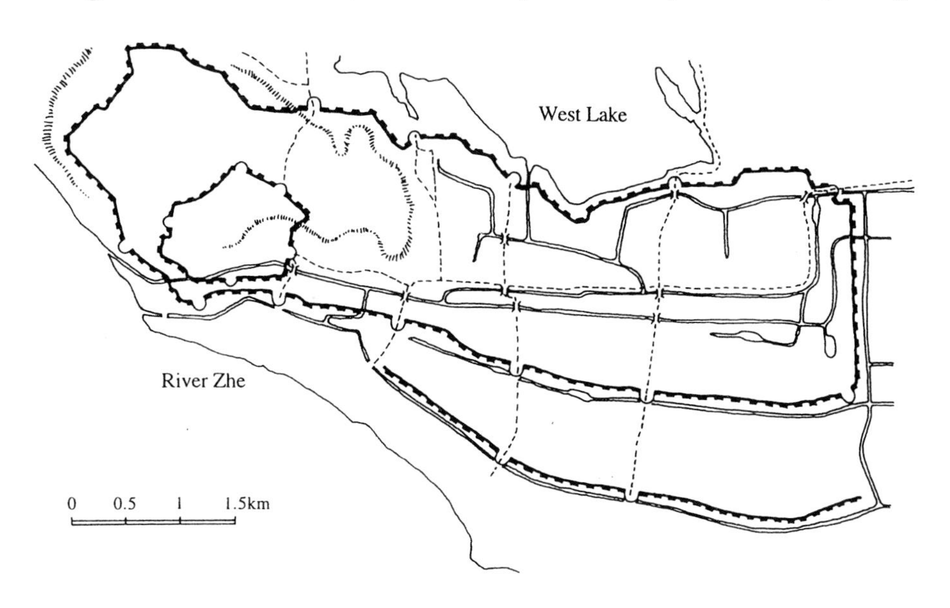

Figure 3.7 Diagrammatic map of the city of Hangzhou. North is to the right of the page. Redrawn from Wright 1977, p. 65, Map 3, by reference to Dong 1982, p. 48, fig. 1-6-3.

their ancestral temples were seldom located in the cities where they held their administrative seats but in their home regions. An official's post and his residence during his assignment were all temporary; what was permanent was his ancestry and the place where his ancestors were buried and worshipped.[21] If the Emperor claimed that his residence, centered in his capital, was "under Heaven" or "within the four seas," the true home of an imperial official could be nowhere but the place from which he originally came into existence. If the imperial capital was regarded as the sacred center ordained by Heaven, from which the Emperor under his ancestors' very eyes ruled the whole world, a regional or local city was perceived as but a node in the imperial administrative network, at which an official was appointed to carry out his duty under the eyes of the Emperor and his officials at the imperial court and from which, after his retirement or dismissal, he would possibly return to his homeland where he was rooted and with which he identified himself. Even if an ancestral temple of an official's family had been set up in the city where he was officiating, it would only have stood for the sake of his family or clan alone, for, like all residents in the city and in its surrounding areas, he was after all a subject of the Son of Heaven.

The symbolic distinction between the imperial capital and all other cities is best exemplified by the words of a Ming scholar named Shen Defu (1578–1642). His *Wanli yehuo bian* contains a record of the 1610 reconstruction of the south gate of the Ming capital city at Beijing, which had been destroyed by fire. Here, Shen quotes the words of Zhang Jiayan, an official in charge of the reconstruction work: "Now the Heavenly Household (*Tianjia*) is going to take the enterprise. This cannot be equated with [those of] the common people (*zhong*)."[22] Elsewhere, Shen makes a similar statement when referring to some restoration work in the palace: "The Heavenly Household's construction projects are hundreds of times more [expensive] than those in the world of the populace (*minjian*)."[23] Any regional or local city was surely included in this "world of the populace," which was held in contrast to the "Heavenly Household," and any construction work associated with the regional or local city was but that of the "common people," no matter how high its level of administration.

I am not trying to deny the existence of cosmological conceptions about the urban form and space of cities. Many cities of long history, especially those constructed as state capitals prior to the imperial era, had embedded in them the imprint of cosmological symbolism of various sources. Suzhou is a good example of this kind of city. Even the cities of later periods often acquired various interpretations in cosmic, or at least prodigious, terms. The essential point here is that the imperial capital was regarded symbolically as *the* city at the center of the cosmos, whereas a regional or local capital was merely *a* city of certain political and economic importance. In terms of cosmological implications, a regional or local city is not to be regarded as the imperial capital writ small, and that the alignment of a system of "progressive" cosmic role and symbolism with the imperial administrative hierarchy does not hold. This understanding is very important for a proper interpretation of the development of regional and local cities in imperial China.

Transformation of Urban Spatial Organization

The third question that derives from reading Murphey's work—whether the cities in the imperial era should be seen as essentially unchanged—is particularly complicated. The answer depends on how the word *essentially* is defined. Murphey's statement is valid if it emphasizes the persistence of the political function of these cities, as I think it probably does, although there are some implications in his writing of unchanging urban form. The point that I would like to make, however, is that a realization of the persisting political role for the cities does not mean that, in China's imperial history, urban changes in many other aspects were negligible. In the following section, I shall demonstrate that these changes significantly transformed the spatial organization of the cities.

Urban Market and Residential Quarters by the Late Tang Period

Many large cities in China experienced profound changes throughout their histories. A notable example is the development of Yangzhou, a city that rose as the central metropolis of the Lower Yangzi region in the late Tang and Northern Song but declined when the imperial capital was moved to Hangzhou in the Southern Song. This process was one of the "regional cycles" of urban growth, during which the economic development, demographic history, and sociopolitical dynamics of the Lower Yangzi region were associated with the buildup of an urban system centered on this particular apex city and with its subsequent (at least partial) breakdown.[24] In the Qing period, Yangzhou again rose as an important regional center.[25] These socioeconomic changes greatly impacted the fortune of this city, which is reflected in the significant variation of its size and form in history, as is shown in Figure 3.8. Change in the overall physical form of other cities may not have been as dramatic as that of Yangzhou, but under the cloak of political-administrative function throughout the dynastic periods, they underwent varying degrees of socioeconomic transformation that altered their regional, or even national, importance.

More important to the present discussion than the fortune of these large individual cities is that their rise and decline, associated with the political and economic dynamics of regional cycles, happened in the historical context of two notable processes of the development of city planning and governing principles as a whole in the urban history of imperial China: the urban revolution that took place from the mid-Tang to the end of the Song and the urban transformation that occurred in the late imperial period in economically more advanced regions. The fundamental metamorphoses of the city structure and the general arrangement of urban space were brought about through these two processes. Since the first process was centered on the collapse of the old ward system of urban market and residence, and since this system derived from the planning doctrines prescribed in the *Zhou li* and largely remained unchanged until the second half of the eighth century, the following is a short description of the main features in the planning of urban markets and residential quarters before the mid-Tang.

The market quarter, in the form of a walled compound usually with four doorways

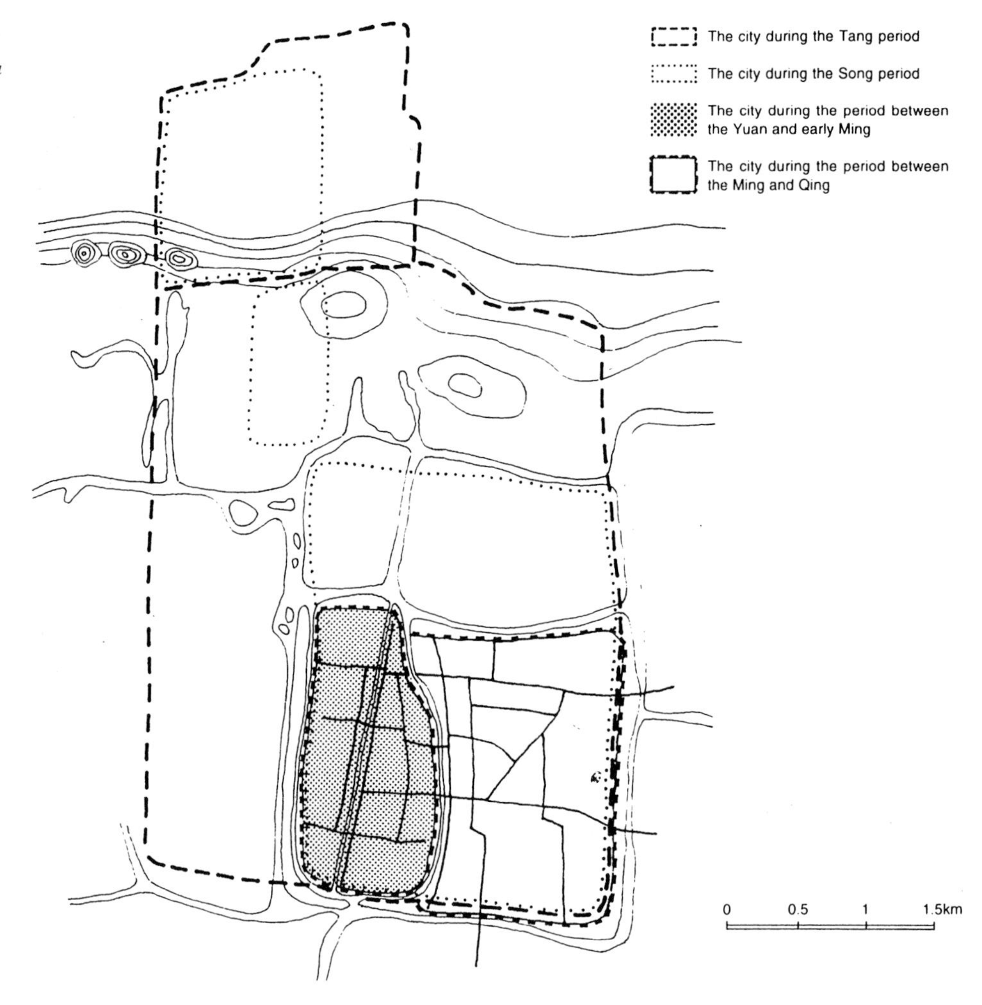

Figure 3.8 Transformation of the urban form of the city of Yangzhou from the Tang to Qing periods. Redrawn from Dong 1982, p. 34, fig. 1-5-9.

open to the main streets of the city and functioning as a venue for not only commercial but social activities,[26] was tightly controlled by the state. From the *Zhou li*, we understand that, within the compound, stalls were strictly arranged in ranks (*si*),[27] while goods displayed on the stalls of each rank were rigorously restricted to specific categories. An altar of earth was probably set up, where sacrifice was regularly made by the *yinli* (female ritual). At the center of the compound, the main administrative office (*sici*) was established in the form of a multistory tower or pavilion (*shilou* or *qiting*) on which a flag would be hoisted when the market was open, and an auxiliary office (*jieci*) was also set up to solve minor disputes over transactions. The market area was organized in three stages during the daytime, namely, the "morning market" (*zhaoshi*), the "great market" (*dashi*) and the "late afternoon market" (*xishi*).[28] Figure 3.9 contains two Eastern Han brick-engraving pictures that clearly depict the spatial arrangement of the market quarter and people's activities in it.

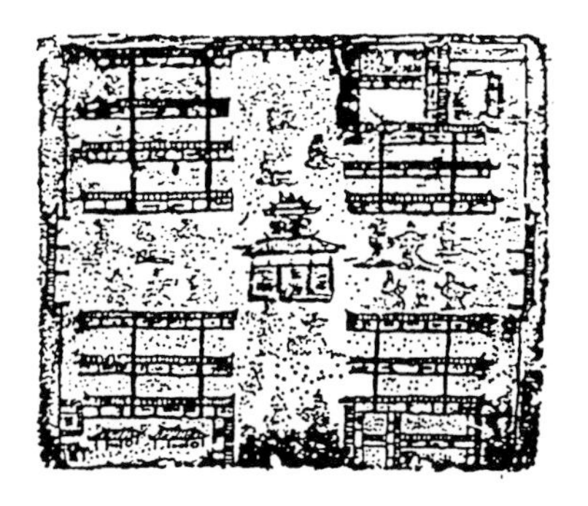

Figure 3.9 Brick-engraving pictures depicting the Eastern Han urban market. Adapted from Liu 1973, p. 57, figs. 1 and 3.

The "Kaogong Ji" does not provide any information about the Zhou planning system of urban residence, but scattered records preserved in other early documents indicate that the city was divided into blocks and that urban residence was organized in the form of walled square or rectangular wards known as *li* (or *lü*),[29] probably with a gate set on each side. Buildings were arranged along alleys (*xiang*) and suballeys (*qu*) within the ward, while an altar of earth was established at its center. Officials (*lizheng* or *lüxu*) were appointed to be in charge of various matters in the ward. No private houses except for those of the high officials were allowed to have entrances opening directly onto the main city roads, and a night curfew was normally imposed.[30] It is also very possible that urban residents were segregated in different wards by class and by profession.[31] The planning system may have had its origin primarily in military considerations, as indicated in the *Zhou li*, where it says that "once the city was in serious trouble, residents were then ordered to stay [close to the officials' posts] in their own wards, so as to stand by, as administrative decrees were pending."[32] Thus every ward would in case of a siege be a stronghold. Figure 3.10 shows the plan of a few residential wards redrawn from a fragment of an engraved scale map of the Tang capital Chang'an dating from A.D. 1080.

Medieval Urban Revolution

Fundamental urban transformation, starting during the second half of the eighth century and culminating during the Southern Song, was probably generated first in the urban market and then directly involved many other sectors of Chinese urban structure, most notably urban residential areas, which gave rise to fundamental changes in urban spatial organization. This is part of what Elvin calls the "medieval revolution in market structure and urbanization."[33] Skinner, on the basis of the works by Twitchett and Shiba,[34] has identified five main features of institutional change at this stage in the transformation of market structure and urbanization, which were accompanied by the increased monetization of taxation and trade; by a growth in the number, wealth, and power of merchants; and by a softening of social and official attitudes disparaging trade and the merchant class: (1) a relaxation of the requirement that each county could maintain only one market, which had to be located in the capital city; (2) the breakdown and eventual collapse of the official marketing organization; (3) the disappearance of the enclosed marketplace and the walled-ward system and their replacement by a much freer

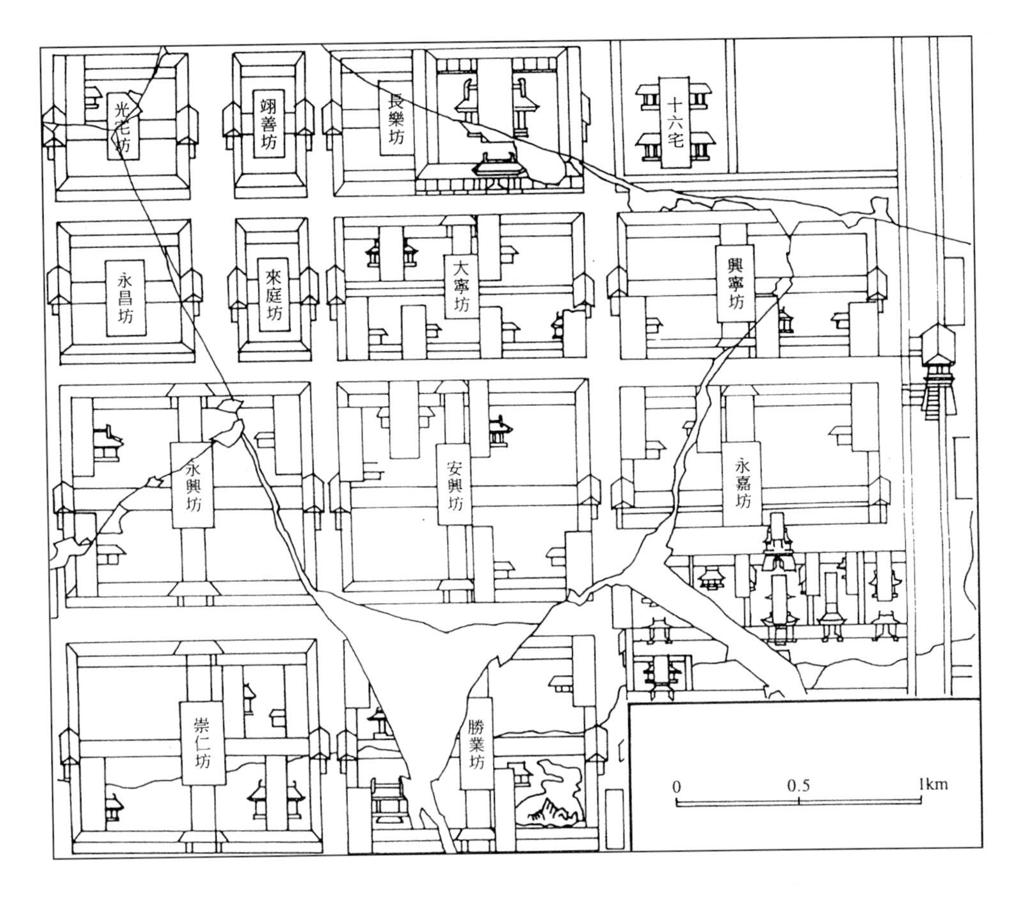

Figure 3.10 Picture map of residential wards redrawn from a fragment of an engraved scale map of Tang Chang'an by Lü Dafang dating from A.D. 1080. Redrawn from Cao et al. 1990, plate 48.

street plan in which trade and commerce could be conducted anywhere within the city or its outlying suburbs; (4) the rapid expansion of particular walled cities and the growth of commercial suburbs outside their gates; and (5) the emergence of great numbers of small and intermediate-size towns with important economic functions.[35]

These changes certainly did not occur suddenly but were part of a gradual process. As Twitchett and He Yeju have pointed out based on such documents as the *Quan Tang wen*, the *Tang huiyao,* and the *Jiu Tang shu*, although a number of shops and stalls had already been built by the mid-Tang in the mid-eighth century around the areas outside the walls of the Eastern and Western Markets in Chang'an, evidence of intensified change is found in the late Tang (ca. A.D. 828–896). Three tendencies breaching the old rules of urban planning and governmental control were representative of the latter period: (1) encroachment was made on the broad public streets by people putting up shops, stalls, and other buildings; (2) shops were built within residential wards with unauthorized doorways opening directly onto city streets; and (3) urban markets were open in prohibited, late evening, hours.[36]

During the Song period, especially in the Southern Song (1127–1279), walled market quarters and residential wards totally disappeared[37] and were replaced by shopping streets of localized business and planned neighborhoods spatially organized and demarcated with streets and alleys. Shops as the principal urban commercial facilities were located wherever it was economically sensible in the city. Figure 3.11 is a street plan of a section of the city of Suzhou taken from a picture map engraved on stone in 1229. It shows, as sharply contrasted with the plan of residential wards in Tang dynasty Chang'an (in Figure 3.10), how significant this change was. Consequently, commercial and residential activities, and thus shops and houses, were no longer segregated from each other, but rather mingled in the web of city streets and alleys. This seems to have been a highly coordinated change in two categories of urban spatial organization, which apparently transformed the city from its highly ritualized nature into one with a fairly high degree of economic and social sophistication. Largely from the results of contemporary urban population studies, and to some extent from ancient descriptions of the splendor and efficiency of Chinese cities, Elvin concludes that China at this time was the most urbanized society in the world.[38] Figures 3.12 and 3.13 present two sections of the scroll-painting *Qingming shanghe tu*, produced in the late Northern Song probably in the early

Figure 3.11 *Street plan of a section of the city of Suzhou, adapted from a picture map engraved on stone in 1229. Courtesy of the Committee of Suzhou Urban and Rural Construction.*

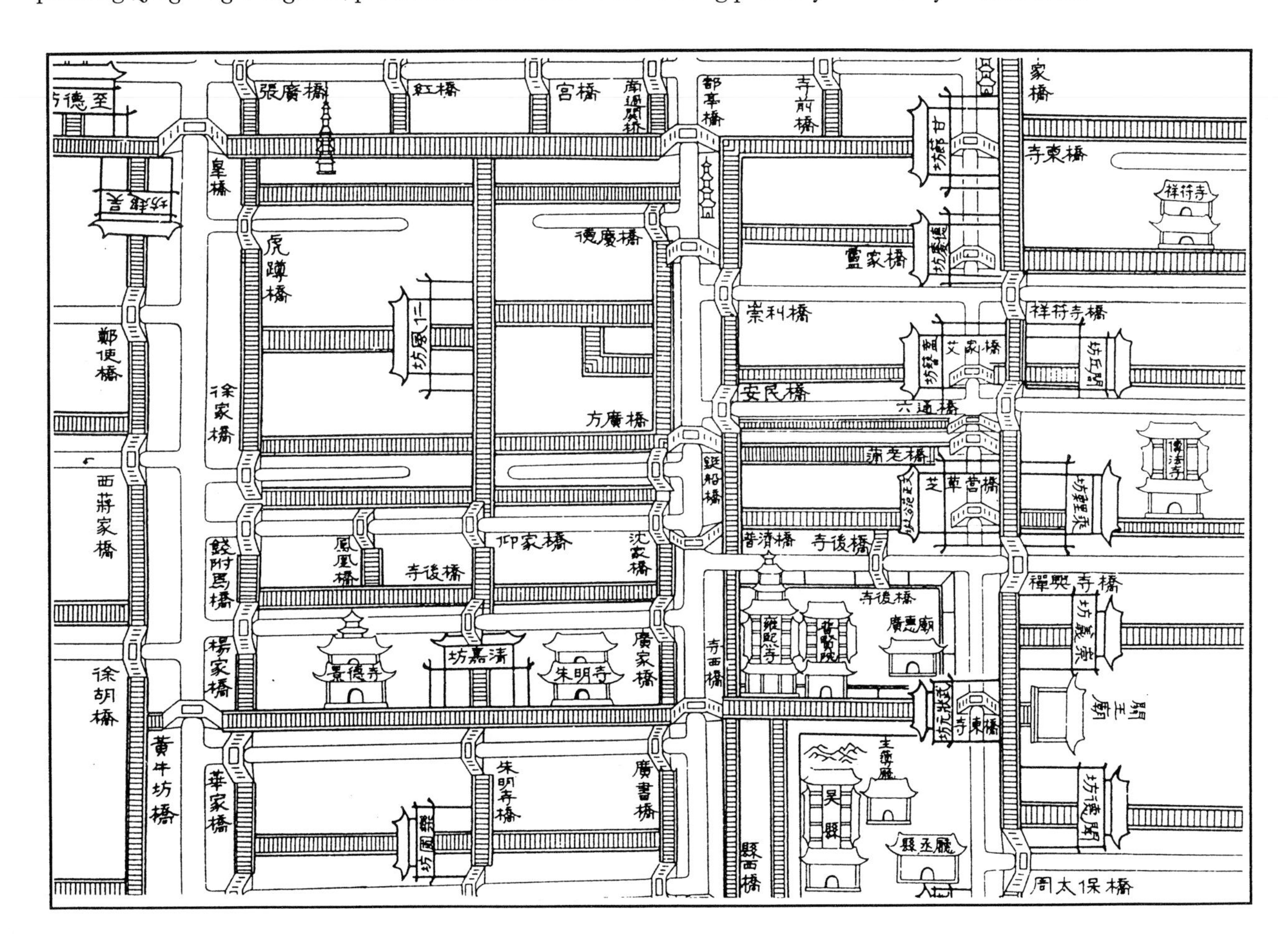

twelfth century, that vividly depicts the bustling urban streets, shops, and houses in and around the Eastern Capital of the Northern Song, Bianliang.[39]

The transformation of urban planning systems during the Tang-Song period by no means took place at a uniform speed across the whole continent. In general, some cities in economically advanced areas and somewhat loosely controlled by the central government experienced earlier and more rapid change than others. During the period when the Tang authorities were trying to ban scattered infringements of the old urban market regulations in Chang'an, shopping streets and market activities in evening hours had already developed in some cities in the Southeast, such as Suzhou and Yangzhou.[40] Moreover, Skinner makes it clear that, official policy aside, the medieval urban revolution had not been completed or even taken place in most of China during medieval times.[41] He sees some justification for periodizing the history of urban and regional development from the Sui reunification on into two great eras, the Tang-Song and Ming-Qing periods, which were separated by a dark age of devolution and depression. He also argues that urban development during the Ming-Qing period was largely an extension and intensification of processes already manifest during medieval times at the cores of the most economically advanced regions and characteristic of a better integration of capitals at various administrative levels and market towns into a single hierarchical system.[42] Elvin has illustrated that there were no more than a dozen cities and towns with markets in the vicinity of Shanghai before A.D. 1470, and the number sharply increased from 1600 onward to around seventy by 1910.[43] Similar patterns of

Figure 3.12 Section of the scroll Qingming shanghe tu *depicting street at one of the gates of the capital city of the Northern Song, Bianliang.*

Figure 3.13 *Section of the scroll* Qingming shanghe tu *depicting life at a crossroad in the city of Bianliang.*

development took place earlier in the core area of Suzhou. Fan Shuzhi, on the basis of the local gazetteers, estimates that by the early seventeenth century, seventy-four cities and towns with markets in the prefecture had already been established.[44] The regional economic centrality of Suzhou was surpassed by the rise of Shanghai only from the second half of the nineteenth century onward, when the modern era of mechanized transport and industry started.[45]

Urban Space in Transformation

The comprehensive and persistent retrenchment of the bureaucratic government's role in all aspects of local affairs, and the gradual replacement of the enclosed marketplace and the walled-ward system by a much freer street plan, led to the practical and conceptual change of public space, notably the street, in the urban area. No term in Han times, to my knowledge, specifically denotes a public road lined with buildings in a city or large settlement of any other kind. In the *Zhou li*, the character *tu*, a general term for road, is employed with certain modifiers to indicate avenues within the royal capital and with other modifiers to indicate roads in the countryside.[46] The character *jie*, later denoting what we know as "street," was defined by the Eastern Han philologist Xu Shen as "a road leading in the four directions,"[47] that is, a crossroads; later it was interpreted by one of his contemporaries, Ying Shao, as "departure from the crossroads."[48] In other words, *jie* could be applied to descriptions of crossroads in both urban and rural settings, and, in this sense, it might not have been differentiated from the general term *qu* ([a road] open in the four directions),[49] which was used before the mid-Tang more often to describe the city road system than was the character *jie*.

The early denotations of these terms clearly reflected the configuration of the urban spatial structure developed in the period up to the mid-Tang. As seen in Figure 3.10, public roads in Sui and Tang dynasty Chang'an were lined by uniform walls enclosing residential wards or the marketplace. These roads effectively helped to divide the city into standard blocks. Wright has pointed out that the division of this kind was implied by the Chinese ritual canons, and, in terms of sociospatial organization, these blocks were meant to control the urban population.[50] Yet practically, the roads were themselves no more than passages for internal traffic. The breakup of city blocks during the period between the mid-Tang and Song led to the transformation of many of these passages into busy streets flanked with shops, restaurants, houses, and the like. Hence I suggest that it was only during the transitional period of urban development beginning from the mid-Tang that *jie* started to carry the full sense of "street" and thus to be used as one of the general terms indicating specific places in large settlements.[51]

This physical and conceptual transformation proves to have been profound and far-reaching in the history of urban development in imperial China. Not only did it function as part of the process of what Skinner calls "a progressive departure from cosmologically proper principles of city planning,"[52] but it also brought a true sense of "public space" into the city: urban space for daily activities in which all residents of and around the city could freely participate. Moreover, streets and alleys became one of the key organizing components in the cognition of the city. Indeed, we find in pre-Ming texts about the city of Suzhou that the location of urban artifacts was invariably recorded by reference to other important structures, such as city gates, important temples, well-known bridges, or neighborhoods (*fang*), whereas in Ming and Qing texts, the location was more likely given by reference to specific streets and alleys. Also, new accounts described distinctive physical features of certain particular streets and alleys and elaborated on their symbolic meanings. Distinctions of this kind seem to indicate the increasing importance of streets and alleys in both physical reality and the people's conception of the city, and this, I believe, should also be regarded as one of the fundamental changes in the cities of imperial China.

Another effect of the medieval urban revolution is the characteristic partitioning of urban space in late imperial time. We have seen that the division of the city into blocks, which effectively produced a functional zoning system, was not only one of the major themes of the canonical prescription of ideal imperial city planning but an actual feature common to most of the cities of appreciable size and importance until the mid-Tang. What Skinner regards as "a long-term secular trend beginning in the T'ang"[53] gradually brought an end to this governmentally imposed and ritualized system. Since Mote's study of Suzhou focuses on the period from not earlier than the ninth century onward, it seems reasonable to assume that his remark that "there were no zones of uniform land use in Chinese cities"[54] is meant to speak for the urban phenomenon only in the second half of the imperial era.

What replaced the old system of the imposed division of the city were districts that could be distinguished by the domination of certain occupations but that were far from socially and functionally homogeneous. After reviewing three areas of discrepancy—the location of business enterprises, socioeconomic differentiation, and population gradients—among descriptive analyses of particular Chinese cities, the generalizations frequently encountered in sinological literature, and the theoretical predictions of urban geographers and sociologists, Skinner presents a fairly comprehensive argument about the nature of social differentiation within late imperial Chinese cities and, in particular, its relation to the partitioning of urban space, which he terms "urban ecology." "It was," he argues after illustrating the situation in Qing dynasty Beijing, "characterized by two nuclei, one the center of merchant activity, the other the center of gentry and official activity." He then sums up in overall perspective some distinctive characteristics of space use between these two districts. The business district was dominated by shophouses that were normally two-story buildings, with quarters that were cramped because of high land values, the normal desire of businessmen to keep nonessential overheads low, and the frugality of sojourners out to save as much as possible of their income. The location of the business nucleus appears to have been determined more by transport costs of the merchants than by convenience of access for consumers, and it was typically displaced from the geographic center of the walled city toward or even beyond the gate or gates affording direct access to the major interurban transport route. The gentry district, on the other hand, was centered around official institutions, such as the *yamen*, Confucian school-temples, and examination halls, and was characterized by a high proportion of residences with spacious compounds and by relatively many complex families.[55]

The situation in Ming-Qing Suzhou appears to have been more complex than that in Beijing. An encyclopedia of 1726 records that since the east area of the prefecture of Suzhou, including the territories of Taicang and Jiading counties, was characterized by high terrain that was unsuitable for paddy field development, cotton was often the main crop and people in that area largely took spinning and weaving as their profession. Consequently, "[residents in] the east part of the city were all engaged in the textile industry," and crowds of laborers of different skills waited to be hired on a daily basis every morning variously at Flower Bridge (Hua Qiao), Guanghua Temple Bridge (Guanghua Si Qiao), and Lianxi Memorial Gateway (Lianxi Fang) in that part of the city. The passage continues regarding other parts of the city:

> Within the city walls, [Wu county] governed with Changzhou [county] the area that was divided into east and west parts.[56] The west part was more boisterous than the east part. . . . The households in the area of Jinchang[57] were all involved in trade and business, whereas its near suburbs were densely occupied by brokers. Within Xu [Gate] and Pan [Gate] were crowded prefectural and county *yamen*.

> [Therefore in this area] more *yamen* clerks resided, and families of letter were concentrated, especially at places in and near the well-regulated neighborhoods.[58]

In Figure 3.14, the diagrammatic plan of the partitioning of urban space in Suzhou indicates that three major districts are distinguishable, namely that of business in the northwest (including its suburbs), which was in the direction of the city's main commercial trade route, that is near the Grand Canal and the west city moat; that of gentry and officials in the southwest, where governmental and cultural establishments were concentrated; and that of family-based textile industry in the northeast, which was largely affected by adjacent rural industrial activities. Certainly a hard and fast line cannot be drawn between these districts, nor were they functionally "purified" quarters. Rather, Suzhou was typical of many other late imperial cities in China in that shops were more dispersed in many parts of the city and the rich and poor residences were more inter-

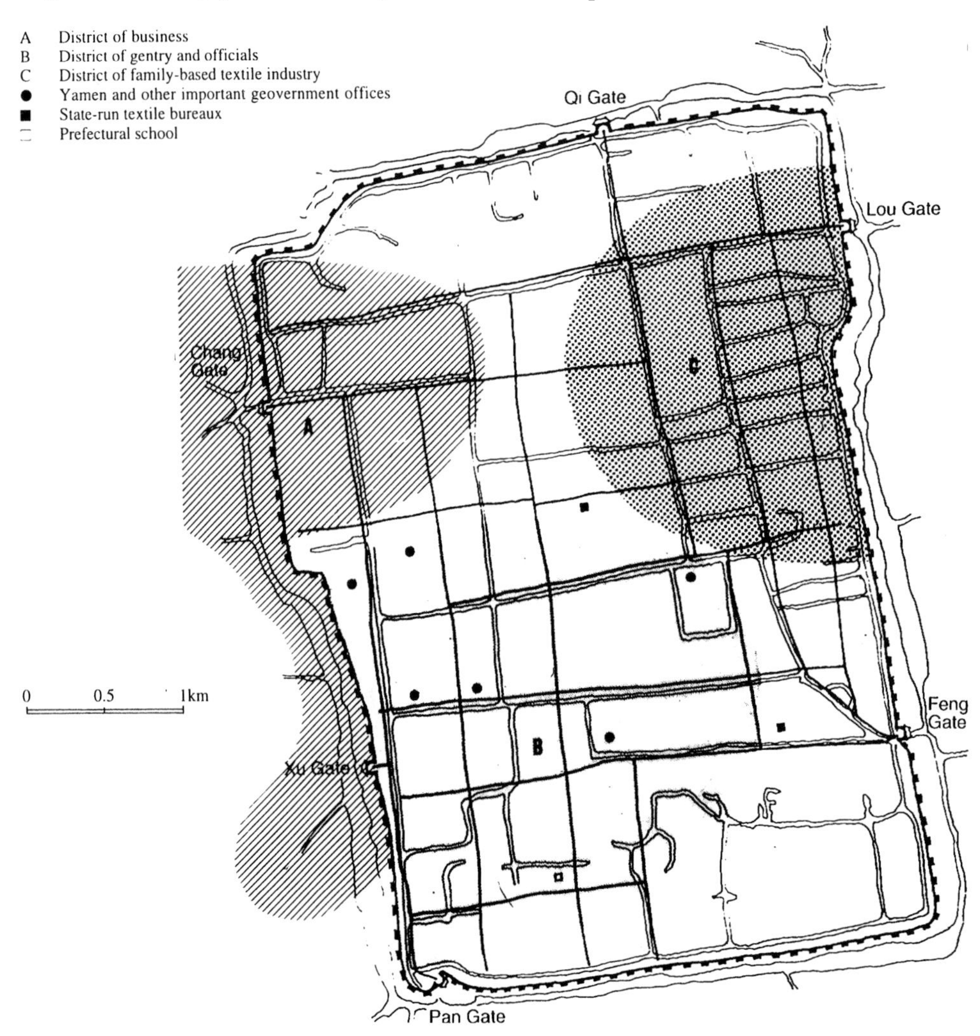

Figure 3.14 Diagrammatic plan of the partitioning of urban space of Suzhou.

mingled than in modern Western cities. Here the reader's attention is drawn to the development of the west suburbs, a process that probably started in the Song but became most intensified in the late imperial period. This development epitomized the enormous urban expansion from the mid-Ming onward. I will return to this phenomenon and its implications later in the next section and in Chapter 5.

Yet the model that Skinner has constructed, approximate as it seems, holds generally for late imperial cities. It differs, as Skinner points out, from the model set forth by Gideon Sjoberg and some other Western scholars[59] in several aspects: first, it had two or more nuclei instead of a single nucleus that *ipso facto* defined *the* city center; second, at least one of the nuclei skewed geographically—in the case of Suzhou, all three functionally differentiated districts were off-center; and third, social status did not decline with distance from the center, nor were the poorest elements necessarily in the peripheries of most imperial Chinese cities, since certain suburbs lay squarely within the business nucleus. Thus the urban sociological periphery in Chinese cities bears no spatial relation to wider concentric circles; instead it was to be found at those corners of the intramural area that were least accessible from the more important gates. It is clearly noticeable from the map of the city of Suzhou contained in the prefectural gazetteer of 1883, (Figure 3.15) that the land in the far southeast, northeast, and northwest was derelict or devoted to agriculture, even though densely populated suburbs must have expanded outside the two gates in the west walls. Another interesting phenomenon in the late Qing period of Suzhou may also serve to strengthen the point: churches and hospitals founded by American protestant and European Jesuit missionaries were mostly located in the southeast part of the city, the quarter that was the least socially prestigious and economically sensible and thus most likely to be utilized by foreign elements.

City and Countryside

As we have seen, the medieval urban revolution that occurred between the mid-eighth and twelfth centuries at the cores of the economically most advanced regions brought about changes in the planning and governing principles of the urban market and residential system. Large cities grew rapidly, often spilling out from their walls into suburbs. Internally, the old system of tightly controlled and segregated walled quarters broke down and was replaced by plans of city streets with a free disposition of commerce, trade, industry, and residence. This process of transformation was further extended and intensified during the Ming and Qing periods, when walled cities and market towns were better integrated into a single hierarchical system and when the development of extramural commercial suburbs of large cities incorporated outlying market towns into enlarged conurbations. Both the physical pattern of urban spatial arrangement and people's conception of the urban world were profoundly transformed. Although the imperial administrative function of cities remained decidedly unchanged,[60] most cities in the late imperial period must have been vastly different from those before the mid-Tang in many important respects, such as their economic function, social organization, arrangement

Figure 3.15 Map of the city of Suzhou contained in the 1883 Suzhoufu zhi, tu 7: *"Sucheng quantu."*

of internal space, and articulation with the rural areas. Changes in these areas were essential as well, I believe, if a city was to be seen as a vital, multiplex phenomenon.

However, Murphey's statement that the traditional Chinese city lasted "essentially unchanged"[61] holds not only in terms of the city's administrative function but also in yet another respect; that is, from a worldwide perspective, the remarkable stability in time of the overall form of many (but not all) cities as defined by their walls. The city of Suzhou provides a perfect example of this characteristic of China's urban history. As we will see later in this chapter and in Chapters 4 and 5, the position of this city's walls and thus its outline shape basically remained unchanged from at least the 1220s onward, whereas its urban expansion was tremendous from that same period. Here an interesting question arises: how should the coexistence of these two seemingly contradictory features be explained? This antithesis has also been noted by Rowe, who speaks of the tension between the realization of the growth of certain cities in the Lower Yangzi and the undeniable long-term stability of city forms.[62] Rowe does not tackle this issue but wisely cautions against accepting easy or one-sided conclusions about it. The following section presents a preliminary answer to this question, which will be fully discussed in Chapter 5.

Urban-Rural Relationships

The underlying assumption of the studies of urban development in the West has been that there exists a clear distinction between city and country because of difference in mode of life, social structure, and means of subsistence. It is the presence of a specifically urban class, which may loosely be termed the bourgeoisie, that has been taken as the defining characteristic of the city. However, China had no urban class comparable to that of the West. Yet, this fundamental social and political distinction between cities in imperial China and their Western counterparts did not conspicuously arise in the pre-Qin period, or the "feudal period," as Balazs calls it, when the cities in China contained "the same basic ideas as come to mind when we think of the rise of the town under Western feudalism, or rather, when we recall the main arguments used in the elaboration of theories on the origin of towns (walls, fortifications, markets)."[63]

A far-reaching transformation of the conception of the city in relation to the countryside took place in China during the period of the Qin unification. In early Zhou times, the character *guo,* which in modern Chinese means "state," "nation," or "country," not only denoted an enfeoffed territory but also meant the walled city where the seat of the head of the fief resided. In political terms, a city of this kind was constructed, or more precisely, *walled*, to defend the authority of a prince or duke over his fiefdom.[64] The opposite of *guo* is *ye,* which literally meant the fields beyond the city's suburbs. Thus, the residents in the walled city were called *guoren* (people in the walled city), and the peasantry living in and cultivating the open fields were known as *yeren* (people in the fields beyond the suburbs), which also connoted "plebeian" or uncivilized men.[65] Thus it may not be too wrong to regard the *guo*, the walled city, as an island of civilization surrounded and sometimes threatened by a sea of less civilized and probably hostile peasantry.[66]

However, as part of the great social change during the period between the breakup of the classical Zhou civilization and the beginning of the imperial era, the conditions allowing a sense of that kind of urban superiority seem to have vanished.[67] Cities became principally an instrument of the imperial government; that is, they were above all political nuclei, nodes in the administrative network, and, in Needham's terms, "they existed for the sake of the country and not vice versa."[68] They did not show what Eberhard calls "the traits of cities in dual societies,"[69] not at least until the Ming and Qing periods, when a sense of urban identification may have emerged among certain groups of residents in the city. Mote maintains that after the Qin unification, Chinese values did not sustain a self-identifying and self-perpetuating urban elite as a component of the population, and probably a unique urban-rural continuum existed both as physical and organizational realities and as an aspect of Chinese psychology; also China achieved in theory and in actual practice what he calls an "open society."[70] He categorically states: "The rural component of Chinese civilization was more or less uniform, and it extended everywhere that Chinese civilization penetrated. It, and not the cities, defined the Chinese way of life."[71]

Mote's arguments touch on the central feature that sets the Chinese experience apart from that of the Western world. However, they seem to constitute a sweeping generalization of a complicated reality and thus may be questioned. There is a slight tendency in them to treat the history of Chinese society as though there were few changes in the entire course of the imperial era. Although the Chinese attained very early, in law and in fact, the rights to own, buy, and sell land freely, it seems, as Eberhard has suggested, that until around A.D. 1000 social mobility was quite restricted in China. The civil war of the tenth century and the economic developments of the eleventh century were periods of greater mobility.[72] We have already seen that fundamental transformation was brought to the cities by the medieval urban revolution that took place from the second half of the eighth century onward. This transformation was accompanied by a marked growth in the numbers, wealth, and power of merchants and by what Balazs calls "the beginning of something quite new: the rise of a new social class in the interstices of the traditional social structure," namely a large group of "upstarts" practicing low-class professions, such as acting, singing, prostitution, fortune-telling, professional storytelling, and juggling.[73] Also concomitant to it was an improvement of spatial (and social) mobility: the collapse of the old residential and market ward system and the spillover of commerce from within the city walls to the suburbs indicate that both urban and rural people were able to change their place of residence and way of life.[74] It seems safer therefore to say that China achieved, in the historical process of the breakup of the classic Zhou civilization, an "open society," in theory at least, whereas it started to become an actual, widespread social practice only from the late Tang onward.[75]

What about the late imperial period? Despite profound differences of opinion on the contours of the historical landscape, historians of China seem agreed that Chinese society underwent significant changes in the course of the Ming dynasty, "changes," as Rawski asserts, "that produced the political, social, and economic institutions of late imperial China."[76] This is largely in accord with Myers' view that "one can argue convincingly that Ming and Ch'ing [i.e., Qing] China experienced changes as profound and far-reaching as those of the Sung [i.e., Song]."[77] One of the characteristic aspects of the period from the mid-Ming on was the multiplication of the market towns, at least in the economically more advanced parts of China such as the Suzhou region, at a rate exceeding that of the population increase.[78] Administrative centers grew with official encouragement, while commercial towns flourished on their own. Although during the late imperial period the trend toward the growth of great cities seems to have stopped or reversed itself, there was a lessening of the contrast between these great cities and the countryside as the relative importance of small to middle-size urban centers increased;[79] and it is reasonable to believe, as do Naquin and Rawski, that now "all Chinese culture was influenced by what was happening in China's towns and cities."[80]

Such a sociological situation—a new phenomenon in Chinese urban history—should not however be seen as a model that sharply distinguishes between urban and rural societies, as it did in Western urban history. This is because by this time, China, and its economically more advanced regions in particular, became something that was truly worthy of the term "open society": the urban and the rural by now formed a kind of organic unity, a unity being evidenced by daily patterns of living in the Suzhou region, daily movements of large number of people into and out of cities. Greater integration of capital cities and market towns into a single hierarchical system, an even distribution of urban population throughout the hierarchy, the interdependence of cities, towns, and villages on each other, and inland communications that were at least as good as and often much better than those of any other part of the world before the railway age,[81] all these "facilitated," to borrow Rawski's words, "the flow of ideas as well as goods between city and countryside."[82] Yet this is not the only reason for the distinctiveness of the late imperial Chinese urban-rural relationship. In fact, cities in China had never embodied the ideas of emancipation and liberty, as cities in Europe did;[83] nor were there secure privileges and autonomy in the administration of them.[84] Naquin and Rawski's careful wording, "what was happening in China's towns and cities," emphasizes localities but does not suggest that urban culture "originated from the social milieu of the independent city residents" who were legally set apart from the country peasants. It was a culture different in many aspects from the rural culture, but not alien to it. In this sense, traditional urban culture in China could be seen as created by the intensive interaction between cities, towns, and villages from the mid-Ming onward.[85] It was undoubtedly an "urban culture," but the use of this term should not confuse the Chinese urban phenomena with those of the West.

The manner of merchant and immigrant influence on the development of China's cities was also very distinct from its European counterparts. The scholar-official's state of China was so entrenched by its ideology and social structure that the merchant class was never able to extract from it liberties, laws, and autonomy for themselves. The abiding ideal measure for Chinese businessmen of climbing up the social ladder was to become assimilated, to be part of the state by becoming, or seeing their children or grandchildren become, scholar-officials themselves.[86] Indeed, by the late imperial period, as Skinner has indicated, "the continual incorporation of assimilat*ing* [Skinner's emphasis] (and hence only partially assimilat*ed* [Skinner's emphasis]) merchants into the urban elite" inevitably affected the cultural tone of cities.[87] Yet the Chinese city, far from being the bulwark of freedom, was always the center of state administration at a certain level, and never developed to a "state within a state," as did many free towns of medieval Europe, where the serf was able to take refuge under the protection of the autonomous bourgeoisie.[88]

Immigrants from various parts of the country brought diverse local subcultural ingredients to the urban environment, which in turn gradually shaped the intensified cultural life of the city. But it is important not to ignore the fact that Chinese culture in the last centuries of imperial rule was not only extremely diverse but also highly integrated.[89] The remarkably high level of cultural integration of late imperial China in comparison with many other peasant societies was another crucial factor in the shaping of its cities. By referring to the situation in nineteenth-century France, Watson emphasizes that, "unlike the French, Chinese leaders did *not* [Watson's emphasis] have to forge a new national culture based on urban models that were alien to the mass of rural people," for "most villagers already identified themselves with an overarching 'Chinese culture,' an abstraction they had no difficulty understanding," and "the general peasantry did not need urban leaders to remind them that they shared a grand cultural tradition."[90] Thus it is hard to regard what developed in the cities of late imperial China as cultures that were as distinct from those of rural societies as their Western counterparts. There certainly developed attitudes and characteristics of consciousness associated with the city, as acknowledged by Mote who ardently depreciates the idea of a general urban-rural dichotomy in Chinese culture. This was particularly so on the popular level.[91]

It would certainly be wrong to assume an urban-rural uniformity and to deny that some of the basic functions of China's cities were absent in villages. But, as Skinner points out, without implying a negligible cultural role for cities of imperial China, Mote's essential point holds; that is, "the basic cultural cleavages in China were those of class and occupation (complexly interrelated) and of region (an elaborated nested hierarchy), not those between cities and their hinterlands."[92] Few would doubt that Murphey's statement is true: in traditional China, "only the continual interchange with the countryside kept the city viable."[93] Since the whole of public life—institutions, construction works, water-control projects, regulations, education—were (at least largely) subjected to government control, and since the cities were invariably the centers of imperial administration, a distinctive phenomenon of urban-rural continuum was manifested in many aspects of Chinese social life. Mote has presented abundant illustrations to corroborate his argument; a large number of them are cogent, while some others are questionable or need further clarification. There are also a few points that Mote has overlooked, as Skinner has appreciated, "in his eagerness to dissociate the Chinese case from the hasty generalizations of synthesizers."[94] Since, disputable as they are, the main issues tackled in Mote's works are crucial for and edifying to my research on Suzhou in imperial history the next three sections will deal with the main points he has made and will serve as the starting point for the present discussion.

Urban and Rural Elements

The Chinese city, as I have argued in the previous section, was an administrative center of an area, not an entity of its own. It possessed no government distinct from that of the surrounding countryside and thus no corporate identity that set it apart from the rural areas. In this respect, I share Mote's argument that the Chinese city had no "civic monuments," no need of a city hall as what Hilberseimer calls "a place of assembly where citizens could exercise their political rights," since it had no "citizens" in that its residents had no legal or social status distinguishing them from rural residents and they were not constituents of different administrative units.[95] As Elvin plainly puts it: "there was little civic awareness as such."[96] Mote also states:

> The Chinese city did not totally lack public squares and public gardens, but it had less need of them because its citizens had, and probably preferred, their small, private, but open and sunny courtyards.[97]

Although I concur in general with this argument, the public squares to which Mote refers[98] are probably only in a physical sense fairly spacious open pieces of ground that may be found occasionally in a very small number of cities. An open piece of ground may have accidentally come into being with the passage of time, and sometimes it may have functioned partially and temporarily as what may be seen as similar to a public square in many historical European cities. Yet it did not function in the way that Paul Zücker sees "as a basic factor in town planning, as the very heart of the city;"[99] nor did it represent an essential element of a typical city or settlement of any other kind in imperial China. This open piece of ground was basically as much contradictory to the political nature of Chinese cities, especially before the late Ming period when an urban identity may have been gained among certain groups of city dwellers, as it was to the psychological attitudes of the Chinese toward sociospatial organization. Although the pragmatic and psychological aspects of the use of public open space will be discussed later in Chapter 6, it needs to be emphasized here that the very few cases of a piece of open ground in the urban area do *not* necessarily indicate that Chinese cities had to a lesser degree a similar need of public squares than their European counterparts, which, as one of the civic urban facilities, characterized cities as distinct from other rural settlements. It should also be noted that public gardens accessible to both urban and rural residents, especially on festivals and holidays, were located in the rural areas around the city as much as within the city walls, and in them natural landscapes were transformed into specific resorts by hydraulic conservancy projects and other scattered constructions.

Another indicator of the absence of Western style urban-rural dichotomy that is noted by Mote is that there were no physical symbols of the religious element of Chinese life comparable to those in the West.[100] Official religion had its important temples in cities, such as the Confucian temples and the temples of city walls and moats (Chenghuang, often loosely translated as "City God"), most of which were patronized by the government and its officials.[101] Yet they did not presuppose professional clergy; nor did they physically or symbolically dominate the cities. Chinese public religion was also sharply different from Western religion in terms of its organization, its financing, and its link with the city as the place where its monuments might attest to its role in society. Buddhist and Daoist temples were licensed by the state, which was often unsympathetic toward them and at times repressive; they could be closed or required to move by imperial authority. Although city temples were often wealthy and ornate, and, in the case of large Buddhist temples, usually had pagodas that were the tallest buildings in the low and sprawling skyline of the Chinese city, they did not dominate the city spiritually or architecturally. A greater number of temples were actually located in rural settings, which were often larger, richer, and more ornate than those in the city.

This feature was clearly evidenced in the area of Suzhou: out of 361 Buddhist temples (including those that had become derelict) in Suzhou prefecture, as recorded in the 1883 prefectural gazetteer, only 87 were located within the walls of the prefectural and county capitals. Similarly, out of a total number of 79 Daoist temples, 33 were located within the walls of these cities.[102] Many other miscellaneous deities in diffused popular religion were worshipped as well, but their temples, much smaller and humbler compared with many Buddhist and Taoist temples, were located both within and outside the city walls. Thus, as Mote rightly asserts, China's cities "were not keystones in an important religious institutional structure—a state within the state as in Europe, or an arm of the state as in ancient Egypt and the Classical and Islamic worlds."[103]

After suggesting that styles of dress, patterns of eating and drinking, means of transportation, and other obvious aspects of daily life did not display characteristic dichotomies between the urban and rural communities, Mote continues to argue that Chinese cultural and economic activities involved both the cities and the countryside, and they were indistinguishable as "urban" and "rural": probably more of the private schools, publishing activities, private libraries and art collections, were located in villages or out-of-the-way rural settings; there were no festivals that could be classified as strictly urban or rural; commercial concentrations, flourishing markets, and industrial production and distribution were often outside city walls but adjacent to major cities, while skilled labor sources were drawn from both within the cities and outside them for hire on very short terms or by the day.[104] Although some of these assertions may be questionable, and exceptions are expected to be found elsewhere, the principal argument is largely tenable that in terms of cultural, industrial, and commercial activities, a hard and fast line can hardly be drawn between the cities and the countryside.

From an architectural point of view, Mote observes that in the essentials of design, in materials used, and in form and ornamentation, Chinese urban structures were indistinguishable from rural structures, and thus the continuum from the city to suburbs to open countryside was embodied in the uniformity of building styles and layout, and in the use of ground space.[105] Skinner apparently disagrees with this observation and points out that Chinese cities did have their distinctive edifices, such as the drum tower and bell tower, the great examination hall, and the elaborate towers at the corners and gates of the city wall.[106] If we are to look into this issue with respect to *architectural styles and building materials*, Skinner seems to have misunderstood Mote's argument. The fact is that the urban structures exemplified by Skinner, although larger and probably more sumptuously ornamented, have proved to have not been so very distinct from other structures in the countryside and have been found to be similar to more humble and rustic examples in some market towns and large villages. Whether certain buildings were supposed to have been located in urban or rural areas is usually indicated by the names given to them rather than by their style. It is also important to note that most of the examples cited by Skinner were associated with the city walls or wall-like structures, and therefore their distinctiveness was gained not by the buildings themselves but by the symbol of the city, the wall. This important point will be qualified later in Chapter 6.

If, however, the issue is to be dealt with in terms of the *functions* of urban structures, the typology of buildings based on their use becomes crucial in distinguishing what should usually be in the walled city and what might not. The following passage by Mote is very pertinent to this point:

> Although certain functions necessary to society had to be located where there were dense populations, there was no necessary pattern governing which functions should be located within the city wall and which outside. The lone exception is the executive level of civil administration itself. Local and regional governments were invariably located within city walls if such existed, and by the later imperial era they existed even at the county level in almost all cases.[107]

The validity of this statement seems to depend on how inclusive the terms "the executive level of civil administration" or "local and regional governments" are with respect to both the institutions and the buildings or building complexes, for invariably the city walls contained not only the offices of regional or local administration (*yamen*), which were in most cases enclosed to form a building complex, but also many other structures that were not themselves administrative offices but were closely associated with some of the daily and annual functions of the government.

Other important examples of typically urban structures are imperial examination facilities, to which Skinner has called our attention, and prefectural and county schools, which were usually combined with the Confucian temples or temples of civilization (*wenmiao*). Also located within the city walls, except for some rare cases like the one in the north suburb of Chengdu prefectural capital, were the temples of Chenghuang, which have been regarded by Feuchtwang as "a spiritual office,"[108] wherein an incoming prefect or magistrate, probably since as early as the beginning of the Ming dynasty, reported himself to the god and swore an oath before taking up office, and then led worship to the god on festivals, on the god's birthdays, and during times of natural disasters. Other structures, such as the prefectural or county storehouses and army barracks, were built in the city proper as well. Yet it should be stressed that all of these urban structures were established for the benefit of the whole jurisdictional area of the regional or local administration, that is, for the city and its surrounding countryside, and they were located within the city walls simply because of their tight link with the governmental functions, which collectively provided the *raison d'être* of regional and local cities in imperial China.

City Walls

There certainly existed a physical sign of definite demarcation of the city from the surrounding countryside: the city walls. It needs to be reiterated that the essential implication of the term *cheng* with regard to city building is "city walls" or "to wall a city."[109] Walls, indeed, have been singularly important to the Chinese. Over and above practical considerations, they draw lines between domains of different categories.[110] Their symbolic and psychological meaning certainly derived from the characteristic way in which the Chinese of ancient times perceived and shaped the world. It points to the ultimate Chinese desire to create and maintain order as much in the minds of the individuals as in society, which should be in accord with both the order of the world and the cosmos. With respect to city construction, this symbolic meaning is fully revealed in the Eastern Han records of the foundation of the city of Suzhou as the Wu capital in the Spring and Autumn period, which I have discussed in Chapter 2. Although great social and political transformation in the imperial era led to profound change in the nature of cities as regional or local administrative centers, a large part, if not all, of that fundamental meaning of walls remained, as did the drive of the Chinese to that social and world order that it reflected. In this sense, Mote argues that city walls of imperial China served the primarily psychological function of marking the presence of the imperial government and did not function as real boundaries in daily life between an urban-within and a rural-without except in rare crisis situations.[111]

Yet I would also suggest that, for many Chinese, the city walls may have further signified a social order in the whole area over which the city-based regional or local government ruled: they conveyed in their prepossessing form a message to all the residents (both the urban and the rural) of the area that various forces were accorded and life went on under the rule of one single government, which was as powerful and reliable as the walls. Let me cite two examples, among many others, that can be seen as supporting my point. In the face of the advancing Manchu forces in 1645, the residents of the city of Jiading, then a subordinate county of Suzhou prefecture, "wept up towards the city wall," as recorded by Gu Gongxie, a local scholar of the eighteenth century.[112] They cried because of the imminent fall of the city and because of the slaughter and plunder that would be likely to ensue. Yet it seems not too far-fetched to interpret this record as implying that the city walls were an emblem for these residents of the existing social order that was about to be overturned. The words of Zheng Yuanyou (1292–1364) of the Yuan in one of his memoirs, recording the reconstruction of Suzhou city walls in 1351, reveals more explicitly the symbolic bond between the city walls as physical artifacts and the social order and security of the region:

> Since the city walls have successfully been constructed today, which can be taken as a work of defense, from now onwards, what defense can be built on lies in the enlightened officials who carry forward the achievements of their predecessors, promulgate moral principles and cultivate the power of the people, so as to unite

> their hearts solidly. [This] will lead to the people of Suzhou loving and respecting the higher as sons and younger brothers love and respect their father and elder brothers. In this way, the people will take *renyi* [benevolence and righteousness] as their shield and *liyue* [ceremony and music] as their armor. Together with these [newly] consolidated city walls and moats, the unity of the people's hearts thus achieved will stand as the natural barrier forever.[113]

This idea was not new. In a collection of texts known as *Guanzi*, variously written between the fifth and first centuries B.C., we read:

> Proper and outer city walls, moats and ditches will not suffice to secure one's defenses. Great strength of arms will not suffice to meet the enemy. Vast territory and wealth will not suffice to hold the masses. Only those who adhere to the true Way [*Dao*] are able to prepare for trouble before it arises. Therefore disasters will not germinate.[114]

By referring to another line in the *Guanzi* that expounded the sequential dependence of the preservation of territory first on walls then grain,[115] Hay argues that walls were seen as an internal differentiation supporting a material definition of the state: agriculture; and he acutely sees this passage quoted from the *Guanzi* as revealing a conception that "through this sequence of dependencies runs the single lineage of ritual and ethical reference."[116] Even though by the late imperial period, the material prosperity of the Suzhou area depended more on commerce, trade, and industry than on agriculture alone, this particular symbolic reference remained.

This is not to say that city walls did not have practical functions, but, as Murphey has indicated, "the walls were as imposing as the rank and size of the city dictated, but in every case were designed to awe and affirm, only secondarily to defend, although of course they might be useful in troubled times."[117] That is, the walls assumed the role of physical barriers between the protected and unprotected areas only in times of real crisis, especially in case of a siege by insurgents. Since a war or a major disorder was usually brought about by rebellions against the current government, cities housing the administrative seats and representing the imperial authority inevitably became scenes of pitched battles or the objects of plunder. Consequently, cities were not necessarily regarded as safe bastions; on the contrary, it was in the countryside where people often sought refuge in times of turmoil.[118] Instances of this are numerous. In an anonymous document, *Wucheng riji* written in the early Qing, for example, this trend of exodus, from the city of Suzhou in the face of the Manchu advance, was repeatedly recorded.[119] Similarly, according to Shen Shouzhi, the magistrate of a county in Henan saved the local government's reserve of food and money and its documents by moving them to the countryside in 1853 in advance of the Taiping rebels' attack.[120]

The city did not have an autonomous citizen army and therefore did not defend itself. Its defenses formed part of the nationwide defense system built by authority of the imperial government.[121] Consequently, defending the city in a practical sense meant upholding the rule of the present government and thus protecting the total administrative territory of which the city was the node and the symbol rather than the area strictly within the walls.[122] Such activity might involve both the residents within the walls and people in the surrounding rural areas. In the summer of 1645 when incompetent officials were fleeing the countryside, it was the largely self-organized rural militia that entered the city of Suzhou and claimed to assume the task of resisting the Manchu conquest.[123] To see it the other way around, an attack on the city signified a direct challenge to the current authority, while sacking the city was equivalent to raping the government, and psychologically as disastrous to the whole jurisdictional area as to the city *per se*. Hence it is fair to say that if the city "existed for the sake of the country and not vice versa," a statement made by Needham that I have quoted earlier, its walls were built for maintaining an awesome sense of the government's presence and the established order and accordingly for the psychological and practical benefit of both the city proper and the surrounding countryside. On this point, Mote makes a felicitous remark on the city walls: "They dignified cities; they did not bound them."[124]

Transformability and Stability of Urban Form

Having said much about the practical and symbolic roles of city walls, I would venture an additional proposition that appears to have a certain degree of validity for some imperial Chinese cities. There is a clear discrepancy between the realization of numerous cases of urban expansion or shrinkage in imperial China, especially from the Tang period onward, and the phenomenon acknowledged by such scholars as Mote and Skinner of the remarkable stability of urban form of some important cities, among which Suzhou is a notable instance. In Figure 3.16, a comparison of maps from 1229, 1797, and 1916,[125] clearly indicates the fact that walls, moats, and the position of city gates[126] are identical; the main streets and canals remain unchanged; many bridges and principal buildings are located on the same sites and bear the same names. While more extensive discussion on the historic process of reconstruction of the city walls, gates, and other structures will be presented in Chapters 4 and 5, it is sufficient for the time being to note that the walls enclosing a site occupied for well over two millennia assumed their present extent and precise location probably during the period between A.D. 626 and 875, if not earlier.

A discrepancy, however, seems to have derived from confusion in the way in which the term *urban form* is to be defined.[127] Let us use the urban development of Suzhou to illustrate this point. To be sure, the stability of "urban form" appears extraordinary only if the morphology of the area determined and, above all, *enclosed* by city walls with gates is meant by that term. It is true that some of the principal structures within the city also bear to some extent this distinctive trait, as we notice from the three foregoing juxtaposed maps that the locations and, in some cases, the names of the structures remained unchanged, such as the Buddhist temples of Baoen in the north, Dinghui in the west, and Ruiguang in the south, all including pagodas; the Daoist temple of Tianqing (later

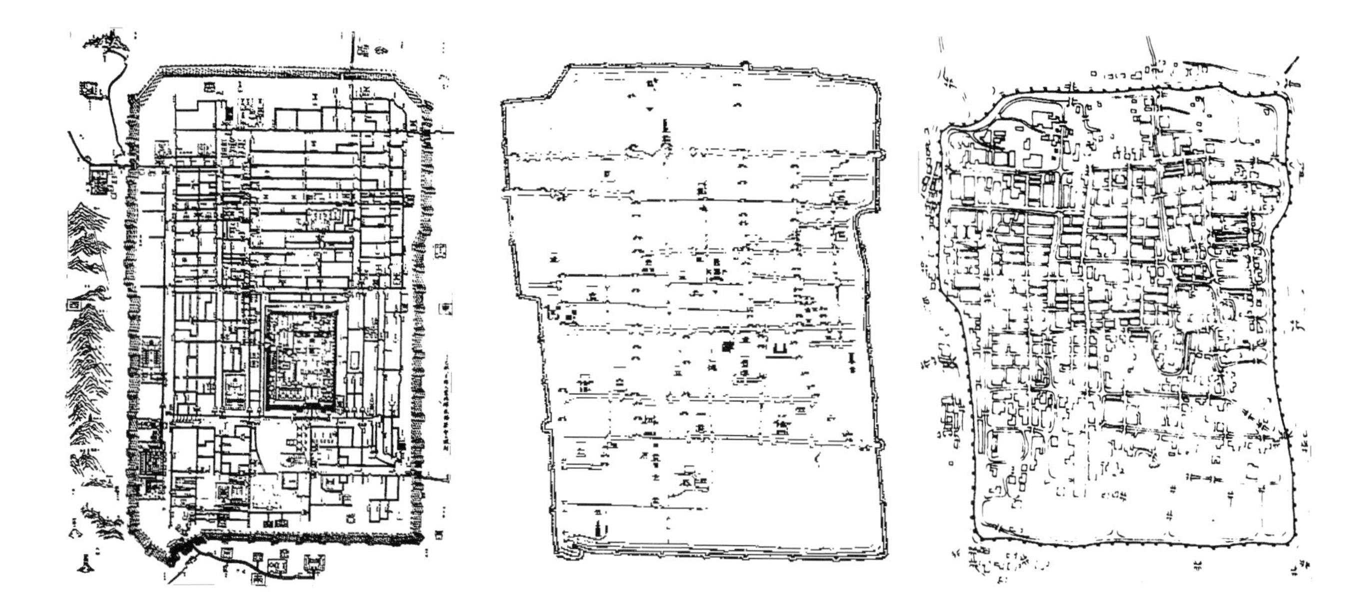

called Yuanmiao and Xuanmiao); the prefectural school-temple (*fuxue*); and the garden of Canglang Ting. Other structures experienced various degrees of alteration, utterly disappearing or being moved to other sites or changing in function and name.

The most notable change that had a profound impact on the internal urban spatial pattern of the city has been the removal of the inner city walls originally built to enclose the local governmental seat, a change that was largely the result of contemporary political requirements.[128] However, what can be said about the western suburban areas that gradually developed into the central business district? They were surely more "urban," in terms of population density, man-made spatial arrangement, and social and economic activities than many parts of the land within the walls, which were either derelict or used as fields to grow crops or vegetables. The growth of these areas thus indicates change, at times slow and at others radical. During the Ming and Qing periods, the city walls were repeatedly restored; and especially in 1662, large-scale reconstruction work on the walls was implemented.[129] Why were additional walls not built to enclose that densely populated business district in the west suburbs, an area that appears to have been very important to the city and prefecture, at least in an economic sense, for a period of four centuries?[130]

It seems clear that it was largely the form and location of the city walls and gates that were responsible for the remarkable continuity and stability of urban form in time. I would therefore hypothesize that this trait of the development of Chinese cities was not only brought about by various material factors, such as any particular city's topographical conditions (the formation of the network of city canals in particular), financial situation, and political decisions,[131] but was also influenced by the Chinese sense of the authority of the past, by the accumulated weight of history, and, above all, by the

Figure 3.16 *Maps showing the stability of the urban form of the city of Suzhou from 1229 to 1916. Left: picture map of the city in 1229, then known as Pingjiang. Adapted from* Zhongguo dabaike quanshu *1988, p. 348. Middle: picture map of the city redrawn from the map engraved on stone in 1797. Courtesy of the Committee of Suzhou Urban and Rural Construction. Right: map of the city of Suzhou drawn on the basis of the survey in 1916. Courtesy of the Committee of Suzhou Urban and Rural Construction.*

dual characteristics of the institutionalization and symbolization of city walls in imperial China. Some support for the argument can be obtained from observing how the construction of city walls was recorded in the imperial periods. It was certainly not uncommon for a traditional Chinese historian to start his section on the evolution of the city walls and moats (*chengchi*) with the opening words that Wang Ao (1450–1524) writes in his *Gusu zhi*: "Wherever there is the need to set up a defense of the state, there must be city walls and moats."[132] It is also not surprising that in all local gazetteers of different historic periods a paraphrased account of the early construction and form of the city is always the opening and often the major part of that section. What seems worth emphasizing, however, is that the successive construction works during later periods are all described as "*re*built" or "*re*constructed" except for the account of the event in 1662, wherein the phase "constructed with alteration" is used.[133] Such typical ways of recording seem to indicate that urban form at the time of the recorded city foundation was conceived as *the* timeless entity which had not, and which should not have, been altered but only renovated. In other words, conceptually and probably physically, as the authors of the *Wuxian zhi* put it, it had long become "the fixed institution from antiquity to the present time."[134]

I have explained why I agree with Mote and Murphey that the city walls signaled the presence of the government. I have also suggested that they symbolized the existence of social and political order and the long tradition that the city boasted. Hence, of utmost importance is what they *stood for* rather than what they enclosed. This conceptual predilection is implied in a passage of commentary in the *Wuxian zhi*:

> For two thousand years those who have come to renovate [the city walls and moats] followed on the heels of one another. Having by turns assumed [the task of] repeated investigation of their predecessors' achievements, [we] understand their good intention: their assiduity came from the realization that the cultural and historic relics [of Suzhou] were second to none in the southeast. This is like valuing the jewels highly but at the same time also being fond of the casket [*bao zhuyu jian'ai qi du*].[135] [Since] they [the city walls] are also one of the principal institutions of the region, who can say that they need not be passed on?[136]

The metaphor of the casket aptly epitomizes how the symbolic role of the city walls far outweighed the practical one: the walls functioned more as a symbol of the existence of the prefecture, and of the solidity and continuity of its social order and cultural achievements than as a physical defense work that only enclosed a tiny (though more concentrated) part of the prefectural territory. In this sense, continuity is visible in those institutional and symbolic values endowed in the walls, and, in the course of remarkable urban expansion driven by economic growth and sociopolitical change, the stability of the city form determined by the walls and gates appears to be in line with the urge of the Chinese to maintain the tradition.

Conclusion

I have presented in this chapter a number of important characteristics of the general development of cities in imperial China. These characteristics indicate that any sweeping generalization about Chinese cities in space and time may lead to oversimplification of their remarkably continuous, and yet highly complex, urban history. They constitute the wider context of that distinctive history, in which the city of Suzhou will be examined more closely in the following four chapters. In order for the reader to keep in mind these general characteristics as the study proceeds, a brief summary of them is necessary.

It is important to reiterate first that it proves to be illusive and misleading to talk about *the* Chinese city either as a constructed ideal type that seemingly provides a set of conclusions in the form of generalizations or as one of the actual cities that symbolizes Chinese culture as a whole. China's cities and the process of their development were highly differentiated in their administrative status, geographical locations, conditions of local economic development, and process of urban construction and transformation. This range of significant width in time and space has led to the realization that, in the words of Samuels, "no one ideal construct can suffice to explain the varied and complex history of urban China."[137] Also, there has not been a single city ever standing as the hub and the symbol of the history and cultural achievements of Chinese civilization. This distinctive phenomenon of urbanization in imperial China has been asserted by Mote in a sweeping comparative manner.[138] He also suggests, as I believe was the case, that the concept of the "provincial" as opposed to the "metropolitan" did not exist in China, especially from Tang times onward, as it did in the cultural life of Europe.[139] Indeed, the cultural and material life of some of the Yangzi Valley provinces was recognized as being superior to that of the capitals and the provinces adjacent to them in the North.

Arguments in this direction are not meant to deny that premodern Chinese cities are in comparative perspective a distinct cultural type nor to neglect the fact that in the national capital, careers were different in character and prestige from those in the provinces and architectural features were often more splendid and imposing. Instead, they stress the necessity that any single city is to be considered as part of a continuous tradition of city building. The city of Suzhou should thus be regarded as a particular instance characterized by unique features wherein the nature of the urban form and space development of China's cities is more or less embedded rather than as a paradigm that inclusively speaks for "the Chinese city" as a whole.

A regional or local walled city was invariably a subcenter of the imperial government; that is, it was a node in the administrative hierarchy. Its managerial role over the territory in which the city was located was embodied in the position of the county magistrate, prefect, or provincial governor, who, through his court and assistants, was officially responsible for everyone and everything within that territory.[140] Yet in terms of cosmological symbolism of the government, a regional or local city was fundamentally differentiated from the imperial capital; it was not the imperial capital writ small. It should not be perceived as a "cosmic center" on a smaller scale. Such a differentiation is indirectly reflected in an interesting remark by Wu Yifeng (1742–1819), a scholar from Changzhou county, on the customary way in which his contemporaries humbly addressed their own home regions:

> Nowadays many an individual calls [his/her home region] "my humble [*bi*] county" or "my humble prefecture" or "my humble province." [This custom] started from [the use of] *biyi* [my humble town] in the *Zuo zhuan*, [which was] probably a self-depreciatory expression. The lone exception is the imperial capital district: it is the place where the Most Revered [*Zhizun*, i.e., the Emperor] is present, and no one dares to use the character *bi* [to refer to it].[141]

Any region, regardless of its administrative level, constituted but a subordinate part of the empire, and its capital was merely *a* city of certain political or economic importance. Under the supreme rule of the Son of Heaven, it was not differentiated from others in cosmological terms. It was the imperial capital (or its district) alone that was symbolically regarded as *the* cosmic, most revered center.

The process of formation and transformation of urban space in China varied across sociogeographical regions. In overall perspective, many local cities on the North China Plain were older, with their rational fortified patterns imposed from above and other urban structures later gradually filling in, than most of the cities in the South, which were later and closer to their unplanned origins, on which some degree of planning was superimposed.

The city of Suzhou in this sense appears to have been one of the few exceptional cases in the southeast region and thus to have shown some traits similar to those of the cities in the North. The enclosed area of the cities under this category was more likely to have been determined so as to match their administrative status than to accommodate their future growth. Thus an evident dichotomized process of development can be detected from these cities, especially from those of economically advanced regions: on the one hand, urban business development from the Tang-Song period onward was skewed toward and very often beyond the city gates, affording direct access to the major commercial trade routes, and on the other hand, city walls were persistently reconstructed on the same site enclosing an area within which many parts remained derelict or as farming land. In other words, there coexisted two seemingly contradictory features of the urban expansion in space and the stability of city form defined by the walls. This distinct phenomenon may be explained by, and at the same time seems to strengthen, a realization of the salient institutional and symbolic role that the city walls played in society, of the characteristic way in which the cities functioned, and of the distinctive relationship between the city and countryside.

The functions of Chinese cities were not peculiar. Setting aside the chicken-or-egg question of whether trade created cities or cities made trade, it can be assumed that a long-standing inseparability of cities and trade existed in Chinese antiquity; and in the imperial era, especially from the Tang onward, domestic commerce, which grew increasingly important, exerted strong influence on the location and growth of cities. It should also be acknowledged that most of China's cities were multifunctional; apart from the most obvious administrative and economic functions, those of the military, transport and communication, religion, cultural life, intellectual activities, and education were also part of the Chinese urban scene. Yet whereas most of the activities of Chinese and Western cities look very similar in a broad view, it is the way in which those activities were exercised that renders the Chinese situation sharply distinctive from that of Europe. This certainly necessitates further extensive examination, but one thing seems worth noting at this stage: because every walled city in imperial China was the administrative center of an area that was largely rural, the city, if seen as a different entity from the countryside, functioned not as much as a locus generating and protecting these activities as a hub within the hierarchically ordered urban system of *organizing* these activities.[142]

I have emphasized that the cities in imperial China were not corporate entities in themselves, with separate legal and political status. They functioned primarily as an instrument of the centralized government and were centers of political and economic power of the empire. Yet paradoxically, these cities, as Elvin phrases it, "played a limited role in pre-modern Chinese political history" in the sense that they were not centers of political change until the traditional fabric was rent by the growth of Western-inspired treaty ports in the late nineteenth and early twentieth centuries.[143] Trade alone in imperial China could not rival administration as an urban foundation, even when some cities' economic centrality had come to far outweigh their administrative status. There was little civic awareness among urban residents and merchant sojourners and no sense of municipal arrogance or power, or the concept of municipal self-government. Consequently, the cities did not show the traits of cities in dual societies.[144]

Of course, the development of this last aspect of China's urban history was a gradual process. If the Qin unification formally brought an end to the urban-rural socio-economic dichotomy, the medieval urban revolution during the Tang-Song period practically made manifest what may loosely be termed an "urban-rural continuum" both as physical and organizational realities and as an aspect of Chinese psychology.[145] Arguments in the direction of urban-rural continuum are not to imply any neglect of those urban aspects that caused Suzhou to be called a "city," nor are they meant to deny those characteristics of cities that were absent from the countryside, but to emphasize that this unique trait of urban-rural relationship was probably one of the crucial factors that rendered China's cities distinct from those of Europe.

This distinctive relationship between the city and the countryside not only manifested itself in evidence from the physical form of cities, the structure and character of cultural activities, the religious establishments, and to some extent the pattern of economic life but was also reflected in building styles and layout, which could be differentiated among regional variations rather than between urban and rural characteristics. In other words, there was rarely such a thing as might be called "urban architecture" in traditional China. Apart from structures that were closely bonded with the walls, such as the gate towers and the drum and bell towers, edifices that were supposed to be located exclusively within the city were identified by names attached to them and sometimes by their grand scale rather than by type, style, and spatial arrangement. Their distinctiveness was essentially associated with the city walls and wall-like structures that were emblematic of the city. More discussions on this characteristic of Chinese architecture will be given in Chapter 6.

CHAPTER 4 The City Walls and Gates

THIS CHAPTER AND CHAPTERS 5 AND 6 FOCUS ON some of the physical aspects of the development of the city of Suzhou in the imperial era. The development of the city walls is given pride of place here because of the physical and symbolic importance of walls in Chinese urban history, which I have argued extensively in previous chapters. I present in it what we know about the walls of the city of Suzhou in the imperial era, by comparing the literary records with city maps which I have so far gathered.

"The Untransferable Terrain"

Little is known about the walls during the period from the fall of the state of Wu to A.D. 876, when the then incumbent prefect, Zhang Tuan, rebuilt them. Although Zhu Changwen (1041–1100) claims that the walls and moats and the names of the gates "continued without change" from the end of Wu, through the ages of the Qin, Han, and Tang, to the Northern Song, scholars of later periods, notably from the Ming onward, seem to have more cautiously suggested that these features of the city "followed their original form" until A.D. 591 when the city was temporarily transferred to a new site.[1] Indeed, tradition has it that for over two and a half millennia the city of Suzhou has remained at exactly the same site on which it was originally built, except for a short transitional period from the Sui to the Tang. Although the Sui had conquered the Southern Chen in the Lower Yangzi valley and reunified China in A.D. 589, the remnant forces of Chen were still actively harassing the new authority around the Suzhou region. According to Zhu Changwen, Yang Su (?–A.D. 606), a Sui minister who was at the time in charge of quelling these local rebellions, saw that the city of Suzhou was vulnerable to a siege because of the unsuitability of the site for establishing tenable defenses, and thus with royal permission he "moved" the city in A.D. 591 to the eastern foot of Mt. Heng, which, as Figure 4.1 shows, is located to the southeast of the old site.[2] Zhu Changwen then gives a more detailed account of this event:

> Yang Su . . . moved the prefectural capital to the foot of Mt. Heng, probably intending to empty the old city. . . . In the early stage when Yang Su transferred the city to Mt. Heng, the artisans used timbers of *zhu* [a kind of oak] as the pillars of the city gates. [Yang] Su noticed and asked the artisans, "These timbers may not be sufficiently strong. How many years could they last?" The artisans said, "Forty years without rotting." "That would be sufficient," [Yang] Su said. "This walled city will be abandoned in fewer than forty years." At the end of the years of the Wude reign-period [A.D. 618–626] [the prefectural capital] was transferred back to the old city, just as he predicted.[3]

What caused the resumed use of the old city is not clear. It is possible that the size and form of the new city, which was hastily constructed, were unsuitable for its practical and symbolic functions as a local governmental center. It is also possible that the new site proved to be poor for communications and transport or prone to natural disasters such as flooding. Yet, whatever the reasons, the significance of such a move to some Chinese scholars seems to have had other implications. This is reflected in Zhu Changwen's comment that those who later reinhabited the old city "probably comprehend the untransferability of the terrain (*dishi zhi buke qian ye*)."[4] It is understandable

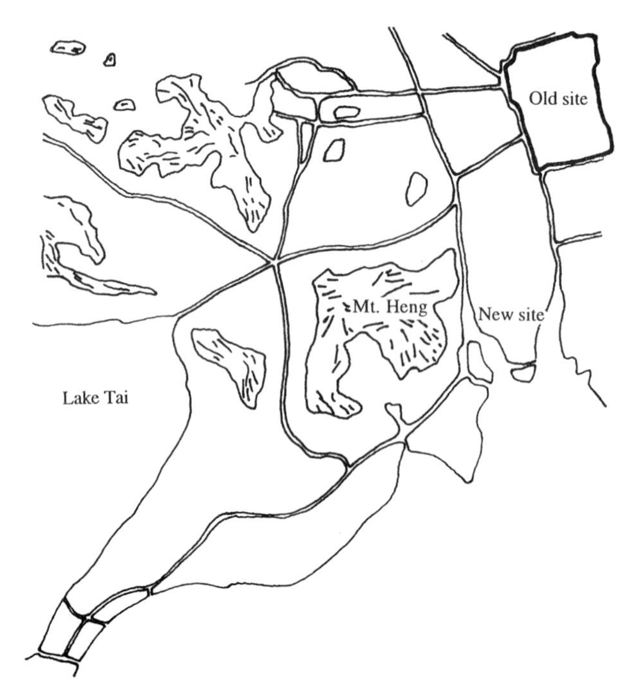

Figure 4.1 Location of the new prefectural city of Suzhou from A.D. 591 to the 620s, speculated on the basis of literary records. This diagrammatic map is adapted from Suzhoufu zhi, tu *2: "Wuxian tu" and* Wuxian zhi, juan *1: "Wuxian zongtu."*

that, after three and a half centuries of disintegration, the nationwide defenses of the newly established Sui authority were fragile and incomplete. The walled city as the symbol of power was more susceptible to siege, and thus its security, as Zhu reasoned, may have been regarded as a priority of governmental practice at that particular time.[5] As a result, the new site, which was supposed to be more militarily tenable, seems to have been preferable.

However, the new site may not have been perceived as an appropriate place for a city of considerable importance but only as an expedient solution during a specific period in history. The prosperity and stability of a prefecture demanded not only the tenability of the site of its capital, which certainly proved crucial at times of crisis, but also that stretch of land with its specific natural features in which local history was embedded. It was around the site of the old city that practical works of irrigation, water conservancy, and transport were concentrated; it was here also that cultural heritage and legends were most densely accumulated. Even more important, the long conceived *raison d'être* of the city's continued location had probably become so deeply rooted in the mind of the imperial officials that the abandonment of the site in the long run could not have been acceptable. Indeed, the city could be "moved" to a new site with all parts of its necessary institutions reestablished there, but it could not move its natural environs, which altogether constituted what this city had been and therefore should be. A city became meaningful and culturally valid to the Chinese only if it was coherently embedded in its natural surroundings where history had been deposited.

At this moment, I have to make a digression because the idea of moving the city may seem a little strange to Westerners. In the West, cities may rise and fall, and capitals may be relocated from one city to another; but a thriving city would not be moved.[6] In other words, the old city that once housed the governmental seat that was moved to another location would not be abandoned utterly and deliberately. Such a practice in the West clearly presupposes the separation of the notion of the city as a physical entity from that of the city as a political instrument, that is, the seat of government of a nation or region; and it is exactly in the conceptual and practical sense of the relationship between the two categories—city and capital—that lies the discrepancy between the Chinese and Western experiences and attitudes.

I have discussed in Chapter 3 how a Chinese city was not a corporate entity of its own but a governmental seat of the region in which it was located; a city as such had to have a set of formal institutions and their physical establishment had to be appropriate to its status and function—the most conspicuous being the city walls which were meant to protect the current authority against rebellions and banditry and to symbolize the presence of the government and social order. Thus, a city as an administrative center not enclosed with city walls was inconceivable to the Chinese; or to put it conversely, a walled city in which governmental functions were essentially absent would be so conceptually absurd as to render it practically unviable to remain a city. In this sense, a walled city and a capital did not fall into two different categories at all; a walled city could only be a capital and vice versa.[7] The physical city largely built with ephemeral materials therefore had to "go" with the capital to whichever new site was chosen by the imperial government, which alone had the authority to do such choosing.

This practice has been abundantly evidenced in the history of Chinese city construction. A site was often left derelict after the capital based on it was transferred elsewhere or abolished, and later may or may not have had another settlement superimposed on it, usually of a much smaller scale and with its spatial structure probably very different from that of the previous one. There were also cases, such as that of Ming and Qing dynasty Hangzhou, which had housed the imperial capital of the Southern Song; and that of Nanjing which was designated as the imperial capital of the Ming between A.D. 1368 and 1421. They ceased thereafter to be the imperial capitals but their spatial structures remained, because they functioned in later times as provincial capitals, and many of the governmental establishments, except for the imperial palatial complex and temples, were thus justifiably kept alive. The prediction by Yang Su in A.D. 591 and the realization of the resumption of the city of Suzhou as the prefectural capital demonstrate exactly the inseparability of the walled city from its status as the regional capital which it was meant to be.

Reconstruction of the Walls

Table 4.1 shows that the first recorded reconstruction of the walls of the city of Suzhou did not occur until the late Tang. We do not know how many times the walls were repaired, if not rebuilt, during the period from the fall of the state of Wu to A.D. 876. It is hard to imagine, however, that in this span of over thirteen centuries no works of wall restoration ever took place, so that the walls of the city could have "followed their original form," a suggestion made by later scholars and probably based on information scattered in some of the poems and rhymed prose-poems prior to A.D. 876. Indeed, the physical features of the city at the time of the Western Jin have been described by Zuo Si (ca. A.D. 250–ca. A.D. 305) in his rhymed prose-poem *Wudu fu*:

> The outer walls [*fuguo*] enclose [the city] *in toto*,
> Heavily built are the middle walls [*cheng*] and consolidated are their corners;
> Open are two sets [land and water] of eight gates [on the middle walls],
> [Connected by a network of] water routes and land roads [in the city].[8]

Except for the outer walls, these features must have continued to exist during the second half of the Tang period, because they are all mentioned in the *Wudi ji* and in some of the Tang poems.[9] We do not know for certain when exactly the city acquired the general form that was to be retained in the later periods of its development, but it is not impossible that this had occurred by the mid-Tang.

During the final years of the Tang, frequent rebellions occurred in the Southeast. As a result, the city of Suzhou met with recurrent sieges and damage. The most notable

Table 4.1 Records of the Construction of the City Walls of Suzhou, by Dynasty

Dynasty	*Year*	*Event*	*Measurement*
Eastern Zhou	514 B.C.	Early Construction[1]	(a) 47 *li* 210 *bu* 2 *chi* in perimeter[2] (b) 37 *li* 161 *bu* in perimeter[3]
Tang	A.D. 876	Reconstruction[1]	12 *li* long north-south; 9 *li* long east-west; 42 *li* 30 *bu* in perimeter[4]
Later Liang	922	Brick and Stone Facing for the First Time[5]	
Northern Song	1110s	Restoration[5]	
	1123	Strengthening of the Brick and Stone Facing	
Southern Song	ca. 1180s	Restoration[5]	
	1223	Reconstruction[1,5]	
	1254	Heightening of the Parapets[5]	
	1259	Restoration[5]	
Yuan	1352	Reconstruction[1,5]	
Ming	ca. Late 1360s	Reconstruction[1]	(a) *Zhou* (perimeter): 34 *li* 53 *bu* 9 *fen*[5] (b) 4482 *zhang* 6 *chi* 5 *cun* in length[6]
	1642	Restoration[7]	
Qing	1662	Reconstruction[1]	(a) *Zhou*: 45 li[8] (b) *chang* (length): 5605 *zhang*[8]
	1729	Repair[9]	
	1730	Repair[9]	
	1838	Repair[9]	
	1860	Repair[9]	

1. Events of relatively more importance.
2. *Yue jue shu, juan* 2, p. 9.
3. Ibid. This figure is the sum total of the lengths of the four sides of the walled city. For more details, see Chapter 2.
4. *Wudi ji*, pp. 14, 111.
5. *Gusu zhi*, juan 16.1–3.
6. Ibid. This figure is the sum total of the lengths of the walls between every two of the six city gates. For more details, see discussion in Chapter 4.
7. *Gtj, ce* 114.62a.
8. *Jiangnan tongzhi, juan* 20.4.
9. *Suzhoufu zhi, juan* 4.5.

of such incidents took place in A.D. 875, when a local military commander, Wang Ying, rose against the Tang government and took the cities of Suzhou and Changzhou.[10] Although the rebels were soon crushed by a Tang task force, the city was severely damaged when pitched battles were fought during the siege. In the following year, the city walls were rebuilt under the direction of the prefect Zhang Tuan.[11] This is the first known recorded reconstruction of the city since it was built in 514 B.C. Yet the significance of this record lies not only in the information it contains about the city form right after the construction work in A.D. 876 but in its descriptions of the city probably *before* that time, including accounts of the number of the rivers, old residential wards, and bridges, all of which were unlikely to have been built from scratch. The walls were strengthened with brick and stone facing in A.D. 922 for the first time.[12]

The area of Suzhou saw few destructive wars during the Northern Song period, and thus only two occasions of moderate repair of the walls are recorded. However, in the wake of the fall of the Northern Song, probably unprecedented damage was inflicted on the city by the Jurchen (Jin) invasion of the region. According to the *Song shi*, on their way back from Lin'an (present-day Hangzhou) in the second month of A.D. 1130, after driving the Song court to the Southeast, the Jurchen cavalry entered the city, and since local officials had already fled, the "soldiers set fire and plundered unrestrainedly."[13] Perhaps due to the political and financial straits in which the Southern Song government was left, the restoration of the damaged infrastructure of the city was not carried out until the middle of the Chunxi reign-period (A.D. 1174–1189), when the prefect Xie Shiji conducted the work at the cost of the remaining sum of four hundred thousand *min* (that is, strings of cash) from the prefectural taxes (*xianyu*). This reconstruction work must have been very incomplete, because only twenty or thirty years later nearly half of the walls had already crumbled or collapsed, and the city moats were largely invaded by marshes. Thus in 1223, supported by the Southern Song prime minister Shi Miyuan (?–1232), who successfully applied for a royal grant to finance the project, the prefects Zhao Rushu and Shen Hao successively directed the restoration of the walls and moats. The work lasted for thirteen months, and the reconstructed walls and moats were regarded by contemporary and later scholars as unsurpassed in the Southeast.[14] The result of this reconstruction work is evidenced by the remarkable picture map of the city, known as the *Pingjiang tu* (picture map of Pingjiang [city]), engraved in 1229 on a stone slab measuring 2.79 meters by 1.38 meters, the map on it measuring 1.97 meters by 1.36 meters (see Figure 4.2).[15]

The Mongol conquerors ordered the leveling of many city walls and the refilling of their moats in the 1280s, early in the reign of the Yuan dynasty Emperor Shizu, Hubilie (known in the West as Khublai Khan).[16] Liu Zhiping and Mote are probably right in seeing this action as removing bastions of Chinese resistance to them, even though it was glossed over by some scholars under the rule of the Yuan as a gesture of confidence.[17] The only evidence of how thoroughly the walls of the city of Suzhou were dismantled at that time comes from Lu Xiong: "many people resided scatteredly on the remains of the walls, and although five [city] gates were left standing, [the walls] were leveled and

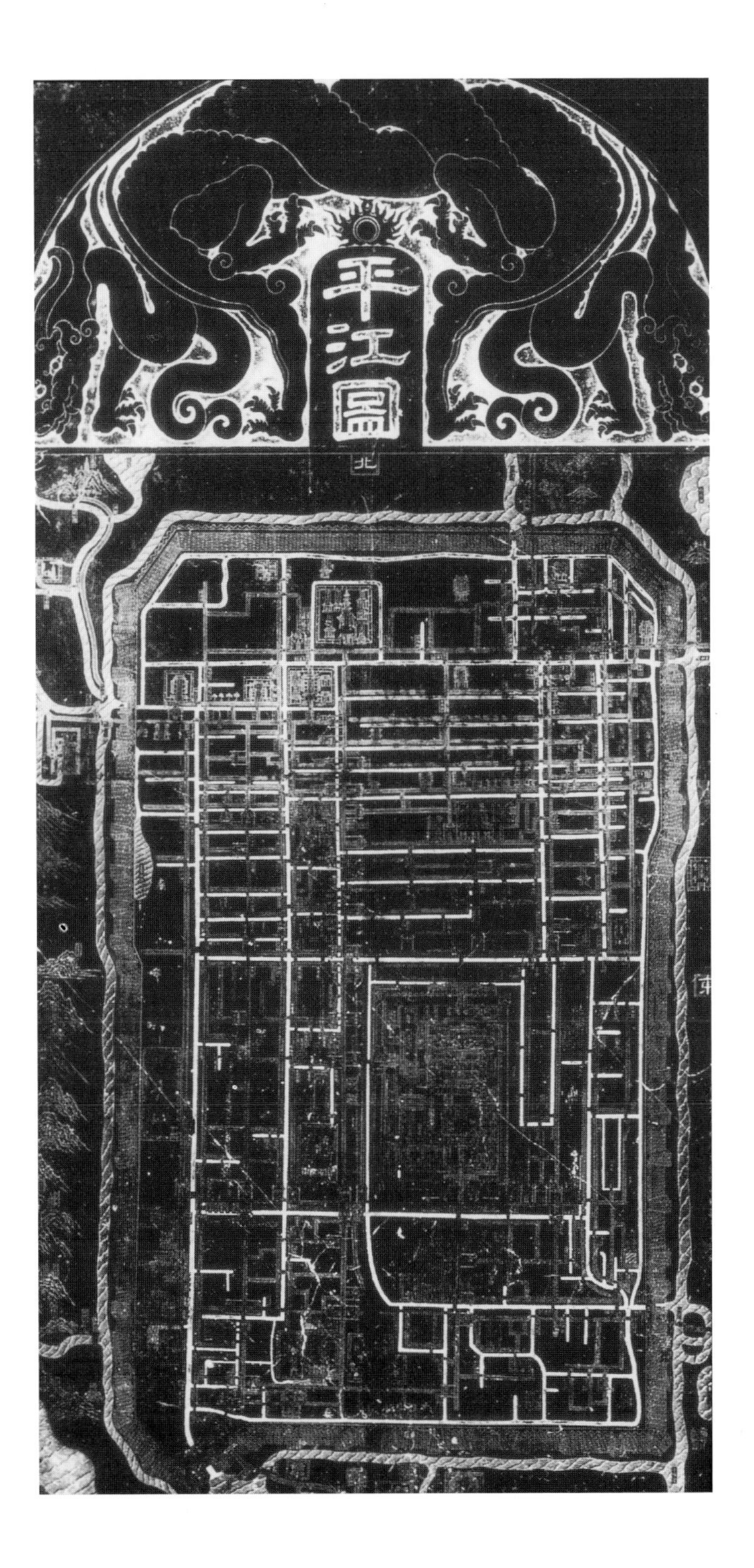

Figure 4.2 *Rubbing of the picture map of the city of Suzhou carved on stone in 1229. Adapted from Cao and Wu 1986, p. 66. This stele is preserved in the former prefectural school attached to the Confucian Temple in the lower left, or southwest, quarter of the city.*

[the city] did not have any physical defense work."[18] This situation did not last long, as in 1352 the Yuan government ordered the rebuilding of city walls in all parts of the country to guard Mongol defenders against Chinese Red Scarf (Hongjin) rebels.[19] Suzhou's walls were rebuilt in the same year. The construction work was carried out by ten thousand laborers under the supervision of the Chinese prefect Gao Lü and two Mongol supervisors, and they also dredged the moats, which became wider and deeper than before.[20] At the completion of the construction of the walls, temples to certain gods were built on top of all the six city gates. This act is interpreted by Zheng Yuanyou as a thankful reply to the gods' gracious protection of the laborers from the harsh heat and at times unbearable rains of the summer.[21]

Clearly, before the Ming, large-scale reconstruction of the walls was usually conducted in the second half of, or even at the end of, each dynastic period. It was only from the Ming onward that such work was carried out in the early period of a dynasty. This phenomenon appears to be in line with the realization that the early Ming dynasty was the great age of Chinese wall building.[22] It may be seen as indicating an ever increased symbolic role that city walls played in society from the early Ming onward, because, in terms of national and regional defense, there is no reason to believe that the military strength of the Ming and Qing empires was less in their early years than that of their predecessors. It is not surprising that the rebuilt city walls of Suzhou in the second half of the fourteenth century, as perceived by Lu Xiong and Wang Ao, in "their height, width, solidity and accuracy surpassed all their precedents."[23] After the Qing consolidated their control over the Southeast, the city of Suzhou was promoted to the provincial capital of Jiangsu, and in 1662, the provincial governor Han Shiqi directed the last complete reconstruction of the walls in the history of Suzhou.[24] From then on, partial repairs continued until the end of the Qing, and walls were left neglected thereafter, later giving way to the development of modern roads and other establishments.

From all these records of reconstruction of the city walls, there is very little information about the actual process of building. In a few cases, documents record the amounts and the sources of money spent on the projects or the total number of laborers summoned to the construction works or, slightly more frequently, the names of the scholar-officials who initiated and supervised them. Yet it seems to be typical in the history of Chinese city building that neither descriptions of the building work were recorded nor technical reports, if any, on plans, engineering, materials, or other features were preserved in historical documents. Is it because architectural skills were not associated with the literati but with the artisans who kept alive what Wright calls "a profoundly conservative architectural tradition"[25] by transmitting these skills and arts through apprenticeship? Or is it because the building process and technical details were long considered part of a fixed convention and there was thus no incentive for the intellectuals to document them? In any event, it is most probably true, as Mote asserts when facing a similar problem in discussing the construction of the city walls of Nanjing in the early Ming,[26] that these details did not command the interest of the Chinese responsible for creating the historical record.

Length and Position of the City Walls

Determining the physical form of the city in a given period basically requires the accurate length and position of its walls at that time. Because of the lack of archaeological findings, the principal sources for information are literary and pictorial records. As indicated in the preceding section, there were at least five occasions on which large-scale reconstruction of the city walls took place from the late ninth century onward. Records of walls' measurements in successive dynastic periods, as far as they are presently available, vary significantly. This variation at first sight suggests that the length and position of the walls changed in the last millennium of the imperial era. Except perhaps for those from the Qing period, wall length and position cannot be directly inferred with any certainty from the morphology of the present city unless historical records are closely examined with contemporary city maps. Such an examination is made difficult not only by the unavailability of either kind of source material for a few different historical periods but also by the ambiguity and inconsistency in some of the records documenting the city of the same period.[27] Despite these difficulties, this problem has to be tackled as vigorously as possible to allow for a more comprehensive study of the development of the urban form of the city of Suzhou.

Table 4.1 shows that after the early construction of city walls in 514 B.C., as recorded in the Eastern Han documents *Yue jue shu* and *Wu Yue chunqia,* no further records of the length of the walls recur in historic documents until the end of the Tang. In the *Wudi ji,* the size of the wall-enclosed area after Zhang Tuan's reconstruction of the city in A.D. 876 is recorded as 12 *li* (approximately 6.048 kilometers by the Tang standard) long from north to south, and 9 *li* (approximately 4.536 kilometers) long from east to west, which would roughly amount to 42 *li,* or about 21.168 kilometers, in perimeter if the general shape of the city is taken as nearly rectangular (the *Wudi ji* indicates that "the city was in the form of the character *ya*") and the irregularity of some sections of the walls is disregarded. Indeed, elsewhere in most editions, the *Wudi ji* records that the city had a wall of 42 *li* 30 *bu* (approximately 21.21 kilometers) in perimeter (*zhou*).[28] Even as an estimate, this figure is considerably larger than the perimeter of the city presently encircled by the city moats, which is around 15 kilometers; and it is not certain how accurately it accounts for the real length of the city walls in the Tang period, because all the Tang establishments are only loosely depicted in the documents of that time and we thus have no information about the precise position of the walls.

The encyclopedia *Taiping huanyu ji* records that the perimeter of the city enclosed by walls was 30 *li* (approximately 16.686 kilometers by the Song standard) at the time of the completion of the document between A.D. 978 and 983.[29] Obviously, this figure again is an estimate. Since there are no other records of wall building between A.D. 876 and 1223, except for strengthening the walls with brick and stone facing in A.D. 922 and partially repairing them in or around the 1180s, it seems plausible to suggest that both the *Wudi ji* and the *Taiping huanyu ji* basically refer to the same walls. The question is, which is closer to their actual measurements? This question may tentatively be answered

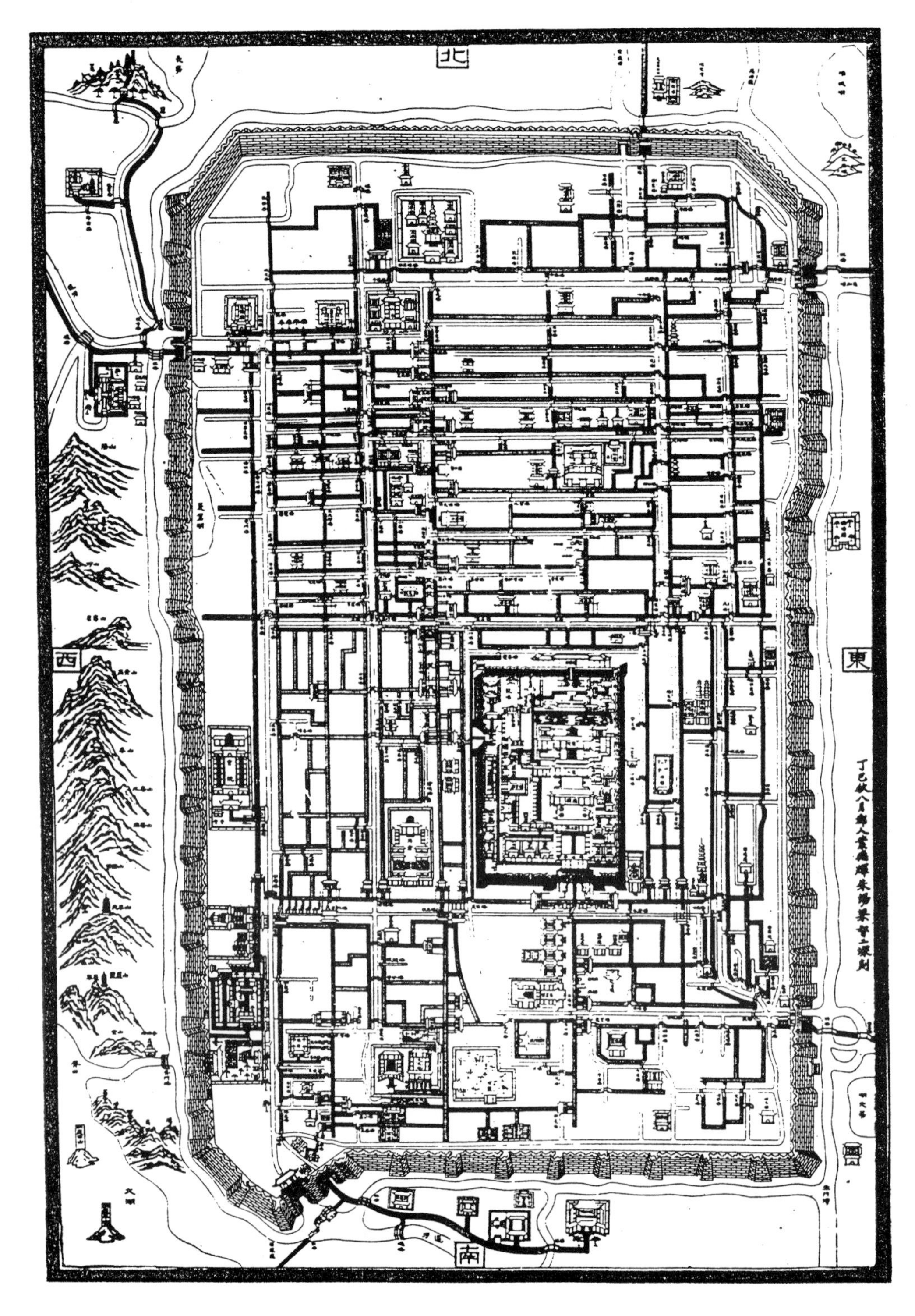

Figure 4.3 Picture map of the city of Suzhou adapted from a rubbing of the 1229 map. Adapted from Zhongguo dabaike quanshu *1988, p. 348.*

by looking at other physical features of the city, especially its network of canals. The whole system of watercourses in and around the city as presented on the 1229 map in Figure 4.3, as we will see later in this section and in Chapter 5, is identical to that produced on maps in subsequent history. Creating such a system demands enormous funds and extensive work, and it most likely was accomplished by stages starting well before the Tang period. Hence, although the construction work in 1223 seems to have been conducted more thoroughly according to the historic records, the position of the walls may not have altered significantly at that time, as there is no reason to assume that the entire water system, which physically determined the form of the city in general, was a new one created in that year. Moreover, since the position of the walls and moats and the overall form of the city shown on the 1229 map, which may be regarded as genuinely reflecting the features of the city right after the 1223 construction, are almost identical to those depicted on later maps, it is very possible that the moderate figure in the *Taiping huanyu ji*, which comes closer to the perimeter of the present city defined by the existing moats, is more accurate than that estimated from the information given in the *Wudi ji*. In that case, the total length of the walls from A.D. 876 on would have been less than 17 kilometers.

The perimeter of the walls in the wake of the reconstruction under the Yuan in A.D. 1352 may not have been recorded,[30] but Zheng Yuanyou, a contemporary local scholar, writes in his memoir: "The four sides of the city walls were oriented like the ones initiated by [Wu] Zixu, and the water gates followed the old ones functioning in the Song except that Xu Gate [blocked during the Song period] was reopened."[31] This passage not only suggests that the form of the city largely remained the same as its predecessor but also implies that the perimeter of the walls was kept similar to that in the Southern Song.

Very detailed measurements of the walls in the early Ming are given in Lu Xiong's *Suzhoufu zhi* and Wang Ao's *Gusu zhi*.[32] Yet, not untypically, three figures that are in considerable discord with each other appear together in the latter, and two appear in the former. In the *Gusu zhi*, for example, the first figure[33] is really a repetition of measurements recorded in the *Wudi ji*: 12 *li* from north to south and 9 *li* from east to west, which would amount to 21.168 kilometers in perimeter by the Tang standard, as noted earlier, or 24.192 kilometers in perimeter by the Ming standard. We may disregard this account for this moment, since its incorporation in the text was more likely to emphasize the continuity of the development of the city form at least from the late Tang onward than to record the actual measurement of the circumference of the walled enclosure, which may have been much smaller.

The second figure in the *Gusu zhi* tells us that "the *zhou* (perimeter)[34] [of the walled city] is 34 *li* 53 *bu* 9 *fen*, . . . that is, 12,293 *bu* 9 *fen*,"[35] its modern equivalent being about 19.669 kilometers when the traditional unit *chi* is converted by the Ming standard. This is certainly a new account. Its liability is perhaps very open to question. The *Wuzhong shuili quanshu*, written in the mid-seventeenth century by Zhang Guowei of the late Ming, contains a detailed picture map of the city of Suzhou showing conditions of his time. It is drawn in four pieces, which all together present the walled enclosure as a square, as shown in Figure 4.4, rather than as an oblong form. This does not mean that the shape of the city at this time was a square, but that the form in the map is misshapen probably because more attention was paid to the courses of rivers and canals of the city. In fact, the same volume also contains another city map drawn in one piece, which aimed at presenting the general form of the city and which clearly indicates that the shape of the city then was similar to its shape in the Southern Song (see Figure 4.5). By comparing the detailed information about the city gates, bridges, temples, and other city establishments in relation to the watercourses contained in these two maps and the 1229 picture map in Figure 4.3, the position of the walls during the Ming period appear to be basically the same as in the Southern Song. Thus the second account of the measurement of the walls in the *Gusu zhi* is still an overstatement if it really meant the perimeter of the walled enclosure.

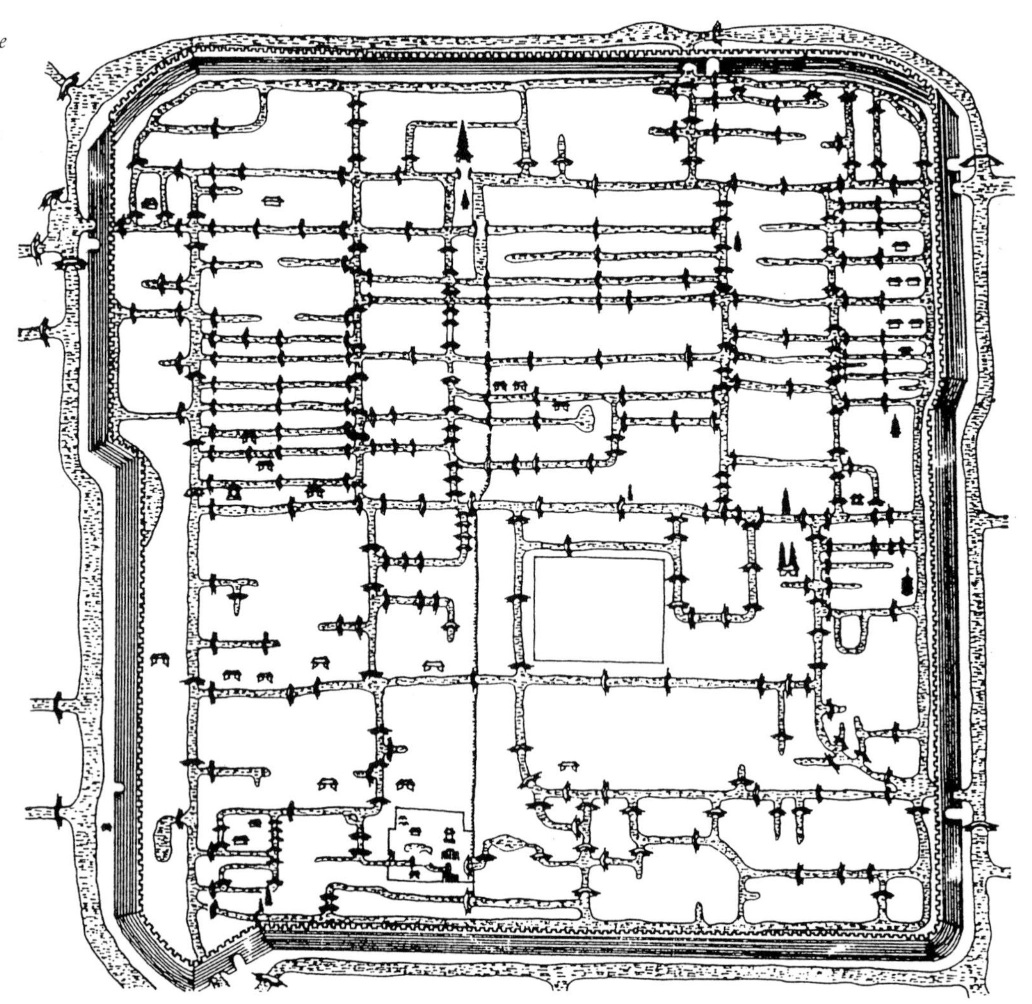

Figure 4.4 *Picture map of the watercourses within the city of Suzhou at the end of the Ming in the mid-seventeenth century. Redrawn from* Wuzhong shuili quanshu, juan *1.7–10*.

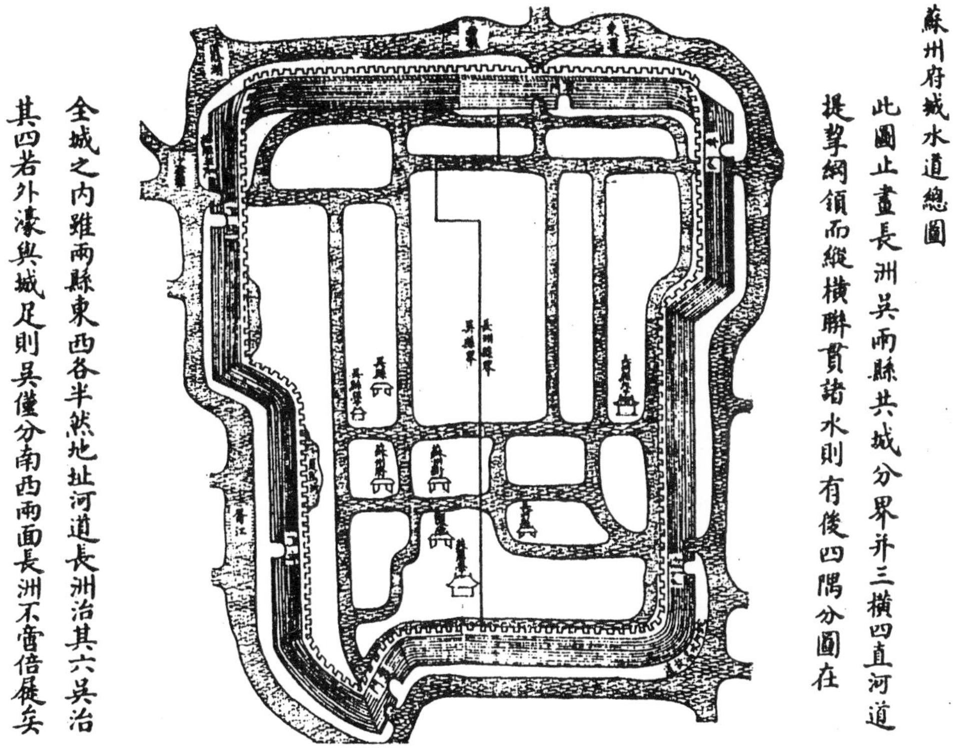

蘇州府城水道總圖
此圖止畫長洲吳兩縣共城分界幷三橫四直河道
提挈綱領而縱橫聯貫諸水則有後四隅分圖在
全城之內雖兩縣東西各半然地址河道長洲治其六吳治
其四若外濠與城足則吳僅分南西兩面長洲不啻倍蓰矣

Figure 4.5 Overall map of the city of Suzhou, as presented in Wuzhong shuili quanshu, juan *1.6.*

The third figure is far more comprehensive than the preceding two in that the distance all around the walls was determined by measuring the wall space between all the gates. The total length (*chang*) of the walls should therefore be 14.344 kilometers, and this figure possibly did not include the measurements of the six city gates.[36] Fortunately, the reliability of this figure and the preceding one can be tested by the record of the lengths of the canals within the city walls, which is provided in the *Wuzhong shuili quanshu*.[37] This record contains measurements of the distance between every two adjacent bridges; and when these segments along the main north-south and east-west canals are added up, it suggests that this last account of the length of the city walls should be regarded as closest to the actual one during the Ming period. In fact, by checking the recorded measurements of the distances along the walls between the gates against those shown on the map of the present-day city, we find that they are remarkably accurate. Thus it is also very likely that this third figure is the most faithful one among all the others from premodern times.[38]

A similar discrepancy is found in the accounts of the length of the walls after their rebuilding in the early Qing in 1662. The *Jiangnan tongzhi*, for example, records two figures: "the *zhou* [perimeter] of the present city walls is forty-five *li* [25.110 kilometers by the Qing standard], and its chang [length], five thousand six hundred and five *zhang* (17.376 kilometers)."[39] A comparison of the city maps of the Southern Song, the Ming, and the mid- and late Qing again indicates that the position of the walls did not change significantly, except that the southeast corner might have bulged a little and that the walls appear to have been more tortuous in the Qing; moreover, since no further large-scale reconstruction works on the walls are recorded from 1662 onward, there is hardly any reason to doubt that the city maps of the mid- and late Qing closely represent the approximate position of the walls in the early Qing. Thus this first account, which is about ten kilometers larger than the actual length of the walls, appears to have been an exaggeration. The second figure, given by the *Jiangnan tongzhi,* seems more reasonable, although it is still about three kilometers larger than the perimeter of the wall-enclosed city during the Ming period. Three possible factors for this discrepancy may be, first, that it was the result of measuring errors by the Qing surveyors; second, the Qing figure, unlike that of the Ming, may have included the measurements of the six city gates; and, third, that the walls were really a little longer during the Qing period, as the southeast section might have stretched further outward and some other sections elsewhere might have featured as more sinuous.

The juxtaposition of two different figures presumably indicating the same thing in the same passage of the Ming texts in question, and the recurrence of a similar pattern of accounts in the Qing documents, induce one to consider that there might have been some particular reasons for these seemingly peculiar accounts of the walls by the Ming and Qing scholars. It seems plausible that this incongruity was caused by the application of different methods of measuring. Liu Jinzao has pointed out in his *Qing xu wenxian tongkao* written in 1921 that the use of *chi* was usually preferable when shorter and more delicate objects were measured, while *li* (usually combined with *bu*) was often applied in the measurement of longer distances, notably road distances.[40] This indicates that the co-existence of two sets of mutually convertible length units may at times have been used with different techniques of measuring a distance. One set with the units *zhang*, *chi,* and *cun* may often have been employed to measurement with a ruler, and the other set with the units *bu* (pace) and *wu*[41] to measurement with counting by steps. Thus, a considerable disparity could have been produced between the result of pacing off the lengths of the city walls and that of measuring them with a ruler. Yet if so, why do the authors of these Ming and Qing documents not comment at all on these obvious disparities?

Still another possible explanation for these differing accounts is that the character *zhou* may not exclusively denote "perimeter" in these Ming and Qing documents. Two words that are frequently used for the description of the extent of a walled city are *chang* and *zhou*. In measurements, *chang* denotes "length" and *zhou* usually means "perimeter" or "circumference." However, since the latter also has the meanings of "all around" and "dense," we may question whether its denotation is as exclusive as that of the former. We should also note that many of the length units used in ancient documents occasionally denote "area" as well, that is, "surface measure." Since most walled cities on the North China Plain appear to have been nearly square in form, their size may sometimes be described with the character *fang* (square in both the sense of "surface measure" and "square shape");[42] while the application of this character to the measurement of the cities in the South would be inaccurate and confusing, because many of them were rectangular, circular or, even more often, irregular in form. It is therefore not totally impossible that the character *zhou*, as a substitute for *fang*, was used to indicate the "area" of the wall-enclosed cities in the South, rather than their "perimeter."

This hypothesis gains a little more support from the textual logic. Since city walls in China almost invariably formed continuous enclosure, the measurement of their "length" was basically equivalent to that of their "perimeter." Thus there was no need simply to juxtapose two sets of figures for the same measurement, but by giving the area of the walled enclosure along with the length of the walls, descriptions of the city form became more informative.[43] This last explanation, however, is still no more than a hypothesis, because in literature not only is it rare that the character *zhou* is used to denote "area" but it is also used in the simultaneous presentation of an account of the area of the walled enclosure and the length of the walls, even though this would sound very logical in our time. These discrepancies are difficult to explain satisfactorily, and the matter must be considered unresolved.[44]

Although the inconsistency in the records of the measurements of the city walls remains puzzling for the time being, two major conclusions can be drawn from the analysis of this evidence: first, at least from the late Tang onward, the length of the walls continuously fell within a range between 25 *li* and 30 *li*, that is, between approximately 15km and 17km; and second, the approximate position of the walls and the basic form of the city that they defined remained unchanged from 1229, or even from the second half of the ninth century, if not still earlier. These two conclusions are verified largely by a comparison of the city maps of the Southern Song, Ming, Qing, and modern periods, with reference to written records of the construction of the city walls. In Figures 4.6, 4.7, and 4.8, three representative city maps produced from 1748 onward are presented so that the reader may collate them with those of the Southern Song (Figure 4.3), the Ming (Figure 4.4) and the late Qing (Figure 3.15). These maps show that images of many constructions such as city gates, bridges, and temples, which bear the same names (occasionally homophones, a result of linguistic change over time) and by which the position of the city walls can be judged, are placed in identical locations in every historic period. This evidence, perhaps insufficient, as it sometimes appears,[45] is corroborated by two facts that are even more convincing: allowing for some minor differences in sinuosity, the overall shape of the city presented on all the maps is characteristically similar, with almost every turn of the walls meticulously indicated; and, more important, the water courses and the points of their confluences both within the walled city and outside are identical. Indeed, since any water control project would have proved to be costly, it is very unlikely that the positions of the existing rivers and canals were altered, but the general pattern of the watercourses nevertheless was maintained.

Before moving onto the structure and configuration of the walls, I would like to discuss two seemingly peculiar aspects of the walls of the city of Suzhou. Of many "irregular" features of the roughly rectangular form of the city, Yu Shengfang noted the varied shapes of the four corners of the walls. Solely on the basis of the plan of the city pre-

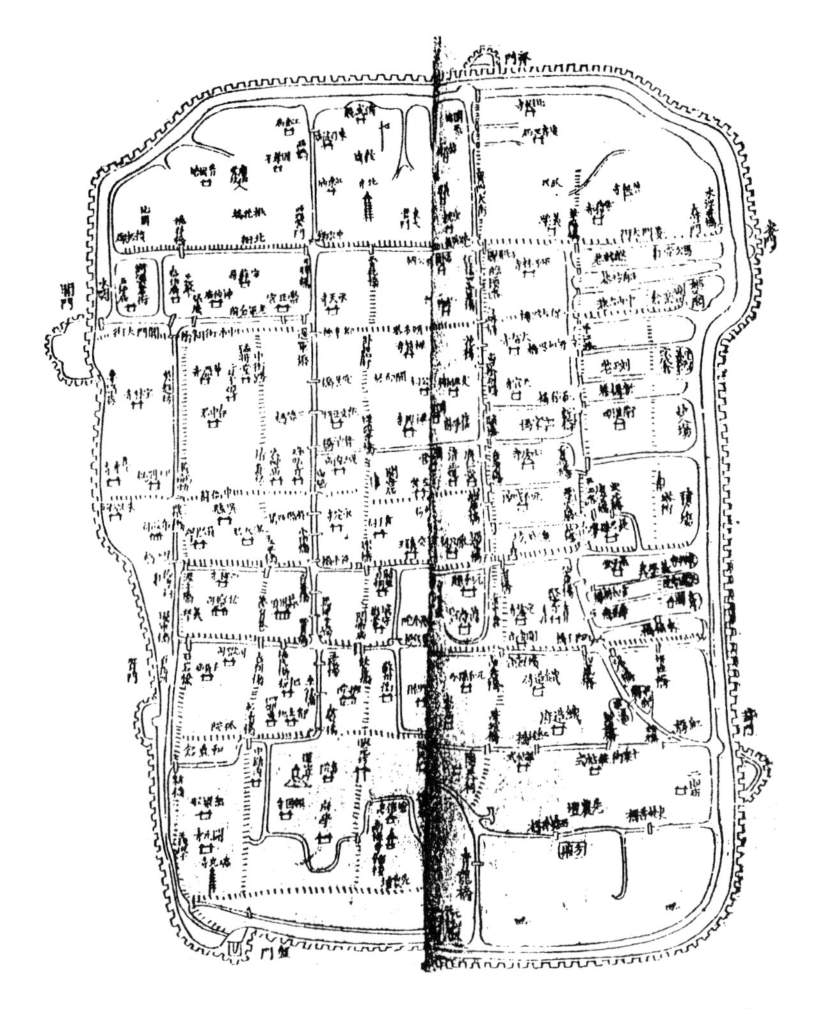

Figure 4.6 Map of the city of Suzhou in the mid–eighteenth century, as presented in the 1748 Suzhoufu zhi. *Adapted from* Shengshi zisheng tu *1986 (page not numbered).*

sented on the 1229 picture map (see Figures 4.2 and 4.3), Yu argues, and Johnston apparently agrees with him, that the northeast and northwest corners were splayed to facilitate water flow in times of flood; the southwest corner was bulged to resist the brunt of the coming flood and to prevent water from rushing into the city; and the southeast corner remained square since at this point the water flowed away from the city.[46] Yet by comparing this map and the maps of later periods, it is reasonable to suspect that the 1229 map may be very much a figurative presentation; that is, the distinct configuration of the walls at the four corners shown on this map only roughly represent the actual features that are portrayed more faithfully by the city maps of later periods.

Even if we assume that the 1229 map represents the city form literally, the conclusion of Yu's analysis still seems questionable. It is my understanding that floods in the Suzhou area, frequent as they were, resulted more from either prolonged heavy rains that outpaced the drainage, leading to the rise of water level, or floods in the Upper or Middle Yangzi regions causing the overflow of Lake Tai to the southwest of the city and its sur-

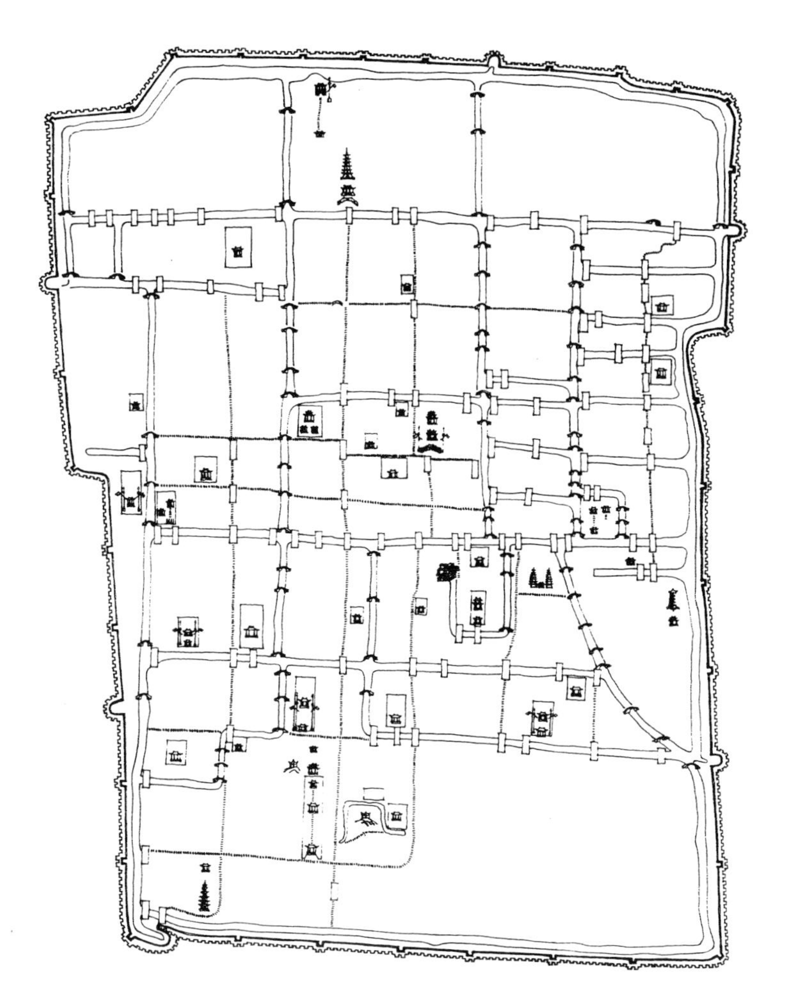

Figure 4.7 Picture map of the city of Suzhou adapted from the map carved on stone in 1797. Courtesy of the Committee of Suzhou Urban and Rural Construction. The stele is preserved in the old Temple of the City Walls and Moats (Chenghuang Miao) in the central left, west, quarter of the city.

rounding rivers, than from the mountain torrents presumed by Yu. In either case, the direction of the drainage was to the east, and thus there was no reason for the northeast corner of the wall to be splayed, since it too was a point where the water flowed away from the city. Moreover, the river leading to Pan Gate at the southwest corner directly connected to the easternmost end of Lake Tai and was therefore a source of incoming floods from the lake. Had the bulging of the southwest corner of the walls been the builders' response to the local conditions of water flows, it would ironically have resulted in increasing the danger of influx of water into the city rather than preventing it. Although some doubts are cast on Yu's argument, I must admit that, with the limited materials presently available, I have not as yet found any alternative and more convincing explanations of these somewhat curious aspects.

Similarly, because of the lack of any information about the activities of building the city walls from the fall of the state of Wu in the early fifth century B.C. to their first recorded reconstruction in A.D. 876 by Zhang Tuan, and because of the insufficiency of data concerning the precise city form until the creation of the picture map of the city, *Pingjiang tu*, in 1229, the questions of how, when, and why the city acquired some of its other characteristic physical features that existed constantly throughout subsequent history are difficult to answer. Paradoxically it is precisely in this difficulty that one may find room for speculation. The city plan at present is oriented 7°54' east of true south,[47] and it is most likely that this was by and large also the case for the city in 1229, or probably earlier, since, as I have argued, the basic form of the city remained unchanged from that time onward. Yu again suggests that, since most buildings in the city were aligned with the city walls, this orientational deviation was deliberately determined so that the prevailing southeast winds would cool the buildings of the city in summer and bring warmth in winter.[48] This is a more than weak explanation indeed. Johnston sees another seemingly more cogent reason for this orientation; that is, that it was probably associated with the situation pointed out by Needham that discrepancies in city alignments in later times may have derived from adherence to the theories of rival schools of geo-

Figure 4.8 *Map of the city of Suzhou drawn on the basis of the survey in 1916. Courtesy of the Committee of Suzhou Urban and Rural Construction.*

mancy after the discovery of magnetic declination during the ninth century.[49] Yet we do not really know whether this orientation of the city was newly obtained during these later periods or simply part of the legacy of the Wu capital city in the late sixth century or at least of the city in the pre-Tang era; nor do we have any descriptions of the specific techniques applied to determine the city's orientation that may have produced slightly different results.[50]

Structure and Configuration of the Walls

The most ancient form of walling in China was that of *terre pisé,* or tamped earth, by which dry earth was rammed into removable elongated box frames at successively higher levels. In ancient China it was customary to use rubble stone without binding material as the foundation of walls and to spread a layer of thin bamboo stems between each *pisé* block so as to hasten thorough drying. Although by the Han period, baked bricks largely replaced the adobe, or sun-dried mud, that was common in late Zhou times, they were usually used in no other structures than graves until the Northern Wei period around the fourth century. In the early Tang, even on such important city walls as the palatial wall of the imperial capital Chang'an, a brick facing was only applied around the gates and corners. However, from the end of the Tang into the Five Dynasties period in the first half of the tenth century, the walls of many large cities in the South were faced entirely with bricks.[51] Suzhou, being one of these cities, acquired a brick facing on its walls for the first time in A.D. 922, as I have mentioned earlier, while the cores of the walls may be construed as having remained earth or rubble.

Like the walls of many other cities in imperial China, the walls of Suzhou did not always rise straight out of the ground or the water-filled moats. They were frequently built on a supporting platform or plinth. It is recorded by Zheng Yuanyou, for example, that three layers of dressed stone blocks were applied to the construction of the plinth of the walls in the late Yuan period.[52] The walls were always battered, that is, sloped markedly inward to the top.[53] Significant variations in the proportion of the batter to the height of the wall may have existed in different regions and during different periods of time, since it was determined by factors such as the strength of the building materials available at the time and place of the construction, the contemporary building technology, and the local conventions of construction work. In the "Kaogong ji" section of the *Zhou li*, it was regarded as the Zhou convention that the proportion of the batter to the height should be 1:6; and this proportion as a principle remained approximately the same throughout subsequent history,[54] even though it was not always strictly followed in many specific cases. As we shall see, this proportion varied significantly in the wall constructions of Suzhou during different periods of time.

The sectional dimensions of the walls of the city of Suzhou in the imperial era were recorded for the first time after they were strengthened in A.D. 922. According to Lu Xiong's quotation from the *Xiangfu tujing*, the walls measured 2 *zhang* 4 *chi* (approximately 7.416 meters by the Song standard) high and 2 *zhang* 5 *chi* (approximately 7.725

Table 4.2 Records of the Sectional Dimensions of the Walls of the City of Suzhou from A.D. 922 Onward.

Dynasty	*Year*	*Measurement*
Later Liang	A.D. 922	2 *zhang* 4 *chi* in height, 2 *zhang* 5 *chi* in thickness.[1, 2]
Yuan	1352	23 *chi* in height, 16 *chi* in breath at the top, 35 *chi* in thickness at the base.[3]
Ming	ca. Late 1360s	2 *zhang* 4 *chi* in height, 1 *zhang* 8 *chi* in breath at the top;[4] 2 *zhang* 3 *chi* in height, 3 *zhang* 5 *chi* in thickness at the base, (parapets) 6 *chi* in height.[2]
Qing	1662	2 *zhang* 8 *chi* in height, 1 *zhang* 8 *chi* in thickness, (parapets) 6 *chi* in height.[5]

1. For conversion of the old Chinese length units into modern ones, see Liu 1980, p. 416.
2. *Gusu zhi, juan* 16.2.
3. *Pxjj*, p. 2a.
4. *Jiangnan jinglüe, juan* 2A.7.
5. *Jiangnan tongzhi, juan* 20.4.

meters) thick at the base.[55] Mote claims that the walls at this time "were enlarged to what is approximately their size throughout subsequent history, that is, about 25 feet high and 25 feet thick at the base."[56] The information I have gathered from the documents of the subsequent dynasties, however, indicates clearly that notable variations existed in the sectional size of the walls. Table 4.2 lists the records of the sectional dimensions of the walls in four dynastic periods from A.D. 922. The proportion of the height to the thickness of the walls in the Tang and probably also in the Song was very close to 1:1; their section in the Yuan and Ming looks to have been shorter and thicker; while in the Qing the walls became much slimmer.[57] The top of the walls was entirely paved with bricks to make a roadway in the late Yuan,[58] and the walls probably retained this feature in later times. In times of peace, the populace had free access to the top of the walls, often simply for pleasure strolling but occasionally for spontaneous public gatherings, as in the case of 1626 when it was thronged with locals protesting the arrest of a respected local official.[59] Only when martial law was imposed on the city in times of real crisis did the top of the walls become a forbidden area. In the autumn of 1653, for example, a rebellion broke out in the coastal areas and threatened the cities of the Yangzi Delta. Soldiers were assigned to the city walls, and ordinary people were prohibited from walking on them.[60]

From the 1229 picture map of the city (see Figures 4.3, 4.9, and 4.10), such features as bastions (*mamian*) and parapets (*nüqiang*) with battlements (*zhidie*) are clearly discernible on the walls, at least the latter two continuously being present throughout subsequent history. The height of the parapets is recorded to have been 6 *chi*, or 1.92 meters in the Ming and 1.86 meters in the Qing. The *Jiangnan tongzhi* even records that the total number of crenellations were three thousand fifty-one in the Qing.[61] Yet the most conspicuous features of the walls must have been the gatetowers. As emphasized by

Needham, Chinese city walls were never complete without their watchtowers and gatetowers, usually single structures of two or three stories.[62] Indeed, apart from the gatetowers of the city of Suzhou, which will be discussed in the following section, there were buildings serving as garrison posts (*pushe* or *wopu*) within a sixteen-meter distance between them on the walls in the Ming. A total of one hundred fifty-seven of them is recorded to have been built on the walls in the Qing, plus fifty-seven watchtowers (*ditai*) on the bastions.[63]

City Gates

It was almost inconceivable for the gates of important cities in the late imperial period not to be topped with gatetowers, except in the case of a number of small county cities and some walled forts on the frontiers. The ubiquity of this practice manifests both the pragmatic and psychological value of the city gates in the history of Chinese city construction. The city gates of Suzhou were indeed so highly regarded that, according to Lu Xiong of the Ming, in the final years of the Northern Song in the 1110s when wall restoration work was conducted, a stone slab was erected at the position of each of the abandoned or blocked gates, on which the name of the gate was engraved in order for it to be remembered.[64]

The special attention paid to the city gates was also reflected in their exquisite, symbolic names. In Chapter 2 I argued that the specific names used for architectural structures functioned as vehicles for linking man's imaginings to real artifacts. The sedulous studies and interpretations of the naming of the city gates of Suzhou were such that this topic invariably occupied considerable space in all local documents and gazetteers; and this predilection culminated in the *Wujun Tujing xuji* written by Zhu Changwen in the eleventh century, in which a whole separate section is exclusively devoted to the explanation of the matter and is thus entitled "Menming" (the names of the gates). Zhu Mu of the Southern Song in his *Fangyu shenglan* published during the period between 1225 and 1264 has noticed that all of the names of the city gates of all states in the Spring and Autumn period were composed of one character only and that Suzhou was the sole city that retained the ancient names of its gates.[65] His contemporary Hong Mai (1123–1202) echoed this observation in his *Rongzhai suibi* and claimed that the name of either a prefecture or a city gate was elegant if it was made up of a single character.[66] From these remarks, one can sense an admiration for the long, continuous history of the city of Suzhou, its refinement over time, and its superior cultural heritage; one can also appreciate the great esteem in which its city gates were held both in reality and in theory.

While acknowledging the tendency of the city of Suzhou to retain these traits through the ages, we should not ignore the fact that change did occur in the number and position of its gates in history. It is revealed in most of the local documents from as early as the Tang period on that scholars were exerting unceasing efforts at investigating the origins and later transformation of the city gates, which must have been regarded as a particularly important part of the prefectural institution and a salient symbol of the local history. These efforts indicate significant change. Whereas the locations and designations of the eight gates of the city at the time of its construction by Wu Zixu in the late Zhou remain a matter of dispute, as has been discussed in Chapter 3, their development in the imperial era, especially from 1229 onward, appears to be much clearer. From Table 4.3, in which the information about the number of the city gates with their names in successive dynastic periods is gathered, we may see that the total number of the gates continued to be eight until as late as the beginning of the Northern Song in the mid-tenth century, although Ping Gate in the north by west was probably abandoned, while a new gate, Feng, in the east by south, was opened after the fall of the state of Wu.

During the early Song period, two gates were blocked and thus only six were in use, and these facilitated both land and water passages. By at least 1084, when old Xu Gate in the west by south had also been blocked, a platform for scenery viewing, Gusu Tai, was constructed as part of a building complex known as the Gusu Guan (Guesthouse of Gusu) built in 1144 by the prefect Wang Huan. This feature is clearly in evidence on the 1229 picture map of the city (Figure 4.9). The reopening of Xu Gate in the late Yuan in 1352, when the city walls were reconstructed, was inspired by a stone slab with the two characters *Xumen* (Xu Gate) engraved on it that was dug out on the spot where the Song dynasty Gusu Guan was located; but this gate remained the only one that did not

Table 4.3 Records of the Number and Names of the City Gates of Suzhou through History.

Dynasty/Year	*Names*	*Total Number*
Eastern Zhou (Late Sixth Century)	Chang, Xu, Pan, She, Jiang, Lou, Qi, Ping	Eight (each twinned for both road and water traffic)[1]
Qin–Tang (Third Century B.C.–A.D. Tenth Century)	Chang, Xu, Pan, She, Jiang, Lou, Qi, Feng (or Ping)	Eight (each twinned for both road and water traffic)[2]
Early Song (Late Tenth–Early Eleventh Century)	Chang, Xu, Pan, Feng, Lou, Qi	Six (each twinned for both road and water traffic)[3]
Song–Southern Song (Mid-Eleventh Century–1279)	Chang, Pan, Feng, Lou, Qi	Five (each twinned for both road and water traffic)[4]
Yuan–Qing (1352–Early Twentieth Century)	Chang, Xu, Pan, Feng, Lou, Qi	Six (each twinned for both road and water traffic, except the Xu Gate)[5]

1. *Yue jue shu, juan* 2, pp. 9 ff.; *Wu Yue chunqiu, juan* 4, pp. 25, 47, *juan* 5, p. 58, and *juan* 10, p. 142; *Wudi ji*, pp. 14 ff.
2. *Wudu fu*; *WTx, juan* A, p. 11; *Wujun zhi, juan* 3, pp. 21 ff., and *juan* 48, p. 626.
3. *Taiping huanyu ji, juan* 91, p. 687; *Baicheng yanshui, juan* 1, p. 1.
4. *WTx, juan* A, p. 12; *Baicheng yanshui, juan* 1, pp. 1–2.
5. *Gusu zhi, juan* 16.3; *Jiangnan tongzhi, juan* 20.4; *Suzhoufu zhi, juan* 4.4–5.

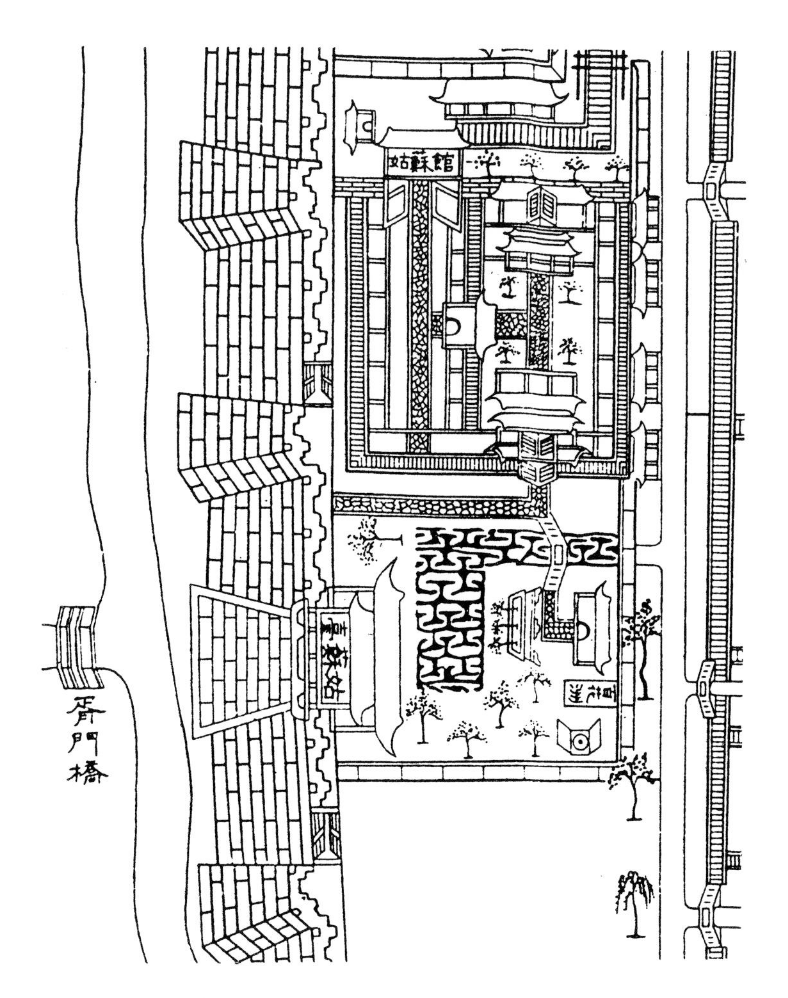

Figure 4.9 *Section of the 1229 picture map of the city of Suzhou showing the details of Gusu Guan (Guesthouse of Gusu) by the blocked Xu Gate along the west city walls. Courtesy of the Committee of Suzhou Urban and Rural Construction.*

accommodate waterborne traffic throughout subsequent dynasties.[67] Few changes are found in the total number of the gates and their positions from 1352 to the end of the Qing, except for the 1356 addition of the semicircular or rectangular counterscarps (*yue-cheng*, the wall in the form of the moon, or *wengcheng*, the wall in the form of an urn).[68]

Structures associated with the city gates became more complicated from as early as the late Yuan. Apart from the gatetowers and counterscarps, there were halls where the officials in charge of the city entrance did their routine duties, barracks with armories for soldiers guarding the gates in case of an emergency, and buildings functioning as guesthouses.[69] The existence of drawbridges started to be recorded in the mid-Ming, if not earlier.[70] Compared with the drawbridges of the other five gates, the drawbridge of Chang Gate was the largest and most splendid, its surface being paved with stone slabs.[71] Although the city gates were closed every night, the keys being kept by the local army commanders, the real task of the officials and soldiers stationed at the gates was, in normal times, as Zheng Yuanyou puts it, "keeping an eye on unusual situations"; in

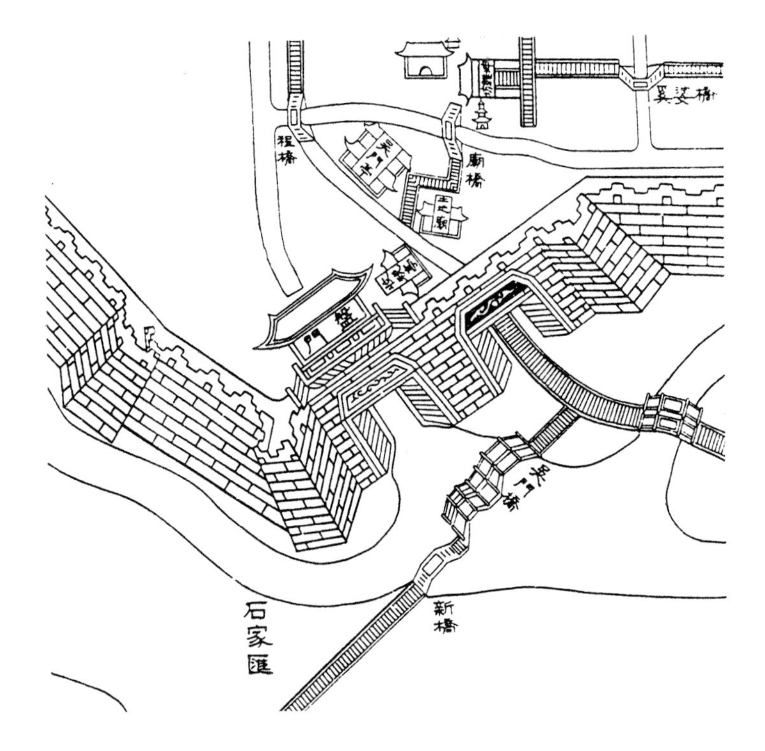

Figure 4.10 Section of the 1229 picture map of the city of Suzhou showing the details of Pan Gate during the Southern Song period. Courtesy of the Committee of Suzhou Urban and Rural Construction.

other words, they were merely part of the deterrents against such serious criminal activities as banditry and robbery, and access to the city was not at all impeded in ordinary circumstances.[72] In fact, partly because of the busy night life in the city and around its west suburbs, the gates must have been closed much later each day than those of the cities in the coastal areas, where threat from pirates was much more serious.[73] Of these six gates, Pan Gate is the only one that survived both the wars in the first half of this century and thereafter the demolition of the walls to give way to modern constructions. Pan Gate was fully repaired in the second half of the 1980s. Figure 4.10 presents the section of the city walls at Pan Gate depicted on the 1229 map; Figure 4.11 shows a diagrammatic plan of the gate with its artificial surroundings drawn in 1983, but which is nevertheless probably close to its actual configuration during the Ming and Qing periods; and Figure 4.12 includes a photograph of the gate taken before the war against the Japanese and a photograph of it after its reconstruction in the 1980s.

As shown in Figures 3.15 and Figures 4.3 through 4.8, the *de facto* disposition of the gates of the city from as early as 1229 onward looks entirely asymmetrical. It has been argued by Yu Shengfang that the asymmetry of the locations of the city gates in later times was a result of topographical conditions of the site and the need to control water flowing eastward in the intramural canal system.[74] This line of argument seems plausible, but it should be noted that it only points to one of many possibilities, none of which is exhaustive. In fact, we cannot be sure whether the locations of the gates from 1229 onward were significantly altered from those of their predecessors. I have argued that the city had a total of eight gates continuously from its foundation to the Tang period. Since each side of the city probably had two gates, it is not unlikely that many of the gates were located fairly symmetrically during that long period. If the locations of the gates after 1229 remained basically the same as in the preceding centuries, is it possible that the canals leading to the gates were dug in phases *after* the gates' positions had long been determined? Should the present asymmetrical effect be regarded more as the consequence of blocking two of the eight gates in the early Song and another after 1144 than as a response of the city planners and builders to the local environment? But Yu's essential points holds. The form of the city of Suzhou does display the traits of flexible arrangement in city building, one of the most notable features being the position of Pan Gate. This conclusion, however, by no means implies a negligible historical continuity in city construction; and any further analysis of the extent of this flexibility necessitates the discovery of more evidence. After all, the city was most probably not rebuilt *ab ovo* at any time in the imperial era.

The gates of the city of Suzhou were in their own right undoubtedly the positions on which not only the defense of the city itself but, by their social and conceptual implication, also the security of the whole prefectural area was concentrated. Unlike many other cities in imperial China, Suzhou did not have a drum tower or bell tower as an independent edifice; it was the gatetowers (occasionally also called *gulou,* or drum tower) during the second half of the Ming and the Qing periods that assumed the function of public time-reckoning, alarm-raising, and command-signaling.[75] They were thus loci from whence the maintenance of social order and security was transmitted. Moreover, if the city walls symbolized the presence of government and its upholding of social order, the city gates by their practical attributes represented the openings through which the

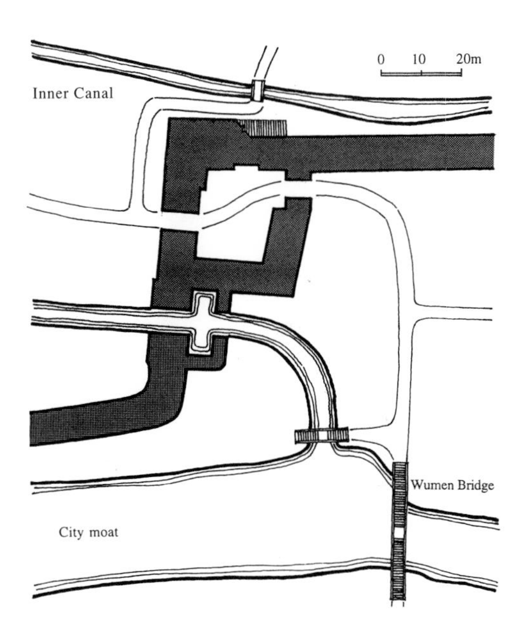

Figure 4.11 Diagrammatic plan of Pan Gate as surveyed and drawn in 1983 by Xu Yinong.

Figure 4.12 Photographs of Pan Gate. Top: in the early twentieth century before the gatetower was destroyed in the Sino-Japanese War (from Cao and Wu 1986, p. 81). Bottom: in 1991, following reconstruction between 1983–1986 (photograph by Xu Yinong).

function of government was carried out: they were the places not only where public injunctions were most often pasted but also where government relief was provided to those stricken by natural calamities.[76]

True, the city gates formed unambiguous passages through which the inside and the outside of the city were divided and connected simultaneously; symbolically, however, they were on some occasions also the thresholds marking out one's homeland from the outside world, regardless of whether one lived in the city or the countryside. A minor incident recorded by Yang Xunji (1458–1546) in his *Su tan* reflects this trait of the city gates. Zhou Boqi (1401–1487), a Jiaxing Confucian scholar of the Ming, teaching at that time in the Suzhou area, voluntarily offered his services to an imperial task force sent out from Suzhou in the late 1440s to quell a rebellion in distant Fujian. It was not at the entrance of the army barracks in the city, nor at any other intersections of the marching-out route, but at Xu Gate by the city moat that he recommended himself to the commander of the troops.[77] Apart from its possible convenience—his residence or place of teaching may have been in the close vicinity—this choice of location indicates that the gate probably represented for him the ideal point of departure from his home for him properly to embark with the expedition force for the remote regions.

As shown in Chapter 2, the theme of symbolism seen as embodied in the construction and naming of the city gates of Helü Dacheng in the Spring and Autumn period was dominated by the conception of the city as a cosmic center. Profound change in the social and political nature of the city from the Qin unification in 221 B.C. on inevitably led to the eclipse of this preeminent theme in the imperial era, although the symbolic characteristics of the city gates persisted. This aspect is best exemplified by the inscriptions on the gates after the reconstruction of the city walls in 1662:

> Chang Gate: "To open up and let in the *qi* ['cosmic breath'] of the Changhe" (*qi tong Changhe*);
> Xu Gate: "The emerald green gathering around [Mt.] Guxu" (*Guxu yongcui*);
> Pan Gate: "The [crisscrossed] land and water routes [resembling] a coiling dragon" (*longpan shuilu*);
> Lou Gate: "The magnificence manifested by the River [Yangzi] and the sea" (*Jianghai yanghua*);
> Qi Gate: "Subjects' hearts [like a myriad of stars] surrounding and protecting the pole-star [i.e., the Emperor]" (*chenxin gongbei*);
> Feng Gate: "Limpid brooks reflecting [the beauties of the prefecture]" (*xiliu qingying*).[78]

These inscriptions were more than just a few poetic phrases attached to the city gates. They conveyed at least two messages concerning the distinctive way in which the city was perceived. First, although some of the ancient cosmological meanings of the gates continued to be appreciated in the imperial era, a fundamental change in their cosmic symbolism is obvious. The notion of the Changhe was still alive, and the heavenly *qi* that was opened up and let in to the city continued to be taken as a blessing. However, Chang Gate was not, as it was at the first time of its construction, seen as representing the Gate of Heaven corresponding to the Gate of Earth symbolized by She Gate, which had by then long been abandoned. Thus the city was no longer treated as being at the center of the universe. In fact, no matter how esteemed the city became, it was in symbolic terms simply *a* regional city, that is, one of the administrative centers of a unified empire, since the true center of the world was, and could only have been, at the imperial capital where the Son of Heaven resided. It was only under the auspices of the Emperor, whose earthly position was equivalent to that of the polestar in Heaven, that the heavenly *qi* could be of benefit to the people of the city and the prefecture. In other words, the heavenly *qi* was no longer regarded as rendering the city cosmically more significant than others but as bringing peace and prosperity to the prefecture as an integral part of the empire.

Second, the city housing the prefectural seat was not perceived as an entity of its own separate from the rural areas that were under the jurisdiction of the prefecture. Although its walls appear to have been physical boundaries between the urban and rural areas, they did not function socially and psychologically as lines of demarcation of the city as contrasted to the countryside, but rather symbolized boundaries of the prefecture, just as the gates were conceptually analogous to the thresholds of the prefectural territory. Indeed, no urban characteristics were reflected at all in the inscriptions on the city gates, and three of them were eulogies of the natural scenery of particular areas in the prefecture, each corresponding to the direction in which a specific gate led. In other words, the attributes of directional and territorial significance of these gates were explicitly revealed in these inscriptions. The role that the city gates played as representing the prefecture's orientation by reference to the four cardinal points was also partly revealed in the course of some seasonal festive rituals that were always a substantial aspect of social life in traditional China. Every year on the day prior to the Beginning of Spring (Lichun), for example, the prefect went with his entourage to the Liuxian (Willow Immortal) Hall just outside Lou Gate in the east to perform the ritual ceremony of the prefecture's entering the new season.[79] A few days later, when the God of Joy (Xishen) was located in the true south, the prefect then led the parade to the prefectural Altar of Mountains and Rivers outside Pan Gate in the south to welcome the god by offering sacrifice to it.[80]

Conclusion

In this chapter, I have attempted to address a number of important points concerning the transformation of the walls of Suzhou and the development of the city form. First, by citing the instance of the temporary transference of the city to a new site in A.D. 591, I have demonstrated that the city and its walls seem to have been an inseparable part of its specific natural setting in which local history was embedded. From this, I have argued that a walled city and a local capital in China's urban history did not practically and conceptually fall into two different categories but were one and the same phenomenon. Second, I have reviewed the history of the reconstruction of the city walls of Suzhou, calling particular attention to the fact that wall construction from the Ming on, sharply in contrast to that in its preceding era, was extensively pursued in the early period of the dynasty. It seems precisely in the late imperial period that the symbolic role of the city walls became more salient. Third, on the basis of written and pictorial materials, I have strongly suggested that from the late Tang onward the length of the city walls of Suzhou may not have altered significantly, falling within the range between fifteen and seventeen kilometers, and that the position of the walls and thus the form of the city defined by them basically remained unchanged, although for whatever the reasons, historical records substantially differ on this point. After a cursory description of the configuration of the wall structures, the last section of this chapter is devoted to a discussion of the transformation of the city gates of Suzhou. As an integral but more salient part of the city walls, their origins, nomenclature, and transformation constantly constituted one of the subjects of great topical interest for local scholars in the imperial era. I have illustrated the continuation of the symbolic nature of the city gates, but at the same time emphasized a profound shift of their symbolism from signifying the city as a cosmic center from which Wu strove for hegemony, to the signifying of its allegiance and homage to the Emperor and central authority.

Since the main purpose of this study is to illustrate some general points about the nature of traditional Chinese cities and an appropriate way of studying them, it is necessary here to make some further suggestions on the significance of city walls in China's urban experience and society in general. Walls in China were undoubtedly of paramount importance not only for cities but also for villages, gardens, temples, houses, and other structures.[81] Yet one should not let this landscape of an apparent continuum of walls, possibly in a hierarchy of their size, configuration, material, and the like, obscure a fundamental distinction between the city walls and walls of other institutions, even though this distinction may have been less obvious in physical form than in conception. In the "Kaogong" part of the encyclopedia *Gujin tushu jicheng*, for example, as in many other similar documents, city wall (with moat) is classified separately from all other kinds of walls, which are gathered under a single category. Although many villages and a number of towns were fortified, their walls, like those of houses and temples, could not be termed *cheng* unless these settlements later became local centers of imperial administration and were thus automatically upgraded to cities, an upgrade that would in many cases be accompanied by reconstruction work to enlarge and strengthen their walls. Therefore, only those walls, often vast in size and sophisticated in configuration, enclosing the proper establishments of imperial government were entitled to this exclusive term. Their significance transcended that of other types of walls; they symbolized authority, order, and of course security.

Yet the city walls' symbolism of protection was not confined to the city itself. Since a regional or local city in the imperial era was invariably the administrative center of the region in which it was located, its walls were perceived by the Chinese as a defense instrument for the entire territory under the jurisdiction of that regional or local government, although technically they were an effective barrier for the city itself in times of siege. This attribute of the walls was explicitly specified by Qin Huitian (1702–1764) in his *Wuli tongkao,* in which he enunciates the necessity of the worship of the god of the city walls and moats (Chenghuang): "The high walls and deep moats [of a city] are the protection (*pinghan*) of a certain region."[82] Similar remarks were made by Zheng Yuanyou of the Yuan on this property of the walls of the city of Suzhou, stressing the importance of the event of their reconstruction in 1351, and by Zheng Ruozeng in the late Ming, who classified cities in accordance with their relative strategic importance: "there are cities that have significant bearings on the vital interests either of a region or of [even a larger territory of] several hundred *li* across."[83] It is worth noting that the term *pinghan* was used in traditional literature more often for its connotation, "important and reliable local officials who defend the state,"[84] than for its literal sense. Thus it would not be unreasonable to interpret Qin Huitian's sentence as equivalent to "the high walls and deep moats of a city represent the presence of local government." Indeed, a *cheng* or *chengshi* in imperial China, which we translate as "a walled city," had to be the capital of a province or prefecture or county; "city" and "capital" were but one concept. A transference of the local government elsewhere would usually have brought the *raison d'être* of the old settlement designated as a *cheng* to an end; and its walls, one of the prerequisites of its former status, would have lost most of their inherent meaning.

A prefecture or county was always identified terminologically with its capital city; for instance, Suzhou prefecture was usually called Suzhoufu[85] and its capital city Suzhoucheng (Walled City of Suzhou), or briefly the *fucheng* (the prefectural walled city). The siting of its capital city was a physical and cultural integration of the city with the local milieu, and the real existence of the city was constituted by its being embedded in its surrounding environs. Except in times of real crisis and at nighttime, the walls of the city of Suzhou did not form a barrier between the city and the countryside. They were the "casket" (see Chapter 3) conceptually extended in space to embrace all the historical and cultural valuables of the prefecture, both within the walls and without. In fact, the cultural relics located outside the city walls were by no means less cherished than those inside. In this sense, not only did the walls symbolize both the presence of the imperial government and the existence of an ideal social order, as I have discussed in the preceding chapter, but they also represented local history and culture, and their form became more important than the actual area they enclosed. Since the city walls were symbols, not physical boundaries, an alteration of them was probably seen as unnecessary and undesirable. In this line of reasoning, I would therefore venture to suggest that this symbolic nature of the city walls, together with a strong sense of the authority of the past constantly at work, was at least partly attributable to the remarkable stability of the city form of Suzhou, defined by the walls, from 1229 onward, and perhaps even much earlier. Homage to the past figured profoundly in Chinese history.

This suggestion, however, by no means implies a denial of the fact that the exact locations of the walls of a number of cities in South China and their specific urban forms were often largely the result of practical considerations concerning the particular local geographical and topographical conditions. The port city of Quanzhou in Fujian is such an example. As Figure 4.13 shows, the irregular form of the city enclosed by the outer walls during the Ming and Qing periods was brought about by the restraints of local watercourses and by the economic expansion of the city from the Song period onward.[86] Another example is the city of Nantong north of Suzhou on the north bank of the River Yangzi. Figure 4.14 shows that a new wall was built after the mid-Ming to enclose the southern suburbs, which were rapidly developing but were very vulnerable to frequent plunder by pirates.[87]

It should be emphasized that the processes of development for Quanzhou and Nantong were not at all isolated instances in Chinese urban history, just as that of the city of Suzhou was not. The transformability of the city forms of Quanzhou and Nantong should be accounted for by a set of local historical, cultural, and geographical conditions that acted as an integral whole; so should the remarkable stability of the comparatively regular city form of Suzhou. Among these conditions, three seem to have figured most in Suzhou's development. First, unlike the other two cities, both being constructed for the first time in the tenth century (Quanzhou in 906, Nantong in 958), the city of Suzhou boasted a much longer history, and consequently the weight of its ancient heritage was enormous. Second, the economic and cultural importance of Suzhou far surpassed that of the other two cities, probably resulting in a more rigorous

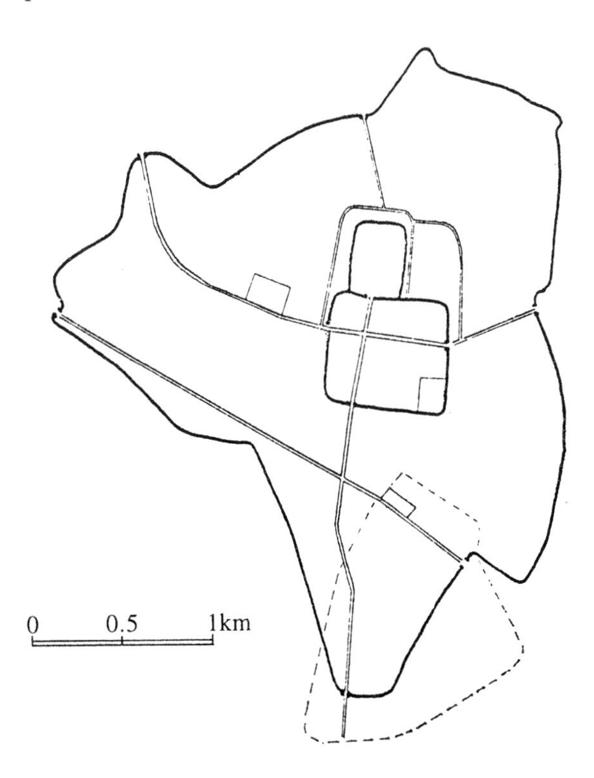

Figure 4.13 *Reconstructed plan of the city of Quanzhou during the Yuan period, around the fourteenth century. Adapted from Dong 1982, p. 55, fig. 1-6-7.*

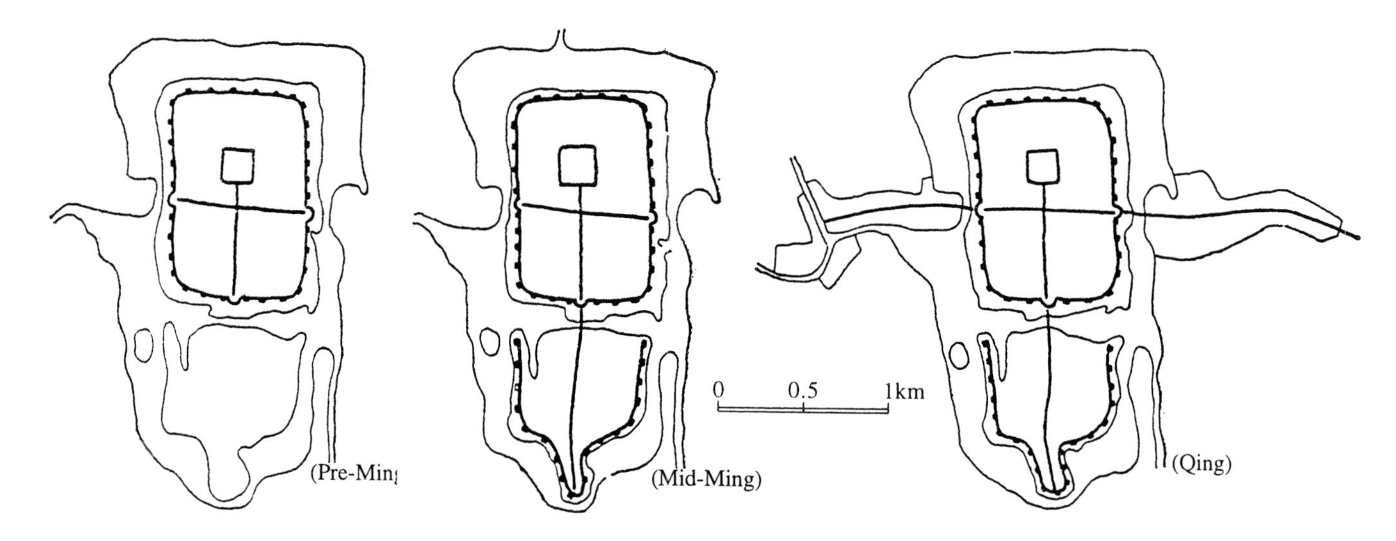

Figure 4.14 Plans of the city of Nantong from the pre-Ming period to the Qing. The southernmost part of the new walls was built after the mid-Ming to protect the south suburbs of the city from pirate attacks and is located right on the north edge of the River Yangzi. Adapted from Dong 1982, p. 101, fig. 1-7-28.

preservation of the city form, which was regarded as a "fixed institution."[88] Third, compared to Quanzhou located by Quanzhou Bay and Nantong by the River Yangzi, Suzhou was an inland city, and thus the pressure of building new walls to protect burgeoning suburbs from pirate attacks was apparently less strong. In any event, the development of the form of the city of Suzhou was a physical manifestation of the Chinese predilection for maintaining what had been achieved in the past. In other words, it may have been exemplary with respect to a tendency in Chinese urban history but not necessarily typical of the usual outcome of this tendency.

As physical structures, the city walls could not last forever; but, in most cases, they were constantly repaired or even rebuilt in such a fashion that their placement and form persisted. Therefore no one would doubt that the city walls "often tell more of the ancient greatness of the city than the houses or temples."[89] Yet for the traditional Chinese, they represented what was seen as constant in the vicissitudes of life. As the most imposing man-made structures apart from the Great Wall in the Chinese landscape, the city walls signified not only the grandeur of the city but also the continuation of a civilization from the past to the future; they were timeless in the midst of temporal change. This Chinese perception of the city walls is revealed by a story told in Tao Qian's (ca. A.D. 372–427) *Sou shen houji*. The story tells how Ding Lingwei, who turned into an immortal crane after having studied the *dao* of immortality on Mt. Lingxu for a millennium, flew back to his home place Liaodong. When a teenage boy attempted a shot at him with an arrow at the city gate, he hovered around and sang a verse before flying into the high skies:

> There is this bird called Ding Lingwei,
> Returning home at last after a thousand years away.
> The city walls are as ever but the people are not the same,
> Why not study immortality among graves after graves?[90]

This verse presents the everlasting quality of the city walls in the Chinese mind alongside the same quality in the immortal and his homeland and in contrast with the transience of human life and society. The city walls are portrayed, though probably unintentionally, as part of the land, and thus part of the eternal universe in which all things change incessantly. Allusion was frequently made to this story in literature of later times. Zhang Dai (1597–ca. 1685), for example, in his nostalgic reminiscence of the old Ming institutions and customs under the newly established Qing rule, deliberately uses the term *chengguo renmin* (the city walls and the people) in the preface of his *Taoan mengyi*,[91] implying the persistence of the memories of his past experiences, as resembling the permanence of the city walls, under the tide of social and political transformation.

CHAPTER 5 Physical Structure of the City

BECAUSE OF THE PAUCITY OF WRITTEN RECORDS and city maps, little is known about the physical structure of the city of Suzhou before the Tang period, except that the city was surrounded by one circle (or perhaps two circles) of walls with eight gates in them, each catering to both road and water traffic, and that, at least from the third century onward, a double system of land and water transport may have started to take shape. We could also conjecture that a government building complex accommodating the prefectural offices, perhaps enclosed by another wall, may have been located near the center of the city. It is from A.D. 876 onward that pieces of information about the city begin to proliferate. On the basis of the *Wudi ji* and a number of Tang poems, for example, it is reasonable to believe that the city, its overall form being a slightly irregular rectangle, had a well-developed network of street and canals, intersected by over three hundred bridges, and the city was divided, though probably unevenly, into as many as sixty residential wards, which were very probably enclosed by walls and strictly controlled by the government. This second feature was common in most of the prominent cities in China until the late Tang.

As discussed in Chapter 3, the medieval urban revolution taking place between the eighth and the twelfth centuries brought about profound change in the spatial organization of many large cities in the economically advanced areas. The most salient features of this change included the disappearance of the enclosed marketplace and the walled-ward system and the emergence of a much freer street plan in which trade and commerce could be conducted anywhere within the city and its outlying suburbs. This urban revolution paved the way for further developments of urban form and space during the late imperial period, developments in areas such as the characteristic partitioning of urban space, the tremendous urban expansion in suburban areas, and the existence of the distinctive antithesis of urban stability and transformability. Suzhou was surely one of the first cities that experienced these transformations. It is on the basis of an understanding of these particular features that I examine more closely in this chapter the general spatial structure of the city of Suzhou.

City Canal and Street System

The area around the city of Suzhou has long been well-known as a land of waters;[1] and the city's extensive canal network and numerous bridges account for its receiving, probably first in Europe and later in modern China, the name "the Venice of the Orient."[2] On the 1229 city map presented in Figure 4.3, it is visually evident that throughout the city a double system of water and road transport prevailed and that the canals and streets, most of them being laid out in alignment with the city walls, either intersected at right angles or paralleled each other. The total length of the canals within the city walls is estimated by Yu Shengfang at about eighty-two kilometers in the Southern Song period, which amounts to 78 percent of the total length of the city streets. On the basis of certain archaeological findings, Yu also speculates that each canal was probably no less than ten meters in width and three to five meters in depth.[3] Apart from the benefit of convenient daily use, firefighting, waterborne transport, and beautification of the landscapes, the canals figured significantly in preventing floods from overrunning the city, as they functioned in time as spillways.[4] In terms of the development of urban form and space, however, this system not only characterized the overall layout of the city from the Southern Song onward but, probably more important for the present research, together with the honorific gateways (*fang*) and bridges, bore the marks of its formation and transformation at earlier stages.

Formation of the City Canals

Few would doubt that the waterway system was the mainstay of the urban spatial structure of the city of Suzhou. In fact, this distinctive urban feature surely had been procured by the city long before the Southern Song period. As was discussed in Chapter 2, in the eyes of the authors of the *Yue jue shu* and *Wu Yue chunqiu*, Helü Dacheng, built in 514 B.C., had eight land gates and eight water gates, and its inner walled enclosure also had two water gates. These seem to imply the existence at that time of multiple rivers within the city walls, although only one river is specified, stretching from Ping Gate to She Gate and twenty-eight *bu* (approximately 40 meters by the Eastern Han standard) in width.[5] The earliest record of the regulation of rivers and canals in the city was made by Zhang Shoujie, the great Tang commentator of the *Shi ji*. He claims that Lord Chunshen dredged four longitudinal and five latitudinal canals north of his palace in the city in the mid-third century B.C., and that these canals continued to exist in Zhang's time.[6] If Zhang's record is reliable, it might have been this water project that laid the foundation of the city's general spatial pattern on which it developed in later times.

The city's water and road transport systems may have begun to take shape, though perhaps only embryonically, at least from the second half of the third century A.D., as revealed in Zuo Si's *Wudu fu* (and as quoted in Chapter 4): "Open are two sets [i.e., land and water] of eight [city] gates, [connected by a network of] water ways and land routes [in the city]." By the late Tang, not only had the basic structure of the watercourses in the city become so fixed—"three latitudinal and four longitudinal" arteries—that the author of the *Wudi ji* felt it necessary to record it in the second half of the ninth century[7] but the canals had already multiplied to such an extent that they became a constant theme in many Tang poems depicting the city of Suzhou of half a century earlier. During his seventeen-month appointment as the prefect of Suzhou from 825 to 826, Bai Juyi once went up to Chang Gate and wrote about what he perceived of the city:

> The city walls of Helü are emerald-green spread with autumn plants,
> The Raven Bridge is red bearing the glow of the setting sun.
> In front of storied buildings everywhere waft the melodies of flutes,
> And by the door of every house are moored ships and boats.[8]

Similarly, in the eyes of Li Shen (772–846), who passed by Suzhou, it was the canals and water traffic that were the representative features of the city:

> In the walls of the Wu capital city amidst mist
> Chang Gate straddles the green water streams.
> Green poplars are in the deep and shallow alleys;
> The boats decorated with carved blue birds are floating backward and forward.[9]

About half of a century later, Du Xunhe (846–ca. 907) recalled the scenery of the city in the late Tang in a brief poem "Songren you Wu":

> Reaching Gusu [i.e., Suzhou] you will see
> People's houses pillowed on the rivers.
> Within the old palatial area little land is vacant,
> Over the rivers small bridges are many.
> Water chestnut fruits and lotus roots are sold in late evening markets,
> And spring boats are loaded with luxurious silken fabrics.
> In the distance I know that wakeful under the moon,
> Homesickness will be accompanied by fishermen's songs.[10]

It is most probable that by the second half of the Northern Song period, the whole network of canals in the city had already come to maturity. In 1084, for example, Zhu Changwen, emphasizing the necessity of the canals in preserving the city from flood, wrote:

> As observed within the city walls, numerous [artery] streams are running through the whole area, taking in and pouring out the water from [Lake] Zhenze [i.e.,

> Lake Tai]. Their tributaries spread out, flanking the [city] roads and streets. Otherwise, perhaps there would be no means of discharging excessive rainwater and settling the residents adequately.[11]

It is true that the unprecedented damage inflicted by the Jurchen cavalry on the city of Suzhou in 1130 was devastating, as Fan Chengda stated a century later, though not without a certain degree of exaggeration, that all buildings except for a couple of temples within the city walls were burned down.[12] It does seem unlikely, though, that the whole existing network of the city canals was destroyed entirely at the same time. This latter statement can be verified, if only inconclusively, by comparing the record of bridges in the city contained in the "Supplement" to the *Wudi ji*, compiled in the Northern Song after 1016, with those presented in the Southern Song picture map of the city carved on stone in 1229 and those contained in the gazetteer *Wujun zhi* published in the same year. Of about one hundred bridges within the city walls that are mentioned by name in the "Supplement,"[13] which amounted to less than one-third of the sum total at that time, up to 95 percent are also either registered in the *Wujun zhi* or appear on the 1229 map.[14] Although some of these remaining bridges, most of which were built of stone, may have been repaired or even reconstructed in the 1220s, their recurrence in the 1229 document and picture map indicates a continuous existence of most of the city canals from the Northern Song to the Southern Song periods.

Thus, even if we assume that the restoration of the city walls and the repair or reconstruction of many other institutions in the 1220s were very thorough and well coordinated, it does not necessarily mean that the double system of water and road transport presented on the 1229 map was, as Yu Shengfang asserts, a brand new creation of the Southern Song, nor is Johnston's suggestion convincing that the whole network of canals had to be built at one and the same time at the inception of city rebuilding.[15] Instead, the evidence presented in the preceding paragraphs suggests that the reconstruction works in the 1220s were conducted on the basis of both the existing network of canals and the spatial pattern of the city, allowing for the addition of some new structures. In the following section, I will further propose that fundamental change in the internal spatial structure of the city of Suzhou was not so much brought about in these few years but came gradually during the second half of the Tang and Northern Song periods, a process closely associated with the so-called "medieval urban revolution," which was discussed in Chapter 3.

City Canals and Urban Spatial Transformation

According to the *Wudi ji*, the city during the Tang period consisted of sixty residential wards (*fang*), one-half of them governed by Wu county and the other half by Changzhou county; the habitations in each ward were divided internally into about five alleys.[16] On the main gate of each of these wards, a horizontal stone slab (*fangbiao*) was installed, on which the name of the ward was engraved. A comparison between the records contained in the *Wudi ji* and *Wujun zhi*, and the pictorial presentation on the 1229 map,

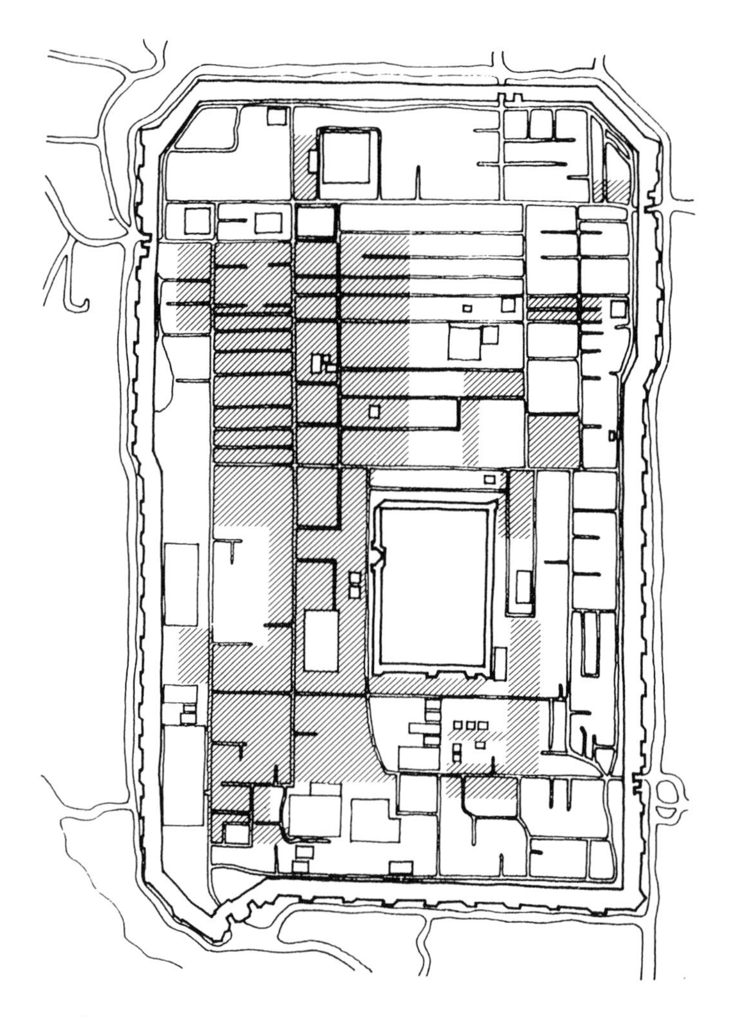

Figure 5.1 The possible disposition of the residential wards in the city of Suzhou during the Tang period, based on the 1229 map of the city.

suggests that these wards were not evenly distributed within the city.[17] Figure 5.1 shows the possible disposition of the wards in the Tang, with them largely clustered around the central inner enclosure housing the prefectural seat and in the north by west and south by west parts of the city. Little information is available about the form of the wards and their internal organization, but it is reasonable to conjecture that, as part of the city planning principle of the Tang, they were probably enclosed by walls and supervised by appointed officials, as were those in many other cities at that time. On the presupposition that the general pattern of the city canal system presented on the 1229 map had taken shape by the mid-Tang, I would further suggest that these residential wards, most of which were perhaps in the shape of a fairly slender rectangle, varied in size and in orientation (either north-south or east-west), as each of them occupied a specific plot of land partitioned by the canals.[18] This is evidenced, though only partly, by the 1229 map, if we are to regard some of the gateways (*fang*) as remnants of the entrances of the residential wards in the early Tang.

By the early ninth century, at the latest, government control over the residential wards must have started to be relaxed. In the 820s Bai Juyi mentions the sixty wards in one poem[19] and tells us in another, "Deng Changmen xianwang," that "by the door of every house are moored sailing boats." Since in the city of Suzhou, canals were equivalent in function to roads, this appears to be in obvious contradiction with the stipulation of the urban system current in the early Tang that no private houses except for those of nobles were allowed to have entrances opening directly onto the city roads. In other words, many, if not all, of the walls of the wards may have ceased bounding residences within the wards to which access had previously been controlled by their common gates. This process of change accelerated in the late Tang. In around the mid-ninth century, for example, Lu Guimeng (?–ca. 881), a native of Changzhou county and a well-known late Tang writer, resided by the Lindun Bridge in the northeast part of the city, a place that his contemporary Pi Rixiu (ca. 834–ca. 883) described as "spacious as a suburb or wilderness though not without the city walls."[20] It is clear that Lu's abode was not located within any of the sixty residential wards recorded in the *Wudi ji*, which indicates a tendency of unrestricted choice of settlement in the city. Accompanying the relaxation of the residential ward control was a relaxation of the market control, as Du Xunhe writes in the second half of the ninth century in his poem quoted earlier, which depicts how not only did "all the houses rest by rivers," but late evening markets where food and vegetables were sold—an activity then still largely prohibited in the imperial capital Chang'an[21]—also became usual in the city of Suzhou.

Substantial change came during the Northern Song period (960–1126). Although the sixty residential wards were still recorded in the *Xiangfu tujing*, a local gazetteer compiled between 1008 and 1016 by Li Zonge but long since lost,[22] by at least the first half of the eleventh century, individuals must have been able to choose freely the location of their abodes, provided their means allowed them to do so. This is not only reflected in Fan Chengda's mention of a couple of places of residence occupied in the 1020s by reference to two bridges rather than to any wards (in his listing of commendable figures in Suzhou history)[23] but substantiated by the fact that a number of scholar-officials, traveling to Suzhou after their retirement or dismissal from office, freely purchased unoccupied plots of land in the city to build houses and gardens.[24] Probably more informative are Zhu Changwen's remarks about Suzhou's residential wards in his *Wujun Tujing xuji* written in 1084: "Recently, most of the *fang* [residential wards] and *shi* [markets] have lost the gate tablets on which their names were engraved [*biaobang*], and people no longer call [these *fang* and *shi*] by their names."[25] This statement suggests that, although the physical entities of the old residential wards at that time may still have been present, their *raison d'être* was not.

In fact, it was during the period between the late Northern Song and the early Southern Song that the denotation of the character *fang* shifted from "residential ward" to "honorific gateway,"[26] one of the semantic changes that signified the complete replacement of the ward system with the system of streets and alleys and thus the fundamental transformation of spatial organization in the city of Suzhou. The result of this transformation is manifested both on the 1229 city map and in the *Wujun zhi*. In Chapter 3, Figures 3.10 and 3.11 contrasted a section of the city plan of Tang dynasty Chang'an, where plots of land were demarcated by the walls of the residential wards, and that of the Southern Song dynasty Suzhou, characterized by its parallel streets and canals, which determined the intramural space. During the Tang and the first half of the Northern Song, each of Suzhou's sixty residential wards, which may to some extent have been equivalent to those of Chang'an, was itself called a *fang;* but probably from the late Northern Song onward, the word denoted any of the honorific gateways, most of them located at the threshold of an old ward but now simply symbolizing a neighborhood or its entrance.

Evidence of this change is found in the *Wujun zhi* in two ways. First, under the entry of many *fang*, *xiang* (alley) is written to indicate the location of the *fang* in question.[27] One should note that, since prior to the late Northern Song the character *xiang* denoted "an alley *within* a residential ward," a *fang* here could mean just a gateway straddling a street or alley. Second, from the texts available to us concerning the city of Suzhou, we understand that Fan Chengda, the author of the *Wujun zhi*, was the first scholar to have used, though still only occasionally, the verb "to erect" (*li*) in recording the building of a new *fang*, a word that is more appropriate for setting up a gateway than a walled residential ward, for which the verbs *jian* and *zuo* (both literally meaning "build" or "construct") are more appropriate and which were used constantly before Fan's time.[28] This semantic change in the character *fang* registers in itself a gradual urban institutional change that led to the fundamental transformation of urban spatial organization from the late Tang to the early Southern Song periods.

Two points that have been developed thus far should be emphasized. The first is a slight digression from, but pertinent to, the main subject of this section. The *fang*, that is, the honorific gateways, presented as independent structures on the 1229 city map, originated from the gates of the old residential wards. It was customary until the Northern Song that, in Suzhou, as in all other cities in China, an honorific name was often conferred by the government on a specific residential ward in honor of the commendable deeds of its individuals or families.[29] This name was then engraved on a stone that was incorporated officially into the gate of the ward, an act known as *biaolü*.[30] The eventual replacement of the ward system by the system of streets and alleys in the early Southern Song, however, did not lead to the cessation of this custom. On the contrary, this practice was freed from the locational limitation concomitant with the establishment of the wards; thus the number of *fang* was increased to sixty-five by Li Shoupeng in 1229.[31] From the Ming period onward, if not earlier, more honorific gateways than ever before were erected.[32] The historic process of the transformation of the *fang* from the residential walled wards, to the symbolic gateways leading to their corresponding residential blocks that were no longer under strict government control, and then to the honorific gateways largely free of any locational restraint, was generated by, and at the same time reflected, the process of change in the physical structure of the city.

The second point I need to emphasize is more central to the present discussion.

Whereas the transformation of urban spatial organization, generated principally by the "medieval urban revolution," proves to have been substantial and far-reaching, in Suzhou this transformation took place largely within the framework of the existing urban physical structure developed over centuries. It is very possible that this framework initially took the position of the city walls and gates as its starting point provided either by the construction of Helü Dacheng in 514 B.C. or by entire city rebuilding—if there was any—in the pre-Tang era. It is certainly true that the geometrically regulated spatial structure of many cities in China, especially those on the North China Plain, was predetermined at the inception of their construction. This should not, however, be taken as a universal model to be applied to explain every Chinese city that evinced such a spatial character, since there were cities of seemingly regular design whose street pattern, watercourses, and residential quarters were jointly a physical outcome of gradual urban development through the centuries. The city of Suzhou was undoubtedly one of them.

I am not entirely sure whether the relatively even quality (though not quantity) of the urban environment over the entire city can be attributed to the application of what Hackett calls the "inherent" method of building cities, which, because of the constant cultural ideal in China's long-lasting civilization, "might well develop naturally in a regular manner without very much of the preliminary thought or decision of a drafted town plan."[33] What I can suggest with some degree of certainty is that, during the period between the beginning of the Tang (or probably even earlier) and the late Northern Song, the network of the city canals was gradually forged in coordination with the division of the city area into the residential wards, the walled market quarters, and government offices and other institutions, which could be regarded as a spatial manifestation of the "classical" urban social organization. Precisely in the second half of this period, that is, from the late Tang to the late Northern Song, the fundamental change in the internal spatial structure of the city was in progress. Thus it was not only at the time when the old residential ward system was prevalent but also through the process of its gradual collapse that the network of city canals eventually came to shape. The formation of this network assisted the spatial arrangement of the residential wards (and the walled markets) as much as it in time helped their disintegration; and at the same time, the canal system itself was the outcome of the establishment of the physical ward system as much as the consequence of the collapse of this system, which epitomized the medieval urban spatial transformation.

City Canals in the Late Imperial Period

Whereas the earliest record of Suzhou's hydraulic works in the imperial era dates back to the Qin dynasty at the end of the third century B.C., frequent and extensive projects started from the early Tang in the first half of the seventh century; and more projects were conducted during the Song period, which were accompanied by a multitude of books, discourses, and memoirs on local water conservancy. Yet among all the relevant documents available, no record of such schemes on the canals within the city walls, except the dredging of the Jinfan Jing in coordination with that of the Grand Canal in

Table 5.1 Chronological Record of Canal-Dredging in the City of Suzhou during the Ming and Qing Periods.

Dynasty / Year	*Year*	*Event*
Ming	1370s	Dredging of One Artery Canal, the Jinfan Jing
(1368–1644)	1493	Full-scale Canal Dredging
	1522	Full-scale Canal Dredging
	1525	Dredging of Seven Sections of the City Canals
	1606	Full-scale Canal Dredging
	1617	Full-scale Canal Dredging
	1630	Dredging of the Canals in Front of the Wu County Offices
Qing	1709	Full-scale Canal Dredging
(1644–1911)	1722	Full-scale Canal Dredging
	1728	Full-scale Canal Dredging
	1739	Full-scale Canal Dredging
	1746	Full-scale Canal Dredging
	1796–1797	Full-scale Canal Dredging
	1835	Full-scale Canal Dredging
	1864	Full-scale Canal Dredging
	1873	Full-scale Canal Dredging
	1890	Full-scale Canal Dredging

Source: *Wsq, juan* 10.34 ff.; *Wumen biaoyin, juan* 1, p. 1; *Suzhoufu zhi, juan* 10.6 ff., *juan* 11.1 ff.; *Wuxian zhi, juan* 43.2 ff.

the west suburbs in 1217 by prefect Zhao Yansu and in the 1370s by prefect Wei Guan, is found before the mid-Ming in 1493.[34] From then on, however, a total of sixteen such undertakings in the city are recorded up to 1890; these are listed in chronological order in Table 5.1. At first sight, the frequent work on regulating the city canals in the course of the last two dynasties seems impressive. Yu Shengfang, for instance, asserts that it indicates the satisfactory accomplishment of the Ming and Qing government's task of maintaining the canal system of the city, an assessment made by equally dividing the period from 1368 to 1890 by fourteen, which averages a comprehensive dredging of the city canals every thirty-seven years.[35] Setting the question of the validity of such an appraisal aside,[36] a closer look at this information, in conjunction with an analysis of the contemporary city maps, otherwise reveals a more complex and interesting situation in the process of city development in the late imperial period.

Starting with the Ming period, from 1229 in the Southern Song onward,[37] there are no recorded works of the regulation of the city canals until the mid-Ming. If we are to ignore partial works in 1525 and 1630, there were only four instances of full-scale canal-dredging in a span of one and a half centuries, from 1493 to the end of the Ming, two of them occurring close to the turn of the sixteenth century and the other two in the early seventeenth century. The layout of the city canals in the late Ming is presented in detail in the city map contained in Zhang Guowei's *Wuzhong shuili quanshu*, the production of which was based on the result of the official survey carried out between 1567 and 1619 (see Figure 4.4). It seems more likely that the survey was part of the two canal-dredging works in the early seventeenth century than that it was a separate work before or after that time. In any event, a comparison between the 1229 map (Figure 4.3) and the late Ming map (Figure 4.4) demonstrates that almost every canal presented on the former reappears on the latter, and some of the unattached canals on the former, especially those in the northeast and, to a lesser degree, the southwest quarters, are shown to have been connected. Thus the watercourses within the city walls in the late Ming were probably slightly longer in total than those in the Southern Song. In fact, the canal system displayed on the late Ming map is the most extensive among those on all other maps of the city of Suzhou from 1229 to the present day. Does this indicate that more attention was paid to the canals in the Ming or that the efforts at attending to them were more effective? Probably both. Yet it would be more interesting in the present discussion to ask whether the well-maintained or even improved city canal system in the late Ming suggests something more of the urban economic and social conditions than of the effectiveness of the local government in attending to its canals. To deal with this last question, we have to move on to the Qing period.[38]

Turning back to Table 5.1, there is no record of full-scale canal-dredging for the period of some two hundred and sixty years from 1229 to 1493. If the written records are largely reliable,[39] one is tempted to conjecture at first sight of the data that the local government in the early Qing may have been more conscious of the need to maintain the city canal system than that in the early Ming, because not only was such a work conducted in 1709, only sixty-five years after the political upheaval of the change of dynasty, a sharp contrast with the interval of one hundred twenty-five years from the beginning of the Ming in 1368, but four more instances immediately followed. When these data are checked more carefully against the contemporary city maps, however, a somewhat more interesting story unfolds. Table 5.1 shows that in the last two hundred and sixty-eight years of the imperial era, six out of ten instances of full-scale canal-dredging occurred in the eighteenth century alone, while five of them were concentrated within a period of thirty-eight years in the first half of that century. It was precisely at the end of this period that the result of a dramatic loss of over a quarter of the canals within the city walls is presented on the city map contained in the 1748 prefectural gazetteer (Figure 4.6). The damage to certain sections of the city canals must have been gradual and probably started from the mid-seventeenth century or some later date.

What, then, does this tell us? As introduced in Chapter 1, Suzhou rose to prominence as what Skinner calls "the regional metropolis" from the early sixteenth century.[40] The physical impact of this economic growth on the city watercourses may not have been felt until the second half of the seventeenth century, when encroachment made by houses and other structures on many of the canals started to pose a serious problem.[41] Thus it seems reasonable to argue that the unusual frequency of the enterprise of canal-dredging in the first half of the eighteenth century—once in less than every eight years on average—was really part of a forced reaction of the local government to the tremendous pressure of urban growth on the city area, especially on those parts that were economically and demographically most sensitive. This argument wins more support when comparing the 1748 city map (Figure 4.6) with that of the late Ming (Figure 4.4) and identifying the areas where the canals were obviously blocked in the mid-eighteenth century (see Figure 5.2). Apart from the far northeast corner, where the loss of a few canals probably resulted from negligence, it was the quarters in the business district close to Chang Gate in the northwest, and in the west part of the district of family-based textile industry adjacent to the business district, that experienced significant loss of canals.

Many of these areas had long been densely populated from the Tang onward, and pressures on them must have increased dramatically since the mid-seventeenth century, while other areas that were scarcely occupied until the early eighteenth century rapidly developed within a period of a century into the most bustling places. The area south of

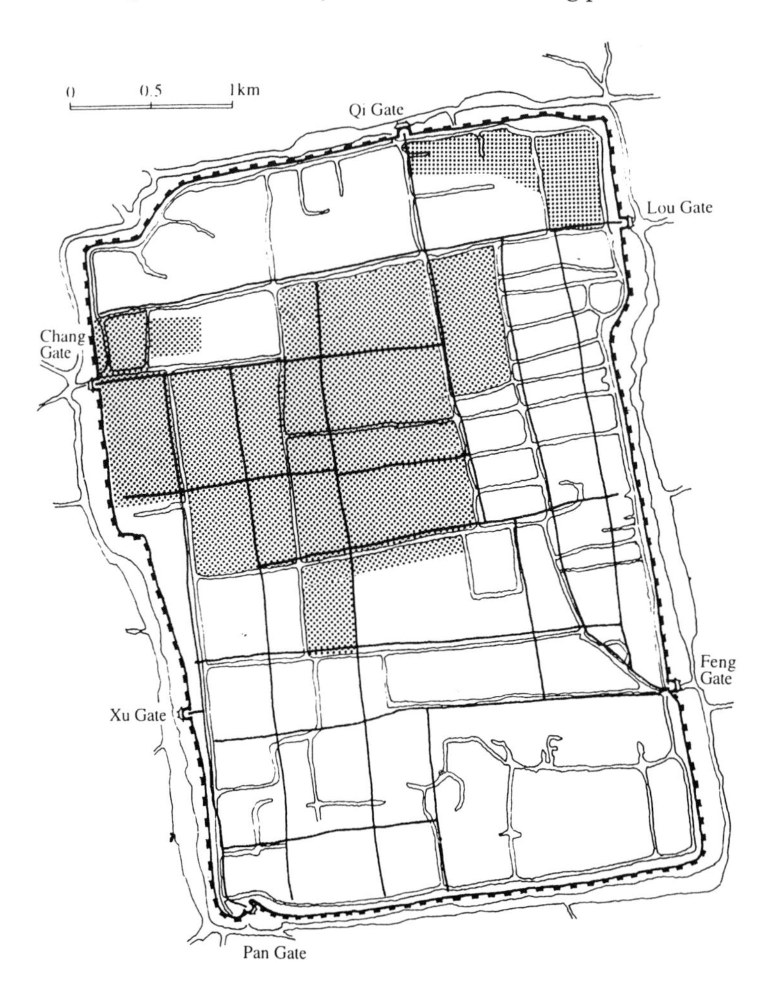

Figure 5.2 Shading on this diagrammatic map of Suzhou indicates areas within the city walls that experienced dramatic loss of canals by 1748.

the Daoist temple Xuanmiao Guan was such an example. Zhang Zilin, an eighteenth-to-nineteenth-century native of Changzhou, speaks in his *Honglan yisheng* of the density of houses and the boisterousness of daily life in that area south of the temple in contrast to the words of another local scholar a century before him who observed that "few residences were located here during the Kangxi reign-period (1662–1722), and what I saw by standing on the [Suijin][42] Bridge was the derelict site of Zhang [Shicheng]'s palaces overspread with wild grasses."[43] The major achievement of the efforts exerted between 1709 and 1746 may therefore be regarded as having reduced the damage of the city canals to the minimum possible.

The problem of the steady decay of the city canals continued in the second half of the eighteenth century. The accumulated damage was such that in 1795, in the eyes of Fei Chun, the provincial governor who inspected the whole city, "over half of the four longitudinal and three latitudinal watercourses were silted or clogged; and the water flow of other small rivers has stopped, some of them having become level land."[44] This prompted the more complete project started in the eighth month of 1796 and finished in the fifth month of the following year at the cost of over 21,596 taels of silver collected principally from private donations rather than government sponsorship. The total length of the canals dredged this time amounted to over 25.237 kilometers, and over 76,026 cubic meters of earth were moved.[45] Although it became impossible for this project to restore the remaining canals to the Ming standard,[46] its success was undeniable: if the undertakings in the first half of the eighteenth century were ironically greeted with the massive loss of the watercourses, this one, followed by those in the ensuing century, effectively prevented the network from deteriorating. Comparing the 1797 and 1883 city maps (Figures 4.7 and 3.15, respectively) and the two produced at the turn of the twentieth century (Figures 5.3 and 5.4) with the 1748 map (Figure 4.6), we find that, apart from the disappearance of two or three small canals by the east city wall, there were no further significant losses in 1797 or thereafter until the end of the Qing.

It is not certain whether these works were conducted more thoroughly, or the attendant control of the canals was tighter, or the pressure of the economic and population growth on the city area lessened as a new equilibrium may have been reached at this stage of urban development. Probably all three factors jointly contributed to this result. My concluding point, however, is that both the pictorial record of the city canals and the written record of the canal-dredging works do not merely reveal how many efforts were made to maintain or improve the city water system and whether these efforts were effective. They also tell us that the geometrically regulated pattern of the watercourses during the Southern Song period, gradually formed over the preceding centuries, was largely a physical outcome of strict government control over city residences and markets, the formation of which were coordinated with the development of these watercourses; that the massive loss of the canals in the first half of the eighteenth century probably resulted from the enormous pressure on certain areas of the city by the unprecedented upsurge of population at that time, the relaxation of government control,[47] and the rapid economic growth beginning from the mid-Ming onward; and that the sustain-

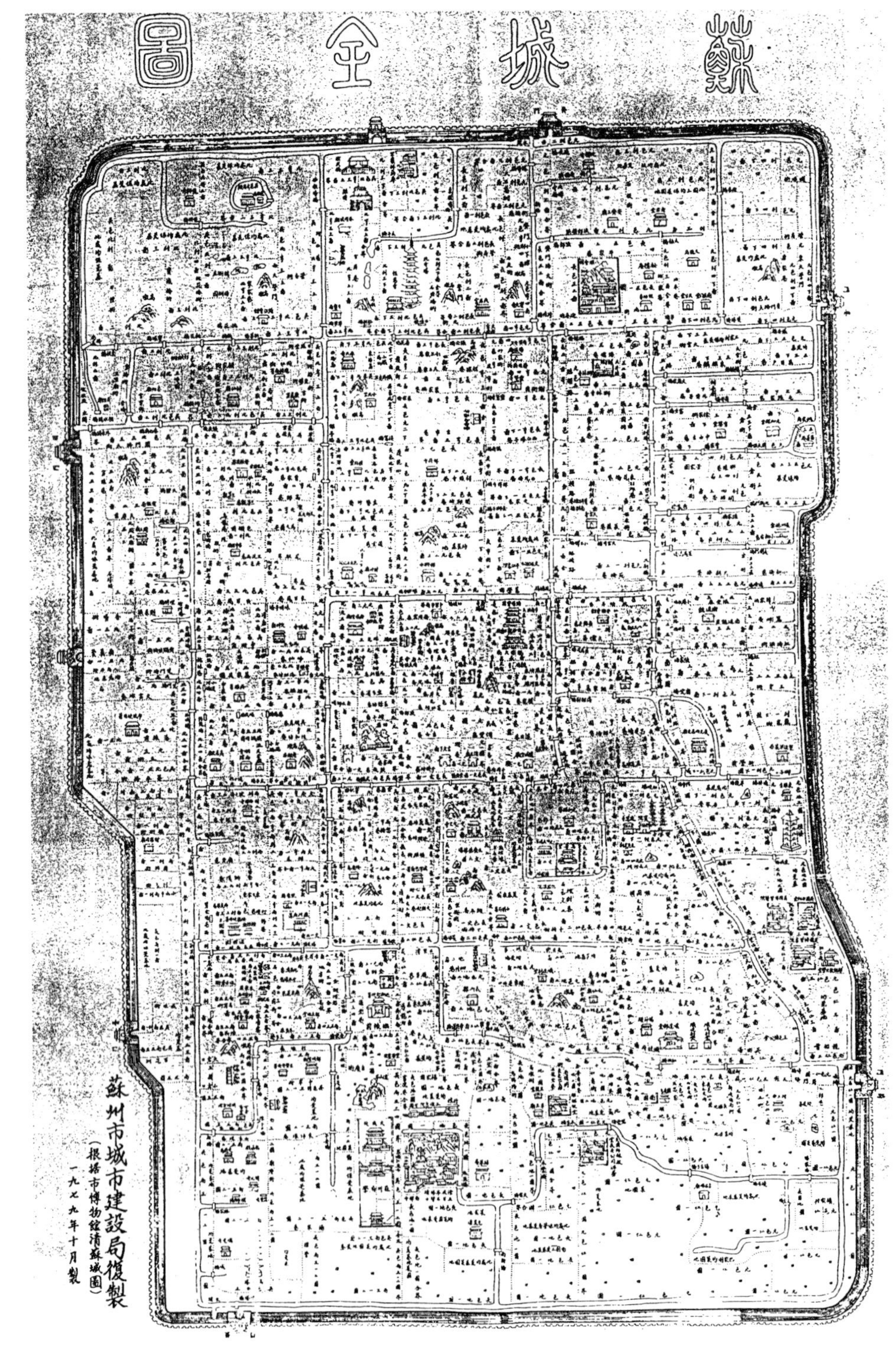

Figure 5.3 Picture map of Suzhou entitled Sucheng quantu *(A Complete Map of the City of Suzhou) produced between 1883 and 1901. Author unknown. Courtesy of the Committee of Suzhou Urban and Rural Construction.*

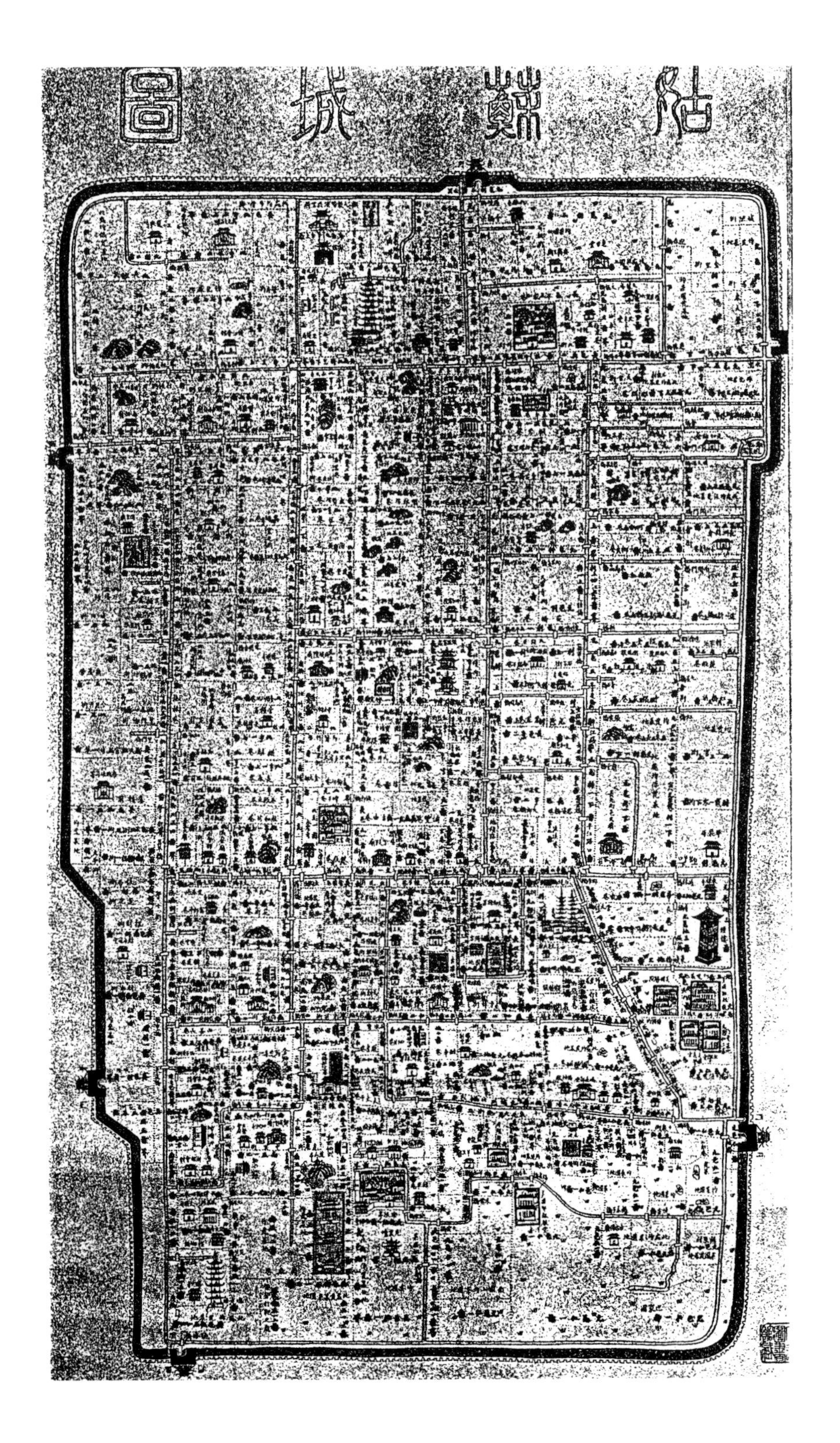

Figure 5.4 Picture map of Suzhou entitled Gusu chengtu *(City Map of Gusu [Suzhou]) produced between 1883 and 1901. Author unknown. Adapted from Liu 1995, plate 35.*

ing of the remaining canals thereafter until the early twentieth century reflects a considerable easing of such pressure and the attainment of a new balance between the economy, population, and urban land use.

The Geometrical Center of the City

By the end of the Northern Song, the medieval urban revolution had substantially transformed the overall spatial structure of the city of Suzhou, but one principal element, the inner walled enclosure at the center of the city housing the prefectural government offices, which was part of the old urban institution, persisted for another two and a half centuries. The origin of this inner enclosure is as yet not clear, but it may have some connection with the planning system of the Wu capital built at the end of the sixth century B.C. In Chapter 2, I suggested that the central area of Helü Dacheng may have been occupied by a walled palatial enclosure (*xiaocheng*) of the king of Wu. By 248 B.C., this building complex must have long been dilapidated, because as Lord Chunshen was enfeoffed in the Wu area by the king of Chu, he had to build his palaces anew in the city.[48] These palatial structures with some later additions became the prefectural offices and the prefects' residence from the Qin period on into the Eastern Han and probably even later, with the exception that in 201 B.C., Liu Jia, a brother of the first Western Han emperor Liu Bang (256–195 B.C.), built a new walled palace known as the Dingcuo Cheng to the north of the *xiaocheng* after he was granted the title of Jing Wang (the king of the Jing [region]).[49] The exact location of the new palatial complex built in 248 B.C. has always been a matter of dispute.[50] However, descriptions of certain official buildings contained in Tang poems and Song documents tell us that a wall-enclosed complex housing the prefectural seat had already been located at the center of the city during the Tang period (A.D. 618–891), if not earlier. Thus I agree with Liu Dunzhen's suggestion that during the Southern Song period the inner walled enclosure shown on the 1229 picture map *Pingjiang tu* was in general merely a reconstruction with a few alterations on the exact site of its predecessors.[51]

This inner enclosure of the Southern Song, shown in Figure 5.5 (cf. Figure 4.3), was much smaller in scale than that at the time of Helü Dacheng, if the *Yue jue shu*'s record of its measurements at twelve *li* (approximately 5.08 kilometers) in perimeter is reliable. By comparing the architectural features and by reference to their names as shown in the city maps of the Southern Song, Ming, and late Qing, we can reasonably contend that the north side of the walls of the inner enclosure in the Southern Song period should have been around present-day Zhangguolao and Qiangengzi Alleys, the west side around Jinfan Road, the south side around Shizi Street, and the east side around Gongyuan Road. This amounts to the perimeter of this rectangular area being only about 2,100 meters (approximately 450 meters by 600 meters). Thus the area enclosed within the walls of the inner enclosure was certainly not, as Johnston claims, slightly larger than the area of the Forbidden City of the Ming and Qing dynasties Beijing, but only a little over a quarter of it.[52]

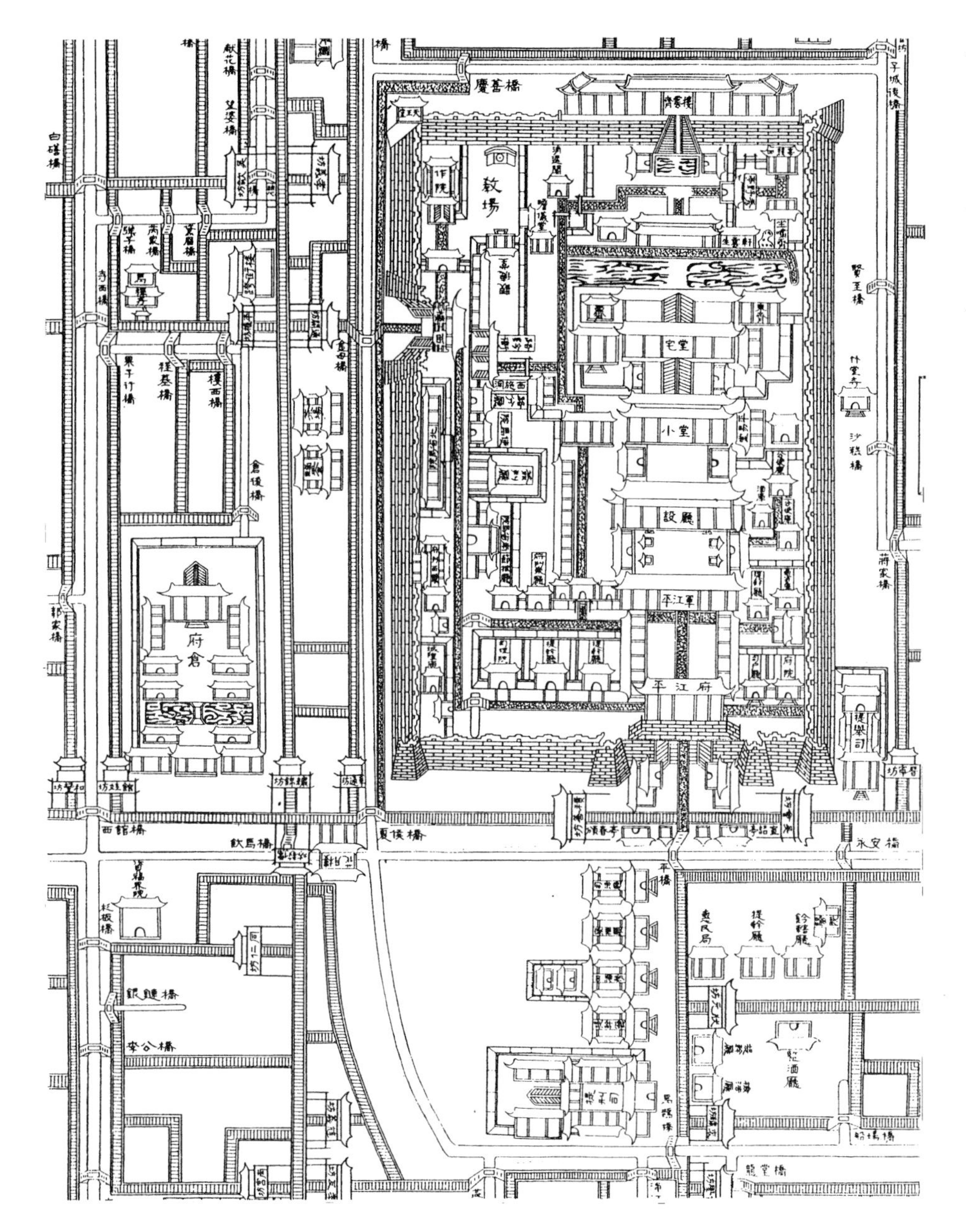

Figure 5.5 The inner walled enclosure housing the prefectural offices of Suzhou in the Southern Song. Adapted from the 1229 city map. On both sides of the axial street running southward from the main entrance of the enclosure are various departments of the prefectural government. The large compound on the west side of the enclosure is the prefectural storehouse.

Yet the grandeur of the inner enclosure of the city of Suzhou as a prefectural capital was remarkable, especially during the Southern Song period. In the early 1130s right after the Song court was driven to the Southeast, Emperor Gaozong (1107–1187) was about to visit Suzhou, known at that time as Pingjiang, and so ordered that palaces be built in the inner enclosure of the city, which had been overrun and seriously damaged by the Jurchen cavalry in 1130. The construction work was completed in 1133, and in the tenth month of the following year, the emperor came to reside in the newly constructed inner enclosure. This new structure may have been reserved as the temporary imperial palace (*xinggong*) for short stays of the emperor away from the capital, until the third month of 1137, when it was converted back to the prefectural government building complex by imperial edict.[53] Whereas the *de facto* administrative status of the city of Suzhou during the early years of the Southern Song may be a matter of dispute,[54] it is certain that at this time it was through the intervention of the central government that the city acquired its physical magnitude and possibly some of the imperial symbolic implications embodied in it, with which the emperor alone was entitled to be associated. This aspect can be seen clearly in Fan Chengda's statement that, since the main hall (*sheting*) of the inner enclosure was intended to function as the formal imperial court, the standard of its form was of the first class as an institution.[55] In other words, the local government did not have, and should not have had, the right to construct any more imposing office buildings, even though it may have had adequate manpower and financial means to do so, unless the construction work was fully endorsed by the emperor and the structures thus built were initially intended for the emperor's exclusive use.

This walled inner enclosure, grandiose as it was, remained the prefectural government building complex from 1137 up to the end of the Yuan in the 1360s. The local warlord Zhang Shicheng took the city as his capital and the inner enclosure as his palace in 1356; but in the face of his defeat by the Ming armies in 1367 after a ten-month siege, he had the inner enclosure burned down. All its structures were turned into ruins.[56] Consequently, the prefectural government office was relocated from the early Ming on a new site in the west part of the city, on the north side of present Daoqian Street, which had formerly been the site of offices of another government agency.

An ill-fated attempt was made in the early 1370s to revert the original site to prefectural government use. The prefect Wei Guan, discontented with the current prefectural government offices, including his official residence, which were cramped and ill-located in a low-lying and damp place, not unnaturally decided to rebuild them on the old site they had occupied throughout history. At the same time, he had an important city artery of water traffic called Jinfan Jing dredged.[57] A well-known poet, Gao Qi (1336–1374), wrote a eulogistic prose essay for the ceremony of "raising the ridge-pole" (*shangliangwen*)[58] on an auspicious day. This act, however, turned out to have been inauspicious indeed. Some colleagues of Wei Guan's surreptitiously reported to the imperial court, alleging that his resuming the site of the ruined palace and dredging the ditch (*fugong kaijing*) held seditious implications. The Hongwu emperor, Zhu Yuanzhang, sent a private watchdog, a censor named Zhang Du, to report on the activities in Suzhou. The charges were then documented that Wei Guan had, in the words recorded by Zhu Yunming (1461–1527), "raised the basis of the obliterated king, and dredged the river of the defeated state" (*xing miewang zhi ji, kai baiguo zhi he*).[59] This accusation led to the immediate arrest and execution of Wei Guan, Gao Qi, and another implicated poet, Wang Yi, in 1374. The killing of Gao Qi was extremely cruel: he was cut in half at the waist (*yaozhan*).[60]

The timing of Wei Guan's reconstruction of the prefectural offices on the site of the old inner enclosure was indeed awkward, especially happening as it did in Suzhou. Not only was it in the early years of Ming rule, when an act suspected of subversive or seditious implications, as Yang Xunji put it in the 1640s, "had to be of serious imperial concern, since [all between] the four seas [i.e., the world] had just begun to be stabilized;"[61] but the fierce resistance of Zhang Shicheng's men against the Ming besiegers of the city made the Hongwu emperor particularly resentful of the Suzhou region and all the more watchful of any signs of anti-Ming feelings. Mote has noted two possibilities in the mentality of the emperor at the moment when he received Zhang Du's report: either he really felt that there was treason afoot in Suzhou, or, violently suspicious of men of learning as he was in general, he reasoned that intimidation, by his swift action of making a terrifying example of his victims, could keep scholar-officials pliable and obedient.[62] Since the inner enclosure was occupied by Zhang Shicheng between 1356 and 1367 as one of his palaces, and Zhang himself at that time took the title of king and was thus the chief enemy of the Hongwu emperor, equating Wei Guan's act of resuming the old site with "reviving the basis of the obliterated" (*xing jimie zhi ji*),[63] though ringing sinisterly cynical to us, may easily have sounded convincing to the emperor.

There were also other interpretations inferred from this construction work, involving yet more remote legends and historic events, which must have aggravated the wrath of the emperor. According to Fan Chengda, there was a legend that the king of Wu used to sail for pleasure in a boat with brocade sails (*jinfan*) on the river that was later accordingly named Jinfan Jing (the water channel of brocade sails).[64] The dredging of this river by Wei Guan was conveniently associated with this legend, "dredging the river of the defeated state,"[65] and thus probably interpreted as betraying his presumed ambition of bidding for power as had the king of Wu. Moreover, Gao Qi in his *Shangliangwen* used the term *longpan huju* (like a coiling dragon and a crouching tiger),[66] to which the emperor must have been very sensitive. This term was immediately reminiscent of the terms used in the assessment of the topographical features of Nanjing attributed to Zhuge Liang (A.D. 181–234), the prime minister of the Shu Han state based in present-day Sichuan during the Three Kingdoms period:

> Mt. Zhong [looks like] a coiling dragon, Mt. Shitou [looks like] a crouching tiger. [Thus this site must be for] the palaces of emperors and kings.[67]

The term later became emblematic of Nanjing as an imperial capital.[68] Thus the use of this term by Gao Qi was probably seen not only as implying that the city of Suzhou was in geomantic terms rivaling Nanjing, which at that time was the imperial capital of the Ming, but also as expressing an ambition of those who were involved in the reconstruction work first to establish a separatist regime based on Suzhou against the Ming authority and later to bid for power over the whole of China in a similar manner to that of Sun Quan, the emperor of the Eastern Wu state, eleven centuries earlier.

To the Hongwu emperor, any such hints or inferences were simply intolerable, and extremely cruel execution was inevitably inflicted upon those who were implicated. It is true that the emperor soon discovered that he had made a great mistake about Wei Guan, one of his most able and devoted servants, and he made public admission of his error and ordered an honorable funeral and burial for him at state expense.[69] Yet the horror of this incident remained, and the site of the destroyed inner enclosure came under a tacit "taboo," as Yang Xunji wrote: "no one, no matter how humble his family was, ever dared to construct a building on it [the site of the old inner enclosure]."[70] Indeed, the city map (see Figure 4.4 earlier in Chapter 4) drawn in the late Ming period in the mid-seventeenth century clearly shows that the site was left entirely vacant. This situation must have lasted until as late as the early Qing, because Xu Song and Zhang Dachun also make a similar statement in their *Baicheng yanshui* published in 1690;[71] and on many of the city maps of the Qing in both the eighteenth and nineteenth centuries, the spot corresponding to the site is invariably marked with the words "disused site of the king's palace," although a few unimportant structures can be seen scattered on it, such as a small private school known as the Pingjiang Shuyuan at the end of the eighteenth century and a martial arts practice hall and a couple of small temples at the end of the nineteenth century.[72]

Could this inner walled enclosure, the most prominent feature in the city and ever more embellished by the reconstruction work in the 1130s, intended to accommodate Emperor Gaozong of the Southern Song during his temporary stays in Suzhou, have been restored after it was destroyed when Zhang Shicheng's army defending the city was finally overwhelmed by the Ming forces in 1367, if its resumption had not been pursued in so untimely a fashion in the first decade of the Ming rule? Such a possibility may have existed; but to conjecture which direction history could have taken, with or without this incident, is less important than to pay attention to the implications that the incident itself carries. The enterprise that Wei Guan undertook—rebuilding the prefectural offices and dredging a clogged artery of water traffic through the city, which we may see as a usual and reasonable act of a responsible official—was interpreted by the Hongwu emperor as a revelation of some seditious plot at work in Suzhou. This interpretation, basically reflecting the contemporary political situation, was nevertheless made entirely in symbolic terms deriving, either directly or indirectly, from both remote legends and recent historic events.

History gave the city, and of course the region it represented, its pride as much as its misfortunes. Every important structure in the inner enclosure, for example, is mentioned in length in the *Wujun zhi*,[73] as indeed in all other local gazetteers, with an account of its origin and reconstruction works and with a record of the deeds of the preceding scholar-officials and other historic events that were associated with it. Paradoxically, it was on the basis of similar sources that the lethal charges were brought against Wei Guan and Gao Qi. Yet more important, this symbolism[74] is not to be regarded simply as a set of rhetorical expressions of the political concerns of the emperor but rather as an integral part of the political and social reality. A reality as such was, as it still is, according to Kertzer, "in good part created through symbolic means;"[75] and creating a symbol or, more commonly, identifying oneself with a popular symbol, became a potent means of gaining and keeping power.

Whether this event is regarded as incidental or inevitable, it did happen; and its physical and psychological effects were far-reaching. Here it is worth reiterating the fact realized by most sinologists that Chinese cities did not play the same historic role as their counterparts in medieval Europe. They were not centers of political or personal freedoms, nor did they possess legal institutions that set them apart from their surrounding countryside. Civic consciousness, as opposed perhaps to a certain regional pride, did not develop among urban inhabitants. There were business centers in or around imperial Chinese cities, of course; and there was merchant influence on the cultural aspects of the urban world. Yet a peculiarly merchant culture did not develop in the cities, nor did the merchants form a powerful class that could seriously challenge the authority of the imperial government, because the cities were never communities of merchants at odds with an alien countryside and its rulers. The basic reason for the divergence between China and Europe was that the continuing existence of a unified imperial structure made independent urban development in China as impossible as the development of a true feudal political and military structure.[76] A regional or local city invariably acted as a political instrument of the state and was but a node in the web of the imperial field administration. Normal bureaucratic measures in curbing the possible concentration of local power, seen by the central authority as a potential source of political threat, included the rule of rapid turnover of incumbents and the rule of "avoidance," keeping an official from serving in his own or even a neighboring province; and the central government undoubtedly remained watchful of the activity and performance of its local agencies, especially those of the areas of political and economic importance.

Building activities were always taken by the Chinese as bearing strong social implications. Any structure in a city had to be located and built in accordance with its hierarchical position in the imperial system. Unless a structure was built with royal consent or, as in the case of the reconstruction of the government halls in the city of Suzhou in the 1130s, for the emperor's exclusive use, any act with a suspicion of transgression was prone to incur grave consequences. If the intervention in the early 1130s from the imperial court of the Southern Song in the rebuilding of the walled inner enclosure had proved to render it magnificent, the intervention this time from the Ming emperor effectively marked the end of any possible reuse of its site ever for the prefectural government offices. Thus even though the cruel conclusion of Wei Guan's attempt to rebuild the prefectural offices on the old site may be perceived as historically fortuitous because of the particular political conditions at that time and the violent and oversuspicious personality of the Hongwu emperor, there was always a tendency for interventions to various degrees from the central government, either in support or in suppression of the activities of its local officials, certainly including building activities. Thus, more strictly speaking, this incident, though taking place in the city and consequently having altered its physical features, did not really happen to the city of Suzhou itself so much as to the whole region of which the city was a symbol and node; and its result, extremely harsh as it was, did not entirely fall outside of the political, social, and cultural context of imperial China.

Partitioning of Urban Space

The removal of the inner walled enclosure and the general disuse of the central area of the city were, as Mote observes, the only large mark that history appears to have left on the physical city in all the centuries from the Southern Song, or even earlier, to the end of the Qing.[77] This, however, probably did not have as much immediate impact on the life of the ordinary people living in and around the city as some other changes might have had, such as blocking a city gate, redeveloping an old street, and dredging a section of the canal network, since this inner enclosure, imposing and centrally positioned as it had been, formerly stood exclusively as a prefectural government establishment that served to represent the prestige of the city and prefecture rather than as a focus of everyday urban activities.[78] Hence it is very unlikely that the inner enclosure ever helped to form any public open space around it that had multiple functions and could thus be identified as what we call the "city center" of many of its European counterparts.[79] Yet one of the long-term effects of the dislodgement of the inner enclosure was that it physically gave way to a new pattern of the partitioning of urban space that gradually came into being from the Ming period onward, which, as has been discussed in Chapter 3, was characterized by three nuclei: the gentry and official district in the southwest part of the city, where governmental and educational establishments were clustered; the business district centered around Chang Gate, northernmost in the west wall, and stretching in the suburbs west of that gate along the Grand Canal; and the district of family-based textile industry focused on the northeast part of the city.

Indeed, if the period from the late Tang to the Southern Song saw the process of transformation of urban space of Suzhou from the old system of the imposed division of the city into walled residential and market quarters into a much freer street plan in which shops and houses mingled together, it was during the Ming period that a concentration of different activities into different areas of the city started to be discernible. A comparison between the city map of the Southern Song and the city maps of the Ming and Qing seems to verify this assertion. Figure 5.6 shows that in 1229 the prefectural government enclosure stood slightly south of the geographical center of the city, its auxiliary offices outside its walls (especially on both sides of the axial route running from its main entrance southward). It also shows the positions of the prefectural school-temple (*fuxue*) and the imperial examination complex (*gongyuan*) of the prefecture, together with the *yamen* of Wu county in the northwest part of the city and of Changzhou county in the northeast. The disposition of these government offices in the Southern Song was already slightly skewed to the southwest of the city. Yet the diagrammatic plan of the city during the Ming and Qing periods, with important governmental establishments marked out in the same manner in Figure 5.7, indicates a notable tendency of further southwestward transference of the government offices at various levels. What exactly caused the concentration of these establishments in the southwest part of the city from the Ming onward is not yet clear, but it may have been facilitated by the removal of the inner enclosure at the beginning of the Ming, the spaciousness and picturesqueness of the southwest quarter of the city,[80] and the convenient access of the government offices to the two city gates in the southwest corner of the walls. It may even have been that the pull of the prefectural school-temple with its admired reputation and prestige[81] upon these governmental establishments also contributed to this process.

It is interesting to note that the state-run textile bureaus (*zhizaoju* and *zhiranju*) of Suzhou prefecture in the Ming and Qing, unlike those in the Yuan, were all located on the peripheries of the district of gentry and officials in the southwest but closer to the district of family-based textile industry in the northeast (see Figure 3.14). These bureaus functioned not only as the places for textile production but also as administrative centers in control of all local activities of this industry. During the Ming period, for example, every household engaged in spinning and weaving had to register itself with the bureaus; and during the Qing, these bureaus also took charge of extracting tax from every loom in family-based textile production.[82] Their special locations therefore seem to have indicated both the governmental nature of these establishments and their direct link with

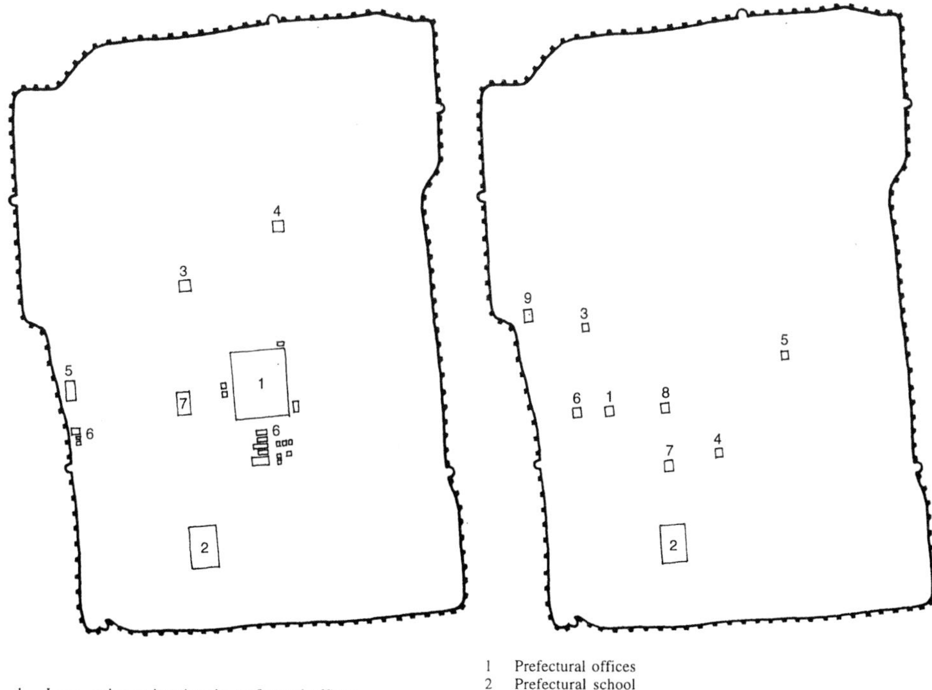

Figure 5.6 (left) The position of the important local government offices in the Southern Song.

Figure 5.7 (right) The position of the important local government offices in the Ming and Qing.

the district of family-based textile industry. An equally informative phenomenon is the location of the prefectural temple of Chenghuang. We understand that this cult provided a ritual link between the popular and the official state religions,[83] and thus represented the common interests of all sections of the city residents and, at least theoretically, the residents of the entire prefecture. Whether by coincidence or as an inevitable outcome of urban development, the prefectural temple of Chenghuang was located from 1370 onward[84] northwest of the junction of present-day Jingde Road and Renmin Road, a place close to all three districts, those of gentry and officials, trade and commerce, and family-based textile industry.

Little is known about how characteristic the urban features of the district of family-based textile industry were as compared to those of other parts of the city. A 1759 painting of the city, *Shengshi zisheng tu* (Scroll of the Flourishing Times)[85] by Xu Yang, however, offers us a rare opportunity to make a fleeting comparison between the architectural

Figure 5.8 *Section of the 1759 scroll* Shengshi zisheng tu *(1986, plate 52) depicting the area around the provincial examination office.*

traits of the business district and those of the gentry and official district. Figures 5.8 and 5.9 are sections of the scroll depicting, respectively, the area around the provincial examination office[86] and the quarter at the north fringe of the gentry and official district. These two pictures show that this district was characterized by the relatively high walls of the residential complexes, more spacious courtyards with gardens, plenty of plants, and the lack of firebreak walls (*fanghuoqiang*) to separate individual buildings attached to each other, suggesting that houses in this area were not as densely built as some in other parts of the city. The streets here appear more filled with people at leisure and with women and children than with busy brokers and salesmen; they are usually flanked by one-story shops that look to have been less ornate than ordinary houses and certainly much humbler than governmental buildings and temples. The shop signs announce those lines of specialized business that were closely associated with academic and official activities.

Figure 5.9 Section of the 1759 scroll Shengshi zisheng tu *(1986, plate 57) depicting the quarter around Shenya Qian Street.*

By contrast, the streets in the business district are much more bustling, as seen in Figure 5.10, containing a section of the scroll depicting Changmen Street at the heart of the business district within the city walls. Packed with traders, the street is flanked by splendid two-story shops catering to a much wider range of business. Firebreak walls were regularly used for separating shops or residential buildings from each other, this area being densely occupied with timber structures. Not surprisingly, fewer gardens and plants are found here than in the gentry and official district, probably because of high land values and the normal desire of traders to keep "nonessential" overheads down. Paradoxically, it was the shops in the vicinity of the gentry and official district but outside the city walls that bear most resemblance to those of Changmen Street. The shops presented in Figure 5.11 are situated to the north of Xu Gate against the outer foot of the city wall, facing the west city moat. This area, that is, along the west moat between Chang Gate and Xu Gate, which was simultaneously a section of the Grand Canal, was called Nanhao (the South Moat)[87] and became an interregional trade center from the mid-Ming onward. Most of the shops there were ornate two-story buildings separated by firebreak walls. They included a few restaurants, teahouses, pharmacies, silk and cloth stores, and bookstores. Figure 5.11 shows that this area also had a stationery shop, a musical instruments shop, a fortune-telling house, a store selling sundry goods from remote regions, and other specialized shops. Transactions of business are shown being briskly conducted inside and outside these shops, the moat functioning as a busy transport route. This section of the scroll vividly displays an atmospheric contrast between the two domains separated by the city wall: the tranquillity and lush green trees inside and the bustling and motley buildings, goods, shop signs, and traders outside.

Michael Marmé rightly points out that "the most striking embodiment of the early Ming prosperity was found outside the city gates, particularly the northwestern Chang Gate."[88] Indeed, the west suburbs extended from Chang Gate westward along the canals to Maple (Feng) Bridge and to Tiger Hill (Huqiu), and later around Xu Gate there were busy areas of trade and commerce in the late imperial era. Tang Yin (1470–1523), a famous poet and one of what were known as the "Four Painters of the Ming," describes the area around Chang Gate in his poem "Changmen jishi":

> Paradise in this world is Wuzhong [i.e., Suzhou],
> Wherein most remarkable is [the area around] Chang Gate.
> Thousands of emerald green sleeves are seen round and about the mansions,
> Millions of gold pieces are flowing along the canals running in east-west directions.
> Have the merchants and businessmen ever taken a break throughout the whole night,
> Who come from the four quarters [of the world] with utterly different dialects?[89]

Apart from the hyperbole natural to poetry, these stanzas do offer us some information about the extent to which the area outside Chang Gate had developed by the early sixteenth century.

Probably a more truthful assessment of this area was provided by Zheng Ruozeng (1505–1508), a native of Kunshan county who produced the *Jiangnan jinglüe*, a document published in 1568 on the defense of the Lower Yangzi region made necessary by the 1550s *wokou* (Japanese pirates) crisis. He writes:

> From Chang Gate to Feng Bridge is a distance of almost ten *li*. On both the north and south bank [of the canal] the residents are as close together as the teeth of a comb, especially on the south bank. None of the goods that are difficult to obtain in the four quarters [of the world] are not found here. Those who pass through are dazzled by its brilliance. Feng Bridge in particular is the spot where merchant ships converge. North of the upper reaches of the River [Yangzi] is where great trade in beans and grain and cotton assembles. It is here that all the

> guests [merchants] from north and south, rest their oars and cast off. . . . Nowhere under Heaven can match Suzhou in its abundance of money and goods, and nowhere in Suzhou can match the Chang Gate [area]. . . . One-tenth of what the pirates are hankering for is within the city walls, while nine-tenths is in this area [outside Chang Gate].[90]

The pressure from the Japanese pirates on the security of this west suburban area was so grave at that time that building another wall to enclose it was once debated. According to Cao Zishou, who was appointed magistrate of Wu county in 1559,

> From Xu Gate and Chang Gate sprawling westward are houses that become as closely lined up like the teeth of a comb as those within the city walls. Most residents in this area are sojourners. A few years ago when the pirates came, advisers [to the local government] suggested building another wall outside the city [in the

Figure 5.10 *Section of the 1759 scroll* Shengshi zisheng tu *(1986, plate 64) depicting Changmen Street.*

west suburbs]; it would be a partial one so that [its two ends] would be attached to the great city walls. But in the end it was not carried out at all.[91]

Cao's contemporary, a native of Changzhou county, Liu Feng (1517–1600), wrote an essay entitled *Changxi zhucheng lun*, discussing in what form the new wall for the west suburbs should be constructed if it really needed construction. Apparently more conscious of preserving the unimpeded accessibility of commercial traffic to the west moat on which, Liu believed, the prosperity and wealth of the region relied, he vigorously argues against the idea of building merely a partial wall, with its westernmost edge reaching Feng Bridge and its two eastern ends attached to the west wall of the city; instead, he suggests that, if people were worried about the defense problem, a completely separate circle of wall should be constructed to enclose the area stretching from Dingjia Alley, about seven hundred meters west of Chang Gate, westward to Feng Bridge, and northward to the whole Shantang. This new independent circle of wall and the old city walls

Figure 5.11 Section of the 1759 scroll Shengshi zisheng tu *(1986, plate 53) depicting the shops against the outer foot of the city walls north of Xu Gate.*

would, he declared, stand facing, protecting each other, and sandwich the strip of land along the west moat so that both could jointly function as a double deterrent to any infiltration into it.[92] Since Liu Feng's concern was only that of the strategic problems in the possible construction of the new wall, he did not propose in what exact form it should be. Nevertheless, from the diagrammatic map of the city of Suzhou and its west suburbs in Figure 5.12, we can see that it would have been a huge project had his proposal been pursued.

Whether because the expense that such a project would have incurred was too great for the local government to spare at that time or because the already significantly mitigated threat of the pirates to this region from the 1560s onward made the officials in charge believe that the project was no longer necessary, neither of the plans ever materialized. Yet it is important to note that, although the two plans were at obvious

variance with each other, as far as the urban form of Suzhou is concerned, there was an implicit agreement between them: the new wall was conceived to be either an auxiliary one "attached to" the old city walls or a totally separate one and was never considered to be an equal and integral part of the old city walls. The latter choice, which the scholar-officials did not consider, would have led to an effective alteration of the shape of the city, an end to the *raison d'être* of some of the urban features of utmost importance, and thus to the tarnishing of many accumulated historical meanings embedded in them, which were altogether indispensable for the city to be identified as the city of Suzhou. If the failure to pursue the building of a new wall to enclose and protect the west suburbs was largely attributable to the practical conditions at that specific time, did not the fact that the possibility of "rebuilding" the west wall of the city by extending it westward never came into the scholar-officials' minds reflect their profound respect, either con-

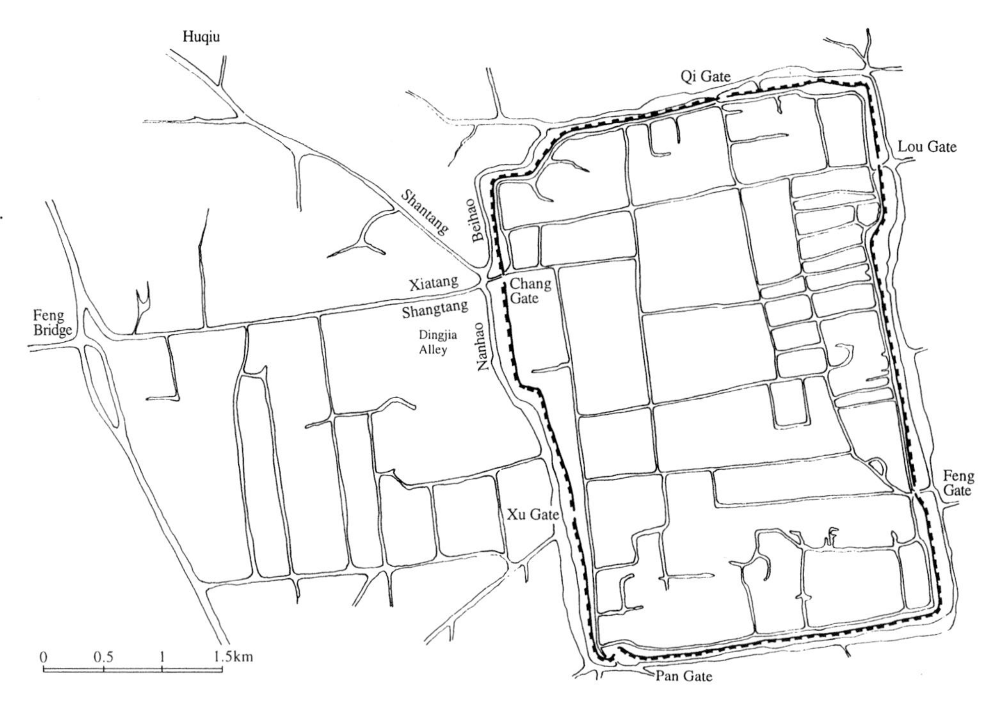

Figure 5.12 *Diagrammatic map of the city of Suzhou and its west suburbs showing the location of a proposed new wall surrounding the west suburbs as described by Liu Feng in the sixteenth century.*

scious or subconscious, for this long established "fixed institution" and their somewhat peculiar sense of history?

The lack of a defensive wall did not hamper the continuous economic centrality of the area outside Chang Gate during the Qing period; and the concentration of regional and interregional trade in this area led to the flourishing of many other lines of business. Elegant restaurants, hotels, teahouses, and the like, massed along the Grand Canal stretching from Chang Gate to Huqiu in the west.[93] Permanent theaters started to be established here from the 1720s or 1730s onward, and by the 1780s over twenty of them were regularly open to the public.[94] It is therefore not surprising that this area was regarded by Cao Xueqin (?–1763) as "uniquely the outstandingly wealthy and dissolute place of the mundane world [*hongchen*]."[95] The importance of the suburbs outside the city gates of Suzhou is epitomized by Shen Shouzhi's remarks. As a Wu county scholar of the late Qing, he records in detail in his *Jiechao biji* events of the fall of the city of Suzhou to the Taiping rebels in the fourth month of 1860. After describing how thoroughly the areas outside the city gates, especially Chang Gate, were plundered and destroyed *before* the city itself was seized, Shen writes in grief, "While the walled city did not fall, its quintessence was utterly annihilated."[96]

Urban Space and City Walls

The order to burn down the houses and shops in the west suburbs was issued by the local Qing official Xu Youren, who was at the time in charge of the defense of the city.

Whether this decision was really tricked out of him and then carried out by the rebel agents who pretended to have led the Qing reinforcements to Suzhou, as Shen Shouzhi claims, or whether it was made simply as an expedient, preemptive measure to destroy any possible shelter that the rebels might have been able to take during the possible siege, is not known. In any event, this act proved to have been a fatal blow to the prosperity of this area and hastened the shift of economic domination from Suzhou to Shanghai. However, the focus of this discussion is on the fact of the continued development of the suburbs west of Chang Gate as the "central" business district for over four centuries during the late imperial period, since it affords me an opportunity to make a further inquiry into the paradoxical phenomenon of the stability of the city form in time in the midst of urban expansion in space and into the relationship between the actuality of Suzhou's urban development and people's, especially the literati's, conception of what the city was or should be. Although the specific process of the development of the city of Suzhou from the mid-Tang onward does not speak for that of all cities in China, and undue sweeping generalization from this case should therefore be avoided, there is no doubt that some of its aspects are nevertheless informative of the tendencies common in Chinese urban history, particularly in that of the economically more advanced regions.

As discussed earlier, the character *cheng* traditionally meant both "city" and "city walls." In Zhou times, however, it was used much more often to indicate the fortifications themselves than what they enclosed. For the city, *guo* (state or city-state), *du* (state capital city), and *yi* (city or simply settlement) were the usual words, the first two of which seem to have more faithfully reflected the nature of the cities in the Eastern Zhou, in the sense that, as Wheatley states, "city and state were coeval" and "the city was the organizing principle of the state, and all generated cities were in their earlier phases city-states."[97] The fundamental political and social change accompanying the conquest of the rival states and the eventual powerfully centralized unification of China by the Qin in 221 B.C. brought to an end the *raison d'être* of the denotation of *guo* as "city-state" as well as *du* as any "city" other than the imperial capital: there came to be only one capital, the imperial one, which itself was not a state, and other cities were merely administrative centers at various levels governed by the central authority. It was the third character, *yi*, which had no connotation of "sovereign state," that continued down to this century to be applied to cities that housed the regional or local imperial government seats. This change is reflected, for example, in the opening passage of the "Chengchi" section in the *Wuxian zhi*, where the terms *mingdu wangyi* (the famous capital and the prestigious city) are used to refer to the city of Suzhou.[98] Here the first term *mingdu* implies the Wu capital, Helü Dacheng, in the late sixth century B.C., whereas the second term *wangyi* indicates the city in the imperial era.

The more accurate word for city, however, was undoubtedly *cheng*, although at times it was used in combination with *yi*, *guo* (outer city walls), or *chi* (city moats). In fact, the use of *cheng*, very often unambiguously denoting "city walls" during the pre-Qin and early imperial periods, later gradually came equally frequently to connote "city," a semantic adjustment abundantly evidenced in comparing the local gazetteers of Suzhou from the Song dynasty onward with those before that time.[99] The preponderant propriety of the application of the term *cheng* over the term *yi* to the city, which in the minds of the Chinese was invariably a center of a certain unit of field administration, lies in the fact that the walls denoted by the former from its origin were always the most basic element of such a city if it was to be regarded as a proper, comprehensive, and coherent institution; walls and local government offices were the two prerequisites of the city.[100] The walls did not mark out any legal distinction between the within and the without. As emphasized in Chapter 3, the city of Suzhou, like other cities in imperial China, did not evince the traits of cities in dual societies, a sociological model that is essentially Western. Such a city was instead what Mote calls "a very open institution,"[101] its residents having no legal or social status distinguishing them from rural residents and probably no sense of themselves as forming a cohesive and self-perpetuating urban group.

Although the city of Suzhou was not a corporate entity of its own but a part of a regional area that was largely rural, of which it was the node and symbol, the area that we regard as "urban" was substantially confined within the city boundaries demarcated by the city walls until perhaps as late as the end of the Yuan in the 1360s. In other words, the reality of the city as a local (and later regional) political and economic center was entirely consistent with the intrinsic meaning of the term *cheng*. From the mid-Ming onward, however, the process of "commerce spilling out of cities," the first sign of which may have appeared in Suzhou and other large cities in the late Tang,[102] dramatically quickened its pace. In the case of Suzhou, the pull of the Grand Canal geographically on commerce eventually resulted in the development of the prosperous west suburbs. At the same time, city systems in the Lower Yangzi region, as in other macroregional cores identified by Skinner, were now more mature and more fully fleshed out than those in the medieval era: capitals and market towns were better integrated into a single hierarchical system, and the total "urban" population was more evenly distributed throughout the hierarchy.[103]

Here we are confronted with two interesting but seemingly conflicting phenomena. Mote correctly points out that, in general, traditionally esteemed "Chinese values did not sustain a self-identifying and self-perpetuating urban elite as a component of the population."[104] Yet during the late imperial period there gradually appeared, as Johnson puts it, "important differences between urban and rural mentalities."[105] These differences were substantial only in the lower levels, while literati culture was probably much the same in country or city,[106] but they *did* nurture the rise of a sort of "urban identification" among certain groups of residents in and around capital cities and large market towns. This change is reflected in the development of certain social customs among urban residents in Suzhou, which were somewhat different, though not in kind, from those among rural residents. The description of the customs in the Southern Song by Fan Chengda in the "Fengsu" ("Folklore and Customs") section of his *Wujun zhi* is characterized by his accounts of those of the city, which show few if any differentiations from those of the countryside. This indicates that it was at that time the regional rather than urban-rural variation of customs that could be discerned. For Gu Lu, by contrast, urban residents' particular ways of behaving during the seasonal festivals in the Qing could be distinguished from those of their country fellows, although such distinctions were apparent only in some of the aspects of social conduct of the ordinary populace rather than in those of the literati and gentry.[107]

On the other hand, it was precisely during the same period that the spatial dichotomy of the urban and the rural, previously marked out by the city walls, became somewhat blurred, as many areas—numerous market towns and the busy suburbs of the city—were so densely populated and commercially activated that they could hardly be regarded as rural. The best example is the area west of Chang Gate and later the area west of Xu Gate, which were certainly no less "urban" than many areas within the city walls in the sense of the term as we use it nowadays. The nonrural traits of the west suburbs in the late imperial period were obviously acknowledged by contemporary scholars as well. In every local gazetteer compiled after the mid-Ming, these areas are referred to by their names, such as Jinchang, Shantang, Shangxiatang (that is, Shangtang and Xiatang), (see Figure 5.12) rather than by the term *jiao* (meaning "areas outside the city walls" and frequently applied to the much less remarked upon east suburbs), which emphasizes the state of being nonurban. What was urban was no longer physically separated by the city walls from what was rural, and the urban-rural continuum became more clearly manifested in space.

Those who saw themselves or were regarded by others as "urban" did not necessarily reside in the area enclosed by the city walls,[108] and their apparent advantage in wealth and sophistication over their country fellows was not gained *de jure* but provided by the competitive urban milieu—as much in the busy suburbs as in the city *per se*—in which luxury consumption, entertainment, improved access to education, economic specialization, opportunities for commercial ventures, and so forth, were more concentrated. In other words, it was the different way of daily life and the different type of social pressure in these areas, emerging along with what Rawski calls "a gradual and long-term trend toward the triumph of the market economy,"[109] rather than any different legal and social status, that forged this kind of urban identification. Thus, the two seemingly conflicting aspects described earlier were in fact merely two congruent sides of the process of urban development in the late imperial period, development which was stimulated by rapid growth of the economy over which, as Rawski notes, direct government controls were steadily more and more relaxed.[110]

This process paradoxically did not, and could not, substantially challenge the scholar-officials' orthodox view of the city, the persistence of which is reflected in the way the city is depicted in the Ming and Qing local gazetteers. Although their "Chengchi" (City Walls and Moats) section emphasizes, as its title signifies, the chronological record of the construction of the city walls and gates, their form, and their measurements, it nevertheless shows a tendency to associate the walls with what they enclosed, a tradition probably started in the Northern Song by Zhu Changwen in his *Wujun Tujing xuji*.[111] This is particularly evidenced in the opening passage of the section in question, where the characteristics of the city's spatial organization, the internal transport system, residential quarters, and bridges are eulogized. On the other hand, the description of the bustling west suburbs is invariably set out in the "Fengsu" (Folklore and Customs) section. For the traditionally minded scholar-officials, and probably also for the populace at large, no matter how densely these areas were populated, how prosperous they became, and how essential the business conducted there was to the city, to the prefecture, and even to the whole nation, they could only be regarded as part of the "local customs" that, compared to those "fixed institutions"—the city walls undoubtedly being one of them (see Chapter 2)—were always transient and thus prone to change.

In the case of Suzhou, our first impression would be that the ideal conception of a city held particularly by scholar-officials in the late imperial period, that is, the area enclosed and represented by the city walls, somewhat diverged from, or lost touch with, the reality of urban development in their times. Yet a closer look at the issue reveals something different. Rawski has summarized a consensus reached by most modern scholars of China "that Chinese society underwent significant changes in the course of the Ming dynasty, changes that produced the political, social, and economic institutions of late imperial China."[112] However, the fundamental imperial ideology and government system persisted; so did the political and social function of regional and local cities as administrative centers. Such a city itself was, as before, not a judicial entity but a symbol and node of the territory of which it was a part, and it was the city walls that physically manifested this symbol in the most conspicuous and meaningful way. In this sense, the topic of the "city" for the authors of local gazetteers was to some extent equivalent to the topic of the institution, history, culture, government, and social order, all of which were symbolized by the city walls.

The more or less notional separation of what we may now see as real urban nature from the limited definition of the city walls during the Ming and Qing periods suggests a greater detachment of their symbolic meanings from their practical functions under the new, specific economic and social circumstances. This resulted in a more conspicuous projection of the symbolism of the city walls; the early stage of this process coincided with "the great age of Chinese wall building" in the first half of the Ming, the true significance of which lies in "the primarily psychological function of reaffirming the presence of the Chinese state" and the reestablishment of proper social order after a century of Mongol rule.[113] Thus, the apparent discrepancy between the scholar-officials' accounts preoccupied with the city and the actual distribution of urban activity and development should therefore be interpreted more as their consistency with the persisting institution of the imperial city system than as any unrealism of conception on their part. By the same token, the paradoxical phenomenon (in many cases) of the remarkable stability of the city form in time in the course of tremendous urban expansion in space may be seen as having been brought about by the distinctive nature of imperial Chinese cities, the characteristic urban-rural relationship, and the symbolic significance of the city walls in society.

Conclusion

In discussing some of the distinctive qualities of Chinese cities, Mote states that "there were no zones of uniform land use" except for small cities that, incapable of supporting a proliferation of commercial activities, had one "main street" or "city center."[114] This assertion would hold only if its application were to be restricted to the cities that had already experienced the fundamental change characteristic of the medieval urban revolution that occurred from the mid-Tang to the Northern Song periods.[115] In the city of Suzhou, as in many other Chinese cities, a sort of "zoning" system must have existed at least until the mid-Tang. The city was divided into residential wards, market quarters, and enceintes exclusively occupied by local government offices, each being enclosed by walls and separated by streets and canals. This division was largely a legacy of the normative principles of city planning in Zhou times, when it evinced as much a ritual nature as its pragmatic function of city residence control. This system most probably reached its maturity in Suzhou by the mid-Tang, after centuries of development in continuous coordination with the gradual establishment of the extensive, geometrically regulated street and canal network, which remained one of the most salient features of the city. It was from the late Tang onward that the city witnessed the beginning of the collapse of this system of rigid urban space division. The effects of this change between the late Tang and the early Southern Song periods were far-reaching indeed, including the replacement of the enclosed marketplaces and the walled residential wards by the free street plan in which shops could be opened anywhere within the city, and signs of the gradual growth of commercial suburbs outside the city gates, especially the areas west of Chang Gate.

What continued to be separated spatially from the rest of the city during the Southern Song and Yuan periods was the inner walled enclosure, the prefectural government offices and the prefect's official residence. If the disappearance of the enclosed marketplaces and the walled residential wards was part of the general process of urban transformation happening in what Skinner regards as "the core areas of the Lower Yangtze,"[116] the removal of this inner enclosure at the beginning of the Ming seems to have been the outcome of specific events taking place in Suzhou alone, events that were nevertheless not at all peculiar to the nature of the cities intrinsically formed in the political and social context of imperial China. Moreover, the replacement of the enclosed marketplaces and walled residential wards seems to have had a profound and all-encompassing impact on urban life and the characteristics of the spatial structure of the city, whereas the removal of the inner walled enclosure did not lead to any significant rearrangement of urban space except that it perhaps indirectly facilitated the concentration of government offices at various levels in the southwest part of the city, which I identify as the district of gentry and officials. Along with the formation of this district came the development of the business district in the northwest around (both inside and outside) Chang Gate and the district of family-based textile industry in the northeast, which formed the basic pattern for partitioning urban space of the city of Suzhou throughout the late imperial period. These three districts were not separated either physically or legally but distinguished in the main by the respective professions of their inhabitants and by the different dominating, but never exclusive, daily activities conducted in them.

The most prominent aspect of this characteristic pattern for partitioning urban space of Suzhou was probably the extensive development of the area outside Chang Gate in the west wall, along the Grand Canal and the outer city moat, which I call the west suburbs. As the area of commercial and banking concentration for over four centuries until 1860, from the mid-Ming it became more of a *de facto* center of interregional trade than the center of business of the city itself. Whereas the concept of "suburbs" in Europe dates back to ancient Rome, it hardly became, except for a few cases, a widely perceived phenomenon before the Industrial Revolution, not only in the sense of being "close to urbs," as the Latin origin of the word (*suburbium*) implies,[117] but also as a spill-out area of the city. The situation in China was markedly different: the burgeoning suburbs as important areas of local, regional, or even interregional trade, from as early as the Northern Song onward, constituted a common feature of all large, and probably many middle-size, cities in the economically advanced regions.

It should be noted that the term *suburb* used here may be somewhat misleading if its Western concept were to be rigidly applied to the Chinese state of affairs. H. J. Dyos, in his studies of Victorian suburbs of London, defines the suburb as "in essence, . . . a decentralized part of a city with which it is inseparably linked by certain economic and social ties."[118] Thus, a modern suburb "is essentially in a dependent relationship to the whole organism of the city, and the complete suburban area of a city performs only part of its total functions."[119] Suburbs in imperial China seem to have shared most of these general traits of a modern suburb, except an important one. The west suburbs of Suzhou, for instance, undoubtedly hinged on the city but developed into a locus of interregional trade and business, were certainly more "central" in economic terms and more bustling in daily life, and thus were more "urban," than most areas within the city walls. Consequently, they were not so much a place containing some facilities for the use of leisure or having "a meaning which was little less than idyllic,"[120] as they were a highly competitive environment where "every inch of land was worth a thousand taels of gold."[121] Nor were they always the places where city residents "could breathe purer suburban air and drink cleaner water";[122] the congestion of shops, warehouses, cotton mills, dye houses, restaurants, teahouses, and other establishments inevitably made these areas more vulnerable to pollution. An official proclamation inscribed on a stele in 1737 tells us, for instance, that the river in front of Huqiu was contaminated by the dye houses, and the contamination was concentrated to such extent by them that its water was utterly multicolored, which prompted the prefectural government to issue an order prohibiting the establishment of any dye house in that area.[123]

A tentative explanation for this probably unique phenomenon in China's urban history has been made. I have repeatedly emphasized in the preceding and present chapters that Chinese cities in the imperial era did not show the traits of the urban-rural dichotomy prevalent in premodern Europe. A city did not form a unity or a world of its own but served the interests of the state. It was not legally separated from its surrounding countryside; nor did it need to boast, as its medieval European counterparts could, "that the majority of its members were free citizens,"[124] because the basic political, social, and cultural cleavages in China, as Skinner notes, were those of class and occupation and of region, not those between cities and their hinterlands.[125] Both the city residents and their country fellows of the same social class were, in principle, "working side by side on a parity." In political, social, and cultural terms, a city in late imperial China was, both psychologically and practically, largely an open institution. Urban components, as long as they were not closely associated with the administration of the imperial government, did not have to be bounded by the city walls. It is therefore very possible that the nature of China's cities and the distinctive urban-rural continuum, both fundamentally determined by the continuing existence of a unified imperial structure, produced a necessary, though not a sufficient,[126] condition for the wide occurrence of this phenomenon in China. It is also probable that the persistence of this nature of the cities in the late imperial period, together with the prominence of the symbolic traits of the city walls, comes to account for the scholar-officials' speciously unrealistic but actually logical insistence on perceiving the city only as something enclosed by the city walls.

CHAPTER 6 Courtyard and Public Urban Space

APART FROM THE CITY WALLS, MOATS, AND GATES, the city was made up of buildings, and the texture of urban space was determined principally by the spatial pattern of individual buildings and building complexes and by the mode in which they formed an integral whole. Our concern with the development of urban form and space of the city of Suzhou therefore does not allow us to ignore them. Numerous works have been produced both in China and in the West on various topics, such as the history of building technology; general features of Chinese architecture; vernacular architecture; individual palace, temple, and residential buildings (or building complexes); architectural details; and social content of building patterns, each constituting a gigantic task in itself. This chapter does not concern these subjects in any comprehensive way, given the serious limitations of space and time that the present research scope imposes and the vastness of these subjects. Instead, it focuses on two issues that seem most pertinent to the subject of this book, the first being the relationship between form types and social functions in Chinese architecture, which constitutes one of the premises for an appropriate way of interpreting architectural features in the city of Suzhou and in other imperial Chinese cities, and second being the significance of the ubiquitous use of the courtyard as the principal form of spatial arrangement in the city (and in all other kinds of Chinese human settlements), with special attention paid to the courtyard of the renowned Daoist temple Xuanmiao Guan as a public urban space.

Form Types and Social Functions in Chinese Architecture

A marked disagreement can be found among scholars of traditional China on whether there existed distinctions of architectural forms between Chinese cities and the countryside. In support of his own persuasive argument for the distinctive urban-rural relationship in China, Mote insists that, in the essentials of design, in building materials used, and in style and ornamentation,

> Chinese urban structures were indistinguishable from rural structures. There is in traditional Chinese architecture no such thing as a "town house" style, a "country church" style, or a "city office" style. The Chinese city did not force structures up into the air like the four- and six-story burghers' houses in old European cities or the tenements of ancient Rome. Nor did the pressure on space gradually remove from the city its courtyards and gardens as it tended to in Renaissance and modern Europe.[1]

These characteristics, Mote argues, were among other aspects of Chinese life evidence of an urban-rural continuum. Skinner, cautioning against neglecting the possibility of a cultural role for China's cities, has his doubts about this kind of statement being entirely true:

> On the more prosaic level of architectural forms, Chinese cities did have their distinctive edifices: the drum tower and bell tower, the great examination hall, and the elaborate towers at the corners and gates of the city wall.[2]

It should not be too difficult to find both statements valid if one takes each particular angle from which the two scholars tackle the issue. Yet the architecture in most premodern societies shows that conspicuous differences in building form are found among the buildings of different social institutions—religious versus secular and public versus private—and between urban and rural structures. In this sense, if we consider this issue from the point of view of the relationship between building forms and types, and their self-contained social functions, the two conflicting arguments will, *pace* Mote and Skinner, turn out to be confusing, if not entirely misleading, in the context of traditional Chinese culture. As I will try to elucidate in the following pages, this is because major differences in Chinese architectural form and style did not lie either in the urban-rural dichotomy or, more importantly, in the differentiation of social institutions. In principle, they did not even reside in the positions of various institutions in the social hierarchy, which were reflected mainly in the modes of ornamentation and the sizes of the structures.

Form and Function

Of the many possible approaches to studying traditional Chinese architecture, the one that prevails in the twentieth century is to classify buildings according to social function. In many contemporary works on Chinese architectural history,[3] we find such common categories as palace buildings, temple buildings (subclassified into those for ancestral worship, state religion, Buddhism, Daoism, and popular cults), residential buildings, garden buildings, and tomb buildings. This approach seems convenient when the works are focused on introducing a series of individual structures scattered in space and time. At the same time, however, it evinces its obvious weakness and fundamental ambiguity.[4] For example, in one of the contemporary works that classifies Chinese buildings into such categories, it is stated that "in general, [the form of] a Buddhist temple building or building compound was nothing but a reproduction of that of a palace or residential building," and "the plan, form, and structure of Daoist temple buildings were basically the same as those of Buddhist temple buildings, except for their lack of pagodas."[5]

The development of this approach in China is much less the outcome of the reflections of modern scholars on Chinese architecture than the uncritical application of Western scholarship. It probably even bears some marks of the creed of Functionalism[6] originating in the late nineteenth century and prevalent in the 1920s, a line of reasoning that hardly corresponds to reality. In his investigation of the meaning of the relationship between the singularity of form and the multiplicity of functions, Aldo Rossi, who calls this creed "naive functionalism," insists that "any explanation of urban artifacts in terms of function must be rejected if the issue is to elucidate their structure and formation."[7] To illustrate his points, he carefully selected a number of large, important urban artifacts in Europe, whose function has changed over time or for which a specific function does not even exist.[8] Yet if we use the word *function* in its broader sense, that is, if we extend it from the pragmatic realm to include ideas and symbols, there should be no doubt that differentiation by social functions of building types that are physically associated with distinctive structural, constructional, spatial, and ornamental forms and styles has been part of the European tradition not only in architectural discourse but also in practice from as early as the Classical period onward. On the theoretical side, Leon Battista Alberti's (1404–1472) formulation seems representative. He advocates in about the mid-fifteenth century in his *De re aedificatoria*, the first book on architecture in Europe since the Augustan architect Vitruvius' *De architectura*, that each of the different parts of the state "should be designated a different type of building." For him, building should first be divided into public and private, with private buildings for the higher members of society being distinguished from those for the lower members; then both public and private should be further subdivided into sacred and profane.[9] On the practical side, even to an unpracticed eye, substantial differences in architectural form are manifest in, for example, Greek temples and domestic buildings, Roman basilicas and baths, and Gothic cathedrals and medieval tenements.

Chinese experience in this field was markedly distinguishable from that of Europe. If the concept of classification according to function, as Rossi argues in the narrow sense of the phrase,[10] is far too superficial in the studies of the premodern Western architecture, it should be regarded as profoundly misleading in the studies of Chinese architecture when issues concerning the structure and formation of buildings or building complexes are to be pursued. By the same token, if in many a European city, one has to be "struck" by the multiplicity of functions that a large building can contain over time and how the functions are entirely independent of the form,[11] this kind of phenomenon, on the contrary, must always have been a taken-for-granted matter in traditional China. Whereas the most marked formal difference is found indeed between the religious and secular structures, and, perhaps to a lesser degree, between the public and private buildings, in premodern Europe and probably in most parts of the world, it was precisely in these areas that there was never any disjunction and dividing line in traditional Chinese (and perhaps also East Asian) architecture. In Suzhou, as in any other area of China, frequent conversion of buildings for different uses, including houses, temples, and government offices, is abundantly evident in the local records and thus must have been a common practice.[12]

The Sacred and the Profane in Chinese Architecture

In this ambiguity, one may certainly see what Needham calls "an outward and visible sign of the fundamental organic and integrated quality of Chinese thought and feeling."[13] Any fruitful inquiry into the *cultural* reasons for it would constitute a special and weighty task, and inevitably call for a series of coordinated studies of the imperial ideology, social psychology, nature of popular beliefs, and so forth. Although I am unable to pursue such a comprehensive task in the present research, it is still worth spending a few words on one important aspect of the issue, that being the problem concerning the characteristic indistinctiveness of building types and forms of the sacred and the profane. In the eyes of Needham, who sees some relation between monumentality in stone and the influence of mystical religion,

> The Chinese mood was essentially secular, loving life and Nature. Hence the gods had to conform, to sit and be worshipped in buildings identical with the halls of families and palaces, or not to be worshipped at all.[14]

One may have to be more cautious about using the word "secular" to define the dominant Chinese attitude toward life, because there is in it a suspicion of applying to the Chinese world the model of the religious-secular dichotomy that has long been adopted in Western scholarship. Nevertheless, even though Needham suggests this only in passing, when he discusses the reasons for the Chinese choice of building materials, the direction he takes is right.

I would take it a step further and argue that the particular traditional Chinese cosmology and world view, a comprehension of which is essential for understanding the range of Chinese culture, should be regarded as the main source of this distinctive property of Chinese architecture. As discussed in Chapter 2, the Chinese, at least among all *traditional* peoples, were apparently unique in having no creation myth;[15] that is, the world and man were regarded as uncreated; they constituted the central features of a spontaneously self-generating cosmos that had no creator, god, ultimate cause, or will external to itself. Consequently, whatever spiritual beings or spiritual forces the Chinese acknowledged and venerated, the limitations imposed by that all-encompassing cosmology were such that no spirit or god could be dignified above all others as something external to the cosmos.[16] Spirits and gods were then regarded as having the same qualities and as being subject to the same processes as all other aspects (including human beings) of Nature; in other words, man and god were equally part of the cosmos. Since the cosmic position of gods was basically the same as, if, indeed, not lower than, that of human beings,[17] there was then no point for an architectonic structure accommodating man to be conceived and constructed differently from a building for the gods.

As for the relationship between the human and the divine, the views representative of the literati's can be found in the *Zuo zhuan*, where it is asserted on several occasions that the people are the masters (*zhu*) of the gods (*shen*) in the sense that the gods' temperament varies in correspondence with the conditions of the people, and thus to promote the people's achievements means simultaneously to be reverent to the gods. Hence even "the sage king first helped the people to make achievements, then offered sacrifices to the gods afterwards."[18] In every aspect of social life, gods were not necessarily given priority of attention by intellectuals and scholar-officials,[19] who as a social group formed the major force in perpetuating a civilization that we now recognize as Chinese. The gods' worldly dwelling may, in a sense, be interpreted as at the mercy of the humans, since they effectively lodged under the human roof. It is very possible, then, that in the Chinese world, the primarily immanent qualities of the divine, the dominance of Confucian humanistic values, and the overwhelmingly worldly concerns may have been three of the main factors that made unnecessary any attempt to build a sacred structure in any specific form that could be sharply differentiated from that of domestic buildings.

Technically, however, Chinese buildings and building complexes were ever ready to cater to as many functions as possible. This high adaptability of the Chinese buildings was inherent in the principles of their structural composition and spatial arrangement. In spite of early knowledge of arch and vault, masonry and brickwork were always confined to terraces, defensive works, walls, tombs, and pagodas;[20] no Chinese house could be a proper dwelling for the living, or a proper place of worship for the gods, unless it were built in wood and roofed with tile.[21] The most typical Chinese building was a rectangular hall on an elevated platform, with its wooden columns joined together in a complex trabeate system, and its walls always curtain walls rather than bearing walls in the support of the structure. Consequently, such a timber frame and the screen walls not only provided large spans, compact supports, maximal unobstructed space, standardization of planning and construction, and flexibility of use but made it possible to expand the basic ground plan in all directions.

Among these traits of Chinese buildings, the standardization of planning and construction needs the most emphasis. In terms of structure, all measurements of a building were derived as multiples of a particular proportion, that is, the cross-section of the horizontal corbel bracket arm (*gong*) in the Song, or the width of the mortise of the bracket (*doukou*) in the Qing, which functioned as a standard module.[22] In individual buildings, the fundamental, repeating unit of space, keyed to the size and scale of human beings, was the *jian*, or bay—the pillar interval—which was manipulated at will to give shape to all buildings and the size of which was predetermined by the standard module.[23] For groups of buildings, the repeating unit of space was the courtyard (*ting*, *yuan*, or *tingyuan*), its measurements being closely associated with those of the buildings adjacent to it, which in principle were arranged, by repetition, to compose, sometimes in a very complex way, a walled compound. The courtyard and gardens, if any, were always an integral part of the building compound rather than something additional and separate. One of the major technical outcomes of these principles of construction was the markedly high adaptability of such structures to diverse uses: since the weight of the roof and structural beams was not supported by the walls, complete freedom was attained for placing doors and windows and a building could be remodeled and, as happened more often, its internal space could be rearranged at will to suit particular purposes without any danger of collapse.

Building Compounds and Social Institutions

Yet it would be wrong to say that all Chinese buildings were uniform and that no differentiation was made with regard to form types in Chinese architecture. Individual buildings that we regard as indigenous Chinese ones[24] were traditionally categorized according to three intertwined criteria: form, location (or sometimes position), and function. Thus in many written works on architectonic structures and building techniques produced in the imperial era, such as the *Yingzao fashi*, *Yuan ye*, and the "Kaogong" section of the *Gujin tushu jicheng*, we are frequently confronted with over a dozen types of buildings,[25] four of which appear most distinguishable to us[26] in terms of their forms: main halls (*dian*, *tang*, and *ting*);[27] halls of two or more stories (*lou* and *ge*);[28] pavilions (*ting*); and galleries or free-standing corridors (*lang*). The spatial functions and patterns of daily use of these structures obviously varied significantly; so did their physical forms, although they were built under the same principle of construction.

However, each of these buildings, apart from a few exceptional cases,[29] did not stand alone as a self-assertive structure independent of other structures but was considered a part of a building compound designated for a certain social establishment,[30] whether it be a palace, a local government office, a school, a house, or a temple. In other words, an individual building, although distinguishable in form from others, should not be perceived as an entity of its own if that means that it is to be taken as a particular structure that in itself exclusively served the purposes, and was thus a physical embodiment, of a particular social institution. Instead, an individual building should be seen as an integral element of a larger composition in which it performed its functions in harmony with other elements. Suppose a building compound was destroyed by fire or in a war and only the main hall survived; this remaining structure would have lost all its practical and social meanings unless some other elements were reconstructed to form a new walled compound of which the hall once again formed a part.

Thus, in terms of social functions, architectural, and especially spatial, integrity existed less in each of the individual structures than in an identifiable group of buildings enclosed by walls. An individual structure was meaningful only if it existed and played its distinctive role in relation to others. Various social establishments—palaces, government offices, temples, schools, and houses—were lodged in such compounds, which resembled each other and were characterized by their elasticity and flexibility of use. That building forms and types should be closely associated with social institutions is basically a European concept; thus the church had its distinctive Christian structures; the municipal government had its town halls; and economically less advantaged citizens had their tenement houses. But it was precisely this kind of formal bond between building types and social institutions that traditional Chinese society lacked.

Building compounds of different social institutions in the built environments of traditional China were of course by no means visually monotonous and indistinguishable. A Chinese person (either a local or a visitor) would usually have no difficulty in telling at first glance whether a compound was a *yamen*, a temple, a house, or a prefectural school. Yet such differentiation in general was not made on the basis of its building form and type. It is true that there were some important formal features of the building compound that functioned as overt indicators of the social rank of the particular institution that it housed, the most notable ones being its magnitude and the form of the roofs of its individual buildings.[31] Every institution was hierarchically positioned in society, this hierarchy being manifested in many features of its buildings. The formal standard of a *yamen* building, for instance, was usually higher than that of many houses of ordinary people and thus could easily be identified. Yet since a certain range of institutions would be designated to the same hierarchical position, there would be little difference between the magnitude and the form of the roofs of the individual buildings of a *yamen* and those of a compound in which an official of a high rank resided or of a large Buddhist or Daoist temple. Thus the basic differences in building form in a certain subcultural region[32] were those of social hierarchy, not those between diverse social institutions.[33]

In very few instances, some slight but symbolically significant changes in the layout of a specific compound of a certain social institution *did* contribute to its distinctiveness;[34] but for the majority of the cases, it was the distinctive mode of ornamentation and arrangement of symbolic objects applied to the compound and the disposition of the particular apparatus pertaining to the social functions of that institution that rendered it visually distinguishable from the compounds of other institutions. To enumerate and analyze comprehensively various conventional modes of these "sublevel" architectural arrangements that helped to reveal the social functions of different building compounds is an important task but falls beyond the scope of the present topic. Suffice it here to mention two conspicuous examples in the Qing dynasty Suzhou. A Buddhist or Daoist temple was most notable for its yellow-painted walls, arched gates at its main entrance (*shanmen*, especially of a large temple), peculiar shapes of some of its windows, and disposition of incense burners and other utensils in its courtyard. From a picture of the Buddhist temple at the foot of Tiger Hill (Huqiu), which is adapted in Figure 6.1 from a section of the 1759 scroll, we can clearly see at least the first three of these features. Figure 6.2 contains another section of the scroll, depicting the compound of the

Figure 6.1 Section of the 1759 scroll Shengshi zisheng tu *(1986, plate 80) depicting the Buddhist temple on Tiger Hill.*

provincial government offices of Jiangsu. As in the case of other local *yamen*, it was characterized by the palings and wooden gates (*yuanmen*) demarcating a prohibited area on the front street; the two pavilions (*chuiguting*) on both sides of the main entrance, where the brass players would perform on ceremonial occasions; and the double flagstaffs flying the banners as part of the insignia of the local authority, on which the appellation of the *yamen* was printed.[35] It was also the atmosphere created by people's activities in and around the compound, linking closely to the social performances of the institution lodged in it, that profoundly reinforced such differentiation.[36]

Urban-Rural Continuum

How should we perceive and interpret traditional Chinese urban buildings and their architectural forms in relation to rural ones? If we insist on the existence of distinctive architectonic structures in Chinese cities, the few examples given by Skinner seem, *prima facie*, to constitute convincing evidence in support of this view. The towers at the corners and gates of the city wall, for instance, when perceived *together with* the walls on which they were standing, could be regarded as distinctive city structures. This is indeed suggested by their Chinese names: *jiaolou* (halls of [usually] two stories at the corners [of the city wall]) and *chenglou* (halls of [usually] two stories at [the gates of] the city wall) or, more accurately, *chengmenlou* (halls of [usually] two stories at the gates of the city wall).[37] Since the character *cheng* was, especially in the second half of the imperial era, an exclusive word for both city walls and cities, buildings called by these names could not be anywhere but on top of the city walls. Paradoxically, however, these Chinese words at the same time imply that each of these structures was perceived less as an integrated whole than as two separate entities—the *cheng* and the *lou*—combined together, which faithfully corresponded to these structures' architectural features. The one- or two-story hall as a part of such a structure was, in terms of building form and style, basically not at all different from those on the ground, existing in various compounds located both within and without the city walls;[38] rather, it was the city wall, standing, and therefore being perceived, as a complete, self-assertive artifact,[39] that rendered them distinct from rural structures.

This argument can be applied to some extent to the drum and bell towers that are found in so many cities in traditional China, although, as independent structures built *ab ovo*, they were absent in the city of Suzhou.[40] A structure of this kind was again the combination of two elements: a multistory (usually two-story) hall and a high raised,

Figure 6.2 *Section of the 1759 scroll* Shengshi zisheng tu *(1986, plate 56) depicting the compound of the provincial government offices and its front street.*

solidly constructed platform on which the hall stood. Their Chinese names, *gulou* (a multistory hall with a drum in it) and *zhonglou* (a multistory hall with a bell), do not signify the separation of the halls from the platforms nor the combination of the two but in essence have derived from and therefore denote the *lou* only, which, in form, style, and materials used, were not different from any other halls. On the other hand, the platforms that elevated the halls, by the same criteria, resembled city walls, and this resemblance was probably the crucial feature that entitled the drum and bell tower to be urban structures. To put it in another way, whether these halls were to be regarded as peculiar structures of the city was not physically determined by their own architectural forms but by the construction of the city-wall-like platforms on which they assumed their functions and from which they acquired their very name "the drum and bell towers."[41] In this sense, the specific cases of using the gate towers as drum towers by the city of Suzhou were entirely consistent with the architectural reality in traditional China. After all, the city walls were the one and only distinctive *type* of architectonic structure that, in name and in fact, symbolized the presence of government and defined cities as places where the government was centered, separate from the open countryside.

As for the examination hall, invariably located in the city, it seems more obvious that this hall was hardly at variance in architectural form and style with the halls of other social functions. From the section of the 1759 scroll presented in Figure 5.8, depicting the quarter of the city of Suzhou around the provincial examination compound, we can see that the examination halls were indistinguishable in general from the buildings along the street outside their compound, although the examination halls appear to be larger and taller than the buildings near by. Even the fact that these particular halls were elongated structures composed of more bays than ordinary ones was not a unique feature: many large private schools located in either urban or rural areas had, in their compounds, structures sharing the same characteristics. As I have acknowledged earlier, all the examples cited by Skinner, especially the drum and bell towers and the towers at the corners and gates of the city wall, were indeed edifices of the city. They facilitated the function of the city and together reflected its nature. Yet as architectural objects, they did not in their form and style represent the city; it would be more true to see this relationship conversely: it was the city, symbolized eminently by its walls, that gave rise to their distinctiveness in name and function. The characteristic property of Chinese architecture in lacking any formal bond between building types and social institutions, fundamentally made impossible and unnecessary the manifestation of any cultural role for China's cities, no matter how significant it was, in the uniqueness of their building forms and styles.

This last argument is crucial for clarifying a possibly problematic line of reasoning revealed in Mote's statement introduced at the beginning of this section. It should be stressed that my slight doubt does not concern the scholar's essential point that a distinctive urban-rural continuum existed in traditional China, nor does it concern the objectivity of his valid observation that the forms and styles of Chinese urban and rural buildings were indistinguishable, which, in general, truly corresponds to the real picture of the architectural landscape of traditional China. Instead, it emerges from the question of whether one could use this observation, though correct in itself, as a piece of evidence on which, to paraphrase Mote, rests the case for the Chinese urban-rural relationship; that is, from the validity of such a statement, expressed also by Mote as "the continuum from city to suburbs to open countryside thus *was embodied in* the uniformity of building styles and layout and in the use of ground space."[42] This line of reasoning fundamentally presupposes that a building would profoundly differ in form and style from others according to its distinctive social functions. Such a presupposition is self-evidently applicable to most cases in the West and many other parts of the world but not to traditional China, because, as I have argued extensively, an absence of formal bond between building types and social institutions long ago became one of the intrinsic traits of Chinese architecture.

A possible logical difficulty would ensue from any forceful application of this presupposition to the social dimension of Chinese architecture. If the uniformity of building forms and styles were to be taken as *ipso facto* evidence of the urban-rural continuum, should it equally be regarded as evidence of a similar "continuum" across diverse social institutions, such as temples, government offices, schools, and houses, each being lodged in a building compound that resembled others in form and style? Or should we expect that there was little to separate these institutions in social-psychological terms? Certain kindred natures were undoubtedly shared by all these institutions; but was not the contrast between a government office in the city and a Buddhist temple in a remote mountain, for instance, more remarkable in their social functions and people's attitudes toward them than the contrast between city and village, whereas the building forms and styles in the city and village were basically the same? Even if we were to see some parallels between the sociopsychological aspects of the urban-rural relationship and the relationship between different social institutions, the uniformity of building forms and styles bore evidence of nothing more essential than the distinctive Chinese conception of the cosmic position of human beings and, in Needham's words quoted earlier, "the fundamental organic and integrated quality of Chinese thought and feeling."

Building in Time

The reader may have noticed that this issue has not explicitly been discussed with respect to the dimension of time. One reason for this is that, because of the paucity of written and pictorial materials, we are far from certain of the way in which the urban space of the city of Suzhou was organized with regard to buildings and courtyard compounds and of the mode in which people were using it in pre-Southern Song times compared to the late imperial era.[43] Changes in urban spatial texture and city life brought about by the medieval urban revolution were so profound that what we have presented in this chapter, being merely a few segments of the whole spectrum of the city in the Ming and Qing periods, should not be taken as speaking for the entire imperial era. Another reason comes from the realization that Chinese architecture as a distinctive system of the art of building, taking form as early as the Han period,[44] evinced a remarkable continuity throughout subsequent history, a continuity evidenced in architectural form and style, in building materials and techniques, and in general principles of construction. On the other hand, few Chinese cities were cities of stone; structures in them were built with relatively ephemeral materials—mostly timber—and often with astonishing speed, resulting in the scarcity in a city, at any historical stage, of buildings that had survived from earlier times. Consequently, they did not show the kind of architectural diversity generated by the succession of historical periods that so much characterized their European counterparts. Instead, Chinese cities were, as purely physical objects, characteristic of what Mote calls "a continuum in time."[45] An understanding of this particular characteristic will further strengthen the first point that I have developed in the preceding section, that is, that a lack of formal bond between building types and social institutions in Chinese architectural tradition was principally responsible for the relative uniformity of building styles and layout in both urban and rural areas.

Mumford's statement that "the city unites times past, times present, and times to come"[46] is undoubtedly applicable to Chinese cases. Yet such unity was achieved, not through the cities' "durable buildings and institutional structures" but through something else. Discussions of this subject by Wright and Mote are highly enlightening. Wright, thirty years ago, presented the imperial capitals of the Han, Sui, and Tang at Chang'an as *urbs ephemera*, compared with imperial Rome, termed an *urbs aeterna*.[47] In the most ephemeral building materials used, the similar techniques of construction employed across a period of seven centuries, and the striking speed with which major building enterprises were carried out, he sees the construction of Chang'an as representing "an architecture of planned ephemerality."[48] This phrase suggests a conscious choice in various modes of construction; and there is indeed ample evidence that Chinese building skills included elements not unlike those of the Greeks and the Romans in areas of engineering, in their understanding of the principles of the arch and the barrel vault, and in their techniques of masonry construction.[49] Wright thus argues that the question why Chang'an was built as an *urbs ephemera* must be asked, not in terms of materials and techniques, but in terms of values and ideas. He answers this question by stressing, among other things, that immortality was sought in "the written word," specifically in the ultimate history of a dynasty that would be compiled by its successor dynasty from carefully kept archives of court and government.[50]

This view is echoed, though in somewhat different terms and with different intent, by Mote in his discussion of the city of Suzhou. Unlike Wright, whose argument may be seen as emphasizing "the Chinese sense of the future" in city construction, Mote pays more attention to "the Chinese sense of the past." China was obsessed with its past to such extent that, in Mote's words, "it studied its past, and drew upon it, using it to design and to maintain its present as has no other civilization." Yet for the Chinese, "the past was a past of words, not of stones." Since Chinese civilization did not lodge its history in the physical entity of buildings, the real past of Suzhou is a past of mind. Its imperishable elements are largely moments of human experience, and the only truly enduring embodiment of the eternal human moments are the literary ones.[51]

Mote illustrates this point by citing and analyzing an entry in the 1883 gazetteer under the heading for the famous Maple Bridge, which dates back to the Tang period.[52] This "psycho-historical material" attaches little importance to the bridge as a physical object, because

> Its reality to them [the Chinese] was not the stones forming its span so much as the imperishable associations with it; those eternal moments realized in words. The physical object is entirely secondary. Anyone planning to achieve immortality in the minds of his fellow men might well give a lower priority to building some great stone monument than to cultivating his human capacities so that he might express himself imperishably in words, or at least be alluded to in some enduring line by a poet or essayist of immortal achievement.[53]

Apart from the city walls, all other artifacts of the city are, or at least could be, accounted for in the same way.[54] In this sense, the city of Suzhou may indeed be thought of as "an ideational tumulus."[55] It was therefore the accumulated verbal artifacts associated with the city of Suzhou, not the physical structures themselves, that united its "times past, times present, and times to come."

The ephemerality of building materials, the homogeneity of building forms, and the lack of formal bond between building types and social institutions did not lead to any physically enduring monuments;[56] nor were they likely to produce any unique individual building that was distinguishable from others in form. The Chinese did not talk about this characteristic; they did not regard physical monumentality and uniqueness as desiderata; they may not even ever have thought of them. In the light of the works by both Wright and Mote, let me cite one particular example to illustrate this point. It comes from Shen Fu's (1763–1808 or after) interesting, though somewhat cynical, remarks on Tengwang Ge, a multistory hall initially built in 659 by the River Gan at present-day Nanchang, and on Wang Bo's (650–726) *Tengwang Ge shixu*, a rhymed prose composition improvised in 671 at the official banquet in that hall, to which Wang, passing by, was invited.[57] Tengwang Ge became famous because of Wang's graceful and euphuistic prose eulogizing the splendor of the hall's surrounding scenery, depicting the grand occasion of the banquet, and voicing the writer's yearning for the realization of his talents.

After visiting the hall en route to Fujian in the late eighteenth century, Shen Fu writes otherwise:

> [We] arrived at Tengwang Ge. [The hall] was just like the *zunjing ge*[58] of our prefectural school moved to the Grand Quay outside Xu Gate. Thus what Wang Zian [i.e., Wang Bo] writes in his prose is not to be believed.[59]

Shen Fu's rejection of Wang Bo's account undoubtedly does not concern the physical aspects of Tengwang Ge, for they are not mentioned in the prose by the Tang writer, except for two short phrases of vivid metaphorical description. Quite apart from that, having been destroyed and rebuilt time and again during the intervening period of twelve centuries, the hall that Shen saw was certainly no longer physically the one referred to by Wang. It may be possible that the setting of the hall did not meet Shen's expectations, which had been fueled by Wang's description of over a millennium earlier. It may also be possible that Shen was at that time in such a despondent mood that the enthusiastic spirit pervading Wang's piece of prose, inspired by the hall and its natural setting and by the event associated with it, could not strike a sympathetic chord in his heart. Yet what is clearly disclosed in Shen Fu's comment is that this Qing intellectual did not consider Tengwang Ge as either a unique or a monumental physical object; what was unique and monumental about it was its reputation gained by its association with specific persons and events, which were all captured in words, and, to a lesser degree, by its unique name and the beauty of its natural setting. Shen Fu also did not regard the *zunjing ge* of the prefectural school as a unique urban structure in terms of its physical form; its urban quality was brought about by its association with the school and likewise by its very appellation. Tengwang Ge was in Shen's eyes not at all different from the *zunjing ge*, as the latter could also well have been located outside the city walls.

The memory of specific associated persons and events were kept alive in literature, which was the real vehicle for commemoration, whereas the physical structures could be rebuilt repeatedly without any danger of losing their historical value and meanings. In short, monumental achievement was made in words. This was categorically stated by Zhu Changwen in 1084 when he found it difficult to determine the origins of many names of the residential wards (*fang*) and the locations of some recorded alleys:

> From these we know that anything that is not written down in words can hardly last long. Thus the art of local record-writing should not be discarded.[60]

The vitality of the city, with all the ideas and memories associated with it, was maintained in the written word; the past reality of the city was psychologically present in the minds of its residents.

Here we may see in the city two somewhat parallel social forces at work perpetuating the memories and making history. One was represented by the scholar-officials or the intelligentsia (in the broadest sense of the word) at large, who incessantly recorded not only the names, dates of construction, and locations of numerous structures but events and moments of experiences or of reflections involving them. Their reality to the Chinese thus became ideas embodied in the most durable forms: in poetry, prose, and all other forms of literature. The intelligentsia seldom paid attention to the physical and technical aspects of these structures, which, to borrow Wright's words, were to the elite "less attractive than those connected with morality, statecraft, history and the arts—subjects of high prestige on which one could write with hope of renown and possibly immortality."[61] It was the artisans and craftsmen who represented the other social force that kept alive a profoundly conservative architectural tradition. Through working manuals and mnemonic craft-rhymes and through apprenticeship, traditional forms and techniques of building were sustained, though undergoing gradual transformation, from one generation to the next. The spiritual reality was perpetuated by the intelligentsia, whereas the physical reality was preserved by the craftsmen. By nourishing and complementing each other, these two realities in their development jointly rendered the city of Suzhou "time free" as a purely physical object.

Temple Courtyard

I have argued that although formal and, perhaps to a lesser degree, typological differentiation in Chinese architecture were naturally associated with the pattern of everyday activities, they did not reflect the organizational and functional distinctions between social institutions. An individual building, seldom standing alone, was differentiated from others within a building compound which was a physical embodiment of a certain institution, and which, in form and style, was similar to other compounds. It was largely the compounds enclosed by walls, not the individual buildings, that gave rise to the characteristic formation of traditional Chinese habitations. One of the obvious consequences of the ubiquity of building compounds was that in the city each compound became a basic component of the urban texture. Spatial arrangement within the compound technically presupposed the development of the courtyard, under the dominance of which individual buildings were physically and conceptually joined together into a whole. Arranging buildings so as to form one, two, or a series of courtyards was more than an ideal measure; it was in fact a norm for the layout of houses and all other social establishments.[62] In Figure 6.3, adapted from the 1229 picture map of the city of Suzhou, are four examples of courtyard compounds, including the prefectural school-temple, the prefectural examination offices, the Gusu Guesthouse, and the Buddhist temple Nengren Si. Figures 6.4 through 6.9 are the plans of a few houses of various sizes within the city, all built in the late imperial period. Without discussing its form, social and symbolic meanings, and pattern of daily use, I should emphasize, as our preoccupation with the subject of urban space determines, that, apart from the streets and alleys, the courtyard was the only kind of open space—both intentionally and conventionally contrived—in the city. Courtyards provided the city residents with abundant pleasant air, sunlight, and vegetation, to be sure. But most of them were in principle private spaces shared only by the members of each family in the case of a dwelling or by the members of each specific social organization in other compounds. The courtyards of Buddhist, Daoist, and popular temples, and that of the temple of Chenghuang, however, retained a public nature.

Temples in Suzhou

Temples in a traditional Chinese city are usually classified into four categories: official, Buddhist, Daoist, and popular,[63] although one often finds that elements of other distinct cults were to some degree incorporated in a temple of one of these four categories. Some of the official temples, such as the Altar to the Gods of Earth and Grain, had their roots in antiquity, while many others were of later development, the most notable ones

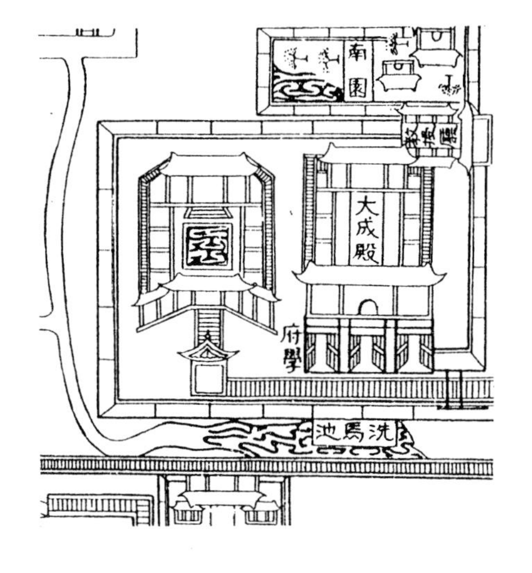

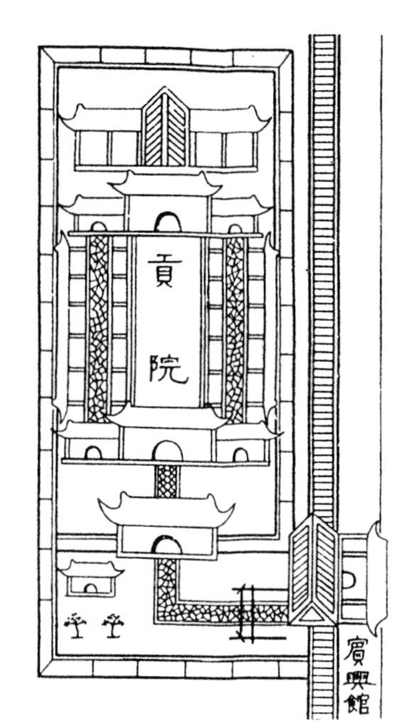

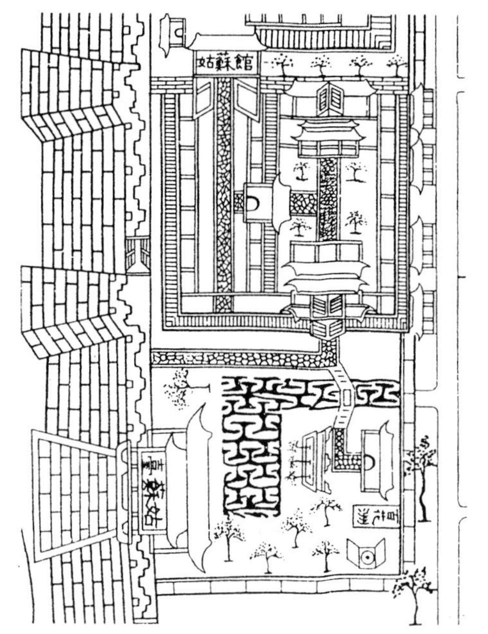

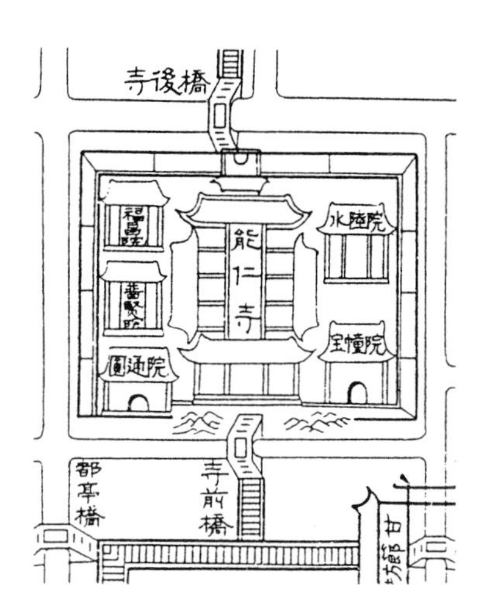

Figure 6.3 Examples of courtyard compounds portrayed on the 1229 city map Pingjiang tu, *including the prefectural school-temple (top left), the prefectural examination offices (top right), the usu uesthouse (bottom left), and the Buddhist temple Nengren Si (bottom right).*

being the Temple of Civil Culture, or Confucian Temple, which was almost invariably located in every prefectural and county school and thus acquired its English name "school-temple"; the temple of Guandi, this name in some cases being a popular one for the Temple of Warfare; and the temple of Chenghuang.[64]

As Buddhist texts poured into China in an unceasing stream from the middle of the second century onward, reaching a maximal influx perhaps in the fifth century, Buddhist temple construction became a conspicuous phenomenon in Suzhou during the Six Dynasties period between the early third century and the late sixth century, when the

Figure 6.4 Plan of the house of the Lu family in Tangjia Alley. Adapted from Suzhou jiuzhuzhai cankao tulu *1958, p. 83.*

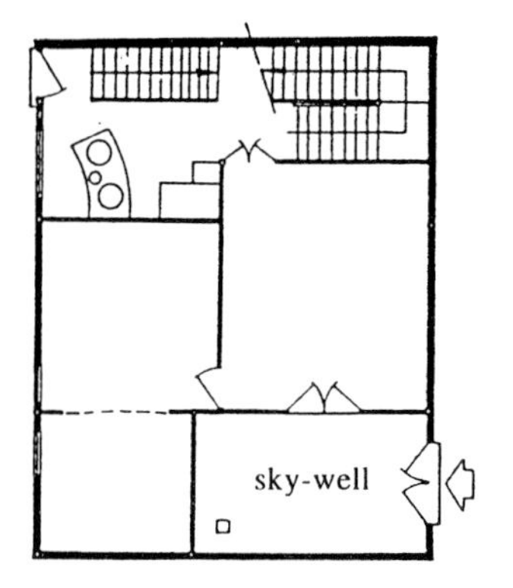

Ground floor

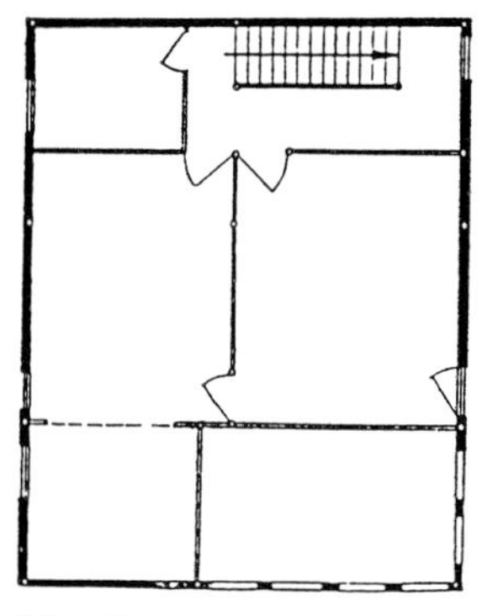

First floor

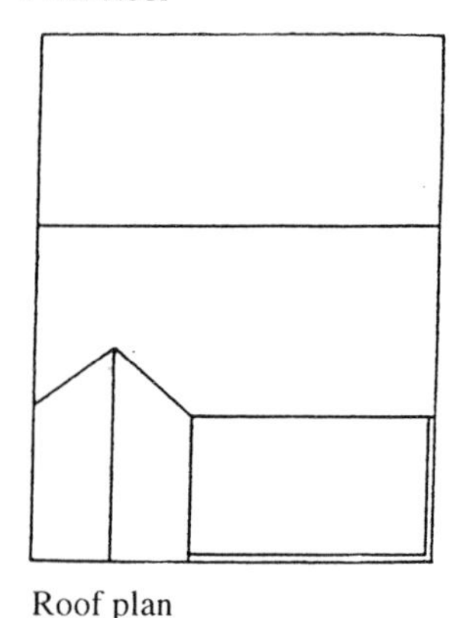

Roof plan

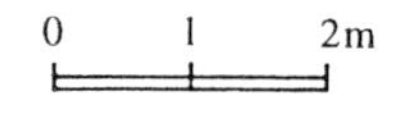

area still remained culturally marginal compared with other parts of Central China. This process particularly intensified during the Southern Liang period (502–557) largely because of the fervent inclinations of Emperor Wu of Liang (464–549) toward Buddhism.[65] It was roughly during the same period that a large number of Daoist temples started to be built in this area as well.[66] This activity continued through the Tang and Song and on up to the end of Qing, even though there were intermittent disruptions brought about by wars and by spells of suppression of Buddhist or Daoist practice by the central authorities.

The origin of a few popular temples dedicated to local men of antiquity, their celebrated virtue, or eminent careers may be traced back to preimperial times; these shrines include Taibo, Zhongyong, and Wu Zixu, although Gu Zhentao in his *Wumen biaoyin* claims that the Temple of the God of Wealth in the East of the River [Yangzi] (Jiangdong Caishenmiao) built in A.D. 239 was the earliest of this kind.[67] It was in the imperial era, especially in its second half, that miscellaneous popular temples proliferated. Some of them accommodated cults that were later shared by or adopted into the religion of the state.

There existed in traditional Chinese society an inextricable link between various cults and social groups, as group interests were usually given religious expression. Thus, the variety of temples in a city, such as Suzhou, reflected the principles of organization on which its social structure rested.[68] Resident bureaucrats and scholars were undoubtedly closely associated with the official temples of the state cult, especially the three Confucian school-temples, those of the prefectural school, the Wu county school, and the Changzhou and Yuanhe joint county school. They supported temples to famous local men of admirable deeds and patronized temples associated with bureaucratic and educational matters.[69] Immigrant or subethnic groups established some specific temples to the deities in the local tradition of their native places; Tianhou Gong (palace of the Empress of Heaven), the shrine of a special cult originated by the coastal people of Fujian province and frequently attended by fishermen and seafaring merchants,[70] was one of such examples, even though its importance in the urban social life in Suzhou may not have been comparable to that of its counterparts in port cities. Occupational groups dedicated a large number of temples to the patron deities or demigods of their callings, many of them being located within the corresponding professional guild compounds.[71] Indeed, one of the two common features of the guild association, religious corporation,[72] typically exemplified the religious nature of social organization in late imperial China. Thus van der Sprenkel's warning against making too sharp a distinction between temples and other types of organization seems very necessary.[73] The location of these temples tended to be in line with the characteristic partitioning of urban space that I have demonstrated earlier; that is, a temple was usually situated in the district in which the specific activities of its patron group were dominant.

However, the reflection of the modes of social organization by the variety of temples in and around the city does not mean that all temples functioned exclusively for the members of the groups that patronized them.[74] Apart from the temples patronized by and functioning strictly for a particular class (notably that of the scholar-officials), subethnic group, or occupational calling, many others were essentially communal in nature, just as most Buddhist and Daoist temples in principle invited participation in their ritual and other activities by all sections of society. Especially in the case of the temples to the Gods of the Earth, they either catered to a specific territory, defined in terms of the deity's jurisdiction,[75] or to their vicinity, with the distance of their influence largely depending on their reputation and scale. Large temples of this kind, in contrast to temples for social groups, were distributed fairly evenly throughout the city and its suburban areas.

The Daoist Temple Xuanmiao Guan

It was the temples of a communal nature that functioned as the loci of urban activities. Among those in the city of Suzhou, the Daoist temple Xuanmiao Guan located slightly north of the geometric center of the city, which was built either in the first half of the

Figure 6.5 Plan of the house of the Zhang family in Ma Dalu Alley. Adapted from Suzhou jiuzhuzhai cankao tulu *1958, p. 84.*

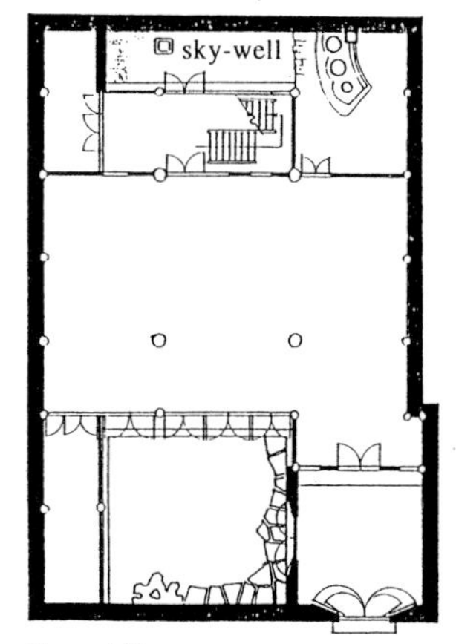

Ground floor

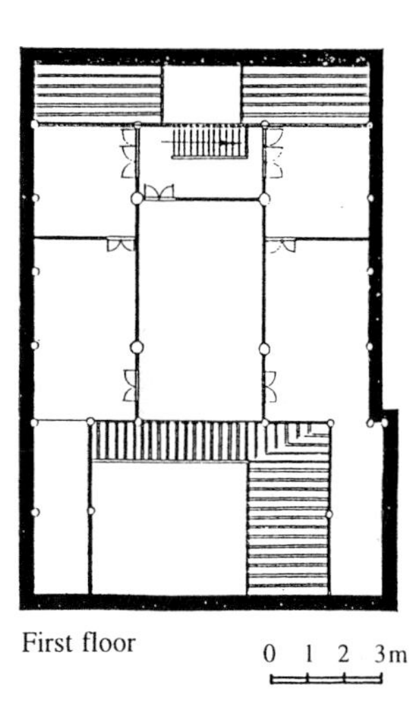

First floor

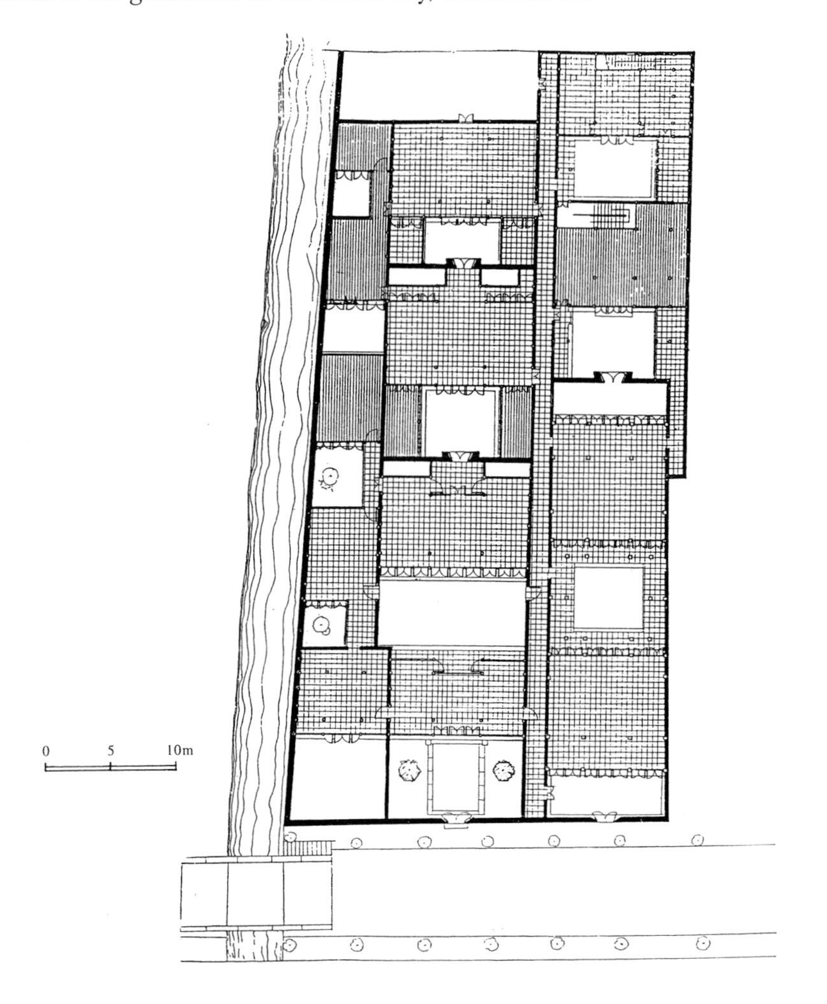

Figure 6.6 Plan of the house of the Chen family in Dongbei Street. Adapted from Suzhou jiuzhuzhai cankao tulu *1958, p. 93.*

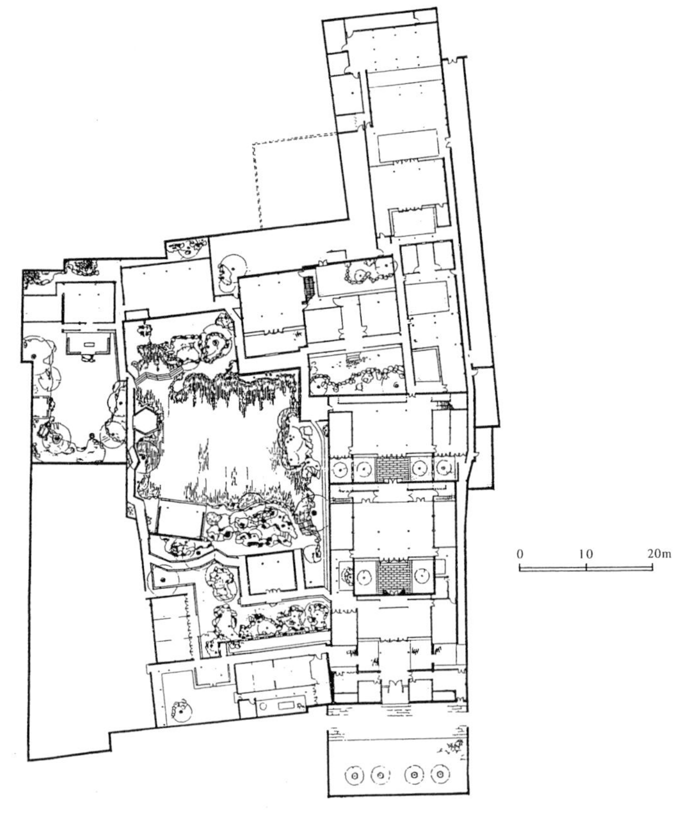

Figure 6.7 *Plan of the garden house Wangshi Yuan (Garden of the Master of the Fishing Nets) in Kuojietou Alley. Adapted from* Suzhou jiuzhuzhai cankao tulu *1958, p. 91.*

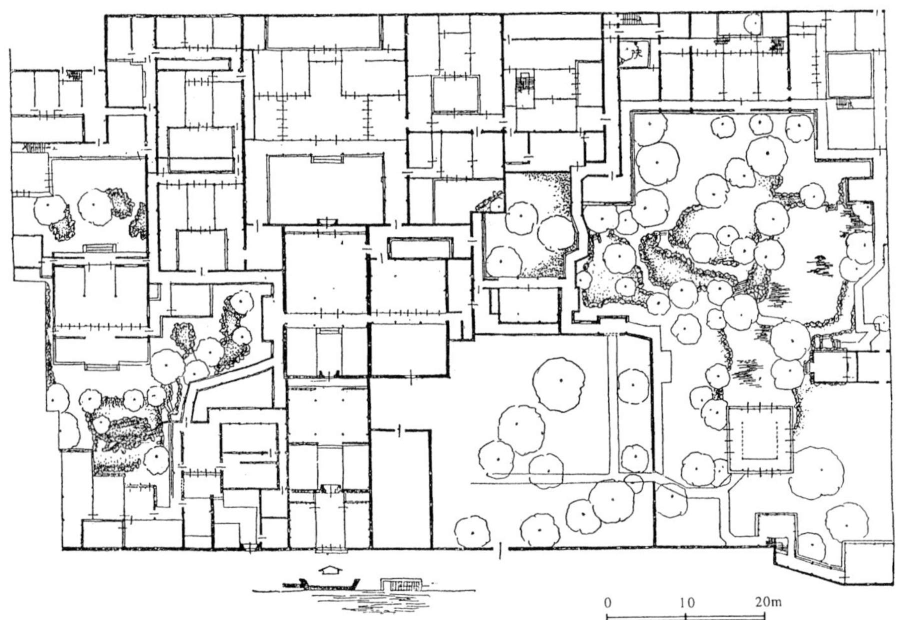

Figure 6.8 *Plan of the garden house of the Liu family, also known as Ou Yuan (Companion Garden) in Xiaoxinqiao Alley. Adapted from* Suzhou jiuzhuzhai cankao tulu *1958, p. 112.*

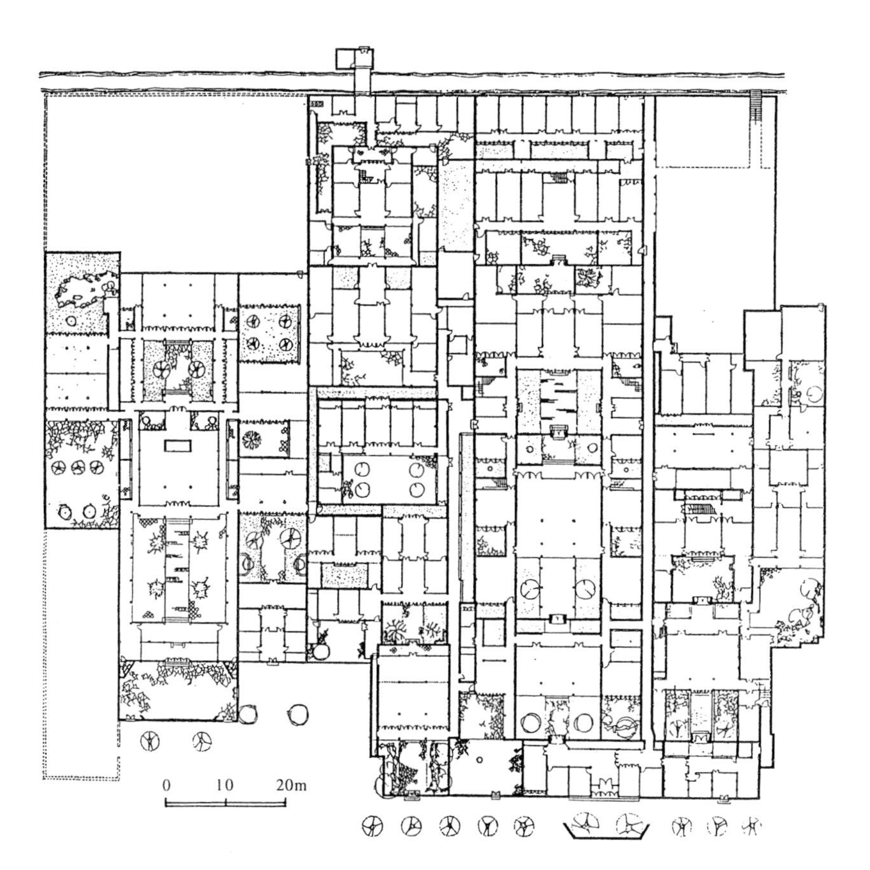

Figure 6.9 Plan of the house of the Lu family in Tianguan Fang. Adapted from Suzhou jiuzhuzhai cankao tulu *1958, p. 162. According to Chen Congzhou (1981, p. 10), this house is the largest in terms of land area covered.*

eighth century or more probably earlier,[76] seems to have been the most important (see Figure 6.10). If Shiba's statement is true that the temples to Chenghuang in many cities provided a ritual link between the popular religion of the city people and the official state cult,[77] it was Xuanmiao Guan that afforded all sections of the people of Suzhou a notable venue where various religious, social, and economic activities were conducted, and thus it functioned as a practical link between the local residents of different class, profession, and place of residence. Figures 6.11 and 6.12 are picture maps of the Xuanmiao Guan found respectively on the 1229 city map and in the *Xuanmiao Guan zhi* (Annals of Xuanmiao Guan) compiled in the first half of the nineteenth century. Figure 6.13 contains photographs of the main hall and gates of the temple in 1991.

Xuanmiao Guan was the largest and most prominent Daoist temple in Suzhou prefecture and probably in the whole Lower Yangzi region. Its reputation was such that several emperors of successive dynasties from the Tang onward bestowed what is called an *e* (a horizontal board with the name of the temple inscribed on it, loosely translated as "placard") in their own handwriting on the temple.[78] Naturally, it held a series of important Daoist rituals and festivals throughout the year, especially those associated with the deities' birthdays as stipulated in the contemporary Daoist doctrines, such as the birthday of the Jade Emperor (Yuhuang) on the ninth day of the first month, the

Figure 6.10 The geographical position of the Daoist temple Xuanmiao Guan.

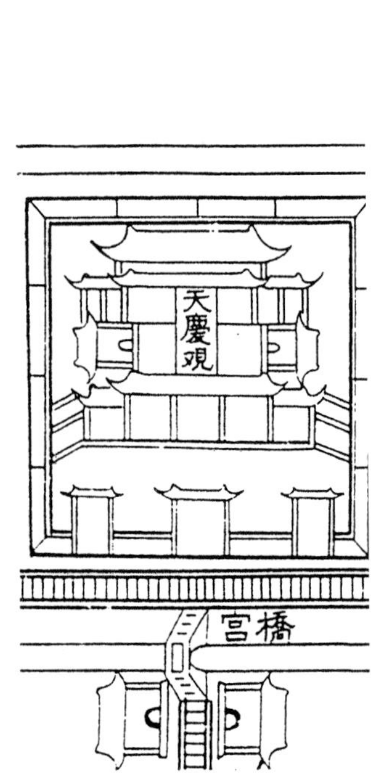

Figure 6.11 Xuanmiao Guan (known as Tianqing Guan during the Southern Song period) as portrayed on the 1229 city map Pingjiang tu.

birthday of the God of the East Mount (Dongyuedi) on the twenty-eighth day of the third month, and the birthday of the God of Thunder (Leizun) on the twenty-fourth day of the sixth month.[79] These occasions attracted a large number of people from both the city and its surrounding towns and villages, who came to the temple to burn joss sticks, worship the deities, and pray for their health, welfare, and success or to redeem a vow to a deity. In fact, Xuanmiao Guan, like some other large Buddhist and Daoist temples in and around the city, was also a place where customary annual rituals were performed, which only loosely fell within the scope of Daoist religion. Gu Lu, a native of Wu county, recorded in his *Qing jia lu* in the first half of the nineteenth century that, during the New Year period, every Buddhist or Daoist temple in the Suzhou area conducted the annual sacrificial ceremony (*suijiao*), "Xuanmiao Guan being the particular one in which people rushed to gather."[80]

On these ceremonial occasions, however, social activities occurring in the temple courtyard were not confined to purely religious matters. From the local documents of the late imperial and Republican periods, we understand that most people, whom Gu Lu prefers to call the *youke* (sightseers or pleasure strollers) rather than the *xiangke* (pilgrims, literally incense guests), were attracted to the temple by the theater, noise, color, and bustle that were much more clamorous during these festivals than in normal times. This was very similar in nature to the temple fairs (*miaohui*) described by Eberhard, who writes: "City people, even the members of the upper classes, go to these fairs, even if they are not at all interested in religion, because here they can make good buys—often 'discoveries'."[81] On such occasions, more stalls were set up in the temple by peddlers to sell various small articles ranging from candles, joss sticks, and New Year pictures to a wide choice of food and drinks, and there were activities such as storytelling, fortune-telling, and variety shows performed by people coming from other regions.[82] Figure 6.14 shows the allocation of the courtyard of the temple to various shops and stalls in 1949.

A Space for Miscellaneous Activities

Xuanmiao Guan's importance to the life of the people of Suzhou, however, was not confined to these communal Daoist ritual ceremonies, annual festivals, and temple market activities, which were functionally associated with each other in one way or another. Diverse social groups also found their interests here. Probably from as early as the Yuan period onward, Xuanmiao Guan became the locus where those who were engaged in spinning and weaving activities frequently congregated. Their earliest professional

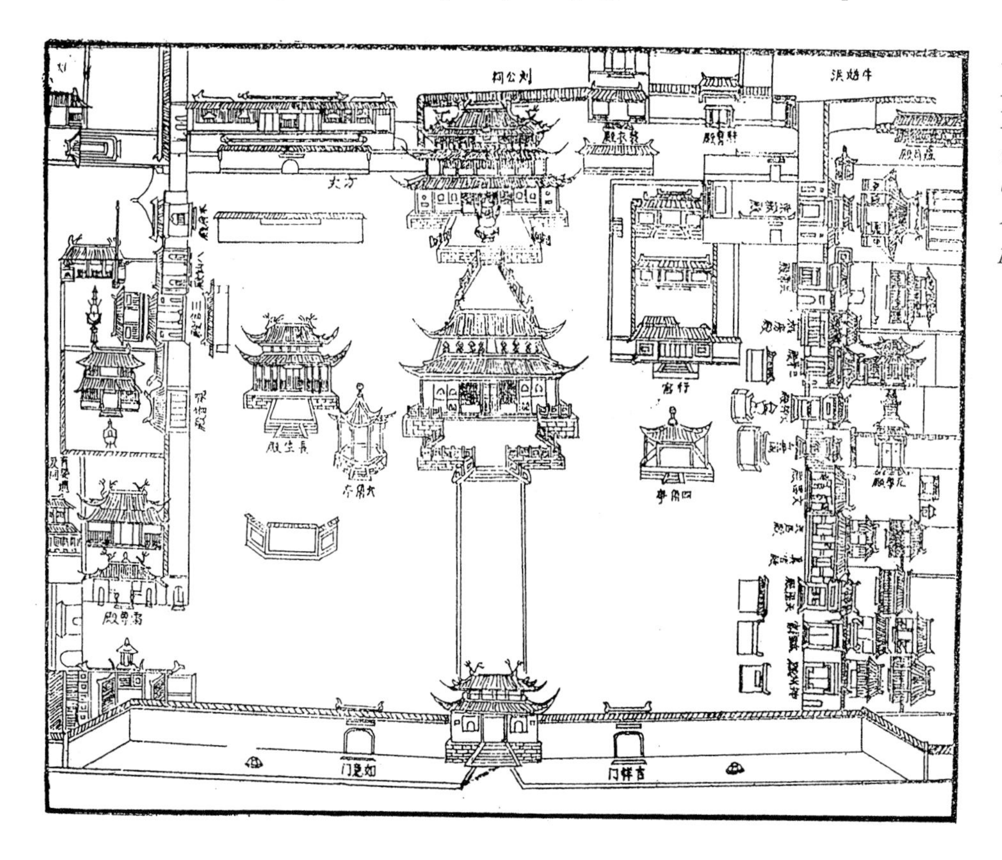

Figure 6.12 Picture map of Xuanmiao uan contained in the Xuanmiao Guan zhi, *compiled in the first half of the nineteenth century. Adapted from "Suzhou Xuanmiao uan zhigao" 1984, pp. 145–146.*

Figure 6.13 Photographs of Xuanmiao Guan. Top: Sanqing Hall. Bottom: two side gates of Xuanmiao Guan. Photographs by Xu Yinong, 1991.

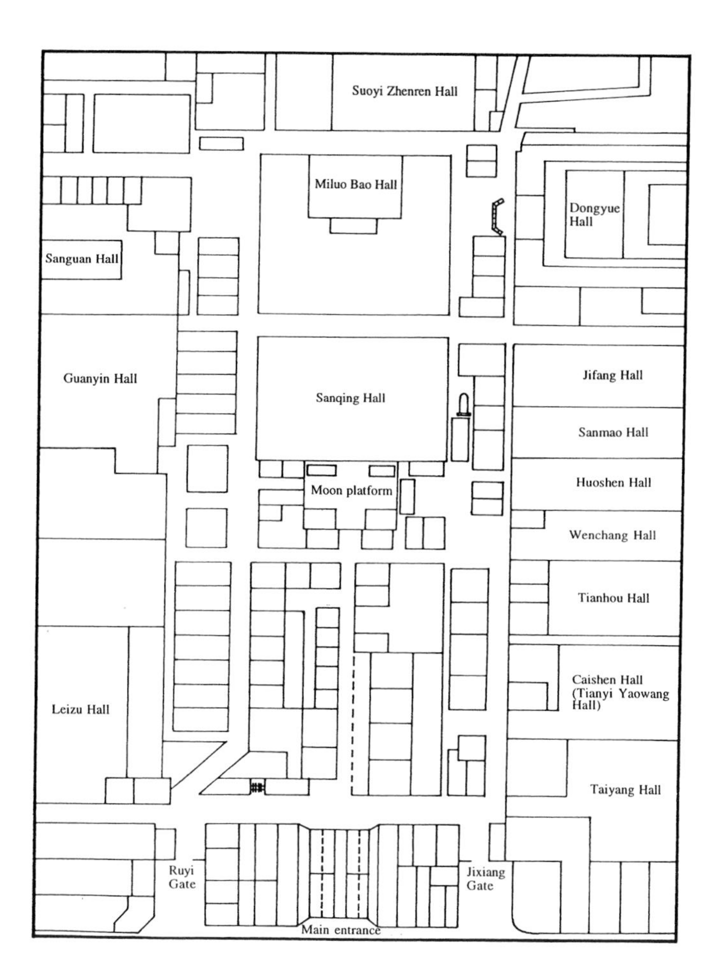

Figure 6.14 Allocation of the courtyard space of Xuanmiao Guan to various shops and stalls in 1949. Adapted from "Suzhou Xuanmiao Guan zhigao" 1984, p. 172.

guild, Jiye Gongsuo (communal association of the textile profession), was founded in Xuanmiao Guan,[83] its main building being the Jifang Dian on the east side of the Sanqing Hall (see Figure 6.12). During the Ming period, according to Jiang Yihua, a Changshu scholar of the sixteenth century, hundreds from the "small [loom] households" (*xiaohu*) boisterously gathered by the entrance of the temple every morning, waiting to be hired by the day by the "large [loom] households" (*dahu*).[84] Other more important events in the field of the textile industry also took place at this temple. In the summer of 1601, for example, a protest led by Ge Cheng, a native of Kunshan, broke out following the imposition of new taxes on production and commerce by the eunuch tax inspector Sun Long. It was at Xuanmiao Guan that the crowds first converged, taking oaths to the god of their profession; they then went on strike, burned down the houses of the tax collectors, and lynched hated local tyrants.[85] In another instance, local authorities, in response to the strike in 1734 by the spinners and weavers working on a day-hire basis, issued an order permanently banning any call to collective strikes. It was again in the Xuanmiao Guan that the stone slab inscribed with this order was placed.[86]

Some other callings had their foot in this temple as well. A wooden image of a Song tanner found in the west corner of the Sanqing Hall was mentioned by Gu Zhentao in his record of the features of Xuanmiao Guan.[87] This may suggest that during the Song period the temple already provided space for some small businesses. But certainly, the temple became in the late imperial period an important place for medical and charitable activities, probably because of the inextricable link between Daoist practice and medicine, as a hall of the Heavenly Physician (*Tianyi*) was also incorporated in the temple.[88] According to the *Wumen busheng* written by Qian Siyuan of the Qing, a widespread epidemic disease broke out in the Suzhou region in 1756 after the severe famine of the preceding year. The prefect urgently set up a temporary field station in Xuanmiao Guan and called upon twenty-five famous men of medicine of the region to treat patients for their illness.[89]

Gentry and officials equally considered the temple as one of the important places for their social interactions.[90] One of the important local customs during the late imperial period was the so-called *baipai;* for this, on New Year's Day the local gentry came to the Sanqing Hall in Xuanmiao Guan, praying to the heavenly gods for blessings for the coming year, before going to the prefectural and county *yamen* to exchange greetings with each other.[91] It may be an overstatement to assert that they all genuinely believed in Daoist religion or any other cults, because this activity had probably long ago become part of social propriety in the gentry/officials circle. Yet at least some of them saw Daoist practice as one of the magical resorts for coping with natural disasters such as drought and flood, as for example in 1438, 1645, 1703, and 1760, when prefects or even provincial governors led their entourage to Xuanmiao Guan to participate in Daoist rituals and pray either for rain or for the cessation of rain.[92]

In addition to these events and activities, which were all associated with Daoist religion or other cults to various extents, there were occasions when the temple Xuanmiao Guan functioned as a place where officials and other leading members of society met to discuss and resolve temporal problems of the city and region. In the early winter of 1633, to reward men of merit and to punish villains, the provincial governor summoned the officials, scholars, and respected elders of the prefecture to Xuanmiao Guan for consultation. Money was awarded to a few well-doers, and, with the consent of those consulted, execution was imposed on four hated scoundrels.[93] When the forces of the Taiping rebels advanced toward Suzhou in 1850, officials and the gentry again chose Xuanmiao Guan as the place where they temporally set up what they called a "joint-relief association" (*xiejiju*) and met regularly, presumably to discuss the defense of the city.[94] These kinds of gathering in the temple may not have been regular ones: a "trial" of criminals was rarely carried out publicly in Suzhou history, and more serious meetings concerning the security of the city would probably be held more often in the *yamen* or, as the case of the meeting in the face of the Manchu advance in 1645, in the Minglun Hall of the prefectural school-temple.[95] Yet these two events do show to a certain degree the temple's utilization for social gatherings in the temporal interest of all residents of the prefecture.

Public Urban Space

The multifarious functions assumed by Xuanmiao Guan as described here may induce an obvious analogy between its temple courtyard and what Norberg-Schulz sees as the most distinct element, or one of the two basic phenomena, of European urban environment, the city square.[96] Yet this temple courtyard should by no means be regarded as the "civic" center in the European sense of the word, even if a civic center in a European city is to be taken "as a place for public business and the display of the trappings of power" rather than as signifying "communal self-government," as interpreted by Kostov, who acknowledges the absence of such a square from the urban fabric of imperial China.[97] Rather, the temple courtyard was a place attracting more than usual people to conduct or participate in a wider than usual variety of activities. These activities, however, formed only a section, and often a small section, of the whole spectrum of the social life of those living in the city and in its nearby countryside.

At least four aspects of the social function of this temple can be enunciated in support of this argument. First, this was not a center of commerce and trade, as the market held here was merely a supplementary instrument of local life. The real interregional and international trade was carried out in the west suburb of the city, especially along the Grand Canal stretching from Chang Gate westward to Feng Bridge and southward forming part of the city moat. Second, it was not a religious center, as the temple of Xuanmiao Guan was merely an independent unit of Daoist establishments, and Daoist religion, like Buddhist religion, did not have an internal hierarchy to fulfill its own organizational needs, and thus the temple existed in what Mote calls "atomized structure."[98] In this sense, Xuanmiao Guan, with the social status of its abbot being no higher than his counterparts in even the most remote areas, was merely one of the discrete temples of the Daoist cult, which coexisted with other numerous diffuse religions, rather than a unit within a diocesan or synodal structure of authority. Third, no government offices were located inside or in the vicinity of Xuanmiao Guan in such a manner that they formed, physically or organizationally, an interrelated part of it.[99] As for merchant and craft associations, different in their relationship with the local authorities from those in medieval Europe, which were usually tightly bound with municipal governments,[100] only one of the guilds of the textile industry was situated in the temple, while three other textile guilds and those of other trades were widely scattered either within or outside the city walls, notably in the west suburbs.[101] Fourth, Xuanmiao Guan was not a place where public facilities were clustered together. Official libraries were in the *yamen* and school-temples, while private libraries were found elsewhere in the city and in the countryside. Scholars came here for pleasure strolling or new discoveries rather than for their career pursuits. There were no equivalents of a European hospital in and around the temple, and the gathering of men of medicine in the temple in 1756 was organized temporarily by the prefect so that efforts could be put together to deal with the unprecedented spread of an epidemic disease. Permanent recreational facilities, such as theaters, were concentrated along the street called Shantang, adjacent to the canal running from

Tiger Hill in the northwest suburb to Chang Gate, whereas only those who did small-scale variety shows and storytelling came to the courtyard of Xuanmiao Guan, particularly during the annual festivals.

Norberg-Schulz, from a phenomenological point of view, insists that the square, functioning as a city center,

> does not necessarily make a particular choice manifest, often it rather condenses what is spread out along the street into one complex but comprehensive image. Choice is thus facilitated, at the same time as the world of the community as perceived as a whole. . . . The square thus appears as a complementary form to the "exterior" of the settlement. The sense of arrival is here fulfilled; what was a promise when the settlement was seen from the outside, becomes an understood world.[102]

This statement to some extent may hold in interpreting the nature of urban space in premodern Europe. But our analysis of the social functions of Xuanmiao Guan has shown that it was anything but applicable to the case of Suzhou (and probably China as a whole), even if we were to regard the temple courtyard as somewhat analogous to a city square in premodern Europe in terms of its unroofed space, its multiple functions, and the centrality of its location in the city. This temple courtyard did not condense what was spread out along the streets into one complex yet comprehensive image but merely displayed a fraction of it. In fact, it was the streets that more fully represented the richness of the urban features of the city of Suzhou and at the same time reflected the different modes of living in their corresponding districts. Diverse choices could be fully facilitated only in the appropriate districts, just as some specific needs could be met in the temple of Xuanmiao Guan. The sense of arrival therefore could be fully fulfilled, not by browsing and meditating upon any single space, but by walking through the representative streets in all three districts of the city and its west suburbs. Only in this way might that which was a promise when the city was seen from the outside—or from afar—start to become an understood world.

Nevertheless, the nearly ubiquitous assumption of multifarious functions (except for those of exclusive official cults) by an important temple in a city or a market town was indeed a conspicuous phenomenon in Chinese urban development during the late imperial period. It seems to have been a natural process in a traditional society that a public religious establishment had a tendency to draw various secular activities to its vicinity, as did important churches in many premodern European towns, since its service cut across all sections of society and consequently the venue afforded people more opportunities for interaction. The scale, reputation, and centrality of Xuanmiao Guan may all have facilitated this process. What appears to have been a typical Chinese experience was that these secular activities could, and in mainland China almost invariably would, take place within the compound of the temple, that is, in the temple courtyard, which was supposed to be part of the sanctuary.

If we keep in mind the most human-centered worldview of the Chinese, which was presented earlier in this chapter, this seemingly odd phenomenon should not be surprising at all. It is also worth noting that the religious and physical attributes of the temple in question directly facilitated the everyday activities in this peculiar way. The social orientation of Daoist and popular cults, and, to some extent, even of the vulgarized Buddhism,[103] was practical and utilitarian in nature,[104] and their rituals and practice were aimed at improving life in this world rather than in the world beyond or at the salvation of the soul. Consequently, many people's belief in them was highly temporary and conditional: they believed in them when they thought that they needed to do so, and they might continue their belief only if their prayer or worship appeared to have been efficacious. Probably because of this practical orientation, the temples of these religions not only tolerated but also encouraged temporal activities within their spatial confinements, which were not at all contradictory to the social purpose of their existence and practice. It was precisely these temples in cities that invariably contained spacious courtyards and at the same time were open to all sections of society.[105] Certainly not everyone approved of this practice. Some vague and infrequent voicings of imperial scholars' repugnance for the temporal invasion of these sanctuaries could be heard. A poem by the Qing scholar Cai Yun, depicting the New Year festivals in Suzhou, is quoted in the *Qing jia lu:*

> To the temple of West Garden outside the city walls and Xuanmiao Guan inside the city walls
> People availing themselves of this idle period and of the bustle and excitement go to enjoy sport and play their fill.
> The pity is that the so wonderful Buddhist edifice and Immortals' Palace
> Have been mixed back into teahouses and wine shops.[106]

Judging from the context of other poems by the same scholar, one may suggest that what was so regrettable to him may not have been so much the seeming profanity as the disturbance of the serenity of the two temples which he himself preferred.

It would be profoundly wrong to assume that the exploitation of the temple courtyard was *caused* by the lack of any open space similar to the city square of premodern Europe that might otherwise have allowed multifarious functions to occur in it. The fact that Chinese cities lacked public open space is noted by many scholars both in China and in the West.[107] Few have tried to explain the reasons for it, but Li Yunhe argues that the early market, usually combined with a public well within the Chinese settlement, originally much the same as in Europe, was later tightly controlled by the central authority, and the materialization of this control—enclosure by walls—undermined the possibility of the emergence of a city square.[108] This argument is certainly an oversimplification of the very complicated issue and can thus hardly be seen as cogent. Its shortcomings probably lie intrinsically more in the validity of the question itself than in the answer. Logically speaking, the question of why the square as a civic center did not arise in premodern Chinese cities appears to be equivalent to the question of why the Chinese never arrived at modern science, which is regarded by Graham as a pseudo-problem, because one generally asks and tries to answer why a phenomenon did occur, not why the same complex set of conditions did *not* come together at some other time and place.[109] The city square appeared in Europe as a *unique* phenomenon, rather than a universal urban feature, depending on a variety of social, political, psychological, and other conditions, and it is pointless to ask in narrow terms why it did not emerge in cities of other parts of the world. Therefore a probably more useful and logical approach to the issue is to ask, as many Western urbanists do,[110] what unique conjunction of factors gave rise to the incorporation of public squares in European cities as early as in Greek civilization, and, likewise, what was the *raison d'être* of wall-enclosed public space in cities of imperial China. It is the second part of the question that concerns us here.

The characteristic mode of the use of temple courtyard as a public urban space in imperial China's cities may be dealt with, though inconclusively, from two perspectives: the sociopolitical relationship between the city and the countryside and the distinctive Chinese concept of socialized space. From the first perspective, European cities in the medieval period were corporate entities of their own. Their city walls "marked off small islands of freedom in a land where all, except the nobility and a relatively few free peasants, were bound to a particular patch of soil and required to work for, and pay heavy dues to, their lord and master." Those living inside the wall were the true townsmen, the burgesses; they "had good reason to look down upon the unfree peasant, the villain, living in some tiny remote village in a one-roomed hut shared with his animals," and "the right to live in the town was jealously guarded, and foreigners were forbidden to be in it except by day."[111] This kind of sociological model that distinguishes sharply between city and village, as Ward points out, is indeed essentially a Western one.[112]

As discussed in preceding chapters, cities in imperial China were not regarded as isolated administrative units but principally as an instrument of the imperial government; in other words, they were administrative centers of the areas in which they were located, which were largely rural. This distinctive urban-rural continuum became ever more the reality during the late imperial period, when the growth of trade stimulated commercial agriculture and handicrafts and spurred expansion of rural markets and when greater integration of the central place hierarchy and growing market participation facilitated the flow of ideas as well as goods between city and country.[113] This situation was more in evidence in the Lower Yangzi core, the most advanced, urbanized, and one of the most densely populated regions during that period. If the square in a city of medieval Europe could be identified as the property of the city itself and as a public place that was maintained by the city authority and to which its citizens psychologically attached themselves, the courtyard of Xuanmiao Guan should then be regarded as the property of the temple, which was nevertheless more than liable to interventions by the imperial authority, and as a public place that was maintained by the abbot of the temple with the patronage of the government and individuals residing either within or without the city and to which residents of the whole prefecture psychologically attached themselves. In this sense, the square in an European city, as part of its corporate entity, was effectively enclosed by city walls, whereas the courtyard of Xuanmiao Guan was symbolically demarcated by the walls of the temple itself yet at the same time open to all sections of society, both urban and rural.

This line of argument, however, does not deny that there were differences between the city and the countryside in imperial China. It simply emphasizes the facts that Xuanmiao Guan, like many other temples of the same nature located within the walls of regional and local capital cities, was not a corporate property of the city of Suzhou itself, partly because the city was not an entity of its own; that access to the temple was not exclusively limited to the people residing within the city walls; and that the necessity for the city walls and temple walls lay at least as much in their practical use as in their symbolic attributes in terms of both separating the within from the without and distinguishing different social institutions. Only one occasion is recorded during which Xuanmiao Guan was used principally by the city residents. According to the *Wuxian zhi*, published in 1933, it was a custom in Suzhou prefecture during the Qing period (probably the Ming as well) that tribute was paid to the heavenly gods every second month, this custom being known as *jie tianxiang* (escorting provisions to heavenly gods). Money was contributed to every local temple to the God of the Earth by families and individuals living in the area that the god governed; then the god's image was carried, in a grand ceremonial parade, to the Daoist temple Shangzhen Guan on Mt. Qionglong in the west of the prefecture, where the sacrificial money was incinerated in a petition for blessings from the heavenly gods for all those living in the prefectural territory. It was in Xuanmiao Guan, however, that the money collected from those residing in the city (perhaps including its near suburbs?) was "sent" to the gods.[114]

Could it be that, because of the prestige of Xuanmiao Guan and its geographical centrality, the ritual ceremony was conveniently conducted here by the city residents without then proceeding to the distant mountain? Or could it be that the interest of the city residents and their way of life were either consciously or unconsciously differentiated from those of the country people, thus requiring that the ritual ceremony be conducted separately for specific blessings from the same gods? In any event, we understand from the context of this record that the ritual ceremony was performed in Xuanmiao Guan not exclusively for people in the city, since the sentence "city residents deliver the money to Xuanmiao Guan" is not equivalent to "only city residents are allowed to deliver the money here." It is also clear that it was the temple of Shangzhen on Mt. Qionglong, not Xuanmiao Guan, that was the more appropriate and effective locality for a ritual ceremony dedicated to the *heavenly* gods. The accounts in the *Wuxian zhi* of the ceremony proceedings conducted on Mt. Qionglong are lengthy and include the statement that the ceremony was intended for the good of the whole prefecture, whereas the collection of money in Xuanmiao Guan is mentioned at the end of the passage with a single short sentence. In fact, the record of this prefectural ritual ceremony in the *Qing jia lu*, on which the description of it in the *Wuxian zhi* is largely based, does not mention any particular preference for the city residents regarding the ceremony.[115] This indicates that this preference probably had not become a common practice by 1830 when the *Qing jia lu* was published.

Looking at the temple courtyard using the Chinese concept of socialized space, it is important to note that the Chinese felt that any space of a considerable size facilitating social interactions in a man-made environment should exist for a certain reason rather than for its own sake; that is, it must not be an independent entity of its own but pertain to a certain institution so as to be explainable and therefore meaningful. The essentiality of the void was appreciated very early in China indeed, as we read in the *Laozi*:

> Thirty spokes share the hub [of a wheel];
> It is on the [center] void that the utility of the vehicle depends.
> Knead clay into a vessel;
> It is on the void that the utility of the vessel depends.
> Pierce doors and windows for a room;
> It is on the voids that the utility of the room depends.
> Therefore benefit comes from what is there;
> Utility from what is not there.[116]

Yet in the Chinese-built environments, any unoccupied area that was not incorporated in a certain building compound was, apart from the cases of streets or alleys, seldom designated by the Chinese with words meaning anything close to that of "space,"[117] that clichéd term of the field of architecture in our time. The equivalent of the term *space* in modern Chinese is *kongjian*, a word that has been "readopted" from Japanese.[118] Characters such as *suo*, *chu*, and *di* all indicate "place" rather than "space"; even the character *chang*, the second component of which the modern word *guangchang* (vast level ground) is composed and which is used to denote "public square," emphasizes the flat surface of an open piece of ground rather than the attribute of a space with boundaries. The absence of a term for *space* in Chinese (and thus possibly of the concept it denotes?) indicates that any area that we call a space had to be specifically designated for its particular function. To put it another way, any confusion of functions in a space was likely to cause psychological discomfort, even though such functions may have been merely nominal. In this sense, it was not impossible that Cai Yun's poem criticizing the invasion by teahouses and wine shops of the two temples also reflected his personal disapproval of the situation in which there was improper mingling of social functions of different categories; and we might expect that he would have had similar complaints had this situation occurred within the structures for other social institutions, such as schools and government offices.

From a Chinese perspective, an architectural space had to be defined nominally *and* physically, so that it could be distinguished both in concept and in reality from other spaces of different categories, defined likewise, and so that the human environments could be maintained in order. The most convenient and probably preferable way to accomplish this materially was to enclose the space with walls. Here we come again to the importance of walls to the Chinese, which is shown by the fact that several words were used to describe their different forms: high walls around courtyards were called *qiang* or *yong;* house walls and part walls, *bi;* low walls, *yuan;* and the inner north-south walls of a building separating the side rooms from the central halls, *xu.*[119] Liu Xi of the Eastern Han elaborates the explanations of these terms except the last one in his *Shi ming:*

> *Bi* connotes *pi* [ward off or keep away]; it is to ward off and resist the wind and cold.
> *Qiang* connotes *zhang* [obstruct]; it is what is used to shield oneself.
> *Yuan* connotes *yuan* [help or aid]; it is what man relies on and thus takes as his protection.
> *Yong* connotes *rong* [to obstruct and shelter]; it is what is used to hide one's body and appearance.[120]

The practical considerations reflected in these explanations were almost universal in human history. What seems to have been distinctive was (and still is) the ubiquity of various kinds of walls in China's landscape.[121] They were not only the first physical structures to be seen when approached from the outside or afar but often the first artifacts of a settlement, and sometimes they were the only ones to be depicted in literature.[122] Walls in China, in fact, became an important part of the vehicle used to distinguish different categories in an ordered human environment, and the social and conceptual function of walls outweighed their physical function of defense and obstruction; that is, they may have physically bounded the spaces that they enclosed, but more importantly they symbolized the manner of classification in the organization of society. Hence, similar to the case of individual buildings *vis-à-vis* building compounds, an unroofed area would be perceived as an active and meaningful space only if it was explicitly attached to or incorporated in the spatial domain of a certain social institution and, more importantly, if it was properly enclosed by walls (usually in combination with buildings), the most common case being that of the courtyard.

This is reflected, for example, in the way the word *guangchang* is used to denote "open level ground" rather than "public square" in its modern sense, in the "New Year" section of the *Qing jia lu* describing socialized spaces in two different locations.[123] The first location is in the courtyard of Xuanmiao Guan. One of the stanzas of the poem "You Guan" (Visiting the Temple) by Fan Laizong of the Qing runs:

> The huge earthly *guangchang* surpasses the Market of Cranes;[124]
> The various heavenly images resemble [those of] the divine palace.

This is obviously a positive description of the courtyard using the word *guangchang*, juxtaposed with the eulogistic analogy of the marvelous halls of the temple. The second location is on the private land of the Zhu family near Wende Bridge outside Chang

Gate. The words that Gu Lu, the author of the *Qing jia lu*, uses concerning it appear to be somewhat negative: "it is merely a *guangchang*," with the inference that such a space, crude as it was in his mind, should not have assumed its function as an open market as it curiously had. Gu Lu's slight implicit contempt (or at least bewilderment) about it is revealed not in the words he uses to account for its location (that is, in the west suburb rather than in the city proper), but in the words he uses for the space itself, "merely open ground," which was for him difficult to define both socially and institutionally. A space like this could hardly have been highly regarded unless it had been properly arranged and preferably enclosed by walls for socially and institutionally categorized functions. The example of these two accounts may be trivial, but the point is not. Whether a space was enclosed by walls concerned not only its conceptual and psychological correctness but also its viability in time. The multipurpose nature of the courtyard of Xuanmiao Guan has persisted along with the courtyard itself to the present day, whereas the function of the open ground near Wende Bridge was very temporary, and the space soon may have been assigned to other uses or occupied by newly built structures.

Conclusion

The main purpose of this chapter is to address how general features of architecture in traditional Chinese cities should properly be interpreted and how public urban spaces were used and why. The reason for incorporating the discussion of the public urban space of Suzhou with the discussion of building compounds and courtyards, instead of combining it with the discussion of the city structure in the preceding chapter, lies in an understanding of the urban and architectural nature of traditional China.

I have indicated that social division was less commonly found between the city and the countryside than in class and occupation, which were manifested in diverse social institutions. The spatial dimension of such social division was, in terms of daily activities, not so much based on the urban-rural dichotomy as on the formation of building compounds under the influence of the courtyard, which were the physical embodiments of different institutions and, at the same time, the basic spatial components of the city. In the architecture of a certain region, however, correspondence between differentiation of social institutions and differentiation of building forms and types was remarkably weak. Individual buildings were classified according to their forms and their spatial functions, but they seldom stood as independent structures that performed a designated social function; instead, they were, or at least should in theory have been, incorporated as integral elements into building compounds that differed from each other principally in ornamentation and yet resembled each other in form and style. In this sense, the uniformity of building forms and styles between the city and the countryside of traditional China should be seen as a display of the typical lack of formal bond between building type and type of social institutions. This lack of connection was not caused by influences emanating from an urban-rural continuum so much as it contributes to the sense or the impression that an urban-rural continuum exists.[125] Any uniqueness of a building was manifested in its location, appellation, and history that was recorded in words rather than in its particular form and style. This appears to be one of the traits of Chinese architecture that sets it apart from Western experience.

It was each of these ubiquitous building compounds, not individual buildings, that acted as a basic unit of spatial organization of the city (or any other kind of human settlements), and the courtyard played an essential role in incorporating all its elements into a coherent whole. This realization leads to the second point that has been developed in this chapter. Apart from that of the streets,[126] any space of notable size that assumed any unambiguous functions in the city most commonly took definite shape in the courtyard. Hence the public urban space. I have cited the example of the use of the courtyard of the Daoist temple Xuanmiao Guan to illustrate that this mode of spatial arrangement was in accordance with both the traditional conception of socialized space and the sociopolitical reality of the city. A purposeful space had to belong, and thus be attached, to a certain social institution physically embodied in a certain building compound. The intramural open spaces without walled compounds consisted of only streets and alleys or vacant land, the latter, apart from constituting part of the area within the city walls, being institutionally not much different from the unoccupied pieces of ground around village houses. Moreover, the city was not a corporate entity of its own; that is, it was not strongly a social institution separated from its surrounding countryside in both jurisdictional and administrative terms. It was the temples, among many other edifices, that formed distinguishable social institutions. Therefore, when we talk about the nonexistence in Chinese cities of public squares, which were essential to most European cities, it is not so much that the city residents "had less need of them" than their European counterparts, as that spaces of this kind were inconceivable and meaningless to them. The courtyards of large temples, characterized by their utilitarian functions in society, became the loci of miscellaneous social activities.

CHAPTER 7 The City in *Fengshui* Interpretations

THIS LAST CHAPTER DEALS WITH THE APPLICATION of *fengshui* (wind and water, often translated as Chinese geomancy)[1] to the city of Suzhou and its urban constructions during the second half of the imperial period. *Fengshui* ideas were indeed an integral part of the urban phenomenon in imperial China, but to what extent and in what way were these ideas applied to city construction and development and what physical and psychological effects have they had on the cities? I shall try to answer these questions through a discussion of several historic features of the city.

The chief mode of *fengshui* application was characterized, not by actual practice in the physical construction of the city at the urban level, but by interpretation of existing diverse aspects of the city, ranging from its geographical location and natural setting to its form, space, and individual structures. In other words, the city was represented in *fengshui* language. The symbols employed in these interpretations derived not only from the *fengshui* manuals but also from popular conceptions and ideas. Because of the collective stance of the imperial scholar-officials toward *fengshui* and, more importantly, the social and ideological context of Suzhou as a regional capital city of imperial China, *fengshui* ideas exerted greater influences on the building activities of local corporate groups than on the city construction at the level of government enterprises. The outcome of the former was usually minor structures with which only small groups of the residents identified themselves, whereas the outcome of the latter determined the form and spatial pattern of the city.

Origins and Principles of *Fengshui*

Fengshui was defined appositely by Chatley as "the art of adapting the residences of the living and the dead so as to cooperate and harmonize with the local currents of the cosmic breath."[2] Its origins are vague, as March has noted, and this leaves room for disagreement.[3] Yet there is no doubt, as Feuchtwang indicates, that the symbolism of town planning and important buildings (and the divination for auspicious dates for the commencement of building) has a history many centuries longer in China than has the *fengshui* of graves and houses, although *fengshui* later shares this symbolism.[4] Although it is true that *fengshui* theories, if we are to take them as a formulated system of ideas that are faithfully denoted by that specific term, found their sources in fragmentary expositions contained in many pre-Han documents and in the recorded ancient architectural activities embodying cosmological conceptions of that age, we should be cautious not to overstretch the evidence to classify all activities of site selection and symbolism of city construction in early Chinese history under the term *fengshui* or its other alternative terms.[5]

It is not at all surprising to find that some *fengshui* proponents of later times attributed its ideas to great antiquity, especially by aligning them with the records of building activities in early Zhou times contained in the Confucian Classics, such as the *Shi jing*, *Shang shu,* and *Zhou li*.[6] Yet hard as the proponents for the early rise of *fengshui* tried to induce vindication from these didactic sources, they would surely have had to admit, as did Bu Yingtian of the Tang and Meng Hao of the early Qing,[7] that what they had were only fragmentary records of the ancients' surveying and divining of building sites, not discourses of anything that can be labeled as *kanyu*, *fengshui,* or *dili.* Also, these same didactic sources were used equally often as evidence by those who vigorously argued against *fengshui* ideas.[8] This point is important in the context of our discussion: the site of Suzhou was possibly chosen initially for geomantic considerations, and the city was built on a set of cosmological symbols, but these are consequently not to be interpreted in *fengshui* terms, even though one may find certain reference made by later *fengshui* promulgators to those events as a source of authority.[9]

The conception of *qi* (cosmic breath) forms the core of *fengshui* theories, and the central theme of these theories is the proper relationship of human dwellings for the living and the dead to the immediate environment and the universe at large. This is a universe animated by the interaction of *yin* and *yang* forces in which *qi* gives character and meaning to a place where a dwelling is sited.[10] Good siting would favor the wealth, health, and happiness of the inhabitants of the settlements and the descendants of those whose bodies lay in the tombs, while ill siting had to be properly adjusted so as to avoid evil effects of a serious nature on them. Conversely, analyses of the sites with knowledge of Chinese geomantic theories would tell the fortune of the site owners. It is this analysis and the art of good siting that is commonly called *fengshui*.[11]

Distinctions existed between the two major schools that employed different sources of ideas and laid stress on different aspects of cosmological and topographical conditions.[12] Considering the complexity of *fengshui* elaboration and practice[13] and the limited purview of this book, I shall quote only two passages by the late Yuan and early Ming writer Wang Wei (1322–1373), who summarizes the distinctive principles of the two schools in his *Qingyan conglu:*

> In later times those who advocated the art of *dili* divided into two schools. One is called the Zongmiao [Ancestral Temple] method, which began in Minzhong [the central area of present-day Fujian]. Its origins go far back, but with Wang Ji of the Song it gained great currency. Its theory focuses on the Planets and the Trigrams [*Xing-Gua*], and on the *yang* positions [*shan*] and directions [*xiang*], and the *yin* positions and directions, so that they are not at odds. By means of exclusive reliance on the Five Planets [*Wuxing*][14] and the Eight Trigrams [*Bagua*], the order of production and conquest is determined. Its doctrine is circulating in Zhejiang and Fujian, but those who presently employ it are very few.
>
> [The other] one is called the Jiangxi method, starting with Yang Yunsong and Zeng Wendi, and especially refined by Lai Dayou and Xie Ziyi. Its theory focuses on landforms and terrains [*xingshi*],[15] and on tracing back where they arise and pursuing where they stop so as to determine position and direction. Special attention is paid to the coordinations of the *long* [dragon], *xue* [cave or lair], *sha* [sand], and *shui* [water],[16] whereas other limitations and refrainments are not considered at all. Its doctrine is current nowadays, and south of the River [Yangzi], everyone follows it.[17]

The former, more often known as the Liqi (principles and cosmic breath) school, emphasized cosmology and attached much importance to the compass, which is regarded by Feuchtwang as "the most complete and comprehensive single body of feng-shui symbols."[18] The latter, on the other hand, emphasized the forms of the landscape, which is overtly signified by its more frequently used name, the Xingshi (landforms and dynamic terrains) school.[19] The former is called, respectively, by Feuchtwang and by March "Cosmology" and "Directions;" the latter, "Earthly Forms" and "Shapes."

There is no doubt that the two schools, in the early periods of their development, were distinct from, and sometimes in fierce opposition to, each other.[20] The Xingshi school was more prestigious than the Liqi school from the Song onward, a situation that is evidenced in the scattered references in non-*fengshui* texts to its application, either practical or interpretative. Theoretically, the Xingshi school should have been more characteristic of direct experience, that is, the immediate response to the whole feeling of a place, whereas the Liqi school could have been more objective, relying on the indications of the compass.[21] In reality, however, each of the two schools had, especially in later times, absorbed ingredients from the other to such an extent that it sometimes becomes difficult to draw a clear and fast line between the two in literature.[22] Thus, places recommended by Liqi could well meet the requirements of Xingshi, and the latter may have been as practical for ordinary poor people as the former.[23]

It is important to note that there were also numerous ideas and beliefs that could be categorized under the title of *fengshui* but were apparently not in accord with either of the two schools. On this phenomenon, Feuchtwang writes:

> The great bulk of evidence of these random symbols is in records, not in [*fengshui*] manuals. From this we may deduce that their inclusion in feng-shui

> interpretations is on a quite different plane from those symbols which form the discourse of the manuals. With the former we are at the most inexpert and popular level of interpretation. Anything the physical environment suggests to you may become significant in the light of appropriate circumstances. The suggestion itself is indeed probably first evoked by those circumstances. . . . On the other hand, the specifically feng-shui symbols . . . occur in any circumstances. Unlike the extraneous symbols, they exist before the specific case. Each case must be interpreted according to at least their crudest principles . . . whereas the case itself suggests the extraneous symbols.[24]

Fengshui interpretations of the city of Suzhou in the late imperial period, as will be presented later in this chapter, are characteristic of a *mélange* of symbols of these two kinds.

Fengshui Advice on Urban Construction of the City of Suzhou

Whereas the great bulk of evidence of the *fengshui* of the city of Suzhou is of a retrospective nature, there occurred in the Southern Song an important event of active *fengshui* advice on the city construction, or, more precisely, on whether two particular city gates that had been blocked should be reopened. This event is recorded by Fan Chengda in his *Wujun zhi*,[25] and the central personage involved was Hu Shunshen (ca. 1081–?), who migrated from Jixi in present-day Anhui to Suzhou in the first half of the twelfth century. There is no doubt that Hu figured prominently in the *fengshui* field: according to Fan Chengda, the book entitled *Jiangxi dili xinfa* (the new method of the Jiangxi Dili [school])[26] and current in the Southern Song was from his hand; and his deeds are included in the biographies of famous *fengshui* specialists in the "Kanyu" section of the *Gujin tushu jicheng*.[27] After surveying the four sides of the city walls, Hu Shunshen wrote an essay between 1144 and 1164[28] entitled *Wumen zhonggao* (sincere advice on the city gates of Suzhou), arguing that both Xu Gate and, more importantly, She Gate should not be obstructed.

As has been discussed in Chapter 4, She Gate remained in use as one of the eight gates of the city probably until the turn of the first millennium, when it was abandoned along with another gate. Xu Gate continued to exist in the early Northern Song, but by 1084 when Zhu Changwen wrote his *Wujun Tujing xuji*, it too had been blocked. Without going into the technical details of Hu's exposition, his points are as follows. Hu started his argument with Mt. Yang,[29] located about thirty *li* to the northwest of the city, which, because of its unmatched height in the Suzhou region, was regarded as supreme among all the nearby mountains, they being simply its offshoots stretching southward. Thus, for Hu Shunshen, the city of Suzhou took Mt. Yang as its primary mountain by the fact that it was located on the vast plain spreading from the foot of the mountain. This assertion wins support, as he sees it, from the fact that the land within the city walls was highest in altitude in the northwest, which was in accord with the location of the mountain in relation to the position of the city. Since the northwest posi-

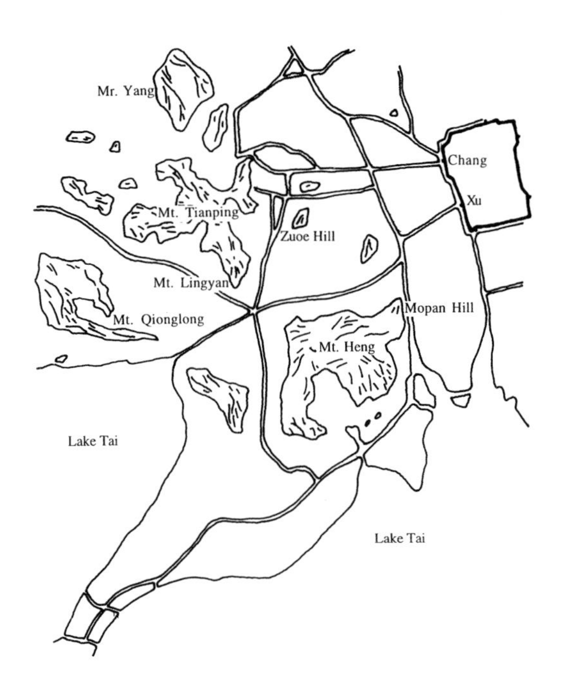

Figure 7.1 Diagrammatic map of the site of the city of Suzhou in relation to Mt. Yang and other nearby major mountains. Based on Suzhoufu zhi, tu *2: "Wuxian tu" and* tu *3: "Changzhou Yuanhe liangxian tu."*

tion corresponded with that of the most noble celestial body, known as the Purple Forbidden Enclosure (*Ziweiyuan*),[30] this particular topographical situation endowed this area with high geomantic qualities. The site of the city, Hu also argued, was located where the topographical influences (*shi*) converged and the topographical forms (*xing*) stopped and coalesced and was thus the place where the immense cosmic breath concentrated (*quanqi zhi di*). Figure 7.1 is a diagrammatic map of the site of the city in relation to Mt. Yang and other nearby major mountains.

The situation of the local waters, Hu Shunshen continued to argue, should be in correspondence with that of the mountains. Although the general pattern of rivers around the city conformed with the *fengshui* principles, there existed serious defects. The stream water coming from the true west represented prosperity, previously flowing into the city through Xu Gate; and the stream water from the southeast represented life, previously flowing into the city through She Gate. The waters of life and prosperity were most crucial for the benefit of the city, "just like the blood and breath (*yingwei*) of a human body."[31] Yet it was precisely these two gates that were blocked by Hu's time, and the grave consequences of this were evident for him in the desolation of the city and, especially, in the devastation that the Jurchen cavalry inflicted on Suzhou in 1130.[32] Of these two gates, She Gate, he felt, was the one in particular that should not be obstructed, because that would deprive the city of its vitality. Hu Shunshen then went on to mention two historic periods in support of this point. At the time of Helü Dacheng, the southeast gate, that is, She Gate, was deliberately closed to signal Wu's resolution to eradicate the state of Yue;[33] consequently, life breaths were cut off and Wu was eventually conquered and subjugated by Yue. In contrast to this severe affliction on the city was its strength and prosperity during the Jin and Tang periods, when all the eight gates—including She Gate—remained in use. Thus, if She Gate were to be reopened, Hu Shunshen concluded, the limpid, refined breaths from the southeast would flow into the city, and its misfortune throughout the recent years would be altered.

The main concern for our discussion is not whether this *fengshui* argument sounds cogent either to the traditional Chinese or to us but what this specific event tells us about the role that *fengshui* ideas and practice played in the construction of the city. Let us first examine what Fan Chengda thought of it. Fan insisted that Hu Shunshen surveyed the city walls "at leisure."[34] It is indeed possible that Hu had some other occupations and thus only used his spare time for this *fengshui* activity; as Feuchtwang suggests, geomancy was at large not considered a profession.[35] Yet it is equally possible that Hu was a fully devoted *fengshui* specialist[36] and therefore actually did not take this matter leisurely. In this latter case, then, Fan Chengda's statement probably reflects his own view on the position of *fengshui* in the daily life of a man of letters; that is, that *fengshui* was no more than a "spare time" matter.[37] There is no doubt that Fan Chengda was sympathetic toward Hu's argument; otherwise he would not have incorporated the entire essay in his work. Yet at the same time he obviously kept his distance from it—he does not overtly express his own opinion about the affair, but records Hu's regret at the eventual failure of the materialization of his ideas: "So rarely did opportunities and human efforts coincide!"[38] Thus the question is which part of the argument really attracted him. I would suggest that Fan's interest lay less in the *fengshui* exposition of the current situation of the city[39] than in the possible restoration of all the eight city gates that were recorded to have been built at the inception of the city's existence and which were open in the Jin and Tang periods—one of the glorious features of the city in the past, which had been kept alive in numerous works of eulogistic poetry and prose.

Turning to Hu Shunshen's argument itself, it is important to note that Hu's advice was not given at the request of the local government nor in fact at the request of any individual officials. He saw the shortcomings of the city in *fengshui* terms; but all that he could do was to write about them, hoping that some officials might one day pay some attention to what he had to say. This is explicitly revealed in his essay: "Those who understand *yinyang* and *fengshui* often sigh at these defects."[40] Hu Shunshen's advice is carefully worded, which is reflected in two passages of his essay. The first concerns whether Xu Gate should be reopened. We understand that, in 1144, the prefect Wang Huan built the Gusu Guesthouse by this gate, which had been disused for about half a century; probably within one or two years, he built on top of the gate the Gusu Platform as part of the guesthouse. As a state guesthouse, it was, in the mind of Fan Chengda, "unsurpassed in grandeur throughout the whole southeast region." State guests were accommodated here on their way to the imperial capital Lin'an. Hu Shunshen was aware of the importance of this establishment; he argued that it would have been beneficial if Xu Gate had not been blocked but immediately acknowledged that the newly constructed guesthouse that stood in the way of the gate was so imposing that it should not be moved. He absolved this uncompromising situation from his *fengshui* requirements by evading the question whether this west gate *should* be reopened. Instead, he tactfully writes:

> Also, the water [that would have run through Xu Gate] merely represents wealth. The water through She Gate . . . represents matters concerning writing and officialdom. In principle this gate is more important and should thus be reopened.[41]

The equation of "life" carried by water from the southeast with "scholarship and imperial office" shifts the scale of the balance of his argument to the side of She Gate. In morality, it conforms with the Confucian ideology; in practice, any offense to the local government is avoided.

The other passage reflecting Hu's caution in putting forward his suggestions is about the advantages and disadvantages of reopening She Gate:

> Nowadays, there are only five gates in use, the other [three] having all been blocked up. The one that should definitely be unobstructed is this unique She Gate. Investigating why it was blocked up, [we find that] the *Tujing*'s[42] explanation is that diverse roads converge to it and consequently defense and inspection are difficult to implement here. Alas! This is the least of considerations. Presently, since his Majesty temporarily resides in Qiantang [i.e., Lin'an],[43] the city of Suzhou should in particular open its southeast gate, so as to uphold the righteousness of Facing and Protecting [*chaogong zhi yi*] [the Emperor].[44]

This line of argument apparently aims at appealing to the imperial scholar-officials for their approval, since it reads as though Hu is concerned not only with the improvement of the fortune of the city, but, more importantly, with the fulfillment of the duty of imperial servants.

Yet in spite of all his efforts, the result was not as Hu Shunshen would have preferred. In 1164, Shen Du, a native of Wukang county, Huzhou prefecture (in the north of present-day Zhejiang), was appointed prefect of Suzhou. According to Fan Chengda, Shen was previously Hu Shunshen's colleague, and, when he learned of Hu's exposition, had much sympathy with it. In the following year, after some locals made a petition to the prefectural authority for it, Shen had his subordinates survey the position of the old She Gate and decided to reopen it in the twelfth month. As everything was ready, those who objected to this idea came forward to argue that the project would cause undue trouble to the populace (*raomin*). "To avoid calumnies," Fan Chengda stated, "[Shen] Du rescinded this project."[45] Exactly ten years later, the prefect Han Yangu was also in favor of the idea of reopening She Gate. He chose in advance an auspicious day for the construction but left office one month before he could start it.[46] In the following century, two other prefects (in the mid-1250s and the late 1260s) who were somewhat interested in this enterprise are mentioned in the *Suzhoufu zhi* compiled in the late fourteenth century by Lu Xiong. But no real attempts were made by them or anyone.[47]

It is clear that because the governmental guesthouse stood in the way of Xu Gate, reopening it was regarded as entirely out of the question; even Hu Shunshen must have known it, notwithstanding his fervent reasoning that the obstruction of this gate effectively cut off the stream of prosperity that would otherwise flow into the city. This seemed to leave only the option of reopening She Gate. For Hu Shunshen, the fact that his idea of reopening She Gate never materialized may have indicated the noncoincidence of opportunities and human efforts; if the prefect Shen Du had not been afraid of criticism, or if the prefect Han Yangu had remained in office for two more months, the gate, so Hu may have thought, would have been reestablished in the light of his exposition. From a historian's point of view, however, the failure in the realization of this *fengshui* idea manifests something more than a simple missed "opportunity," for one could well argue that the social and ideological milieu of the governing body of the prefecture of which the city was a node and symbol hardly produced the conditions that would bring this *fengshui* idea to physical realization in the city construction, even though the sporadic events mentioned here may have indicated that fortune was turning Hu Shunshen's way.

There is no doubt that, among the prefects of Suzhou through the ages, Shen and Han were in the minority in being interested in this *fengshui* proposal. Within the period of eleven years from the beginning of Shen's tenure of prefectural office to Han's dismissal, for example, there were a total of twelve scholar-officials appointed to the post.[48] It is hardly surprising that throughout the subsequent history of Suzhou, only two prefects are recorded as having paid any attention to this matter. The point is even better illustrated by the series of actions taken by Shen Du in association with the proposal, which is recorded in more detail by Fan Chengda. This prefect was sympathetic toward the idea partly because, as Fan Chengda emphasizes, he had once worked together with Hu Shunshen; that is, their personal rapport increased the chance that the prefect would make a decision in favor of Hu's opinion.[49] Yet Shen was cautious enough not to show publicly any inclination to pursue the scheme until the spring of the following year when a petition for it was made to him. Once opposition to the scheme emerged, he immediately revoked the planned project. What seems more informative is the accusation that the project was "causing trouble to the populace."

The fundamental purpose for people to employ *fengshui* in building activities was undoubtedly to secure the good fortune of their families or communities. Taken a step further, one could acknowledge the fact that, in the traditional Chinese setting, as Freedman has observed, there was more involved than a mere desire to procure good fortune: there was a moral obligation to seek a future of happiness for those for whom one is responsible.[50] In the case of construction work in the prefectural city, it was certainly the prefect who was responsible for the welfare of the people of the prefecture and whose moral obligation it was to seek a future of happiness for them. However, as I will argue extensively later in this chapter, both the prefect's personal, though not untypical, stance with regard to *fengshui* and the social and ideological context of the local government that was centered at the city hardly made the desire to bring about good fortune by means of *fengshui* a morally sound one.

Like so many other prefects of Suzhou in history, Shen might have felt no qualms about pursuing reconstruction of the city walls, restoration of gate towers, dredging of city canals, and building of other structures of the city. On such occasions, he may have shown much consideration for the populace by taking certain measures to limit the distress that the construction work might inflict on them, in the hope of then being praised for his righteous, humane ways of performing his governmental duties by his fellow officials and, more importantly, by later historians. This kind of deed was indeed regarded as one of the most commendable and is frequently recorded in the local gazetteers of Suzhou. But none of such deeds have bearings on *fengshui*. By contrast with these, the charge of "causing trouble to the populace" raised against the scheme of reopening She Gate in the light of *fengshui* ideas was so serious to the prefect that he had to cancel it outright. It was not the scale of the construction but its association with *fengshui* that rendered the charge inexorable. No other measures seem to have been considered as adequate either to reverse the prospective accusation against him or to mitigate the immediate distress to the populace, even though *fengshui* was understood by everyone who thought of it as producing long-term beneficial effects.[51]

Fengshui Interpretations of the City of Suzhou

Fan Chengda's description of the events in the mid-twelfth century and the mid-thirteenth century, centered on Hu Shunshen's argument concerning the geomantic situation of the city gates of Suzhou, is, to the best of my knowledge, the first written record of the city in history containing explicit *fengshui* ideas. From then on, particularly during the late imperial period, more accounts of the site and form of the city in the light of *fengshui* appeared occasionally in both the prefectural gazetteers and, particularly, the casual writings of the local scholars. Yet unlike the first instance which is of active (but vain) *fengshui* advice on city construction, seeking to change the fortune of the city and the prefecture, the accounts of later times are all retrospective interpretations of the city using miscellaneous *fengshui* ideas and symbols. Since many of these random symbols are basically found, not in *fengshui* manuals, but in local records, they appear to be at what Feuchtwang calls "the most inexpert and popular level of interpretation."[52] Moreover, by combing all the relevant local documents produced from the Yuan period onward that are presently at my disposal, I find that recorded *fengshui* accounts of the city, though very limited in number, range from interpretations of its grand geographical conditions all the way down to interpretations of individual structures in and around the city, and these written sources are so scattered and diverse in nature that their ideas do not form a consistent system as a whole. Because of this, only three major examples of *fengshui* interpretations of the city will be discussed in this section: topographical conditions, the overall city form, and the conformation of city space. Attention is paid not so much to the *fengshui* notions themselves as reflected in these interpretations as to the way they entered and were treated in the elite circle.

Topographical Conditions

Apart from Hu Shunshen's work, no monographs on the *fengshui* conditions of the setting of the city of Suzhou are available to us, but it is most probable that written works of this kind were in circulation during the late imperial period. In Wang Ao's (1450–1524) time, for example, *fengshui* expositions of the topographical conditions of Suzhou had developed sufficiently for him to draw upon them in his description of the city's natural surroundings. The opening passage of the two sections entitled "Mountains" in his *Gusu zhi*, a gazetteer of Suzhou compiled in 1506, reads:

> The mountains in the Suzhou area are fascinatingly beautiful; and the fine qualities of the Southeast are all concentrated here. The specialists in *dili* [texture of the earth] say that they originate from Mt. Tianmu and sprout from Mt. Yang. From Mt. Yang [the mountain range] splits into Mt. Hua and Mt. Lu, tortuously via Mt. Tianping, and terminates at Mt. Lingyan; another branch grows from Mt. Qionglong and then turns eastward, terminating at Mt. Lengjia and the mountains in Lake [Tai].[53]

This statement is an explanation of the geographical situation of the mountains in the Suzhou region made in part on some of the expositions by the specialists in *fengshui*. Such expositions apparently are closely associated with the theories of the Xingshi (landforms and terrains) school.

Mountain ranges were denoted by the Xingshi school by the figurative term *long* (dragon), or *longmai* (dragon vein). The identification of the hierarchy of the *long* was made in association with the classification of rivers, which were always perceived as flanking the *long* on both sides. Three great primary "dragons" or "stems" (*gan*) in China and its contiguous regions were identified from the *fengshui* point of view so that the geographical positions of the cities could be assessed and argued about: the three arterial mountain ranges—north, middle, and south—were believed to have all originated from Mt. Kunlun in the northwest and to have been demarcated by four major watercourses, namely, the River Yalu in the north, the Yellow River and the River Yangzi in the middle, and the South Sea in the south.[54] As Figure 7.2 shows, this perception has been diagrammatically depicted in the "Zhongguo san da gan tu" (a map of the three great stems in the Middle Kingdom), which is contained in the *Sancai tuhui* compiled in 1609 by Wang Qi and his son Wang Siyi. The same perceptive and methodological principle was applied at every level of the hierarchical system of the "dragons"; that is, as March states, the main "dragons" were seen as dividing and subdividing into lower-order stems and branches (*zhi*), affecting progressively smaller areas and fewer people and being less and less potent.[55] Thus a settlement was supposed to be built at the place where the *qi* of the "dragons" concentrated, for it was here that the influences of the mountains and waters merged, the *yin* and *yang* forces harmoniously converged, and the "affections" (*qing*) of Nature were concentrated and nurtured. A place that held an immense quantity of *qi* was considered to be suitable for the establishment of a state, provincial, or prefectural capital, while the place with meager *qi* provided the site for a county capital, a market town, or a village.

The mountain ranges in the Suzhou area are probably seen by the *fengshui* theorists as originating from Mt. Tianmu in the northwest of Zhejiang, which forms the major part of one of the prominent branches of the "south stem" (*nan gan*) or the "south dragon" (*nan long*) and from which the mountains in the entire Lower Yangzi region are believed to have arisen.[56] Mt. Yang is important to Suzhou in *fengshui* terms because, as we have seen in Hu Shunshen's elaboration in the preceding section, it is from this mountain that all others in the region derive as its offshoots. However, the "Mountains" section of Wang Ao's *Gusu zhi*, like that of any other gazetteers, deals with the locations, names, natural features, and cultural relics of these mountains together with the historic events associated with them. It does not apply any specific *fengshui* terminology, such as *long* or *longmai*, to its account of the mountains; nor does it aim at assessing the *fengshui* situation of the city's natural setting. It simply borrows the *fengshui* explanation of the mountain ranges without paying any attention to matters regarding "fortune" (in the widest sense of the term), which is the central concern of any geomantic theories. In other words, unlike Hu Shunshen's *Wumen zhonggao,* which analyzes and evaluates the *fengshui* situation of the city as determined by its surrounding topographical features, the passage in Wang Ao's work only adopts the part of *fengshui* theories

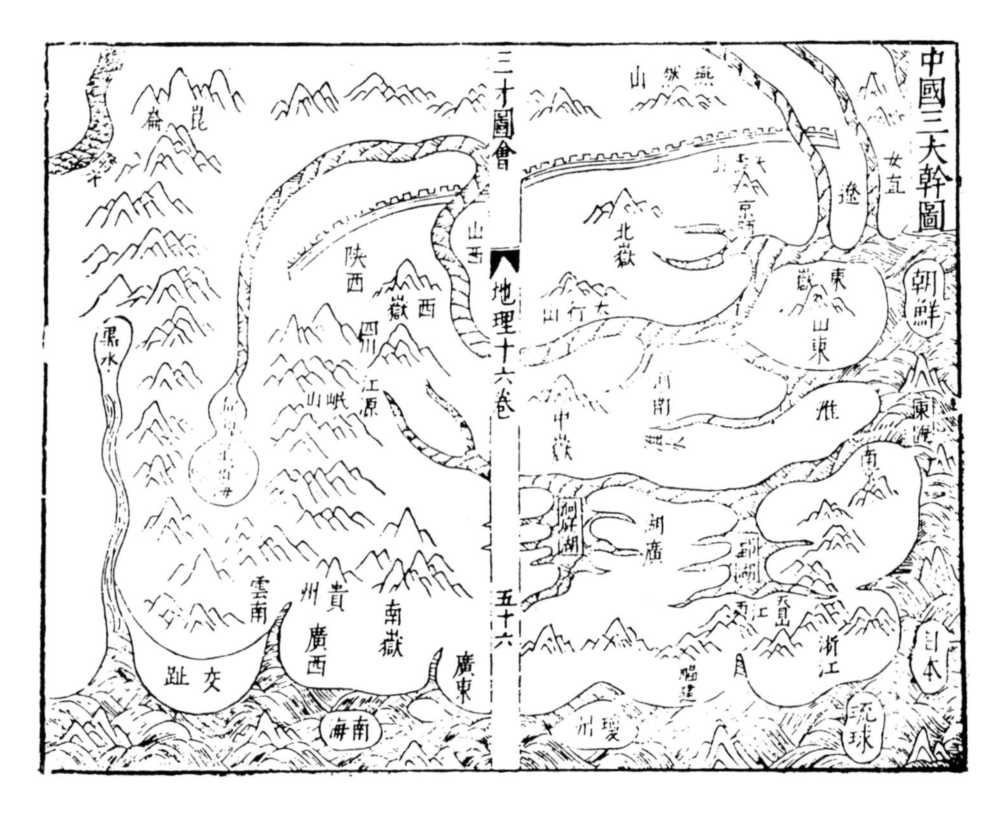

Figure 7.2 "Zhongguo san da gan tu" (literally, map of the three great stems in the Middle Kingdom), contained in Sancai tuhui, juan *16.56.*

that appears to be close to what we know as geographical description but leaves out of it any value judgment on the appropriateness of these specific mountainous conditions and the geomantic fortunes they are supposed to carry for the city and the whole prefecture, which is the crucial part of *fengshui* as a form of divination.

Not only did the existence of *fengshui* ideas about Suzhou's mountains continue in the Qing period, but different versions may have competed with each other. This is partly evidenced in Zhang Zilin's *Honglan yisheng*, a casual record of Suzhou written in 1822. Zhang's work contains a passage in which some contemporary *fengshui* interpretations are cited in a similar manner to, but in more detail than, Wang Ao's words quoted earlier:

> Among all the mountains in the Suzhou region, Mt. Qinwang[57] is the primary one [*zhen*]. Within the area of one hundred *li*, the winds, clouds, thunder, and rain all come from it. The mountain range develops southward from the west, including for instance Mt. Qionglong, Mt. Lengjia, Mt. Tianping, and Mt. Hua, meandering and rising and falling like a roving dragon [*youlong*], and settles at Mopan Hill[58] to form the *xue* [cave or lair]. . . . The specialists in landforms [*xing jia*] say that [the situation of] the city of Suzhou is determined by three dragon ranges [*longmai*]. Generally speaking, the one in the northwest comes from Mt. Jiulong and Mt. Hui, the one in the southwest from Mt. Tianmu, Mt. Lang, and Mt. Dongting, and the one in the true north links with Mt. Yu.[59]

As in the passage from the *Gusu zhi*, no assessment of the geomantic conditions of Suzhou's mountains is made by Zhang Zilin, but he is apparently more enthusiastic about *fengshui* ideas than Wang Ao,[60] for he consistently uses some of the technical terms from *fengshui* vocabulary, such as *zhen*, *long*, *longmai,* and *xue*. Three interesting points can be made by reference to Wang and Zhang's passages. First, the ideas as to where Suzhou's mountains were generated are slightly different in the two versions. In the quotation from Wang Ao, the local mountain ranges are said to arise from Mt. Tianmu alone, whereas the version adopted by Zhang Zilin states that they are formed by three "dragon ranges" coming from three different directions, only one of which Mt. Tianmu represents. Thus it is very reasonable to suggest either that the *fengshui* interpretations of Suzhou's topographical situation may not have emerged from a single source, or that during the second half of the late imperial period they had further developed to such an extent that some of them were no longer entirely consistent with each other.

The second point centers on the *fengshui* term *xue*. The idea that the *xue* is formed at Mopan Hill, as Zhang Zilin cites, possibly from some *fengshui* works current at his time, appears to be far from conforming with a favorable geomantic situation. The *xue* was supposed to be the exact spot where the cosmic breaths of life were concentrated and thus the one where a settlement or a tomb should be located. Yet as Figure 7.1 shows, the city is situated northeast of Mopan Hill, the southwesternmost of its walls being over four and a half kilometers away from this ideal spot. Although Zhang Zilin does not include in his citation any value judgment on this actual situation, the site of the city can hardly be seen as preferable according to this particular *fengshui* interpretation. Here we are presented with a more conspicuous contradiction between different versions of *fengshui* ideas, as we recall Hu Shunshen's argument that the site of the city is the place where the cosmic breaths concentrate; from this we can assume that he may have regarded it as the *xue*, even though he does not use this specific term.

The third point concerns the use of the character *zhen*. This character, denoting "to weigh (or hold) down," has many derivative meanings. In the present context, it is sufficient to mention only those connotations that seem relevant to its application to the description of mountains, namely "to stabilize" and "to pacify." One of the *fengshui* notions is that "among the mountains and valleys of a particular region, there must be one that is the highest and largest as its *zhen*, which is accordingly termed 'the ancestor mountain' [*zushan*]";[61] that is, the character *zhen* means the primary mountain when it is employed in the *fengshui* accounts of local topographical conditions. As the principal point of reference, it is believed to be able to "stabilize" and "pacify" the land of a given region. Yet unlike the other three *fengshui* terms that Zhang Zilin uses, *zhen* not only has an ancient root for its specific connotation as "primary mountains" but, more importantly, finds its place in some of the Confucian Classics. The Han scholar Kong Anguo, commenting on a sentence in the *Shang shu*, states: "The most famous and particularly large mountain of every region was taken as its *zhen*."[62] This statement is entirely consistent with the passage in the *Zhou li* about the designation of the most important mountain in each of the nine regions as a *zhen*.[63] Thus it seems certain that the term found its way into the *fengshui* theories without any significant alteration of its meaning when it was applied to the descriptions of a region's mountains.

It is precisely in the use of *zhen* in its sense as a primary mountain that we are confronted with markedly conflicting opinions between imperial scholars and *fengshui* advocates. We have seen that, in *fengshui* terms, Mt. Yang was continuously regarded as the primary mountain, or *zhen*, of the Suzhou region. Yet those who produced the local gazetteers from the Northern Song onward held different views on it. Zhu Changwen, for instance, writes in his *Wujun Tujing xuji* published in 1084:

> Mt. Tianping is . . . majestic and particularly lofty; surrounded by a group of other mountain peaks, it is the *zhen* of the prefecture. Its vegetation is graceful and verdant; it is lovely to observe.[64]

In the same volume, he also insists that Mt. Heng, to the east foot of which the city of Suzhou was temporarily "moved" around the turn of the seventh century, "pacifies" (*zhen*)[65] the southwest of this region, because, situated by Lake Tai in the west and controlling the Yue region in the south, it was the strategic point at the time of the conflict between the rival states of Wu and Yue.[66] One and a half centuries later, Zhu Mu takes up both of the two ideas in his *Fangyu shenglan* written in 1240, whereas Fan Chengda pays great attention only to the former in his *Wujun zhi* published in 1229.[67] All of the

Suzhou gazetteers compiled during the Ming and Qing periods follow these ideas presented by local historians rather than those from the *fengshui* interpretations. Lu Xiong in his early Ming *Suzhoufu zhi* goes even further, selecting Mt. Qionglong as yet another *zhen* of the prefecture, due to its magnificent height and depth.[68]

There is no doubt that the spiritual sense of the term *zhen*[69] is as strong in the historians' descriptions of the mountains as in the *fengshui* interpretations. But their perceptions never coincide. One of the main reasons for this discrepancy is, I would hypothesize, that the criteria for a mountain to be seen as the primary one in the Suzhou region are profoundly different in the minds of the local historians than in the minds of *fengshui* advocates. For the historians, a mountain that deserved to be called a *zhen* should not only be lofty but, more importantly, have the unsurpassed natural beauty that could inspire all the writers and poets who visited it to write about it. Mt. Tianping and, to a lesser degree, Mt. Qionglong, were two such mountains. As for Mt. Heng, *zhen* was applied to it because of its strategic position during a specific historic period. Yet for the *fengshui* theorists, it was the physically highest mountain in a given region that should be designated as the *zhen*. In this case, Mt. Yang, 338 meters above sea level, is indeed the highest in the Suzhou region; Mt. Tianping, by contrast, reaches to an elevation of only 221 meters. Therefore, we may say that, in one sense, the *fengshui* idea of the *zhen* when applied to mountains appears more strictly geographical, that is, more objective in terms of measurement and location, whereas the historians' views are more subjective in terms of literary inspiration. In another sense, *fengshui* theorists could to some extent detach themselves from strictly practical considerations, probably because they believed that their concerns were of long-term geomantic importance, whereas historians seem to have been ready to use the term *zhen* in their accounts of the topological features in light of strategic and military conditions.

City Form

In the *fengshui* of building, especially in the *fengshui* notions derived from the Xingshi theories, most cases represent what Freedman calls "the significance of resemblances."[70] The *Pingjiang jishi*, a casual work written by Gao Lü probably in the early 1350s when he was the prefect of Suzhou, provides us with such an example:

> The city wall of Suzhou, as the old story tells us, was built by [Wu] Zixu at the time of King Helü of Wu. Thus it is called Helü Cheng. . . . The city is in the form of the character *ya;* the common people do not know this, taking it otherwise, as the form of a tortoise[shell].[71]

The discord between the elite's perception of the form of the city and the populace's interpretation of it is revealed here most explicitly. For Gao Lü and those who produced the local gazetteers of Suzhou, the city should be properly seen and depicted as assuming the form of a particular ideogram, an idea that had been formed at least as early as the Tang period when the *Wudi ji* was written and that was continuously emphasized in all the gazetteers up to the Republican era. Yet for the common people, the use of the tortoiseshell to describe the form of the city was naturally more acceptable: it employed a figural language that could more easily be understood and expressed than the written language, and the meanings of this symbolic image had long formed part of the built-in notions of all the Chinese.

Hence, although the tortoiseshell symbolism of the city of Suzhou perhaps did not come from the *fengshui* manuals, it derived, to borrow Freedman's words again, "from the trained fancy of ordinary minds."[72] Like the case of the carp and net symbolism of Quanzhou cited by Freedman, the tortoiseshell here is an "extraneous" symbol. It could not have occurred in just any circumstances, as the standard *fengshui* symbols forming the discourse of the manuals do, but existed only on the basis of the specific conditions of the city of Suzhou (and the city of Chengdu). This perception of the city form is at what Feuchtwang sees as "the most inexpert and popular level of interpretation,"[73] although it was most unlikely to have emerged directly from the uneducated masses, since the majority of the residents in and around the city may not have had access to the city maps that were crucial for the conception of this idea.

Gao Lü does not tell us whether such a reading into the form of the city presages good or ill fortune for the city and prefectural residents, but we could reasonably expect that the tortoise, regarded by the Chinese as one of the Four Spiritual Animals (Siling),[74] was taken as a favorable symbol for the city and the prefecture.[75] This is in fact indirectly expressed in an elaborate account of the siege of the city by the Ming forces in 1367 and contained in the "Taifu shoucheng" section of Yang Xunji's (1458–1546) *Wuzhong guyu:*

> The Grand Mentor [Taifu], Wuning, Prince of Zhongshan [Zhongshan Wuning Wang], who was actually the marshal [of the Ming forces] at that time, had the city completely surrounded. Those who were within the city walls sustained [the attack] for nine months. . . . After the long siege, Wuning could not take the city. There was someone, perhaps an advisor, who suggested: "The city of Suzhou is in the form of a tortoise[shell]. It becomes more impregnable if it is attacked simultaneously from all the six positions [i.e., the six city gates]. It would be better to select one position only and attack it suddenly and fiercely, then it would be broken."[76]

Although the siege eventually ended with the victorious Ming army entering the city, the defense was seen as unusually strong because of the particular shape of the city walls, interpreted symbolically in the light of that popular *fengshui* idea. In military terms, this does not seem like a sound explanation of the fall of Suzhou: while Zhang Shicheng's men fought unusually tenaciously in defense of the besieged city, the Ming attacking battalions were so overwhelming that their onslaught on all the six gates[77] would have forced the dispersion of Zhang's soldiers along a wide front, thus weakening the strength of the defense, the collapse of which was marked by the Ming general Xu Da's (1332–1385) entrance into the city through Feng Gate and his assistant's, Chang Yuchun's (1330–

1369), entrance through Chang Gate. However, this is not a discourse on military strategy and tactics, nor a strictly historical record of the battle. What is communicated in Yang's statement is the popular *fengshui* conception of the event that was seen to be influenced by the geomantic conditions of the city.

The section in Yang Xunji's work continues with an account of the ensuing event, which may not strictly concern *fengshui* ideas but nevertheless shares *fengshui*'s main characteristics:

> The Prince of Wuning then led the soldiers and entered [the city through] Chang Gate, . . . without slaughtering a single civilian [in the city]. At the same time, the Duke of Xinguo [Xinguo Gong], infuriated by not being able to break the defense of the city for a long time, declared that once the city fell, [everyone,] even any three-year-old child, should be cut into three pieces. As Xinguo led his soldiers, entering [the city through] Feng Gate, they killed whichever city residents they encountered. When informed of this act, Wuning sent a dispatch rider to confront Xinguo's army and ordered: "Whoever kills those who have surrendered will be executed." Then Xinguo's army stopped the killing. . . . Feng Gate was where Xinguo initially entered [the city]; to date a hundred years have passed since then, but the area is still desolate. Wuning entered [the city through] Chang Gate, and thus it is now a prosperous area unsurpassed by all other gates.[78]

From a historian's point of view, this story is an even poorer document than that of the preceding passage; but in sociological terms, when its content is compared with its historic information, it can probably be seen as revealing an interesting side of the mentality of those who created this story and those who shared their feelings.

From the historiographical works produced during the Ming and early Qing periods, we learn that, unlike Chang Yuchun, Xu Da was especially well known for his disciplined military actions in all parts of China and that his armies were so well disciplined that the fall of the city of Suzhou was accompanied by no looting or pillaging.[79] What appears yet more curious and fascinating concerns the Ming army commanders mentioned in the preceding passage, namely, Wuning, Prince of Zhongshan, and the Duke of Xinguo. Who are these two personalities? According to the *Huang Ming benji*, *Huangchao ping-Wu lu,* and *Ming shi*, on the return of the triumphant Ming task force, the title of "Duke of Xinguo" was conferred on Xu Da and the title of "Duke of Eguo" (Eguo Gong) was given to Chang Yuchun. When Chang died of sudden illness in 1369, the emperor bestowed the posthumous titles of "Prince of Kaiping" (Kaiping Wang) and "the Loyal and Mighty" (Zhongwu) on him. After Xu died in 1385, he was given the posthumous titles of "Prince of Zhongshan" and "the Mighty and Peaceful" (Wuning).[80] It is clear, then, that the two characters referred to in the *Wuzhong guyu* are in fact one and the same person, Xu Da, whose identity is intentionally[81] split into two. The character who is said to have led the army through Feng Gate, allegedly inflicting misfortunes on the city then and in the years to come, is referred to by one of Xu Da's titles gained in his lifetime, right after he captured the city of Suzhou; the other character, who is said to have led the army through Chang Gate, which was believed to have presaged the prosperity of the city, is alluded to by Xu Da's posthumously bestowed titles.[82]

Why? We certainly cannot be sure of reading precisely the thoughts of those who elaborated the story, but I would hypothesize that what is expressed is their ambivalent attitudes toward the overthrow of Zhang Shicheng's regime by the Ming forces and its lasting effects. Many people of Suzhou may not have believed that the Mandate of Heaven had shifted to the Ming; they fought against the enemy armies indomitably and were said to remain loyal to Zhang Shicheng even years after the fall of the city.[83] Their enmities against early Ming rule were aggravated by the banishment to the arid Huai areas of thousands of the local rich and men who had held office under Zhang and by the new, punitive taxes imposed on the Suzhou region, which, as Gu Gongxie says, averaged ten times higher than those elsewhere in the empire.[84] On the other hand, the new local government, having replaced that of Zhang Shicheng, was, as Mote insists, "efficient, well-organized, and thorough—all of the things that the Chang Shih-cheng [i.e., Zhang Shicheng] rebel regime had failed to be."[85] More important, it was the Ming period, especially after the imperial capital was formally transferred from Nanjing to Beijing in 1421, that witnessed the steady rise of Suzhou, eventually becoming the dominant metropolis in the entire Lower Yangzi region.[86]

Thus, by the mid-Ming, bitter memories of the harsh treatment of Suzhou by Zhu Yuanzhang may still have lingered on, whereas the increasing wealth and prosperity there, epitomized by the development of the area at Chang Gate, was hardly deniable. What is communicated in this fabricated story of the Ming armies entering the city is therefore a perception of the combination of the good and ill fortunes that had been brought on Suzhou during the turbulent second half of the fourteenth century. This history of the region in these decades is somewhat "condensed" to the single event in 1367. Xu Da is logically taken as the symbol of the victorious Ming forces; the prosperity that ensued from the early fifteenth century around Chang Gate is interpreted as heralded by the favorable side of Xu Da's action, whereas the enduring plight around Feng Gate is explained as foreboded by the imagined atrocious side of Xu's action.[87] The sharp contrast between the conditions of the two areas, symbolizing the complicated fate of Suzhou at that time, is referred to as a consequence of the different bearings of the Ming victory and subsequent rule. Here, though, from a discussion of the popular geomantic notion of the city form we have digressed to note a psychological projection of the political, social, and economic life of the people of Suzhou in the first half of the Ming period, whereas the *fengshui* interpretations of the city are more centrally pertinent to our topic.

Conformation of City Space and Principal Structures

The next example of *fengshui* interpretations of the city of Suzhou comes from the casual works of two nineteenth-century local scholars, namely Zhang Zilin's *Honglan Yisheng,* written in 1822, and Shen Shouzhi's *Jiechao biji,* probably written in the 1860s. Unlike the preceding case in which the key symbol, the tortoiseshell, stands basically extraneous to the discourse of *fengshui* manuals, the one that follows is hinged on the dragon, a standard and most commonly used symbol of the Xingshi school. "Dragons," Freedman notes, "are themselves the outward expression of the favorable mystical forces animating a landscape."[88] In our case, however, this symbolic creature is perceived by an identification, not of the natural topographical conditions, but of the particular conformations of the space and principal structures of the city.

Let us begin with the passage in Zhang Zilin's work:

> Hulong [protective dragon] Street[89] runs straight from south to north through the city. The specialists in landforms [*xingjia*] have indicated that the street is the dragon's body; the North Temple Pagoda[90] is its tail; the prefectural school is its head; the Twin Pagodas[91] are its horns, taking in the cosmic breath from the *chenxun* [i.e., east by south] direction; the double wells in front of the main gate of the prefectural school are its eyes; and its nearby land is its brain, because it produces [a special kind of] peppermint whose fragrance is not too pungent but very delicate, like the aroma of *longnao* [borneol, but literally "dragon's brain"], and thus being called *longnao* peppermint.[92]

This is a retrospective *fengshui* interpretation not only elaborated from the configuration of some of the principal urban structures but also facilitated by the appellations of certain places in the city.[93] Figure 7.3 indicates the positions of some of the city structures involved in this interpretation, which shows that the dragon image seen by the *fengshui* advocates has little to do with these real structures. It is in fact an example of "projection of the imagination," to borrow Feuchtwang's words,[94] aimed principally not at foretelling the future of the city, but, in the manner of recollection, at verifying its success in the past.

It is worth noting that the key inspirational element for this interpretation is the prefectural school-temple located in the south by west of the city. The topic gains more interest if we review various versions of the account of the initial founding of the school from the Northern Song onward. Both Zhu Changwen and Fan Chengda record that, in 1035, Fan Zhongyan (989–1052), a prominent scholar-official of the Northern Song, "separated out a corner of the land of the South Garden as its site and then had it established" after having successfully petitioned in a memorial to the emperor concerning this matter.[95] The site, picturesque as it must have been, was a convenient choice, but no geomantic considerations are mentioned or even implied by either of the two scholars. By 1506, when Wang Ao finished his *Gusu zhi*, a new version of the event appeared. In *juan* 24, entitled "School," the record reads basically the same as those of the two Song writers, but an interesting interlinear note is interpolated:

> The area [where the school is located] is at the South Garden previously possessed by Qian Yuanliao, Prince of Guangling.[96] His Honor [i.e., Fan Zhongyan] acquired a corner of it on which he intended to build his own house. A geo-

> mancer claimed that [this was a place where] highly respected officials would frequently be produced. His Honor said, "How can my family's nobility be as preferable as the nobility of all the people of Suzhou? This [more preferred nobility] will be limitless." Hence he took [the area] as [the site of] the school.[97]

From the historic point of view, the story of Fan Zhongyan's initial intention of building a house on this site must be a fabrication,[98] as most probably is the geomancer's advice. Yet for the people of Suzhou, this account was surely as credible as the one that is historically verifiable, its credibility being largely due to the traditionally admired deeds of Fan Zhongyan, which are epitomized in the famous motto expressed in his *Yueyang Lou ji:* "Be concerned before anyone else in the world, and enjoy oneself only after everyone else finds enjoyment." Because of the alleged high geomantic quality of the site and the paramount importance of the prefectural school to the success of the

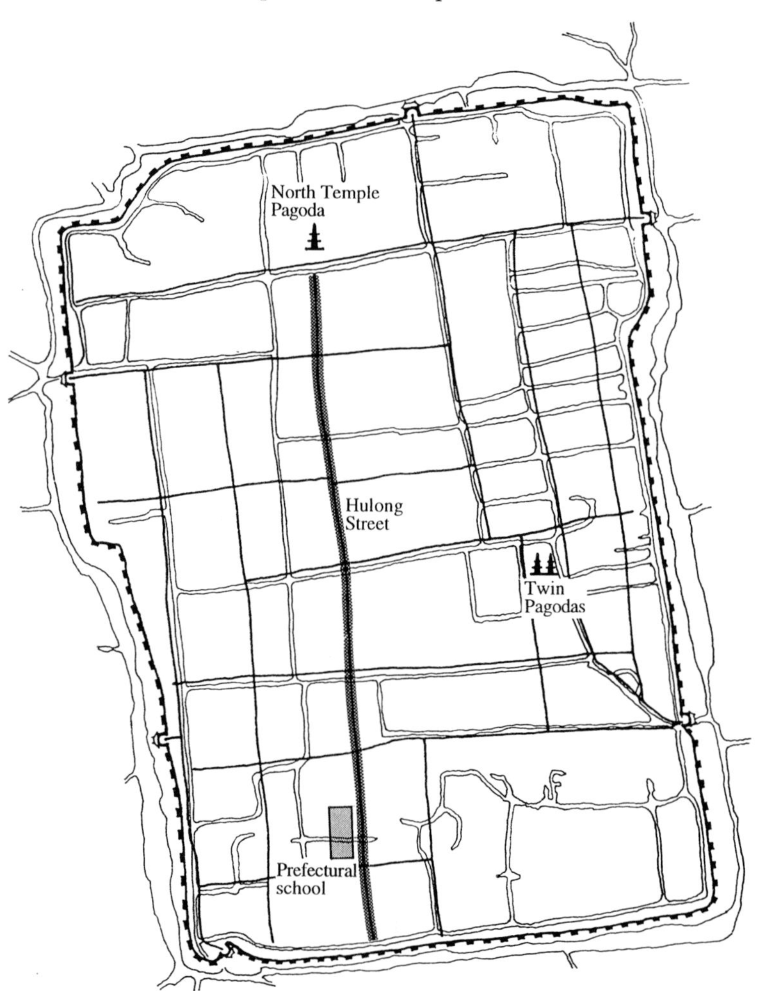

Figure 7.3 *Positions of the main urban structures involved in the cognition of the dragon image in the city.*

local candidates in the imperial examinations, by Zhang Zilin's time it was conveniently identified as the dragon's head, and the rest of the objects were elaborated accordingly to form a seemingly consistent symbolic system.

Zhang Zilin does not include in his work any explicit value judgment on this *fengshui* situation of the city. It is Shen Shouzhi who pays more attention to this matter. In his *Jiechao biji*, Shen writes:

> I do not have much belief in *fengshui* theories. Yet there are also cases in which they cannot be defamed. Our Suzhou's success in the imperial examinations is unmatchable among other provinces. During the Qianlong and Jiaqing reign-periods [1736–1795 and 1796–1820], the success was at its peak. . . . Hulong Street in the city, over ten *li* long, taking the prefectural school as the dragon's head and the North Temple Pagoda as the dragon's tail, has a bearing on the *fengshui* situation of the whole city. It has been known from the past that this street is unsuitable for tunneling or digging, for it has been feared that such kind of acts would impair the dragon range. In the mid-Daoguang reign-period [1821–1850], . . . the area [near the Guandi Temple by Hulong Street] was cleaned up, and the twin wells there were dredged and sunk, and wooden railings were installed around them for the convenience of the residents in drawing water. From then on, successful candidates in the examinations at both the provincial and the national levels became fewer and fewer. In the one at the national level in 1850, it actually went so wrong [for Suzhou] that all its candidates failed. The blame [for these failures] started to be laid on the dredging of the wells, which impaired the dragon range. A few members of local gentry petitioned the authority to have them filled in and blocked up, but the situation remained unchanged and their effort did not bear any fruit. Consequently, the city has now been occupied by the bandits [i.e., Taiping rebels]. I wonder whether there will be anyone discussing this matter again [i.e., filling the wells] once the city is recovered.[99]

Unlike Zhang Zilin, who wrote his *Honglan yisheng* at the time when Suzhou was still prosperous, Shen Shouzhi lived during the period when life in Suzhou had taken a dramatic down-turn; in particular, he witnessed the fall of the city to the Taiping rebels and all the ensuing misfortunes. Thus, in contrast to Zhang, who pays attention to the interpretation of the favorable *fengshui* situation of the city, Shen inevitably gives more of his mind to regretting the unwanted "interference" with this situation, which he sees as accounting for all the mishaps that Suzhou experienced from the mid-nineteenth century onward.

Applicability of *Fengshui* Ideas to Urban Constructions

How much and in what way was *fengshui* important in the formation and transformation of regional or local cities like Suzhou? This is a very large question, in the sense that every city was more or less a unique case with regard to the specific historic conditions under which it was built and developed. It would therefore be unwise to make hasty generalizations. It should be recognized that the time and process of the establishment of a city may render it characteristic of different sources of cosmological ideas.[100] I would therefore only hypothesize that, although *fengshui* ideas widely influenced the site selection, site adjustment, and construction of tombs, houses,[101] gardens, villages, and, possibly to some extent, imperial capitals, it should not be taken for granted that the apparently omnipresent practice of *fengshui* was equally active in the planning and construction of regional and local cities.

Before presenting analyses and arguments in support of my hypothesis, it is important to acknowledge that my inquiries are based entirely on literary evidence. Latent problems may ensue from this approach, since the information provided by the surviving written documents is often misleading, as their authors were most likely to have been biased to various extents against ideas and even historical facts that they found hard to accept. What would be more reliable for the study of the materialization of ideas is archaeological and remaining physical evidence. Here, however, lies the difficulty fairly specific to the investigation of the application of *fengshui* to building activities during the periods that are remote from our time: since the social function of *fengshui* as a way of conceiving, perceiving, and dealing with reality was basically psychological and ritualistic in nature, and since its loosely defined prescriptions and regulations could be manipulated to such extent that they left the way open to diverse, and often contradictory, interpretations of particular situations,[102] it is, at least in most cases, impossible to determine on physical evidence whether and to what extent, if any, *fengshui* operated in any building project. Hence, despite all their inherent shortcomings, the surviving written documents seem to be the only sources on which we can possibly rely.

The influence of *fengshui* on the physical construction of the cities was less in literary evidence than its influence on other architectural activities in imperial China. Those students who wish to insist on the ubiquity of *fengshui* in traditional building activities may feel frustrated when they find it extremely difficult to obtain consistent and reliable literary records about *fengshui*'s influence on the construction of regional and local cities. *Fengshui* theories have been very richly documented. Many of their discourses enunciate where and how a city *should* be planned and built according to their principles, but many fewer real cases of cities as evidence in support of these theories are mentioned than those of houses, gardens, villages, and tombs. The accounts about how a city was actually built with *fengshui* considerations, scattered and very small in number as they are, usually appear in local gazetteers or casual notes (*biji*). Since many of these accounts were probably written centuries after the events to which they refer, their reliability is very questionable.[103] Apocryphal accounts have always been troublesome to all academic approaches. Yet this problem seems to have been more serious in the case of *fengshui*, and especially in the case of its influence on the physical forms of cities. The cause of the intensity of this problem concerning the influence of *fengshui* on city constructions appears to be twofold: first, the scarcity of actual cases in which cities were built on *feng-*

shui schemes, or at least, the lack of contemporary records of such events, and, second, the apparently abstruse nature of *fengshui* theories making more room for various elaborations.

Since *fengshui* as a set of cosmological ideas has its social, political, and cultural implications, two related lines of reasoning may be taken to support my hypothesis. One of them concerns the social attitudes toward the influence of *fengshui,* that is, we may ask how much enthusiasm the governing individual or group of people of the community had for *fengshui* ideas. In his discussion of the cosmology of Chinese imperial capitals, Wright insists that "despite its ancient pedigree and the approval of Chu Hsi [i.e., Zhu Xi], *feng-shui* and the 'emanation' theory associated with it did not become an integral part of the dominant Confucian ideology or of its subideology of the city. It was introduced into later city planning not by the scholar-officials but by their often restive masters, the emperors of China."[104] To extend this observation from the field of imperial city construction to the whole of society, one is inclined to suggest that, apparently omnipresent as they were, *fengshui* ideas and, especially, practice, were not entirely approved openly by the majority of the scholar-officials and classically educated intellectuals, who as a group consciously made efforts to perpetuate the elite culture of imperial China.[105] This is certainly an overgeneralized statement, because the social reality of imperial China was much more complicated than a simple, sharp division of the population into three groups, the emperors and the populace at the two ends and the intellectuals in the middle.[106] Yet there is not space enough here to pursue in detail an analysis of this kind, nor would my knowledge and the materials at my disposal be equal to the task if there were. My discussion therefore has to dwell on the general perspective outlined earlier, and the subsequent conclusions in many cases are drawn on an *ex silentio* basis.

There were those who were deeply skeptical about the legitimacy of *fengshui* or even vigorously objected to it on a Confucian moral ground.[107] Individuals with such uncompromising outlook may not have been many in society, even though their scholarly activities formed what Needham calls a "skeptical tradition" in history.[108] The majority of Chinese intellectuals may have paid certain attention to *fengshui* ideas, perhaps partly due to the fact that the underlying principles of *fengshui* were in conformity with the long-lasting worldview of the Chinese people and that many of its ideas and symbols derived, through elaboration and sometimes distortion, from ancient cosmic conceptions that were the backbone of the orthodox cosmology; but they were reluctant to accept it fully,[109] especially on its pragmatic ground, even though they apparently did not categorically deny *fengshui* ideas in their cosmological sense. This kind of stance is usually reflected in their casual writings. In his *Su tan*, the Ming scholar-official Yang Xunji, for instance, tells us an interesting story of this kind. The father of his friend, a Mr. Wang, was one of the assistants of the prefect of Dongping in the 1440s. During the dredging of a river, a stone slab was found in an excavated ancient tomb, with an epitaph suggesting, in *fengshui* terms, that five hundred years later a prefectural assistant whose family name was Wang would save the tomb from being flooded away. Shortly after he moved the tomb, out of curiosity, to another site according to this somewhat prognostic passage, he was promoted to prefect. Yang Xunji continues:

> He then said with a smile: "The ancients only suggested that I would be a prefectural assistant. Now I have taken hold of the official seal [of the prefecture]. Have I gained excessively?" He continued his officialdom until he died.[110]

Another example of this kind of attitude toward *fengshui* is revealed in a passage by Wei Guangfu (ca. 1789–1853), a Changzhou holder of the *shengyuan* degree and a locally well-known poet, according to the *Suzhoufu zhi*.[111] He was seemingly interested in *fengshui* ideas and symbols. In his *Wenjian chanyou lu*, a casual piece of writing rather than a *fengshui* manual, he discusses some of the *fengshui* principles in fairly positive terms but at the same time caustically criticizes any excessive elaboration of its ideas. He bluntly states that "any day when it is bright, the air is fresh, and the wind and sunshine are genial, is the auspicious moment [for burial]," as opposed to the practice of choosing a propitious time according to *fengshui* elaborations.[112] More interesting is his scornful remark on the popular attribution of a few *dili* discourses to Liu Ji (1311–1375), a prominent minister of the Ming founder Zhu Yuanzhang:

> This is especially ridiculous. Just think. The land under Heaven being as vast as it is, how could it all be surveyed piece by piece! Besides, [Liu Ji] was whole-heartedly assisting Taizu [i.e., Zhu Yuanzhang] in conquering the world. Exploits and documents were so many that not a single day was free [for him]. How could he have had any spare time to do unimportant, leisurely things as those![113]

The point is not whether Liu Ji really wrote *fengshui* works—the *Kanyu manxing*, for example, is most probably from his hand—but what Wei Guangfu thought of it, his writings unmistakably reading uncritical of *fengshui* itself. For Wei, *fengshui* remained "unimportant" in political and social life, and talking about it or writing on it was simply a leisure activity that should not interfere with one's governmental duties.

Both Yang Xunji and Wei Guangfu were Suzhou scholars, but their attitudes toward *fengshui* ideas and practice are probably not far from representing the general stance of the majority of imperial scholars in the whole country. Even those who were not only sympathetic toward *fengshui* ideas but also in direct service of the emperors often maintained a cautious attitude. The remarks by one of the imperial inspectors (*zhongcheng*), Zhu Jian, in his memorial to the Ming throne in 1449, seem to have exemplified their ambivalent stance. While arguing in the light of *fengshui* ideas the advantages and disadvantages of some of the recently constructed buildings in the palatial complex in Beijing, he declares,

> [We] must not whole-heartedly believe in the art of Yinyang (*yinyang zhi shu*), yet [we] could not entirely denounce the accounts of Dili (*dili zhi shu*) either.[114]

Shen Shouzhi's remarks in his *Jiechao biji* on the *fengshui* interpretation of the city of Suzhou, to which we will have occasion to return, is made in a tone strikingly similar to Zhu Jian's.

One may find that, among numerous imperial and local documents, examples like the ones cited so far are relatively few indeed; but the opposite cases are many fewer. Citing documents either supporting or disputing *fengshui* ideas, however, by no means implies that importance should be attached to whether the classically educated men actually believed in *fengshui*, a line of inquiry that would miss the point here. On this issue, Freedman rightly warns us that "beliefs and disbeliefs are expressed in a context, and one can too easily fall into the trap of gathering evidence in the contexts of skepticism."[115] Some of the local scholar-officials' indifference or, in some cases, repugnance, to pursuing any project of city construction in light of *fengshui* theory may not always indicate their total lack of belief, or more often, interest, in it. There is no doubt that *fengshui* occupied what Freedman calls "a highly ambiguous status in the world of the educated."[116] This ambiguity was brought about not only by the ambivalent stance of the majority of individual intellectuals toward *fengshui* but also by their different backgrounds of education and self-cultivation; in other words, the educated must not be regarded as all standing on an intellectually undifferentiated plane. As Rawski writes in cautioning against overgeneralizing this highly complex issue,

> Educated men were not necessarily creative intellectuals, and many must have adhered to beliefs in what we call the popular realm. We close a potentially important area of inquiry if we draw a sharp line between educated and uneducated that correlates with belief systems.[117]

It seems reasonable to assume, for instance, that not every one of them would have objected to the undertakings of a *fengshui* scheme in the building of his private houses, of the tombs of his parents or grandparents, or of his home village (if he originally came from a rural community), even though he could, at the right place and the right time, well have raised a voice in opposition to such undertakings in city construction.[118]

The question central to the present discussion is whether and to what extent the classically educated men accepted *fengshui* as an "ideology," to borrow Feuchtwang's word, that provided interpretations of the world as well as shaped actions within it. The evidence that I have assembled suggests that *fengshui* ideas, with their inherent divinatory implications, perhaps never took a significant position in the mentality of the majority of these members of society. Since it was precisely those intellectuals who were appointed to regional and local governmental posts, we could hardly expect them in most cases to have encouraged the application of *fengshui* in the construction of the cities in their charge. This is evident in various records of the city of Suzhou, which document how the local scholar-officials, on occasions of building activities at the level of individual buildings, bridges, or honorific gateways, either condemned the errors in the name of *fengshui* or forcefully implemented schemes that were seen by some as incongruous with *fengshui* interpretations. One can hardly say that all of them were unfamiliar with its language—some of them may have been conversant with it, while others must have known some of it[119]—nor that they rejected the orthodox cosmology that underlay *fengshui*—on the contrary, the orthodox cosmology constituted the very foundation of their world view.[120] But this is not the same thing as accepting *fengshui* itself, a set of geomantic ideas elaborated on the basis of the orthodox cosmology for the *purpose* of procuring present and future wealth, health, and happiness, that is, good fortune in the broadest sense of the word.

Yet to argue that imperial scholar-officials' reluctance to accept *fengshui* in full was responsible for *fengshui* having much less influence on the planning and building of regional and local cities than on the construction of houses, tombs, villages, and gardens may turn out to be problematic. Like the question of beliefs and disbeliefs, the extent of its acceptance was socially contextual. This leads to the other, more important, line of reasoning that I take to support my hypothesis: the walled cities on which the local governments were based did not form the kind of social context that would have promoted, as did those of houses or villages and, to a lesser degree, market towns and perhaps imperial capitals, the application of *fengshui* to their building projects.

Here the discussion is limited to two aspects of regional or local cities in imperial China that set the social context of these cities apart from those of other social categories. The first aspect is urban social formation. Chinese society was largely based on family values; within the family or, to some extent, familylike structure, decisions and actions taken by the leaders for the welfare of its members, right or wrong, were usually tolerated by outsiders and the authorities.[121] Within such a domain, a scholar-official could have acted on *fengshui* ideas without any concern about serious criticism that would cost his official career or, at least, tarnish his reputation. The cities, however, were not the personal properties of the scholar-official. They never developed the distinctive institutions or any degree of autonomy with regard to the state, which would have been possible only within the looser, feudal matrix.[122] The population of the city did not form a corporate, self-identifying, and self-perpetuating group who otherwise shared a common interest and, more importantly, a sense of common origin but was basically a sum total of individuals, each of whom was closely linked with the village from which the family had originated and where its ancestral temple stood.[123] In brief, unlike family systems, the cities were open institutions. Consequently, any decision or action taken by a county magistrate, a prefect, or a provincial governor that was of public nature was open to attack by others. This may have been one of the specific conditions of the cities that deterred those scholar-officials who were sympathetic toward *fengshui* from allowing it to determine concrete actions in city construction.

The second aspect is the social milieu of the governing body of the city. On the one hand, unlike tombs, houses, villages, and, to some degree, the imperial capitals, which encompassed the governing individual's or group's personal, enduring possessions in both practical and symbolic terms, cities were never personal possessions of the regional and local governmental officials, nor could any prominent family or group of people in them make a personal claim to them. Thus, even if an imperial official was a devotee of *fengshui*, he would seem to have had much less personal will to implement its ideas in the physical transformation of the city as a whole than in the realm of similar activities in his family or lineage. On the other hand, China in the second half of the imperial period was principally what Johnson calls "a grammatocracy: the learned ruled," where a single elite controlled all national institutions.[124] Local governments in particular were such institutions in which scholar-officials clustered; the construction of cities as imperial administrative centers was exclusively the concern of the members of the cultural elite, except for very few cases when the emperors personally intervened.

A perception of landscape that was closely associated with *fengshui* ideas and language may have been very widely shared by many members of the elite during the Ming, as Clunas argues.[125] Yet the denunciation of *fengshui* practice and, perhaps to a lesser degree, its theories, would have become more conspicuous in the social milieu of the local government than in that of many other institutions. Under the close scrutiny from his classically educated peers, a scholar-official had to be extra scrupulous in matters associated with geomancy, and his personal inclination toward *fengshui* ideas was inevitably restrained within such a particular social context.[126] We should certainly acknowledge that it was Chinese cognition in general that the geomantic fate of a prefecture or county was held to derive not only from the siting of its capital city but its form and spatial pattern, for a capital city was always regarded as the node and the symbol of the total administrative territory. But what the construction of capital really symbolized as, above all, the establishment of the rule of the imperial government and the consolidation of social order, both of which remained at the core of the elite culture perpetuated by the imperial scholar-officials as a whole.

This is not to say cities were never consciously constructed and their sites never consciously or subconsciously chosen based on *fengshui* ideas. The practice of *fengshui* was more active in the far southeast region than in other areas of China, and thus literary evidence is relatively more likely to be found in the local documents of the areas of present-day Zhejiang, Jiangxi, Guangdong, Fujian, and Taiwan provinces. In his study of the formation of cities in Taiwan, Lamley, for example, has mentioned the appearance in local gazetteers of references to divination and geomancy in accounts of wall construction in three northern Taiwanese cities, namely Xinzhu, Yilan, and Taibeifu, and has emphasized the particular importance of *fengshui* considerations in the layout of Yilan, although he does not tell us how reliable these references are likely to be for learning about the actual process of the construction of these cities.[127] The site of the prefectural city of Wenzhou, according to the *Zhejiang tongzhi*, was determined by Guo Pu; similarly, Gu Gongxie claims in his *Xiaoxia xianji zaichao* that the prefectural city of Huzhou (present-day Wuxing in Northern Zhejiang) was planned geomantically by Guo Pu.[128] Yet could these accounts produced nearly one and a half millennia after the alleged events be trustworthy in historiographical terms?

Among the cities in the Suzhou region, only the building of the county city of Kunshan is said to have been associated with *fengshui;* the choice of its site was probably made in consideration of the *fengshui* of Mt. Ma'an.[129] But we do not know when exactly the event occurred—it might well go back to the Qin period—nor are we sure whether this is again a retrospective explanation. In fact, written records of city construction under the *fengshui* influence, regardless of their reliability, are very few indeed, and this paucity itself comes to support the major point that I have so far developed: theoretically, as many geomantic documents advocate, *fengshui* should have operated in man-made construction of all kinds and continuously at each stage of the planning or growing processes right down the scale—from the settlement as a whole to all individual buildings—yet in practice, as the actual guidelines, it functioned less actively in the construction of a regional or local city than in many other architectural activities and less often on the overall urban structure than on smaller scales of spatial arrangement in and around the city. Even if we are to avoid sweeping generalization, it would probably be safe to insist that the physical applications of *fengshui* ideas, if any, are more likely to be found in the far south than the north. The city of Suzhou is located in between them; *fengshui* is not, as abundant evidence has shown in the preceding two sections, recorded to have been influential in the physical outcome of any urban construction projects there.[130]

Freedman has drawn a general picture of the application of *fengshui* in the Chinese social landscape:

> In fact, *feng-shui* is applicable to any unit of habitation, so that from the single house at one end of the scale to the society as a whole there is a hierarchy of nesting units each with its *feng-shui* and subject also to the *feng-shui* of all the higher units to which it belongs. That is to say, localized lineages, villages, cities, districts, and provinces have each their geomancy; it may derive from the chief place (for example, the capital of an administrative unit) or the chief building (for example, the ancestral hall of a localized lineage) of the unit in question.[131]

The applicability of *fengshui* in the cities is indeed beyond all question. The point is rather of the manner of application; that is, in what way should we appropriately regard *fengshui* ideas as an integral part of the urban phenomenon in imperial China?

Wright has noted when he refers to the experience of city building in the South before the Sui reunification, the fact that for cities, *fengshui* "seems to figure more in the retrospective writings of later scholars than in the actual choice of site."[132] This observation, I believe, can be extended to the second half of the imperial era and thus epitomizes the probable historical fact that in most cases the *fengshui* of the city existed in retrospective interpretation and perception rather than as guiding principles in actual urban construction. Such interpretations and perceptions, on the one hand, facilitated the *fengshui* specialists' assessment of any existing city's geomantic conditions with regard to its security, prosperity, and sometimes superiority over those in its surrounding areas and, on the other hand, provided the residents of the city with new schematic ingredients for them to construct a metaphysical conception of the city and thus to maintain in them a sense of psychospiritual balance. I have shown in the preceding two sections how *feng-shui* ideas were employed in the interpretations and perceptions of the city of Suzhou, but they were seldom contained in the official history of the region.

It should also be emphasized that *fengshui* encompasses merely *a* set of cosmological ideas that were elaborated on the basis of various sources from ancient texts, which matured probably during the Han period, rather than *the* Chinese system, as Meyer remarks (possibly offhandedly),[133] which *ipso facto* would encompass all kinds of cosmological conceptions found in ancient or traditional architectural activities in China. The fact is that most instances of the occurrence of *fengshui* symbols in other contexts could be collected. It would be most erroneous to describe them as symbols coming exclusively from the *fengshui* scheme. On the contrary, the prevalence of concepts including the Five Elements, *yin* and *yang*, the Eight Trigrams, and so forth, and the symbolization of Heaven and Earth, the seasons and the four quarters, were independent facets of a widely accepted cosmology. The *fengshui* scheme should therefore be understood, as Feuchtwang rightly emphasizes, "as a point in the development of Chinese metaphysical thought around which such concepts and symbols have clustered and been arranged."[134] By the same taken, it would be misleading to categorize under the title of *fengshui* either various modes of archaic cosmological symbolism or the canonical rituals and the imperial ideology of city building.

Other cosmological or metaphysical conceptions of cities found in local customs of later imperial times should also be carefully distinguished from *fengshui*, even though they might occasionally have been expressed in certain *fengshui* terms or absorbed a few of its various notions. If there was an all-encompassing cosmology, it was then part of the enduring worldview of the Chinese people, under the sway of which various modes of applicational systems, including *fengshui*, coexisted. Thus, some imperial scholars might have described some cities by using terms that were closer, or even identical, to those employed in *fengshui* theories, but it does not necessarily mean that these scholars' perception of the cities were influenced by *fengshui* ideas, and, conversely, a description of this kind actually reflected the persistent worldview with which *fengshui* ideas, and hence most of its terms, were largely in accordance.[135] After all, most cosmological terms were borrowed into the *fengshui* elaboration and were not in its exclusive use.

Fengshui and the City

Earlier in this chapter, I demonstrated that, at least from the Southern Song period on, the city of Suzhou at its urban level was inextricably involved with diverse *fengshui* ideas. There is however no evidence of *fengshui* influence on any construction works that would have had significant impact on the overall form and spatial pattern of the city. Apart from Hu Shunshen's recommendation in the mid-twelfth century that She Gate be reopened in the light of his reading of the geomantic situation of the siting of the city, which proved to be a vain attempt, all the records of *fengshui* application to the city in later periods are characteristic of retrospective interpretation.[136] These cases reflect that not only the competing versions of expert *fengshui* ideas but also the notions of the elite and the geomantic interpretations at popular level all dwelled on what Freedman calls "a central theme in Chinese metaphysics—man's place in nature and the universe"[137] —and shared the fundamental view of being in tune with the universe. These cases also show that in the course of time these different ideas, notions, and interpretations drew elements from each other to such an extent that none of them can be treated entirely on its own. Yet incongruity between them is obvious and significant, and consequently *fengshui* practice in building activities in and around the city could not but operate in a very complicated situation.

I also argued in the preceding section that, since an ambivalent attitude toward *fengshui* and other popular "superstitions" was built into Chinese administration and the outlook of civil servants, and since the local government body and the social structures of the city did not form a context that would foster *fengshui* practices, the inapplicability of its ideas to the physical construction of the city is hardly surprising. That is not to say, however, that no building activities in the city ever fell under *fengshui* influence. In fact, the phrase *buju* (choose and divine a dwelling-place) and *buzhai* (choose and divine a house) are frequently used in numerous local documents referring to gentry families' choice of the site of their urban residence. Although the character *bu* in these contexts may have long been a formal term only denoting "choose" and may have been detached from its ancient meaning of fortune-telling, we cannot entirely rule out the geomantic implications of these phrases. Constructions in and around the city by local lineages, guilds, and the like were also inclined to be influenced by *fengshui* ideas. A notable example, the building of honorific gateways (*fangbiao*) during the late imperial period, appears in Gu Zhentao's statement in his *Wumen biaoyin*:

> The honorific gateways [in praise] of the sons of filial piety and the women of chastity and filial piety, . . . [their builders] being so often deluded with *fengshui* [requirements] [*huo yu fengshui*], were either built into the walls [of houses] or covered with a roof; there were also many that collapsed and were abandoned. Their fundamental significance of public commendation has utterly been lost.[138]

It should not be too unreasonable to surmise that other kinds of building activities conducted by local corporate groups were in a similar situation.

What, then, were the situations of building activities that fell in between these two levels; or, what would have happened, for instance, to an operation of the nongovernment enterprises with regard to the collective interests of the urban residents, in which *fengshui* ideas were involved? I would like to cite an informative and well-documented case, the building of Wannian (ten thousand years) Bridge across the city moat outside Xu Gate, to answer this question and to illustrate how *fengshui* usually may have exerted its influence on building activities in an urban milieu. The first record of Wannian Bridge appears in a passage contained in the prefectural gazetteer compiled in the second half of the Kangxi reign-period (1662–1722), which is quoted in the 1883 *Suzhoufu zhi:*

> Five of the prefectural city gates each has a guarded water passage and a bridge straddling across the city moat, facilitating traffic. Only Xu Gate does not. It has been said that it faces Zuoe Hill which looks like a lion in form.[139] Building a bridge [there] is not suitable, for it would evoke the malicious influences [*zhengning zhi shi*] from the hill [to the city]. . . . During the Jiajing reign-period [1522–1566], there were those who went against [the interest of] the multitude and built a bridge [there]. [Consequently,] the city suffered repeated natural disaster and disturbances by Japanese pirates. Later, the residents demolished it.[140]

It is not certain whether the story of the building and the subsequent demolition of the bridge in the sixteenth century is a historical fact, but the city maps contained in both the *Gusu zhi*, completed in 1506, and the *Wuzhong shuili quanshu*, written in the 1630s—that is, the maps produced, respectively, before and after this event—show that among the six gates of the city, Xu Gate was the only one that did not have a nearby bridge across the moat.

The passage continues by narrating the following event of the early Qing, likewise centered on an attempt at constructing a bridge at this location:

> In the twenty-eighth year of the Kangxi reign-period [i.e., 1689], Shen Zaikuan from Wujiang [county] suddenly proposed to build the bridge and solicited contributions from all sides. Those who sought to make profit [from it] rushed to chime in with him.[141] Just as the timbers for the bridge were ready, fire spread over the area around Nanhao [the city moat between Chang Gate and Xu Gate] and burned down a thousand houses. Within a few days, fire broke out repeatedly. The specialist in landforms, Xu Changshi, petitioned the interested parties, explaining in detail the topographical forms and influences [of this area] in an irrefutable way: "The city moat is over thirty *zhang* [approximately 100 meters] in width; [consequently] the bridge must be built extremely high and steep so that grain barges can pass through. Within the city walls, store-houses and prisons are all located in the southeast, and should one stand on the bridge, the situation here could be spied from outside the city walls. This would run counter to the principles of establishing strategic security." Those who were building the bridge hated it [i.e., Xu Changshi's exposition], and led the way with many people to smash his house. The police inspector heard of this [and reported it?]. The provincial authority charged its subordinate department with making inquiries and arrests and as usual was about to punish the major criminals so as to put an end to [any similar criminal acts in] the future.[142]

The building of this bridge was clearly a private project. It was initiated and financed entirely by individuals and independent parties, and profits were expected to be gained from it. Probably not a few people voiced their opposition to this project, for there would otherwise have been no need for its supporters to attack the residence of Xu Changshi,

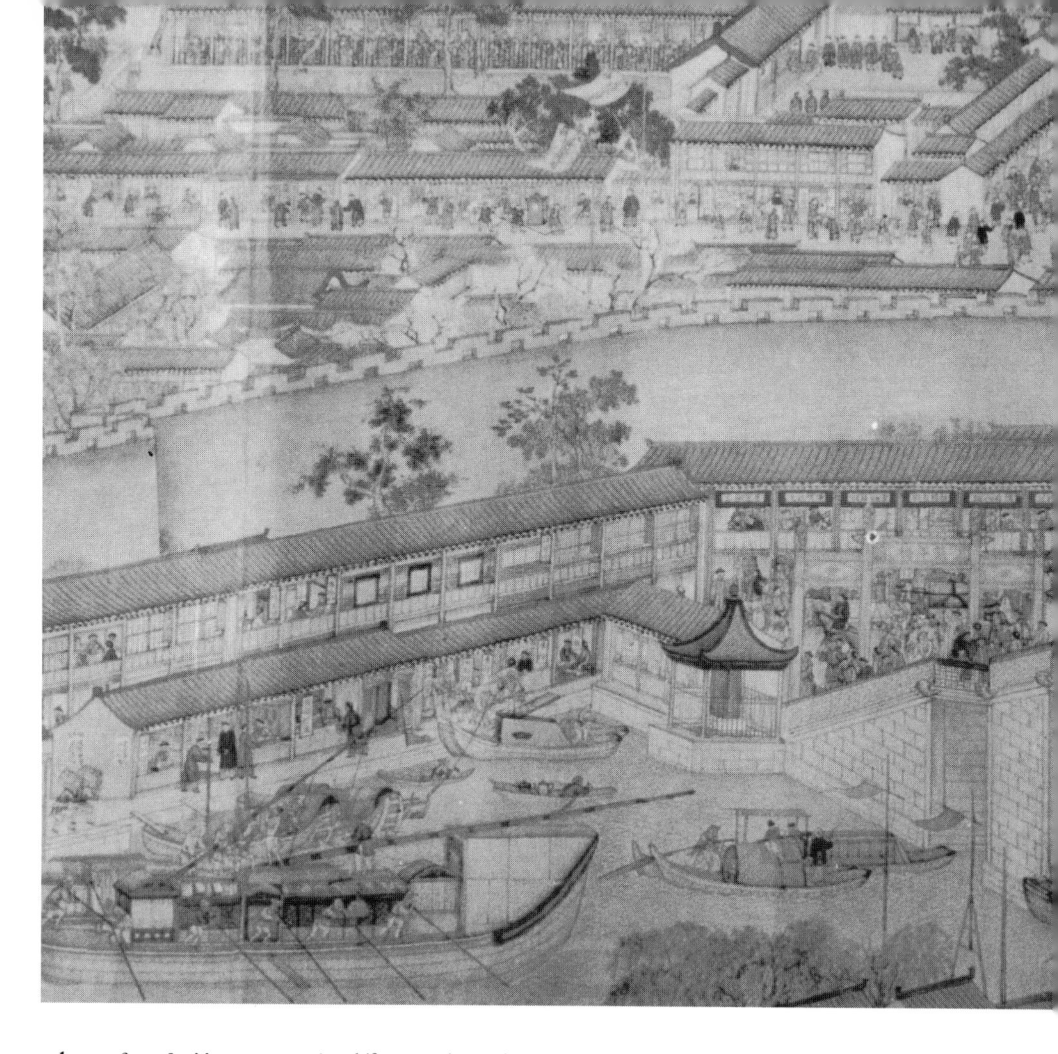

whose *fengshui* interpretation[143] must have been seen as effectively inciting widespread objection to the project. Only when the situation eventually developed into cases of civil litigation, and even criminal acts, did active intervention from the local government occur. The current provincial governor then summoned the magistrates of Wu and Changzhou counties for their opinions, and they proposed five provisions, the most important two being that charges against those who damaged Xu Changshi's house should not be pressed and that it was not appropriate to build the bridge. The dispute was finally settled when the governor ordered that the building materials be transported to the Wu county school for the repair of its buildings and the attempt to build the bridge dropped. The government's indifference to the project is clear, but it is not certain whether the reason for the local government's decision to stop the project was that contemporary officials were influenced by *fengshui* ideas, or, more probably, that tension between the two conflicting sides was so strong that building the bridge at that time had become a highly sensitive or even inflammatory issue. Nevertheless, as we shall see next, these officials and their successors in the following fifty years were criticized by

Figure 7.4 Section of the 1759 scroll Shengshi zisheng tu *(1986, plate 49) depicting Wannian Bridge across the city moat outside Xu ate.*

later scholars for being "deluded" into believing in *fengshui* and not pursuing this enterprise.

The bridge was eventually built in 1740 by the incumbent prefect Wang Dexin, at the cost of ten thousand six hundred taels of silver, all coming from private donations. The construction started on the second day of the fourth month and was completed in the same year on the first day of the eleventh month. The bridge measured slightly over one hundred meters in length, seven and a half meters in width and about eleven meters in height. These figures are all recorded in the memoir written by Xu Shilin, the provincial governor in that same year, and are also contained in the 1883 *Suzhoufu zhi*.[144] Figure 7.4 is a picture of the bridge drawn by Xu Yang in his *Shengshi zisheng tu* produced in 1759. In his memoir, Xu Shilin also describes how troublesome it was before the bridge was constructed, for over ten thousand people had to wait to be ferried across the moat every day. He then provides us with a valuable record of two different explanations of the reasons for the absence of a bridge outside Xu Gate, which he learned from the local records and from the locals whom he interviewed in person:

> One explanation is that in the preceding dynasty there was a huge plate-girder bridge [*jubanqiao*],[145] but it was destroyed a long time ago. The people were afraid of the heavy labor [of rebuilding it], and thus this task remained unaccomplished. Another explanation is that the ferrymen, secretly wanting to retain it [i.e., their ferry job], passed their intention off as the sayings of the specialists in landforms. They claimed that [building a bridge here] would be detrimental to [the interests of] the gentry and officials and led the latter to provoke [fear of it] in each other. [The latter] did not investigate this, but all alike believed it. This state of affairs has carried on and on until today. If we study this [*fengshui* idea] carefully, then [we know that it] took the lie of Zuoe Hill as being hideous and thus emanating noxious breaths [*shaqi*]; [that] fortunately the water [of the city moat] was restraining them; [and that] a bridge would invite the noxiousness straight into the city, which would be ominous in every way. Alas! This is a delusion as well.[146]

The first explanation does not concern *fengshui* at all, and, to some extent, is apparently preferred by Xu Shilin. It reveals that the lack of success in building the bridge before 1740 may not have been the outcome of opposition from any geomantic point of view. The second explanation attributes such a failure to the *fengshui* influence. But the blame on the ferrymen for concocting the *fengshui* interpretation in the first place might at first glance seem very unfair to them. It is not difficult to find that the *fengshui* interpretation of the geomantic situation around the site where the bridge was intended to be built is well constructed. For instance, in the *Zang shu*, one of the classics of *fengshui* theories, we read: "The breaths will disperse when carried by the wind, and will stop when reaching the edge of the water."[147] This statement applies to the breaths of both benign and malignant nature. The water of the city moat was therefore seen as stopping the noxious breaths emanated from Zuoe Hill, whereas a bridge would help them flow into the city. It is unlikely that such an expert view could have originated from the ferrymen, although they might naturally have taken it as a convenient weapon in their struggle to retain their means of livelihood. Nevertheless, the second explanation also suggests that other factors, both social and economic, were, or at least were believed to be, at work on this matter.

Resistance to the pursuit of this enterprise was undoubtedly further fueled by *fengshui* interpretations. It is true that in traditional Chinese society, conflicts between parties of different interests often took place in the name of *fengshui*. For the Chinese, good fortune was a quantum and one's neighbor's increment was one's own decrement, because happiness and prosperity were seen not as limitless; they formed a fixed fund from which each person had to strive to draw for oneself the maximum at the expense of others. It is for this reason that *fengshui* is seen by Freedman as an instrument of competition.[148] Competitions of this kind are indeed abundantly evidenced in both premodern literature and modern scholarship.[149] Some of them have resulted in physical settlement; some have remained as unmaterialized ideas; and some have been presented merely as retrospective interpretations. My concern here is precisely with the workings of a similar competition in the urban milieu around that same city gate of Suzhou. I should first note that what happened around the building of a bridge at Xu Gate was not between parties of different geomantic interests but apparently between those who paid attention to the *fengshui* effects of this project and those who did not. Thus the point at issue was neither which of the rival *fengshui* interpretations was more acceptable nor whether one party's action for its own *fengshui* benefit would impair others' geomantic situations, but whether any particular *fengshui* interpretation in opposition to the project in this specific context was convincing or should be considered at all.

One would probably rightly expect that *fengshui* ideas used in disputes of this kind were likely to lead to effective actions and to bring about concrete physical results, either positive or negative, in the contexts of local corporate entities, that is, families, clans, or professional and native-place associations.[150] Yet the area around Xu Gate formed an urban milieu where the population was made up of residents who were heterogeneous in terms of genealogy, occupation, class and native-place identity. Neither the consensus nor the collective will of those who objected to the project was sufficiently strong to put their *fengshui* argument into physical effect. It was therefore not impossible that, even with the *fengshui* opposition at work, the construction of the bridge as a private enterprise might have been accomplished earlier than 1740 if the matter had not deteriorated into a riot in the 1689 case; or if (in other cases) sufficient funding had been available not only for the acquisition of building materials but for recompensing the builders adequately so that their heavy labor could be offset; or if, indeed, there was explicit government support of the project. The success of the effort in 1740 seems to have verified this analysis.

How was this enterprise thought of by the local scholars (and, to some extent, possibly by commoners as well) of later periods? Gu Gongxie, for example, writes in 1785 a version of the story current in his time and makes a few personal comments on it:

> Outside Xu Gate of the [city of the] Suzhou prefecture, there was once a drawbridge. Tradition has it that, during the Jiajing reign-period [1522–1566], Yan Song [1480–1567],[151] fond of its white stones, moved it to Jiangxi. I once passed by Fenyi,[152] and saw a bridge [there]. [It was made of] purple stones, not white stones. For over two hundred years from then on, those who entered into government office in Suzhou were deluded with *fengshui* ideas, which claimed that the bridge would connect the noxious breaths from the mountains to the west, and disasters of the dikes of Lake [Tai] bursting were bound to happen. [Yet] there were those people, coming and going [at this point], who were drowned when the ferry boat was capsized. Many schemed to build a bridge, but failed repeatedly. It was not until the fifth year of the Qianlong reign-period [i.e., 1740] that the prefect, His Honor Wang Dexin, having cogently refuted the heresies, generously took charge [of the project] by himself. Within a year, the task was accomplished. The bridge was named Wannian [ten thousand years]; the virtue of His Honor, together with this bridge, will surely be everlasting and immortal.[153]

Fifty years later, Gu Zhentao also devoted a passage to this event and its historic background in his *Wumen biaoyin*, which reads similarly to that of Gu Gongxie's but with a lightly different wording.[154] For these two scholars, and possibly also for the many others from whom they extracted their versions of the story, only Yan Song and the officials who let themselves be "deluded" with *fengshui* were to blame for the absence of a bridge at this location before 1740; other social and economic factors were entirely negligible. The story of Yan Song in connection with the bridge in Ming time was, as Gu Gongxie has implied, a fabrication. Yet by equating those officials' inaction in the matter of building the bridge, allegedly because of *fengshui* influence, to Yan Song's despicable, selfish deeds, the criticism became particularly harsh indeed. In the minds of Gu Gongxie and Gu Zhentao, *fengshui* thoughts themselves were probably tolerable; it was the social context that mattered. Government officials should never allow such "superstitious" ideas to interfere with any enterprise that was meant to function to the benefit of the public.

Conclusion

In this chapter, I have argued that, because of the collective ambivalent attitudes of the imperial scholar-officials towards *fengshui,* and because of the social context of the local government and urban society, city constructions as part of the local administration[155] seldom fell under geomantic influences. In other words, at the level of government building projects, *fengshui* influence was kept to a minimum. On the other hand, *fengshui* was often applied to various features of the city in the form of retrospective interpretations rather than as a guide for their construction. Scholar-officials might occasionally borrow *fengshui* ideas in their descriptions of the city, but they often preferred a cautious wording in doing so. The reader may remember that Fei Chun, the provincial governor in 1795, wrote a memoir recording the successful project of city canal-dredging in that same year. The memoir contains the following passage eulogizing the conditions of the newly dredged water courses in the city:

> Because of the vastness and grandness [*pangbo weiqi*] of the city of Suzhou, the channels that flow through it make it fertile and well-watered [*gaorun*]. [The channels] mingled with one another as in the arteries and veins, bringing their waters where they are most valued; [these waters] are directed along their natural courses, and at the same time facilitate the movement of water traffic. [They are] like the circulation of the blood and breath [*yingwei*] in a human body,[156] removing what is stagnant, and maintaining the unimpeded flow of their currents; [in consequence] there is nothing [in the city] that is not pleasantly ordered, and nothing that is not peacefully at ease. While at this point I certainly am not disposed to consult the views of "specialists in landforms" [i.e., geomancers], their principles nonetheless can literally be believed by many.[157]

Fei Chun talks eloquently about the benefit of waters to the city by borrowing the rhetorical metaphors that sometimes were used to express *fengshui* principles,[158] but at the end explicitly dissociates himself from the art of *fengshui*. It is unlikely that he would have allowed *fengshui* practice to get in the way of his government actions, certainly including carrying out a canal-dredging project of this kind.

Indeed, most members of the scholar bureaucracy disdained the ideas of the *fengshui* specialists, and would not allow their interpretations of signs and portents to influence official planning or other decisions on the work of city construction and maintenance. But even such officials might write about city construction matters using metaphors which shared or even borrowed elements of *fengshui* formulas. The geomantic ideas were ubiquitous, "in the air," influencing the way many people spoke or described both natural and artificial features, and even these scholar-officials had to recognize those ever-present elements of popular thought and speech. But all applications of geomantic ideas to actual cities were "after the fact," mere elements of shared everyday culture, and consequently they were very useful, virtually unavoidable when describing what actually existed, after the fact.

At the level of building activities of local corporate groups, such as families, lineages, and native-place and professional associations, however, *fengshui* influences on their physical results either in the city or in the countryside were supposedly strong, even though written evidence of this is not particularly rich.[159] More complex and volatile situations thus often occurred when construction projects fell between the level of local corporate groups and the level of local government. They were the ones around which the two domains intertwined. The building of Wannian Bridge was such a case in which a plethora of social, economic, and psychological factors, including *fengshui*, were at work on the whole process of construction, from the initial scheme to its aftermath, whereas the determining role in its eventual outcome was played by active intervention from the local officials. The history of this project and all the elaborate stories that evolved around it are not only informative of the case itself but also suggestive of other cases at the highest and lowest levels of building activities. It is for this reason that I have paid special attention to this case.

I conclude this chapter by referring once again to one of Freedman's observations on the hierarchical system of *fengshui* application,[160] which I have cited earlier (p. 226). In terms of *fengshui* interpretation, Freedman's point holds indeed. I have shown that interpretations may have taken the form of contemporary assessment of the geomantic situation of a given setting, or advice on some particular building projects that would hopefully produce favorable geomantic effects, or objection to them, they being seen as a threat to the geomantic conditions of a certain area, or simply retrospective views on the geomantic quality of a settlement.

When we talk about the *fengshui* influence on building activities that was supposed to produce conspicuous physical effects, however, unquestioningly following this line of reasoning would be far too simplistic an assessment. Based on the evidence presented in this chapter, it is my *a priori* hypothesis that both the general ambivalent stance of the scholar-officials towards *fengshui*, and, more important, the particular social and ideological context of walled cities on which local governments were founded may effectively have restrained any hypothetical role that *fengshui* could possibly have played in building activities at an urban level. The hierarchy of imperial administration and the hierarchy of lineage (and lineage-like association) did not dwell on the same plane, and, in its political, social, and psychological nature, the city, being a local administrative center, was profoundly different from houses and villages. The case of the building of Wannian Bridge demonstrates that *fengshui* influences on the physical outcome of construction projects at the level of local corporate groups were probably strong, but more complex and volatile situations are likely to have existed in the projects that fell between this lower level and the level of local governmental duties.

Throughout this work I have attempted to separate historical truth from the accumulation of pseudo-historical lore concerning the way in which cities were created, took form, and were transformed. Following the opening chapter that introduces the historical background of the city of Suzhou, Chapter 2 sifts the deep layers of accumulated ancient legend and myth to present a verifiable albeit more spare outline of the city's origins than is to be found in either the traditional historiography or in any of the recent writings. Chapter 3 clarifies a number of more purely historical issues where diverse readings of the historical documentation have persisted. Chapters 4, 5, and 6 explain a number of functional and organizational aspects of later imperial China's urban life, as seen in the preeminent example of Suzhou. Finally Chapter 7 takes up one of the most persistent problems of cultural misunderstanding in an attempt to critically define the place of *fengshui* concepts in the various levels of private and public life. This chapter continues the earlier chapters' discrimination between fact and fancy, here in an area of popular culture that has assumed a large explanatory role even in the recent writings of Chinese and Western social scientists. Their over-generalizations about all of Chinese civilization from their focal interests in popular culture have contributed much to our understanding at many points, but in this instance, their views must be modified. My views too may err, but I hope that by critically examining the long history of this great ancient urban center as a representative example, a clear and coherent picture emerges of China's experience with urbanism.

Conclusion

After decades of admirable efforts by scholars from China, Japan, and the West, the academic field of history now may be less conspicuously surrounded by the "mystifying miasma" of Eurocentric attitude than thirty-five years ago, when Arthur F. Wright wrote an article entitled "Viewpoints on a City."[1] However, writings on China's urban history, from an architectural point of view in particular, still fall far short in the proportion of number to its importance in the history of world civilization. It is my hope, therefore, that this book will encourage more scholarly works on this vast, fascinating subject. As I emphasized at the beginning of the book, by taking the city of Suzhou as a specific case, I have attempted to address a number of significant features of city building and development in order that a sound historical approach to the study of Chinese cities may emerge.

My inquiry into the formation and transformation of the city of Suzhou begins at the conceptual inception of its history in 514 B.C., when the city was said to have been built for the first time as the state capital of Wu. This early "history" may properly be seen as a construct devised by the authors of Eastern Han documents to express the historical struggle for survival between the states of Wu and Yue. Two related features of this construct are especially relevant to the present study. One is the physical aspect of the city. The accounts of this feature may have been made on the basis of what had been transmitted to these authors and their own perceptions of the city in their time. Another, and more central, feature is the idea of the city having been built as a cosmic center. This symbolic aspect probably had combined elements drawn from both the local traditions and the culture of Central China as it had evolved from as early as Shang times and involved the cosmological synthesis of the Han. Yet for a study of urban history, people's conception of a city is often no less significant than its physical reality. In fact, the authenticity of this symbolic theme of the earliest construction of the city was never challenged in subsequent dynastic periods; rather, it proves to have been particularly important for its influence on the thinking of later ages, directly manifested in some aspects of the fully historical Suzhou. It is for this reason that I have maintained a positive attitude in my interpretation of it.

Constructing city walls and founding a capital city were described as having been achieved by the rulers of the states of Wu and Yue as the first, and crucial, step toward an idealized order, an order of both social and cosmic significance. The cosmic scheme is enunciated by the author of the *Wu Yue chunqiu* as realized in two principal measures. One is that the builder of the Wu capital, Wu Zixu, constructed the great city walls by "following the forms manifested in Heaven and the process taking place on Earth." The eight land gates of the city were built to symbolize the eight winds from Heaven and the eight water gates to imitate the eight intelligent attributes of Earth. In this manner, the city can be interpreted as having condensed and represented the universe. The other measure is the symbolic correspondence between two important, individual gates, namely Chang Gate, symbolizing the Gate of Heaven in the northwest, and She Gate symbolizing the Gate of Earth in the southeast. The directional attributes of this symbolism must have been closely associated with some mythical accounts of an ancient cosmological idea that derived from direct observation of the topographical and celestial phenomena of the geographical location in China.

However, in interpreting any cosmological symbolism of the building of cities or other kinds of human settlements, it is of utmost importance to caution against neglecting a fundamental point that sets the Chinese experience apart from that of many other ancient civilizations, that is, the distinctive notion of Chinese cosmogony. Although an interpretation of the transformation of a territory into a cosmos through a ritual repetition of the cosmogony[2] may, to some extent, be applicable to Chinese experience as well, it can hardly be seen as an act of "recreation," since for the ancient Chinese, the world and its myriad things existed not because they were created by the gods, as Eliade generalizes for the "archaic societies;"[3] they were simply uncreated. The world and man were regarded as constituting the central features of a spontaneously self-generating cosmos. There was indeed a paradigmatic model for the building of the city, but it was not "the creation of the universe by the gods." What the builders strove for, as the author of the *Wu Yue chunqiu* sees it, was to construct a city, the form of which could be believed to be both imitating the form of the universe and representing the center of the cosmos. By doing so, it was hoped that an ideal order would be established within the city and the state, which would coordinate the Way of Heaven and Earth, jointly constituting the eternal Way of the cosmos.

The idea of the city as a cosmic center lost its relevance to its occupants once the state of Wu was destroyed by Yue in 473 B.C. This was particularly so from the Qin unification in 221 B.C. onward, when China became a centralized empire administered by an appointed bureaucracy of literati, and the system of cities underwent profound changes. A city, which previously was a state capital and therefore could have represented a self-contained political power struggling for survival against others, became by this time principally an instrument of the imperial government. Consequently, a fundamental distinction evolved between the imperial capital and regional or local cities: any cosmological symbolism was only overtly retained and perpetuated in the building of the former as the cosmic pivot of the four quarters, at which the Son of Heaven resided. On the other hand, a city was not a corporate entity of its own that could be legally separated from its surrounding countryside, but functioned as a center of imperial administration, its jurisdiction being over a regional area that was largely rural and in which the city was a part. Thus from the beginning of the imperial era, the city in China did not show the traits of cities in dual societies, and there existed what we may loosely call "an urban-rural continuum."

However, the *raison d'être* for cities invariably being centers of the imperial administration should not lead to the *a priori* assumption that they were no more than government offices writ large, that they were uniform in plan, and that they lasted essentially unchanged for two millennia. Many cities were also prominent centers of production, trade, and commerce. Their economic and administrative functions demanded each other's support at a certain stage of development. Given the vastness of the Chinese empire, the form, spatial structure, and urban life of cities were in fact markedly different from region to region, and from one city to another in the same region. As for the planning principles, the cities, especially those in the economically more advanced areas, experienced profound institutional changes over time. Most notable transformations were first brought about by the medieval urban revolution that took place between the second half of the eighth century and the twelfth century. The best examples of this transformation are the breakdown of the government-controlled walled-ward system of residential and market quarters in the city, the freer street plan in which trade and commerce could be conducted anywhere within the city or its outlying suburbs, and the rapid expansion of particular walled cities and the commercial spillover outside their gates. During the late imperial period, further relaxation of government control and the intensification of market economy gave rise to the functional partitioning of urban space in large cities, the rapid growth of commercial suburbs, and the integration of capital cities and numerous market towns into a single hierarchical system of information, production, and distribution.

The city of Suzhou in the imperial era was an important one of such cities. For the existence of this city, as for that of all others to which the term "city" can be applied, the city walls constituted, or at least should have constituted, a basic prerequisite. Conversely, a settlement that did not house an office of imperial administration was not supposed to be enclosed by the kind of fortifications that, in both measurement and building technique, were to be seen as equivalent to city walls. Thus when the prefectural government of Suzhou was temporarily transferred to a new site in A.D. 591, the old city had to be "emptied." The city walls and the imperial government were institutionally and conceptually inseparable: the existence of the former was required by the latter and at the same time affirmed the presence of the latter.

The important growth of the city of Suzhou started in the ninth century, when the demographic center of China began to shift to the Yangzi provinces. The recorded history of the repeated reconstruction of the city walls dates from that same period. Yet the earliest city maps available to us date from as late as 1229. These maps form an invaluable source of pictorial evidence, supplemented by written information, on which an examination of the transformation of the city can be based with greater certainty. By collating the city maps with literary records, I have demonstrated that, at least from 1229 onward, the position of the city walls and thus the overall form of the city (defined by its walls) remained basically unchanged. The existing network of city canals and moats, both forming a fixed framework in which the city was embedded, must have been a crucial factor in its remarkable morphological stability. Yet this stability of the city form was paradoxically accompanied by a process of steady urban growth, the most notable feature of which was the rapid spatial expansion along the Grand Canal in the west suburbs from the fifteenth century onward, an expansion driven by trade and commerce. In a modern sense, these bustling suburbs became more "urban" than most areas enclosed by the city walls. It was only in 1860 that the prosperity of these suburban areas was disastrously brought to an end by the Taiping Rebellion.

The specious contradiction between stability of city form and urban growth is most overtly epitomized by an event that happened in the mid-sixteenth century. Under the heavy pressure from the repeated invasions and pillages by the Japanese pirates in the 1550s, a few local government advisors once considered building a new wall that would have enclosed the prosperous west suburban area. But this wall never materialized. More significantly, the record of this event is never included in any of the official documents—principally the gazetteers—purporting to be the proper history of Suzhou. To explain this incongruity between the walled city and what was urban according to the modern criteria, I have offered the following rationale. On the one hand, in theory during the first half of the imperial period, and in practice from the Song dynasty onward, the Chinese city functioned as an open institution and fostered the development of an urban-rural continuum. Both may jointly have generated a necessary, though not a sufficient, condition for the phenomenon of the free development of prosperous suburbs. On the other hand, the symbolic meaning of the city walls appears to have been particularly strong for the scholar-officials who were indisputably responsible for any decision on the building of city walls. The walls, in their eyes, not only affirmed the presence of the imperial government and the existence of a social order but also signified the continuation of a civilization from the past to the future. Since it was what the city walls stood for, not necessarily what they enclosed, that was of the utmost importance in the minds of the scholar-officials, the restoration of the city walls always remained central to the local government, and any construction that would have conspicuously altered their perception of the city may not have been regarded as desirable.

The symbolism of the city walls and gates had a seemingly similar version in ancient times. I have shown that the construction of the walls of the earliest city can be interpreted as signifying the establishment and maintenance of an ideal order that could be kept in accord with the order of the cosmos. The construction of the gates is seen as a measure both to draw a parallel between the form of the city and the form of the universe and to symbolize an alignment of the city with the axis of the cosmos. The essential implication of this early symbolism was therefore the building of the city as a cosmic center, a theme that was entirely in conformity with the circumstances in the state of Wu, which was striving for power in contest against its rival states. Under the sociopolitical conditions of imperial China, however, the emphasis of the symbolism shifted profoundly from the city being treated as the center of the cosmos to the centrality of the imperial government and the social order that it had established and to the loyalty of the region to the Son of Heaven residing in the imperial capital, which was the single, incontestable pivot of the four quarters.

The most marked change in the physical city of Suzhou in all the centuries from the Southern Song period to the end of the Qing is the removal of the inner walled enclosure in the early years of the Ming, previously housing the offices of the local government. The attempt at rebuilding this structure in the early 1370s, destroyed when Zhang Shicheng's army defending the city was defeated in 1367 by the Ming forces, brought about catastrophic consequences to the fortune of the prefect Wei Guan and two other reputed local poets. While the event may be seen as historically fortuitous because of the particular political conditions at that time and the oversuspicious personality of the Hongwu emperor, it nevertheless carries some significant implications that fall well within the general political, social, and cultural context of imperial Chinese history. A city was principally an instrument of the imperial government, not an autonomous, corporate entity, nor a center of political or personal freedom. On the other hand, building activities were of strong sociopolitical relevance. Thus the main point, derived from the analysis of this specific event, is that there was always a tendency for interventions from the central authority in the activities of its local officials, certainly including building activities. This kind of intervention could be made in pragmatic as much as in symbolic terms.

Another prominent physical feature of the city of Suzhou was the network of its canals. The city was characterized, probably from as early as the second half of the third century A.D. onward, by a parallel system of waterways and roads. I have emphasized that, as far as the present diachronic study of the urban form and space is concerned, these canals in their development appear to be more important in revealing how the city was transformed through history. On the basis mainly of Tang and Song literary descriptions and records of the canals and the bridges, I have suggested that, in the late Tang in the ninth century, the network of urban water traffic was probably already maturely formed, and it largely determined the spatial structure of the city. I have also pointed out the possibility that what is presented on the 1229 city map, which registers the result of the contemporary large-scale restoration of the city walls and the reconstruction of many other governmental institutions after the severe damage of the city by Jurchen cavalry in 1130, may basically have been the spatial structure that continuously developed from the late Tang period. In other words, the reconstruction works in the 1220s were conducted on the basis of both the existing framework of canals and the urban spatial pattern that was delineated by the canals. I have suggested that the formation of the network of city canals assisted the spatial arrangement of the residential and market wards before the late Tang as much as it in time helped their disintegration, and at the same time it was itself as much the outcome of the establishment of the physical ward system as the consequence of the collapse of this system epitomizing the medieval urban spatial transformation.

The availability of a great multitude of historic accounts of the city canals, records of canal-dredging, and city maps, from the late imperial period has enabled me to draw some more affirmative conclusions. The data collected from a number of historic documents tell us that during the entire Qing period, that is, the last two hundred and sixty-eight years of the imperial era, six out of ten instances of full-scale canal-dredging occurred in the eighteenth century alone, while five of them were concentrated within a period of thirty-eight years in the first half of that century. This is in sharp contrast to such activity in the Ming, when there were only four instances of full-scale canal-dredging during the entire two hundred seventy-six years of this dynasty. Yet we are also informed by the city maps of both the Ming and Qing periods that precisely at the end of the first half of the eighteenth century over a quarter of the city canals were lost, whereas at the end of the Ming, the canal system was slightly more extensive than the one that had existed in 1229. On the basis of this information, I have argued that the unusual frequency of the canal-dredging enterprises in the first half of the eighteenth century was part of a forced reaction of the local government to the tremendous pressure of urban growth that had occurred for two centuries and was aggravated by a sharp increase in Suzhou's population in that same century.

If the geometrically regulated pattern of the watercourses during the Southern Song period, gradually formed over the preceding centuries, was largely a physical outcome of strict government control over city residences and markets that developed in coordination with the development of the watercourses, the massive loss of the canals in the first half of the eighteenth century probably resulted from the enormous pressure on certain areas of the city that was brought about by the unprecedented upsurge of population at that time, the marked relaxation of government control, and the rapid economic growth from the mid-Ming onward. In support of this argument, I have identified the areas that had experienced significant loss of canals by the mid-eighteenth century. We should bear in mind that urban space had gradually, and largely spontaneously, developed into three districts during the Ming period: the business district in the northwest (including the west suburbs), the gentry and official district in the southwest, and the district of family-based textile industry in the northeast. The majority of the areas where canals were blocked were the quarters of the business district close to Chang Gate in the northwest and part of the district of family-based textile industry adjacent to the business district. These areas were obviously economically and demographically most sensitive.

An examination of the mode of arranging public urban space in the city of Suzhou as exemplified by the miscellaneous public use of the Daoist temple Xuanmiao Guan has been conducted in conjunction with discussions of building form and style and the relationship between building compounds and social institutions rather than with discussions of the urban structure. The reason for this choice comes from my observation that, apart from city streets, canals, and bridges, public urban space in Suzhou, as in most traditional Chinese cities, principally took the form of the courtyard, which was an integral part of the building compound. Institutionally and conceptually, there were few public open places that can be perceived as equivalent to the city square in European cities. With an acknowledgment of the danger in attempting to answer the pseudo-question of why the traditional Chinese city lacked the square as a civic center, I have concentrated on trying to explain what were the conjunctural factors that gave rise to this particular phenomenon in the city of Suzhou, which was most probably representative of the general Chinese experience.

This has been approached tentatively from two perspectives. One is the sociopolitical relationship between the city and the countryside. Since the city was not an administrative unit itself but part of a regional area that was largely rural, Xuanmiao Guan, like all other temples located in the urban area, was certainly not regarded as a property of the city. Access to this temple and its courtyard, symbolically demarcated by its own walls, was maintained both institutionally and psychologically by all sections of society, urban as much as rural. Its locality and spaciousness were the main determinants of its public functions. The second perspective used to examine the mode of arranging public urban space in Suzhou is the distinctive Chinese concept of socialized space. I have noted that for the Chinese, any space of a considerable size facilitating social interactions in a man-made environment was not an independent entity of its own but had to pertain to a certain institution in order to be explicable and therefore meaningful. The realization of this kind of functional pertinence was characterized by defining the space not only nominally but physically, so that this particular space could be distinguished both in concept and in reality from other spaces of different categories defined likewise and so that the human environments could be maintained in order. The most effective and most explicit means of physically defining an urban space was the use of walls, and the most ubiquitous and common space defined by this means was that of courtyards.

I have insisted that, in terms of architectural form and style, buildings in a traditional Chinese city can hardly be differentiated from buildings in its surrounding countryside. Structures that appear to be distinctively "urban," such as the city gate towers, the corner towers, the drum tower, and bell tower, were in fact a combination of one- or two-story halls with the city walls or high raised, wall-like platforms on which the halls stood. The architectural form and style of these halls were not at all distinguishable from those on the ground; it was the city walls and wall-like platforms that rendered these particular "urban structures," in many cases (but not always), distinct from rural buildings. I have also argued extensively that the lack of discernible difference between the forms and styles of Chinese urban and rural buildings should be seen as indicating an absence of formal bond between building types and social institutions in Chinese architectural experience rather than as providing evidence of the urban-rural continuum. This attribute of Chinese architecture was developed not only by its technological tradition but also by the characteristic worldview of the Chinese people.

The last, but equally important, area of my inquiry into the formation and transformation of the city of Suzhou is the application of *fengshui* (or Chinese geomantic) ideas to its urban development. The main concern of this study has lain in the question of to what extent and in what way *fengshui* ideas were applied to the urban construction and development of the city of Suzhou in the imperial era and how significant this approach of inquiry may prove in studies of traditional urban China. In order to answer these questions properly, I classified all the available literary records of *fengshui* ideas and activities that are associated with the city at an urban level into two categories: the *fengshui* influences on the physical construction works, either successful or unsuccessful, and interpretations of the natural setting, form, and space of the city in *fengshui* terms.

There is in the first category only one instance revealed in the historical records, namely the event in the mid-twelfth century of active *fengshui* advice on whether two particular city gates that had been blocked should be reopened in a quest to change the fortune of the city and the prefecture for the better. My close analysis of this event led to the conclusion that the eventual failure of this *fengshui* attempt was somewhat inevitable in the specific circumstances of the city and, in particular, of the prefectural government at that time, circumstances which, however, may not have been uncommon to those of other cities and local governments in imperial China. On the second category, three examples, all characteristic of retrospective interpretation or assessment of the city, have been cited and analyzed. They indicate that not only the competing versions of expert *fengshui* ideas but also the notions of the elite and the geomantic interpretations at the popular level all dwelt on a central theme in Chinese metaphysics—man's place in Nature and the universe—and share the fundamental view of seeking to be in tune with the universe. These different ideas, notions, and interpretations drew elements from, but at the same time contradicted, each other to such an extent that none of them can be treated entirely on its own.

In consideration of the role of *fengshui* in the history of the city of Suzhou, what is really most striking is the lone recorded instance of its active advice on urban construction and its failure in contrast to the relative multitude of retrospective interpretations of the city. I have offered a hypothetical two-part explanation for this phenomenon. First, the ambiguous attitudes toward *fengshui* on the part of the classically educated scholars, who collectively monopolized the government of imperial China at all levels, limited its influence on urban constructions; second, and more importantly, walled cities on which the regional or local governments were based, did not form the kind of social context that would have promoted the application of *fengshui* ideas to their prominent building projects. I have subsequently suggested that, in theory and as the geomantic specialists advocate, *fengshui* should have operated in man-made environments of all kinds, continuously at each stage of the planning or growing processes, from a large city as a whole to all individual buildings or other constructions; yet in practice, *fengshui* was applied much more often as part of the retrospective evaluation of a regional or local city's siting and the evolution of its form than as the actual guidelines of construction projects at an urban level.

In order to support this argument and to illustrate to what extent *fengshui* ideas may have worked in the urban context of Suzhou, I have taken the issue a step further by examining in detail the example of the building of Wannian Bridge across the west city moat outside Xu Gate. This has then led to a tentative conclusion that, at the level of the building activities of local corporate groups, *fengshui* influences on their physical results were supposedly strong; more complex and volatile situations were often more likely to have resulted when construction projects, such as the building of Wannian Bridge, fell between the level of local corporate groups and the level of local government. Thus, a plethora of social, economic, and psychological factors, including *fengshui,* were at work on the whole process of construction, but the eventual outcome was determined by the active intervention of the local government.

Abbreviations *(used in the Notes and Bibliography)*

Ch	*Ci hai*
Cj	*Congshu jicheng*
Cy	*Ci yuan*
Gjc	*Guoxue jiben congshu*
Gtj	*Gujin tushu jicheng*
MQSgbj	*Ming Qing Suzhou gongshangye beike ji*
Pxjj	*Pingjianglu xinzhu juncheng ji*
Sc	*Sibu congkan*
SPck	*Song Pingjiang chengfang kao*
Sq	*Siku quanshu*
Sz	*Shisanjing zhushu*
Tjls	*Tianxia junguo libing shu*
Wsq	*Wuzhong shuili quanshu*
WTx	*Wujun Tujing xuji*
Xxx	*Xiaoxia xianji xuancun*
Xxz	*Xiaoxia xianji zhaichao*
Zj	*Zhuzi jicheng*

Notes

Introduction

1. This book uses Pinyin for romanizing Chinese words. In the context of imperial China's urban history, I use the term *city* for any walled urban nucleus having functioned as a regional or local center of imperial administration. A local, economic center that did not overtly have this administrative function is accordingly called a "market town." The name of a city in imperial China was usually identical to the name of an administrative unit-region, whether it was a prefecture or a county, which was largely rural, in which the city was situated and over which the city-based local government ruled. The name of Suzhou, for instance, designated the prefectural city as well as the prefecture. I therefore explicitly make a distinction between the two meanings whenever I use this name, except for the cases in which what is referred to is quite obvious to the reader. Suzhou acquired many other names at different historic periods. To avoid confusion, I make a point of using *Suzhou* to refer to the city and the prefecture in the imperial era, because, having been the official appellation during the entire Ming and Qing periods, and presently being the name for the modern city, it is the most current one. Other names are mentioned wherever it seems historically appropriate.
2. For representative works of this kind, see Mote 1973; Murphey 1984.
3. Braunfels 1988, p. 1.
4. Ibid.
5. The paucity of knowledge about China's urban history, and the insufficient awareness of its importance to the studies of the urban history of the world, are partly reflected, for instance, in the place of the description of Chinese cities in A. E. J. Morris' *History of Urban Form: Before the Industrial Revolutions*. The emphasis of this work is understandably placed on European urban history and, to a lesser degree, on the development of cities in the United States. Its first edition of 1972 is a text of 258 pages (including Appendices), whereas descriptions of a few Chinese cases, based entirely on the works of Andrew Boyd (1962) and Nelson I. Wu (1968), are only given two pages in one of the Appendices. The book has continuously been enlarged in the second and third editions of it (1979, 305 pages; 1994, 413 pages), but its part on the Chinese cities remains basically the same in length and position and based on the same sources of reference. In terms of the entire urban history of the world, the proportion of attention given to the Chinese experience seems regrettable.
6. See, for example, Samuels 1978, pp. 713–714; Rowe 1993, p. 1.
7. Hillier and Hanson 1984, p. 9. They insist: "Through its ordering of space the man-made physi-

cal world is already a social behavior. It constitutes (not merely represents) a form of order in itself, an order that is created for social purposes, whether by design or accumulatively, and through which society is both constrained and recognizable."

8. Ibid., p. 22.

Chapter 1: Historical and Cultural Background

1. The Wu tribe (and later, state) was also known as Gou-Wu. The character *gou* was, according to Yan Shigu (81–64), applied only as a transliteration by the aborigines, and had a similar phonetic function to the character *yu* of Yu-Yue, another name of the Yue tribe. See *Han shu*, *juan* 28B, p. 1667, Yan's commentary. Cf. Du Yu (222–284) and Kong Yingda's (74–648) commentaries on *Zuo zhuan*, *juan* : "Ding th year [o B.C.]", p. 437.
2. The region extending from the River Yangzi southward to the River Xin'an in Zhejiang province.
3. *Dushi fangyu jiyao*, *juan* 24, p. 1099.
4. Chen et al. 1988, pp. 91–9 .
5. Granet 1930, p. 31.
6. Chang 1986, p. 39 ; Zhou 1988, p. 237.
7. *Beiyinyangying* 1993.
8. Zhou 1988, pp. 237–241; Lin 1988, pp. 2 1–2 4.
9. Chang 1986, p. 396; Lin 1988, p. 2 7; and Chen et al. 1988, pp. 30 –307.
10. Danfu gave the Zhou a political identity and was thus posthumously granted the title of Zhou Taiwang (the Zhou's earliest and greatest king or the Zhou's patriarch king).
11. According to the *Shi ji* (*juan* 4, p. 11 and *juan* 31, p. 144), the head of the Zhou tribe, Danfu, raised three sons: the eldest Taibo, the second Zhongyong, and the youngest Jili. Danfu had the intention of passing on his position to Jili, whose son, Chang, later King Wen, was born with cosmically auspicious signs (*shengrui*). Taibo, therefore, came with Zhongyong to the Wu area, and both had their hair cut and bodies tattooed and wore dress identical to that of the aborigines in order to signify that they had become alien to the Zhou culture and could thus no longer inherit the Zhou title. "Once Taibo came to Jingman, he entitled his own [newly established tribelike group] Gou-Wu. The aborigines appreciated Taibo's righteousness, and over one thousand households followed him and came under his rule, having him assume the title of Taibo of Wu." Translations of Chinese texts here and hereafter are the author's unless otherwise specified. Cf. Creel 1970, p. 122, note 80.
12. Wheatley 1971, p. 171.
13. *Shi ji*, *juan* 31, p. 144 , with Pei Yin's commentary, and p. 1448.
14. Wheatley 1971, pp. 112, 162–164; Zhang 1984, p. 14.
15. Bai-Yue, also known as Yue, is a general name for the myriad ancient tribes spread across the region to the south of the middle and lower River Yangzi.
16. Cf. *Guo yu*, *juan* 20, p. 633; *Lüshi chunqiu*, *juan* 23: "Zhihua," p. 300; *Han shu*, *juan* 28B, p. 1668.
17. *Shuowen jiezi*, 13A.24; *Taiping yulan*, *juan* 170, p. 831. This is most overtly signified by the character *man*, its lower part, *hui*, originally meaning "poisonous snake." By the same token, the people in the north were called *di*, "progenies of the dog"; the people in the east were called *he*, "progenies of the cat family"; the people in the west were called *qiang*, "progenies of the goat." See *Shuowen jiezi*, 4A.17; 9B.17 and 10A.14. This set of designations of the barbarians as the descendants of certain animal species did not represent for the Han Chinese a system of totemism. In totemism, as Geertz (1973, p. 3 3), when commenting on the work of Lévi-Stauss, *La Pensee Sauvage*, stated, "a logical parallel is (quite subconsciously) postulated between two series, one natural and one cultural," and the relationship between a particular clan and its neighbors is "analogous to the perceived relationship between species." The Chinese case, however, is different. Whereas it differentiated in an explicit, metaphorical way the barbarians from the Han Chinese in Central China, such a differentiation was obviously not made on equal terms. Thierry (1989, pp. 78, 79)

insists that the basis of the difference between the Han Chinese and the barbarians was not originally of an ethnic nature but rested on a relationship to civilization, since for the Chinese there was civilization and the void. So in this case, "the graphic classification of the name of each type of Barbarian under a radical marking his animal nature is an ontological necessity"; and "this denial of the humanity of others evolved over the centuries, but it underlay the relations that the Chinese formed with their neighbors."

18. Cf. *Shuo yuan*, *juan* 12, pp. 302–303; *Han shu*, *juan* 28B, pp. 1669, 1670 with Ying Shao's commentary; *Huainanzi*, *juan* 1: "Yuandao xun," p. 6.
19. Creel (1970, pp. 224–225, note 118, p. 361, note 159) casts some doubts on whether the Zhou in Taibo's time were any more advanced in culture than the people of the Wu area. Chang (1986, pp. 398–399), however, based on archaeological findings, suggests that "the rise of some of the Western Zhou civilizations in the Lower Yangtze Valley may have been brought about by an elite class who established there a local technological and societal pattern after the North China model." He sees the story of Taibo and Zhongyong in its broad outline and the archaeological facts as having jointly established the process of acculturation in this region by the Western Zhou civilization.
20. An informative event, for example, was recorded in the *Zuo zhuan*, (*juan* 22: "Xuan 8th year [601 B.C.]," p. 1873) when Chu, allying with Wu and Yue, sent an expedition against Shu and Liao. Du Yu comments, "It was said that as Chu was powerful, Wu and Yue obeyed it." See also Creel, 1970, p. 224; Chen et al. 1988, p. 169.
21. Cf. *Zuo zhuan*, *juan* 26: "Cheng 7th year [584 B.C.]," p. 1903; *Shi ji*, *juan* 31, p. 1448. See also Granet 1930, pp. 92–93. Ironically, as Creel (1970, p. 224) observes, the people of Wu learned their lessons so well that they were soon not only a match for Chu, but within a century had become a more serious threat to the north than Chu had ever been.
22. *Zuo zhuan*, *juan* 54: "Ding 4th year [506 B.C.]," pp. 2133–2137; *Shi ji*, *juan* 31, p.1466.
23. *Zuo zhuan*, *juan* 53: "Zhao 32nd year [510 B.C.]" with Du's commentary, p. 2127; *Shi ji*, *juan* 31, p. 1446.
24. *Zuo zhuan*, *juan* 55: "Ding 5th year [505 B.C.]," p. 2139; *Shi ji*, *juan* 31, p.1467. Granet (1930, p. 93) holds that it was this attack by Yue to the rear of Wu that put an end to the latter's success.
25. *Zuo zhuan*, *juan* 56: "Ding 14th year [496 B.C.]," pp. 2150–2151; *Shi ji*, *juan* 31, p. 1468; *juan* 41, p. 1739–1740.
26. *Zuo zhuan*, *juan* 57: "Ai 1st year [494 B.C.]," pp. 2154–2155; *uo yu*, *juan* 21, p. 644.
27. *uo yu*, *juan* 20, p. 633. Wu Zixu was most conscious of the danger that Yue posed to Wu. Opposing Wu's campaign against the distant state of Qi in the north, he insisted that Wu should pay major attention to the potential threat from Yue in the south, because to Wu, he reasoned metaphorically, Yue was like a serious disease in the internal, vital organs of a human body, whereas Qi should be regarded merely as a case of skin illness. Cf. *Zuo zhuan*, *juan* 58: "Ai 11th year [484 B.C.]," p. 2167; *uo yu*, *juan* 19, p. 597; *Shi ji*, *juan* 31, p. 1471, *juan* 41, p. 1743, and *juan* 66, p. 2179.
28. *Zuo zhuan*, *juan* 60: "Ai 22nd year [473 B.C.]," p. 2181. The *Shi ji* (*juan* 41, p. 1745) contains an interesting passage of Fan Li's advice to the king of Yue when the remnants of Wu were bottled up on Mt. Gusu to the west of its capital city. At this point, Goujian was disposed to clemency, just as Fuchai was at the time when Yue had been entirely at the mercy of Wu. Fan Li said:

   > In the events of Guiji [where Yue was pinned down by Wu], Heaven bestowed Yue on Wu. Wu did not take it. Now Heaven bestows Wu on Yue. How can Yue go against the mandate of Heaven? . . . When one does not take what Heaven gives, one exposes oneself to disaster.

   Then Goujian proceeded to the attack and eventually had Fuchai killed. See also *uo yu*, *juan* 19, p. 627, *juan* 20, p. 639, and *juan* 21, p. 657 for similar passages. Granet (1930, p. 31) sees this as a good example of "realist politics" under the guise of the ancient rhetoric of the wise ministers of the states situated on the borders of Central China.
29. *Shi ji*, *juan* 78, p. 2394.

30. The area of Suzhou was converted only occasionally to an enfeoffment for very short periods before the end of the Tang dynasty.
31. *Shi ji*, *juan* 129, p. 3270.
32. Lü 1983, p. 1078. The term "San Wu" as the name of an area has evoked many interpretations, which I shall not enumerate here. For further information, cf. *Wujun zhi*, *juan* 48, pp. 620–621; *Ch* 1980, p. 1 ; *Cy* 1988, p. 16. No matter how controversial the issue is, it is certain that the term denotes an important area in the Southeast and that Suzhou prefecture was an important part of it. According to the *Song shu* (*juan* 4, p. 1 40), after a relatively peaceful period (from the early fourth century to the mid-fifth century) in the Southeast, "if [one prefecture in the region] enjoyed a year of harvest, then [the people of] several prefectures could forget about starvation." In the *Zizhi tongjian* (*juan* 163: "1st year of Dabao [reign-period] [A.D. 0]," p. 04), we read, "Since the Jin family crossed the River [Yangzi], San Wu has been the richest and most populous [region]; tribute, taxes and merchants have all come from this area." Even after the devastation inflicted upon this area by what Chinese historians call the Houjing zhi luan (the rebellion led by Hou Jing, A.D. 48– 2), the San Wu region was still highly esteemed for its agricultural advantages, as the first emperor of the Southern Chen considered: "San Wu, as the heart of the territory, used to be called a rich and fertile land. Although sometimes wars and famines have occurred there, it is still an area of abundance and prosperity" (*Chen shu*, *juan* 2 , p. 318).
33. Progress in agriculture in the Lower Yangzi plain was not only promoted by waves of southeastward immigrants who introduced to this region the more advanced technology of cultivation and irrigation long developed in Central China but also based upon the superior economic conditions of the region, "conditions," as Mote (1973, p. 44) concisely puts it, "favorable both to a higher margin in agriculture and a cheaper and more convenient distribution using water transport." In fact, the advantage of this land of waters has been emphasized by many imperial Chinese scholars. An assessment of it by Sima Qian is that Suzhou in Qin and Han times "had rich resources of sea salt, bronze ore in Mt. Zhang, and the benefit of the Three Rivers and the Five Lakes; [thus it was] also a major city in the South-east" (*Shi ji*, *juan* 129, p. 3267). In the *Sui shu* (*juan* 31, p. 887) we read that the area with its "rivers, lakes and fertile soil has the plenitude provided by the waters and flat lands. Precious and rare goods are gathered here, and thus merchants and businessmen converge here." In 1070, Jia Dan (1038–1103), in his memorial presented to the emperor, points out: "[If we] should say that none of the benefits of all-under-Heaven can surpass that of the watered paddy-fields, then none of the beauties of the watered paddy-fields can surpass those of Suzhou" (*Wujun zhi*, *juan* 19, p. 262). Fan Chengda (1126–1193) even claims that "[The area of] the River Song and Lake Tai, a land of crisscrossing waters, can certainly boast itself first under Heaven" (*Suzhoufu zhi*, *juan* 2.19).
34. Sun 1983, p. 284; cf. Eastman 1988, p. 9.
35. Han Yu (768–824), in the introduction to one of his poems, indicates that "nowadays nine-tenth of the taxes from all-under-Heaven are levied on the region south of the Yangzi" (*Han Changli wenji jiaozhu*, *juan* 4, p. 231). Although the proportional figure he used is certainly an artistic hyperbole, it does however point to the fact that, in the words of Du Mu (803–ca. 8 2), "today the world takes the region around the River Yangzi and River Huai as its lifeblood" (*Quan Tang wen*, *juan* 7 3, p. 34 9). As for the importance of Suzhou prefecture, Bai Juyi (772–846) claims that "nowadays most of the state expenditure comes from the region south of the Yangzi; and amongst the prefectures of this region, Suzhou is the largest" (*Quan Tang wen*, *juan* 666, p. 3001). Similar accounts were given in 814 by Yuan Xi in his "Suzhou cishi xieshang biao" (*Quan Tang wen*, *juan* 693, pp. 31 0–31 1).
36. Emperor Suzong of the Tang in 7 8 established two administrative regions in the Southeast, namely the Zhejiang Xidao (the west circuit of the River Zhe) and the Zhejiang Dongdao (the east circuit of the River Zhe). The two regions were sometimes collectively called Liang-Zhe (the two Zhe).
37. *Wujun zhi*, *juan* 1, p. . According to the *Xin Tang shu* (*juan* 37, p. 960 and *juan* 2, pp. 13 1–13 2),

the annual Inland Revenue from 780 on was just over 30,000,000 *min* (=*guan*) collected from 328 prefectures. Thus, the amount of tax levied on the Liang-Zhe region counted as 22.2 percent of the annual Inland Revenue.

38. Gernet (1982, p. 319) holds that this "was undoubtedly one of the great events in this period of the history of East Asia."
39. Cf. *WTx*, *juan* C, pp. 2– ; *Wujun zhi*, *juan* 19, pp. 260–292.
40. *Wujun zhi*, *juan* 0, p. 660.
41. Marmé 1993, p. 17. During the Tang period, Suzhou prefecture was believed to be second to none in the west circuit of the River Zhe (*Wujun zhi*, ibid.). Yet at least by the eleventh century, Suzhou could no longer rival Hangzhou in its economic development under the Northern Song and much less the Song capital at Kaifeng. During the Southern Song period (1127–1276), the gap separating Hangzhou from Suzhou widened as the former was designated as the "temporary" capital. See Marmé 1993, pp. 17–19.
42. Within a period of fifteen years from 127 to 1290, the registered population of the prefecture rose from 329,603 households to 466,1 8 (*Suzhoufu zhi*, *juan* 13.2–3).
43. Marmé 1993, pp. 2 –26.
44. Mote 1962; cf. Dreyer 1982. The property of the big landowners of the Jiangnan region was classified as official land and taxed ten to fifteen times as heavily as private land. Suzhou prefecture alone was assessed for one-tenth of the state's land tax, most of it being applied to official land at a rate of 30 to 70 percent of the crops' value, even though the wealthy families may not have fully complied with it. In the fourth month of 1380, a 20 percent reduction of taxes was decreed, but even after this the land tax remained exorbitant. Cf. Liang 1980, p. 43 , Table ; Chan 1988, p. 190.
45. Marmé 1993, p. 30. He also notes that Suzhou's ability to prosper while paying such heavy taxes depended from the outset on the thoroughly commercialized character of the local economy. "The prefecture," he argues, "was as much the victim of its economic maturity as of its political indiscretions."
46. Suzhou also boasts a long history of superior textile productivity. After the Eastern Jin period, according to the *Song shu* (*juan* 4, p. 1 40), textile industry in the Southeast was developed to the extent that "the abundance of its silk floss and wadding, cloth and silk fabrics has provided clothes for the whole world." Cotton only came to be widely cultivated in this region during the Yuan, but its production expanded most quickly in Ming times.
47. Skinner 1977a, p. 17.
48. These figures are obtained from Liang 1980, pp. 401–413, Table 77; p. 43 , Table .
49. *Dushi fangyu jiyao*, *juan* 24, p. 1098.
50. Skinner 1977a, pp. 11, 2 , 28.
51. Skinner (1977a, pp. 16–17) has succinctly summarized the temporal pattern of urban development in the Lower Yangzi after the medieval urban revolution. During the phase of late Tang and Northern Song, the relatively complex urban system that developed was focused on Yangzhou as the central metropolis. The designation of Hangzhou as the Southern Song capital caused the urban structure to be reoriented further southward to the imperial capital. Nanjing came to play the central role after the fourteenth century as the Ming founder vastly enlarged the city as his political base, this being followed by the longer and somewhat more dramatic developmental cycle during the period between the sixteenth and the nineteenth centuries, in which Suzhou rose to prominence as the regional metropolis. The cycle from the late nineteenth century onward was intimately associated with the rise of Shanghai. Yet Skinner also notices that even before and after its heyday as the Lower Yangzi's central metropolis, Suzhou maintained its standing as a commercial and political center of major importance.
52. Elvin 1973, p. 268.
53. Ibid., p. 318. In Elvin's words, "nowhere in the world of 1800 was the hierarchy of urban central places so maturely developed as in the more advanced parts of China."

54. The cotton industry, for example, was probably the largest single industry in China in late imperial times (Elvin 1973, p. 270), but the spinning and weaving of cotton were not conducted in the city but in the rural areas (*tj, ce* 115.24b). Similar features could also be found in other industries. In the early Ming period, the silk industry was largely controlled by the government through its official establishment of weaving production located in the city, but from the mid-sixteenth century onward, private weavers proliferated, and their productivity was based probably not much more in the city than in the countryside (Duan and Zhang 1986, pp. 1–92). This, together with some other characteristics of industrial production and distribution, leads to Elvin's (ibid., p. 277) apparently paradoxical proposition that in late imperial times "the Chinese countryside was both overindustrialized and overcommercialized."
55. Liang 1980, pp., 273–279, Table 88.
56. Ibid., p. 14, Table 4; p. 26, Table 8.
57. Naquin and Rawski 1987, p. 152.
58. Skinner 1977a, p. 19. Skinner (ibid., pp. 17–23) argues that the reasons for this tendency were, in the face of population growth and territory expansion, a secular decline in governmental effectiveness from mid-Tang on to the end of the imperial era, and a steady reduction in basic-level administrative central functions from one era to the next, so as to keep coordination and control within the capabilities of the agrarian state. Yet Eberhard (1962, p. 268) suggests that "typically, the other cities [than imperial capitals] of classical China stopped growing when they had reached an 'optimum' size because the government would need, in a heavily inhabited area, to create a new administrative center which would draw population away from the old center." He then explains further: "the Chinese government . . . broke up units which had grown too much, creating two districts out of one. We do not yet know where, in terms of population, the 'optimum' was. Over time, Chinese skill in administration grew (especially since Sung time), but at the same time, higher efficiency was desired" (ibid., p. 268, note 1). It seems that Eberhard is talking about the regions that were economically most advanced.
59. *Wuxian zhi, juan* 49.3.
60. Mote 1973, p. 39. Skinner (1977a, p. 29) however, makes a more cautious estimate of the population of the city of Suzhou at seven hundred thousand in the 1840s, a view that has later been shared by Naquin and Rawski (1987, p. 152).
61. Du Bose 1911, pp. 62–63; Mote 1973, p. 42.
62. Mote 1973, p. 42.
63. *Han shu, juan* 28, p. 1667. See also *Taiping huanyu ji, juan* 91, p. 686, quotation from the *Junguo zhi*.
64. *Sui shu, juan* 31, p. 887.
65. *WTx, juan* A, pp. 10–11. See also *Wujun zhi, juan* 2, pp. 8, 13, for Fan Chengda's accounts in the Southern Song period.
66. Cf. *Ch* 1980, p. 1747; *Cy* 1988, p. 1247; Yang 1987, pp. 459, 460–461; Xu 1991, pp. 799–800, 802. Gernet (1982, p. 257) insists, however, that this new method could not have been properly organized in a systematic way until the year 669.
67. Gernet 1982, p. 304.
68. *Wujun zhi, juan* 4, p. 28–31.
69. Ho 1962, pp. 226–237; Wakeman, Jr. 1975, pp. 19–24.
70. Elman 1984, pp. 59, 121.
71. Ibid., pp. 12, 142, 147.
72. Wang 1985, pp. 409–416.
73. Cf. *Wujun zhi, juan* 2, p. 13; *usu zhi, juan* 13.1–3.
74. *Shuyuan zaji, juan* 13, p. 156. The translation is adapted from Clunas 1996, p. 21, with some modifications to the last sentence.
75. *ui Zhuan ji, juan* 6, p. 351.

76. *Chaolin bitan, juan* , p.113.
77. *Xxz, juan* A.27a–b.
78. Mote 1973, p. 7.
79. "Jiuri yanji zuiti junlou jiancheng Zhou Yin er panguan," in *Quan Tang shi, juan* 444, pp. 4968–4969.
80. "Qiyunlou wanwang outi shiyun jiancheng Feng shiyu Zhou Yin er xielü," in *Quan Tang shi, juan* 447, pp. 033– 034. Chang'an was the imperial capital of the Tang.
81. Mote 1973, pp. 48, 49.
82. This refers to the period from 978, when the Wu-Yue regime (907–978) surrendered to the Northern Song, to the time when Zhu Changwen wrote this passage.
83. *WTx, juan* A, pp. 6–7.
84. Frances Wood (199) argues that Marco Polo never traveled further than the Black Sea and Constantinople, let alone lived in China for seventeen years. Some of the blindingly obvious exotic features of China—the Chinese script, the Great Wall, tea, or foot-binding—that Marco Polo somehow failed to notice, or at least to comment on, indicate to Wood that he never set foot in the place. It seems possible that his accounts of many parts of China may have been lifted from a Persian or Arabic guidebook, but no such book, if one existed, survives. Yet one thing is certain, as Wood admits, whatever its provenance, Marco Polo's travel book remains a rich and useful source for thirteenth-century China.
85. Manzi, a derogatory term used by the Mongols for the southern Chinese subjects of the Song. The character *man* was previously used by the Han Chinese for the people in the south.
86. The number of the bridges within the city is exaggerated here by twenty times.
87. Ross and Power 1931, pp. 232–233. See also Balazs' (1964, pp. 66–100) discussions of Chinese cities by reference to Marco Polo's accounts.
88. Marco Polo was later nicknamed Il Milione for his habit of exaggeration.
89. At the beginning of the Yuan period, the city walls, over fifteen kilometers in circumference, were ordered to be dismantled. Marco Polo's account that the city had "a circuit of sixty miles," apart from exaggeration, must have included many areas that were on the outskirts of the city.
90. *Yupu zaji, juan* , p. 42.
91. *P'yohaerok*, 2.21. See also Santangelo 1992, pp. 2–3; 1993, pp. 82–83. For a full translation of *P'yohaerok* in English, see Meskill 196 .
92. Johnston 1983, p. 203.
93. Elsewhere, Oliphant (1970, pp. 198, 206) has made similar statements that "in the city . . . the lanes of water . . . like those of Venice, opened up in divers [*sic*] directions," and that the most remarkable feature he could catch in passing "was the numerous canals intersecting it in every direction, spanned, rialto fashion, by high single arches, and with houses rising out of the water as in Venice."
94. Oliphant 184 , p. 84.
95. By this, the author must have been referring to the west suburbs of Suzhou, the commercial center of the Jiangnan region during the late imperial period.
96. This must have been Chang Gate, the northern gate in the west wall.
97. Oliphant 184 , p. 8
98. Du Bose 1911. Cf. Mote 1973, pp. 4 –48.
99. Du Bose 1911, p. 1.
100. Mote 1973, p. 4 .
101. This bridge is called Baodai Qiao (Treasure-girder Bridge). First built in 806, it is located about three kilometers south of the city of Suzhou. It is mentioned by Laurence Oliphant (1970, pp. 212–213), who, being told that the bridge had ninety arches, correctly counted fifty-three himself.
102. Du Bose 1911, pp. 7–8.
103. Ibid., p. 39.
104. Ibid., pp. 39–40.

Chapter 2: The City in Its Beginning

1. Schwartz 1985, pp. 20–30. For an extensive discussion of the origin of Tian, see Creel 1970, pp. 493–506.
2. Wheatley 1971, p. 135.
3. Dong 1982, p. 52. For a report on the archaeological findings of an old water gate at the site of Qi Gate, see Ding and Mi 1983.
4. For a bibliographical guide to these two documents, see Lagerwey 1993; Schuessler and Loewe 1993.
5. Sivin 1995, p. 6.
6. Wright 1977; Wheatley 1971.
7. I borrow this word from Wheatley 1971, p. 411.
8. For the authenticity, date, and character of the *Zhou li*, see Wright 1977, p. 46; Boltz 1993, pp. 24–25.
9. *Zhou li, juan* 10, p. 66. Translation of the second half of this passage by Wright (1977, p. 47) with modifications. For a French translation, see Biot 1851, vol. 1, p. 201.
10. Wright 1977, p. 47.
11. *Zhou li, juan* 1, p. 1. Translation by Wright (1977, p. 46) with modifications. See also Biot 1851, vol. 1, p. 1.
12. Wright 1977, p. 46. This appears to be in line with the Chinese conception of civilization that the Virtue of the Son of Heaven spreads out over the four quarters of the world, civilizing the regions close by and gradually losing its effectiveness as it gets farther away from the center. The ideal city was regarded as a cosmic center that reproduced the order of the wider cosmos. In doing so, the capital city, where the king resided, linked Heaven and Earth. The royal capital, duplicating the cosmic order, drew forth the power of that order into the city and state on earth. Schwartz (1985, p. 37) argues that since the dominant religious orientations in ancient China had formed, in the first instance, a religious base for an extraordinary, powerful conception of universal kingship and, by extension, for the early emergence within the high culture of the concept of a total all-embracing social and cosmic order, it was then the person of the king who linked Heaven and Earth, and matters which had been divined before were now routinely in the power of the king to control. The ordered city, expressive of his position at the pinnacle of the social hierarchy and as the pivot of the four quarters, ensured just rule, and likewise the just rule protected the ordered city and the cosmos it represented. This conception is clearly expressed in a passage in the *Lüshi chunqiu* (*juan* 17: "Shen shi," p. 211) declaring that the Son of Heaven should be at the pivot of the concentric system:

    > In antiquity, he who had come to rule selected the center under Heaven to establish his state, then selected the center of the state to establish his palace, and then selected the center of the palace to establish the Ancestral Temple. The land of a thousand square *li* under Heaven was regarded as a state, and therefore [it was] ruled at the pivot, and that is [the king's] duty.

    This idea is epitomized in the *Mengzi* (*juan* 13A, p. 102), which states that it should be the exemplary ruler's role "to stand in the center under Heaven and stabilize the people within the four seas." In the ode "Minlao" (*Shi jing*, Mao #253 [*juan* 17/4: "Da ya"], p. 280) which was allegedly written by Duke Shaomu to remonstrate sarcastically with King Li (?–828 B.C.) of Zhou upon his tyrannical government, we read,

    > The people are indeed heavily burdened
    > And it is time for them to repose awhile.
    > Show favor to this Central Kingdom [Zhongguo]
    > So as to placate the four quarters.
    >
    > (Translation by Wheatley [1971, p. 445] with minor modifications)

It was an attribute of the king to be at the center; in turn, it was also an attribute of the center to be occupied exclusively by the king.

13. *Zhou li*, *juan* 24, pp. 164–167; *juan* 41, p. 289, with the commentaries of Zheng Xuan (127–200) and of Jia Gongyan of the seventh century A.D.
14. Wright 1977, p. 47.
15. Ding (the Pegasus α, β), also known as Shi or Yingshi, literally means "constructing buildings." Both Zheng Xuan and Kong Yingda (74–648) explain that as the constellation Ding reached the middle of the sky, it was at the middle of the tenth month when winter started and when it was the proper time for constructions; this is perhaps the reason for the constellation's having been named Yingshi (*Shi jing*, Mao # o [*juan* 3/1: "Guo feng"], pp. 47–48). The ritually sanctioned season for the construction of a city, according to the "Yueling" section of the *Li ji* (*juan* 16 and 17), was the second month of autumn; and the repair of walls and gates was to be made in the first month of winter. The coincidence of the timing of city construction and repair work with the relatively slack season in the farming year seems more than incidental, as Wheatley (1971, pp. 182–183) has suggested. Kong, when commenting on the *Zuo zhuan* (*juan* 10: "Zhuang 29th year [66 B.C.]," p. 80), explicitly explains that any construction work should be accomplished in the interval between busy seasons in farming, and even after the winter solstice, the coming year's farm work should be prepared and constructions should thus not be pursued any further. The proper or improper timing of constructions was in fact mentioned again and again in the records of such writings as the *Zuo zhuan*.
16. *Shi jing*, Mao # o (*juan* 3/1: "Guo feng"), p. 47. Translation adapted from Wheatley 1971, p. 426. For different renderings, see Legge 1960, vol. 4, p. 81; Waley 1937, p. 281.
17. Wheatley 1971, pp. 423–42 .
18. Needham 19 9, pp. 266–267.
19. *Zhou li*, *juan* 41, p. 289. For different renderings, see Wheatley 1971, p. 426; Steinhardt 1990, p. 33. For a French translation, see Biot 18 1, vol. 2, p.   3.
20. Needham 19 9, p. 230.
21. *Lun yu*, *juan* 2, p. . Translation by Legge 1967, vol. 1, p. 14 with minor modifications.
22. Here I paraphrase Diana Eck (1987, p. 3), who speaks of a general pattern of building a city at a cosmic center.
23. *Zhou li*, *juan* 41, p. 289. Translation by Wheatley (1971, p. 411) with minor modification. For a different rendering, see Steinhardt 1990, p. 33. For a French translation, see Biot 18 1, vol. 2, p.   6.
24. Wheatley (1971, pp. 411, 414) suggests that the text of the "Kaogong ji" might have incorporated a confusion between the postulated nine meridional and nine latitudinal avenues of the city and the nine units of the well-field system; and thus, a group of four units fulfilling the role of the central tract occupied a quarter, rather than a ninth, of the total area, which was subdivided into sixteen quarters, rather than nine. By referring to this passage, He Yeju (198 , pp. 43–44; 48– 1) maintains that the city is subdivided into nine units, with the central tract—the palace complex occupying a ninth of the total area. He insists that the subdivision is realized by only two sets (1 set = 3 avenues) of meridional and latitudinal avenues, leaving the central meridional one as the main north-south axis and the central latitudinal one as an auxiliary east-west axis. The proportion of the central tract, that is, the royal palace (*gong*), to the area of the city (*cheng*), is explicitly indicated in the *Shang shu dazhuan* (*juan* 3, p. 3) of the Han: "The *cheng* has sides of 9 *li*, and *gong* has sides of 3 *li*."
25. Granet 1930, pp. 243–244. Balazs (1964, p. 68) explicitly speaks of the "rural origin" of such spatial organization. For discussions of the well-field system, see Granet 1930, pp. 149–1 0; Wheatley 1971, pp. 132–134, 20 , note 11 and He 198 , pp. 39–42. Those discussions are mainly based on the descriptions in the *Mengzi*, *juan* A, pp. 38–39; and in the *Zhou li*, *juan* 11, p. 711 and *juan* 1 , pp. 102–103.
26. The assumption of "heaven round, earth square" (*tianyuan difang*) is of great antiquity. It was, for example, expounded in the *Huainanzi* and some other writings and incorporated in one of the

ancient astronomical theories, that of the Gai Tian school. For an introduction to and discussion of the school, see Needham 1959, pp. 212–213.

27. *Shang shu*, *juan* 6, pp. 34 ff. Needham (1959, p. 500) regards this section as the oldest Chinese geographical document.
28. *Shi ji*, *juan* 74, p. 2344. Zou Yan (ca. 305–240 B.C.) refers to the Middle Kingdom by the name the "Spiritual Region of the Red Continent" (Chixian Shenzhou). Thus, the area of China was also named the "Central Region" (Zhongzhou) or the "Central Earth" (Zhongtu). For a discussion of the cosmological significance of the idea of the Nine Provinces, see Henderson 1984, pp. 66–68.
29. In the "Kaogong ji" we read, for example, that "the market and the royal court of audience each occupies an area of one *fu*," with Zheng Xuan and Jia Gongyan explaining that "each occupied one hundred square *bu*." This measurement is identical with that of the well-field system. Cf. *Zhou li*, *juan* 11, pp. 73 ff. and *juan* 15, pp. 102–103.
30. Wright 1977, p. 48. Cf. Granet 1934, chap. 3, especially pp. 173–174.
31. Cf. *Li ji*, *juan* 23, pp. 203–205; *Zuo zhuan*, *juan* 9: "Zhuang 18th year [676 B.C.]," p. 71.
32. *Zhi* was an area unit for the measurement of city walls. One *zhi* equaled three *zhang* in length by one *zhang* in height.
33. *Zuo zhuan*, *juan* 2: "Yin 1st year [722 B.C.]," p. 14. Cf. Legge 1960, vol 5, p. 5.
34. *Han shu*, *juan* 73, p. 3127.
35. *Zhou li*, *juan* 41, p. 289. Biot 1851, vol. 2, p. 556.
36. Wright 1977, p. 39.
37. *Zuo zhuan*, *juan* 10: "Zhuang 28th year [666 B.C.]," p. 80. Translation adapted from Legge 1960, vol. 5, p. 115. The ritualized activities at the *zongmiao* are repeatedly recorded in the *Zuo zhuan*.
38. *Li ji*, *juan* 12, pp. 104 ff.
39. *Yi Zhou shu*, *juan* 5/48, p. 78.
40. *Li ji*, *juan* 25, p. 221.
41. See, for example, *Zuo zhuan*, *juan* 54: "Ding 4th year [506 B.C.]," p. 433.
42. *Zuo zhuan*, passim. Hence it is not surprising that "the ruin of the Altar of Earth and Grain" was simply an expression designating the extinction of the state in question.
43. *Yi Zhou shu*, *juan* 4/32, p. 47. See also the commentary by Jia Gongyan on the first sentence of the "Xiao zongbo" section in the *Zhou li*, *juan* 19, p. 128.
44. The original meaning of the Chinese character *tian* (later meaning "heaven" or "the sky"), according to Xu Shen's (ca. A.D. 58–147) definition, is man's head, or, in some circumstances his forehead or the top of his head (*Shuowen jiezi*, 1A.1 and 9A.1). Duan Yucai (1735–1815) commented, ". . . it meant the top of a man, and was extended to connote all which were high. . . . Thus *tian* was also extended to indicate all occupiers of the superior position, such as the king compared to his subjects, the father compared to his sons, the husband compared to his wife" (*Shuowen jiezi zhu*, *pian* 1A.2). This concept is scattered throughout ancient literature, a few examples of which follow. For the line in the ode "Bai zhou" (*Shi jing*, Mao #45 [*juan* 3-1: "Guo feng" section], p. 44), "Oh, mother! Oh, *tian*!" Mao explains: "By *tian* was meant father." For a line in another ode, "Dang" (Mao # 255 [*juan* 18-1: "Da ya" section], p. 285), "*Tian* grants [the people of Yin] arrogant and befuddled dispositions"; he explains, "Here *tian* is the ruler." And it is recorded in the *Yi li* (*juan* 30, p. 162), "Hence the father is his son's *tian*, and the husband is his wife's *tian*."
45. This concept was omnipresent in ancient times. For example, cf. the odes "Wen Wang" and "Da ming" in the *Shi jing* (Mao #235 [*juan* 16/1] and Mao #236 [*juan* 16/2]: "Da ya").
46. Granet (1930, p. 241) holds that the two institutions were formerly one and the same.
47. *uo yu*, *juan* 19, pp. 619, 622. A parallel, if not universal, concept has been revealed in the *Chronicum Laurissense breve*, written about 800, which says that in the course of one of his wars against the Saxons (772), Charlemagne destroyed the temple and the sacred wood of their "famous Irminsul" in the town of Eresburg. See Eliade 1959, p. 35. This appears to correspond with the idea that, as the city was constituted ritually, it had a more than physical existence; when it was conquered, it

had to be ritually unmade and disestablished, as Rykwert (1989, pp. 70–71) suggests, who also gives a number of such recorded events in the Roman world, ancient Greece, and Shechem.

48. *Zuo zhuan, juan* 36: “Xiang 2 th year [48 B.C.],” p. 282. Cf. Wheatley 1971, p. 431; Wright 1977, p. 40.
49. Wheatley, ibid.
50. Wright, ibid., p. 49.
51. *Zhou li, juan* 14, pp. 96–97.
52. Graham 1989, pp. 227, 331.
53. *Zhou li, juan* 7, p. 47.
54. Wright 1977, p. 49.
55. Pragmatic theories of city planning had been developed by the end of the Warring States period, among which the most representative is found in the *Guanzi*. It advocates that the scale, size, and name (title) of the city should be adjusted according to its population and the surrounding cultivated land it relies on, rather than to its enfeoffed hierarchical title of enfeoffment only (*Guanzi, juan* /13: “Ba guan,” p. 74). As for the site and layout of the city, it states,

    > In any case of establishing a state capital, situate it either at the foot of a great mountain, or above [the bank of] a broad river. Avoid placing it so high as to approach the drought [level], thus sufficient water is available. Avoid placing it so low as to approach the flood [level], thus [excessive use of] canals and embankments are spared. Take advantage of the resources of Heaven and adapt yourself to the benefit from Earth. Hence the inner and outer city-walls need not accord with the compasses and square, nor its roads with the level and marking line.
    >
    > (*Guanzi, juan* 1/5: “Cheng ma,” p. 13. Translation adapted from Rickett 1985, p. 116, with some modifications.)

    Whereas these expositions seem to have presaged the later urban development in the south of China, where the geographical conditions are much more complex than those in the North, they may prove to have been complementary ideas to the canonical principles of the early city form. From the philosophical point of view, does not this apparent contradiction of ideas reflect Graham’s (1989, p. 370) observation that “it is as though Chinese civilization has been careful to preserve a certain latitude in the organization of its cosmos, in order that throughout its long history originality and creativity should never die out”? In symbolic terms, however, the *Guanzi* (*juan* 18/ 7: “Duo di,” p. 303) also expounds that “the Son of Heaven should reside at the center.”
56. *Zhou Yi qianzaodu, juan* A.2.
57. Sivin 199 , p. 18.
58. The trend for princes and dukes of all states to reject the Zhou king’s authority and ambitiously to seek hegemony over China was visible in the construction of their capitals. Most capital city planning at that time exceeded the restrictions imposed by the Zhou’s institutional rituals (*jianyue*), which were intended to reflect the princes’ and dukes’ feudal rank and duty, and thus breached the once rigid regulations of the hierarchical system. For the restrictions in hierarchical order, cf. *Zuo zhuan, juan* 2: “Yin 1st year [722 B.C.],” p. 14; *Li ji, juan* 23, pp. 203 ff. For a discussion, see He 1986, pp. 26–28.
59. For the details of the event, see *Zuo zhuan, juan* 2: “Zhao 27th year [1 B.C.],” p. 414; *Shi ji, juan* 31, p. 1463, *juan* 86, pp. 2 16–2 18.
60. See, for example, Shang 1988; Xiao 1988. The only information about the Wu settlement prior to the building of Helü Dacheng comes from a largely fictional account in the *Wu Yue chunqiu* (*juan* 1, pp. 3–4). Scholars of later periods speculated that the location of the settlement was at Meili [southeast of present-day Wuxi]. See, for example, *Wujun zhi, juan* 3, p. 20.
61. Xiao 1988, pp. 28–30.

62. There are, for example, a total of 483 military actions mentioned in the *Zuo zhuan,* which covers a span of about 240 years (starting from 722 B.C.). See He 1986, p. 55.
63. *Zuo zhuan, juan* 52: "Zhao 26th year [516 B.C.]," p. 411. Cf. Legge 1960, vol. 5, p. 716. Wheatley (1971, p. 398) argues: "It follows from the functional criterion of urbanism adopted in this work that city and state were coeval, indeed the city was the organizing principle of the state, and all generated cities were in their earlier phases city-states. . . . the process of crystallization of urban forms at the same time brought into being the earliest state institutions." Cf. Graham 1989, p. 300.
64. *Yue jue shu, juan* 7, p. 49. In his bibliographical guide to the text of the *Wu Yue chunqiu,* Lagerwey (1993, p. 473) writes: "The very choice of venue was dictated by a pessimistic cosmological consideration; for the south-east is, in the words of the *Wu yüeh ch'un ch'iu,* the *ti hu,* the Door of the Earth, i.e. the cosmic drain."
65. *uanzi, juan* 18/57: "Duo di," p. 303.
66. *Wei Liaozi, juan* 1/2.2.
67. A similar idea is revealed in the alleged proposal by Fan Li to the king of Yue for relocating the Yue capital:

> Now that the great king intends to establish the state and to build the capital, in order to annex the territories of the rival states, if the capital were not situated on the level plain from which the four quarters can be reached, how would the enterprise of hegemony be pursued?
>
> (*Wu Yue Chunqiu, juan* 8, p. 107)

68. We find the same term used by Xun Qing (*c.* 313-238 B.C.) as the criterion for the site of the capital with the advantages of strategic tenability, convenience of transport, beautiful scenery and rich natural resources. See *Xunzi, juan* 11/16: "Qiangguo," p. 202.
69. "The Three Rivers (Sanjiang)," according to Fan Chengda means the Rivers Song, Dong, and Lou, which ran through the Wu territory, although other interpretations are not to be excluded. "The Five Lakes (Wuhu)" is probably another name for Lake Tai. See *Wujun zhi, juan* 48, pp. 622–626.
70. *Suzhoufu zhi, juan* 2.19.
71. *Wu Yue chunqiu, juan* 4, p. 25. Ji Yuyi (1988, pp. 38–40) has made a rather bold suggestion that deviates from the traditionally received interpretation of the phrase. He argues that the character *shui* (water) is a wrong word, erroneously transcribed from the character *he* (crops), and thus the character *chang* (to taste or try) here does not mean "to inspect or examine" but denotes a special sacrifice in autumn. Therefore, this phrase, in his view, should be interpreted as "to survey the terrain of the land and offer sacrifice to the gods [before the construction of the city]." While this suggestion is very interesting, at the present time it is given as only a reference to await further proofs rather than as an *a priori* conclusion.
72. A passage from the *Shang shu* (*juan* 15, p. 99) states: "King Cheng . . . intended to build his palace at Luo, [therefore he] ordered the Duke of Shao to survey [*xiang*] [the area where] his palace was to be built." Kong commented, "*Xiang* means to survey the area and to divine it."
73. *Han shu, juan* 49, p. 2288.
74. *Yue jue shu, juan* 2, p. 9.
75. Ji 1988, p. 34. The accounts of its size vary in other documents of later periods. For example, in the *Wudi ji* (p. 14), a local record book of Suzhou written from the Tang period onward, it is recorded as 45 *li* 30 *bu* in perimeter. Fortunately, however, the measurements of the four sides of the *dacheng* are also recorded in detail in the same volume of the *Yue jue shu* (p. 9): the south side measures 10 *li* 42 *bu* 5 *chi*; the west, 7 *li* 112 *bu* 3 *chi*; the north, 8 *li* 226 *bu* 3 *chi*; and the east, 11 *li* 79 *bu* 1 *chi*. Thus, the perimeter of the *dacheng* must have been 37 *li* 161 *bu* (approximately 15.88km by the Eastern

Han standard). This measurement can be further verified if another record in the same volume (p. 10) is taken into account: the central street of the city from Chang Gate to Lou Gate is 9 *li* 72 *bu* long and from Ping Gate to She Gate, 10 *li* 75 *bu*.

76. *Yue jue shu*, *juan* 2, p. 10. In the *Yi Zhou shu* (*juan* 5/48: "Zuo Luo," p. 77), the outer city wall of the Zhou royal capital at Luoyang is recorded as being "a square with sides of 72 *li*," that is, 288 *li* in perimeter, which is eight times that of the city proper. This account has been challenged by scholars of later dynastic periods and seems impossible in consideration of the geographical conditions in Luoyang and the economic resources of those times. See, for example, Sun Yirang's (1848–1908) commentary in *Zhou li zhengyi*, *juan* 83, p. 3424; He 1985, p. 61; Ji 1988, p. 35. Generally speaking, the proportion of the length of the *cheng* perimeter to that of the *guo* perimeter during the Warring States period, according some other writings such as the *Mengzi* (*juan* 4A, p. 29) and the *Zhanguo ce* (*juan* 4, pp. 465 and 467), appears to have ranged from 1:1.4 to 1:2.3. This proportion has been attested by archaeological evidence. See He 1985, p. 62. Thus the outer city wall of the Zhou royal capital at Luoyang, for example, probably measured 68 to 70 *li* in perimeter and was erroneously transcribed. See Ji 1988, p. 36.
77. The figures in the *Wu Yue chunqiu* and the *Wudi ji* are read respectively as 10 *li* and 8 *li* 660 *bu*, which is regarded by Ji Yuyi as the consequence of scribal errors as well. Cf. *Yue jue shu*, *juan* 2, p. 10; *Wu Yue chunqiu*, *juan* 4, p. 25; *Wudi ji*, p. 14.
78. *Yue jue shu*, *juan* 2, p. 10. A few characters describing the height of the walls are missing in some of the editions of this work. Since this height recorded in the other sources appears to have been extraordinary in proportion to its thickness, the accuracy of this account becomes doubtful. For a discussion of the proportion of the height to the thickness of the city walls in the Spring and Autumn period, see He 1985, pp. 65–67.
79. See note 32 for this chapter.
80. The walled inner enclosure has been speculated to be either at the very center of the city or slightly east of center. See, for example, Qu 1991, p. 221; Ji 1988, pp. 43–44.
81. Qu Yingjie (1991, pp. 211–225), contradicting the traditionally accepted supposition, holds that in the early stage of the city's development Ping Gate and Qi Gate were really in reverse positions. He also argues that the city was built in imitation of the capital city of Chu at Ying. Yet his argument is equally not based on archaeological evidence but solely on assumption.
82. In some circumstances, the Ancestral Temple and the Altar of Earth and Grain are referred to as representing the existence of the state and city. But I am disposed to regard the mentions of these two features in the documents in question as a twofold implication, that is, of the existence of the state and city, and of the two city structures per se.
83. See *Wu Yue chunqiu*, *juan* 3, pp. 10 and 17, *juan* 4, pp. 32 and 36; *Yue jue shu*, *juan* 1, pp. 6–7, *juan* 2, p. 11. These sources imply that there was a well-organized market in the Wu capital before its reconstruction in 514 B.C. The market in the reconstructed capital was later also known as the Market of Cranes (Heshi) and the bridge nearby as the Crane-Dancing (Hewu) Bridge due to an event mentioned in the *Wu Yue chunqiu*.
84. *Wu Yue chunqiu*, *juan* 4, p. 25.
85. *Zhou Yi*, *juan* 8: "Xici" B, p. 74. Translation by Legge 1899, p. 382, with minor modifications. Similar accounts can be read in the *Huainanzi*, *juan* 20, p. 351.
86. *Wu Yue chunqiu*, *juan* 4, p. 25.
87. Ibid. An interpretation of the term *bacong* is worth attempting. The character *cong* means "sensitivity of hearing," which can be extended to denote "learning something and thus being intelligent" (*Ch* 1980, p. 1822; *Cy* 1988, p. 1377). It also can imply "window," as the *Shi ming* (*juan* 5, p. 18b) explained: "*Chuang* [window] embodies the meaning of *cong*. From the inside [through the window] to peek to the outside is [to become] wise." In some documents of later times, such as the *Wudi ji* (p. 14) and the *Wujun zhi* (*juan* 3, p. 20), we read, "Eight water gates [were built] to

imitate the Eight Trigrams [*bagua*] of Earth." Ji Yuyi (1988, pp. 40–41) has suggested, again boldly, that the character *cong* was erroneously transcribed from *ji*. I see this suggestion as too radical to be accepted for the moment.

88. *Wu Yue chunqiu, juan* 8, pp. 106–107.
89. The concept appears not only in the *Lüshi chunqiu* (the authenticity of which as a pre-Qin text, as Carson and Loewe [1993, p. 324] indicate, is generally accepted) but also in the *Zuo zhuan*.
90. Ji Yuyi (1988, p. 40) suggests that, whereas the city is not recorded as having followed in this aspect the form of the ideal capital for the Son of Heaven prescribed in the *Zhou li*—it contained not twelve but only eight gates—the application of the symbols for the eight winds, of which the Son of Heaven probably used to have the exclusive title, appears to have signified the ambition of the king of Wu. In the *Zuo zhuan* (*juan* 3: "Yin th year [718 B.C.]," pp. 2 –26) for example, it is recorded that Duke Yin, offering sacrifices in the Temple of Zhongzi and presenting the spirits with dancing performances, asked his advisers about the proper number of the dancers. They replied, "The Son of Heaven uses eight [lines in square, that is, sixty-four dancers], princes and Dukes use six [lines in square, that is, thirty-six dancers], senior officials use four [lines in square, that is, sixteen dancers], and junior officials use two [lines in square, that is, four dancers]. The dancing is to promote the eight winds by virtue of the rhythms of the eight musical sounds, therefore [the application of the number of dancers] should be in degression from eight [lines in square]."
91. *Wu Yue chunqiu, juan* 8, p. 107.
92. See, for example, *Huainanzi, juan* 1, p. 3, with Gao's commentary. See also Needham's (19 9, pp. 2 9–262) discussion of the celestial phenomenon of the Purple Palace from the astronomical point of view.
93. The analogy between the Purple Forbidden Palace and the imperial court was more fully elaborated in the later dynastic periods. In the *Sanfu huangtu* (p. 8), for example, it is recorded that the palaces of the First Emperor (Shi Huangdi [2 9–210 B.C.]) of Qin allegedly imitated the Purple Forbidden Palace so as to symbolize his absolute power. The *Wu Yue chunqiu* (*juan* 8, pp. 107–108) also presents an interesting conversation between the king and Fan Li, who reported to the king after the completion of the construction of the capital:

> "As a minister I constructed the city which corresponds to Heaven. It even retains the likeness of Mt. Kunlun." The king of Yue said, "I have heard that Mt. Kunlun is the pillar of Earth. It reaches august Heaven above and therefore has the *qi* [cosmic breath] prevalent in the whole world; it is rooted in deep Earth and therefore receives [the natural resources and qualities] from the limitless realms. It nourishes what is sacred and produces what is divine; it immensely nurtures the High God's residence. Therefore the [Five] Emperors resided in the *yang* area on it, and the Three Kings lived at the pivot of it. My state is at the periphery of Heaven and Earth, and on the far southeast guyrope of Earth, and the Big Dipper is in the extreme north. . . . How can it be compared with those which are endowed with regal magnificence?" Fan Li said, "My lord has only noticed what is extrinsic without recognizing what is intrinsic. I have constructed the city corresponding to the Gate of Heaven, and the *qi* has been concentrated in deep Earth [on which the city stands]. The image of the great mountain has been established, and Mt. Kunlun has thus been [symbolically] produced. [All these will ensure] the hegemony of Yue."

From such early documents as the *Shanhai jing*, *Huainanzi*, *Shui jing zhu,* and *Bowu zhi*, we learn that Mt. Kunlun was believed to be the capital of the High God on earth (*Di zhi xiadu*). Its pinnacle reaches heaven, and thus it is the center of the world, where myriad deities and gods reside, including the goddess Xi Wang Mu (Queen-Mother of the West). It is also the mystical mountain where the Underworld (*Youdu*) can be entered. In addition, there is a bronze pillar on the mountain, so high as to penetrate the sky and therefore named the Pillar of Heaven (*Tianzhu*). Since the capital of Yue, a marginal state on the fringes of classical China, was believed to have been built as a replica of this cosmic mountain, it could then be interpreted as having constituted the preeminent link between Earth and Heaven necessary for acquiring the paramount cosmic power for its survival and glory.

94. *Wu Yue chunqiu, juan* 4, pp. 24–25.
95. Note the dual denotations of the character *guo*: state *and* walled capital city.
96. Gugong Danfu. See Chapter 1.
97. *Wu Yue chunqiu, juan* 8, pp. 106–107.
98. See, for example, *Shuowen jiezi*, 5B.10-11.
99. Gun is the semilegendary emperor Yu's father. He failed to regulate the rivers and watercourses and was therefore killed by Shun at Mt. Yu.
100. This passage is missing in the currently preserved *Wu Yue chunqiu*. I cite this passage from *Chu xue ji, juan* 24, p. 565. Note the ambiguity of the word *shou*, as it could be interpreted either as "to protect" or as "to watch over and prevent from escaping or rebelling." The *Taiping yulan* (*juan* 193, p. 933) too preserves this passage from the *Wu Yue chunqiu*, but the wording is slightly different: "Gun constructed the *cheng* so as to defend the ruler, built the *guo* so as to settle [*ju*] the people, and these are the origin of the city walls [*chengguo*]."

    For a study of the origins of the city walls in China, see Miyazaki 1957.
101. Eliade 1959, p. 49.
102. It is in this line of thought that, in his study of ancient Near Eastern religion, Henri Frankfort (1948, p. 3) wrote a passage that seems largely applicable to the experience of the ancient Chinese as well:

    > The ancients, however, experienced human life as part of a widely spreading network of connections which reached beyond the local and the national communities into the hidden depths of nature and the powers that rule nature. The purely secular—in so far as it could be granted to exist at all—was the purely trivial. Whatever was significant was imbedded in the life of the cosmos, and it was precisely the king's function to maintain the harmony of that integration.

103. *Zuo zhuan, juan* 9: "Zhuang 14th year [680 B.C.]," p. 69. Translation adapted from Legge 1960, vol. 5, p. 92.
104. *Zuo zhuan, juan* 10: "Zhuang 32nd year [662 B.C.]," p. 81.
105. Granet (1930, pp. 237, 239) has correctly noted that, for the Chinese, the walls were "the most sacred part of the town," and that "the divinity of the town is lodged in the gates and walls."
106. As a verb, it also meant both "to construct a city" and "to construct city walls."
107. *Shuowen jiezi zhu, pian* 13B.29; *Zuo zhuan, juan* 6: "Huan 6th year [706 B.C.]," p. 48. Cf. Legge 1960, vol. 5, p. 48.
108. See Du Yu and Kong Yingda's commentaries on this passage from the *Zuo zhuan*, ibid.
109. *Shuowen jiezi*, 5B.10–11; cf. 3B.10 for the definition of the character *du*. Xu Shen also claims that *guo* is the archaic form of *yong*, which denotes city walls (*chengyuan*) (*Shuowen jiezi*, 13B.10). Mao in his commentaries on the odes "Huang yi" (*Shi jing*, Mao #241 [*juan* 16/4: "Da ya" section], p. 254) and "Song Gao" (Mao #259 [*juan* 18/3: "Da ya" section], p. 298) defines *yong* as *cheng*. Duan Yucai explains that *cheng* emphasizes what is contained within the walls, while *yong* emphasizes the material wall that physically contains. See *Shuowen jiezi zhu, pian* 13B.29.
110. On the one hand, in the *Yue jue shu* (*juan* 8, p. 58), the wall of the inner enclosure (*xiaocheng*) is said to have measured 2 *li* 223 *bu* (approximately 1.16 kilometers by the Eastern Han standard) in perimeter, while the city proper (*dacheng*) had a wall of 20 *li* 72 *bu* (approximately 8.56 kilometers) in perimeter; and on the other, no outer city wall (*guo*) is recorded as ever having been constructed. In the *Wu Yue chunqiu* (*juan* 8, p. 107), the inner city wall measures 1,121 *bu* in perimeter.

111. *Shui jing zhu*, *juan* 40, p. 7 . A *que* is one of the two ornamented columns erected outside the main gate of a royal palace or tomb. The reversal of the "proper" orientation of the Yue capital is mentioned in the *Wu Yue chunqiu* (*juan* 8, p. 107) as well.
112. *Shi ji*, *juan* 67, p. 2197.
113. When defining the character *huang*, Xu Shen explained in his *Shuowen jiezi* (14B.): "[City moats] with water are called *chi*; without water, *huang*."
114. If the quality of the local earth was not satisfactory for the walls to be strong and durable, better earth would be conveyed from other regions, as recorded in the *WTx* (*juan* C, p. 6): "It was said that Wu Zixu, after leading the army to attack Chu, conveyed earth from Danyang and Huangdu to [re-]construct [the city wall], probably in order to give it extra strength."
115. Cf. Graham 1989, p. 3 9; Shaughnessy 1993, p. 221.
116. *Zhou Yi*, *juan* 2: "Tai," p. 17.
117. Eliade 19 9, p. 22.
118. Ibid., p. 31.
119. Mote, 1971, pp. 17–18, 19. A similar statement made by Needham (19 6, p. 82) more than a decade earlier runs:

> The Chinese world-view depended upon a totally different line of thought. The harmonious co-operation of all beings arose, not from the orders of a superior authority external to themselves, but from the fact that they were all parts in a hierarchy of wholes forming a cosmic pattern, and what they obeyed were the internal dictates of their own natures.

Graham (1986, pp. 30 ff.; 1989, pp. 12, 203, 332 ff.) also plainly states that there is no cosmogonic myth in pre-Han literature, merely a blank of prehistory before the first, legendary emperors; that the myriad things were universally conceived as not created but generated by Heaven or by Heaven and Earth; and that the most developed cosmogony in early Chinese literature, in the *Huainanzi* and *Zhou Yi*, for instance, is characterized by the conception of the cosmos as evolving by division along a chain of binary oppositions.

120. Eliade 19 9, pp. 6– 7.
121. Needham 19 6, p. 290.
122. Ibid.
123. *Zhou Yi*, *juan* 7, p. 70; *juan* 8, p. 7 . Similar passages can be read in many other documents, for example, *Mozi*, *juan* 1/6: "Ciguo," pp. 17–18 and *juan* 6/21: "Jieyong" B, p. 104; *Huainanzi*, *juan* 13: "Fanlun sun," p. 211 and *juan* 19: "Xiuwu sun," p. 331; and *Li ji*, *juan* 21, p. 188.
124. Granet 1930, p. 238.
125. As in Helü Dacheng, where towers are said to have been built on top of two of the eight land gates in the wall of the city proper, and on top of all three land route gates and one water gate in the wall of the inner enclosure. See *Yue jue shu*, *juan* 2, pp. 9, 10.
126. See, for example, Mote 1971, p. 49; Schwartz 198 , p. 92.
127. For an explanation of the names of other gates, see Xu 1996, pp. 89–92.
128. *Wu Yue chunqiu*, *juan* 4, p. 2 . The term *changhe* has two denotations. It denotes one of the eight winds from Heaven, believed to be coming from the northwest. It is also the name of the first gate leading to Heaven and thus the gate of the celestial Ziweigong (Purple Forbidden Palace). See, for example, *Shuowen jiezi*, 12A.3, 13B.3.
129. *Wu Yue chunqiu*, *juan* 8, p. 107.
130. In his *Chu ci zhangju* (*juan* 1, p. 1), Wang Yi of the Eastern Han explains, "*Changhe* is the Gate of Heaven." Translation of the stanza adapted from Hawkes 198 , p. 74.
131. *Shuowen jiezi*, 12A.3. This generalization is more symbolically significant than confusing, in that every house, temple, or city could be regarded by archaic man as the cosmos in which he actually lived, and the gate or door of his abode could then be analogous to the Gate of Heaven and

his abode could be a replica of the universe. The multiple homologies, among cosmos, land, city, temple, palace, and house, emphasized the same fundamental symbolism: each one of these images expresses the existential experience of being situated in an organized and meaningful world.

132. It seems to have been only in later periods that the term *changhe* was used in the naming of other cities' gates in the west by north of their walls, such as that of the city of Luoyang during the Jin and of the city of Yangzhou during the Tang, and in denoting the main gate of an imperial palace. Cf. *Wen xuan, juan* 21: 5th poem of "Yong shi" by Zuo Si [ca. 250–305], with Li Shan's [ca. 630–689] commentary, p. 297; *Jiu Tang shu, juan* 17A, p. 518; *Sanfu huangtu*, p. 21.
133. *Wu Yue chunqiu, juan* 4, p. 25. It is possible that the naming of this gate was associated with the theme of the snake in the local customs. In the *Taiping yulan* (*juan* 183, p. 890), a passage from the *Junguo zhi* is quoted: "The Qiu Gate is Wu's great city gate." According to the *Shuowen jiezi* (13A.22), the *qiu* is a small dragon (*longzi*) with horns. The snake is also one of the twelve animals (*shengxiao*) that respectively correspond to what are known as the twelve Earthly Branches (*dizhi*) and with the positions in twelve directions. Cf. *Lun heng*, "Wu shi" and "Yan du" sections. The "Yan du" section (p. 224), for example, states, "*Chen* corresponds to dragon, *si* corresponds to snake, and the positions of *chen* and *si* are in the southeast." Whether the idea of correlating the *shengxiao* and *dizhi* with positions/directions emerged before the building of Helü Dacheng, or at the time of Zou Yan in the third century B.C., or later in the Han, I do not yet know.
134. *Wu Yue chunqiu, juan* 8, p. 107.
135. *Huainanzi, juan* 3: "Tianwen xun," p. 35. Translation by Chatley (cited in Needham 1959, p. 214), with minor modifications. Also cf. *Lun heng*: "Tan tian," p. 105; *Bowu zhi, juan* 1, p. 9.
136. *Zhou li, juan* 10, p. 66.
137. Kertzer 1988, p. 2.
138. In 506 B.C., Wu's army joined with Cai's forces to initiate a major attack on Chu. Within ten days, Chu's capital was captured and the king of Chu fled to Yun, where he remained until Qin dispatched a relief army to help Chu. See *Zuo zhuan, juan* 54: "Ding 4th year [506 B.C.]," pp. 431–435 and *juan* 55: "Ding 5th year [505 B.C.]," pp. 437–438.
139. *Wu Yue chunqiu, juan* 4, p. 25.
140. Cf. *Han shu, juan* 76, p. 3230, with Yan's commentary; *Shui jing zhu, juan* 40, p. 755; *SPck, juan* 5, p. 226, with quotations from the *Luoyang jiujing*.
141. *Zuo zhuan, juan* 10: "Zhuang 25th year [669 B.C.]," pp. 77–78.
142. *Zuo zhuan, juan* 7: "Huan 14th year [698 B.C.]," p. 55.
143. Similarly, it was also at the cosmic center that the king of Yue, after completing his capital, was said to have chosen the auspicious day and moment to restart his government in the Hall of Light (*Mingtang*), so that the centrality of his position could be ensured. See *Wu Yue chunqiu, juan* 8, p. 109. The cosmic spot in space and the cosmic point in time coincided to verify the authority of the king and thus guarantee the fate of the state.
144. *uo yu, juan* 19, pp. 619 and 622. See *Wu Yue chunqiu, juan* 10, p. 136 for a similar passage.
145. *Wuxian zhi, juan* 18C.1. Emphasis is mine.
146. *WTx, juan* A, p. 6.

Chapter 3: Cities in the Imperial Era

1. Not a single capital in Chinese history ever achieved the ideal city form based on the archetypal cosmological symbolism that was supposed to be followed rigorously. Only the Ming capital or, as Liu Zhiping (1987, p. 8) asserts, the Yuan capital, at present-day Beijing was in very close accord with the canonical cosmology of city building. This aspect has extensively been discussed by Wright (1977). For a history of the planning of Chinese imperial capitals, see Steinhardt 1990.
2. For representative studies of the origins of the *xian*, see Lü 1985, pp. 410–444 (a work first published in 1929); Bodde 1938, pp. 135–139, 238–243; Creel 1964; Wheatley 1971, pp. 179–182.

3. See, for example, Gernet 1982, pp. 64–6 , 106; Fairbank 1992, p. 6.
4. Skinner 1977d, p. 304.
5. They were the *yamen* of Wu, Changzhou, and Yuanhe counties. Wu county was the earliest one, established in 222 B.C.; the seat of Changzhou was set up in 696 to govern half of the territory of Wu county. This situation remained for over a millennium until 1724, when part of the territory of Changzhou county was put under the jurisdiction of the newly established county Yuanhe. See, for example, *Suzhoufu zhi, juan* 2.10-2.
6. In this article, Murphey critically reviews China's urban development in three selected historical stages: first, what he calls "the traditional/imperial model;" second, the Western presence in the treaty-port cities around the turn of this century; and, third, the urbanization from the Communist revolution onward. He concludes by arguing that, in the midst of political and economic changes, Chinese society will remain distinctive, and so will the cities that it builds and shapes.
7. Murphey 1984, p. 188. See a similar statement in one of Murphey's earlier papers (19 4, p. 3 3) in which the author treats the cities as centers of change on the basis of comparisons between Europe and China.
8. Murphey 1984, p. 190.
9. The form and layout of the local cities is also depicted by Needham (1971, pp. 71–73) in a similarly undifferentiated way, together with a diagrammatic plan of an ideal case. Some general descriptions of the internal spatial organization of Chinese cities by Murphey, on the other hand, appear more questionable, in the sense that not only are urban features characteristic of different historical periods and of different regions mixed up, but some elements of other civilizations, such as the "plaza" (the application of this particular word to Chinese cities is probably an off-handed use of language), are also included.
10. Murphey 19 4, p. 3 3.
11. Mote 1977, pp. 107–108. This classification is certainly a simplified schema. Mote (ibid.) also makes it clear that all Chinese cities were in some sense "hybrid," for they were in varying degrees multifunctional throughout imperial time, with the two most clearly identifiable functions being the economic and the administrative (or "dynastic," or "political-military"), either of which demanded the support of the other at a certain stage of development.
12. Considering the vast territories that Chinese culture penetrated and the variety of regional and local subcultural traditions, the arrangement of regions with regard to different pace and characteristics of urban development is a complicated task. Whereas Skinner (1977a, p. 11) has divided the territory of agrarian China, except Manchuria and Taiwan, into eight macroregions "as the 'natural' vessels for territorially based socioeconomic systems," the conventional, simplified dichotomization of the regions into the North and South would be sufficient for the present argument. The noncontemporaneity of the construction of the city walls and the establishment of local governmental seats, closely associated with regional variation in social and economic development, was a common phenomenon in many parts of the country. Chen Zhengxiang (1983, pp. 9–60) argues that in a city's development, either of two events, the construction of walls and the establishment of governmental seats, may have occurred long before the other. In the regions of strategic importance or of constant wars, the construction of the walls of a city was usually well in advance of the establishment of a governmental seat, while in the relatively peaceful and secure regions like the Southeast, the building of walls may have come much later than the establishment of a government seat.
13. Liu 1987, p. 9.
14. This presentation preference is also acutely noted, though with somewhat different intent, by Steinhardt (1990, pp. 146–147) when she discusses the planning of Hangzhou as the imperial capital of Southern Song, then known as Lin'an:

> The city's actual scheme may be considered irrelevant to the historical record. The Chinese imperial city is supposed to be geometrically perfect. In a case such as Lin'an,

in which it was not, illustrations like those from *Xianshun* [*sic*] *Lin'an zhi* amend fact so that the capital will appear perfect for posterity. Thus the heavenly approved and classically sanctioned plan could transcend transitory earthen timbers and mud-brick walls joined by man. The prepared drawings for *Lin'an zhi* assured that when the material remains of Song Lin'an could no longer be found, the city plan, although fictitious, would ever after be recorded, perceived, and certified as an ideal Chinese imperial city.

15. Meyer 1991, p. 2.
16. For analyses of the architectural aspects of the Altar of Heaven in the southern suburb of Beijing, cf. Liu Dunzhen 1980, pp. 347–354 and Liu Zhiping 1987, pp. 15–17. For a description of the ceremonies associated with it, see Cameron and Brake 1965, pp. 117–200, and for a discussion of its religious significance and the legends associated with it, see Meyer 1991, pp. 79–99, 137–143.
17. *Shi jing*, Mao #205 (*juan* 13/1: "Xiao ya" section), p. 463.
18. A related aspect should be stressed, which also reflects the basic difference between the imperial system and the feudal system of the early Zhou. I have mentioned in Chapter 2 that the accomplishment of any enfeoffment was to be symbolized by a prince or duke's taking a handful of earth from the part of the King's Altar to the Gods of the Earth and Grain in the direction of the relevant enfeoffed land. No similar rituals were conducted when an imperial official was about to take up his allocated post.
19. Schwartz 1985, pp. 20–21.
20. This nature of Chinese cities has been mentioned or studied by many Western scholars. Cf., for example, Eberhard 1962, pp. 228, 267; Gernet 1970b; Needham 1971, pp. 71–72; Elvin 1973, pp. 22, 177; Mote 1970, pp. 42–43, 1973, pp. 37–38, 1977, pp. 102–110; Murphey 1954, 1984. It brought about some unique urban features and the specific way that the cities functioned, as discussed elsewhere in this book.
21. The distinction between an official's home and the place where he held office is also emphasized by Elvin (1978, p. 85) from a different direction.
22. *Wanli yehuo bian*, *juan* 6, p. 174.
23. Ibid., *juan* 19, p. 487.
24. Skinner 1977a, pp. 16–17.
25. Finnane 1993.
26. For a parallel in this respect between China and ancient Greece and Rome, see Wheatley 1971, p. 178.
27. The term *si* retains several connotations that are related in one way or another to the ancient market: display; exposing bodies in the market after execution; and stalls, shops, or workshops. See *Ch* 1980, p. 1963.
28. In the "Sishi" section of the *Zhou li* (*juan* 14, p. 96), we read:

    The great market is held at midday, [and in it] commoners are the main participants. The morning market is held in the early morning, [and in it] merchants are the main participants. The afternoon market is held in the late afternoon, [and in it] male and female peddlers are the main participants.

    During the "great market" hour, transactions had to be conducted in the central part of the compound; during the "morning market" hour, in the eastern part; and during the "late afternoon market" hour, in the western part.
29. Both *lü* and *li* meant a unit of residential organization, which contained twenty-five households, and applied to both urban and rural settlements. Cf. Mao's commentary on the ode "Jiangzhongzi" (*Shi jing*, Mao #76 [*juan* 4.2: "Zheng feng"], p. 337); *Zhou li*, *juan* 10, p. 69 and *juan* 15, p. 102. As they came to indicate physical structures, the term *li* mainly denoted a residential ward, while *lü* also connoted one of its gates. See *Ch* 1980, pp. 881, 1963; *Cy* 1988, pp. 1711, 1766. In Tang times,

the term *fang* was used to denote residential wards. See *Jiu Tang shu*, *juan* 48, p. 2089. For a study of the *li* and *fang* systems, see Miyazaki 1962a.

30. For a brief description of this feature, particularly in the Tang period, see Balazs 1964, pp. 68–69.
31. This discrimination seems to be in conformity with the advocacy recorded in the *Yi Zhou shu* (*juan* 2/12, p. 2) that "nobles and officials should not mix with artisans and merchants."
32. *Zhou li*, *juan* 12, p. 79. Cf. Zhao 1988, p. 44.
33. Elvin 1973, pp. 164–178. Elsewhere, Elvin (1978, p. 79) writes about the changing roles for the cities: "Up to this time [between about 900 and 1200], the large centers had been predominantly cities of administrators and consumers, and the circulation of wealth and goods had depended primarily on the pumping mechanism provided by taxation. Now they also became commercial and industrial centers, in degrees varying from case to case."
34. Twitchett 1966, 1968; Shiba 1970. Cf. Shiba 1966.
35. Skinner 1977, pp. 23–24.
36. Twitchett, 1966, pp. 231–233; He 1986, pp. 20 –206. This intensified process of change can be detected from documentary accounts that the Tang authorities from time to time made efforts to restore the conventional urban planning and regulation system.
37. Shiba 1970, p. 127; Liu 1980, pp. 163–166.
38. Elvin 1973, p. 177.
39. For a study of the Northern Song capital, see Kracke 197 .
40. Some of the poems by contemporary writers reveal the situation in these two cities. "Zongyou Huainan" by Zhang Hu (?–after 849) reads that in Yangzhou "[along] the ten-*li* long street, markets and shops are adjacent to each other" (*Quan Tang shi*, *juan* 11, p. 846), while Wang Jian (ca. 766–ca. 830), in his description of the city in "Yekan Yangzhou shi," says "a thousand lamps from the late evening market illuminated the blue clouds" (ibid., *juan* 301, p. 3430). As for the city of Suzhou, Du Xunhe (846–ca. 907) also mentions the late evening market in his "Songren you Wu" (ibid., *juan* 691, p. 792).
41. Skinner 1977a, p. 26.
42. Ibid. pp. 27–28.
43. Elvin 1977, pp. 470–471, Maps 2–6. The area that later became known as Shanghai was under the jurisdiction of Suzhou prefecture until A.D. 939.
44. Fan 198 , p. 399.
45. Skinner 1977a, p. 17.
46. See, for example, *juan* 41, p. 290.
47. *Shuowen jiezi*, 2B.11.
48. See quotations from the *Fengsu tongyi* in *Taiping yulan*, *juan* 19 , p. 943.
49. Cf. *Er ya*, *juan* , p. 32; *Shuowen jiezi*, 2B.11.
50. Wright 196 , p. 671.
51. This is partly reflected in the change of the meaning of the character *jie*. In the *Yiqie jing yinyi* (*juan* 4, p. 1 6), compiled in the mid-Tang or after by the Buddhist monk Hui Lin, a quotation from the late seventh century document, *Shengkao qieyun*, by Zhang Jian reads: "*Jie* [denotes] the passageways within cities." This seems to suggest that the character by then was applied *exclusively* to the description of the urban environments. Yet the assumption of the term *jie* to indicate busy roads of a certain width and length within a *particular* city was not necessarily determined by the timing or the extent of the occurrence of such transformation in the region but was often closely associated with the specific path of the city's development, since Chinese civilization lodged its history mainly in the written word rather than in architectural artifacts. In the city of Suzhou, for example, the application of *jie* did not take place until the early Ming period, whereas it had been widely used in Northern Song Kaifeng and Southern Song Hangzhou.
52. Skinner 1977a, p. 28.
53. Ibid., p. 2 .

54. Mote 1973, p. 59.
55. Skinner 1977e, pp. 527–538.
56. The account in this encyclopedia is a citation from earlier local documents and thus does not include the periods after the event that the county of Changzhou was further divided in 1724 to establish the county of Yuanhe, the seat of which was also to be in the city.
57. This is the area around (both inside and outside) Chang Gate in the north by west walls. The term *Jinchang* derived from the name of an old pavilion, known as Jinchang Ting, outside Chang Gate.
58. *tj, ce* 115.24b–25b.
59. Sjoberg 1960. The concept represented by Sjoberg's model seems to have been generally, if not totally, accepted by Kostof 1991, p. 27. The feature of cities having two (or, as in the case of Suzhou, three) nuclei is not peculiar to Chinese experience. See Hohenberg and Lees 1985, p. 33.
60. A recognition of the persistence of the administrative functions of cities by no means implies that the government role in marketing, commerce, and social regulations lasted unchanged. There was in fact a trend of gradual, and yet marked retreat of government control over these affairs, beginning in the mid-Tang and lasting to the late imperial period, although it was punctuated by the periodic reimposition of controls. Cf. Skinner 1977a, pp. 24–25; Rawski 1985a, pp. 5–6.
61. Murphey 1984, p. 188.
62. Rowe 1993, p. 2.
63. Balazs 1964, pp. 66, 68.
64. Zhang Guangzhi (1983, p. 110) explicitly points out that in Chinese antiquity, "city construction was not merely an activity of architecture but also an activity of politics." Elsewhere, he (Chang, 1976, pp. 68–69) makes a similar statement. Such an activity, that of defense, is clearly conveyed by the way in which the pictographic elements compose the character *guo: yu* was an archaic pictograph denoting the enfeoffed territory, which consisted of the elements *ge* (dagger-ax), *wei* ([archaic] circle or to encircle) and a dash ([archaic] earth or land), and thus, according to Xu Shen, also indicated the defense of the [enfeoffed] land with weapons. Duan Yucai holds that since the character *yu*, also having a broad sense of protecting one's belongings, became insufficient to convey the exclusive meaning of the enfeoffed territory, as the feudal system was more intensively implemented, another *wei* was added to encircle the character *yu* so as to make the denotation more specific. See *Shuowen jiezi zhu*, *pian* 6B.9–10, 11; *pian* 12B.39.
65. Cf. *Cy* 1988, pp. 310, 1714.
66. For a discussion of the sharp distinction between the city and countryside in the Shang and Zhou civilizations, see Trewartha 1952, pp. 69–70.
67. For the revolutionary transformation of Chinese social and political system around the period of the Qin unification, see Mote 1977, pp. 102–130.
68. Needham 1971, p. 72.
69. Eberhard 1962, p. 267.
70. Mote 1977, pp. 103–104. Elsewhere, Mote (1973, p. 54) states, "Patterns of social interaction between rural and urban social elements were those of profound mutual involvement. There may have been a trend toward concentration of the elite in cities as places of domicile in the later imperial era, but it was at best a trend; throughout the traditional period in Chinese social history, the elite was widely diffused in space, and psychologically oriented toward as many rural ties as urban ones." Indeed, from all Chinese documents, we find that individuals, notably the intellectuals, usually identified themselves or were identified by others as coming from certain regions, prefectures or counties, regardless of whether their home places were urban or rural.
71. Mote 1977, p. 105. He offers an interesting metaphor to illustrate the point:

> It [the rural component of Chinese civilization] was like the net in which the cities and towns of China were suspended. The fabric of this net was the stuff of Chinese civilization, sustaining it and giving it its fundamental character. . . . China's cities

> were but knots of the same material, of one piece with the net, denser in quality but not foreign bodies resting on it.

72. See, for example, Fairbank 1992, pp. , 102; Eberhard 1962, p. 30.
73. Balazs 1964, p. 72.
74. Mote (1977, p. 103) has emphasized the generally favorable Chinese attitude toward peasantry, which must also have affected the development of Chinese cities. "Chinese civilization," he writes, "may be unique in that its word for 'peasant' has not been a term of contempt—even though the Chinese idea of a 'rustic' may be that of a humorously unsophisticated person." The humorous side of this attitude has been vividly illustrated by Cao Xueqin (?–1763) in the description of Granny Liu (Liu Laolao) in his *Honglou meng*. Mote (1977, p. 106) has, in acknowledging sophistication and skills in dealing with complex situations represented by the city, also noticed the circumstance under which even a learned gentleman who knew both city and country life well (but probably preferred the latter) might declare himself a mere "country fellow," a "rustic simpleton," as a gesture of conventional humility before the rich and the prominent or even before his intellectual peers and old neighbors who happened to be in office. In fact, the Chinese word for "peasantry" has often been a term of admiration in a moral sense. Among the traditionally received "four classes of people" (*simin*), *shi* (gentry or literati), *nong* (peasantry), *gong* (craftsmen), and *shang* (merchants), peasantry stood in second place behind gentry, who were educated people in government service or candidates for service and whose families were at the same time usually landlords and thus were closely related to both land and civilization. Cf. Feng 198 , pp. 23–24; Eberhard 1962, pp. –6.
75. For social mobility by the second half of the imperial era, see P. T. Ho 1962. It is also suggested by Elvin (1973, p. 2) that the disappearance of the "manorial order," as he calls it, led to greatly increased social mobility and to greater geographical mobility during the Ming and Qing periods. Eberhard (1962, p. 264) lays more stress on families as social units with regard to social mobility. He argues that not every individual had the same chance of moving up into the top level of society and concludes that the process of social mobility has to be conceived of as "a movement of families rather than a movement of individuals" if a long-term social rise is to be seen to have occurred. Yet Mote (1977, p. 103) has adroitly emphasized, "Whether large numbers actually participated in either kind of mobility is less important than the psychological fact that such mobility was possible."
76. Rawski 198 a, p. 3.
77. Myers 1974, p. 274. Wakeman, Jr. (197 a, p. 2), emphasizes that "the entire period from the 1 os to the 1930s constituted a coherent whole" and that continued processes of development "stretched across the last four centuries of Chinese history into the republican period."
78. Elvin 1973, p. 268. Elvin (ibid., p. 277) suggests that "one can argue the paradoxical proposition that the Chinese countryside was both overindustrialized and overcommercialized [sic]." Huang Xingzeng (1490–1 40), a scholar of Wu county, records what he observed in the Suzhou region in a passage also cited in part by Elvin:

    > The large villages and famous towns invariably developed shops that sold every kind of commodity, so as to monopolize the profits; and those who carried goods on their backs between the towns and villages were all in distress. Thus money accumulated [amounts to] millions. To this day, most members of the gentry in the Suzhou area take trade and business as their priority.
    >
    > (*Wufeng lu*, pp. 5–6. Except for the last two sentences, translation by Elvin [1973, p. 268] with minor modifications.)

79. Elvin 1973, p. 178.
80. Naquin and Rawski 1987, p. . Rawski (198 a, p. 8) has argued that, in the Lower Yangzi core,

absentee landlordism was a prominent development during the late Ming and Qing periods. Elsewhere (ibid., pp. 9, 28), she states more explicitly that the trend to urban residence among large landlords and other elites from villages stimulated urban culture.

81. Skinner 1977a, p. 28; Ward 1985, pp. 173–174.
82. Rawski 1985a, p. 9.
83. By the period of late Ming and Qing, cities, unlike what Balazs (1964, pp. 70, 78) claims, undoubtedly became a sort of "magnet" for the countryside, "the center of attraction," although they did not pull the rural people toward their political and economic freedom.
84. Rowe (1993, p. 13) asserts that by the late imperial period "an autonomous urban culture" had evolved. One of the examples that he uses to support this view is what he calls "the 1720 Suzhou public security reform," an incident discussed by Santangelo (1992, pp. 34, 35; 1993, pp. 112, 113). Yet according to the main source of this incident, a regulatory document carved on a stone stele in 1720 (*MQSgbj* 1981, pp. 68–71), the "private" policing structure was set up in Suzhou by the managers or contractors of the textile industry (*baotou*), under the recognition of the local government, to restrict the immigrant calenderers (*chuaijiang*) from leaving their workshops (*chuaifang*) at night and from committing themselves to other undesirable activities. It was indeed an "urban" problem. But this policing structure only aimed at tackling the problems of the calenderers, and its patrol area was mostly confined to the workshops rather than extending to the city at large. Thus it would be overstretching the evidence to call it "a style of urban societal self-policing." For a study of Suzhou's calendry, see Terada 1972, pp. 337–410.
85. This includes, for instance, the trend to assimilate merchants into the urban elite, which affected its cultural tone, and the great subcultural variety and heightened cultural awareness among city residents that were brought about by organization on the basis of the subcultural origin of the immigrants from other parts of China and by intergroup competition and confrontation. See Skinner 1977c, p. 269.
86. See, for example, Balazs 1964, p. 23.
87. Skinner 1977c, pp. 268–269.
88. Balazs, ibid. On the towns of medieval Europe, Mumford (1961, p. 236) writes over thirty years ago:

> By fighting, by bargaining, by outright purchase, or by some combination of these means the towns won the right to hold a regular market, the right to be subject to a special market law, the right to coin money and establish weights and measures, the right of citizens to be tried in their local court, under their local laws and ordinances, and not least, as before noted, the right to bear arms. These powers, which had once been pre-empted by the citadel, now belonged to the city, and each citizen bore a responsibility for exercising them.

None of these rights were gained by Chinese cities.

89. This was the direct consequence of two facts enunciated by Johnson et al. (1985, Preface, p. xi):

> At the beginning of our period [ca. 1550], the population of China had already passed the 100 million mark, and by the last quarter of the eighteenth century it was approaching 300 million. At that time France, the largest nation in Europe, would have ranked third among the provinces of China, and England would have been one of the smallest, surpassing only remote Yunnan, Kweichow [i.e., Guizhou], and Kuangsi [i.e., Guangxi]. Demographically, China was not a France or an England—it was a Europe. But while Europe was divided into a multitude of nations growing ever more distinct from each other linguistically, economically, socially, and culturally, China was a single polity, and had been since the late sixth century (with interruptions during the Five Dynasties and Southern Song periods).

Although the nature of the integration of diverse elements into a single complex cultural system is very hard to account for, it has to be taken as axiomatic, as Johnson et al. suggest, since if not, "the whole idea of Chinese culture dissolves—'China' is reduced to the semantic triviality of 'Asia' " (ibid., p. xiii).

90. Watson 198 , p. 292. The role played by the regional elite in society was also sharply in contrast to that of the French:

> In China, by contrast, local elites shared a common cultural tradition (fostered by a standardized educational curriculum) and were anxious to participate in the affairs of state. They could, in the process, retain their regional identities as long as they were loyal to the idea of a unified whole. Chinese national-level authorities were themselves likely to have strong ties to kinsmen in the countryside and, hence, allegiance to the center did not necessarily preclude loyalty to one's region. In this sense China may have been unique.
>
> (Ibid., p. 293.)

91. Mote 1977, p. 117. Johnson (198 a, p. 7) seems more affirmative on this when he states that "rural oral culture probably differed substantially from urban oral culture, while literati culture was probably much the same in country or city." The self-identification of some groups of urban residents were indeed evidenced in many popular novels, such as *Jinping mei* and *Honglou meng*.
92. Skinner 1977c, p. 269.
93. Murphey 1984, p. 192. Elsewhere, Murphey (ibid., p. 190) also states: "The close interdependence of city and countryside was far more explicitly recognized, and indeed welcomed, in China than elsewhere."
94. Skinner 1977c, p. 268.
95. Mote 1973, p. 4; 1977, p. 114. Cf. Hilberseimer 19 , p. 90.
96. Elvin 1978, p. 87.
97. Mote 1977, p. 116.
98. This statement is presumably an example of Mote's cautious writing, since in his earlier work on Suzhou (1973, p. 8), he has explicitly indicated that "China's cities have no town halls, hence no town squares."
99. Zücker 19 9, p. 1.
100. Mote 1977, pp. 114–11 .
101. On the nature of the imperial cult, Mote (ibid., p. 114) emphasizes that it was the private business of the emperor. Its important physical monuments included the Imperial Ancestral Temple, the Altar of Land and Grain and the Altar of Heaven. They were located only in and around the imperial capital. Since the present study is about the regional and local cities, I shall bypass this part of the discussion. His statement that "China had no sacred cities or holy public shrines" (ibid.) may not be taken as a denial of the cosmic role of imperial capitals, but as a stress on the dissociation of the Chinese case from that of Europe, ancient Egypt, and the Classical and Islamic worlds.
102. *Suzhoufu zhi*, *juan* 39–44.
103. Mote 1977, p. 11 .
104. Mote 1973, p. 8; 1977, pp. 117–118. The contrast between the luxury of life provided for the wealthy in the city of Suzhou and the meager conditions in the remote countryside was revealed in an interesting incident which was morally deplored by Shen Shouzhi, a nineteenth-century local scholar. When the news reached Suzhou of the fall of Jiujiang, a city located over five hundred miles away in the south west, all the gentry families immediately fled to the countryside; but later at the time when the nearby cities of Jinling, Yangzhou, and Zhenjiang were taken by the rebels, these families unexpectedly returned to the city simply because the country life was unbearable for them. See *Jiechao biji*, p. 8.

A total of ninety-five schools (including both public and private and both existing and derelict), for example, is recorded in the area of Suzhou prefecture in 1883, while only thirty-nine of them were located within the walls of the prefectural and county capitals (see *Suzhoufu zhi*, *juan* 25–27). Although it is evidenced in the *Suzhoufu zhi* that prominent schools were more likely located within these cities of the prefecture, the fact that more of the most nationally renowned *shuyuan* in history were in the countryside seems to indicate that the situation may have been different in nationwide perspective.

Festivals were indeed usually classified as part of the nationwide, regional, or local customs.

We have seen that the bustling industrial and commercial areas of the city of Suzhou were outside the gates called Chang and Xu, from which direct access was available to the Great Canal as the major trade route.

105. Mote 1977, pp. 115–116. Although this observation apparently offers an illustration of the trait of urban-rural continuum, it seems to me that the architectural uniformity (in a loose sense of the word) within a certain region in China found its deeper implications in buildings or building complexes across functions and locations rather than across urban and rural areas. A discussion of this will be given in Chapter 6.
106. Skinner 1977c, p. 269.
107. Mote 1973, p. 54.
108. Feuchtwang 1977, p. 601. For a study of the cults of Chenghuang, or "City God," during the Tang and Song periods, see Johnson 1985b.
109. *Cheng* might indicate a walled settlement that we regard as a city; it might also mean a walled stronghold. It is therefore the common feature of walls of considerable size and certain configuration that really counts.
110. For a brief discussion of the significance of the walls in general in Chinese life, see Meyer 1991, p. 4.
111. Mote 1973, p. 54; 1977, p. 104. The psychological function of the walls of Nanjing and of other cities in Ming times after the harsh century of Mongol domination was, in Mote's words, that of "reaffirming the presence of the Chinese state." He reinforces his argument by claiming that "the Great Wall itself had little tactical significance" and asking in a rhetorical manner, "was its true significance not that of its psychological effect on the enemy, and conversely on the Chinese defender?" (ibid., p. 137). Meyer (1991, p. 4), too, has talked briefly about the symbolic gesture of the building of the Great Wall, but with a different emphasis. For studies of the Great Wall, see Aoki 1972, Uemura 1974, Waldron 1990.
112. *Xxz*, *juan* A.19a–b.
113. *Pingjianglu xinzhu juncheng ji*, *juan* 9.2b–3a. It also reminds us of an old proverb still widely in use, "the unity of the people's hearts makes walls" (*zhongxin chengcheng*) (*uo yu*, *juan* 3, p. 131), which certainly indicates the belief that "unity is strength," and hence the tenability of the city and its surrounding areas relies on the solidarity of people's minds. Another interesting incident also exemplifies this concept. At the end of the Song, defenders of Changzhou gallantly resisted attack by the Mongol army for over one month, while the officials at Suzhou simply surrendered in advance of any attack. This incident was then metaphorically referred to in the phrase "Pingjiang [i.e., Suzhou] [had] walls of iron but people of paper; Changzhou [had] walls of paper but people of iron" (see *aiyu congkao*, *juan* 35, p. 776; *Suzhoufu zhi*, *juan* 145.53).
114. *uanzi*, *juan* 1/1: "Mumin," p. 3. Translation by Rickett (1985, p. 57), with minor modification.
115. "The preservation of territory depends upon city walls; the preservation of city walls depends upon arms. The preservation of arms depends on men, and the preservation of men depends on grain. Therefore, unless a territory is brought under cultivation, its city walls will not be secure." (*uanzi*, *juan* 1/3: "Quanxiu," p. 7. Translation by Rickett [ibid., p. 95] with minor modification.)
116. Hay 1994a, pp. 13–14. On this subject, Hay (ibid., p. 14) remarks: "Discontinuities are always given meaning by continuity, and continuities are always signaled by discontinuities."

117. Murphey 1984, p. 189.
118. A proverb (though slightly different in wording) has been mentioned by Mote (1977, p. 104), Elvin (1978, p. 87) and Chen Zhengxiang (1983, p. 74): "Major disorder occurred in the cities; minor disorders occurred in the countryside" (*daluan zaicheng, xiaoluan zaixiang*).
119. *Wucheng riji, juan* A, *passim*.
120. *Jiechao biji*, pp. 26–27.
121. Mote 1977, p. 114.
122. Murphey (1984, p. 190) from a reverse direction, acutely points out that the local capital city was responsible for the defense as well as the administration of the jurisdictional territory as a whole, and not merely for the defense of its own walled base. "It was," he writes succinctly, "truly a *center* [*sic*], not an isolated or discrete intrusion."
123. *Wucheng riji, juan* A, p. 20 .
124. Mote 1977, p. 138.
125. This juxtaposition of city maps of Suzhou of different periods of time is produced under the inspiration of the ingenious overlay of the map made in 1229 and an aerial photograph made in 194 initially by Mote (1973, pp. 40–41) and later borrowed by Skinner (1977a, pp. 14–1).
126. Xu Gate in the west wall by south was abandoned during the early Northern Song but restored to use in 13 2 (see *Gusu zhi, juan* 16.2).
127. I have noted earlier Rowe's (1993, p. 2) identification of some tension between Mote's conclusion of a remarkable long-term stability of urban form of Suzhou and its urban growth from the Ming onwards. Here, what Mote means by "urban form" seems to be what was defined by the city walls, as he also acknowledges the development of commerce outside the city, in the suburbs to the west of the city of walls, extending along the Grand Canal; whereas Rowe refers to all the parts that were "urban" in quality, including the busy suburbs and the nearby market towns which are seen as incorporated into "a greatly enlarged metropolitan area."
128. See Chapter   for details of the incident.
129. See, for example, *Suzhoufu zhi, juan* 4.3–4.
130. During the 1 os *wokou* (Japanese pirates) crisis, proposals for building new city walls to enclose the west suburb were put forward, but did not materialize. See Chapter   for details.
131. In the case of Suzhou, the existing network of city canals also played a significant role in its morphological stability in time. We will have occasions to return to this in Chapters 4 and .
132. *Gusu zhi, juan* 16.1.
133. See, for example, *Suzhoufu zhi*, ibid. Ironically, from a comparison of the city maps of the Southern Song, Ming, and Qing periods, we know that the city form enclosed and determined by the walls was obviously *not* altered by the construction work of this time. See Chapter 4.
134. *Wuxian zhi, juan* 18C.1.
135. For a better understanding of the meaning this phrase conveys, a few words are needed here about the artistic use of an old proverb that derives from a story told in the *Han Feizi* (*juan* 11/32: "Waichu shuo" Left A, pp. 198–199) compiled in the third century B.C. A man from the state of Chu came to Zheng to sell a precious pearl that was contained in a lavishly ornamented casket. Curiously, a man of Zheng bought the casket but gave back the pearl, which was supposed to be sold. The proverb *maidu huanzhu* (buying the casket and returning the pearl) has later come to denote "to attend to trifles to the neglect of essentials." Likewise, although it is the cultural achievements and historic relics of the Suzhou region that were the essential and precious things, the city walls as the symbolic casket, instead of being treated as trifles, were equally highly regarded.
136. *Wuxian zhi, juan* 18C.1.
137. Samuels 1978, p. 713; cf. Skinner 1977a, p. .
138. Mote 1977, pp. 101–102: "No single great city has either dominated Chinese civilization in the way that Rome and Constantinople dominated phases of Roman history or typified Chinese civilization in the way that Paris and London typify for us the French and the English civilizations."

Mote (ibid.) then offers two explanations for this phenomenon: (1) China has been too vast a cultural and political area for three millennia or more to have been dominated by one city; and (2) Chinese civilization has not granted the same importance to typically urban activities that other civilizations have, and thus the Chinese have never felt the impulse to create one great city that would express and embody their urban ideals, nor has the urban sector in the aggregate typified or dominated the tone of Chinese life.

139. Mote 1977, p. 118.
140. As Murphey (1984, p. 189) has noted, in practice it was impossible for the local government officials based in cities to carry out close administration of so large a population, the great majority of it being rural-agricultural: "Unofficial, but often powerful, local gentry and peasant village elders or clans managed the bulk of rural . . . affairs. It was a closely ordered society, . . . [and] the combined force of family, clan, gentry, and nearly universally accepted Confucian morality kept order remarkably well in what we may call a largely self-regulating society."
141. *Dengchuang conglu*, *juan* 1.6a.
142. "These activities," Mote (1977, p. 110) writes, "all existed within the particular dynamics of Chinese society, were ordered by Chinese government, and expressed Chinese cultural values."
143. Elvin 1978, p. 85. Elvin (ibid., p. 88) also has noted that no rebellion against the imperial regime ever originated in the cities apart from a few strikes by urban workers after the seventeenth century and occasional closures of the market by merchants as a form of political pressure. But these could not seriously have toppled the imperial government, and would certainly not have challenged the basic nature of the existing order. For a comparative study of the city as a center of change between China and Europe, see Murphey 1954.
144. Similarly, no rivalry between cities in aesthetic or religious projects developed in the way in which the cities of medieval and Renaissance Europe did.
145. Another process of important change in China's urban system is observed by Skinner (1977a, p. 28). The regional city systems that developed in the Tang-Song period were immature and uneven, in the sense that cities and market towns were only very imperfectly meshed into an integrated system, and the urban population as a whole was concentrated in the largest cities. In contrast, city systems of the Ming-Qing period were more mature and more fully fleshed out, in the sense that cities and market towns were better integrated into a single hierarchical system, and the total urban population was more evenly distributed throughout the hierarchy.

Chapter 4: The City Walls and Gates

1. Cf. *WTx*, *juan* A, p. 5; *usu zhi*, *juan* 16.1.
2. *WTx*, *juan* A, p. 5. The *Wudi ji* (p. 32) claims that the city was moved in A.D. 589. Cf. *WTx*, *juan* B, p. 41; *Suzhoufu zhi*, *juan* 6.1.
3. *WTx*, *juan* C, p. 58.
4. Ibid., *juan* A, p. 5.
5. Ibid.
6. The unfamiliarity of this notion to Westerners was brought to my attention by the late C. B. Wilson in 1992 through personal communication. This phenomenon, however, seems to have been common in Far Eastern countries. Nara in Japan, for example, was officially established in A.D. 710 as Heijo-kyo, the "capital city of peace." Yet the capital was moved again in 784, and the physical form of the city and of its architecture was thereafter gradually buried beneath the mud of the paddy fields that spread over the ruins of the city. See Coaldrake 1991, pp. 37–38.
7. Although many villages and a number of towns were encircled by walls, these walls, however, as those of a house, temple, or garden, were not termed *cheng*, which at once denotes both "city" and "city walls." Only those walls of vast size that acquired certain somewhat institutionalized configurational elements and, above all, enclosed the proper establishments of imperial govern-

ment, were entitled to be called by this exclusive term. This is partly reflected in Lu Xiangsheng's (1600–1639) casuistic assessment of the walls of the county cities of Yunyang prefecture in present-day Hubei. One of his reports to the emperor on the defense of the prefecture runs:

> The seven cities under the jurisdiction of Yun[yang] were all first [hastily] walled in the Chenghua reign-period [1465–1487]. With stones piled up along [the contours of] the hills, they were then [forcefully] called "city walls." Within [each of them] no more than a few hundred households inhabit, and they thus cannot match the villages of other prefectures.
>
> (*Lu Xiangsheng shudu*, *juan* 1, p. 3.)

In another report (ibid., pp. 11, 12), Lu emphasizes that these walls did not reach one *zhang* in height, nor did any of them enclose an area of one *li* across, housing a maximum of two to three hundred families, and thus the settlements should really not be worthy of the term "county cities."

8. *Wudu fu*, p. 12. My rendering of this passage is different from that by Knechtges 1982, p. 39 .
9. Cf. Liu Yuxi's (A.D. 772–842) "Bai sheren cao zhang ji xinshi you youyan zhi sheng yinyi xichou" (*Quan Tang shi*, *juan* 360, p. 4060), Xu Hun's (the first half of the ninth century) "Song Yuanzhou shangren gui Suzhou jianji Zhanghou" (ibid., *juan* 36, p. 6113), and Bai Juyi's (A.D. 772–846) "Jiuri yanji zuiti junlou jiancheng Zhou Yin er pan'guan" (ibid., *juan* 444, pp. 4968–4969). Note that the eight gates may not have been entirely in accord with those of the city at the time of its early construction. A full discussion of them is presented later in this chapter.
10. See, for example, *Zizhi tongjian*, *juan* 2 2: "2nd year of the Qianfu reign-period [A.D. 87]," pp. 8178–8179.
11. Cf. *Wudi ji*, p. 111, and "Supplement," p. 113; *WTx*, *juan* 3, p. 6.
12. *WTx*, ibid. The earliest source of this information comes from a passage quoted by Lu Xiong of the Ming in his *Suzhoufu zhi* from Li Zonge's *Xiangfu tujing*, which was written in the 1010s but has long been lost. See *SPck juan* , p 220.
13. *Song shi*, *juan* 26, p. 476. As a witness, Qian Mu, a local scholar, gives a very detailed account of the event in his *Shoufu Pingjiang ji*, written on the twentieth day of the fourth month, 1130:

    > On the twenty-fifth day [of the second month, 1130], . . . the Jin soldiers having entered [the city] through Pan Gate, plundered governmental offices and residents' houses of their treasures and children and women, and looted state storehouses of their goods in stock. [They] set [the city] extensively on fire, with smoke and flame being seen two hundred *li* away for five days and nights. At the beginning of the third month, [the Jin soldiers] left the city from Chang Gate. Those residents who managed to escape from the city amounted to only two or three out of ten, while those who failed to do so and were thus slaughtered amounted to six or seven out of ten. . . . Innumerable dead bodies were scattered about on streets and alleys, and in rivers and canals. The noise of wailing thundered the skies. Since antiquity, no disturbance could match the harshness of this one.
    >
    > (Cited in *Huizhu lu*, "Hou lu," *juan* 10, pp. 202–206.)

14. Cf. *SPck*, *juan* , p. 220, quotations from Lu Xiong's *Suzhoufu zhi*; *Gusu zhi*, *juan* 16.2; *Baicheng yanshui*, *juan* 1, pp. 1–2.
15. The map was engraved by Lü Ting and two other local cartographers, Zhang Yuncheng and Zhang Yundi, probably on the instructions of the prefect Li Shoupeng, who at the time conducted a series of construction works in the city and promoted the publication of *Wujun zhi*. Cf. *Wujun zhi*, "Preface" by Zhao Rutan; *SPck*, "Preface." The construction works carried out in the period between 1224 and 1229 are also reflected on the picture map. After his scrupulous examination and

comparison of contemporary documents and the map, Wang Jian concludes that the official establishments and temples built by the end of the summer of 1229 are all shown on the map, while those built thereafter are not. For a discussion of the content of this map, see Wang 1990, pp. 50–55.

16. *usu zhi*, *juan* 16.2.

17. Liu 1987, p. 8; Mote 1973, p. 53. Zheng Yuanyou (1292–1364), for example, writes in his *Pingjianglu xinzhu juncheng ji (Pxjj)*, p. 1b: "Emperor Shizu united all under Heaven. [He] took the land between the Four Seas as his abode, and the six domains [*liuhe*, i.e., Heaven, Earth and the Four Quarters] as his palaces. [Therefore he] did not set up defense at those trifling city walls."

18. *SPck*, *juan* 5, pp. 220–221, quotations from Lu Xiong's *Suzhoufu zhi*. The character *dang* reads a little ambiguously here, as two of its meanings are relevant in the context. It denotes "level" and accordingly modifies the omitted word "walls"; it also denotes "damaged" or "destroyed" and thus modifies either the omitted word "walls" or the word "gates" in the preceding sentence. Since in the following passage of the same document there appears the phrase "built the walls and dredged the moats," to refer to the reestablishment of the city defense, I find that the former meaning of *dang*, that is, "level," is more to be favored.

19. Cf. *Yuan shi*, *juan* 42, p. 899; *usu zhi*, *juan* 16.2.

20. Cf. *Pxjj*, p. 1b–2a; *SPck*, *juan* 5, p. 221, quotations from Lu Xiong's *Suzhoufu zhi*.

21. *Pxjj*, p. 2a. A special temple dedicated to Wu Zixu was built on top of Xu Gate. See *Zhongxiao anhui Xianshengwang miao bei*, pp. 1a–2b.

22. Cf. Liu 1987, p. 8; Mote 1977, p. 137; Dong 1982, p. 68; and Chen 1983, p. 71. This was evidenced in the numerous records about wall building in the imperial capitals, in regional and local capital cities, in military forts on the frontiers, and more conspicuously, in the work on the Great Wall.

23. See, for example, *usu zhi*, *juan* 16.2.

24. Cf. *Jiangnan tongzhi*, *juan* 20.4; *Suzhoufu zhi*, *juan* 4.4.

25. Wright 1977, p. 73.

26. Mote 1977, p. 133.

27. To my knowledge, this problem has not been considered by Western students of Suzhou's history nor, for whatever reasons, seriously dealt with by modern Chinese scholars. Cao and Wu (1986, pp. 50, 69, 77, 80), for example, evade this difficulty not only by simply repeating the figures stated in some of the ancient documents without any critical analysis of their contradictory aspects but also by making some groundless assertions about the scale of the city.

28. Cf. *Wudi ji*, pp. 14, 111. One exception to the record of the circumference of the city wall can be found in the *Xuejin taoyuan* edition, where it is recorded as 45 *li* 30 *bu*.

29. *Taiping huanyu ji*, *juan* 91, p. 687.

30. Cao and Wu (1986, p. 69) claim that the perimeter of the walls at this time was 45 *li*, without giving any source of reference. Yet the description of other details of the wall reconstruction in their work indicates that they have relied on the sources no more than I do, and according to the versions of these documents available to me, no mentions of the perimeter of the walls are found at all. Mote (1962, p. 43) asserts: "The new wall built in the late Yuan period was forty-seven *li*, or about sixteen miles in circumference." Likewise, no source of reference is provided.

31. *Pxjj*, p. 2a.

32. See quotations in *SPck*, *juan* 5, p. 221; *usu zhi*, *juan* 16.2–3.

33. The priority of this set of figures here is not in accordance with the order of its appearance in the original text in question but simply for the convenience of the present discussion.

34. We assume for the moment that the character *zhou* denotes perimeter and will later return to this possibly questionable assumption.

35. 1 *li* = 360 *bu*, as 1 *bu* = 5 *chi* from the early Tang onward. Cf. Needham 1971, p. 7, note g; Liu 1980, p. 416.

36. The length of the wall between Chang Gate and Xu Gate is recorded in the *usu zhi* (*juan* 16.2–3) as 639 *zhang* 5 *chi;* that between Xu Gate and Pan Gate as 388 *zhang* 7 *chi;* that between Pan Gate

and Feng Gate as 1,118 *zhang;* that between Feng Gate and Lou Gate as 864 *zhang* 2 *chi;* that between Lou Gate and Qi Gate as 80 *zhang;* and that between Qi Gate and Chang Gate as 892 *zhang* 2 *chi* *cun*. Thus the sum total is 4,482 *zhang* 6 *chi* *cun*.

37. *Wsq*, *juan* 7.1–11.
38. About half a century after the compilation of Wang Ao's *Gusu zhi* in 1 06, Zheng Ruozeng (fl. 1 0 –1 80) echoes in his *Jiangnan jinglüe* (*juan* 2A.6–7) Wang Ao's statement that "the perimeter [of the walled city] is 12,293 *bu* 9 *fen*," but adds that "in total, it is forty-five *li*" and that the section belonging to Wu county is twenty-two *li* and the section belonging to Changzhou county is twenty-three *li*. These figures added by Zheng Ruozeng must be disregarded not only because they represent a measurement that is far out of proportion to the possible actual size of the area enclosed by the city walls but, unlike Wang Ao's account, they are entirely inconsistent with the figure using the length unit *bu*, which Zheng possibly adopted from the *Gusu zhi*. Roughly during the same period of time, Cao Zishou, the magistrate of Wu county in 1 9, wrote a short discourse entitled *Wuxian chengtu shuo* concerning the city walls of Suzhou. Although Cao claims, as does Zheng Ruozeng, that the wall was forty-five *li* in circumference, he also indicates that the city measured five *li* (approximately 2.88 kilometers) wide from east to west and seven *li* (approximately 4.032 kilometers) long from north to south. This comes very close indeed to the third figure presented in the *Gusu zhi* and thus probably to the actual measurements of the length of the city walls as well.
39. *Jiangnan tongzhi*, *juan* 20.4.
40. Liang 1980, p. 27.
41. 1 *bu* = 0. *wu*. There is little doubt that these units, though convertible in any certain period of time and sometimes used in mixture, are more compatible with each other within their own set than with those of the other set. This pattern is visible not only in the frequency of its practical use but also in many idiomatic phrases, as we read, for example, in the *Guo yu* (*juan* 3, p. 123): "[The capacity of] the eye to measure by observing does not exceed the scope of *buwu* and *chicun*."
42. See, for example, *Yandu congkao*, *bian* 1/2, pp. 10, 14, for the accounts of the walls of the Liao and Yuan capital cities at Beijing, collected from various historical documents. It should be noted, however, that the use of *fang* in the account of the size of the city appears in most cases to have been in the manner that the figures following the character are the length of each side of the square, as the "Kaogong ji" section of the *Zhou li* describes the canonical royal Zhou city as "a square with sides of nine *li* (*fang jiu li*)." The territorial area of the Central Kingdom was also accounted for with the character *fang*, as was sometimes that of other regions. Practically, this was a method of "cutting off from the long to supplement the short (*jiechang buduan*)"; conceptually, it was in line with the notion that since the earth was square, so should be regulated territories.
43. This hypothesis is proposed by Xu Jialu, professor of classical Chinese, through personal communication in 199 . Using this hypothesis, we may examine the measurements of the city walls of Suzhou recorded in the Ming documents. Let us again take the statement in the *Gusu zhi* (*juan* 16.2–3), for example: "the *zhou* [of the walled city] was 34 *li* 3 *bu* 9 *fen*, that is, 12,293 *bu* 9 *fen*," and "the total [length of the wall] is 4,482 *zhang* 6 *chi* *cun*." Taking the character *zhou* as indicating area measurement of the city in a close rectangular shape, we may assume that the length of the city's short side, that is, east-west side, was around *li* (approximately 2.88 kilometers by the Ming standard) and that of its long side, that is, north-south side, was around 7 *li* (approximately 4.032 kilometers); both are fairly close to the dimensions of the present area encircled by the remains of the city moats. As the area of the city, they approximate 3 square *li*, which is roughly in accord with the figure in the *Gusu zhi* for the *zhou* of the walled city; while the sum of their doubles, 24 *li*, is equivalent to about 4,220 *zhang*, or 42,200 *chi*, as 1 *li* = 180 *zhang* and 1 *zhang* = 10 *chi*, which is also close to but about 2,000 *chi* (approximate 0.6 kilometers) smaller than the other figure given by the *Gusu zhi* for the total length of the walls. The 2,000 *chi* difference seems explainable: it probably comprises the length of the walls that formed the counterscarps outside the six city gates. When the same hypothetical method is applied in the Qing measurements, we obtain a similarly

proportional result between the figure presumably representing the area of the walled enclosure and the figure representing the length of the walls. They roughly correspond to each other when the measurements are converted either way, except that there exists a larger difference, about 7,000 *chi* (approx. 2.17 kilometers), between the recorded length of the walls and the length estimated by reference to the presumably recorded area. Is it possible that this difference comes from not only the inclusion of both the length of the wall sections that functioned as semicircular or square counterscarps outside those six city gates (*yuecheng*) but from the extra measurements possibly brought about by the meandering of the walls in the Qing?

44. Confronting a similar problem when considering the length of the city wall of Nanjing, Mote (1977, pp. 134–136) has noted that the historical records and even the modern descriptions all differ on this point, although as the wall stands today, it is essentially the fourteenth-century wall built by the Ming founder in the second half of the fourteenth century, and that this kind of discrepancies in records "tends to leave some doubt about all traditional measurements, even when corroborated in very recent studies."
45. One may be fastidious and cast some doubt on this evidence by insisting that, since many of these artifacts were in fact reconstructed time and again, with their original names persistently applied to them, their recurrence on these maps in the same positional relationship with the city walls and gates does not necessarily mean that they were rebuilt on the exact locations of their predecessors.
46. Yu 1980, p. 18; Johnston 1983, p. 200.
47. This result was obtained in 1978 by the Surveying Team of Suzhou Bureau of City Construction Control. See Yu 1980, pp. 19 and 20, note 9.
48. Yu, ibid., p. 19.
49. Cf. Johnston 1983, p. 200; Needham 1962, pp. 312–313.
50. Paul Wheatley (1971, p. 426) summarizes a few techniques used by the Chinese in early times for the orientation of cities. One was the determination of a north-south axis by bisecting the angle between the directions of the rising and setting of the sun. This procedure is recorded in the "Kaogong ji" section of the *Zhou li* (for quotations from it, see Chapter 2), the use of which is suggested by Wheatley as having been attributable to the layout of those cities with a more or less accurate orientation. Another technique was that the north-south axis was determined by reference to the celestial pole, the result of which was prone to an orientation of a few degrees east of the true north, because not only as a result of precession does the celestial pole move along the arc of a circle having the pole of the ecliptic for its center, but also the pole stars in Zhou times were a few degrees distant from the celestial pole. A third technique current from the Han period onward was the use of a primitive form of compass known as *zhinan* (the south-pointing [instrument]), which may also have been responsible for cities' orientational discrepancies, since declination was easterly until Song times, after which the compass needle began to show a westerly declination. For a discussion of magnetic declination and the compass needle in China, see Needham 1962, pp. 301–313.
51. Liu 1980, pp. 63, 97, 154.
52. *Pxjj*, p. 2a.
53. Needham (1971, p. 46) sees a contrast here between this Chinese practice and that of the medieval West, where the walls of castles are often seen as perpendicular.
54. *Zhou li*, *juan* 42, p. 295. See, for example, *Yingzao fashi* (*juan* 3, p. 55) for the officially stipulated proportion in the Song period. For discussions of this work in English, see Glahn 1975, 1981, 1984.
55. *SPck*, *juan* 5, p. 220. Since the *Xiangfu tujing* was written in the Song dynasty, the measurements are converted accordingly by the Song standard as 1 *chi* = 0.309m.
56. Mote 1973, p. 53.
57. Cf. *Pxjj*, p. 2a; *usu zhi*, *juan* 16.2; *Baicheng yanshui*, *juan* 1, pp. 1–2; *Jiangnan tongzhi*, *juan* 20.4; *tj*, *ce* 114.61b–62a; *Wumen biaoyin*, *juan* 1, p. 1; and *SPck*, *juan* 5, pp. 220–221. Xu Song (1617–1690) and Zhang Dachun (1637–1702) have claimed in their *Baicheng yanshui* (ibid.) written in the early

Qing that the walls in the Yuan measured 3 *zhang* 3 *chi* high. In terms of the sectional proportion of the walls, this account seems more logical, although it conflicts with that given in *Pxjj* produced much earlier, in the late Yuan. The account of the thickness of the walls in the Qing reads a little ambiguously in all contemporary documents available to me, in that it has not been explicitly indicated whether the account means the thickness at the base or at the top. In the *Jiangnan tongzhi* the character *guang* (width) is used to depict the thickness of the walls, which conveys a strong sense of the measurement on the top of the walls; whereas in the other documents the character *hou* (thickness) is used, which implies the measurement at the base.

58. *Pxjj*, p. 2a.
59. See, for example, *Su tan*, p. 1 . *Suzhoufu zhi*, *juan* 147.33–34.
60. *Wucheng riji*, *juan* C, p. 236.
61. *Gusu zhi*, *juan* 16.2; *Jiangnan tongzhi*, *juan* 20.4.
62. Needham 1971, p. 46.
63. *Gusu zhi*, *juan* 16.3; *Jiangnan tongzhi*, *juan* 20.4.
64. See *SPck*, *juan* , p. 221, with quotations from Lu's *Suzhoufu zhi*. Cf. *Gusu zhi*, *juan* 16.2.
65. *Fangyu shenglan*, *juan* 2.1 .
66. *Rongzhai suibi*, "Xubi," *juan* 8, p. 316.
67. Cf. *Taiping huanyu ji*, *juan* 91, p. 687; *Wujun zhi*, *juan* 3, p. 23, *juan* 7, p. 9 ; *Gusu zhi*, *juan* 16.2; *Baicheng yanshui*, *juan* 1, pp. 1–2; *Suzhoufu zhi*, *juan* 4.4– .
68. *Baicheng yanshui*, *juan* 1, p. 2.
69. Cf. *Pxjj*, p. 2a; *Jiangnan tongzhi*, *juan* 20.4; *Suzhoufu zhi*, *juan* 4. .
70. *Gusu zhi*, *juan* 16.2.
71. *Wucheng riji*, *juan* B, p. 221.
72. *Pxjj*, p. 2a; Cf. *Gusu zhi*, *juan* 16.3; *Jiangnan tongzhi*, *juan* 20.4; *Suzhoufu zhi*, *juan* 4. .
73. According to Shen Fu (1763–1808 or after), a native of Suzhou, the city gates of Suzhou were closed well after midnight and were opened no later than five in the morning (*Fusheng liuji*, *juan* 1, pp. 2, 21; *juan* 3, p. 40). He was so used to the late hour of gate closing of his home city that, in the mid 1780s when he sojourned briefly in the city of Guangzhou on the southern coast, he was once unexpectedly shut out of this unfamiliar city at about nine o'clock after a late drink with his friends in the suburb (ibid., *juan* 4, pp. 71–73). Even in 164 , the year of turbulent transition from the Ming to the Qing rule over the Suzhou area, after two months of being closed, Chang Gate was opened from as early as three in the morning to as late as seven in the evening by order of the Qing general Tu Guobao, whereby officials and soldiers at the gate were instructed not to hinder travelers and peddlers but only pay attention to bandits. See *Wucheng riji*, *juan* B, p. 216.
74. Yu 1980, p. 19. This line of reasoning is followed by Johnston 1983, p. 200.
75. *Wucheng riji*, *juan* A, pp. 207, 208. According to the *Wuxian zhi* (*juan* 29B.7) and *Baicheng yanshui* (*juan* 1, p. 73), the south gate of the inner enclosure, known as Qiaolou, functioned as a drum/horn (*gujiao*) tower from as early as the Tang period, although it was only in 1149 that a more accurate clepsydra (*kelou*) was installed in it. Yet in 1366 the buildings of the inner enclosure, taken over by Zhang Shicheng to serve as one of his palaces, were totally destroyed in the fighting accompanying the entry into the city of the Ming forces led by Xu Da (1332–138). Only a section of the dilapidated walls around the south gate was left, whereupon later in the first half of the Ming, an official drum was placed to sound the night watches, thereby gaining it the popular name Gulou.
76. See, for example, *Wucheng riji*, *juan* C, p. 232; *Xxz*, *juan* A.44b.
77. *Su tan*, pp. 8–9. The usual name of Zhou Boqi was Zhou Ding, Boqi being his given title. This event is also briefly mentioned in *Yupu zaji*, *juan* , pp. 36–37.
78. *Wumen biaoyin*, *juan* 1, p. 1. For the origins and transformations of some of these inscriptions, cf. "The *Locus Classicus*" and "Symbolism of the City Gates" sections in Chapter 2.
79. *Qingjia lu*, *juan* 1, p. 1. Ceremonies of similar kind conducted in the east suburbs are found in many other parts of China. See Song and Li 1991, p. 240 .

80. *Qing jia lu*, ibid., p. 17. This was believed to occur on the days *ding* and *ren*, the Ten Heavenly Branches being used to designate the sequence of days. For more information about this god and its rotational locations, see *Qinding xieji bianfang shu*, *juan* 7.21-2; Zong and Liu 1987, pp. 660–661.
81. For a remark on the ubiquity and essentiality of walls in Chinese community, see Sirén 1929, p. 557.
82. *Wuli tongkao*, *juan* 45.55.
83. *Pxjj*, p. 2b; *Jiangnan jinglüe*, *juan* 1A.27.
84. Cf. *Ch* 1980, p. 1074; *Cy* 1988, p. 492.
85. This term could also mean "the city of Suzhou" often with an emphasis on "the administrative offices of the prefecture of Suzhou in its capital," or even on "the prefect" or "the prefect's administration."
86. Dong 1982, pp. 53–57; *Zhongguo lishi wenhua mingcheng cidian*, 1985, p. 406. This process of development appears to have been somewhat similar to that of many medieval cities in continental Europe, where, as Morris (1994, pp. 98–99) concludes, the consequence of horizontal growth of a city like Florence was marked in each stage by the construction of a new wall to include newly developed but previously undefended "suburbs." In discussing the city of Florence, Braunfels (1988, pp. 51–52) explicitly asserts that the growth of the city found its expression in the building of the city walls.
87. Dong 1982, pp. 101–103.
88. See quotations from the *Wuxian zhi*, *juan* 18C.1 in Chapter 2.
89. Sirén 1929, p. 557. Some locals may have regarded the city walls as emblematic of their home places. Gao Qi (1336–1374), who may have resided in the northern part of the city within the walls (Mote 1962, p. 38) or outside but at least in their close vicinity, was one of such personalities. Among many of his poems associated with the Feng (maple) Bridge over three kilometers west of the Suzhou city walls, two contain similarly contrasting perceptions of the distant city walls and the Hanshan Buddhist Temple in the close vicinity of the bridge. The first one was written in 1368 at the Feng Bridge, where the poet spent the night aboard his canal boat on his journey to the Ming court in Nanjing:

    Crows caw at this frosty moonlight night, hollow and forlorn,
    Turning back my head I see the city walls still not far.
    Truly a first night of many of longing for home,
    Distant bell-tolls, a lone boat, lodging by Maple Bridge.

    ("Jiangfu Jinling shichu Changmen yebo," in *Hanshan Si zhi*, *juan* 3, pp. 82–83)

    The second poem, written in 1370 at the same point on his return journey after almost two years service at court, has the following lines:

    From far off I see the city's walls, and still doubt that it's really so.
    I can't make out the green hills; only faintly glimpse the old pagoda.

    . . . .

    The temple is hidden in the sunset haze, but the raven's call is here;
    With the autumn stream and the empty bridge, and the fledging ducks flying.

    ("Gui Wu zhi Fengqiao," in *Hanshan Si zhi*, *juan* 3, p. 82. The English translation of these stanzas by Mote 1962, p. 182)

    Here, for Gao Qi, the distant city walls were always viewed as clear and close, in contrast to the nearby Buddhist temple shrouded in the sunset haze, with its bell tolling distantly. Although this perception is very much in conformity with the worldly attribute of the city walls as compared to the seclusive nature of a Buddhist temple, the expression of Gao Qi's personal attachment to the city walls seems particularly strong.

90. *Sou shen houji, juan* 1, p. 1.
91. *Tao'an mengyi*, pp. 117–118.

Chapter 5: Physical Structure of the City

1. Needham (1971, pp. 211–212) holds that "the Chinese people have been outstanding among the nations of the world in their control and use of water" and that "if there was one feature of China which impressed the early modern European travelers there more than any other, it was the great abundance of waterworks and canals." The area of Suzhou was regarded by imperial scholars as the best in its beneficial availability and use of waters. See, for example, *Suzhoufu zhi, juan* 2.19–20.
2. Cf. Mote 1973, p. 43 where he uses the term "the Venice of China;" Liao and Ye 1984, p. 3 9. Such an analogy, probably associated with Marco Polo's alleged visit to Suzhou in the 1280s, is certainly helpful to those Westerners who are not familiar with Suzhou for their obtaining a rough idea about what the city was like. Yet if one were to be fastidious and to compare the two cities in terms of their age, population, and stability in time, one could justifiably argue that calling Suzhou "the Venice of the Orient" might be less appropriate than calling Venice "the Suzhou of the Occident."
3. Yu 1980, p. 16.
4. In Suzhou the average annual rainfall is around one thousand one hundred millimeters, with 40 to o percent of it in summer. Cf. *Zhongguo lishi wenhua mingcheng cidian* 198 , p. 2 0; Cao and Wu 1986, p. .
5. *Yue jue shu, juan* 2, p. 10.
6. *Shi ji, juan* 78, pp. 2394–239 .
7. *Wudi ji*, p. 111.
8. "Deng Changmen xianwang," in *Quan Tang shi, juan* 447, p. 021.
9. "Guo Wumen ershisi yun," in *Quan Tang shi, juan* 481, p. 474.
10. Ibid., *juan* 691, p. 792 .
11. *WTx, juan* 1, pp. –6.
12. *Wujun zhi, juan* 12, p. 172.
13. Since there are a few cases in the record where a name either simultaneously denotes two bridges or is a repetition of one already mentioned, the exact number is hard to determine.
14. *Wudi ji*, "Supplement," pp. 128–129, 131, 144; *Wujun zhi, juan* 17, pp. 234–243. Cf. *WTx, juan* B, pp. 23–26. There is no doubt, as the *Wudi ji* (p. 111) records, that the city of Suzhou had well over three hundred bridges during the Tang period, most of them built of wood, with their banisters painted red. During his seventeen-month tenure of office as the Suzhou prefect, Bai Juyi writes in his poem "Zhengyue sanri xianxing" (*Quan Tang shi, juan* 447, p. 026) that in the city, "With red banisters are three hundred and ninety bridges." His contemporary Liu Yuxi speaks otherwise of three hundred and seventy bridges when repaying Bai's courtesy with a poem (*Quan Tang shi, juan* 3 6, p. 4003). The number of the bridges must have remained similar if not larger, as Zhu Changwen and another Song scholar-official Yang Bei claim, in the Northern Song and probably throughout the following centuries. By Zhu Changwen's time (1041–1098), most of the bridges had eventually come to be built of stone. See *WTx, juan* B, p. 23; *Wujun zhi, juan* 17, p. 234.
15. Yu 1980, p. 16; Johnston 1983, p. 203.
16. *Wudi ji*, p. 111. We are informed by this document that the city contained over three hundred *xiang* (alleys in a residential ward).
17. Cf. *Wudi ji*, pp. 100–103; *Wujun zhi, juan* 6, pp. 69–71.
18. It is not impossible that a few small canals may have channeled their ways *through* some of the wards, which accordingly should have had appropriate water gates on their walls to control access, although there are no records of such kinds of apparatus available to us. Yet the majority of the

canals must have run only in between the wards so as to have functioned as routes of public transport. We do not know whether a large number of canals were dug or rearranged to be accommodated to the already established ward system, or whether instead many wards were adapted to the gradually regulated canal system. This question may be of chicken-and-egg nature in the history of the city of Suzhou, but the two systems surely must have been coordinated from time to time.

19. "Jiuri yanji zuiti junlou jiancheng Zhou Yin er pan'guan," in *Quan Tang shi*, *juan* 444, pp. 4968–4969. Part of this poem has been quoted in Chapter 1.
20. *WTx*, *juan* B, pp. 24–25. Cf. *Wujun zhi*, *juan* 9, p. 114, and *juan* 17, p. 234.
21. Twitchett 1966, p. 232; He 1986, p. 210.
22. Cf. *WTx*, *juan* A, p. 8; *Wujun zhi*, *juan* 6, p. 69.
23. *Wujun zhi*, *juan* 25, pp. 364, 365.
24. The poet Su Shunqin (1008–1048), traveling to the Suzhou area in the 1040s after his dismissal from office in the imperial capital Kaifeng, bought a piece of land east of the prefectural school, a long deserted spot full of small hills, ponds, and lush plants and having no houses round it, which he perceived as "not at all resembling those within the city walls." He then constructed on it the renowned Surging Waves Pavilion. Cf. *Canglang Ting ji*; p. 187; *WTx*, *juan* C, p. 64; *Wujun zhi*, *juan* 14, p. 187. Similarly, Cheng Shimeng, a native of the prefecture of Suzhou, bought an unoccupied plot east of the Buddhist Ruiguang Temple and built on it his own house in the first half of the eleventh century. See *WTx*, ibid.
25. *WTx*, *juan* A, p. 8.
26. Needham (1971, pp. 69, 142), on the basis of the works of some Western scholars before him, insists that this kind of structure, "the triumphal gateway" as he calls it, derived from the Indian *torana*, familiar from Sanchi at which four of them surround the first-century B.C. *dagoba* or *tope*, facing the quarters of the world. Liu Zhiping, (1987, p. 42) however, holds that it had its source in ancient China itself and originated from both the *hengmen*, "a kind of gates with a timber crossbar," as Yan Shigu (581–645) explains it, and the *huabiao*, a kind of ceremonial column probably developed from the archaic totemic pillars marking each of the specific tribes. See *Han shu*, *juan* 73, p. 3110. Whatever the truth of the matter—whether it be a gift from Indian to Chinese architecture or the outcome of a slow intrinsic evolution—the supersession of the gates of residential wards by honorific gateways, from the late Northern Song to the early Southern Song, was undoubtedly one of the emblematic aspects of the process of medieval urban transformation in Suzhou.
27. *Wujun zhi*, *juan* 6, pp. 69 ff.
28. *Wujun zhi*, *juan* 6, p. 72. Even when mentioning that the sixty-five *fang* in 1229 were the works of the prefect Li Shoupeng, Fan Chengda still uses the verb *zuo* (build or construct). In almost all of the local gazetteers from the Ming onward, however, the verb *li* (erect) is invariably used in the records of the building of *fang* in later times. More interesting is that Lu Xiong of the early Ming, in his *Suzhoufu zhi* compiled in the late fourteenth century, first argues that *fang* in antiquity meant "residential wards" and then, on the basis of Fan Chengda's record, as many others have done in their writings, refers to the 1229 event but replaces the verb *zuo* with *li*. See quotation in *SPck*, section preceding *juan* 1, p. 2. Cf. *Suzhoufu zhi*, *juan* 5.3. This reveals Lu's and others' acute understanding of the change in the denotation of the character *fang*.
29. There were also cases in which the name of a ward derived from a historic or legendary event. Yet it was because a *fang* was often set up in later times to honor an individual or family's praised moral or righteous conduct that it is now loosely translated as an "honorific gateway."
30. See, for example, *Cy* 1988, p. 1529.
31. *Wujun zhi*, *juan* 6, p. 71.
32. In his *Wumen biaoyin* (*juan* 12, pp. 161 ff.), for example, Gu Zhentao (1750–?) lists over two hundred honorific gateways erected in and around the city of Suzhou from the Ming period to his time. Two notable changes characterized these activities: first, unlike that in the Southern Song, the erection of many gateways was financed and conducted by local gentry or wealthy individuals

rather than solely by the local government; and second, the location of the new gateways was no longer limited to the area enclosed by the city walls but extended to the rural areas. Taking the record in the *Suzhoufu zhi* (*juan* .1ff.) of the building of *fang* in Wu, Changzhou, and Yuanhe counties, the seats of all of which were located in the city of Suzhou, we also find that 29 percent of the gateways were located either in the suburbs or in the more distant areas of the countryside. These changes, in fact, came entirely in concurrence with social developments in late imperial China, that is, further relaxation of government controls over social and economic activities, and increased ties between the city and countryside.

33. Hackett 19 0, p. 91.
34. Cf., for example, *Gusu zhi*, *juan* 12.1 ; *Wsq*, *juan* 10.21; *Ming shi*, *juan* 140, p. 4002.
35. Yu 1986, p. 38. Yu holds that there were fourteen recorded canal-dredgings during this period of time. Whether this results from his intentional exclusion of the two instances of partial work (1 2 and 1630) or from his omission of certain pieces of information, I do not know.
36. An appraisal of the local efforts at regulating the city canals during a certain period of time demands not only an analysis of the whole set of political, social, and economic conditions but a comparative assessment between the effectiveness of the actions taken by the local government or groups in response to this set of conditions during this particular period and that in other times and places.
37. It is reasonable to assume that the reconstruction of the city in the 1220s was accompanied by extensive canal-dredging, although no written record of this has been found so far.
38. It should be emphasized that this discussion following the sequence of dynasties does not imply dividing the history of canal regulation in the city of Suzhou into dynastic slices, although dynastic cycles at times did exert tremendous influence on local conditions and resources.
39. Since records of a number of water-control projects outside the city from the thirteenth to the fifteenth centuries appear in the same sources, it seems possible that the instances of the dredging of the city canals, if any, may not have been judged by the contemporary local historians significant enough to deserve being recorded.
40. Skinner 1977a, p. 17.
41. *Chongjun Suzhou chenghe ji*, p. 30 . This problem may have been aggravated in the eighteenth century by a sharp increase in Suzhou's population, which coincided with an increase of the nationwide population to unprecedented levels.
42. The street in front of Xuanmiao Guan, known from the Qing to the present day as Guanqian Street, was formerly called Suijin Street. Thus the bridge in front of the main entrance of the temple was sometimes called Suijin Bridge, although its proper name was Gong Bridge in the Song and Ming and Guan Bridge in the Qing.
43. *Honglan yisheng*, *juan* 1, p. 3a.
44. *Chongjun Suzhou chenghe ji*, p. 306.
45. Ibid., p. 306; *Sujun chenghe sanheng sizhi tushuo*, p. 309.
46. The official figure obtained during the period between 1 67 and 1619 for the width of the city canals ranges from about 6.4 meters to 12.8 meters. See *Wsq*, *juan* 7.1ff. Yet even after the 1796 canal-dredging, as Sheng Linji acknowledged in 1797, the average width of the canals had been halved, and their full width was impossible to restore (*Sujun chenghe sanheng sizhi tushuo*, ibid.).
47. Even in the process of the full-scale city canal-dredging between 1796 and 1797, according to Fei Chun, the government did not simply tear down all the houses overhanging or encroaching the canals but, by "weighing up public convenience and individual benefit," accordingly cleared the canals of those which appeared most inconvenient to the public transport system. See *Chongjun Suzhou chenghe ji*, p. 306.
48. *Shi ji*, *juan* 78, pp. 2394–239 .
49. *Yue jue shu*, *juan* 2, p. 18.
50. According to Zhang Shoujie of the Tang, a commentator of the *Shi ji*, Lord Chunshen "constructed in the city another walled structure to the northwest of the *xiaocheng* and resided in it" (*Shi ji*, *juan*

78, p. 2394). This proposition is accepted by Qu Yingjie (1991, pp. 221–222), who further suggests that the Dingcuo Cheng built in 201 B.C. might also have been located on the site of Lord Chunshen's palace. Yet more scholars seem to have preferred the proposition that Lord Chunshen's palace was built on the site of the *xiaocheng*, which, later usually known as *zicheng* (inner walled enclosure), continued to be used as the site of the prefectural offices until the end of the Yuan in the 1360s. Cf., for example, *WTx, juan* A, p. 13; *Wujun zhi, juan* 6, p. 1; *Baicheng yanshui, juan* 1, pp. 72–73; Wen 1988, pp. – 6.

51. Liu 1980, p. 168. Since a very large number of Tang poems were associated with various architectural structures in the government building complex, a full reference to them appears to be unnecessary here. Refer to *Wujun zhi, juan* 6, pp. o ff., where some of the poems are quoted.
52. Johnston 1983, p. 21 . The area enclosed within the walls of the inner city of Suzhou was about 270,000 square meters. The area enclosed within the walls of the Forbidden City of Beijing is, according to Liu Dunzhen (1980, p. 281), 726,600 square meters (960 meters x 760 meters), whereas Johnston (1983, p. 222, note 30) maintains that it is 80, 00 square meters, but without providing any reference for this figure. As for the measurements of Suzhou, Johnston has presumed the plan of Suzhou on the *Pingjiang tu* to be on a reasonably accurate scale and thus the size of every structure depicted on it to be close to that of the real one. This presumption is very problematic because, like the picture maps of many other cities, this plan depicts important urban structures by means of elevational images, and thus indicates precision in their positions and orientations rather than in their dimensions. If we were to accept Johnston's presumed measurements, any large five-bay building in the inner enclosure would have been around 170 meters in length (that is, the span of one pillar-interval or bay [*jian*] would have been around 34 meters), which is obviously too much out of proportion.
53. Cf. *SPck, juan* 3, p. 147, quotations from Lu Xiong's *Suzhoufu zhi*; *Baicheng yanshui, juan* 1, pp. 72–73; *Suzhoufu zhi, juan* 21.2.
54. It is claimed in the *Zhongguo dabaike quanshu* (1988, p. 346, entry "Pingjiangfu cheng") that during the period between 1131 and 1162, Emperor Gaozong intended to relocate his capital at Pingjiang, and the city was therefore rebuilt in accordance with the requirements of an imperial capital. Yet no reference to this statement is given, nor has any evidence been found to support it. A more cautious suggestion made by Wang Jian is that Pingjiang functioned in the Southern Song as a *de facto* auxiliary imperial capital (*peidu*), and thus institutionally its spatial layout and structural organization were the same as those of the capital Lin'an. See *SPck, juan* 3, p. 1 7 and *juan* 4, p. 200.
55. *Wujun zhi, juan* 6, p. 1.
56. Cf. *Huangchao ping-Wu lu*, A, pp. 128–132, C, p. 147; *Baicheng yanshui, juan* 1, p. 73; *Suzhoufu zhi, juan* 21.2–3.
57. There are considerable discrepancies among various accounts of this river. Fan Chengda holds that Jinfan Jing was the inner moat of the city of Suzhou (*Wujun zhi, juan* 18, p. 2 7), whereas Wang Ao in his *Gusu zhi* (*juan* 33.20) states that it was the moat of the inner walled enclosure, although he immediately contradicts himself by indicating that this river stretched in the north-south direction west of Le Bridge, which was located in the middle section of Wolong Street, present-day Renmin Road. The majority of the Ming and Qing scholars nevertheless seem to have agreed on the position of Jinfan Jing as being between Han Bridge and Xianghua Bridge. Cf., for example, *SPck, juan* , p. 261, with quotations from Lu Xiong's *Suzhoufu zhi* and Yang Xunji's *Wuyi zhi*; *Wumen biaoyin, juan* 1, p. .
58. For a biography of Gao Qi, see Mote 1962. Mote (ibid., pp. 234–236) holds that Gao Qi died because he wrote a customary congratulatory poem "On Raising the Roof Beams of the Prefectural Hall," although he also acknowledges the possibility that the poet composed a prose essay on the same occasion, which, as he believes, does not survive. However, the documents at my disposal all indicate that Gao Qi's death was triggered by the latter, because it contains the term *longpan huju* (like a coiling dragon and a crouching tiger).

59. *Ye ji, juan* 1, p. 516.
60. For detailed information about this event, see *Ming shi, juan* 140, p. 4002 and *juan* 285, p. 7328; *Wuzhong guyu*, pp. 2b–4a; *Ye ji, juan* 1, p. 516; *Pengchuang leiji, juan* 1, pp. 4b–5a; *Baicheng yanshui, juan* 3, p. 195; *Xxz, juan* C.1b–2a; Mote 1962, pp. 234–240.
61. *Wuzhong guyu*, p. 3b.
62. Mote 1962, p. 238.
63. See *Ming shi, juan* 140, p. 4002. Cf. *Ye ji, juan* 1, p. 516, for a slight variation of wording.
64. *Wujun zhi, juan* 18, p. 257.
65. The period of Helü Dacheng, said to have been built in 514 B.C., was short-lived, and the state of Wu was finally conquered by Yue in 473 B.C. See Chapters 1 and 2.
66. *Baicheng yanshui, juan* 3, p. 195; *Xxz, juan* C.2a.
67. See *Taiping yulan, juan* 156, p. 758, quotations from the *Wu lu*. In the former document (ibid.) it is also quoted from the *Wu lu* and *Jiangbiao zhuan* that around 220 B.C., the First Emperor of Qin, during his tour of inspection to Guiji prefecture, visited the site of Nanjing, which was then called Jinling (gold tumulus). Being informed by a specialist in observing *qi* (*wangqizhe*) that the terrain of Jinling possessed the *qi* of kingship, he had part of the range of the East Hill (*donggang*) cut away so as to break up this potential threat and ordered the seemingly auspicious name Jinling to be changed to Moling (fodder mound), which sounds much more humble. Four hundred years later, Sun Quan, who took Suzhou as one of his substantial bases, was persuaded by Zhang Hong with the same geomantic argument to transfer his capital to Nanjing.
68. Huang Wei, a local scholar, quotes in his *Pengchuang leiji* (*juan* 1, p. 5a), written in the mid-Ming, another scholar's comments on this event: "Gao was the top poet in the early period of the empire and conversant with [things in] the past and present, but [curiously] he did not know that *huju longpan* is an old symbolic name for the capital, and thus that it should not be applied to an ordinary city. [When one] intended to have him condemned, the pretext had been there."
69. See, for example, Mote 1962, p. 240.
70. *Wuzhong guyu*, pp. 3b–4a.
71. *Baicheng yanshui, juan* 3, p. 195. Cf. also the quotation in the preceding section from the *Honglan yisheng* on the unattended state of this site around the turn of the eighteenth century.
72. The geometrical center of the city may have regained some degree of symbolic importance from 1717 when the provincial governor Wu Cunli supervised the construction of Wanshou Gong (Palace of Eternal Life) on the east side of the site of the old inner walled enclosure, it being a palace in which formal prostration to the emperor was performed. See *Suzhoufu zhi, juan* 21.1.
73. *Wujun zhi, juan* 6, pp. 50 ff.
74. Here, as does Kertzer (1988, pp. 1–14; p. 185, note 6), who talks about symbolism in politics, I follow Geertz' (1973, p. 91) broad use of the concept of the symbol. A symbol thus refers to "any object, act, event, quality, or relation which serves as a vehicle for a conception," and the conception is the meaning of the symbol.
75. Kertzer 1988, p. 5.
76. Elvin 1973, p. 177.
77. Mote 1973, p. 39.
78. The manner of urban social management may have varied from one city to another, and probably from the mid-Ming on, and surely during the Qing period, marked institutional change in this regard occurred in most cities. See Skinner 1977e, pp. 547–548. Yet it seems safe to recognize that at least up to the beginning of the Ming, the involvement in regional or local governance of urban residents in any form of organization had been rare, and even during the eighteenth and nineteenth centuries the scale and area of such involvement were still very limited in the largest cities like Suzhou serving as regional administrative centers.
79. Johnston (1983, p. 215) asserts that the open space in front of the main gate of the inner city "was

an important civic space." Yet in every sense of the term "civic," this can hardly have been the case. First, since the city was not a corporate entity of its own, in theory any open space within the walls was not exclusively associated with citizens legally identified as the inhabitants of the city. Second, even if the inhabitants of the city might in practice have had more frequent access to this space, few public establishments were grouped together here for their use, and the official temples, library, garden, and the like were all situated behind gates of the walled, forbidden enclosure. Third, although the public might have had the limited right to pass through this area, it was not a space in which they could participate actively in any political or social activity. The city of Suzhou, like all other cities in imperial China, *did* have some sorts of public open space, and these will be described in Chapter 6 in a discussion about temple courtyards in the city.

80. In the mid-tenth century, the ruling Qian family of the Wu-Yue state, built in this part of the city a huge garden known as Nanyuan (the South Garden). Cf. *WTx*, *juan* A, pp. 1 –16; *Wujun zhi*, *juan* 14, pp. 189–190. By the Northern Song period, the southeast quarter of the city was still very much characterized by its natural scenery, which attracted many officials and scholars to reside here. Su Shunqin (1008–1048), as I have mentioned earlier, when traveling to Suzhou after his dismissal from office, saw the natural landscape of the quarter as "utterly unlike those within the city walls." He was so impressed by it that he bought a piece of land east of the prefectural school and built the famous Surging Waves Pavilion. See *Canglang Ting ji*, p. 187.
81. Fan Zhongyan (989–10 2), one of the famous paragon scholar-officials, assigned to Suzhou as a prefect in 103 , successfully applied to the Song imperial court to establish the prefectural school on the southeast corner of the old South Garden. See *WTx*, *juan* A, p.12; *Wujun zhi*, *juan* 4, p. 28. Zhu Changwen claims that this was the first time in history that Suzhou had its formal prefectural school and that the influence of this establishment was such that a few years later, an imperial edict was issued for all prefectures and counties in China to set up similar schools. See Zhu's memoir contained in *Wujun zhi*, ibid., pp. 28 ff. These statements may later have inspired the saying that "the institution of [prefectural and county] schools throughout China started from Wu prefecture." See *Suzhou yuanlin*, 1991, p. 213. Whereas this may be an overstatement, it is beyond any doubt that the prefectural school of Suzhou was recognized as the best in Southeast China. See, for example, memoirs by scholars from the Song period on in *Suzhoufu zhi*, *juan* 2 .6 ff.
82. Duan and Zhang 1986, p. 16; *Ch* 1980, p. 1162.
83. Shiba 1977, p. 424; Feuchtwang 1977, *passim*.
84. This temple was located within the inner walled enclosure, in its northwest corner, during the Southern Song period.
85. The scroll is also known as *Gusu fanhua tu* (Scroll of Gusu's [i.e., Suzhou's] prosperity).
86. The office was formally known as Anchashi Sishu and popularly called Nietai, and it was in charge of inspection of local government, judicial commissions, and local imperial examinations.
87. This name was probably derived from taking Chang Gate as the reference point, as the moat north of the gate was called Beihao (North Moat).
88. Marmé, 1993, p. 36.
89. Quoted in *Suzhoufu zhi*, *juan* 4.9.
90. *Jiangnan jinglüe*, *juan* 2A.60.
91. *Wuxian cheng tu shuo*, p. 12a.
92. *Changxi zhucheng lun*, pp. 12a–b.
93. See, for example, *Tongqiao yizhao lu*, *juan* 10, pp. 143 ff.
94. Before the early eighteenth century, dramas were played in this area on large boats on the canals, initially to serve the relevant deities during specific festival periods but later mainly to entertain the public. It was during the Yongzheng reign-period (1723–173) that the first theater on land was built on the estate known as Guoyuan. See *Xxz*, *juan* C.20b–21a.
95. *Honglou meng*, *hui* 1, p. 4.

96. *Jiechao biji*, pp. 9–10. For more information about this event, see Ke Wuchi's *Louwang yongyu ji*, p. 38, and the Appendix of the 1980 edition of the *Tongqiao yizhao lu*, with quotations from Tian Huisheng's *Jinti yishi* in Xie Guozhen's *Memoir*.
97. Wheatley 1971, p. 398.
98. *Wuxian zhi, juan* 18C.1.
99. Cf., for example, *Yue jue shu, juan* 2; *Wu Yue chunqiu, juan* 4; *WTx, juan* A, pp. 5–7; *usu zhi, juan* 16.1, especially the opening passage; *Suzhoufu zhi, juan* 4.1, especially the opening passage. This change proves to have been the case for both the regional or local cities and the imperial capital, which additionally acquired the exclusive title *du* or *jing*. In the present study, however, I have to restrict my focus to the regional or local cities.
100. There were other emblems of the establishment of an administrative city, such as the Altars of the Earth and Grain and other natural features, that may have claimed a longer history than others, notably the Confucian school-temple and the temple of Chenghuang, which became more or less the normative features of a city in the second half of the imperial era, although they did not come together to be incorporated in its all-encompassing institution at the same time. Temples of popular religion, some of which were later shared by or adopted into the state religion, were located as much in the city as in the countryside, just as were Buddhist and Daoist temples. As for the economic aspects, few would doubt Feuchtwang's (1977, p. 583) assertion that "in only very rare cases would a city have been purely administrative." Yet the development of its economic functions was more of the *de facto* than of the *de jure* element of an administrative center.
101. Mote 1973, p. 54.
102. Skinner 1977a, p. 25.
103. Ibid., p. 28; 1977b, *passim*.
104. Mote 1977, p. 102. Skinner (1977c, p. 267) shares this view by stating that "China stands out among traditional agrarian societies in having an elite that was by no means predominantly urban."
105. Johnson 1985a, p. 71.
106. Ibid., p. 37.
107. *Qing jia lu, passim*. One of the interesting examples of this distinction is revealed in Gu Lu's account of the annual celebration of the birthday of the god Dongyue Di (Emperor of the East Mountain). Since those who came to burn incense in the god's temples—located either in the countryside or in the Xuanmiao Guan in the city of Suzhou—were mostly from the rural areas, this worship was humorously called *caoxie xiang* (incense of straw sandals) (ibid., *juan* 3, p. 84). Although not all peasants necessarily wore straw sandals, the use of this term by the urban residents immediately identified themselves as differentiated from the rustic and economically disadvantaged yokels.
108. As discussed in Chapter 3, by the beginning of the imperial era in the late third century B.C., the conditions allowing the sharp division into distinct urban and rural cultures seem to have vanished, as had the use of the opposing terms *guoren* (inhabitant of the walled capital city) and *yeren* (inhabitant in the fields beyond the suburbs) in their original senses. Consequently, there was no equivalent word in imperial China for "citizen" or "burgher" in the European sense of "inhabitant of a city or town" until the beginning of modern times. The terms that came closer to denote city residents were the ones composed of the character *shi* (market), such as *shimin*, *shiren*, *shiyong*, *shijingtu*, and *shijing zhi chen*, all emphasizing more the nature and social class of the trading profession (and, to a lesser degree, the handicraft profession) than urban-rural distinction. It is true that, simply because markets were more often formed in and around the cities, these terms were usually applied to those residing in the city, but this does not mean that a resident of a market town or a business suburb of a city would not be called by these terms nor that it was proper to refer to an intellectual living in the city as such.
109. Rawski 1985a, p. 6.

110. Ibid., pp. –6.
111. Interestingly, it is in the "Chengchi" section of the *Wuxian zhi* compiled in the Republic in 1933 that the topic is strictly limited to the walls *per se*.
112. Rawski 198 a, p. 1.
113. Mote 1977, p. 137. Cf. also Chapter 4 of this book.
114. Mote 1973, p. 9.
115. A cautious wording is preferred here because of the fact of the noncontemporaneity of the effects of the medieval urban revolution in the various cities of China. See Skinner 1977a, p. 26; see also Chapter 3 of this book.
116. Skinner 1977a, p. 26.
117. The Chinese character *jiao*, denoting "the area immediately outside the city," came close in Zhou times to sharing this sense of the Latin term. See, for example, *Er ya*, *juan* 7, p. 0. This meaning is reflected in the two components of the character: the one on the left, *jiao*, means "join" or "cross," which derived etymologically from "the crossing of one's legs"; the one on the right, *yi*, means "city" or, more generally, "settlement." See *Shuowen jiezi*, 6B.10, 10B.4. Thus the pictograph may be interpreted as depicting the area where the city and the wild countryside intermingle.
118. Dyos 1961, p. 22.
119. Ibid., p. 24.
120. Ibid., pp. 22–23.
121. *Xxz*, *juan* B.13a.
122. Dyos 1961, p. 23.
123. *MQSgbj* 1981, pp. 71–73.
124. Mumford 1961, p. 271.
125. Skinner 1977c, p. 269.
126. Another necessary condition was the development of market economy. It was precisely the political and social transformation from the mid-Tang onward, characterized by the gradual retreat of government control over the economy, the improved social mobility, and the economic growth, that created this condition.

Chapter 6: Courtyard and Public Urban Space

1. Mote 1977, pp. 11 –116.
2. Skinner 1977c, p. 269.
3. Cf., for example, Liu 1980, *passim*; *Zhongguo jianzhu shi* 1982, pp. 6–1 1; Liu Zhiping 1987, pp. 7–28; Liu 1989, *passim*.
4. Even if we apply this approach to European architecture, there is still a possibility of its divesting architectural form of all its symbolic values, aesthetic dimensions, and cultural significance and reducing building type to a single scheme of organization of special activities and to a diagram of circulation routes.
5. *Zhongguo jianzhu shi* 1982, p. 87.
6. This creed is expressed in the slogan "form follows function," its invention being usually credited to Louis Henry Sullivan (18 6–1924). Yet to be fair, as Norberg-Schulz (1980b, p. 180) has noted, a study of Sullivan's writings (for example, *Kindergarten Chats*) and buildings shows that he interpreted the words "function" and "form" liberally.
7. Rossi 1982, p. 46. Rossi qualifies this statement immediately:

> This does not entail the rejection of the concept of function in its most proper sense, that is, as an algebra of values that can be known as functions of one another, nor does

it deny that between functions and form one may seek to establish more complex ties than the linear ones of cause and effect (which are belied by reality itself). More specifically, we reject that conception of functionalism dictated by an ingenuous empiricism which holds that *functions bring form together* and in themselves constitute urban artifacts and architecture.

8. Buildings that could have served different purposes certainly were not limited to large, important ones. Some of the ancient Greek domestic buildings at Delos, for example, are noted by Watkin (1986, pp. 40–41) for their informal and asymmetrical planning; and "with its flexibility and simplicity this type was adaptable to a range of functions including inn, factory, school, or hotel as in a block south of the theater." Yet these lines of argument should not be taken as implying the negligibility of the phenomenon that some types of buildings *did* have their exclusive use, such as the cathedral, the form of which is explicitly expressive of Christian concepts, ideas, and symbols.
9. Alberti 1988, pp. 93, 117, 189. Note that at the same time as he distinguishes the various types of buildings, Alberti (ibid., p. 5) stresses the necessity of inquiring whether the same type of lineaments could be applied to several different uses.
10. That buildings can be explained only in terms of function, and the ties between function and form are the linear ones of cause and effect. See Rossi 1982, pp. 46–48.
11. Ibid., p. 29.
12. Of the twenty-one Buddhist temples mentioned in the *Wudi ji*, pp. 89 ff., for instance, sixteen are recorded to have been converted from houses. Yet it should also be noted that China did not entirely lack buildings constructed in particular form and for exclusive use. The pagoda, for instance, derived form the Indian *stupa*, was in most cases a necessary part of a large Buddhist temple. In the late imperial period, however, it was also often built as a free-standing structure on a suitable hill in the countryside, principally for geomantic purposes, as its popular name *fengshui ta* implies, and thus totally detached itself from its original Buddhist meaning. The Temple of Heaven was probably a better example of a structure of architectural unambiguity between form and use. But it was after all a lone structure unique for any time in imperial China.
13. Needham 1971, p. 70.
14. Ibid., p. 90, note a.
15. Unless we use the word *creation* in the more general sense of "genesis."
16. Mote 1972, p. 12. For discussions on the distinctiveness of Chinese cosmogony and cosmology, and their contents, cf., for example, Needham 1956; Mote 1971, 1972; Henderson 1984; Graham 1989. While emphasizing the distinctiveness of Chinese cosmology, Mote (ibid., pp. 13–14) does not ignore the existence of differences between popular religion and the religious elements preserved in the documents of the Great Tradition. For early periods, he suggests that any theistic tendencies in popular religious practices must have been greatly weakened by the failure (or inability) of the Great Tradition to support them on the higher level of rationalization. For later periods, he believes that the active possibility of social mobility kept the different levels of cultural life coherent and congruent, if not truly identical in quality and character, and the capacity of a Great Tradition to exert the influence of broadened versions of its essential characteristics on the popular culture was greater in China than in closed societies. Watson (1985, pp. 292–293) presents, though from a different angle, a similar point on the phenomenon of a remarkably high level of cultural integration in late imperial China, as compared with that of nineteenth-century France. To treat popular religion merely as a mirror image of the religious dimension of the elite culture would certainly be far too simplistic. But the prevalent influence of "the genuine Chinese cosmology" on the general tone of people's material and spiritual life is beyond any doubt. As for the process of interactions between Chinese and foreign cultures, Mote (ibid., p. 7) insists that other fundamentally different cosmogonies presenting the idea of a creation and a creator external to the created world, when encountered by the Chinese, made no significant impression on the

Chinese mind. Their own indigenous conception of the world, shared subsequently by all Chinese schools of thought on the level of the Great Tradition, and having pervasive influence throughout the entire society, has been developed throughout the continuous cultural history of the Chinese with no modification save its refinement and detailed articulation. Although vulgarized Buddhist notions of transmigration and karma found their niche in the popular culture, the Chinese worldview that kept people's attention on life here and now nevertheless remained unchallenged.

17. It is our understanding that Confucianism in the course of its development remained (and probably will still continue to be) the principal guide to Chinese civilization. It was, in Needham's (19 6, p.) words, "a doctrine of this-worldly social-mindedness." Mote (1971, p. 4) goes further to suggest that "the absolute primacy of humanistic ethics in a man-centered world may be taken as the ultimate touchstone of Confucianism." Indeed, in Chinese thought, Man was always given a preeminent position as compared to the other myriad categories of things and beings in the world. It is explicitly stated, for instance, in Xu Shen's *Shuowen jiezi* (10B.2) that Man is one of the three primary powers of the cosmos: Heaven, Earth, and Man. As Freedman (1979a, p. 191) points out, although Man "may not be as important as Heaven and Earth, he is an essential element in the trinity." It is interesting and important to note that Xu's statement was probably derived from a similar line in the *Laozi* (*Laozi zhu*, 2 , p. 14), the first complete and self-contained work of Daoism. As the chief rival philosophical school of Confucianism, Daoism offers complementary views of life to those of Confucianism and thus presents another side of the Chinese mind. Yet of many other mutually shared characteristics and views, the "worldliness" in the sense that human beings (emphasizing either their social properties in the case of the Confucians or their natural properties in the case of the Daoists) are held as fundamental to the cosmos as Heaven and Earth, is one that both schools have in common.

18. *Zuo zhuan*, *juan* 6: "Huan 6th year [706 B.C.]," p. 17 0; cf. *juan* 10: "Zhuang 32nd year [662 B.C.]," p. 1783 and *juan* 14: "Xi 19th year [641 B.C.]," p. 1810.

19. This attitude of the literati toward gods in relation to people is more vividly revealed, to varied extents and in various manners, in their leisurely records of historic events and remarks on them. Yang Xunji, for example, records an interesting story about a Ming scholar-official named Zhou Wenxiang who was fond of visiting Buddhist temples:

> Every time he arrived at the main hall of a temple, he prostrated himself in front of the Buddha [image]. When he was censured for it by others, [Zhou] Wenxiang replied with a smile, "If we consider him [Buddha] in terms of age, he is about two or three thousand years older than I am. Would not even he deserve some tribute?"
>
> (*Su tan*, p. 8.)

For those "other" people, this habit of Zhou's was absurd enough to be scoffed at. For Zhou himself, on the other hand, whether he seriously believed in Buddhism, he had to defend his habit slyly in secular terms of respect for the elders, a universal norm of morality in traditional China. In another direction, Yu Yue (1821–1907), in his *Chaxiangshi congchao*, expresses his views on the relationship between humans and the gods by quoting another scholar's remarks on the proliferation of cults derived from some of the fabled figures in Ming fiction:

> From this [the proliferation of the new cults] we know that the gods accord with the will of the people, and there is no actual need for their existence. (*Chaxiangshi congchao*, *Si chao*, *juan* 20, pp. 1807–1808.)

20. From as early as the Northern Song onward, masonry was also applied to bridges. "The prevailing styles and modes of Chinese architecture," Mote (1973, p. 63, note 18) suggests, "appear to rep-

resent choices made in consciousness of alternatives." This seems to correspond to Rapoport's (1969, p. 24) nicely phrased point as he argues against technological determinism of building form: "The determinist view neglects the *idea* of the house; just because man can do something does not mean that he will."

21. Needham 1971, p. 65. We may recall that, when the king of Yue, Goujian, spent his three-year hostageship in Helü Dacheng, he was said to have hostilely been accommodated with his wife and his chief minister, Fan Li, in a stone house (*shishi*) rather than in an appropriate timber abode. See Chapter 1 of this book.
22. None of the modulars of variable absolute size were ever out of scale with human beings; by this working norm, right proportion was safeguarded and relational harmony preserved, whatever the magnitude of the structures. Compared with Le Corbusier's "modular," Needham (1971, p. 67) believes that the harmonious assembly of units each fixed to the human scale is even more deeply Chinese, because it was universally, not occasionally, practiced in Chinese civilization, and thus was a working norm rather than an aesthetic theory. It produced "the sober humanism of the Chinese style." The module was of relative dimensions having a certain range of actual measurements so as to be applied to buildings of different sizes and importance. In Song times, for instance, it was classified into eight grades; in the Qing, eleven grades. For the Song and Qing systems, cf., for example, Glahn 1981, pp. 169–170; 1982, pp. 27–32; 1984; *Zhongguo jianzhu shi* 1982, pp. 170, 190; *Zhongguo gujianzhu xiushan jishu* 1983, pp. 15–16; *Zhongguo dabaike quanshu* 1988, pp. 30, 117–120; Ma 1997, pp. 8–15.
23. The character *jian* is currently composed of two elements: one is for the "door" (*men*), the other for "the sun" (*ri*), which was placed inside the former. In earlier times, however, the element inside was *yue*, "the moon," instead of *ri*. According to Duan Yucai, its connotations, including that of "bay," were probably derived from its original, basic denotation of "crevice" (*Shuowen jiezi zhu*, *pian* 12A.12). Xu Kai (920–974) once interpreted the character *jian* in a semantic sense: "When the door is closed at night and the moonlight is seen [from inside], it is certain that there is a crevice [between the door and the wall]"; see *Shuowen jiezi*, 12A.5. One may be tempted to suggest in the light of Xu Kai's interpretation that the concepts of the relationship between Heaven and Earth, between Nature and Man, between time and space, and between the outside and the inside, were all embedded in *jian* as the basic spatial unit of Chinese buildings. Cf. Xu 1989, p. 71.
24. This statement leaves aside the pagoda derived from the ancient Indian *stupa*, the technical principles of which were, as Needham (1971, pp. 140–141) puts it, "really only the extension of the techniques of all building to a particular specialized field." For the evolution of the pagoda, see Seckel 1964, pp. 103–132; 1980.
25. As Liu Zhiping (1987, p. 37) has indicated, discernible distinction among some of those types of buildings in their form and function, such as *xuan*, *xie*, *zhai*, and *guan*, gradually became blurred in the late imperial period.
26. When Rapoport insists in his *House Form and Culture* (1969, pp. 8–9)—an "original work," as Knapp (1989, p. xi) calls it, of interpretation of the ways in which people around the world organize and use space—that in "primitive" and peasant societies, "there is no separation among man's life, work, and religion, and very little differentiation, if any, between the sacred and the profane," one should find no difficulty in sharing his point of view. But when he extends from this to state that, in contrast to the high specialization in most fields of modern societies, "lack of differentiation in the forms and construction of buildings is an expression of the general lack of differentiation typical of primitive and even peasant societies" and that this characteristic of no, or limited, differentiation also applies to the way in which space is used, one is bound to question the validity of his argument. Rapoport's latter statements obviously represent an evolutionary view of "a process of differentiation that changes from primitive to vernacular and then to industrial vernacular and modern," a judgment of the modes of life of traditional societies according to the standard of classification in the context of our, or modern, societies. The fact is, however, that people

of primitive societies (in the "traditional" rather than "less civilized" sense of the word) differentiate and classify myriad things in no less complex manners than, but simply different from, ours. In the *Er ya* (*juan* 5, p. 31), a dictionary first compiled in Zhou times, for example, each of the four corners of a room is differentiated from the rest with a peculiar name, a classification that we now lack but that had meanings and values in itself for the ancients, reflecting their way of perceiving and conceiving the world and of using space. Thus, if we are to understand the life—including architecture—of a traditional people, it is imperative to interpret its various aspects in *their* terms rather than to account for its speciously mooted "incapacity" to come up with the "vantage point" of ours. It is also worth pointing out in passing that the diversity of architectural forms (and styles) of our times is not the only outcome of the "process of differentiation in building types and spaces, the building process, and the trades involved" (Rapoport 1969, p. 8); the interaction between technological progress and cultural freedom, fueled by a widening appreciation of self-expression and individualistic creativity, has also led to this unique phenomenon of modern (especially Western) societies.

27. *Dian* was denominative only of the main halls of imperial palaces and of the important halls of temples. The main halls of houses, ancestral temples, local government offices, and gardens were instead called *tang* or *ting*. See Liu 1987, pp. 33–36.
28. Liu Zhiping (1987, pp. 31–32) insists that *lou* and *ge* basically were not different from each other in form and structure, but *lou* were usually used for human accommodation, whereas *ge* were often for storage. Apart from the cases, such as small houses in particular, in which choice was limited by unfavorable conditions, the structures over one story were invariably placed in unimportant positions and often away from the main axis of the compound.
29. Notable cases included such structures as the drum and bell towers in many cities, the towers at the corners and gates of the city wall, and watchtowers in some towns and large villages. Although free-standing pavilions and pagodas were often found in the countryside or scenic spots, they certainly did not constitute by themselves any social institutions, nor did the small, shabby individual buildings scattered in the rural areas, serving as the shrines of certain local deities.
30. An individual building of a certain type in the compound of one particular social institution often varied significantly in spatial function, this variation being closely associated with the pattern of its distinctive daily use, from a building of the same type in the compound of another social institution. As has been mentioned earlier, the internal spatial arrangement of a "hall" in a Buddhist temple was markedly different from that in a domestic building complex. But their architectural form and structure remained the same.
31. Although no official text is found in the pre-Tang era on the codes of regulating the hierarchical standard of buildings according to the residents' social rank, one is probably not wrong in assuming the existence of this kind of stipulations in the early imperial period. From the Tang onward, however, sumptuary laws are recorded to regulate not only by the number of pillar intervals, the sizes of the buildings in which commoners, nobles, and officials of different ranks were entitled to dwell, but also the modes of their ornamentation and materials for decoration. Roofs constituted one of the most salient elements of Chinese buildings. In fact, such great emphasis was placed on the roof that a range of form types were developed to signify the importance of an individual building. For an illustration of various types of roofs, see Liu 1980, pp. 15–16, figures 8-1, 8-2; for a brief description of a number of form types of the roof, see Liu 1987, pp. 105–108.
32. One should certainly not ignore the regional differences in building forms. Indeed several fairly unique types of domestic buildings can be found, such as the cave dwellings excavated in the loess hillsides in northwest China and the fortified three- or four-story clan community houses of the Hakka (Kejia) people in Fujian, built on the basis of either rectangular or circular plans, with their inward-facing individual family "apartments" looking down on a central communal courtyard. But the majority of Chinese domestic buildings undoubtedly shared the same planning, structure, and construction principles and thus retained similar forms, although they usually evinced character-

istic regional styles reflected in details such as the curvature of the roof or the materials applied to the facing of the building wall. Hence even if we were to extend the statement to refer to the entire Chinese cultural sphere, the argument would still largely hold. It is also interesting to note that the higher the social rank of an institution, the less distinctive was the regional style shown in the buildings of the compound that housed that institution.

33. The pagoda was indeed a unique type of structure that could have come to be one of the prime elements signaling a Buddhist temple. However, many a Buddhist temple did not actually have a pagoda; moreover, as has been stated earlier, such a structure in the late imperial period was often built free-standing in the countryside, probably for geomantic purposes, and thus had nothing to do with Buddhism in terms of its peculiar social and religious functions.
34. A good example was the prefectural or county school-temple, which was often marked by the placement of the honorific gateways (*lingxingmen*) in its main courtyard near the entrance, the possible employment of the semicircular ponds (*panchi*), and the inward-opening colonnaded galleries flanking the courtyard, in which steles were installed to commemorate admired scholars of the past. Yet again, the principle of the spatial arrangement and the building forms of the compound were basically the same as others.
35. One should not disregard the function of the huge *paie*, that is, a wooden or metal board (loosely translated as "placard") fixed on the lintel of the front gate of a compound (except that of ordinary houses) and the front door of each of its main halls, on which the name or title of the compound or the hall was inscribed. This alone was certainly not of any help to the illiterate but would have proved very informative for the men and women who could read.
36. Even in everyday ordinary times, the toll of the temple bells, the peculiar percussion of the tapping of the "wooden fish" (*muyu*), the sound of chanting, and the smoke and smell of the burning incense would immediately suggest to any passerby that a Buddhist temple was probably not far away. By the same token, the runners, guards, executioners strolling in official costumes, the noise of summoning and dispatching servants, and placards displayed on the walls and palings would unmistakably proclaim the compound in front of one's eyes a *yamen*.
37. It should be noted that, in many cases, these *lou* were only one-story halls. Probably because they were in early times often halls of two or more stories, or because they stood on the lofty walls instead of on the level ground, the word *lou* was invariably used for them regardless of the number of their stories. All the gate towers of the city of Suzhou were called *lou*, whereas on the 17 9 scroll, of the four gates Xu Yang portrayed, only the one above Chang Gate was a two-story hall.
38. The towers on the city walls were unsurprisingly "elaborate" structures. But there is no reason to assume that they were more elaborate than the main buildings of large temples in rural areas and remote mountains; even if they were, which was not the case in reality, should the extent of elaboration be considered as a criterion for differentiating building types?
39. Although it was felt that the gates of important cities should preferably be topped with gate towers or, as the Chinese called them, *chengmenlou*, this practice was far from a mandatory one throughout history. Among the gates of the city of Suzhou before the late Yuan, probably only two had ever had such *lou*. The 1229 city map registered just one gate on which a tower is portrayed. It should be noted that, in various texts produced during the pre-Ming period, such as the *Yue jue shu*, *Wudi ji*, *Wujun Tujing xuji*, *Wujun zhi*, and *Pingjiang jishi*, this information is revealed to us not by the kind of statement as "which gates do *not* have *lou*" but by statements as "which gate *does* have a *lou*." This point is important, for, although the gates with towers built on them were admired by the imperial scholars, the towers were considered noteworthy and, *a posteriori*, may not have been regarded as an obligatory element for the former. It was from 13 3 onward, when the city walls of Suzhou were rebuilt, that its gates were all topped with *lou* (see Chapter 4). Hence even if the practice of constructing a *lou* above every city gate became normative, which we can assume only with little certainty, it only happened in the late imperial period.

40. The tower of the south gate of the ruined inner enclosure in the early Ming and the towers over the gates of the city walls in the late Ming and early Qing were successively used as, and called, drum towers. See Chapter 4.
41. Structures that had similar functions to the drum and bell towers of the cities can be found in some market towns. They were certainly much less elaborate than their urban counterparts, and, more important, they were often raised not on solid platforms but on wooden stilts. A good example of these can be found at the center of a market town Chengcun, of Chongan county in the north of Fujian. See Guan 1988, p. 8, fig. 1.
42. Mote 1977, pp. 116, 119. The emphasis in italics is mine.
43. We do not know, for example, exactly how domestic buildings and courtyards were arranged within a residential ward enclosed by walls, nor do we have sufficient knowledge about the everyday activities in Xuanmiao Guan and other temples in the Tang and earlier.
44. Liu 1980, p. 2.
45. Mote 1977, p. 117. Mote (ibid., pp. 116–117) emphasizes this point by referring to Mumford's (1938, p. 4) observations on the cities of Europe:

> The Chinese city did not possess visible "diversity of its time-structures." Time did not challenge time in the eyes of a wanderer in a city street in traditional China. In China there was no danger of the past not preserving itself; but neither did the architectural monuments remind one of the past, because architecturally the present was never strikingly new or different. No Chinese building was obviously datable in terms of period styles. No traditional Chinese city ever had a Romanesque or a Gothic past to be overlaid in a burst of classical renascence, of a Victorian nightmare to be scorned in an age of aggressive functionalism. In that sense, the Chinese city did not escape "the tyranny of a single present," but neither did it consider "a future that consists in repeating only a single beat heard in the past" to be monotonous.

It is important to note that it would be wrong to regard Chinese architecture as invariable in time. "Continuity" indicates change rather than stagnation. To the eye of a trained architect or archaeologist, a building of the Tang period would be evidently different in its form, structure, and ornamentation from a building of the Ming or Qing. For authentication of old Chinese buildings, see, for example, Qi 1981. Yet Mote's essential point holds, especially as he carefully weighs his words by adding such adverbs as "strikingly" and "obviously," because such changes came so gradually that visible diversity of time-structures could hardly have been detected by the contemporary Chinese.
46. Mumford 1961, p. 98.
47. Wright 1965. pp. 676–679.
48. Ibid., p. 677.
49. Wright believes that there are two corollaries to this architecture of planned ephemerality, namely, that the city of Chang'an contained, apart from the basic plan, very few buildings that survived from earlier times as tangible links with the past and that memories were not perpetuated in permanent structures within the city. My slight uneasiness is prompted precisely by these implications of Wright's phrase "an architecture of planned ephemerality" (and by Mote's somewhat similar but less explicit lines of reasoning). In spite of some progress made in the past two decades, we still know very little about how the Chinese architectural system was originally formed (see, for example, Qi 1983; Thorp 1983, 1986). Yet in the minds of the Chinese, trabeate timber structures for the living had long become a norm, the only choice that the Chinese were given by their deep-rooted, seemingly unchallengeable tradition. This fact is revealed by the passages in many ancient texts, such as the Great Appendix ("Xici zhuan") of the *Zhou Yi*, *Mozi*, *Huainanzi*, all talking in a similarly didactic manner about how the ancient Sage Kings initiated the construction of timber buildings for their subjects. For us, the knowledge and techniques of masonry construc-

tion possessed by the Chinese, along with those of timber construction, retrospectively present a range of options to the builders; but for the Chinese who were supposed to conform to ancient tradition, such options did not really exist. Their capability of building in stone does not mean that they *could* under ordinary conditions apply such techniques to structures for the living. Mote (1973, p. 63, note 18), in supporting his similar point, cites a temple (but actually the main hall in that temple) in Suzhou, which employed masonry to enclose large spaces under barrel vaults and thus acquired its popular name "beamless hall" (*wuliang dian*). But does not this name itself tell us that the hall was to the locals abnormal, as the name might well equate with "the hall that should have beams but does not"? Thus what the construction of Chang'an represents may not be so much "an architecture of planned ephemerality" as "an architecture of *determined* ephemerality." Such ephemerality is not, however, determined by materials and techniques but by values and ideas; this corresponds with Wright's argument referred to in note 0.

50. Wright (196 , pp. 678–679) brings to our attention not only different psychological impacts of the Chinese and the Roman histories on their distinctive approaches to city building but also some other ways in which hopes of personal glory in ages to come found expression in the building projects of the Chinese emperors.
51. Mote 1973, pp. 0– 1.
52. *Suzhoufu zhi*, *juan* 33.11-2. The bridge became important in history because the eighth-century poet Zhang Ji wrote a poem, "Fengqiao yebo" (Mooring at night at Maple Bridge), concerning it. The entry, like so many others with the notable exception of the one under the heading for the city walls, is principally of psychological and historical value rather than its objective and descriptive nature. It includes the location of the bridge, a discussion of the evolution of its name, the time of the construction of the present bridge, the time of its rebuilding and the name of the builders, and a small anthology of poems, starting with Zhang Ji's. We are not told of its building materials, its measurements, or its appearance, nor are we informed of its physical existence from Tang times up to 1770. It is the discussion of its name and the inclusion of the poems associated with it that are significant. The importance of names for the Chinese in general has been touched on in Chapters 2 and 4. As for the poems, in Mote's (1973, p. 2) words, they "all capture moments of experience or of reflection involving the bridge, but even more, involving the earlier poems inspired in some indirect way by the bridge."
53. Mote 1973, pp. 2– 3.
54. The length of an entry in a gazetteer depends on the importance of the structure to which it refers. For the least important one, often only its location is mentioned, then, as the structure's historical or social weight increased, other information might be added, such as an account of when and by whom it was built and rebuilt, legends or historical events associated with it, and an anthology of poems and prose essays.
55. For Mote (1973, p. 3), the literary remains are to Suzhou as the forum is to Rome. Indeed, from them every educated Chinese could reconstruct a real city of Suzhou in his mind. A substantial and usable rebuilt architectonic structure was usually more desired, especially one that was brought back to "the appearance in old times," than an antique wreck, a preference evidenced in numerous memoirs of reconstruction works. Mote may also be right by assuming that even the ordinary man in the street must likewise have lived with an awareness of much of that ideally real city as well as with the physical remnants of the city's long history.
56. Here emphasis is put on the term *monument* in its original sense of "memorial" or monumentum, not in its derivative sense of "a notable building or site."
57. *Wang Zian ji zhu*, *juan* 8, pp. 229–23 .
58. A two-story hall for keeping classical documents.
59. *Fusheng liuji*, *juan* 4, p. 70.
60. *WTx*, *juan* A, p. 8. It is interesting to note that Zhu Changwen wrote his work at the time when the collapse of the residential ward system was in its final stages, but the passage shows that he

did not pay any attention to the physical form of the wards or the physical form of their gates, nor did he express any uneasiness at their changes.

61. Wright 1977, p. 34.
62. This does not claim that building compounds and their courtyards formed an even spatial texture in the real city, which would be not only a simplistic but a very wrong kind of perception, especially in reference to the late imperial period. The size of the courtyard varied significantly, the range of this variation being dictated by the social importance of the compound and, more decisively, by the economic status of the institution. This was most obvious for houses. In the city of Suzhou, the wealthy and the high ranking officials' houses could comprise a series of courtyards, the largest measuring well over ten meters across, and, in many cases, spacious gardens (see Figures 6.6 through 6.9); the houses of the economically and socially less advantaged residents might contain only one or two courtyards as small as four square meters (see Figures 6.4 and 6.5); and many of the urban poor, numbering, if Skinner's (1977e, p. 537) estimate is applicable to Suzhou, between a tenth and a fifth of the entire urban population, did not actually have a courtyard of their own at all. There were also shop-residences along the streets of business areas, each occupying a deep plot with a narrow frontage, filled by two-story buildings arranged in between tiny courtyards, or "sky-wells" (*tianjing*). The front, outward-opening rooms were employed as shops, the rear parts as storage; the upper floor was reserved as the living space for the occupants and apprentices. These structures were probably developed from the Southern Song onward, when trade and commerce started to be conducted freely within the city or its outlying suburbs after the collapse of the ward system. Thereafter, they became a common feature in both cities and market towns in South China. Moreover, although a sharp separation between the neighborhoods of the well-off and city slums was not a typical city phenomenon in traditional China, the residences of the rich and the poor were not evenly intermingled either: some of the houses, or more accurately, hovels and shacks, of the latter may have squeezed themselves in the remnant spaces of the populated neighborhoods, but the majority of them were more likely to be found in the peripheral areas of the three professional nuclei and the isolated corners of the walled city.
63. See, for example, Feuchtwang 1977, p. 582. I should emphasize that this section does not aim at a comprehensive investigation of the temples in Suzhou but only deals with the manner of the use of urban open space for multiple purposes and its social implications by focusing on the specific case of the Daoist temple Xuanmiao Guan.
64. For a detailed discussion of the cults of Chenghuang during the Tang and Song periods, see Johnson 1985b.
65. See, for example, *WTx, juan* B, p. 30.
66. Wen Liding (1988, p. 57), on the basis of the information contained in the 1883 *Suzhoufu zhi* and 1933 *Wuxian zhi*, states statistically though inconclusively, that out of the approximately 450 Buddhist and Daoist temples ever built in the Suzhou area, 107 are recorded as having a history dating back to the Six Dynasties period, while 73 were probably built between A.D. 503 and 557.
67. *Wumen biaoyin, juan* 10, p. 125.
68. For a discussion of this phenomenon in the city of Ningbo, see Shiba 1977, p. 422.
69. See, for example, *Baicheng yanshui, juan* 1–3, *passim.*
70. For a discussion of the origins and later development of the cult dedicated to the goddess Tianhou, see Watson 1985, pp. 292–324.
71. A few temples of this kind in Suzhou are listed in the *Wumen biaoyin, juan* 9, pp. 122 ff.
72. Golas' (1977) work on the early Qing guilds demonstrates that, of the two universal features among the earliest guilds, religious corporation and native-place particularism, the former was more resistant to change, whereas the latter gradually evolved along economic or professional lines rather than in accordance with strong regional interests.
73. Van der Sprenkel 1977, p. 615.
74. It is a paradoxical phenomenon that numerous temple cults coexisted in a vast country that revealed

a recognizable cultural unity. James L. Watson (198 , p. 293) has acutely observed this problem, before showing, in the specific case of the promotion of Tianhou, how the state intervened in subtle ways to impose a kind of unity on regional and local-level cults:

> At first sight, it is easy to gain the impression that Chinese temple cults are a manifestation of cultural anarchy rather than integration. Literally thousands of deities were worshipped in temples of every conceivable description throughout the empire. In most parts of China religious activities were not organized by a professional clergy. Local people built their own temples, installed their own deities, and ran their own festivals. On closer examination, however, it becomes apparent that the state intervened in subtle ways to impose a kind of unity on regional and local-level cults. The mass of peasants were seldom even aware of the state's intervention. A surprisingly high degree of uniformity was attained through the promotion of deities that had been sanctioned by the Imperial Board of Rites and recognized by the emperor himself.

75. The territorial definition of these temples by no means meant a social exclusion of those who were not residents of the area or neighborhood in question. Skinner (1977e, p. 48) points out that, whereas the associations hinged on *tudi* deities were inward looking, with their annual feast limited to association members, the sectors or wards of the city centered on deity temples were outward looking, their festivals designed to attract visitors from other wards and to provide occasions for hosting kinsmen, fellows from the same native place, business associates, and friends residing elsewhere.
76. According to the "Supplement" of the *Wudi ji* (p. 13) and the *WTx* (*juan* B, p. 27), the temple was built between A.D. 713 and 741 in the Tang and was then known as Kaiyuan Guan or Kaiyuan Gong. Fan Chengda of the Southern Song, indicating only that this temple was the continuation of the Tang dynasty Kaiyuan Guan, asserts that some of the things in the temple in his time that had survived the wars could be dated back to the Six Dynasties period between the early third century and the late sixth century, implying that the date of the initial establishment of the temple was well anterior to the Tang period. Most of the later documents, especially those in the Ming and Qing, explicitly state that the temple was constructed for the first time in A.D. 276 in the Western Jin, when it was called Zhenqing Daoyuan. See, for example, *Baicheng yanshui*, *juan* 3, p. 192. The name of the temple changed, not unusually, many times in history, as dynasty succeeded dynasty and reign succeeded reign. In chronological order they are: Zhenqing Daoyuan (from A.D. 276), Kaiyuan Guan (or Kaiyuan Gong) (from 728), Yuqing Daoguan (from the 990s), Tianqing Guan (from 1009), Xuanmiao Guan (from 129), Zhengyi Conglin (from 1371), Yuanmiao Guan (from the 1640s), and Xuanmiao Guan (from the end of the Qing on).
77. Shiba 1977, p. 424. A similar view is presented by Feuchtwang (1977, *passim*), who sees the position of the City God cult as a point of transformation between the official and the popular religions.
78. See, for example, *Baicheng yanshui*, *juan* 3, pp. 192–193; *Suzhoufu zhi*, *juan* 41.16–17.
79. *Qing jia lu*, *juan* 1, p. 2 , *juan* 3, p. 84, *juan* 6, p. 141; *Wuxian zhi*, *juan* 2A.12 ff.
80. *Qing jia lu*, *juan* 1, p. 13. Less important temples involved in this specific annual event were the Buddhist North Temple (Bei Si, its formal contemporary name being Bao'en Si) at the north end of the city, and West Garden Temple (Xiyuan Si, its formal contemporary name being Jiezhuanglü Si). The tradition of this annual ceremonial activity until the Qing period seems to have been that the event was held more often in Buddhist temples than Daoist temples. Cf. *Wujun zhi*, *juan* 2, pp. 13–1 ; *Qing jia lu*, *juan* 1, pp. 13–16. Gu Lu has specifically indicated that by his time the number of people attending the New Year ceremony held in North Temple had declined, while an open area around Wende Bridge outside Chang Gate (half-way to Feng Bridge)—an integral part of the bustling business district—was developed as an area where people gathered during the New Year period.

81. Eberhard 1962, p. 243. Markets in Xuanmiao Guan did not take place only during these festivals, although they initially occurred in the form of "temple fairs." At the early stages of the Xuanmiao Guan market, only scattered stalls were set up temporarily in the temple courtyard on festival days; but as more and more pilgrims and, in particular, tourists came to visit the temple year-round, the market gradually became permanent, as the temple let either some of its buildings as shops or pieces of land in its courtyard to various retailers to build makeshift booths, the rent being paid monthly to the temple. See "Suzhou Xuanmiao Guan zhigao," 1984, p. 171.
82. See, for example, *Qing jia lu, juan* 1, pp. 13–16. Gu Lu depicts in detail the variety shows performed in the temple during the New Year period as those coming from distant Fengyang (in present-day Anhui province), Jiangyin (in present-day North Jiangsu province), and Jiangxi. See *Qing jia lu*, ibid. A scholar by the name of Wuai Jushi writes in one of the prefaces to the *Jingshi tongyan* compiled by Feng Menglong (1574–1646) and published in 1624: "I just listened to [the story of] the *Sanguo zhi* told in Xuanmiao Guan." This indicates that there had already been storytelling activities in the temple as early as the late Ming period.
83. *Wumen biaoyin, juan* 5, p. 63.
84. See quotation in Duan and Zhang 1986, p. 11.
85. For the details of this event, see *Suzhou zhizaoju zhi, juan* 12, pp. 105–106; *Suzhoufu zhi, juan* 94.4–5, *juan* 147.21–22; Chen Jiru's epitaph ("Wu Ge Jiangjun mubei") for Ge Cheng inscribed on Ge's tombstone in 1673, contained in *MQSgbj* 1981, pp. 383–384; Duan and Zhang 1986, pp. 181–184. For descriptions of it in Italian, see Santangelo 1992, pp. 25–27; and in English, Santangelo 1993, pp. 102–104.
86. Cf. *Wumen biaoyin, juan* 11, pp. 148–149; *MQSgbj* 1981, pp. 15–17.
87. *Wumen biaoyin, juan* 5, p. 59.
88. *Baicheng yanshui, juan* 3, p. 193. The charitable Yuying Tang ("hall of infant-rearing"), for example, was built in the temple in 1674, where infants deserted by destitute families were taken care of. See ibid., p. 194; *Wumen biaoyin, juan* 5, p. 60. In the east vicinity of the temple, there long existed a well-known pharmacy owned by the Qian family, who specialized in curing rare diseases, which was in legend associated with the deeds of some Daoist immortals. See *Wumen biaoyin*, ibid., p. 62.
89. See quotation in *Suzhoufu zhi, juan* 149.7.
90. The earliest recorded event reflecting the affinity between scholars and the temple is dated back to the 780s when the abbot Zhang Chengde became close friends with Lu Guimeng (?–ca. 881), a native of Changzhou and one of the famous writers of the Tang dynasty. See *Baicheng yanshui, juan* 3, p. 192. According to Fan Chengda, in 1249 the prefect Zheng Lin invited forty-two (including himself) imperial university students to a banquet in the Hall of "Spring Rain" (*chunyu*) after they had formally paid their respects to each other in Xuanmiao Guan in their order of reputation and seniority. See *Wujun zhi, juan* 2, pp. 17–18. Gu Zhentao recorded that there were three small temples in Xuanmiao Guan dedicated to some earlier local officials for their merit and integrity. See *Wumen biaoyin, juan* 5, p. 60. The attention paid to this temple by scholar-officials was such that it was constantly repaired or reconstructed under the supervision of local officials and occasionally with financial support from the imperial court. Cf. *Baicheng yanshui, juan* 3, pp. 192–194; *Suzhoufu zhi, juan* 41.16.
91. *Qing jia lu, juan* 1, p. 4. Cf. *Baicheng yanshui, juan* 3, p. 193.
92. See, for example, *Wucheng riji, juan* B, p. 217; *Baicheng yanshui, juan* 3, p. 193; *Xxz, juan* B.15b–16a, *juan* C.16b; *Xxx*, pp. 41–42. Yet it should be noted that their "belief" was often highly *conditional*, in the sense that it depended on the efficacy of the deities and the morality of the rituals. In other words, for scholar-officials and ordinary people, to heed religious ordinances and to participate in religious practice were plainly acts for practical reasons rather than for the salvation of their souls. If the deities were seen as efficacious, they would be rewarded; if not, punishment would often be inflicted on them. In two of the cases mentioned earlier, once rain did come after the ceremonies, the officials in question either donated part of their salaries to have the temple repaired or directed

the restoration of the statues of the deities. This practical stance seems to have been typical of officials and scholars in imperial China. Li Bai (701–762), in his eulogistic epitaph to the deeds of the prefect of Ezhou, records that at the time of a severe flood caused by prolonged, torrential rain, the prefect went to the temple of Chenghuang and warned the deity sternly: "Should the rain not stop in three days, I am obliged to cut down the tall trees [in the temple courtyard] and set your temple on fire" (see *Li Taibai quanji*, *juan* 29, p. 1361). An incident of student protest in 1711 Suzhou is another example of Chinese intellectuals' ambivalent attitude toward religion. Suspecting that the results of the first level imperial examination (*xiangshi*) were fraudulent, over a thousand students, converging on Xuanmiao Guan, carried from the temple the image of the Wulushen (worshipped by the populace as the deity of wealth; see *Qing jia lu*, *juan* 1, pp. 22–23), taking it to the prefectural school-temple and locking it up in the Minglun Tang (the hall in which human relationships are illuminated) (see *Xxz*, *juan* B.16b–17b). This punishment was inflicted on the deity probably on the assumption that the deity had "allowed" the corrupt officials in charge of the examination to gain money by fraud at the expense of many talented students' future careers. This was certainly a sarcastic act, its innuendo being against the officials in question. However, had the students really been pious believers, they would hardly have treated the deity so rudely and had it "reeducated" in secular terms. The students bothered to pay so much attention to the deity probably because many other members of society believed in it; for the students, it became a useful tool for other purposes.

93. *Suzhoufu zhi*, *juan* 147.38–39.
94. *Jiechao biji*, p. 8. Yet these panelists, according to Shen Shouzhi, the author of the *Jiechao biji*, were either corrupt officials or the profligate offspring of the rich who were not at all interested in defending the city but merely took the meetings as additional opportunities for drinking and empty talk.
95. *Wucheng riji*, *juan* A, p. 202.
96. Norberg-Schulz 1971, p. 84; 1980a, pp. 6, 9. It should be noted that city squares in medieval Europe certainly did not have to be of a geometrically square shape but were open "places" that acted as settings for churches, guildhalls, town halls, or other prominent buildings. Gerald Burke (1976, p. 18 note) offers an apt explanation for the use of this term:

> In town-planning jargon the word "place" is taken to correspond with the French *place*, German *platz*, Italian *piazza* etc., i.e. "an open space in city or town usually surrounded by buildings." The English word "square" is nearest in meaning though a "place" is not necessarily four-sided or right-angled.

A similar clarification is put forward by Jere Stuart French (1983, p. 23):

> A square can be square, hence its English name. But the various names derived from Latin (*platea;* place or widened street), are more cautious, and refer to location rather than shape: *Place* (French), *Piassa* (Italian), *Praça* (Portuguese), *Plaza* (Spanish), *Plateia* (Greek).

It should also be noted that, although the persistence of the existence of city square has been a tradition of many European cities, the social meaning and concept of the square varied significantly in time and space. A discussion of the urban space of Suzhou in the imperial era by reference to traditional European cities does not mean a sweeping generalization of this European urban phenomenon.

97. Kostof 1992, p. 1 3.
98. Mote 1977, p. 11 .
99. The Ming state-run textile factory-bureau (Zhizaoju) was located in the southwest, two alleys away

from the temple, and during the Qing period it was reconstructed and called by the locals North Bureau (Beiju) so as to distinguish it from the new one set up in 1646 in the southeastern part of the city. The location of this bureau, however, was probably largely determined by the partitioning of urban space and was thus only physically adjacent to the temple, without a strong sense of mutual incorporation of the two establishments.

100. See, for example, Mumford, 1961, p. 271.
101. See, for example, *Wumen biaoyin*, *juan* , p. 63, *juan* 9, pp. 122–123.
102. Norberg-Schulz 198 , pp. 60–61.
103. Elliot (19 , p. 26) holds that the greatest positive contribution of Buddhism to Chinese religious ideas was that of attaining Enlightenment, and thereby salvation, through the merit of the Bodhisattvas. Yet like Daoism, Chinese Buddhism has also tended to manifest two very different facets. One is the scholarly, mystical Buddhism of the reputable monks and masters. The other facet is represented by a more "corrupt" Buddhism, which has contributed greatly to popular beliefs and has, in turn, absorbed many religious practices of an unorthodox nature.
104. This practical orientation of religion was fundamentally determined by the general Chinese worldview that was mentioned earlier; but it may also have had some connection with the Chinese attitude toward reason, which is summarized by Graham (1989, p. 7): "reason is for questions of means; for your ends in life listen to aphorism, example, parable, and poetry." The lasting effect of this attitude in China was "to convince everyone except the Mohists that problem-solving without useful purpose is a pointless frivolity." Graham also indicates that in the temporal sphere, it was those inventions that generally seem to be ones not obviously *useful* that the Chinese neglected (ibid., p. 316).
105. Some of the official temples (for example, Confucian temples), schools, imperial examination complexes, and *yamen* also had large courtyards of their own, but access to them was very exclusive.
106. *Qing jia lu*, *juan* 1, p. 1 .
107. See, for example, Mote 1973, pp. 8– 9; Kostof 1992, p. 1 3; Li 1982, pp. 404–40 ; Liu 1990, p. 119.
108. Li, ibid.
109. Graham 1989, p. 317.
110. Zücker (19 9, pp. 19–20) for example, explains the emergence of the square in Europe in sociological, aesthetic, and philosophical terms:

> Only within a civilization where the anonymous human being had become a "citizen," where democracy had unfolded to some extent, could the gathering place become important enough to take on a specific shape. This sociological development was paralleled by an aesthetic phenomenon: only when a full consciousness of space evolved and at least a certain sensitive perception of spatial expansion began to spread—one may compare the essentially frontal sculpture of Egypt and Mesopotamia with the roundness of Greek classical sculpture—only then could the void before, around, and within a structure become more than a mere counterpart to articulated volume. . . .
>
> . . . To one who believes in the primacy of ideas, there seems no doubt that the growing concept of man in relation to his environment and the awareness of the human scale gave a stronger impetus to the shaping of space within the town than the merely socio-functional need for a gathering place. One may even play with the idea that both trends are not simply coincidental but go back to one last cause: the sanction of reason as the guiding principle of human life, which Greece contributed to the history of man.

All these factors must jointly have contributed to the emergence and probable conventionalization of the square in ancient Greek cities, although it seems doubtful whether we could take "the sanction of reason as the guiding principle of human life" as the ultimate cause of the development of this distinctive urban feature. It is our understanding that Confucianism, developing as a school of thought from approximately the turn of the fifth century B.C., thereafter remained the principal guide to Chinese civilization and from the Han dynasty onward became the official doctrine of the bureaucratically run society. Characterized by its rationalism, Confucianism, as Mote (1971, p. 45) argues, takes the absolute primacy of humanistic ethics in a man-centered world as its ultimate touchstone; it is "a humanism—the most unequivocal the world has known" (ibid., p. 71). Chinese civilization, however, did not generate in its cities an equivalent to the public open space in the European urban environment. Therefore one may have to take a more cautious line over this issue: it is perhaps the specific content of the "guiding principle of human life" that had really mattered.

111. Healy 1968, p. 13.
112. Ward 1985, p. 173.
113. Rawski 1985a, p. 9.
114. *Wuxian zhi*, *juan* 52A.13.
115. *Qing jia lu*, *juan* 2, p. 56. Nor is it mentioned by Zhou Zhenhe, when recording the ceremony in his *Suzhou fengsu* (part 3, pp. 34–35) published in the late 1920s.
116. *Laozi*, chapter 11, p. 6.
117. The term *space* refers here to its narrower sense of limited areas unoccupied by buildings or other physical objects rather than to its sense of the unlimited three-dimensional expanse in which all things are located. The latter is denoted by the Chinese character *yu*, as we read in the *Mozi* (*juan* 10/40, p. 194): "*Yu* encompasses all different places." The development of the denotation of *yu* is closely associated with that of the character *zhou*, both jointly epitomizing interesting Chinese time-space concepts. The equivalent of the term *cosmos* in the Chinese language is *yuzhou*; its two characters literally mean "eaves" and "ridgepole" (see *Huainanzi*, *juan* 6: "Lanming sun," p. 93, with Gao's commentaries). At the same time, as their etymologies imply, they have a strong sense of "space" and "time," respectively (see *Shuowen jiezi zhu*, *pian* 7B.7, *pian* 12B.15). This is explicitly stated in the *Huainanzi* (*juan* 11: "Qisu sun," p. 178): "Moving back to the past and forth to the present are called *zhou*; the four quarters and from above to below are called *yu*." It is equally clearly explained, though with somewhat different intent, in the text of *Zhuangzi*, *juan* 6/23: "Geng sang chu," p. 151: "That which has reality, and in which there is no fixed place to settle in, is *yu*. That which has endless continuity, and in which there is no beginning and end to search for, is *zhou*."
118. Liu et al. 1984, p. 190. Wang Li (1980, pp. 528–529) shows how the elements of the Chinese language have taken deep root in Japanese, the ideographs of Japanese being basically borrowed from ancient Chinese. "The Chinese ideographs in Japan," he writes, "have held a similar position to Greek and Latin in European countries. They can be used as the basis on which new Japanese words are constructed." *Kongjian* is one of the words in Japanese (*kukan*), derived from ancient Chinese, that have been given a different shade of meaning and borrowed back into Chinese. I use the term *re-adopted* here simply because I am as yet not clear whether this kind of loanword, of which the component characters are of Chinese origin, should strictly speaking be identified in linguistic terms as "borrowed" from Japanese.
119. Cf. *Er ya*, *juan* 5, p. 31; *Shuowen jiezi*, 9B.6. This wall is located on either the east or west side of a building, separating the east or west *xiang* (side room) from the central *tang* (main hall). Guo Pu (A.D. 276–324) explains when commenting on the *Er ya* that "as such it distinguishes [in an orderly way] the inside from the outside."
120. *Shi ming*, *juan* 5, p. 15b.
121. For comments on the ubiquity of walls in China by Western scholars, see Sirén (1929) and Meyer (1991, pp. 4–5).
122. This predilection can be sensed, for example, in *Shi jing*, Ode "Hongyan," Mao #181 [*juan* 11/1: "Xiao ya" section], pp. 431–432; Ode "Mian," Mao #237 [*juan* 16/2: "Da ya" section], pp. 509–512.

123. *Qing jia lu*, *juan* 1, pp. 1 –16.
124. The Market of Cranes was a legendary market area in the city of Suzhou at the time of the Wu state around 00 b.c. For the legend, see *Wu Yue chunqiu*, *juan* 4, p. 36.
125. The wording of this sentence was suggested by F. W. Mote through personal communication.
126. The Tang gazetteer *Wudi ji*, p. 111, tells us that the city of Suzhou had "over three hundred alleys (*xiang*)," whereas it makes no mention of any city streets or roads. Prior to the Northern Song period, the character *xiang* was, as I have indicated in Chapter 3, denominative only of the alleys within a walled residential ward. Does not this reflect the preconception of the author that any features that lacked institutional attachment were not worth mentioning, even if they were as important as the streets of the city?

Chapter 7: The City in Fengshui *Interpretations*

1. For a discussion of the inappropriateness in the application of the term *geomancy* to the Chinese case, see March 1968, p. 2 3, note 2; Bennett 1978, pp. 1–2.
2. Chatley 1917, p. 17 . This definition is also quoted by Needham 19 6, p. 3 9.
3. March 1968, p. 260. J. J. M. de Groot (1897, p. 938), for instance, holds that its elementary principles were practically applied already in Zhou times. Needham (19 6, pp. 3 9–363; 1962, p. 240) takes a more cautious stance by arguing that although it developed during the Warring States period when Zou Yan's (ca. 30 –240 b.c.) correlative cosmology and philosophic magic were flourishing, in Wang Chong's (a.d. 27–ca. 97) time the system had developed sufficiently for him to argue against it. In the *Shi ji* (*juan* 127, p. 3222), Needham reminds us, a class of diviners known as the *kanyu jia* is mentioned along with six other classes of diviner; whereas the bibliography of the *Han shu* (*juan* 30, pp. 1768, 1774) mentions two books that may be relevant to *fengshui*, namely, the fourteen-volume *Kanyu jingui* (Golden Box of *Kanyu*) and the twenty-volume *Gongzhai dixing* (Terrestrial Conformations for Palaces and Houses), but both are long since lost. Needham (19 6, p. 360) further suggests that its consolidation took place in the Three Kingdoms period (a.d. 220–280) when Guan Lu (a.d. 209–2 6) probably wrote about it. Both the *Sanguo zhi* ("Wei shu," *juan* 29, pp. 811–829) and the *Sanguo yanyi* (*hui* 69, pp. 3 ff.) mention Guan Lu in length. Wright's (1977, p. 4) statement on this subject appears more unambiguous: although various ingredients of the system can be traced back to the Zhou, "the origins of *feng-shui* are to be found in the systematic organicism that was characteristic of the Han synthesis"; and the subtradition during the late Zhou, Qin, and Han of manipulating the Five Elements system and the symbols of the *Zhou Yi*, and of the practice of surveying the ambience or emanations (*qi*) of a site or situation to determine its favorable or unfavorable character, "persisted and was fused with *feng-shui* theories in the a.d. third or fourth century."
4. Feuchtwang 1974, p. 16. March (1968, p. 260), apparently agreeing with Feuchtwang on this issue, writes: "Burial geomancy seems to have arisen later than the geomancy of city and building sites. . . . Earlier evidence is fragmentary and seems to show merely the existence of a diffuse vitalism, or some other element of thought later taken up by geomancy." It is also certain that during the periods of the Eastern Jin (a.d. 317–420) and the Southern Dynasties (420– 89), *fengshui* theory and practice were greatly promoted in Southeast China. Two important books that are still extant were produced during this period of time in the South. One is the *Zang shu* ascribed to Guo Pu (276–324), which is regarded now as containing the first known appearance of the word *fengshui* as the specific term denoting this elaborated system. The other is the *Huangdi zhaijing* attributed to Wang Wei of the Liu Song dynasty. Wright (1977, p. 4) even speculates that it was in the South and in this period of time that the system of *fengshui* became loosely appended to the imperial cosmology of the city. In any case, during later imperial periods, the leading forces of development of *fengshui* always came from the South.
5. Other terms to some degree equivalent to, or closely associated with, *fengshui* are *kanyu*, *xingfa*

(method of configuration), and *dili* (texture of the earth). Among them *kanyu* is probably the earliest. Its two characters originally denote, respectively, "the bulging part of the earth [*ditu*]" and "chariot" (*Shuowen jiezi*, 13B.8; 14A.16) but later jointly signify "Heaven and Earth." One of the earliest appearances of the combination of the two characters in this sense seems to be in the *Huainanzi* (*juan* 3: "Tianwen xun," p. 51), where it may indicate the order of Heaven and Earth. Later, Xu Shen explains explicitly that "*kan* means the *dao* of Heaven; *yu* means the *dao* of Earth," as cited by Yan Shigu when commenting on *Han shu* (*juan* 30, p. 1769), and by Li Shan when commenting on Yang Xiong's *anquan fu* in the *Wen xuan* (*juan* 7, p. 111). Zhang Yan of the Three Kingdoms period, however, defines *kanyu* as "the general name for Heaven and Earth," which is cited again by both Yan Shigu (*Han shu, juan* 87A, p. 3523) and Li Shan (ibid.). The word *kanyu* by the Han period was associated with the *xingye* (stars/planets and field) system. *Xingye* is undoubtedly a system of great antiquity, the principal idea of which is the correspondence between the spatial sections of the heavens (*fenxing*) and the spatial divisions of the earthly field (*fenye*), and between the movement of the heavenly bodies in one celestial section and the vicissitudes in the corresponding terrestrial division; and, based on such correspondence, auspicious or inauspicious signs in the world of man can be interpreted. Cf. *Huainanzi, juan* 3: "Tianwen sun," p. 50; *Shi ji, juan* 27, p. 1330; Zheng's commentary on *Zhou li, juan* 26, p. 819. Zheng mentions a long-lost book that was titled with the very term *kanyu* and contained in it an advocacy of the notion of the so-called Twelve *Ci* (the twelve sections of the heavens along the zodiac) that corresponded to the earthly states in the late Zhou period. Thus, both Fang Yizhi (1611–1671) and Yuan Mei (1716–1798) emphasize the appropriation in later times of this word in the system of *fengshui*. Cf. *Tong ya, juan* 12, pp. 456–457; *Suiyuan suibi, juan* 18, p. 321.

6. See, for example, *uanshi dili zhimeng*, 1/3.52a.
7. *Xuexin fu, juan* 1, p. 2a, with Meng's commentary.
8. See a number of exemplary works reserved in *tj, ce* 476.59b ff.
9. See, for example, *Zang jing yi*: "Nanjie ershisi pian" section, no. 21.8a.
10. It is for this reason that Bennett (1978, p. 2) insists on the use of the word *siting* as a "neutral English designation" for *fengshui*.
11. Feuchtwang 1974, p. 2.
12. This division has been noted in Western scholarship by Needham (1962, pp. 242, 282), Eitel (1979, p. 77), March (1968, p. 261), Feuchtwang (1974, pp. 17–18) and Bennett (1978, pp. 2–4), among others.
13. For details of *fengshui* theories, see Feuchtwang, ibid. Cf. Needham 1956, p. 359; March, ibid., pp. 253–267; Freedman 1971, pp. 118–154; 1979a; 1979b; Bennett, ibid.
14. The Five Planets correspond to the Five Elements and all their correlates. This correspondence is depicted in the *Shi ji* (*juan* 27, p. 1342) as associated with that between heaven and earth: "In the sky there are the Five Planets, on earth there are the Five Elements. Thus in the sky there are arrays of stars and planets, and on earth there are divided territories."
15. The term *xingshi* may, in some other contexts, also be interpreted as "topographical forms and influences" or "the power/significance of circumstances."
16. The *long*, also known as the *longmai* (dragon vein), appears to be a figurative term denoting mountain ranges characteristic of both continuous and directional display. In the *uanshi dili zhimeng* (1/10.55a), we read that "identifying mountains as dragons is to symbolize the rising and falling features in their form and influence" and that "the whole body of a dragon is taken as a metaphor of the living forms of mountains." The conception of the continuous and directional attribute of mountain ranges through which the cosmic breath circulates was probably associated with the idea presented by the passage in the *uanzi* (*juan* 14/39, p. 236) about the *qi* of the earth flowing in vessels comparable with those in the body of man and animals. Needham (1956, p. 42, note d) suggests that, if this passage is not a later interpolation, it must be one of the earliest statements of the theory underlying *fengshui*. The *xue* indicates the exact spot where a settlement or a tomb should be located, for it is here that the influences of the mountains and waters merge, the *yin* and

yang forces harmoniously converge, and the "affections" (*qing*) of Nature are concentrated and nurtured. See, for example, *Zang jing yi*, *pian* 2.16. Two extended meanings of the term *xue* are informative of its *fengshui* connotation. One is the impulse point, or *foramen*, of a human body, on which acupuncture can be practiced; the other is the point of origin and return. See *Ch* 1980, p. 1791. The *sha* denoted the setting of a site, that is, the overall layout of the hills and mountains surrounding the prospective settlement. The *shui* meant all kinds of bodies of waters—springs, streams, ponds, rivers, lakes—and was regarded by *fengshui* specialists as the blood veins of the "dragons," running through their bones (i.e., rocks or stones), flesh (i.e., earth and soil), skin (i.e., grass and straws) and hair (i.e., trees). See, for example, *Qingnang haijiao jing*, 4.43b.

17. *Qingyan conglu*, pp. 8–9. See also *Gaiyu congkao*, *juan* 34, pp. 732–733 for a similar account by Zhao Yi (1727–1814).
18. Feuchtwang 1974, p. 96.
19. March (1968, p. 261) suggests that these two principal schools emerged after Guo Pu. It should be emphasized that, in many cases of *fengshui* practice and, more often, interpretation, we find that it is difficult to draw a clear line even between the Xingshi and the Liqi applications, and specific situations were sometimes dealt with in the light of both approaches.
20. The attitude of Zhu Xi (1130–1200) toward the *fengshui* applications of his times to some extent exemplifies the conflicting relation between the two schools. Wright (1977, p.) has stated that Zhu Xi "was a particular enthusiast of *feng-shui*." However, he was seemingly enthusiastic only about the theory and practice of the Xingshi school, while he vigorously denounced those of the Liqi school. Obstinate refusal of the Liqi school is also found in the section entitled "Dishu zhengxie bian" of the *Bianlun sanshipian* written by Meng Hao, incorporated in his *Xuexin fu zhengjie* (12a–b) produced around 1680, where he branded all discourses of the Liqi school as "heresies"; its principle is useful, as Meng implies in the "Luantou tianxing Liqi bian" section of his work (10b–11a), only if it is to be seen and treated not as a set of ideas separated from that of the Xingshi but as an inferior part of the Xingshi theory.
21. March 1968, p. 263.
22. This pheonomenon is also emphasized by Bennett (1978, p. 4).
23. Cf. March, ibid.
24. Feuchtwang 1974, p. 171.
25. *Wujun zhi*, *juan* 3, pp. 24–27.
26. Note that this title reads as if Hu Shunshen followed the Jiangxi method, that is, the doctrine of the Xingshi school. Yet the terminology and theories he employs in his arguments about the city of Suzhou betray the fact that he principally espoused the doctrine of the Liqi school or a combination of the two. This is probably what the words "new method" in the title of the book mean.
27. *Gtj*, *ce* 476. 8a.
28. Hu mentions the newly constructed Gusu Guesthouse, which was built in 1144, and thus the essay must have been written in or after that year; and since in 1164 the prefect was considering Hu's ideas as presented in the essay, it must have been finished and circulated by that time. Cf. *Wujun zhi*, *juan* 3, pp. 23, 26 and *juan* 7, p. 9 .
29. According to Gu Yuanqing, a Ming scholar from Changzhou county, Mt. Yang was regarded as the primary mountain (*zhen*) of Suzhou. In relation to the position of the city, the mountain faces the *yang* direction (i.e., southeast), and that was how it gained its name. See "Preface" of the *Yangshan xinlu*, quoted in the *Suzhoufu zhi*, *juan* 7.1.
30. See Chapter 2 for an explanation of this celestial body and its cosmological meanings.
31. *Wumen zhonggao*, p. 2 .
32. See Chapter 4 for the details of this event.
33. Note that the *Wu Yue chunqiu* (*juan* 4, p. 2), *Wudi ji* (p. 1), and *WTx* (*juan* A, p. 12) record that it was the gates on the east side of the city, not the southeast one, that were said to have been closed as a gesture of hostility. Hu Shunshen obviously alters this information to illustrate his point.

34. *Wujun zhi, juan* 3, p. 24.
35. Feuchtwang 1974, p. 176.
36. Since Hu Shunshen wrote, as far as we know, nothing but an acclaimed *fengshui* discourse and the advice on the city gates of Suzhou, it seems unlikely that he was just a humble *fengshui* practitioner who had to use his spare time to carry out the survey. Although *fengshui* may not have been Hu's professional livelihood, the fact that he went to the effort of choosing a geomantically appropriate day suggests that he took the surveying of the city walls very seriously.
37. We will see later in this chapter a similar view expressed six hundred years later by Wei Guangfu (ca. 1789–1853) in his remark on the current attribution of some *fengshui* works to Liu Ji (1311–1375).
38. *Wujun zhi, juan* 3, p. 27.
39. We should note that Fan also incorporates in his *Wujun zhi* (*juan* 38, p. 543) an essay by someone else criticizing the choice of the site of the county seat of Kunshan made by "yielding to the *fengshui* situation of Mt. Ma'an," and regarding all the administrative difficulties as the consequences of this choice, since the county seat was located far too askew in the northwest part of its territory.
40. *Wumen zhonggao*, p. 25.
41. Ibid.
42. *Xiangfu tujing*, written by Li Zonge in the 1010s, but which has long been lost.
43. The city of Hangzhou (named Lin'an in the Southern Song) was designated euphemistically as a temporary capital (*xingzai*) in 1138 by the battered remnants of the Song court after the Jurchen conquest of the North China Plain. For a detailed study of Southern Song Lin'an, see Gernet 1970a.
44. The Southern Song capital is located to the southeast of the city of Suzhou. Because of the awkward topographical conditions of Hangzhou, the *de facto* Principal Gate of the imperial palace was located in the north, which was at odds with the canonical principle of imperial city planning requiring that the palace city should face south, as did the Son of Heaven. For the conception of *chaogong*, cf. Chapter 4, where I have discussed a similar phrase inscribed on Qi Gate. Quotation from *Wumen zhonggao*, p. 26.
45. *Wujun zhi, juan* 4, p. 26.
46. Ibid., pp. 26–27.
47. See quotations in *SPck, juan* 5, p. 226. It is interesting to note that the event in the mid-1250s was started by a petition from a few wealthy sojourners (*yugong*) rather than by the natives.
48. See *Wujun zhi, juan* 11, pp. 149–150.
49. Unfortunately, we are not certain whether this was one of the actual reasons for Shen's willingness to adopt Hu's proposal or an excuse made for him by Fan Chengda, who perhaps believed that Shen's judgment should not easily have been influenced by *fengshui* ideas unless some intimate social connection had been involved.
50. Freedman 1979b, p. 328.
51. Freedman (ibid., p. 330) reminds us that, from our point of view, there is no objective test of a geomancer's success in his craft: "*Feng-shui* works on a long time-scale; nobody expects quick results, although they are very pleased to have them, and everybody is prepared to put down to a geomancer's credit the happy consequences that follow many years after his labors."
52. Feuchtwang 1974, p. 171.
53. *usu zhi, juan* 8.1, p. 208.
54. See, for example, *Han long jing*, p. 1; *Kanyu manxing*, p. 59a; and *uangyou zhi, juan* A, pp. 210–212.
55. March 1968, p. 257.
56. Cf. *uangyou zhi, juan* A, pp. 210–211; *Sancai tuhui, juan* 16.57–58. Wang Shixing (1547–1598) explicitly states that "the San Wu region is the tail of the 'south dragon,' and the *qi* of the dragon terminates as it enters the sea" (see *Wuyue youcao, juan* 3, p. 65). Apart from those in the Suzhou area, the mountains around Hangzhou and Huzhou, for example, are likewise traced by the *fengshui* theorists back to Mt. Tianmu (see *Kanyu zazhu*, p. 64a, b).
57. There are two well-known mountains under this name. One is in the north of present-day

Zhejiang, which is too far away from Suzhou to be considered relevant to our discussion. The other is located in the southwest of Jiangyin county under the jurisdiction of Changzhou prefecture. Yet, about seventy kilometers away in the northwest from the city of Suzhou, it is much smaller in both height and depth than many of the mountains in the Suzhou region and thus unlikely to be the one that Zhang Zilin talks about. Moreover, according to the *Suzhoufu zhi* (*juan* 7.26), there is still another small hill named Qinwang within the territory of Suzhou prefecture. It is located thirty *li* south of the city of Kunshan, a subordinate county of Suzhou situated to the east of the prefectural city. However, from the context of Zhang's description, we know that the mountain to which Zhang refers could not possibly be this one; instead, it is possible that what he means is Mt. Qinyuhang, that is, Mt. Yang standing to the northwest of the city. But we are as yet not at all certain about this.

58. Mopan Hill is the popular name for Chamo Hill located at the northeast edge of Mt. Lengjia.
59. *Honglan yisheng, juan* 4.1a.
60. The information that we have about Wang Ao and, in particular, Zhang Zilin is not sufficient for us to say whether their attitudes toward *fengshui* vary significantly. Likewise, we could not conclude with any certainty that their possibly different educational background and definitely different social status had contributed to their different views; nor are we sure whether it is the genres of their writings—one is a gazetteer, and the other is a casual notebook—that determine the different tones of their wordings. Yet it is interesting to note that in the "Fanli" (Guide [to the Use of the Book]), Zhang claims: "Any unfounded statement is not recorded." Since his book contains not only the passage that I have just quoted but also some others on the *fengshui* of burial and on the principal urban spatial pattern (which we will see in detail later on), geomantic matters must have been regarded by him as fairly legitimate and important. In contrast, on very few occasions is anything in connection with *fengshui* mentioned in the *Gusu zhi*.
61. *Zang jing yi*, "Nanjie ershisi pian" section, 1.6a. Cf. ibid., *pian* 6.2a.
62. *Shang shu, juan* 3, p. 128.
63. *Zhou li, juan* 33, pp. 862–863. Zheng Xuan (A.D. 127–200) explains in his commentary that "*zhen* are the famous mountains that help to maintain the unique property of the land."
64. *WTx, juan* B, p. 44. This idea appeared even earlier, in one of Su Shunqin's (1009–1048) poems, quoted by Fan Chengda in his *Wujun zhi, juan* 1 , p. 207.
65. Here the term is used as a verb.
66. *WTx, juan* B, p. 41.
67. Cf. *Fangyu shenglan, juan* 2.3, 4; *Wujun zhi, juan* 1 , p. 207.
68. Quoted in *SPck, juan* , pp. 249, 2 2. Fan Chengda sees Mt. Qionglong as the most notable for its height and depth, but he does not apply the term *zhen* to it. See *Wujun zhi, juan* 1 , p. 208.
69. The term in the similar spiritual sense is used in many other contexts. We are told, for example, that the treasured golden horizontal board (*jinbaopai*) in the Daoist temple Xuanmiao Guan, bestowed by Emperor Zhenzong (reigned 998–1022) of the Northern Song, was what would forever "pacify" the place (*Wujun zhi, juan* 31, p. 4 6); that the brick pagoda of the Buddhist temple on top of Mt. Lingyan, so lofty as to be able to support the canopy of Heaven, could "pacify" the land for a long time (ibid., *juan* 32, p. 482); that the old lower millstone and well in Mamopan Alley were "pacifying" the neighborhood and thus should not be moved (*Wumen biaoyin, juan* 7, p. 86); and that the temple dedicated to the aquatic deities near Qilin Alley was built in the early Ming to "pacify" the evil dragons (ibid., *juan* 10, p. 139). In these contexts, *zhen* is somewhat equivalent to the term *ya* (to subdue [the evil forces]), as we read in the *Wudi ji* (p. 20): "Pan Gate, . . . on it being carved wooden coiling dragons, pacified [*zhen*] this place and subdued [*ya*] Yue."
70. Freedman 1979b. p. 319.
71. *Pingjiang jishi*, p. 7.
72. Freedman, ibid.
73. Feuchtwang 1974, p. 171.

74. The other three spiritual animals are the Lin (imaginary deerlike animal with one horn and scales on its body), Feng (phoenix), and Long (dragon). See *Li ji*, *juan* 22, p. 1425. These four animals are occasionally also called the Four Auspicious Animals (Sirui). See, for example, *Wujun zhi*, *juan* 44, p. 591. Note that Suzhou folklore has it that there are four auspicious things in the region, one of them being the White Tortoise (ibid., p. 590).
75. Suzhou is not the sole case in which the symbol of the tortoise was favorably applied to a settlement or a tomb. The building of the city walls of Chengdu, the provincial capital of present-day Sichuan, is another example involving the tortoise. Legend has it, as the *Sou shen ji* (*juan* 13.2) claims, that Zhang Yi (?–310 B.C.), the prime minister of the state of Qin, was commissioned to build the city walls in 311 B.C.:

> The walls collapsed repeatedly. Suddenly, a huge tortoise emerged from the river and crawled to the southeast corner of the walls of the inner enclosure before it died. [Zhang] Yi consulted a wizard [*wu*] on this. The wizard suggested building the walls along [the tracks left by] the tortoise. The walls were then constructed successfully. Thus [the city] is called Guihua Cheng [the city evolved from a tortoise].
>
> (Cf. *Yuanhe junxian tuzhi*, *juan* 31, p. 768.)

Even now, the city of Chengdu is still known as "the City of Tortoise" (Guicheng). Yet another example can be cited from the *Wumen biaoyin* (*juan* 10, pp. 128–129) published in 1834. The terrain of a Ding family's tombs at Shedu in Changzhou county was seen as being in the form of a tortoise. It was allegedly given as a favor by a friend who was a specialist in *fengshui*, and, eventually, a successful imperial official was produced in the family.
76. *Wuzhong guyu*, pp. 1a–b. It is interesting to note that although this embroidered version of the event is cited in both the *Suzhoufu zhi* (*juan* 146.12) and *Wuxian zhi* (*juan* 78.14), it remains part of the sections entitled "Zaji," that is, "Miscellaneous Notes," rather than being incorporated into the "orthodox" history of Suzhou.
77. From the *Ming shi* (*juan* 125, p. 3725) and *Huangchao ping-Wu lu* (B, p. 144), we know that the Ming armies were stationed at eleven positions around the city.
78. *Wuzhong guyu*, pp. 2a–b.
79. In the *Ming shi* (*juan* 125, pp. 3725–3726), we read:

> As the city was about to be captured, [Xu] Da made a request of [Chang] Yuchun: "Once the troops enter [the city], I will camp on the left [i.e., east] side [of the city], and your Excellency will camp at the right [i.e., west] side [of the city]." He then issued an order to all the army officers and soldiers: "Whoever plunders the civilians will be executed; whoever damages their buildings will be executed; and whoever finds himself twenty *li* away from the camp will be executed." Thus after the armies entered [the city], the people of Suzhou lived in peace and security as before.
>
> At that time, among famous generals, [Xu] Da and [Chang] Yuchun were definitely held in esteem. . . . Yuchun was agile and brave [in battles], daring to penetrate deep [into enemy lines]; while Da was especially proficient in strategy. Yuchun would not capture a city without slaughtering; Da never inflicted any disturbance on [the places] where he had reached.

See also the similar account of the event in the *Huangchao ping-Wu lu* (C, p. 148) and the remarks by Mote 1962, p. 138.
80. *Huangchao ping-Wu lu*, C, p. 148; *Ming shi*, *juan* 125, pp. 3726, 3730, 3735, 3736.

81. Since Yang Xunji was a highly acclaimed local scholar of the Ming, who had produced many valuable works on Suzhou's history, customs, and the like, it is most unlikely that he could have mistaken Xu Da (with all his titles) for any other individual.
82. In the eleventh month of 1370, Xu Da was appointed to an additional honorary position, that of Grand Mentor, but it is not a title of honor.
83. Mote (1962, p. 140) indicates that they concealed Zhang Shicheng's two little sons to prevent their capture by Ming agents and secretly made sacrifices to Zhang's memory. There are also stories revealing the lingering feelings of the people of Suzhou. We are told that years after Suzhou was captured, the people there still mentioned Zhang Shicheng by the name "King Zhang" and were grateful to him, even for his eventual surrender to the Ming army to spare the residents further suffering. Cf. *Shuyuan zaji, juan* 3, p. 33; *Ye ji*, p. 518. We are also told how much Zhu Yuanzhang, then supposed to be hailed as the "Son of Heaven," was astonished and angered by an old woman calling him under her breath "old chap" (*laotour*) on the street of Nanjing, compared to the people of Suzhou referring to Zhang Shicheng, a defeated and executed "bandit" in the emperor's eyes, as "King Zhang" (see *Jiansheng yewen*, p. 57).
84. See *Xxz, juan* C.1a–b. The best known, and probably the extreme case, of the casualties of the aftermath of the Ming conquest were Gao Qi and Wang Yi. See Chapter 5 and Mote 1962, pp. 234–243. The imposition of punitive tax on the Suzhou region is recorded in the *Ye ji* (p. 517):

> Taizu [i.e., Zhu Yuanzhang] was exasperated at the city of Suzhou's not having submitted for a long time, and resentful of the people who adhered to the bandit [i.e., Zhang Shicheng]. In addition, they were in bond with the wealthy and thus resisted for them to the end. For these reasons, he ordered the seizure of all the rent registers of the powerful families by the relevant government agencies and had the [new] fixed tax made equal to the amount [calculated on the basis of these rent registers]. Consequently, the taxes levied on Suzhou were especially heavy, probably in order to punish the maladies of one time, and in later times they would be relaxed.

Yet the exceptionally heavy tax quotas persisted down to the late nineteenth century. See Chapter 1; cf. Marmé 1993, p. 27.

85. Mote 1962, p. 108.
86. Marmé (1993, p. 32) suggests that even "the results of early Ming policies were not necessarily detrimental to the interests of Suzhou as a collectivity."

> However unwelcome to the individual involved, the exile of elite and artisan families—a practice which affected natives of Suzhou more often than it had those of most other places—had the unintended effect of creating an unusually dense and well-developed network of particularistic contacts in every corner of the empire. Such networks played a critical role, particularly in trade, throughout the late imperial period.

87. Still another fictitious account of the event is found in *Pengchuang leiji, juan* 1.1a–b. It does not put the two personalities into one figure but makes a switch of them as if Xu Da, not Chang Yuchun, entered the city through Chang Gate.
88. Freedman 1979b, p. 319.
89. The street was in the position of present-day Renmin Road, dividing the urban territories of Wu and Changzhou counties during the imperial period. This street had most probably not acquired a name consisting of the character denoting "dragon" by Lu Xiong's time in the second half of the fourteenth century, when it was simply called "the Great Street" (Dajie) (see *SPck, juan* 1, p. 11).

But by the early Qing, it may have started to be known by the name Wolong (reclining dragon) Street, which was later changed to Hulong Street after one of the Qing emperors' Southern Inspection Tours.

90. The North Temple Pagoda (Beisi Ta), located at the north end of Hulong Street and seventy-six meters tall, was the highest building in premodern Suzhou and in South China, second only to the "Porcelain Pagoda" of Nanjing, the latter being destroyed during the Taiping Rebellion in the mid-nineteenth century. The temple to which it is attached is formally known as Baoen Si, founded early in the third century A.D. For a brief chronological account in English of the history of its reconstruction, see Mote 1973, p. 0.
91. The Twin Pagodas are located about one hundred meters east of Hulong Street. The temple to which they are attached was first built in 861.
92. *Honglan yisheng, juan* 4.7a.
93. Although we cannot entirely exclude the possibility that the name of the street, seen as symbolizing the dragon's body, was given based on this *fengshui* idea, I prefer to suggest that the street had been named prior to the writing of the *fengshui* interpretation. I have explained that the street may have acquired a name involving "dragon" in the early Qing, especially in the second half of the seventeenth century. It seems very likely, on the other hand, that this *fengshui* interpretation was made not earlier than the Qianlong reign-period (1736–179) or even the Jiaqing reign-period (1796–1820), because, given the fact that this interpretation is a retrospective one in nature, the visible "effects" of this set of favorable geomantic conditions on the local community—notably the success of the locals in the imperial examinations—refer only to these two periods, as we will see later in the passage cited from Shen Shouzhi's work.
94. Feuchtwang 1974, p. 242.
95. *WTx, juan* A, p. 12; *Wujun zhi, juan* 4, p. 28.
96. Qian Yuanliao was the sixth son of Qian Liu (8 2–932), the founder of the Wu-Yue Kingdom (907–978) based on Hangzhou.
97. *Gusu zhi, juan* 24.1. A similar passage appears, in a slightly different wording and again as an interlinear note, in Xu Song and Zhang Dachun's *Baicheng yanshui* (*juan* 1, p. 7) published in 1690.
98. Not only is there little evidence of it found in the Song documents, but the story reads differently in diverse versions in the Ming. Qian Gu (1 08–?), for example, presents in his *Wudu wencui xuji* (*juan* 4.14, commentary on Wang Ruyu's *Suxue ba yong*) a somewhat different and seemingly even more embroidered story:

    > His Honor Wenzheng [i.e., Fan Zhongyan] had a garden house in the south of the city. A geomancer suggested that [the place] would frequently produce highly respected officials. His Honor said: "Rather than having it remain in [the possession of] one private family, it would be better if it were to be shared publicly by a whole prefecture." Then he charitably gave up the house and set up the present school.

    Gu Zhentao (17 0–?) in his *Wumen biaoyin* (*juan* 6, p. 74) talks about yet another version of the story:

    > Wenzheng originally opened up [part of] the land of the South Garden and built his own house. On second thought, he said, "Rather than having it for one private family, it would be better to have it shared publicly with the whole prefecture." Then he . . . converted it to an alms-house (*yizhai*).

    Here the prefectural school is not even mentioned.
99. *Jiechao biji*, p. .

100. A considerable number of cities, as is the case with Suzhou, boast their alleged foundation as state capitals or other kinds of settlements in the Zhou period, and it is very possible that these cities were established on a cosmic scheme of one kind or another. The systems of cosmological symbolism employed in these cities manifest distinctive local beliefs and conventions as well as the extent to which the local traditional cultures interacted with that of the Zhou; but, as I have stated earlier, these systems could not be labeled with the name of *fengshui,* which was developed centuries later, even though *fengshui* advocates might have found these early examples of city construction illuminating and appealing, with their authority from the past. Other regional or local cities, of which probably very few were constructed from scratch, were usually established—notably by means of constructing walls and with some degree of planning—at the sites of the settlements of natural growth. To gather and analyze information about whether many of these existing settlements were initially built on *fengshui* or any other cosmic schemes is of course a painstaking task, and neither the limited space nor time allow me to take this up in the present study. If their early constructions did follow the *fengshui* principles, I wonder whether the original *fengshui* or other cosmological schemes in these settlements, on which the later plannings were superimposed, would still convey the same meanings to their residents of these newly established cities; if so, how much were these meanings inherited; and if not, whether they simply went into oblivion or were transformed into some new implications pertinent to the cities. At this stage of the research, I have to leave these questions unanswered.
101. If Freedman's (1971, p. 125) assertion that *fengshui* was not for the poor and humble proves to have been the case, any sweeping generalization about the influence over the construction of tombs and houses has to be carefully avoided.
102. For an emphasis on this point, see Ruitenbeek 1993, pp. 38, 58–61; Clunas 1996, p. 183.
103. Even those who wrote passages of this kind often emphasized their uncertainty by putting at the beginning of them terms like "it is said that" or "some people thought that."
104. Wright 1977, p. 55. Since Wright's argument concentrates on the imperial capitals, I regard the terms "city planning" here as not including that of other types of cities.
105. Freedman (1979b, p. 316) holds that the practitioners of *fengshui* were in one sense a part of the elite. Elsewhere, he is more cautious:

> The sources are too vague for us to say exactly how the ranks of the geomancers were filled, but we may well suspect that the typical geomancer was either a failure of the imperial examination system (as was often the doctor, the schoolmaster, and the scribe) or the product of a literate family not yet ripe for the standing of the elite.
>
> (Ibid., p. 324.)

In brief, the geomancer's social status was of an intermediate kind (ibid., p. 435, note 9). He was "a kind of literatus"; at least he was "literate" (ibid., p. 329). But a literate man was not necessarily a part of the elite. In his study of communication, class, and consciousness in late imperial China, Johnson (1985a, p. 37) has made it clear that the appropriate figure for thinking about the literate realm is not a network but a hierarchy, and the most meaningful subdivisions of this realm were related to class. It was principally the gentry group, consisting of active and retired officials at the upper level, those qualified to hold office in the middle—civil and military *jinshi* and *juren*, *gongsheng* by examination and purchase (in the late imperial period), and holders of *shengyuan* and *jiansheng* in the lower reaches—that I refer to as the elite. It was also these members who were able to make, or assist in making, effective decisions on city construction works. A number of *fengshui* theorists and advocates, such as Guo Pu and Liu Ji, were undoubtedly members of the educated elite. Yet the majority of its practitioners probably were, because of their limited education, merely "moderately literate," to borrow Johnson's (1985a, p. 38) words, in the sense that, although they could write, they might not be capable of using writing to order and record their thoughts in highly subtle and allusive ways.

106. Johnson (198 a, *passim*) has made it clear that social structure during the Ming and Qing periods was extremely complex and that we ought to pay attention to the factors relating to both position in the systems of communication and position in the structure of dominance if we are to determine whether an individual's consciousness could be taken as representing a certain group's collective mentalities. Studies on people's attitudes towards *fengshui* are no exception.
107. Wright (1977, p.) mentions skeptics among the Song Neo-Confucians, notably Zhang Zai (1020–1268) and Sima Guang (1019–1086). In fact, objection to *fengshui* did not only come from the Neo-Confucians. To mention a few more scholars in the history of imperial China, Wang Chong of the Eastern Han rigorously argued against it in his *Lun heng*, and Zhang Juzheng (1 2 –1 82) of the Ming dynasty and Xiong Bolong of the early Qing dynasty scathingly criticized its doctrines. See Zhang 1994, pp. 39–43 for a brief summary of those opinions against *fengshui*.
108. See Needham's discussion of the Chinese skeptical tradition (19 6, pp. 36 –39).
109. For those who did accept it, many preferred to dissociate themselves from it by including cautious wordings in their writings, such as the Ming scholars Wang Qi and Wang Siyi. In their *Sancai tuhui* (*juan* 16.60) compiled in 1609, their fervent adoption of *fengshui* ideas on many occasions betrays the fact that they take its expositions as being acceptable. Yet after talking about the overall geographical conditions of China entirely in *fengshui* terms, they emphasize that "*kanyu jia*'s words certainly must not utterly be stuck to, but . . . neither should their books be cast away all together. . . . Although the filial sons and benevolent men did not entirely follow . . . vulgar [*fengshui*] ideas, its general principles were kept clear in their mind. [For this reason,] the analysis in *fengshui* terms is retained for the moment."
110. *Su tan*, p. 8.
111. *Suzhoufu zhi*, *juan* 89.31.
112. *Wenjian chanyou lu*, pp. 1–2.
113. Ibid., p. 2.
114. *Tianfu guangji*, *juan* 21, p. 277.
115. Freedman 1979a, p. 191.
116. Freedman 1979b, p. 316.
117. Rawski 198 b, p. 402.
118. Although I do not yet have any information of this kind, the assumption should not be too wrong. To gather and analyze such information would take us an important step forward toward a better understanding of the possible different attitudes of a given scholar-official toward *fengshui* in different social contexts.
119. According to Shen Defu, at the beginning of the Wanli-reign period in the 1 70s, the site of the imperial tomb was decided at Dayu Hill. Opposition on account of *fengshui* to this decision emerged so seriously that the Wanli emperor "was deluded with it." An official in charge of this matter had to "read the *Xuexin fu* overnight so as to be prepared to argue with the oppositions" in the following day. See *Wanli yehuo bian*, *juan* 20, p. 1 . This official was obviously not familiar with *fengshui* theories and its language, but he had the ability to learn it very quickly.
120. Clunas 1996, pp. 180, 181.
121. Spence (1990, p. 12), in discussing the Qing penal system, cites an extreme case, originally given in *Law in Imperial China* (Cambridge: Harvard University Press, 1967, p. 390) edited by Derk Bodde and Clarence Morris, in which a father killed his son by burying him alive:

> The Ministry of Punishments carefully reviewed the facts and concluded that the governor had acted wrongly in sentencing the father to be beaten for the crime. Fathers who killed sons should be beaten only if they had acted "unreasonably," argued the ministry. In this case, the son had used foul language at his father, an act

that deserved the death penalty: "Thus, although the killing was done intentionally, it was the killing of a son who had committed a capital crime by reviling his father." The father was acquitted.

122. Elvin 1973, p. 22.
123. Needham 1971, pp. 71–72; Mote 1977, p. 102. See also Chapter 3 of this book.
124. Johnson 1985a, pp. 47–48.
125. Clunas 1996, p. 183.
126. Freedman (1979b, p. 324) admits that, from the point of view of the elite, a practitioner of *feng-shui* was tainted by his attachment to the popular and the "extra-bureaucratic," in contrast with the local government, which was the unquestionable "intra-bureaucratic."
127. Lamley 1977, pp. 208, 706 note 125.
128. *Zhejiang tongzhi*, *juan* 24.23; *Xxz*, *juan* A.2b. A passage from the prefectural gazetteer of Huzhou is quoted in *Zhejiang tongzhi*, *juan* 23.16, stating that Guo Pu once intended to move the prefectural office eastward, and it was his daughter who, expert in *fengshui* as well, proposed successfully that he should not do so.
129. *Wujun zhi*, *juan* 38, p. 543.
130. One should also not neglect the possibility that, since the majority of the local scholar-officials were likely to have been conversant both with the *fengshui* theories and with its technical terminology, it may, at the unconscious level, have affected to various extents the process of urban constructions. A realization of this possibility, however, does not rebut my central argument that *fengshui* exerted its influence less strongly on the building of cities as a government enterprise than on the building of tombs, houses, villages, and the like.
131. Freedman 1979b, pp. 318–319.
132. Wright 1977, p. 55.
133. Meyer 1991, p. 41.
134. Feuchtwang 1974, p. 174.
135. Freedman (1974, p. 39) has tackled a similar issue with somewhat different intent:

> At first sight, the baroque elaboration of popular feng-shui may seem to contrast sharply with the austere religious imagination of the elite; but on closer inspection it becomes evident that both sets of beliefs are products of the same assumptions and manipulate versions of the same concepts.

136. It is worth noting that, although the city during the imperial period was time and again interpreted in *fengshui* terms, no evidence of elaboration of this kind is found in explicit relation to the recorded cosmological symbolism in the initial construction of the Wu capital in the late sixth century B.C. It is hard to tell whether the reason for the absence of such a connection is that the *fengshui* specialists of later periods may have had considerable doubts as to this particular symbolism portending good fortunes, for the state of Wu was destroyed by Yue within half of a century after the construction of its capital, or that, since this symbolism emphasized the cosmic centrality of the city and expressed the ambition of the king of Wu to seek hegemony over the whole of China, no one dared to associate his *fengshui* ideas with it.
137. Freedman 1979a, p. 191.
138. *Wumen biaoyin*, *juan* 12, p. 161.
139. The name of the hill, literally meaning "precipitous," was gained from its particular configuration. For the same reason, it was also known as Lion Hill (Shizi Shan).
140. *Suzhoufu zhi*, *juan* 148.25.
141. This statement seems to suggest that this enterprise was profitable, probably as a consequence of charging of tolls.
142. Ibid., *juan* 148.25–26.

143. Ironically, Xu Changshi's exposition does not appear to have a particularly strong basis in *feng-shui* theories and is certainly sharply different from the one concerning the form of Zuoe Hill cited earlier.

144. Ibid., *juan* 33.14.

145. What Xu Shilin refers to here as the "plate-girder bridge," having temporarily existed in the Ming, could have been the same one that was allegedly built in the period 1 22–1 66.

146. Ibid. It is worth noting that, although both this record and the one made in the Kangxi reign-period are contained in the local gazetteers, the former is arranged in one of the last sections entitled "Miscellaneous Notes" and may therefore not have been regarded by the compilers as a piece of reliable information; the latter, by contrast, is contained in the interlinear note in the entry "Wannian Bridge" in the section entitled "Bridges," which is one of the sections dealing with official history.

147. *Zang shu*, *neipian*, p. .

148. Freedman 1979b, pp. 322, 329.

149. Freedman (ibid., p. 319) holds that "between coordinate units—between houses in one village, between villages, between towns, and so on—there may be rivalry issuing in geomantic quarrels, one side accusing the other of harming its *feng-shui* and taking countermeasures, . . . But geomancy may also be involved in the relations between entities at different levels of the hierarchy, such that a capital city may harm one of the nearby villages in its jurisdiction." In principle, I agree with Freedman. Where cities are concerned, however, we may have to be more cautious about it. This point is best illustrated in the Quanzhou case cited by Freedman himself, which has also been relished by so many anthropologists before and after him: the prefectural city of Quanzhou, like a carp in shape, was said to have erected two pagodas to foil its netlike neighboring city. See de Groot 1897, p. 977. To be sure, the story is a later invented myth, not a historical fact. The two pagodas were first built in 86 and 916, respectively, prior to the initial construction of the city walls in the 940s or 9 0s; and it was probably not until the Yuan period (1279–1368) that the city, after centuries of expansion, assumed the form of a carp. But my point centers on the hierarchical relationship between the city of Quanzhou and its neighboring city referred to in the story, the capital city of Yongchun county, a county under the jurisdiction of Quanzhou prefecture. In other words, Yongchun was a city administratively subordinate to Quanzhou. Since the geomantic fate of the territory, a given administrative unit, was for the Chinese held to derive from the site and form of its capital, Yongchun's fortune was determined by the *fengshui* situation of its county city, whereas Quanzhou's fortune, including of course that of Yongchun, was determined by the *fengshui* situation of its prefectural city. Thus in theory at least, interpretations of taking measures to counter any harmful influences from neighboring cities could only occur down the hierarchical levels, not the other way around.

150. There is some written evidence of this in the Suzhou area. Let me cite one example. Xu Qi (ca. 1828–?), a Changzhou scholar in the late Qing, records in the early 1880s that his grandfather's grandfather paid a high price for a piece of land to the south of the market town of Fuli (that is, the town of Luzhi, 2 kilometers to the southeast of the city of Suzhou) and intended to build on it a family mourning hall (*bingshe*). However, this attempt did not succeed in the face of opposition from the neighboring village, the inhabitants of which were "deluded with *fengshui* teachings." See *Shanhushe diaotan zhaichao*, p. 7.

151. At that time, Yan Song was a Great Mentor in the Ming court, notorious for his manipulation of state affairs and embezzlement of army provisions.

152. Fenyi, the native place of Yan Song, is located in the west of Jiangxi.

153. *Xxz*, *juan* B.12a–b.

154. *Wumen biaoyin*, *juan* 7, p. 8 . Gu Zhentao does not imply a denial of the story that Yan Song moved the bridge away to Jiangxi. He also indicates that the memorial gateway built in front of the bridge (see Figure 7.4), *qiaofang*, as he calls it, was the first of this kind in the Suzhou area.

But the most interesting difference between the accounts by these two scholars is that, whereas Gu Gongxie only criticizes the government officials with being deluded with *fengshui*, Gu Zhentao explicitly blames both the officials and the commoners on that same ground. This difference, by reference to the other parts of their books, seems to suggest varied levels at which the two scholars regarded *fengshui* as justifiable. It is possible that for the former *fengshui* may have been part of the "popular superstitions," and thus (perhaps condescendingly) there was held to be no need to criticize the common people for their belief. For the latter, it was the social contexts, not any categorization of people, that determined whether *fengshui* practice should be denounced—I have noted earlier that Gu Zhentao records approvingly a case of the *fengshui* of burial but scorns geomantic concerns in the building of the honorific gateways. Yet one thing is certain: both scholars share the view that *fengshui* should be condemned if it interferes with government enterprises or any other projects that are supposed to function in the interest of the public.

155. From the mid-nineteenth century onward, there were signs of active participation of the local gentry and professional associations in the management of the city affairs, but the local government's role in urban construction works remained predominant.
156. Note that Hu Shunshen used this phrase in his assessment of the *fengshui* situation of the city of Suzhou.
157. *Chongjun Suzhou chenghe ji*, p. 306.
158. The fact is that in this passage, Fei Chun did not use any specific *fengshui* terminology.
159. It should be noted that the majority of the records of this kind are contained in the documents produced in the Ming and Qing periods, which suggests proliferation of *fengshui* practice in the city in the late imperial era. This may have something to do with the medieval urban revolution that freed private urban building activities from previously strict government control.
160. Freedman 1979b, pp. 318–319.

Conclusion

1. Wright 1965.
2. See, for example, Eliade 1959, pp. 30–31.
3. Ibid., p. 165.

Glossary

Anchashi Sishu 按察史司署
Anhui 安徽
bagua 八卦
Bai Juyi 白居易
baipai 拜牌
Bai-Yue 百越
baji 八極
Baodai Qiao 寶帶橋
Baoen Si 報恩寺
baotou 包頭
bao zhuyu jian'ai qi du 寶珠玉兼愛其櫝
Beihao 北濠
Beiju 北局
beimian chengchen 北面稱臣
Bei Si (Ta) 北寺（塔）
Beiyinyangying 北陰陽營
bi 壁
bi 敝
Bianliang 汴梁
biaobang 標牓
biaolü 表閭
biji 筆記
bingshe 丙舍
biyi 敝邑
bu 步
buju/zhai 卜居/宅
Bu Yingtian 卜應天
Buzhou 不周
Cai 蔡
Cai Yun 蔡雲
Canglang Ting 滄浪亭
caoxie xiang 草鞋香
Cao Xueqin 曹雪芹
Cao Zishou 曹自守
Chamo 茶磨
Chang 閶
Chang 昌
chang 長
chang 常
chang 場
chang 嘗
Changhe 閶闔
Changmen 閶門
Changshu 常熟
Chang Yuchun 常遇春
Changzhou 長洲
Changzhou 常州
Chao 朝

Chao Cuo 晁錯
chaogong zhi yi 朝拱之義
Chen 陳
chen 辰
cheng 成
cheng 城
chengchi 城池
Chengcun 城村
Chengdu 成都
chengguo 城郭
chengguo renmin 城郭人民
Chenghua 成化
Chenghuang 城隍
chenglou 城樓
chengmenlou 城門樓
chengmin 成民
chengshi 城市
Cheng Shimeng 程師孟
chengyuan 城垣
Chen Jiru 陳繼儒
chenxin gongbei 臣心拱北
chenxun 辰巽
chi 尺
Chixian Shenzhou 赤縣神州
Ch'oe Pu 崔溥
Chongan 崇安
Chongqing 重慶
Chu 楚
chu 處
chuaifang 踹坊
chuaijiang 踹匠
chuiguting 吹鼓亭
Chunshen 春申
Chunxi 淳熙
chunyu 春雨
Ci 次
cong 聰
cun 寸
dacheng 大城
dahu 大戶
Dajie 大街
daluan zaicheng, xiaoluan zaixiang 大亂在城，
小亂在鄉
dang 蕩
Danyang 丹陽
Dao (*dao*) 道
Daoguang 道光
Daoqian 道前
dashi 大市
Da Situ 大司徒
Dayu 大峪
di 地
di 狄
dian 殿
Dihu 地戶
dili 地理
dili zhi shu 地理之書
Ding 定
ding 丁
Dingcuo Cheng 定錯城
dingguo licheng 定國立城
Dinghui 定慧
Dingjia 丁家
Ding Lingwei 丁令威
dishi zhi buke qian ye 地勢之不可遷也
ditai 敵臺
ditu 地突
dizhi 地支
Di zhi bacong 地之八聰
Di zhi xiadu 帝之下都
Dong 東
donggang 東岡
Dongguan 冬官
Dongping 東平
Dongting 洞庭
Dongyuedi 東嶽帝
Dong Zhongshu 董仲舒
doukou 斗口
du 度
du 都
Duan Yucai 段玉裁
Du Mu 杜牧

Du Xunhe 杜荀鶴
Du Yu 杜預
e 額
Eguo Gong 鄂國公
Ezhou 鄂州
Fan Chengda 范成大
fang 坊
fangbiao 坊表
fanghuoqiang 防火牆
fang jiu li 方九里
Fan Laizong 范來宗
"Fanli" 凡例
Fan Li 范蠡
Fan Zhongyan 范仲淹
Fei Chun 費淳
Feng 葑
Feng 鳳
Feng Menglong 馮夢龍
Feng(qiao) 楓（橋）
fengshui 風水
fengshui ta 風水塔
fengsu 風俗
Fengyang 鳳陽
fenxing/ye 分星/野
Fenyi 分宜
fu 夫
fu 府
Fuchai 夫差
fucheng 府城
fugong kaijing 復宮開涇
fuguo 郛郭
Fujian 福建
Fujiao 夫椒
Fuli 甫里
Fu Xi 伏羲
fuxue 府學
Gai Tian 蓋天
Gan 贛
gan 幹
Ganquan fu 甘泉賦
Gao Lü 高履
Gao Qi 高啟
gaorun 膏潤
Gaozong 高宗
ge 閣
Ge Cheng 葛成
Gong 宮
gong 宮
gong 工
gong 栱
Gonggong 共工
gongsheng 貢生
Gong Wei 龔煒
Gongyuan 公園
gongyuan 貢院
Gongzhai dixing 宮宅地形
Goujian 句踐
Gou-Wu 句吳
guan 貫
guan 館
guan 觀
guang 廣
guangchang 廣場
Guanghua Si Qiao 廣化寺橋
Guangxi 廣西
Guangzhou 廣州
Guan Lu 管輅
Guanqian 觀前
Gugong Danfu 古公亶父
Gu Gongxie 顧公燮
Gui(hua)cheng 龜（化）城
Guiji 會稽
Guizhou 貴州
gujiao 鼓角
gulou 鼓樓
Gu Lu 顧祿
Gun 鯀
guo 國
guo 郭
Guo Pu 郭璞
guoren 國人
Guoyuan 郭園

Gusu 姑蘇
Gusu Guan 姑蘇館
Gusu Tai 姑蘇臺
Guxu 姑胥
Guxu yongcui 姑胥擁翠
Gu Yuanqing 顧元慶
Gu Zhentao 顧震濤
Gu Zuyu 顧祖禹
Han 憨
Hangzhou 杭州
Hanshan 寒山
Han Shiqi 韓世琦
Hanxue 漢學
Han Yangu 韓彥古
Han Yu 韓愈
he 禾
he 貉
Heijo-kyo 平京城
Helü 闔閭
Helü Dacheng 闔閭大城
Henan 河南
Heng 横
hengmen 衡門
Hengtang 横塘
Hetu kuodi xiang 河圖括地象
hongchen 紅塵
Hongjin 紅巾
Hong Mai 洪邁
Hongwu 洪武
hou 厚
Hou Jing zhi luan 侯景之亂
Hua 華
huabiao 華表
Huai 淮
huang 隍
Huangdu 黃瀆
Huang Xingzeng 黃省曾
Huaqiao 花橋
Hubei 湖北
Hubilie 忽必列
Hui 惠
hui 虫
hui 虺
Hui Lin 慧琳
Hulong 護龍
huogeng shuinou 火耕水耨
huo yu fengshui 惑於風水
Huqiu 虎丘
Hushu 湖熟
Hu Shunshen 胡舜申
Hu Yinglin 胡應麟
Huzhou 湖州
ji 極
Jia Dan 郟亶
Jiading 嘉定
Jia Gongyan 賈公彥
jian 建
jian 間
Jiang 將
Jiangbiao zhuan 江表傳
Jiangdong Caishenmiao 江東財神廟
Jianghai yanghua 江海揚華
Jiangnan 江南
Jiangsu 江蘇
Jiangxi 江西
Jiangxi dili xinfa 江西地理新法
Jiang Yihua 蔣以化
Jiangyin 江陰
Jiang Yong 江永
jiansheng 監生
jianyue 僭越
jiao 交
jiao 郊
jiaolou 角樓
Jiaqing 嘉慶
Jiaxing 嘉興
jie 街
jiechang buduan 截長補短
jieci 介次
jie tianxiang 解天餉
Jiezhuanglü Si 戒幢律寺
Jifang Dian 機房殿
Jili 季歷
Jin 晉

jinbaopai 金寶牌
Jinchang 金閶
Jinfan Jing 錦帆涇
jing 京
jingtian 井田
Jing Wang 荊王
Jinling 金陵
jinshi 進士
Jiujiang 九江
Jiulong 九龍
jiuzhou 九州
Jixi 績溪
Jiye Gongsuo 機業公所
jubanqiao 巨板橋
jun 郡
juren 舉人
Kaifeng 開封
Kaiping Wang 開平王
Kaiyuan Guan/Gong 開元觀/宮
Kangxi 康熙
kanyu 堪輿
kanyu jia 堪輿家
Kanyu jingui 堪輿金匱
"Kaogong ji" 考工記
Kejia 客家
keju 科舉
kelou 刻漏
Ke Wuchi 柯悟遲
Kong Anguo 孔安國
kongjian 空間
Kong Yingda 孔穎達
Kunlun 崑崙
Kunshan 崑山
Lai Dayou 賴大有
Lang 狼
lang 廊
laotour 老頭兒
Le 樂
lei 雷
Leizun 雷尊
Lengjia 楞伽
Li 厲
li 立
li 里
li 禮
Liang-Zhe 兩浙
Liangzhu 良渚
Lianxi Fang 濂溪坊
Liao 蓼
Liao 僚
Liaodong 遼東
Li Bai 李白
Lichun 立春
Li Daoyuan 酈道元
Lin 麟
Lin'an 臨安
Lindun 臨頓
lingxingmen 櫺星門
Lingxu 靈虛
Lingyan 靈巖
Liqi 理氣
Li Shan 李善
Li Shen 李紳
Li Shoupeng 李壽朋
Liu Bang 劉邦
Liu Feng 劉鳳
liuhe 六合
Liu Ji 劉基
Liu Jia 劉賈
Liu Jinzao 劉錦藻
Liu Laolao 劉姥姥
Liu Xi 劉熙
Liuxian 柳仙
Liu Yuxi 劉禹錫
liyue 禮樂
lizheng 里正
Li Zonge 李宗諤
long(mai) 龍(脈)
longnao 龍腦
longpan huju 龍蟠虎踞
longpan shuilu 龍蟠水陸
longzi 龍子
Lou 婁
lou 樓

Lu 魯
Lu 盧
Lu 鹿
lü 閭
Lu Guimeng 陸龜蒙
Luo 雒
Luoyang 洛陽
Luoyang jiujing 洛陽舊經
Lu Rong 陸容
Lü Ting 呂梃
Lu Wenchao 盧文弨
Lu Xiangsheng 盧象昇
Lu Xiong 盧熊
Luzhi 甪直
Ma'an 馬鞍
maidu huanzhu 買櫝還珠
mamian 馬面
Mamopan 馬磨盤
Manzi 蠻子
Maqiao 馬橋
men 門
Meng Hao 孟浩
"Menming" 門名
miaohui 廟會
min 緡
mingdu wangyi 名都望邑
Minglun Tang 明倫堂
mingshen 明神
Ming sijia 明四家
mingtang 明堂
Minzhong 閩中
Moling 秣陵
Mopan 磨盤
Mudu 木瀆
muyu 木魚
Nanchang 南昌
nan gan/long 南幹/龍
Nanhao 南濠
nanman 南蠻
Nantong 南通
Nanyuan 南園
Nara 奈良
neizai 內宰
Nengren Si 能仁寺
Nietai 臬臺
Ningbo 寧波
nong 農
nüqiang 女牆
paie 牌額
Pan 盤
panchi 泮池
pangbo weiqi 旁魄蔚跂
peidu 陪都
Pei Yin 裴駰
pi 辟
Ping 平
pinghan 屏翰
Pingjiang 平江
Pingjiang Shuyuan 平江書院
Pingjiang tu 平江圖
Pingyao 平遙
Pi Rixiu 皮日休
po-Chu 破楚
pushe 鋪舍
Qi 齊
qi 氣
Qian 錢
Qianfu 乾符
qiang 羌
qiang 牆
Qiangengzi 前埂子
Qian Gu 錢穀
Qian Liu 錢鏐
Qianlong 乾隆
Qian Mu 錢穆
Qian Siyuan 錢思元
Qiantang 錢塘
qiaofang 橋坊
Qiaolou 譙樓
Qilin 麒麟
qing 情
Qin Huitian 秦蕙田
Qinwang 秦望
Qinyuhang 秦餘杭

Qionglong 穹窿
qiting 旗亭
qi tong Changhe 氣通閶闔
qiu 虯
Qiu Ying 仇英
Qiyun Lou 齊雲樓
Qu 渠
qu 曲
qu 衢
quanqi zhi di 全氣之地
Quanzhou 泉州
que 闕
Qu Yuan 屈原
raomin 擾民
ren 人
ren 壬
Renmin 人民
renyi 仁義
ri 日
riying 日景
rong 容
Ruiguang 瑞光
Sanjiang 三江
Sanqing (Dian) 三清 (殿)
San Wu 三吳
sha 砂
shan 山
shang 商
shangliangwen 上梁文
Shangtang 上塘
Shangzhen Guan 上真觀
shanmen 山門
Shantang 山塘
Shanxi 山西
Shaomu 召穆
Shaoxing 紹興
shaqi 煞氣
She 社
She 蛇
Shedu 射瀆
sheji 社稷
shen 審
Shen Defu 沈德符
Shen Du 沈度
Shen Fu 沈復
Shengkao qieyun 聲考切韻
Sheng Linji 盛林基
shengrui 聖瑞
shengxiao 生肖
shengyuan 生員
Shen Hao 沈皞
Shen Shouzhi 沈守之
Shen Xu 申繻
Shen Zaikuan 沈在寬
Shen Zhou 沈周
sheting 設廳
Shi 室
shi 仕
shi 市
Shi Huangdi 始皇帝
shijingtu 市井徒
shijing zhi chen 市井之臣
shili 市吏
shilou 市樓
shimin 市民
Shi Miyuan 史彌遠
shiren 市人
shishi 石室
Shitou 石頭
shiyong 市庸
shizheng 市正
Shizi 十梓
Shizi Shan 獅子山
Shizu 世祖
Shoumeng 壽夢
Shu 舒
shui 水
Shun 舜
si 巳
si 肆
Sichuan 四川
sici 思次
Siling 四靈
Sima Guang 司馬光

simin 四民
Sirui 四瑞
sishi 司市
Song 淞
Songxue 宋學
Su-Hu shu, tianxia zu 蘇湖熟，天下足
suijiao 歲醮
Suijin 碎錦
Sun Long 孫隆
Sun Quan 孫權
suo 所
Su Shunqin 蘇舜欽
Suzhou 蘇州
Suzong 肅宗
Tai 太
Taibeifu 臺北府
Taibo 太伯
Taicang 太倉
Taifu 太傅
Taigu 太古
Taiping 太平
Taizu 太祖
tang 堂
Tang Yin 唐寅
Tao Qian 陶潛
Tengwang Ge 滕王閣
Tianhou Gong 天后宮
Tian Huisheng 天悔生
Tianmen 天門
Tianmu 天目
Tianping 天平
Tianqing (Guan) 天慶（觀）
Tianqi zhi shui 天氣之數
tianshang tiantang, dixia Su-Hang 天上天堂，地下蘇杭
Tianshun 天順
Tianyi 天醫
tianyuan difang 天圓地方
Tian zhi bafeng 天之八風
Tianzhu 天柱
ting 亭
ting 廳
ting (yuan) 庭（院）
tu 涂
tu 土
tugui 土圭
Tu Guobao 土國寶
tushen 土深
Wang Ao 王鏊
Wang Bo 王勃
Wang Chong 王充
Wang Dexin 汪德馨
Wang Huan 王喚
Wang Ji 王伋
Wang Jian 王建
Wang Mingqing 王明清
Wang Qi 王圻
Wang Qi 王錡
wangqizhe 望氣者
Wang Ruyu 王汝玉
Wang Shixing 王士性
Wang Siyi 王思義
Wang Wei 王褘
Wang Wei 王微
Wang Yi 王逸
Wang Yi 王彝
Wang Ying 王郢
Wanli 萬曆
Wannian 萬年
Wanshou Gong 萬壽宮
Wei 渭
Wei 衛
Wei Guan 魏觀
Wei Guangfu 韋光黻
Wende 文德
wengcheng 甕城
wenmiao 文廟
Wenzheng 文正
Wen Zhengming 文征明
Wenzhou 溫州
wokou 倭寇
Wolong 臥龍
wopu 窩鋪
Wu 吳

Wuai Jushi 無礙居士
Wuchang 武昌
Wu Cunli 吳存禮
Wude 武德
Wuhu 五湖
Wujiang 吳江
Wukang 武康
wuliang dian 無梁殿
Wu lu 吳錄
Wulushen 五路神
Wumen busheng 吳門補乘
Wuning 武寧
Wupai 吳派
Wutai 五臺
Wuxi 無錫
Wuxing 吳興
Wuxing 五星
Wu Yifeng 吳翌鳳
Wu-Yue 吳越
Wuzhong 吳中
Wu Zixu 伍子胥
xian 縣
xiang 向
xiang 巷
xiang 相
xiang 廂
Xiangfu tujing 祥符圖經
Xianghua 香花
xiangke 香客
xiangshi 鄉試
xiang-Tian fa-Di 象天法地
xiangtu changshui 相土嘗水
xianyu 羨餘
xiaocheng 小城
xiaohu 小戶
Xiatang 下塘
xie 榭
Xie Guozhen 謝國楨
xiejiju 協濟局
Xie Shiji 謝師稷
Xie Ziyi 謝子逸
xiliu qingying 溪流清映
xingfa 形法
xinggong 行宮
Xing-Gua 星卦
xingjia 形家
xing jimie zhi ji 興既滅之基
xing miewang zhi ji, kai baiguo zhi he 興滅王之基, 開敗國之河
xingsheng 形勝
Xingshi 形勢
xingshi 形勢
Xinguo Gong 信國公
xingye 星野
xingzai 行在
Xinzhu 新竹
Xiong Bolong 熊伯龍
Xishen 喜神
xishi 夕市
Xi Wang Mu 西王母
Xiyuan Si 西園寺
Xu 胥
xu 序
xuan 軒
Xuanmiao Guan 玄妙觀
xuanshi 選仕
Xu Changshi 徐昌時
Xu Da 徐達
xue 穴
Xu Hun 許渾
Xu Kai 徐鍇
Xumen 胥門
Xun Qing 荀卿
Xu Qi 許起
Xu Shen 許慎
Xu Shilin 徐士林
Xu Song 徐崧
Xu Yang 徐揚
Xu Youren 徐有壬
ya 亞
ya 壓 or 厭
Yalu 鴨綠
yamen 衙門
Yang 陽

Yang Bei 楊備
Yangshan xinlu 陽山新錄
Yang Su 楊素
Yang Xiong 揚雄
Yang Xunji 楊循吉
Yang Yunsong 楊筠松
Yangzhou 揚州
Yan Shigu 顏師古
Yan Song 嚴嵩
Yao 堯
yao 妖
yaozhan 腰斬
ye 野
yeren 野人
yi 邑
Yilan 宜蘭
Yin 隱
Yingshao 應劭
Yingshi 營室
yingwei 營衛
yinli 陰禮
yinyang zhi shu 陰陽之術
yizhai 義宅
yong 墉
Yongchun 永春
Yongzheng 雍正
Youdu 幽都
"You Guan" 游觀
youke 游客
youlong 游龍
Yu 羽
Yu 禹
Yu 虞
yu 宇
yu 或
Yu-Yue 於越
Yu Yue 俞樾
yuan 垣
yuan 院
yuan 援
Yuanhe 元和
yuanmen 轅門
Yuanmiao (Guan) 圓妙（觀）
Yuan Xi 元錫
Yue 越
yue 月
yuecheng 月城
Yueyang Lou ji 岳陽樓記
"Yufu" 輿服
yugong 寓公
Yuhuang 玉皇
Yun 鄖
Yunnan 雲南
Yunyang 鄖陽
Yuqing Daoguan 玉清道觀
Yuying Tang 育嬰堂
"Zaji" 雜記
Zeng Wendi 曾文迪
zhai 齋
Zhang 章
zhang 丈
zhang 障
Zhang Chengde 張誠德
Zhang Dachun 張大純
Zhang Dai 張岱
Zhang Du 張度
Zhangguolao 張果老
Zhang Guowei 張國維
Zhang Hong 張紘
Zhang Hu 張祜
Zhang Ji 張繼
Zhang Juzheng 張居正
Zhang Shicheng 張士誠
Zhang Shoujie 張守節
Zhang Tuan 張摶
Zhang Yan 張晏
Zhang Yi 張儀
Zhang Yuncheng 張允成
Zhang Yundi 張允迪
Zhang Zai 張載
Zhang Zilin 張紫琳
Zhao Rushu 趙汝述
zhaoshi 朝市
Zhejiang 浙江

Zhejiang Dongdao/Xidao 浙江東道/西道
zhen 鎮
Zheng 鄭
Zheng Lin 鄭霖
zhengning zhi shi 猙獰之勢
Zheng Ruozeng 鄭若曾
Zhengtong 正統
Zheng Xuan 鄭玄
Zhengyi Conglin 正一叢林
Zheng Yuanyou 鄭元祐
Zhenjiang 鎮江
Zhenqing Daoyuan 真慶道院
Zhenze 震澤
Zhenzong 真宗
zhi 支
zhi 雉
zhidie 雉堞
zhiranju 織染局
zhizaoju 織造局
Zhizun 至尊
Zhong 鍾
zhongcheng 中丞
Zhongguo 中國
"Zhongguo san da gan tu" 中國三大幹圖
Zhongshan Wuning Wang 中山武寧王
Zhongtu 中土
Zhongwu 忠武
zhongxin chengcheng 眾心成城
Zhongyong 仲雍
Zhongzhou 中州
Zhongzi 仲子
zhou 周
zhou 宙
Zhou Boqi 周伯器
Zhou Wenxiang 周文襄
Zhu 朱
zhu 築
zhu 櫧
zhu 主
Zhuanxu 顓頊
Zhu Changwen 朱長文
Zhuge Liang 諸葛亮
Zhu Jian 朱鑒
Zhu Mu 祝穆
Zhu Xi 朱熹
Zhu Yuanzhang 朱元璋
Zhu Yunming 祝允明
Zhu Zichang 朱子昌
zicheng 子城
Zigong 子貢
Zigong 紫宮
Ziweigong/yuan 紫微宮/垣
zongmiao 宗廟
Zou Yan 鄒衍
Zu 祖
Zuili 檇李
zunjing ge 尊經閣
zuo 作
Zuoe 岝㟧
Zuo Si 左思
zushan 祖山

Bibliography

Asian Language References

Aoki Tomitaro 青木富太郎 (1972). *Banri no chojo* 万里の長城 (The Great Wall). Tokyo: Kondo shuppansha.

Baicheng yanshui 百城煙水 (Myriad Things and Events in a Hundred Cities [description of the Suzhou region]). Xu Song 徐崧 (1617–1690) and Zhang Dachun 張大純 (1637–1702). Early Qing, 1690. Nanjing: Jiangsu guji chubanshe, 1986.

Baihu tongyi 白虎通義 (Comprehensive Discussions at White Tiger Lodge). Ban Gu 班固 (A.D. 32–92). Eastern Han. Commented on in the early 1830s by Chen Li 陳立 (1809–1869) in the edition *Baihu tong shuzheng* 白虎通疏證 (Commentary on and Verification of the *Baihu tong*). Beijing: Zhonghua shuju, 1994.

Beiyinyangying–Xinshiqi shidai ji Shang Zhou shiqi yizhi fajue baogao 北陰陽營: 新石器時代及商周時期遺址發掘報告 (Beiyinyangying: Report on the Excavations of the Remains of the Neolithic, Shang and Zhou Periods). Beijing: Wenwu chubanshe, 1993.

Bin tui lu 賓退錄 (Record Made After the Guests Departed). Zhao Yushi 趙與時 (1175–1231). Song, 1224. Shanghai: Shanghai guji chubanshe, 1983.

Bowu zhi 博物志 (Record of the Investigation of Things). Zhang Hua 張華 (A.D. 232–300). Jin, ca. A.D. 270–290. Verified by Fan Ning 范寧 in the edition *Bowu zhi jiaozheng* 博物志校證 (Verification and Rectification of the *Bowu zhi*). Beijing: Zhonghua shuju, 1980.

Canglang Ting ji 滄浪亭記 (Memoir on Canglang Ting [Garden]). Su Shunqin 蘇舜欽 (1008–1048). Northern Song, 1040s. In *Wujun zhi* (see citation), *juan* 14, pp. 187–188.

Cao Wanru 曹婉如 et al., eds. (1990). *Zhongguo gudai ditu ji: Zhanguo—Yuan* 中國古代地圖集: 戰國—元 (A Collection of Ancient Chinese Maps: The Warring States Period—Yuan Dynasty [476 B.C.–A.D. 1368]). Beijing: Wenwu chubanshe.

Cao Zifang 曹子芳 and Wu Naifu 吳奈夫, eds. (1986). *Suzhou* 蘇州. Beijing: Zhongguo jianzhu gongye chubanshe.

Changxi zhucheng lun 閶西築城論 (On Building the City Walls West of Chang [Gate]). Liu Feng 劉鳳 (1517–1600). Ming, 1550s. In *Tjls* (see citation), *juan* 5, pp. 12a–b.

Chaolin bitan 巢林筆談 (Jotted Conversations from the Nested Bush). Gong Wei 龔煒 (1704–?). Qing, 1765; *Subian* 續編, 1769. Beijing: Zhonghua shuju, 1981.

Chaxiangshi congchao 茶香室叢鈔 (Collected Excerpts of the Tea-Fragrance Study). Yu Yue 俞樾 (1821–1907). Late Qing, Preface 1883. Beijing: Zhonghua shuju, 1995.

Chen Congzhou 陳從周 (1981). "Suzhou jiu zhuzhai" "蘇州舊住宅" (Old Houses in Suzhou). *Tongji daxue xuebao (zengkan): Jianzhu wenhua* (1981): 5–21.

Chen Guoqiang 陳國強 et al. (1988). *Baiyue minzu shi* 百越民族史 (Ethnological History of Baiyue). Beijing: Zhongguo shehui kexue chubanshe.

Chen Mingda 陳明達 (1981). Yingzao fashi *damuzuo yanjiu* 營造法式大木作研究 (Research on "Great Carpentry" in the *Yingzao fashi*). 2 vols. Beijing: Wenwu chubanshe.

Chen shu 陳書 (History of the Chen Dynasty [A.D. 557–589]). Yao Silian 姚思廉 (A.D. 557–637). Tang, 636. Beijing: Zhonghua shuju, 1972.

Chen Zhengxiang 陳正祥 (1983). *Zhongguo wenhua dili* 中國文化地理 (Chinese Cultural Geography). Beijing: Sanlian shudian.

Chongjun Suzhou chenghe ji 重浚蘇州城河記 (Memoir on the Redredging of the City Rivers of Suzhou). Fei Chun 費淳. Qing, 1797. In *MQSgbj*, pp. 305–307.

Chu ci 楚辭 (Elegies of the Chu [State]). Compiled by Liu Xiang 劉向 (ca. 77–6 B.C.). Warring States to Han. Commented on in Eastern Han by Wang Yi 王逸 in the edition *Chu ci zhangju* 楚辭章句 (Annotation of the *Chu ci*). *Sq* ed. Shanghai: Shanghai guji chubanshe, 1987.

Chu xue ji 初學記 (Notes Taken at the Entry into Learning [encyclopaedia]). Xu Jian 徐堅 et al. Tang, A.D. Beijing: Zhonghua shuju, 1962.

Ci hai 辭海 (Ocean of Words). Shanghai: Shanghai cishu chubanshe, 1980.

Ci yuan 辭源 (Sources of Words). Rev. ed. Beijing: Shangwu yinshuguan, 1988.

Dengchuang conglu 鐙窗叢錄 (Collected Records by the Illuminated Window). Wu Yifeng 吳翌鳳 (1742–1819). Qing. *Hanfenlou miji* ed. Taibei: Taiwan shangwu yinshuguan, 1967.

Ding Jinlong 丁金龍 and Mi Weifeng 米偉峰 (1983). "Suzhou faxian Qimen gu shuimen jichu" "蘇州發現齊門古水門基礎" (Discoveries of the Foundation of the Old Water Gate at the Site of Qi Gate of Suzhou). *Wenwu* 5 (1983): 55–59.

Dong Jianhong 董鑒泓, ed. (1982). *Zhongguo chengshi jianshe shi* 中國城市建設史 (A History of Chinese City Construction). Beijing: Zhongguo jianzhu gongye chubanshe.

Dong Jianhong 董鑒泓 and Ruan Yisan 阮儀三 (1981). "Qingdai de piaohao zhongxin chengshi—Pingyao Taigu" "清代的票號中心城市—平遙太古" (The Central Cities for Banking in the Qing Dynasty—Pingyao and Taigu). *Tongji daxue xuebao (zengkan): Jianzhu wenhua* (1981): 22–26.

Dongjing menghua lu 東京夢華錄 (Record of the Dreamlike Past in the Eastern Capital [Kaifeng]). Meng Yuanlao 孟元老. Southern Song, twelfth century. Beijing: Zhongguo shangye chubanshe, 1982.

Duan Benluo 段本洛 and Zhang Qifu 張圻福 (1986). *Suzhou shougongye shi* 蘇州手工業史 (A History of Suzhou's Handicraft Industry). Nanjing: Jiangsu guji chubanshe.

Ducheng jisheng 都城紀勝 (The Wonders of the Capital City [Hangzhou]). Zhao 趙. Southern Song, thirteenth century. Beijing: Zhongguo shangye chubanshe, 1982.
Dushi fangyu jiyao 讀史方輿紀要 (Essentials of Geography for Reading History). Gu Zuyu 顧祖禹 (1631–1692). Early Qing, ca. 1672. Beijing: Zhonghua shuju, 1955.
Er ya 爾雅 (Literary Expositor [dictionary]). Compilers unknown. Zhou material, stabilized in Qin and Western Han. *Sz* ed. Beijing: Zhonghua shuju, 1980.
Fan Shuzhi 樊樹志 (1985). "Shiyi zhi shiqi shiji Jiangnan nongye jingji de fazhan" "十一至十七世紀江南農業經濟的發展" (Economic Development of the Jiangnan Agriculture from the Eleventh to the Seventeenth Centuries). In *Zhongguo fengjian shehui jingji jiegou yanjiu* 中國封建社會經濟結構研究 (Beijing: Zhongguo shehui kexue chubanshe, 1985), pp. 384–405.
Fangyu shenglan 方輿勝覽 (Grand Vision of the Great World [geography]). Zhu Mu 祝穆. Song, A.D. 1240. *Sq* ed. Shanghai: Shanghai guji chubanshe, 1987.
Feng Youlan 馮友蘭 (1985). *Zhongguo zhexue jianshi* 中國哲學簡史 (A Brief History of Chinese Philosophy). Chinese translation by Tu Youguang 涂又光 from the English ed. (New York: Macmillan & Co.: 1948). Beijing: Beijing Daxue chubanshe.
Fujian tongzhi 福建通志 (Comprehensive Gazetteer of Fujian). Chen Shouqi 陳壽祺 et al. Qing, rev. ed. 1871. Taibei: Huawen shuju, 1968.
Fusheng liuji 浮生六記 (Six Chapters of a Floating Life). Shen Fu 沈復 (1763–1808 or after). Qing, ca. 1820s–1830s. Only the first four chapters extant. Tainan: Wenguo shuju, 1991.
Gaiyu congkao 陔餘叢考 (Collection of Studies after Work in the Cultivated Field). Zhao Yi 趙翼 (1727–1814). Qing, 1750. Beijing: Zhonghua shuju, 1963.
Gao Yongyuan 高泳源. "Gudai Suzhou chengshi jingguan de lishi dili toushi" "古代蘇州城市景觀的歷史地理透視" (A Historical Geography Perspective on the Urban Landscape of Early Suzhou). *Lishi dili* 7 (1990): 62–71.
Gongyang zhuan 公羊傳 (Gongyang's Commentary). Gongyang Gao 公羊高. Zhou, Compiled between 722 and 481 B.C. *Sz* ed. Beijing: Zhonghua shuju, 1980.
Guangyou zhi 廣遊志 (Records of Wide Travelling). Wang Shixing 王士性 (1547–1598) . Ming. In *Wang Shixing dili shu sanzhong* (see *Guang zhi yi*), pp. 210–229.
Guang zhi yi 廣志繹 (Records and Investigation of General Geography). Wang Shixing 王士性 (1547–1598). Ming. In *Wang Shixing dili shu sanzhong* 王士性地理書三種 (Shanghai: Shanghai guji chubanshe, 1993), pp. 230–402.
Guanshi dili zhimeng 管氏地理指蒙 (Mr. Guan's Geomantic Indicator). Attrib. Guan Lu 管輅 (A.D. 209–256). Ascribed to the Three Kingdoms, A.D. third century but probably Tang, A.D. eighth century. In *Gtj* (see citation), *ce* 474.50b–475.33b.
Guan Zhaoye 關肇鄴 (1988). "Jiji de chengshi jianzhu" "積極的城市建築" (Positive Urban Buildings). *Jianzhu xuebao* 240 (August 1988): 8–11.
Guanzi 管子 (The Book of Master Guan). Compilers unknown; attributed to Guan Zhong 管仲. Zhou and Western Han. Commented on in Qing by Dai Wang 戴望 in the edition *Guanzi jiaozheng* 管子校正 (Rectification of the *Guanzi*). *Zj* ed. Beijing: Zhonghua shuju, 1954.
Gui Zhuang ji 歸莊集 (Anthology of Gui Zhuang). Gui Zhuang 歸莊 (1613–1673). Late Ming to early Qing. Shanghai: Shanghai guji, 1984.
Gujin tushu jicheng (*Gtj*) 古今圖書集成 (Imperial Encyclopaedia of Ancient and Modern Books).

First ed. by Chen Menglei 陳夢雷; revised ed. by Jiang Tingxi 蔣廷錫. Qing, 1726. Taibei: Wenxing Shudian, 1964.

Guo Moruo 郭沫若, ed. (1979). *Zhongguo shigao ditu ji: Shang ce* 中國史稿地圖集：上冊 (Atlas Attached to a Draft Chinese History: *ce* A). Shanghai: Ditu chubanshe.

Guo yu 國語 (Discourses on the States). Attributed to Zuo Qiuming 左丘明. Late Zhou. Shanghai: Shanghai guiu chubanshe, 1978.

Guochao diangu 國朝典故 (Institutions and Anecdotes in the [Ming] Dynasty [encyclopaedia]). Deng Shilong 鄧士龍. Ming, ca. early seventeenth century. Beijing: Beijing Daxue chubanshe, 1993.

Gusu zhi 姑蘇志 (Gazetteer of Gusu [Suzhou]). Wang Ao 王鏊 (1450–1524). Ming, 1506. *Sq* ed. Shanghai: Shanghai guji chubanshe, 1987.

Han Changli wenji jiaozhu 韓昌黎文集校注 (Collated and Annotated Anthology of Han Changli). Han Yu 韓愈 (A.D. 768–824). Compiled in 1907 by Ma Qichang 馬其昶 (1855–1930). Shanghai: Shanghai guji chubanshe, 1986.

Han Feizi 韓非子 (The Book of Master Han Fei). Han Fei 韓非 (ca. 280–233 B.C.). Zhou, early third century B.C. Commented on in late Qing by Wang Xianshen 王先慎 in the edition *Han Feizi jijie* 韓非子集解 (Collective Interpretations of the *Han Feizi*). *Zj* ed. Beijing: Zhonghua shuju, 1954.

Han long jing 撼龍經 (Manual of Shaking the Dragon). Attributed to Yang Yunsong 楊筠松. Tang. *Sq* ed. Shanghai: Shanghai guji chubanshe, 1987.

Hanshan Si zhi 寒山寺志 (Annals of the Hanshan Temple). Ye Changchi 葉昌熾 (1847–1917). Late Qing Preface, 1911. Nanjing: Jiangsu guji chubanshe, 1990.

Han shu 漢書 (History of the Western Han Dynasty [206 B.C.–A.D. 9]). Ban Gu 班固 (A.D. 32–92). Eastern Han. Commented on in Tang by Yan Shigu 顏師古 (A.D. 581–645). Beijing: Zhonghua shuju, 1962.

He Yeju 賀業鉅 (1985). *Kaogong ji yingguo zhidu yanjiu* 考工記營國制度研究 (A Study of the System of City Construction in the *Kaogong ji*). Beijing: Zhongguo jianzhu gongye chubanshe.

He Yeju 賀業鉅 (1986). *Zhongguo gudai chengshi guihua shi luncong* 中國古代城市規劃史論叢 (Collective Discourses on the History of Ancient Chinese City Planning). Beijing: Zhongguo jianzhu gongye chubanshe.

Honglan yisheng 紅蘭逸乘 (The Red Orchid [Record] of the Omissions in [Suzhou] Gazetteers). Zhang Zilin 張紫琳. Qing, 1822. Suzhou: Jiangsu shengli Suzhou tushuguan, 1932.

Honglou meng 紅樓夢 (The Dream of the Red Chamber). Cao Xueqin 曹雪芹 (?–1763 or 1764). The last forty chapters attributed to Gao E 高鶚 (ca. 1738–1815). Beijing: Renmin wenxue chubanshe, 1964.

Hou Han shu 後漢書 (History of the Later Han Dynasty [A.D. 25–220]). Fan Ye 范曄 (A.D. 398–445); monograph chapters by Sima Biao 司馬彪 (?–ca. 306). Liu Song, A.D. 450. Beijing: Zhonghua shuju, 1965.

Huainanzi 淮南子 (The Book of Huainan). Written by the group of scholars gathered by Liu An 劉安 (179–122 B.C.). Western Han, ca. 120 B.C. *Zj* ed. Beijing: Zhonghua shuju, 1954.

Huangchao ping-Wu lu 皇朝平吳錄 (A Record of the Conquest of the Wu [Region] by the August [Ming] Empire). Writer unknown. First half of Ming. In *Guochao diangu* (see citation), *juan* 6, pp. 127–155.

Huangdi zhaijing 黃帝宅經 (The Yellow Emperor's House-Siting Manual). Wang Wei 王微. Liu Song, A.D. fifth century. *Sq* ed. Shanghai: Shanghai guji chubanshe, 1987.

Huang Ming benji 皇明本紀 (Record of the Essential Deeds of the Imperial Ming Court). Writer unknown. First half of Ming. In *Guochao diangu* (see citation), *juan* 2, pp. 15–48.

Huizhu lu 揮麈錄 (A Record of Flicking Whisk [Record of the Song institutions and political events]). Composed of four parts: "Qianlu," "Houlu," "Sanlu," and "Yuhua." Wang Mingqing 王明清 (1127–?). Southern Song, 1166–1197. Beijing: Zhonghua shuju, 1961.

Ito Chuta 伊東忠太 (1943). *Toyo kenchiku no kenkyu* 東洋建築の研究. (Studies of East Asian Architecture). Tokyo: Ryuginsha.

Ji Yuyi 姬郁逸 (1988). "Chunqiu shiqi Gusucheng yingjian zhidu chutan" "春秋時期姑蘇城營建制度初探" (Preliminary Study of the Building Institution of the Capital Suzhou in the Spring and Autumn Period). In *Wu wenhua lunwen ji* (see citation), pp. 33–53.

Jiangnan jinglüe 江南經略 (Tactics and Strategy [of Defense] in the Jiangnan Region). Zheng Ruozeng 鄭若曾 (fl. 1505–1580). Ming, 1568. *Sq* ed. Shanghai: Shanghai guji chubanshe, 1987.

Jiangnan tongzhi 江南通志 (Comprehensive Gazetteer of Jiangnan [Province]). Huang Zhijun 黃之雋 et al. Qing. Rev. ed., 1737. Taibei: Jinghua shuju, 1967.

Jiangsu sheng ditu ce 江蘇省地圖冊 (Atlas of Jiangsu Province). Guangzhou: Guangdongsheng ditu chubanshe, 1990.

Jiansheng yewen 翦勝野聞 (The Best Features Clipped from the Unofficial Stories). Xu Zhenqing 徐禎卿 (1479–1511). Ming. In *Guochao diangu* (see citation), *juan* 3, pp. 49–66.

Jiechao biji 借巢筆記 (Notes Taken in a Borrowed Nest). Shen Shouzhi 沈守之. Late Qing, ca. 1860s. Suzhou: Jiangsu shengli Suzhou tushuguan, 1940.

Jingshi tongyan 警世通言 (Comprehensive words to admonish the world). Compiler Feng Menglong 馮夢龍 (1574–1646). Ming, 1624. Shanghai: Shanghai guji chubanshe, 1987.

Jinping mei 金瓶梅 (Plum in the Golden Vase). Writer unknown; attributed to Xiaoxiao Sheng 笑笑生. Ming, ca. 1678, first known date of publication. Taibei: Lianjing chuban shiye gongsi, 1978.

Jin shu 晉書 (History of the Jin Dynasty [A.D. 281–420]). Fang Xuanling 房玄齡 (579–648) et al. Tang, A.D. 644–648. Beijing: Zhonghua shuju, 1974.

Jiu Tang shu 舊唐書 (Old History of the Tang Dynasty [A.D. 618–896]). Liu Xu 劉昫 et al. Tang and the Five Dynasties, A.D. 945. Beijing: Zhonghua shuju, 1975.

Kaizuka Shigeki 貝塚茂樹 (1962). "Chugoku kodai toshi ni okeru minkai" "中国古代都市に於ける民会" (Popular Assemblies in Ancient Chinese Cities), *Tohogaku ronshu* 2 (March 1962): 34–39.

Kanyu manxing 堪輿漫興 (Agreeable Geomantic Aphorisms). Liu Ji 劉基 (1311–1375). Ming, ca. 1370. In *Gtj* (see citation), *ce* 475.59a–63a.

Kanyu zazhu 堪輿雜著 (Miscellanies of Geomancy). Attributed to Li Sicong 李思聰. Song, eleventh century. In *Gtj* (see citation), *ce* 475.63a–65a.

Kaogong ji tu 考工記圖 (Illustrated Commentary on the *Kaogong ji*). Dai Zhen 戴震 (1723–1777). Qing. *Gjc* ed. Taibei: Taiwan shangwu yinshuguan, 1968.

Laozi zhu 老子注 (Commentary on the *Laozi*). Wang Bi 王弼 (226–249). Cao Wei. *Zj* ed. Beijing: Zhonghua shuju, 1954.

Li ji 禮記 (Record of Rites). Ed. Dai Sheng 戴聖. Western Han, ca. 50 B.C. *Sz* ed. Beijing: Zhonghua shuju, 1980.

Li Taibai quanji 李太白全集 (Collected Works of Li Taibai). Li Bai 李白 (701–762). Beijing: Zhonghua shuju, 1977.

Li Yunhe 李允鉌 (1982). *Huaxia yijiang: Zhongguo gudian jianzhu sheji yuanli fenxi* 華夏意匠：中國古典建築設計原理分析 (Cathay's Idea: Design Theory of Chinese Classical Architecture). Hong Kong: Wideangle Press.

Liang Fangzhong 梁方仲 (1980). *Zhongguo lidai hukou, tiandi, tianfu tongji* 中國歷代戶口田地田賦統計 (Statistics on Households, Cultivated Land and Taxation in China's Successive Dynasties). Shanghai: Shanghai renmin chubanshe.

Liao Zhihao 廖志豪 and Ye Wanzhong 葉萬忠 (1984). "Suzhou shihua" "蘇州史話" (An Introduction to the History of Suzhou). In *Mingcheng shihua* 名城史話 (An Introduction to the History of the Famous Cities), *ce* B (Beijing: Zhonghua shuju), pp. 341–388.

Lin Liugen 林留根 (1988). "Shilun Wu wenhua de duoyuan xing" "試論吳文化的多元性" (On the Pluralistic Nature of the Wu Culture). In *Wu wenhua lunwen ji* (see citation), pp. 251–260.

Liu Dunzhen 劉敦楨, ed. (1980). *Zhongguo gudai jianzhu shi* 中國古代建築史 (A History of Ancient Chinese Architecture). Rev. ed. of 1966. Beijing: Zhongguo jianzhu gongye chubanshe.

Liu Zhengyan 劉正琰 et al. (1984). *Hanyu wailaiyu cidian* 漢語外來語詞典 (A Dictionary of Loan Words in the Chinese Language). Shanghai: Shanghai cishu chubanshe.

Liu Zhenwei 劉鎮偉, ed. (1995). *Zhongguo guditu jingxuan* 中國古地圖精選 (A Selection of China's Ancient Maps). Beijing: Zhongguo shijieyu chubanshe.

Liu Zhiping 劉致平 (1987). *Zhongguo jianzhu leixing ji jiegou* 中國建築類型及結構 (Form types and Structure in Chinese Architecture). Teaching manuscript in 1930s. Beijing: Zhongguo jianzhu gongye chubanshe.

Liu Zhiping 劉致平 (1990). *Zhongguo juzhu jianzhu jianshi—Chengshi, zhuzhai, yuanlin [Fu: Sichuan zhuzhai jianzhu]* 中國居住建築簡史—城市、住宅、園林〔附:四川住宅建築〕(A Brief History of Chinese Residential Architecture—Cities, Houses, Gardens [Appended: Residential Architecture of Sichuan]). Supplement to 1950s ed. by Wang Qiming 王其明. Beijing: Zhongguo jianzhu gongye chubanshe.

Liu Zhiyuan 劉志遠 (1973). "Handai shijing kao—Shuo Dong Han shijing huaxiangzhuan" "漢代市井考—說東漢市井畫像磚" (A Study of Urban Markets in the Han Dynasty—Interpretation of Brick Reliefs of Urban Markets in the Eastern Han). *Wenwu* 3 (1973): 52–57.

Louwang yongyu ji 漏網喁魚集 (Collection of the Gasping Fish That Escaped from the Net). Ke Wuchi 柯悟遲 (ca. 1809–?). Late Qing. Beijing: Zhonghua shuju, 1959.

Lü Simian 呂思勉 (1983). *Liang Jin Nanbeichao shi* 兩晉南北朝史 (A History of the Two Jin [Dynasties] [A.D. 265–420] and the Northern and Southern Dynasties [A.D. 420–589]). First published in 1948 (Shanghai: Kaiming shudian). Shanghai: Shanghai guji chubanshe.

Lü Simian 呂思勉 (1985). *Zhongguo zhidu shi* 中國制度史 (A History of Chinese Institutions). Rev. ed. of *Shixue congshu* 史學叢書 (Shanghai, 1936). Shanghai: Shanghai jiaoyu chubanshe.

Lu Xiangsheng shudu 盧象昇疏牘 (Lu Xiangsheng's Reports and Memorials [to the Emperor]). Lu Xiangsheng 盧象昇 (1600–1639). Hangzhou: Zhejiang guji chubanshe, 1984.

Lun heng 論衡 (Discourses Weighed in the Balance). Wang Chong 王充 (A.D. 27–ca. 97). Eastern Han. *Zj* ed. Beijing: Zhonghua shuju, 1954.

Lun yu 論語 (Analects). Compiled by disciples of Confucius. Zhou (State of Lu 魯), ca. 465 to 450 B.C. *Sz* ed. Beijing: Zhonghua shuju, 1980.

Lüshi chunqiu 呂氏春秋 (Lü's Spring and Autumn Annals). Written by the group of scholars gathered by Lü Buwei 呂不韋 (?–235 B.C.). The end of the Warring States. *Zj* ed. Beijing: Zhonghua shuju, 1954.

Ma Bingjian 馬炳堅 (1997). *Zhongguo gujianzhu muzuo yingzao jishu* 中國古建築木作營造技術 (Technology of Timberwork Construction in Chinese Ancient Architecture). Beijing: Kexue chubanshe.

Mengliang lu 夢梁錄 (A Record of the Dream of the Past). Wu Zimu 吳自牧. Southern Song, early thirteenth century. Beijing: Zhongguo shangye chubanshe, 1982.

Mengzi 孟子 (The Book of Master Mencius). Meng Ke 孟軻 (ca. 372–289 B.C.). Zhou, ca. 290 B.C. *Sz* ed. Beijing: Zhonghua shuju, 1980.

Ming Qing Suzhou gongshangye beike ji 明清蘇州工商業碑刻集 (*MQSgbj*) (A Collection of Stele Inscriptions Concerning Industry and Commerce in the Ming-Qing Suzhou). Nanjing: Jiangsu renmin chubanshe, 1981.

Ming shi 明史 (History of the Ming Dynasty [1368–1644]). Zhang Tingyu 張廷玉 (1672–1755) et al. Qing, 1739. Beijing: Zhonghua shuju, 1977.

Miyazaki Ichisada 宮崎市定 (1957). "Chugoku jokaku no kigen isetsu" "中国城郭の起源異説" (Hypothesis on the Origin of the Inner and Outer Cities Walls in China), *Ajiashi Kenkyu* 1 (1957): 50–65.

Miyazaki Ichisada 宮崎市定 (1962a). "Kandai no risei to Todai no josei" "漢代の里制と唐代の坊制" (The Han *Li* System and the Tang *Jo* System), *Toyoshi kenkyu* 21, no. 3 (1962): 271–294.

Miyazaki Ichisada 宮崎市定 (1962b). "Rokucho jidai Kahoku no toshi" "六朝時代華北の都市" (Cities of Six Dynasties in North China), *Toyoshi kenkyu* 20:2 (March 1962): 53–74.

Mozi 墨子 (The Book of Master Mo). Mo Di 墨翟 (ca. 468–376 B.C.) and disciples. Zhou, ca. fourth century B.C. Commented on in late Qing by Sun Yirang 孫詒讓 (1848–1908) in the edition *Mozi jian gu* 墨子閒詁 (Interpretation of the *Mozi*). *Zj* ed. Beijing: Zhonghua shuju, 1954.

Pengchuang leiji 蓬窗類紀 (Classified Record by the Wicker Window). Huang Wei 黃暐. Ming, ca. 1520s. *Hanfenlou miji* ed. Taibei: Taiwan shangwu yinshuguan, 1967.

Pingjiang jishi 平江紀事 (Stories of Pingjiang [Suzhou]). Gao Lü 高履 (i.e., Gao Deji 高德基). Yuan, ca. 1360. *Sq* ed. Shanghai: Shanghai guji chubanshe, 1987.

Pingjianglu xinzhu juncheng ji (*Pxjj*) 平江路新築郡城記 (Memoir on the Renewed Reconstruction of the City Walls of Pingjiang [Suzhou] Prefecture). Zheng Yuanyou 鄭元祐 (1292–1364). Yuan, 1350s. In *Qiao-Wu ji* (see citation), *juan* 9.1a–3a.

P'yohaerok 漂海錄 (Record of Drift over the Sea). Ch'oe Pu 崔溥 (1454–1504). Seoul: Kyoyangsa, 1996.

Qi Yingtao 祁英濤 (1981). *Zenyang jianding gujianzhu* 怎樣鑒定古建築 (How to Authenticate Ancient Buildings). Beijing: Wenwu chubanshe.

Qi Yingtao 祁英濤 (1983). "Zhongguo zaoqi mujiegou jianzhu de shidai tezheng" "中國早期木結構建築的時代特徵" (Periodization and Characteristics of Early Chinese Timber Buildings). *Wenwu* 4 (1983): 60–74.

Qiao-Wu ji 僑吳集 (Collective Works Produced When Sojourning in Wu). Zheng Yuanyou 鄭元祐

(1292–1364). Yuan, 1360; recompiled in 1496 by Zhang Xi 張習. Taibei: Guoli zhongyang tushuguan, 1970.

Qinding xieji bianfang shu 欽定協紀辨方書 (Imperial Compendium of Coordinated Classification of Directions). Wang Yunlu 王允祿, ed. Qing, 1790. *Sq* ed. Shanghai: Shanghai guji chubanshe, 1987.

Qing jia lu 清嘉錄 (Record of Customs and Folklores in the Suzhou Region). Gu Lu 顧祿. Qing, 1830. Nanjing: Jiangsu guji chubanshe, 1986.

Qingming shanghe tu 清明上河圖 (Along the River[-bank] on the Qingming Festival [picture scroll]). Zhang Zeduan 張擇端. Late Northern Song, ca. early twelfth century. Beijing: Renmin meishu chubanshe, 1979.

Qingnang aozhi 青囊奧旨 (Profound Principles of the Blue Bag [i.e., Geomancy or Divination]). Attrib. Yang Yunsong 楊筠松. Tang, ca. A.D. 880. In *Gtj* (see citation), *ce* 475.34b–475.37b.

Qingnang haijiao jing 青囊海角經 (Ocean-Corner Classic of the Blue Bag [i.e., Geomancy or Divination]). Attributed to Guo Pu 郭璞 (A.D. 276–324); probably anonymous at the end of Tang. In *Gtj* (see citation), *ce* 474.27a–49a.

Qingyan conglu 青巖叢錄 (Qingyan's [i.e., Wang Wei's] Collected Records). Wang Wei 王禕 (1322–1373). Early Ming. *Xuehai leibian* ed. Taibei: Taiwan wenyuan shuju, 1964.

Qu Yingjie 曲英傑 (1991). *Xian-Qin ducheng fuyuan yanjiu* 先秦都城復原研究 (A Study of Reconstruction of the State Capitals in the pre-Qin era [before 221 B.C.]). Harbin: Heilongjiang renmin chubanshe.

Quan Tang shi 全唐詩 (Complete Anthology of Tang Poems). Compiled by Peng Dingqiu 彭定求 et al. Qing, seventeenth to early eighteenth centuries. Beijing: Zhonghua shuju, 1960.

Quan Tang wen 全唐文 (Complete Anthology of Tang Writings). Compiled by Dong Gao 董誥 (1740–1818), et al. Qing, 1814. Shanghai: Shanghai guji chubanshe, 1990.

Rongzhai suibi 容齋隨筆 (Miscellanies of the Rong Study [collection of extracts from literature, with editorial commentaries]). Hong Mai 洪邁 (1123–1202). Southern Song, late twelfth century to early thirteenth century. Shanghai: Shanghai guji chubanshe, 1978.

Saeki Tomi 佐伯富 (1966). "Kinsei Chugoku no toshi to noson" "近世中国の都市と農村" (Cities and Villages of China in Recent History [during the Song to Qing periods]), *Rekishi kyoiku* 14:12 (December 1966): 66–72.

Sancai tuhui 三才圖會 (Collective Illustration of the Three Gifts [Heaven, Earth, and Man] [encyclopaedia]). Wang Qi 王圻 and Wang Siyi 王思義. Ming, 1609. Shanghai: Shanghai guji chubanshe, 1988.

Sanfu huangtu 三輔黃圖 (Description of the Three Districts in the Capital). Writers unknown. Not later than A.D. third century. *Cj* ed.

Sanguo yanyi 三國演義 (Romance of the Three Kingdoms). Traditionally attributed to Luo Guanzhong 羅貫中 (ca. 1330–ca. 1400). Early Ming. Beijing: Renmin wenxue chubanshe, 1957.

Sanguo zhi 三國志 (Chronicles of the Three Kingdoms). Chen Shou 陳壽 (A.D. 233–297). Western Jin, ca. A.D. 290. Beijing: Zhonghua shuju, 1959.

San li tu jizhu 三禮圖集注 (Collective Illustrated Commentary on the Three Books of Rites [*Yi li*, *Zhou li*, and *Li ji*]). Nie Chongyi 聶崇義. Song, mid-ninth century. *Sc* ed.

Shang shu 尚書 (Book of Documents). Writers unknown. Tenth century B.C. to ca. A.D. 320. *Sz* ed. Beijing: Zhonghua shuju, 1980.

Shang shu dazhuan 尚書大傳 (Great Commentary on the *Shang shu*). Attributed to Fu Sheng 伏生. Western Han, second century B.C. *Sc* ed.

Shang Zhitan 商志醰 (1988). "Wuguo ducheng de bianqian ji Helü jiandu Suzhou de yuanyou" "吳國都城的變遷及闔閭建都蘇州的原由" (The Changes of the Wu Capital and the Reason for Helü's Moving the capital to Suzhou). In *Wu wenhua lunwen ji* (see citation), pp. 1–13.

Shanhai jing 山海經 (Classic of Mountains and Seas). Writers unknown. Zhou and Western Han. Collated and annotated by Yuan Ke 袁柯 in the edition *Shanhai jing jiaozhu* 山海經校注 (Collation of and Annotation to the *Shanhai jing*). Shanghai: Shanghai guji chubanshe, 1980.

Shanhushe diaotan zhaichao 珊瑚舌雕談摘鈔 (Excerpts from Coral Tongue's Elaborations and Idle Talks). Xu Qi 許起 (ca. 1828–?). Late Qing, 1885. Suzhou: Jiangsu shengli Suzhou tushuguan, 1939.

Shengshi zisheng tu 盛世滋生圖 (The Scroll of the Flourishing Times [Suzhou in the mid-eighteenth century]). Xu Yang 徐揚. Qing, 1759. Beijing: Wenwu chubanshe, 1986.

Shiba Yoshinobu 斯波義信 (1966). "10–13 seiki ni okeru Chugoku toshi no tenkan" "10–13世紀に於ける中国都市の転換" (Transformation of Chinese Cities in the 10th–13th Centuries), *Sekaishi kenkyu* 14 (January 1966): 22–37.

Shi ji 史記 (Historian's Record). Sima Qian 司馬遷 (ca. 145 or 135–? B.C.). Western Han, ca. 104–91 B.C. Beijing: Zhonghua shuju, 1959.

Shi jing 詩經 (Book of Odes).Writers/compilers unknown. Zhou, ninth to fifth centuries B.C. *Sz* ed. Beijing: Zhonghua shuju, 1980.

Shi ming 釋名 (Explanation of Names [dictionary]). Liu Xi 劉熙. Eastern Han, ca. A.D. 100. Commented on in 1896 by Wang Xianqian (1842–1917) in the edition *Shi ming shuzheng bu* 釋名疏證補 (Commentary on and Verification of the *Shi ming* with supplements). Shanghai: Shanghai guji chubanshe, 1984.

Shoufu Pingjiang ji 收復平江記 (Record of the Recapture of Pingjiang). Qian Mu 錢穆. Southern Song, 1130. In *Huizhu lu*, "Hou lu" (see citation), *juan* 10, pp. 202–206.

Shui jing zhu 水經注 (Commentary on the Waterways Classic). Li Daoyuan 酈道元 (466 or 472–527). Northern Wei, early A.D. sixth century. Shanghai: Shanghai guji chubanshe, 1990.

Shuowen jiezi 説文解字 (Analytical Dictionary of Characters). Xu Shen 許慎 (ca. A.D. 58–147). Eastern Han, A.D. 121. Beijing: Zhonghua shuju, 1963.

Shuowen jiezi zhu 説文解字注 (Annotations to the *Shuowen jiezi*). Duan Yucai 段玉裁 (1735–1815). Qing, 1815. Shanghai: Shanghai guji chubanshe, 1981.

Shuo yuan 説苑 (Garden of Discourses). Liu Xiang 劉向 (ca. 77–6 B.C.). Han, ca. 20 B.C. Rectified by Xiang Zonglu 向宗魯 in the edition *Shuo yuan jiaozheng* 説苑校正 (Rectification of the *Shuo yuan*). Beijing: Zhonghua shuju, 1987.

Shuyuan zaji 菽園雜記 (Miscellaneous Notes of the Leguminous Garden). Lu Rong 陸容 (1436–1494). Ming. Beijing: Zhonghua shuju, 1985.

Song Pingjiang chengfang kao (*SPck*) 宋平江城坊考 (Textual Enquiry into the Song Dynasty Pingjiang City and Its Environs). Wang Jian 王謇 (1888–1969), 1925. Nanjing: Jiangsu guji chubanshe, 1986.

Song shi 宋史 (History of the Song Dynasty [960–1279]). Tuotuo (Toghto) 脱脱 and Ouyang Xuan 歐陽玄 (1273–1357). Yuan, ca. 1343. Beijing: Zhonghua shuju, 1977.

Song shu 宋書 (History of the Liu Song Dynasty [A.D. 420–479]). Shen Yue 沈約 (A.D. 441–513). Liang, A.D. 480s. Beijing: Zhonghua shuju, 1974.

Song Zhaolin 宋兆麟 and Li Lulu 李露露 (1991). *Zhongguo gudai jieri wenhua* 中國古代節日文化 (Festival Culture in Ancient China). Beijing: Wenwu chubanshe.

Sou shen houji 搜神後記 (Supplementary Reports on Spiritual Manifestations). Attributed to Tao Qian 陶潛 (365 or 372–427). Jin 晉, late fourth or early fifth century. Beijing: Zhonghua shuju, 1981.

Sou shen ji 搜神記 (Reports on Spiritual Manifestations). Gan Bao 干寶. Jin, early fourth century. *Sq* ed. Shanghai: Shanghai guji chubanshe, 1987.

Sui shu 隋書 (History of the Sui Dynasty [A.D. 589–618]). Wei Zheng 魏徵 (A.D. 580–643) et al. Tang, 636. Beijing: Zhonghua shuju, 1973.

Suiyuan suibi 隨園隨筆 (Miscellanies of Suiyuan). Yuan Mei 袁枚 (1716–1789). In *Yuan Mei quanji* 袁枚全集 (Nanjing: Jiangsu guji chubanshe, 1993), *ce* 5.

Sujun chenghe sanheng sizhi tushuo 蘇郡城河三橫四直圖説 (Explanation of the Map of the Three Latitudinal and Four Longitudinal Rivers in the Prefectural City of Suzhou). Sheng Linji 盛林基. Qing, 1797. In *MQSgbj* (see citation), pp. 309–311.

Sun Jingzhi 孫敬之 (1983). *Zhongguo jingji dili gailun* 中國經濟地理概論 (On the Economic Geography of China). Beijing: Shangwu yinshuguan.

Su tan 蘇談 (Stories of Suzhou). Yang Xunji 楊循吉 (1458–1546). Ming. *Xuehai leibian* ed. Taibei: Taiwan wenyuan shuju, 1964.

Suzhou fengsu 蘇州風俗 (Customs in Suzhou). Zhou Zhenhe 周振鶴. First published in ca. 1928. Shanghai: Shanghai wenyi chubanshe, 1989.

Suzhoufu zhi 蘇州府志 (Gazetteer of Suzhou Prefecture). Li Mingwan 李銘皖 and Feng Guifen 馮桂芬. Late Qing, 1883. Taibei: Chengwen chubanshe, 1970.

Suzhou jiuzhuzhai cankao tulu 蘇州舊住宅參考圖錄 (Collection of Reference Illustrations of Old Houses in Suzhou). Shanghai: Tongji Daxue textbook, 1958 (restricted circulation).

"Suzhou Xuanmiao Guan zhigao" "蘇州玄妙觀志稿" (A Manuscript of the Annals of Suzhou's Xuanmiao Guan). *Suzhou shizhi ziliao xuanbian* 蘇州史志資料選編, *ce* 3 (1984, restricted circulation), pp. 142–184.

Suzhou yuanlin 蘇州園林 (Suzhou's Gardens). Shanghai: Tongji Daxue chubanshe, 1991.

Suzhou zhizaoju zhi 蘇州織造局志 (Annals of Suzhou's Textile Bureau). Sun Pei 孫珮. Qing, ca. 1686. Nanjing: Jiangsu renmin chubanshe, 1959.

Taiping huanyu ji 太平寰宇記 (Taiping Reign-Period General Description of the World). Yue Shi 樂史 (930–1007). Northern Song, A.D. 976–983. Taibei: Wenhai chubanshe, 1963.

Taiping yulan 太平御覽 (Taiping Reign-Period Imperial Encyclopaedia). Edited by Li Fang 李昉 (925–996) et al. Song, A.D. 983. Beijing: Zhonghua shuju, 1960.

Tanaka Tan 田中淡 (1983). "Jujiro ni tatsu hoji rokaku" "十字路に立つ報時樓閣" (Towers for Keeping Time at the Crossroads), *Chyamus* no. 5 (1983): 20–22.

Tan Qixiang 譚其驤, ed. (1982). *Zhongguo lishi ditu ji* 中國歷史地圖集. Shanghai: Ditu chubanshe.

Tao'an mengyi 陶庵夢憶 (Dream Recollections of the Past by [Zhang] Tao'an). Zhang Dai 張岱 (1597–ca. 1685). Late Ming to early Qing. Hangzhou: Xihu shushe, 1982.

Terada Takanobu 寺田隆信 (1958). "SoSo chiho ni okeru toshi no mengyo shonin ni tsuite" "蘇松地方に於ける都市の棉業商人について" (Concerning Cotton Industry Merchants in the Cities of the Suzhou and Songjiang Region), *Shirin* 41:6 (November 1958): 52–69.

Terada Takanobu 寺田隆信 (1972). *Sansei shonin no kenkyu* 山西商人の研究 (Studies of Shanxi Merchants). Kyoto: Toyoshi Kenkyukai.

Tianfu guangji 天府廣記 (Extended Record of the Heavenly Prefecture [Prefecture of Shuntian]). Sun Chengze 孫承澤 (1592–1676). Early Qing, ca. 1671. Beijing: Beijing guji chubanshe, 1984.

Tianxia junguo libing shu (*Tjls*) 天下郡國利病書 (Advantages and Disadvantages of Prefectures and Principalities under Heaven). Gu Yanwu 顧炎武 (1613–1682). Qing, 1662. *Sc* ed.

Tongqiao yizhao lu 桐橋倚棹錄 (Records Written on a Boat by the Tong Bridge). Gu Lu 顧祿. Qing, 1842. Shanghai: Shanghai guji chubanshe, 1980.

Tong ya 通雅 (General Explanation of Words and Sentences in Ancient Texts). Fang Yizhi 方以智 (1611–1671). Ming and Qing, finished 1636, printed 1666. In *Fang Yizhi quanshu* 方以智全書, *ce* 1. Edited by Hou Wailu 侯外廬. Shanghai: Shanghai guji chubanshe, 1988.

Uemura Seiji 植村清二 (1974). *Banri no chojo* 万里の長城 (The Great Wall). Tokyo: Sogensha.

Umehara Kaoru 梅原郁 (1966). "Sodai no chiho toshi" "宋代の地方都市" (Local Cities in the Song Dynasty), *Rekishi kyoiku* 14:12 (December 1966), 52–58.

Wang Li 王力 (1980). *Hanyu shigao* 漢語史稿. (Draft History of the Chinese Language). Rev. ed. of 1956. Beijing: Zhonghua shuju.

Wang Qianjin 汪前進 (1990). "Nan Song beike *Pingjiang tu* yanjiu" "南宋碑刻平江圖研究" (A Study of the Southern Song Stele—The Map of Pingjiang). In Cao et al. (1990) (see citation), pp. 50–55.

Wang Xun 王遜 (1985). *Zhongguo meishu shi* 中國美術史 (A History of Chinese Art). Shanghai: Shanghai renmin yishu chubanshe.

Wang Zian ji zhu 王子安集注 (Commentary on the Collective works of Wang Zian [i.e., Wang Bo, 650–726]). Jiang Qingyi 蔣清翊. Qing, second half of nineteenth century. Shanghai: Shanghai guji chubanshe, 1995.

Wanli yehuo bian 萬曆野獲編 (Random Gatherings of the Wanli Reign-Period). Shen Defu 沈德符 (1578–1642). Late Ming, preface 1606; supplemented in 1710s by Shen Zhen 沈振. Beijing: Zhonghua shuju, 1959.

Wei Liaozi 尉繚子 (The Book of Master Wei Liao). Attributed to Wei Liao 尉繚. Warring States. *Sq* ed. Shanghai: Shanghai guji chubanshe, 1987.

Wei Songshan 魏嵩山 (1988). "Gudai Wu liguo de fayuandi jiqi jiangyu de bianqian" "古代吳立國的發源地及其疆域的變遷" (On the Original Location of the Wu State and Its Territorial Changes). In *Wu wenhua lunwen ji* (see citation), pp. 111–122.

Wei Zhonghua 魏仲華 and Xu Bingruo 徐冰若, eds. (1986). *Shaoxing* 紹興. Beijing: Zhongguo jianzhu gongye chubanshe.

Wenjian chanyou lu 聞見闡幽錄 (Disclosing Records of the Things Heard and Seen). Wei Guangfu 韋光黻 (ca. 1789–1853). Qing. Suzhou: Jiangsu shengli Suzhou tushuguan, 1939.

Wen Liding 聞立鼎 (1988). "Zhanguo zhi Wudai Suzhou chengshi jianshe de fazhan" "戰國至五代

蘇州城市建設的發展" (Development of Suzhou City Construction from the Warring States Period to the Five Dynasties [475 B.C.–A.D. 979]). In *Wu wenhua lunwen ji* (see citation), pp. 54–67.
Wen xuan 文選 (General Anthology of Prose and Verse). Edited by Xiao Tong 蕭統 (A.D. 501–531). Liang. Beijing: Zhonghua shuju, 1977.
Wucheng riji 吳城日記 (Diary on Wu City [Suzhou]). Writer unknown. Early Qing, seventeenth century. Abridged and commented on by Ye Tingguan 葉廷琯 in late Qing. Nanjing: Jiangsu guji chubanshe, 1985.
Wudi ji 吳地記 (Record of Wu Region). Original writers unknown. Compiled by Lu Guangwei 陸廣微. Late Tang, with "Houji 後集" (Supplement) and interpolations by scholars down to the Southern Song. Nanjing: Jiangsu guji chubanshe, 1986.
Wudu fu 吳都賦 (Rhymed Prose Poem on the Capital of Wu State [Suzhou]). Zuo Si 左思 (ca. 250–305). Jin, ca. A.D. 270. In *Wen xuan* (see citation), juan 5. 1–27.
Wudu wencui 吳都文粹 (The Best of Literature from [the Area of the old] Wu Capital). Zheng Huchen 鄭虎臣. Southern Song, thirteenth century. *Sq* ed. Shanghai: Shanghai guji chubanshe, 1987.
Wudu wencui xuji 吳都文粹續集 (A Continuation of the *Wudu wencui*). Qian Gu 錢穀 (1508–?). Ming, 1565. *Sq* ed. Shanghai: Shanghai guji chubanshe, 1987.
Wufeng lu 吳風錄 (A Record of the Customs of Wu [Suzhou]). Huang Xingzeng 黃省曾 (1490–1540). Ming. *Xuehai leibian* ed. Taibei: Taiwan wenyuan shuju, 1964.
Wujun Tujing xuji 吳郡圖經續記 (*WTx*) (Supplementary Notes to the *Xiangfu tujing* on the Wu Prefecture). Zhu Changwen 朱長文 (1041–1098). Northern Song, 1084. Nanjing: Jiangsu guji chubanshe, 1986.
Wujun zhi 吳郡志 (Topography of Wu Prefecture). Fan Chengda 范成大 (1126–1193). Song, 1192–1193; addenda, 1229–1255. Nanjing: Jiangsu guji chubanshe, 1986.
Wulin jiushi 武林舊事 (Old Stories of Wulin [Hangzhou]). Zhou Mi 周密 (1232–1298). Southern Song, thirteenth century. Beijing: Zhongguo shangye chubanshe, 1982.
Wuli tongkao 五禮通考 (Comprehensive Investigation of the Five [Categories of] Rites). Qin Huitian 秦蕙田 (1702–1764). Qing, 1761. *Sq* ed. Shanghai: Shanghai guji chubanshe, 1987.
Wumen biaoyin 吳門表隱 (Description of the Concealed Things and Events in the Wu Region). Gu Zhentao 顧震濤 (1750–?). Qing, 1834. Nanjing: Jiangsu guji chubanshe, 1986.
Wumen zhonggao 吳門忠告 (Advice on [the Building of] the Wu [Suzhou] City Gates). Hu Shunshen 胡舜申 (ca. 1081–?). Southern Song, first half of twelfth century. In *Wujun zhi* (see citation), *juan* 3, pp. 24–26.
Wu wenhua lunwen ji 吳文化論文集 (Collected Discourses on Wu Culture). Guangzhou: Zhongshan Daxue chubanshe, 1988.
Wuxian cheng tu shuo 吳縣城圖說 (Illustrated Discourse on the City Walls of Wu County). Cao Zishou 曹自守. Ming, ca. 1559–1560. In *Tjls* (see citation), *juan* 5, pp. 11b–12a.
Wuxian zhi 吳縣志 (Annals of Wu County). Wu Xiuzhi 吳秀之 and Cao Yunyuan 曹允源. 1933. Taibei: Chengwen chubanshe, 1970.
Wu Yue chunqiu 吳越春秋 (Spring and Autumn Annals of the Wu and Yue [States]). Zhao Ye 趙曄 (fl. A.D. 40). Eastern Han. Nanjing: Jiangsu guji chubanshe, 1986.
Wuyue youcao 五嶽遊草 (Manuscripts on the Travels to the Five [Primary] Mountains). Wang

Shixing 王士性 (1547–1598). Ming, preface 1591. In W*ang Shixing dili shu sanzhong* (see entry for *Guang zhi yi*), pp. 19–209.

Wuzhong guyu 吳中故語 (Old Stories of Suzhou). Yang Xunji 楊循吉 (1458–1546). Ming. In *Shuofu xu* 説郛續 (A Continuation of the *Shuofu* [Encyclopaedia]), *jiu* (i.e., *juan*) 14, compiled by Tao Ting 陶珽 and printed by Li Jiqi's 李際期 Wanwei Shantang 宛委山堂 in 1646.

Wuzhong jiushi 吳中舊事 (Old Wonders of the Wu Region). Lu Youren 陸友仁. Yuan. *Sq* ed. Shanghai: Shanghai guji chubanshe, 1987.

Wuzhong shuili quanshu 吳中水利全書 (*Wsq*) (Complete Book of the Water Conservancy of the Wu District). Zhang Guowei 張國維. Ming, ca. 1630s to 1640s. *Sq* ed. Shanghai: Shanghai guji chubanshe, 1987.

Xianchun Lin'an zhi 咸淳臨安志 (Gazetteer of Lin'an during the Xianchun Reign-Period [1265–1275]). Qian Yueyou 潛説友. Southern Song. Taibei: Chengwen chubanshe, 1970.

Xianqing ouji 閑情偶寄 (A Casual Deposit of Leisurely Moods). Li Yu 李漁 (1611–1680). Qing, 1671. Hangzhou: Zhejiang guji chubanshe, 1985.

Xiao Menglong 肖夢龍 (1988). "Wuguo de Sanci Qiandu Shitan" "吳國的三次遷都試探" (On the Three Transferences of Wu's Capital). In *Wu wenhua lunwen ji* (see citation), pp. 14–32.

Xiaoxia xianji xuancun (*Xxx*) 消夏閑記選存 (A Selection from Leisurely Writings to While the Summer Away). Gu Gongxie 顧公燮. Qing, preface 1785. Suzhou: Jiangsu shengli Suzhou tushuguan, 1940.

Xiaoxia xianji zhaichao (*Xxz*) 消夏閑記摘抄 (Excerpts from Leisurely Writings to While the Summer Away). Gu Gongxie 顧公燮. Qing, preface 1785. Shanghai: Shanghai shangwu yinshuguan, 1917.

Xihu laoren fansheng lu 西湖老人繁勝錄 (Record of the Prosperous Past by the Old Man of West Lake). Writer unknown. Southern Song. Beijing: Zhongguo shangye chubanshe, 1982.

Xihu youlan zhi 西湖游覽志 (Record of the Area around the West Lake). Tian Rucheng 田汝成 (ca. 1503–?). Ming. *Sq* ed. Shanghai: Shanghai guji chubanshe, 1987.

Xin Tang shu 新唐書 (New History of the Tang Dynasty [A.D. 618–896]). Ouyang Xiu 歐陽修 (1007–1072), Song Qi 宋祁 (998–1061) et al. Song, 1060. Beijing: Zhonghua shuju, 1975.

Xuexin fu 雪心賦 (Rhymed Prose from Snow-Pure Heart). Attributed to Bu Yingtian 卜應天. Tang. Annotated by Meng Hao 孟浩 in 1680 in the edition *Xuexin fu zhengjie* 雪心賦正解 (Rectified Interpretation of the *Xuexin fu*). Xinzhu: Zhulin yinshuju, 1989.

Xu Jialu 許嘉璐, ed. (1991). *Zhongguo gudai lisu cidian* 中國古代禮俗辭典 (A Dictionary of Ancient Chinese Etiquette and Customs). Beijing: Zhongguo youyi chuban gongsi.

Xunzi 荀子 (The Book of Master Xun). Xun Kuang 荀況 (courtesy name Xun Qing 荀卿) (ca. 313–238 B.C.). Warring States, ca. 240 B.C. Commented on in late Qing by Wang Xianqian 王先謙 (1842–1917) in the edition *Xunzi jijie* 荀子集解 (Collective Interpretations of the *Xunzi*). *Zj* ed. Beijing: Zhonghua shuju, 1954.

Xu Yinong 許亦農 (1989, 1990). "Zhongguo chuantong fuhe kongjian guannian" "中國傳統复合空間觀念" (Composite Space Concepts in Traditional Chinese Architecture). *Jianzhushi* 36 (December 1989): 67–87; 38 (July 1990): 71–96, 37; 39 (June 1990): 67–82.

Yandu congkao 燕都叢考 (Collected Works on the Study of the Capitals at Yan [Beijing]). Chen

Zongfan 陳宗蕃 (1879–1954). 3 *juan*: *juan* 1, 1930; *juan* 2 and 3, 1931. Beijing: Beijing guji chubanshe, 1991.
Yang Jinding 楊金鼎, ed. (1987). *Zhongguo wenhua shi cidian* 中國文化史詞典 (A Dictionary of Chinese Cultural History). Hangzhou: Zhejiang guji chubanshe.
Yao Chengzu 姚承祖 (1986). *Yingzao fayuan* 營造法原 (Building Techniques and Their Sources). Teaching manuscript in 1920s to 1930s. Restructured and amended by Zhang Zhigang 張至剛 in 1937. Beijing: Zhongguo jianzhu gongye chubanshe.
Ye ji 野記 (Unofficial Record). Zhu Yunming 祝允明 (1460–1526). Ming, preface 1511. In *Guochao diangu* (see citation), pp. 492–600.
Yi li 儀禮 (Ceremonies and Rituals). Writers/compilers unknown. Spring and Autumn to Warring States. *Sz* ed. Beijing: Zhonghua shuju, 1980.
Yingzao fashi 營造法式 (Building Standards). Li Jie 李誡 . Song, 1097; printed 1103. *Gjc* ed. Taibei: Taiwen shangwu yinshuguan, 1956.
Yiqie jing yinyi 一切經音義 (Sounds and Meanings of words in All Classics). Hui Lin 慧琳. Tang, ca. first half of ninth century. Supplemented in the Liao by Xi Lin 希麟. Shanghai: Shanghai guji chubanshe, 1986.
Yiwen leiju 藝文類聚 (Literary Records Collected and Classified). Ouyang Xun 歐陽詢 (557–641). Tang, A.D. 624. Shanghai: Shanghai guji chubanshe, 1982.
Yi Zhou shu 逸周書 (Lost Books of the Zhou). Authors unknown. Zhou, ca. third century B.C. *Gjc* ed. Taibei: Taiwen shangwu yinshuguan, 1956.
Yongle dadian 永樂大典 (Great Encyclopaeodia of the Yongle Reign). Xie Jin 解縉 (1369–1415) et al. Ming, 1408. Beijing: Zhonghua shuju, 1960.
Yu Shengfang 俞繩方 (1980). "Woguo gudai chengshi guihua de yige jiezuo—Song Pingjiang (Suzhou) tu" "我國古代城市規劃的一個傑作—宋平江（蘇州）圖" (A Masterpiece of Ancient Chinese City Planning—The City Map of Song Pingjiang [Suzhou]). *Jianzhu xuebao* (January 1980): 15–20.
Yu Shengfang 俞繩方 (1986). "Cong Suzhou lun Zhongguo chengshi guihua de shuixi wenti" "從蘇州論中國城市規劃的水系問題" (A Discussion of the Issue of Waterway Systems in China's City Planning). *Jianzhu xuebao* 217 (September 1986): pp. 37–42.
Yuanhe junxian tuzhi 元和郡縣圖志 (An Illustrated Gazetteer of the Prefectures and Counties during the Yuanhe Reign-Period [806–820]). Li Jifu 李吉甫 (758–814). Tang, 813. Beijing: Zhonghua shuju, 1983.
Yuan shi 元史 (History of the Yuan [Mongol] Dynasty [1206–1367]). Song Lian 宋濂 (1310–1381) et al. Ming, ca. 1370. Beijing: Zhonghua shuju, 1976.
Yuan ye 園冶 (The Craft of Gardens). Ji Cheng 計成 (1582–?). Ming, 1631. Collated by Chen Zhi 陳植 in the edition *Yuan ye zhushi* 園冶注釋. Beijing: Zhongguo jianzhu gongye chubanshe, 1981.
Yue jue shu 越絕書 (Book of the Unique Events of Yue [State]). Yuan Kang 袁康 and Wu Ping 吳平. Eastern Han. Shanghai: Shanghai guji chubanshe, 1985.
Yupu zaji 寓圃雜記 (Scattered Records from the Yu Garden). Wang Qi 王錡 (1433–1499). Ming, preface 1500. Beijing: Zhonghua shuju, 1984.
Zang jing yi 葬經翼 (Complementary Interpretations of the Burial Classic). Miao Xiyong 繆希雍 (?–

1627). Ming. With *Nanjie ershisi pian* 難解二十四篇 (Twenty-four Passages on Difficult Issues); probably later additions. In *Gtj* (see citation), *ce* 476.1a–8b.

Zang shu 葬書 (Burial Book). Attributed to Guo Pu 郭璞 (A.D. 276–324). Ascribed to the Eastern Jin, A.D. fourth century. *Sq* ed. Shanghai: Shanghai guji chubanshe, 1987.

Zhang Guangzhi 張光直 (Chang Kwang-chih) (1983). *Zhongguo qingtong shidai* 中國青銅時代 (Bronze Age China). Beijing: Sanlian shudian.

Zhang Huijian 張慧劍 (1986). *Ming Qing Jiangsu wenren nianbiao* 明清江蘇文人年表 (A Chronicle of Scholars from Jiangsu [Province] during the Ming and Qing periods). Manuscript completed in 1965. Shanghai: Shanghai guji chubanshe.

Zhang Rongming 張榮明 (1994). "Daoyan: kanyu yuanliu jiqi fazhan" "導言：堪輿源流及其發展" (Introduction: the Origin of *Kanyu* and Its Development). In Gu Jie 顧頡, ed., *Kanyu jicheng* 堪輿集成 (Encyclopaedia of *Kanyu*), *ce* 1. Chongqing: Chongqing chubanshe.

Zhanguo ce 戰國策 (Strategems of the Warring States). Writer unknown. Edited in late Western Han by Liu Xiang 劉向 (ca. 77–6 B.C.). Shanghai: Shanghai guji chubanshe, 1985.

Zhao Liying 趙立瀛 (1988). "Lun Tang changan de guihua sixiang jiqi lishi pingjia" "論唐長安的規劃及其歷史評價" (On the Ideas of the Planning of the Tang Chang'an City and Its Historical Assessment). *Jianzhushi* 29 (1988): 41–50.

Zhejiang tongzhi 浙江通志 (Comprehensive Gazetteer of Zhejiang [Province]). Shen Yiji 沈翼機 et al. Qing, revised ed. 1736. Taibei: Jinghua shuju, 1969.

Zhongguo dabaike quanshu: jianzhu yuanlin chengshi guihua 中國大百科全書：建築園林城市規劃 (China's Encyclopaedia: Architecture, Landscape Architecture and Urban Planning). Beijing: Zhongguo dabaike quanshu chubanshe, 1988.

Zhongguo gujianzhu xiushan jishu 中國古建築修繕技術 (Techniques of Restoration of Ancient Chinese Buildings). Beijing: Zhongguo jianzhu gongye chubanshe, 1983.

Zhongguo jianzhu shi 中國建築史 (A History of Chinese Architecture). Beijing: Zhongguo jianzhu gongye chubanshe, 1982.

Zhongguo lishi wenhua mingcheng cidian 中國歷史文化名城詞典 (A Dictionary of the Famous Chinese Cities of History and Culture). Shanghai: Shanghai cishu chubanshe, 1985.

Zhongwu jiwen 中吳紀聞 (Record of Things Heard in the Wu Region). Gong Mingzhi 龔明之. Southern Song, 1174. *Sq* ed. Shanghai: Shanghai guji chubanshe, 1987.

Zhongxiao Ganhui Xianshengwang miao bei 忠孝感惠顯聖王廟碑. Zheng Yuanyou 鄭元祐 (1292–1364). Yuan. In *Qiao-Wu ji* (see citation), *juan* 11.1a–2b.

Zhou Daming 周大鳴 (1988). "Shilun xian-Wu wenhua de shehui fazhan licheng" "試論先吳文化的社會發展歷程" (On the Social Development Process of Pre-Wu Culture). In *Wu wenhua lunwen ji* (see citation), pp. 237–250.

Zhou li 周禮 (Record of the Rites of Zhou). Compilers unknown. Western Han, perhaps containing some material from Late Zhou. *Sz* ed. Beijing: Zhonghua shuju, 1980.

Zhou li zhengyi 周禮正義 (Annotation of the *Zhou li*). Sun Yirang 孫詒讓 (1848–1908). Late Qing. Beijing: Zhonghua shuju, 1987.

Zhou Yi 周易 (Book of Changes of the Zhou). Compiler unknown. Zhou with Western Han additions. *Sz* ed. Beijing: Zhonghua shuju, 1980.

Zhou Yi qianzaodu 周易乾鑿度 (Penetration of Qian of the *Zhou Yi*). Writers unknown. Han, ca. first century B.C. *Sq* ed. Shanghai: Shanghai guji chubanshe, 1987.

Zhu Guanhua 朱觀華 (1984). "Suzhou Daojiao Lishi Gaikuang" "蘇州道教歷史概況" (A General Survey of the History of Daoism in Suzhou). In *Suzhou shizhi ziliao xuanbian, ce* 3 (1984, restricted circulation), pp. 126–141.

Zhuangzi 莊子 (The Book of Master Zhuang). Zhuang Zhou 莊周 (ca. 369–286 B.C.). Zhou, ca. 290 B.C., with later additions. Commented on in late Qing by Wang Xianqian 王先謙 (1842–1917) in the edition *Zhuangzi jijie* 莊子集解 (Collective Interpretation of *Zhuangzi*). *Zj* ed. Beijing: Zhonghua shuju, 1954.

Zizhi tongjian 資治通鑑 (Comprehensive Mirror to Aid Government [403 B.C. to A.D. 959]). Sima Guang 司馬光 (1019–1086). Song, 1084. Beijing: Guji chubanshe, 1956.

Zong Li 宗力 and Liu Qun 劉群 (1987). *Zhongguo minjian zhushen* 中國民間諸神 (Various Popular Gods in China). Shijiazhuang: Hebei renmin chubanshe.

Zuo zhuan 左傳 (Zuo's Commentary). Zuo Qiuming 左丘明. Zhou, compiled between 430 and 250 B.C., with additions and changes by Confucian scholars of the Qin and Han. *Sz* ed. Beijing: Zhonghua shuju, 1980.

Western Language References

Aijmer, Göran (1968). "Being Caught by a Fishnet: On Fengshui in South-eastern China." *Journal of the Hong Kong Branch of the Royal Asiatic Society* 8 (1968): 74–81.

Alberti, Leon Battista (1988). *On the Art of Building in Ten Books*. Trans. of *De re aedificatoria* by Joseph Rykwert, Neil Leach, and Robert Tavernor. Cambridge, MA: The MIT Press.

Balazs, Etienne (1964). *Chinese Civilization and Bureaucracy: Variations on a Theme*. Trans. by H. M. Wright and ed. by Arthur F. Wright. New Haven and London: Yale University Press.

Bennett, Steven J. (1978). "Patterns of the Sky and Earth: A Chinese Science of Applied Cosmology." *Chinese Science* 3 (1978): 1–26.

Biot, Edouard (1851). *Le Tcheou-li*. 2 vols. Paris: Imprimerie nationale.

Bodde, Derk (1938). *China's First Unifier: A Study of the Ch'in Dynasty As Seen in the Life of Li Ssu (280?–208 B.C.)*. Leiden: E. J. Brill.

Boltz, William G. (1993). "*Chou li* 周禮." In Loewe 1993 (see citation), pp. 24–32.

Braunfels, Wolfgang (1988). *Urban Design in Western Europe: Regime and Architecture, 900–1900*. Trans. by Kenneth J. Northcott from the 1976 edition under the title *Abendländische Stadtbaukunst: Herrschaftsform und Baugestalt*. Chicago: University of Chicago Press.

Burke, Gerald (1976). *Townscapes*. Middlesex: Penguin Books.

Buxbaum, David C., and Frederick W. Mote, eds. (1972). *Transition and Permanence: Chinese History and Culture*. Seattle, WA: University of Washington.

Cameron, Nigel, and Brian Brake (1965). *Peking: A Tale of Three Cities*. New York and Evanston: Harper & Row.

Carson, Michael, and Michael Loewe (1993). "*Lü shih ch'un ch'iu* 呂氏春秋." In Loewe, ed. 1993 (see citation), pp. 324–330.

Chan, Hok-lam (1988). "The Chien-wen, Yung-lo, Hung-hsi, and Hsüan-te reigns." In Mote and Twitchett, eds. 1988 (see citation), pp. 182–304.
Chang, Kwang-chih (1976). *Early Chinese Civilization: Anthropological Perspectives.* Cambridge, MA and London, England: Harvard University Press.
Chang, Kwang-chih (1983). *Art, Myth, and Ritual: The Path to Political Authority in Ancient China.* Cambridge, MA and London, England: Harvard University Press.
Chang, Kwang-chih (1986). *The Archaeology of Ancient China.* 4th ed., revised and enlarged. New Haven and London: Yale University Press.
Chang, Sen-dou (1961). "Some Aspects of the Urban Geography of the Chinese Hsien Capital." *Annals of the Association of American Geographers* 51, no. 1 (March 1961): 23–45.
Chang, Sen-dou (1963). "The Historical Trend of Chinese Urbanization." *Annals of the Association of American Geographers* 53, no. 2 (June 1963): 109–143.
Chang, Sen-dou (1977). "The Morphology of Walled Capitals." In Skinner, ed. 1977 (see citation), pp. 75–100.
Chatley, H. (1917). "Fêng Shui." In Samuel Couling, ed., *The Encyclopaedia Sinica* (Shanghai: Kelly and Walsh), p. 175.
Cheng, Anne (1993). "*Ch'un ch'iu* 春秋, *Kung yang* 公羊, *Ku liang* 穀梁 and *Tso chuan* 左傳." In Loewe, ed. 1993 (see citation), pp. 67–76.
Clément, Pierre (1983). *Les Capitales chinoises, leur modèle et leur site.* Paris: L'institut Français d'Architecture.
Clément, Sophie et al. (1982). *Architecture du paysage en Asie orientale.* Paris: L'institut Français d'Architecture.
Clunas, Craig (1996). *Fruitful Sites: Garden Culture in Ming Dynasty China.* Durham, NC: Duke University Press.
Coaldrake, William H. (1991). "City Planning and Palace Architecture in the Creation of the Nara Political Order: the Accommodation of Place and Purpose at Heijo-kyo." *East Asian History* 1 (June 1991): 37–54.
Creel, Herrlee G. (1964). "The Beginnings of Bureaucracy in China: The Origin of the Hsien." *Journal of Asian Studies* 23, no. 2 (1964): pp. 155–183.
Creel, Herrlee G. (1970). *The Origins of Statecraft in China.* Vol. One: *The Western Chou Empire.* Chicago: The University of Chicago Press.
De Groot, J. J. M. (1897). *The Religious System of China*, Vol. 3. Leiden: E. J. Brill.
Dreyer, Edward L. (1982). *Early Ming China: A Political History, 1355–1435.* Stanford, CA: Stanford University Press.
Dreyer, Edward L. (1988). "Military Origins of Ming China." In Mote and Twitchett, eds. 1988 (see citation), pp. 58–106.
Du Bose, Hampden C. (1911). *A Handbook to Soochow, the Capital of Kiangsu.* Shanghai: Kelly & Walsh.
Durkheim, Émile, and Marcel Mauss (1963). *Primitive Classification.* Trans. from the French ed. *De Quelques Formes Primitives de Classification* (Année Sociologique, 1903) and ed. with an introduction by Rodney Needham. London: Cohen & West.

Dyos, H. J. (1961). *Victorian Suburb: A Study of the Growth of Camberwell.* Foreword by Sir John Summerson. Leicester: Leicester University Press.

Eastman, Lloyd E. (1988). *Family, Fields, and Ancestors: Constancy and Change in China's Social and Economic History, 1550–1949.* New York and Oxford: Oxford University Press.

Eberhard, Wolfram (1962). *Social Mobility in Traditional China.* Leiden: E. J. Brill.

Eberhard, Wolfram (1967). *Settlement and Social Change in Asia.* Hong Kong: Hong Kong University Press.

Eck, Diana L. (1987). "The City as a Sacred Center." In Smith and Reynolds, eds. 1987 (see citation), pp. 1–11.

Eitel, E. J. (1979). *Feng Shui, or The Rudiments of Natural Science in China.* 3rd ed. Bristol: Pentacle Books.

Eliade, Mircea (1959). *The Sacred and the Profane: The Nature of Religion.* Translated from the French ed. by Willard R. Trask. New York: Harcourt Brace Jovanovich.

Elliot, Alan J. A. (1955). *Chinese Spirit-Medium Cults in Singapore.* Department of Anthropology, the London School of Economics and Political Science.

Elman, Benjamin A. (1984). *From Philosophy to Philology: Intellectual and Social Aspects of Change in Late Imperial China.* Cambridge, MA: Council on East Asian Studies, Harvard University.

Elvin, Mark (1973). *The Pattern of the Chinese Past.* London: Eyre Methuen Limited.

Elvin, Mark (1977). "Market Towns and Waterways: The County of Shang-hai from 1480 to 1910." In Skinner, ed. 1977 (see citation), pp. 441–473.

Elvin, Mark (1978). "Chinese Cities since the Sung Dynasty." In Philip Abrams and E. A. Wrigley, eds., *Towns in Societies: Essays in Economic History and Historical Sociology* (Cambridge: Cambridge University Press, 1978), pp. 79–89.

Fairbank, John King (1992). *China: A New History.* Cambridge, MA: The Belknap Press of Harvard University Press.

Feuchtwang, Stephan (1974). *An Anthropological Analysis of Chinese Geomancy.* Vientiane and Paris: Vithagna.

Feuchtwang, Stephan (1977). "School-Temple and City God." In Skinner, ed. 1977 (see citation), pp. 581–608.

Finanne, Antonia (1993). "Yangzhou: A Central Place in the Qing Empire." In Johnson, ed. 1993 (see citation), pp. 117–149.

Frankfort, Henri (1948). *Kingship and the Gods: A Study of Ancient Near Eastern Religion as the Integration of Society & Nature.* Chicago: The University of Chicago Press.

Freedman, Maurice (1971). *Chinese Lineage and Society: Fukien and Kwangtung.* London: Athlone Press.

Freedman, Maurice (1974). "On the Sociological Study of Chinese Religion." In Arthur P. Wolf, ed., *Religion and Ritual in Chinese Society* (Stanford, CA: Stanford University Press, 1974), pp. 19–41.

Freedman, Maurice (1979). *The Study of Chinese Society: Essays by Maurice Freedman.* Selected and introduced by G. William Skinner. Stanford, CA: Stanford University Press.

Freedman, Maurice (1979a). "Chinese Geomancy: Some Observations in Hong Kong." In Freedman, 1979, pp. 189–211.

Freedman, Maurice (1979b). "Geomancy." In Freedman, ed. 1979, pp. 313–333.
French, Jere Stuart (1983). *Urban Space: A Brief History of the City Square.* 2nd ed. Dubuque: Kendall/Hunt Publishing Company.
Geertz, Clifford (1973). *The Interpretation of Cultures.* New York: Basic Books, Inc.
Gernet, Jacques (1970a). *Daily Life in China: On the Eve of the Mongol Invasion 1250–1276.* Translated by H. M. Wright. Stanford, CA: Stanford University Press.
Gernet, Jacques (1970b). "Note sur les villes chinoises au moment de l'apogée islamique." In A. H. Hourani and S. M. Stern, eds. *The Islamic City* (Oxford: Bruno Cassirer), pp. 77–85.
Gernet, Jacques (1982). *A History of Chinese Civilization.* Translated by J. R. Foster from the French edition of 1972 under the title *Le Monde Chinois* (Paris: Librairie Armand Colin). Cambridge: Cambridge University Press.
Glahn, Else (1975). "On the Transmission of the Ying-tsao fa-shih." *T'oung Pao* 61 (1975): 232–265.
Glahn, Else (1981). "Chinese Building Standards in the 12th Century." *Scientific American* 244, no. 5 (May 1981): 132–141.
Glahn, Else (1984). "Unfolding the Chinese Building Standards: Research on the *Yingzao fashi.*" In Nancy Shatzman Steinhardt, ed., *Chinese Traditional Architecture* (New York: China Institute, 1984), pp. 47–57.
Golas, Peter J. (1977). "Early Qing Guilds." In Skinner, ed. 1977 (see citation), pp. 555–580.
Goodrich, L. Carrington, ed. (1976). *Dictionary of Ming Biography 1368–1644.* New York and London: Columbia University Press.
Graham, A. C. (1986). *Yin-Yang and the Nature of Correlative Thinking.* Occasional Paper and Monography Series No. 6. Singapore: The Institute of East Asian Philosophies, National University of Singapore.
Graham, A. C. (1989). *Disputers of the Tao: Philosophical Argument in Ancient China.* La Salle, IL: Open Court Publishing Co.
Granet, Marcel (1930). *Chinese Civilization.* Translated by Kathleen E. Innes and Mabel R. Brailsford. London: Kegan Paul, Trench, Trubner & Co., Ltd.
Granet, Marcel (1934). *La pensée chinoise.* Paris: La Renaissance du livre.
Granet, Marcel (1975). *The Religion of the Chinese People.* Translated from the French edition of 1922 by Maurice Freedman. New York: Harper & Row, Publishers, Inc.
Hackett, Brian (1950). *Man, Society and Environment: The Historical Basis of Planning.* London: Percival Marshall.
Haeger, John Winthrop, ed. (1975). *Crisis and Prosperity in Sung China.* Tucson, AZ: University of Arizona Press.
Hawkes, David (1985). *The Songs of the South: An Ancient Chinese Anthology of Poems by Qu Yuan and Other Poets.* Harmondsworth, England: Penguin Books, 1985.
Hay, John, ed. (1994). *Boundaries in China.* London: Reaktion Books.
Hay, John (1994a). "Introduction." In Hay, ed. 1994, pp. 1–55.
Healy, Seán (1968). *Town Life.* London: B. T. Batsford.
Henderson, John B. (1984). *The Development and Decline of Chinese Cosmology.* New York: Columbia University Press.

Hilberseimer, L. (1955). *The Nature of Cities: Origin, Growth, and Decline, Pattern and Form, Planning Problems*. Chicago: Paul Theobald & Co.
Hillier, Bill, and Julienne Hanson (1984). *The Social Logic of Space*. Cambridge: Cambridge University Press.
Ho, P. T. (1962). *The Ladder of Success in Imperial China*. New York: Columbia University Press.
Hohenberg, Paul M., and Lynn Hollen Lees (1985). *The Making of Urban Europe, 1000–1950*. Cambridge, MA: Harvard University Press.
Johnson, David (1985a). "Communication, Class, and Consciousness in Late Imperial China." In David Johnson et al. 1985, pp. 34–72.
Johnson, David (1985b). "The City-God Cults of T'ang and Sung China." *Harvard Journal of Asiatic Studies* 45, no. 2 (December 1985): 363–457.
Johnson, David, Andrew J. Nathan, and Evelyn S. Rawski, eds. (1985). *Popular Culture in Late Imperial China*. Berkeley and Los Angeles, CA: University of California Press.
Johnson, Linda Cooke, ed. (1993). *Cities of Jiangnan in Late Imperial China*. Albany: State University of New York Press.
Johnston, R. Stewart (1983). "The Ancient City of Suzhou: Town Planning in the Sung [*sic*] Dynasty." *Town Planning Review* 54, no. 2 (1983): 194–222.
Kertzer, David (1988). *Ritual, Politics, and Power*. New Haven and London: Yale University Press.
Knapp, Ronald G. (1989). *China's Vernacular Architecture: House Form and Culture*. Honolulu: University of Hawai'i Press.
Knechtges, David R. (1982). *Wen xuan, or Selections of Refined Literature*. Vol. 1: *Rhapsodies on Metropolises and Capitals*. Princeton, New Jersey: Princeton University Press.
Ko, Dorothy (1994). "Lady-scholars at the Door: The Practice of Gender Relations in Eighteenth-Century Suzhou." In Hay, ed. 1994 (see citation), pp. 198–216.
Kostof, Spiro (1991). *The City Shaped: Urban Patterns and Meanings Through History*. London: Thames and Hudson Ltd.
Kostof, Spiro (1992). *The City Assembled: the Elements of Urban Form Through History*. London: Thames and Hudson Ltd.
Kracke, Jr., E. A. (1955). "Sung Society: Change within Tradition." *Far Eastern Quarterly* 14 (1955): 479–488.
Kracke, Jr., E. A. (1975). "Sung K'ai-feng: Pragmatic Metropolis and Formalistic Capital." In Haeger, ed. 1975 (see citation), pp. 49–77.
Lagerwey, John (1993). "*Wu Yüeh ch'un ch'iu* 吳越春秋." In Loewe, ed. 1993 (see citation), pp. 473–476.
Lamley, Harry J. (1977). "The Formation of Cities: Initiative and Motivation in Building Three Walled Cities in Taiwan." In Skinner, ed. 1977 (see citation), pp. 155–209.
Le Blanc, Charles (1993). "*Huai nan tzu* 淮南子." In Loewe, ed. 1993 (see citation), pp. 189–195.
Legge, James (1899). *I Ching, Book of Changes*. In *Sacred Books of the East Series,* Vol. 16. Oxford: Clarendon Press.
Legge, James (1960). *The Chinese Classics*. 5 vols. Hong Kong: Hong Kong University Press.
Legge, James (1967). *Li Chi: Book of Rites*. 2 vols. Edited, with Introduction and study guide, by Ch'u Chai and Winberg Chai. New Hyde Park, NY: University Books.

Levi-Strauss, Claude (1962). *La pensée sauvage*. Paris: Plon.
Liu, Laurence G. (1989). *Chinese Architecture*. London: Academy Editions.
Loewe, Michael, ed. (1993). *Early Chinese Texts. A Bibliographical Guide*, Early China Special Monograph Series, No. 2. Berkeley: The Society for the Study of Early China and the Institute of East Asian Studies, University of California.
March, Andrew L. (1968). "An Appreciation of Chinese Geomancy." *Journal of Asian Studies* XXVII, no. 2 (February 1968): 253–267.
Marmé, Michael (1981). "Population and Possibility in Ming (1368–1644) Suzhou: A Quantified Model." *Ming Studies* 12 (Spring 1981): 29–64.
Marmé, Michael (1993). "Heaven on Earth: The Rise of Suzhou, 1127–1550." In Linda Cooke Johnson, ed. 1993 (see citation), pp. 17–45.
Meskill, John (1965). *Ch'oe Pu's Diary: A Record of Drifting Across the Sea*. Tucson, AZ: The University of Arizona Press.
Meyer, Jeffrey F. (1987), "Traditional Peking: The Architecture of Conditional Power." In Smith and Reynolds, eds. 1987 (see citation), pp. 114–133.
Meyer, Jeffrey F. (1991). *The Dragons of Tiananmen: Beijing as a Sacred City*. Columbia, SC: University of South Carolina Press.
Morris, A. E. J. (1994). *History of Urban Form: Before the Industrial Revolutions*. 3rd ed. Essex: Longman Scientific & Technical.
Mote, F. W. (1962). *The Poet Kao Ch'i 1336–1374*. Princeton, NJ: Princeton University Press.
Mote, F. W. (1970). "The City in Traditional Chinese Civilization." In James T. C. Liu and Wei-ming Tu, eds. *Traditional China* (NY: Prentice-Hall, 1970), pp. 42–49.
Mote, F. W. (1971). *Intellectual Foundations of China*. New York: Alfred A. Knopf.
Mote, F. W. (1972). "The Cosmological Gulf Between China and the West." In Buxbaum and Mote, eds. 1972 (see citation), pp. 3–21.
Mote, F. W. (1973). "A Millennium of Chinese Urban History: Form, Time, and Space Concepts in Soochow." *Rice University Studies* 59, no. 4 (Fall 1973): 35–65.
Mote, F. W. (1977). "The Transformation of Nanking, 1350–1400." In Skinner, ed. 1977 (see citation), pp. 101–153.
Mote, Frederick W., and Denis Twitchett, eds. (1988). *The Ming Dynasty, 1368–1644, Part 1. The Cambridge History of China, Vol. 7*. Cambridge: Cambridge University Press.
Mumford, Lewis (1938). *The Culture of Cities*. New York: Harcourt, Brace.
Mumford, Lewis (1961). *The City in History: Its Origins, Its Transformation, and Its Prospects*. London: Secker & Warburg.
Murphey, Rhoads (1954). "The City as a Center of Change: Western Europe and China." *Annals of the Association of American Geographers* 44, no. 4 (December 1954): 349–362.
Murphey, Rhoads (1984). "City as a Mirror of Society: China, Tradition and Transformation." In John A. Agnew, John Mercer, and David E. Sopher, eds. *The City in Cultural Context* (Boston: Allen & Unwin), pp. 186–204.
Myers, Ramon H. (1974). "Transformation and Continuity of Chinese Econom ic and Social History." *Journal of Asian Studies* XXXIII, no. 2 (February 1974): 265–277.

Naquin, Susan, and Evelyn S. Rawski (1987). *Chinese Society in the Eighteenth Century.* New Haven and London: Yale University Press.

Needham, Joseph (1956). *Science and Civilization in China,* Vol. 2. Cambridge: Cambridge University Press.

Needham, Joseph (1959). *Science and Civilization in China,* Vol. 3. Cambridge: Cambridge University Press.

Needham, Joseph (1962). *Science and Civilization in China,* Vol. 4, Part I. Cambridge: Cambridge University Press.

Needham, Joseph (1971). *Science and Civilization in China,* Vol. 4, Part III. Cambridge: Cambridge University Press.

Norberg-Schulz, Christian (1971). *Existence, Space & Architecture.* New York: Praeger Publishers.

Norberg-Schulz, Christian (1980a). *Genius Loci: Towards a Phenomenology of Architecture.* New York: Rizzoli International Publications, Inc.

Norberg-Schulz, Christian (1980b). *Meaning in Western Architecture.* Rev. ed. New York: Rizzoli International Publications, Inc.

Norberg-Schulz, Christian (1985). *The Concept of Dwelling: On the Way to Figurative Architecture.* New York: Rizzoli International Publications, Inc.

(Oliphant, Laurence) L.B.O. (1845). "Excursion to the City of Súchau." *The Chinese Repository,* Vol. XIV: From January to December (1845), pp. 584–587.

Oliphant, Laurence (1970). *Elgin's Mission of China and Japan.* Introduction by J. J. Gerson. Ely House, London: Oxford University Press.

Peterson, Willard J. (1982). "Making Connections: 'Commentary on the Attached Verbalisations' of the Book of Change." *Harvard Journal of Asiatic Studies* 42, no. 1 (1982): 67–116.

Polachek, James (1975). "Gentry Hegemony: Soochow in the T'ung-chih Restoration." In Wakeman, and Grant, eds. 1975 (see citation), pp. 211–256.

Rapoport, Amos (1969). *House Form and Culture.* Englewood Cliffs, NJ: Prentice-Hall, Inc.

Rawski, Evelyn S. (1985a). "Economic and Social Foundations of Late Imperial Culture." In Johnson et al., eds. 1985 (see citation), pp. 3–33.

Rawski, Evelyn S. (1985b). "Problems and Prospects." In Johnson et al., eds. 1985 (see citation), pp. 399–417.

Rickett, W. Allyn (1985). *Guanzi,* Vol. 1. Princeton, NJ: Princeton University Press.

Ross, Sir E. Denison, and Eileen Power, eds. (1931). *The Broadway Travellers: The Travels of Marco Polo.* Trans. from the text of L. F. Benedetto by Professor Aldo Rocci. London: George Routledge & Sons, Ltd.

Rossi, Aldo (1982). *The Architecture of the City.* Translated from the Italian edition entitled *L'architettura della citta* by Diane Ghirardo and Joan Ockman. Cambridge, MA: The MIT Press.

Rowe, William T. (1993). "Introduction: City and Region in the Lower Yangzi." In Johnson, ed. 1993 (see citation), pp. 1–15.

Ruitenbeek, Klaas (1993). *Carpentry and Building in Late Imperial China: A Study of the Fifteenth-Century Carpenter's Manual* Lu Ban jing. Leiden: E. J. Brill.

Rykwert, Joseph (1989). *The Idea of a Town.* Cambridge, MA: MIT Press.

Samuels, Marwyn S. (1978). "Review Article: The City in Late Imperial China." *Journal of Asian Studies* XXXVII, no. 4 (August 1978): 713–723.

Santangelo, Paolo (1992). "Alcuni aspetti di vita urbana: Suzhou, una metropoli 'moderna' fra il XVI e il XVIII secolo." *Ming Qing yanjiu* (Settembre 1992): 1–45.

Santangelo, Paolo (1993). "Urban Society in Late Imperial Suzhou." Translated by Adam Victor. In Johnson, ed. 1993 (see citation), pp. 81–116.

Schuessler, Axel, and Michael Loewe (1993). "*Yüeh chüeh shu* 越絕書." In Loewe, ed. 1993 (see citation), pp. 490–493.

Schwartz, Benjamin I. (1985). *The World of Thought in Ancient China.* Cambridge, MA: The Belknap Press of Harvard University Press.

Seckel, Dietrich (1964). *The Art of Buddhism.* Translated by Ann E. Keep. New York: Crown.

Seckel, Dietrich (1980). "Stupa Elements Surviving in East Asian Pagodas." In Anna Libera Dallapiccola, ed., *The Stupa: Its Religious, Historical and Architectural Significance* (Wiesbaden: Franz Steiner Verlag, 1980), pp. 249–259.

Shaughnessy, Edward L. (1993). "*I Chou shu* 逸周書 (*Chou shu*)." In Loewe, ed. 1993, pp. 229–233.

Shaughnessy, Edward L. "*I ching* 易經 (*Chou I* 周易)." In Loewe, ed. 1993 (see citation), pp. 216–228.

Shiba, Yoshinobu (1970). *Commerce and Society in Sung China.* Translated by Mark Elvin. Ann Arbor: University of Michigan Center for Chinese Studies.

Shiba, Yoshinobu (1975). "Urbanization and the Development of Markets in the Lower Yangtze Valley." In Haeger, ed. 1975 (see citation), pp. 13–48.

Shiba, Yoshinobu (1977). "Ningpo and Its Hinterland." In Skinner, ed. 1977 (see citation), pp. 391–439.

Sirén, Osvald (1929). "Chinese Architecture." In *Encyclopaedia Britannica,* 14th ed., Vol. V, pp. 556–565.

Sivin, Nathan (1995). "State, Cosmos, and Body in the Last Three Centuries B.C." *Harvard Journal of Asiatic Studies* 55, no. 1 (June 1995): 5–37.

Sjoberg, Gideon (1960). *The Preindustial City: Past and Present.* Glencoe, IL: Free Press.

Skinner, G. William, ed. (1977). *The City in Late Imperial China.* Stanford, CA: Stanford University Press.

Skinner, G. William (1977a). "Introduction: Urban Development in Imperial China." In Skinner, ed. 1977, pp. 3–31.

Skinner, G. William (1977b). "Regional Urbanization in Nineteenth-Century China." In Skinner, ed. 1977, pp. 211–249.

Skinner, G. William (1977c). "Introduction: Urban and Rural in Chinese Society." In Skinner, ed. 1977, pp. 253–273.

Skinner, G. William (1977d). "Cities and the Hierarchy of Local Systems." In Skinner, ed. 1977, pp. 275–351.

Skinner, G. William (1977e). "Introduction: Urban Social Structure in Ch'ing China." In Skinner, ed. 1977, pp. 521–553.

Smith, Bardwell, and Holly Baker Reynolds, eds. (1987). *The City as a Sacred Center: Essays on Six Asian Contexts.* Leiden, The Netherlands: E. J. Brill.

Spence, Jonathan D. (1990). *The Search for Modern China.* London: Century Hutchinson.

Steinhardt, Nancy Shatzman (1990). *Chinese Imperial City Planning.* Honolulu: University of Hawai'i Press.

Thierry, François (1989). "Empire and Minority in China." In Gérard Chaliand, ed., *Minority Peoples in the Age of Nation-States*. Translated by Tony Berrett; foreword by Ben Whitaker (London: Pluto Press), pp. 76–99.

Thorp, Robert L. (1983). "Origins of Chinese Architectural Style: The Earliest Plans and Building Types." *Archives of Asian Art* 36 (1983): 22–39.

Thorp, Robert L. (1986). "Architectural Principles in Early Imperial China: Structural Problems and Their Solution." *The Art Bulletin* 68, no. 3 (September 1986): 360–377.

Trewartha, Glenn T. (1952). "Chinese Cities: Origins and Functions." *Annals of the Association of American Geographers* 42, no. 2 (March 1952): 69–93.

Twitchett, Denis (1966). "The T'ang Market System." *Asia Major*, n.s., 12, no. 2 (1966): 202–248.

Twitchett, Denis (1968). "Mercant, Trade and Government in Late T'ang." *Asia Major*, n.s., 14, part 1 (1968): pp. 63–95.

Van der Sprenkel, Sybille (1977). "Urban Social Control." In Skinner, ed. 1977 (see citation), pp. 609–632.

Wakeman, Jr., Frederic (1975). "Introduction: The Evolution of Local Control in Late Imperial China." In Wakeman and Grant, eds. 1975 (see citation), pp. 1–25.

Wakeman, Jr., Frederic, and Carolyn Grant, eds. (1975). *Conflict and Control in Late Imperial China*. Berkeley, Los Angeles: University of California Press.

Waldron, Arthur (1990). *The Great Wall of China: From History to Myth*. New York: Cambridge University Press.

Waley, Arthur (1937). *The Book of Songs*. London: George Allen & Unwin, 1937.

Ward, Barbara E. (1985). "Regional Operas and Their Audiences: Evidence from Hong Kong." In Johnson, et al., eds. 1985 (see citation), pp. 161–187.

Watkin, David (1986). *A History of Western Architecture*. London: Barrie & Jenkins.

Watson, James L. (1985). "Standardizing the Gods: The Promotion of T'ien Hou ("Empress of Heaven") Along the South China Coast, 960–1960." In Johnson, et al., eds. 1985 (see citation), pp. 292–324.

Watt, John R. (1977). "The Yamen and Urban Administration." In Skinner, ed. 1977 (see citation), pp. 353–390.

Wheatley, Paul (1971). *The Pivot of the Four Quarters: a Preliminary Enquiry into the Origins and Character of the Ancient Chinese City*. Edinburgh: Edinburgh University Press.

Wood, Frances (1995). *Did Marco Polo Go to China?* London: Seckel and Warburg.

Wright, Arthur F. (1965). "Symbolism and Function: Reflections on Changan and Other Great Cities." *Journal of Asian Studies* XXIV, no. 4 (August 1965): 667–679.

Wright, Arthur F. (1965a). "Viewpoints on a City: Changan (583–904): Chinese Capital and Asian Cosmopolis." *Ventures* 5, no. 1 (1965): pp. 15–23.

Wright, Arthur F. (1977). "The Cosmology of the Chinese City." In Skinner, ed. 1985 (see citation), pp. 33–73.

Xu Yinong (1996). "The City in Space and Time: Development of the Urban Form and Space of Suzhou until 1911." Ph.D. Dissertation. University of Edinburgh.

Zücker, Paul (1959). *Town and Square: From the Agora to the Village Green*. New York: Columbia University Press.

Index

References to illustrations are in **boldface.**

About the Author

YINONG XU, who is currently Joukowsky Postdoctoral Fellow in the Department of History of Art and Architecture at Brown University, holds Bachelor's and Master's Degrees in architecture from Tsinghua University in Beijing. He received his Ph.D. in architectural and urban history from the University of Edinburgh in 1997. His articles on architectural history have appeared in academic journals. *The Chinese City in Space and Time* is his first book.